READINGS IN RENAISSANCE WOMEN'S DRAMA

Readings in Renaissance Women's Drama collects together for the first time the key critical commentaries and historical essays – both classic and contemporary – on Renaissance women's drama. The essays cover the following playwrights:

- Joanna Lumley
- Elizabeth Cary
- Mary Sidney
- Mary Wroth
- Jane Cavendish and Elizabeth Brackley
- Margaret Cavendish

Specifically designed to provide a comprehensive overview for students, teachers and scholars, this collection combines

- key critical commentaries on drama by women in the Early Modern period, by writers and critics such as Ben Jonson, Virginia Woolf and T. S. Eliot
- specially-commissioned new essays by some of today's most important feminist critics
- a preface and introduction explaining the selection and contexts of the materials
- a bibliography of secondary sources

Readings in Renaissance Women's Drama is the most complete sourcebook for the study of this revelatory and growing area of enquiry.

S. P. Cerasano is in the English Department at Colgate University, and **Marion Wynne-Davies** is in the English Department at the University of Dundee. They co-edited *Renaissance Drama by Women*, published by Routledge, 1996.

READINGS IN RENAISSANCE WOMEN'S DRAMA

Criticism, history, and performance 1594–1998

Edited by S. P. Cerasano and Marion Wynne-Davies

London and New York

First published 1998
by Routledge
11 New Fetter Lane, London EC4P 4EE

Simultaneously published in the USA and Canada
by Routledge
29 West 35th Street, New York, NY 10001

Typeset in Galliard by RefineCatch Limited, Bungay, Suffolk
Printed and bound in Great Britain by
TJ International Ltd, Padstow, Cornwall

British Library Cataloguing in Publication Data
A catalogue record for this book is available from the British Library

Library of Congress Cataloging in Publication Data
Readings in renaissance women's drama: criticism, history, and performance, 1594–1998 / edited by S. P. Cerasano & Marion Wynne-Davies.
p. cm.
Includes bibliographical references and index.
1. English drama – Women authors – History and criticism.
2. English drama – Early modern and Elizabethan, 1500–1600 – History and criticism. 3. Women and literature – England – History – 16th century. 4. Women and literature – England – History – 17th century.
5. English drama –17th century – History and criticism.
6. Renaissance – England. I. Cerasano, S. P. II. Wynne-Davies, Marion.
PR658.W6R43 1998
822′.3099287 – dc21 98–6670
CIP

ISBN 0–415–16443–5 (pbk)
ISBN 0–415–16442–7 (hbk)

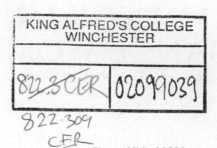

FOR THE NEXT GENERATION:
MADDY, RICHARD, AND ROBERT

CONTENTS

PREFACE

Readings in Renaissance Women's Drama addresses a wide variety of cultural and literary interests relating to women's drama in England from the late sixteenth to the mid-seventeenth centuries. It was initially conceived as a collection of critical readings that would serve as a companion volume to the dramatic texts presented in the editors' earlier volume, *Renaissance Drama by Women* (Routledge, 1996). However, it quickly became apparent that – as in that former volume – it was important to construe the sense of women's dramatic activity as broadly as possible, to further the exploration of the ways in which women participated in theatrical culture not only as authors and translators, but also as patrons, performers, and even as part-owners of one particular public playhouse, the second Fortune. Additionally, in Part I (Early Commentaries) the editors have traced the critical heritage that informed Renaissance women's drama previous to 1950 so that this might foreground the more contemporary critical commentaries in the collection.

In compiling *Readings in Renaissance Women's Drama* the editors have thought primarily about the needs of readers who are approaching this area of inquiry for the first time. As a sourcebook it is intended to provide an overview of key issues and observations. As such, and also because this burgeoning field is fast becoming much more complex than any single collection can represent, the volume includes an extensive bibliography of secondary sources. By the time that this collection appears in print the bibliography will doubtless be out of date; however, if nothing else it suggests the richness that so many critics, historians and, more recently, theatre directors have discovered in Renaissance women's drama, and it will provide some useful suggestions for further study.

Moreover, the present volume is a mixture of reprinted and newly written essays. The essays appearing here for the first time chart fresh territory that will contribute much to the conversation that will inform future scholarship; while the reprinted essays remind us how privileged scholars have previously been, both to listen to and to participate in the exciting conversation that has established Renaissance women's drama as a dynamic area of inquiry. Consequently, it is hoped that *Readings in Renaissance Women's Drama* will stimulate a broad audience among readers of many levels and backgrounds – from those who are already engaged in the scholarship surrounding this field to those who wish to begin their learning; and from those who are interested specifically in Renaissance drama and theatre history to those in women's studies and cultural studies more generally.

ACKNOWLEDGEMENTS

S. P. Cerasano wishes to thank the many colleagues and friends who generously contributed to this volume. This collection is a tribute to their continuing interest in the field of Renaissance women's drama and the erudition with which it is being approached. She especially acknowledges the institutional support extended by Jane Pinchin (Dean of the Faculty), Chris Vescey (Director, Humanities Division), the Colgate University Research Council, and the Colgate Humanities Development Fund. The staff of the Public Record Office and Mr A. C. L. Hall (the Wodehouse Library, Dulwich College) have also been generous in their assistance. The London Goodenough Trust (Ms Val Martin, the Registrar), which provided housing for the period when part of this collection was assembled, is especially to be thanked. Clara Lantz (Department of Romance Languages, Colgate University) provided timely assistance and technical life support in the preparation of many essays that were reprinted for this volume. Not least of all, the editorial staff at Routledge have offered remarkable insight and steadfast support, especially Talia Rodgers. Marion Wynne-Davies remains a much-appreciated and a much-respected friend. Others, too numerous to name here, will know that they too deserve praise and thanks.

Marion Wynne-Davies would like to thank all those who have contributed to this volume; their co-operation, scholarship and efficiency have speeded the volume along. She would also like to thank those colleagues and friends with whom she has discussed Renaissance drama by women over the past three years, in particular, Michael Brennan, Hero Chalmers, Danielle Clark, Emma Clark, Elizabeth Clarke, Elaine Hobby, Mary McNally, Rebecca de Monte, Nicole Pohl, Diane Purkiss, Victor Skretkowitz, Sophie Tomlinson, and Sue Wiseman. In addition she wishes to thank the library staff of Dundee Library, St Andrews University Library, the British Library, the University of Nottingham Library and the Bodleian Library for their invaluable assistance; Gwen Hunter and Ann Bain for their generous secretarial assistance; and the editorial staff at Routledge for their usual expertise and courteous efficiency, in particular Talia Rodgers. Finally, on a more personal note, she wishes to acknowledge the support and affection offered by her husband, Geoff Ward, and their two sons, Richard and Robert, and, most of all, by her friend and co-editor, S. P. Cerasano.

PERMISSIONS

The editors are grateful to the following authors and publishers for their willingness to reprint materials:

Elaine V. Beilin's essays on Elizabeth Cary and Joanna Lumley first appeared in Beilin, *Redeeming Eve: Women Writers of the English Renaissance* (Princeton, NJ: Princeton University Press, 1987), pp. 153–76.

David M. Bergeron's 'Women as Patrons of English Renaissance Drama' first appeared in Guy Fitch Lytle and Stephen Orgel (eds) *Patronage in the Renaissance* (Princeton, NJ: Princeton University Press, 1981), pp. 274–90.

Nancy Cotton's 'Renaissance Noblewomen' is taken from her *Women Playwrights in England, c. 1363–1750* (Lewisburg, PA: Bucknell University Press, 1980), pp. 27-54.

Margaret J. M. Ezell's '"To Be Your Daughter in Your Pen": The Social Functions of Literature in the Writings of Lady Elizabeth Brackley and Lady Jane Cavendish' is reprinted from the essay of the same title published in *Huntington Library Quarterly* (*HLQ*) 51 (1988), pp. 281–96. It is reprinted with the kind permission of the Henry E. Huntington Library.

Margaret W. Ferguson's 'The Spectre of Resistance: *The Tragedy of Mariam (1613)*' is a reprinted version of the essay by the same title as printed in David Scott Kastan and Peter Stallybrass (eds) *Staging the Renaissance: Reinterpretations of Elizabethan and Jacobean Drama* (London: Routledge, 1991), pp. 235–50.

Margaret P. Hannay's 'Patronesse of the Muses' first appeared in ch. 5 of her *Philip's Phoenix: Mary Sidney, Countess of Pembroke* (Oxford: Oxford University Press, 1990), pp. 106–42.

Jean E. Howard's 'Women as Spectators, Spectacles, and Paying Customers' is reprinted from the version of the essay that appeared in David Scott Kastan and Peter Stallybrass (eds) *Staging the Renaissance: Reinterpretations of Elizabethan and Jacobean Drama* (London: Routledge, 1991), pp. 68–74.

Tina Krontiris's 'Mary Herbert: Englishing a Purified Cleopatra' is reprinted from ch. 3 of her *Oppositional Voices: Women as Writers and Translators of Literature in the English Renaissance* (London: Routledge, 1992), pp. 64–78.

Barbara Kiefer Lewalski's 'Resisting Tyrants: Elizabeth Cary's Tragedy' first appeared in her

Writing Women in Jacobean England (Cambridge, MA: Harvard University Press, 1993), pp. 179–211.

Margaret Anne McLaren's 'An Unknown Continent: Lady Mary Wroth's Forgotten Pastoral Drama, *Love's Victory*' first appeared in Anne Haselkorn and Betty Travistky (eds) *The Renaissance Englishwoman in Print* (Amherst, MA: University of Massachusetts Press, 1990), pp. 276–92.

Sophie Tomlinson's '"My Brain the Stage": Margaret Cavendish and the Fantasy of Female Performance' appeared initially in Claire Brant and Diane Purkiss (eds) *Women, Texts and Histories 1575–1760* (London: Routledge, 1992), pp. 134–63.

Gary Waller's '"Like One in a Gay Masque": The Sidney Cousins in the Theaters of Court and Country' is taken from his chapter of the same name in *The Sidney Family Romance: Mary Wroth, William Herbert, and the Early Modern Construction of Gender* (Detroit, MI: Wayne State University Press, 1993), pp. 231–45.

All of the other essays have been written especially for this collection.

INTRODUCTION

S. P. Cerasano and Marion Wynne-Davies

Recalling the dismal fate of Virginia Woolf's fictional playwright, Judith Shakespeare, we might be prompted to ask why Early Modern women such as Mary Sidney, Elizabeth Cary, Mary Wroth and the Cavendish sisters dared to write a play at all? It has long been common knowledge that no women acted on the English stage during the Renaissance and, it has long been assumed, that no women wrote plays in that period either; indeed, even after the post-1970s incursion of Early Modern female authors into the canon, their contributions were seen to be either in poetry or prose. But female dramatists did exist. Some women translated plays written by men: Joanna/Jane Lumley's *Iphigenia at Aulis* (Lumley herself used both 'Jane' and 'Joanna' and these names have been used by different critics; in general, 'Jane' seems to be preferred, Elizabeth I's *Hercules Oetaeus* and Mary Sidney's *The Tragedy of Antonie.* Others wrote original dramas: Elizabeth Cary's *The Tragedy of Mariam* is the first tragedy written by an Englishwoman, Mary Wroth's *Love's Victory* (*c.*1620) is the first comedy, while the two plays of Elizabeth Brackley and Jane Cavendish, together with the dramatic compositions of Margaret Cavendish, serve as a transition to the productions of the first professional woman dramatist, Aphra Behn. However, perhaps the most surprising facet of this late-twentieth-century 'discovery' of the Early Modern woman dramatist is that they were perfectly well known in their own period and were the subject of numerous panegyric commentaries. Examples of these, such as the poems written by Samuel Daniel and John Davies of Hereford, are included in the Early Commentaries (Part I of this book). Indeed, even in 1752 when George Ballard wrote his *Memoirs of Several Ladies of Great Britain* he includes chapters on all the women mentioned in this collection, with the exception of Jane Cavendish. It is from the mid-eighteenth century therefore that the Early Modern woman dramatist completes her descent into obscurity, and she remained a dim and forgotten figure until the resurgence of interest in women writers that accompanied the growth in female consciousness at the start of the twentieth century. This renewed interest uncovered the neglected texts and several of the plays, *Antonie*, *Iphigenia at Aulis*, *Mariam* and *The Concealed Fancies*, were published for the first time in modern editions. Critical attention remained lacking, however, the most well-known commentary from this period being T. S. Eliot's somewhat reductive analysis of Mary Sidney's oeuvre and influence. Finally, in the 1980s, as the influence of feminist criticism permeated successive periods and genres, Early Modern women playwrights began to be recognised once again and their work has been the focus of an increasing number of scholarly editions and critical re-evaluations. What this brief history of drama by Early Modern women makes clear is that the late twentieth century did not discover Sidney, Cary, Wroth and the others, but *re*discovered them. Moreover, without the contemporary panegyric verse, Ballard's comprehensive list and the initial excavations by early-twentieth-century scholars, the present critical pieces would not, and could not, have been written. As such, the Early Commentaries part of this book demonstrates a broad continuity of interest, with a few chronological lacunae, from the sixteenth century to the present day.

Part II of this book examines Contexts and Issues. One of the first present-day critics to treat Early Modern women dramatists as a group was Nancy Cotton in her pathbreaking *Women Playwrights in England c.1363–1750*, gathering them together as 'Renaissance noblewomen'. This social positioning has become an inevitable focus for subsequent critics who have concentrated on the court, as does Leeds Barroll in his essay 'The Arts at the English Court of Anna of Denmark', and the country house, as in Marion Wynne-Davies's '"My seeled chamber and dark parlour room": the English country house and Renaissance women dramatists'. This does not mean that there were no women from lower social groups writing plays or involved in some form with dramatic productions, but simply that any possible published or manuscript material has yet to be identified. It is important to recall that in the 1970s it was generally believed that *no* women, noble or otherwise, from the Early Modern period wrote plays, so the field of excavation must be considered as developing rather than as concluded. However, because of the overwhelming lack of primary dramatic texts, many critics have chosen to focus upon the ancillary roles of women to Renaissance theatre, such as patronage (David M. Bergeron's 'Women as patrons of English Renaissance drama'), spectatorship (Jean E. Howard's 'Women as spectators, spectacles, and paying customers') and the ownership of theatres (S. P. Cerasano's 'Women as theatrical investors: three shareholders and the second Fortune Playhouse'). Yet, although the plays of Early Modern women dramatists have only been *re*discovered since the late 1970s, such has been the impact of these texts that they have already been performed in the theatre. Thus, as Gweno Williams explains in her essay, '"Why may not a lady write a good play?": plays by Early Modern women reassessed as performance texts' that, although not originally intended for performance, the plays themselves have proved vital, stimulating and surprisingly 'modern' in a late-twentieth-century theatrical context.

Because of a general lack of contextualising documentation for Early Modern women's plays, the dramatic function of these early texts is often difficult to excavate. Still, to understand the role of the woman dramatist in the English Renaissance it is imperative to address the question of whether or not the earlier material was written for performance or whether the plays were simply exercises in translation and/or composition. While there exists at present no hard evidence to settle the argument one way or the other, internal evidence from the texts and manuscripts may, to a certain extent, be used to answer the question. It is clear from the scholarly nature of the works that Lumley and Elizabeth I were primarily interested in translating from the original Latin without ever intending the texts to be used as the basis for performance. Sidney's and Cary's plays similarly contain no material which would suggest the necessity of dramatic action, although the vogue for closet drama would have allowed for the plays to have been read aloud in a private house. The Countess of Pembroke's 'academy' at Wilton produced a number of these closet plays and not all were written by women; Samuel Daniel's *Tragedy of Cleopatra* and Thomas Kyd's *Cornelia*, being two prominent examples. It is possible that Elizabeth Cary spent some time at Wilton and would have been encouraged by Mary Sidney's example to produce her own closet drama, like the Countess's constructed for her companions within the sheltered interior of that cultural domicile. Plays written for the pleasure of an intimate coterie are, of necessity, more personal, more 'closeted', and it is hardly surprising that several critics have identified autobiographical elements in *Antonie* and *Mariam*. Still, the possibility of contemporary allusion is increased when the dramatist is writing about and for his or her own family. This becomes apparent when looking at the other plays referred to in this book: Mary Wroth, Jane Cavendish, Elizabeth Brackley and Margaret Cavendish all draw upon their familial group to create characters and narrative events. Moreover, it is clear that Wroth's *Love's Victory* and Jane Cavendish and Elizabeth Brackley's *The Concealed Fancies* and *A Pastorall* were meant to be performed and not simply read aloud as was the case with the plays of the previous generation of women dramatists. The change is apparent in several ways: first, the alteration in genre, from the long declamations of neo-Senecan tragedy to the swift action of romantic comedy, encouraged movement about a stage and interaction between characters. Second, the later plays facilitate a layering of awareness accessible only through staging; for example, Wroth positions characters at the front and rear of a performance site, while Cavendish and Brackley use the aside to great comic effect. Finally, and most importantly, the later texts contain stage directions informing us when characters enter, exit and, on one occasion, descend from the sky! Not only were *Love's Victory, The Concealed Fancies* and *A Pastorall* about the dramatists' families, not only were they created for those families' pleasure, but also they were written to be performed by those same familial groups. As further detailed research is undertaken upon individual authors and plays such deductions will become more common, opening out the field of criticism on Early Modern women dramatists towards discussion and debate.

The third part of this book focuses upon separate women dramatists and their plays, following a chronological line from Elizabeth I to Margaret Cavendish. Carole Levin's essay, '"We princes, I tell you, are set on stages": Elizabeth I and dramatic self-representation', explores how, as a queen, Elizabeth had constantly to project herself in a quasi-dramatic context, and it was this self–consciousness which emerged in her translation of Seneca's *Hercules Oetaeus*. Both criticisms of Joanna/Jane Lumley's *Iphigenia at Aulis*, Elaine V. Beilin's 'Joanna Lumley (1537?-1576/1577)' and Stephanie Hodgson-Wright's 'Jane Lumley's *Iphigenia at Aulis*: *multum in parvo*, or, less is more', comment upon the importance of gender, in a spiritual and political context, in the play, revealing that the text is far more than a classroom revision exercise. Similar sophistication and originality are uncovered by Margaret P. Hannay's 'Patronesse of the muses' and Tina Krontiris's 'Mary Herbert: Englishing a purified Cleopatra' in their analyses of Mary Sidney/Herbert's translation *The Tragedy of Antonie*. Indeed, the works of these first three authors demand a careful and considered understanding of the concept of 'translation', for each woman altered her source material to fit her gender's and her period's specific discourses.

The next two women dramatists considered here, Elizabeth Cary and Mary Wroth, both built upon the earlier women writers with their safer choice of translation, producing, respectively, the first original tragedy and comedy to be written in English. The two essays which focus on Cary's *The Tragedy of Mariam*, Margaret W. Ferguson's 'The spectre of resistance: *The Tragedy of Mariam* (1613)' and Barbara Kiefer Lewalski's 'Resisting tyrants: Elizabeth Cary's tragedy', acknowledge the intense complexity and powerful imaginative force of the play, underlining the fact that Cary's work is one of the key Senecan tragedies to be written at the start of the seventeenth century. Mary Wroth's comedy, *Love's Victory,* has not received the same amount of critical attention as Cary's *Mariam*, mainly because it was available, until recently, only in a single complete manuscript and an expensive limited edition. This comparative lack of attention is dealt with by Margaret Anne McLaren in her pathbreaking essay, 'An unknown continent: Lady Mary Wroth's forgotten pastoral drama, "Loves Victorie"'. A more detailed account is available in Gary Waller's '"Like one in a gay masque": the Sidney cousins in the theaters of court and country'. With both plays becoming available in a number of different editions, such obscurity is now, we hope, a thing of the past.

The final three women dramatists to be considered here are all, perhaps somewhat surprisingly, from the same family: the two sisters, Jane Cavendish and Elizabeth Brackley, wrote two plays, while their stepmother, Margaret Cavendish, wrote almost twenty plays, although none were intended as contemporary performance texts. While it is important to acknowledge the influence of William Cavendish, the first Duke of Newcastle, father to Jane and Elizabeth and husband to Margaret, it is no longer adequate to view his male influence as dominating, controlling and superior. When examining the works of all four – William also wrote plays – what becomes apparent is a mutual dramatic discourse which liberated both female and male voices, and which clearly demonstrates that seventeenth-century women dramatists were not radical or 'odd' individuals, nor did they form a separate and reclusive group, but were an integral part of Early Modern dramatic discourses. The two essays on the Cavendish sisters, Margaret J. M. Ezell's '"To be your daughter in your pen": the social functions of literature in the writings of Lady Elizabeth Brackley and Lady Jane Cavendish' and Alison Findlay's '"She gave you the civility of the house": household performance in *The Concealed Fancies*', strongly affirm that their dramatic writings cross gender boundaries and that our late-twentieth-century reception of their plays should be open to such collaborative interpretations. However, of all the women dramatists included in this book the last, Margaret Cavendish, is perhaps the most well known, and criticism on her work is, correspondingly, more profuse and established. As such, Sophie Tomlinson in '"My Brain the Stage": Margaret Cavendish and the fantasy of female performance' and Julie Sanders in '"A woman write a play!": Jonsonian strategies and the dramatic writings of Margaret Cavendish; or, did the Duchess feel the anxiety of influence?', both adopt radical positions which challenge previously held views on the Cavendish oeuvre: Tomlinson redefines the idea of female 'performance' in pre-Restoration drama, while Sanders demands that the influence of male authors upon their female counterparts must be acknowledged. However, alongside the early and sustained recognition of Margaret Cavendish's work there has existed a seam of commentary which has defined Margaret Cavendish as fantastic, eccentric and even mad. It is no longer necessary to refute such claims. For example, even if Cavendish's psychological 'normality' is in question, such instability has never been regarded as detrimental to male authorship. More importantly, however, the allegations of oddity, particularly in relation to her identity as an Early Modern woman playwright, are no longer sustainable or excusable.

As the new millennium approaches we are now able to recognise that Margaret Cavendish is simply one of a number of Renaissance women dramatists whose works were recognised and admired in their own day, and whose plays have since been rediscovered and enjoyed as literary texts, as the source of critical commentaries, and as dramatic productions in the public theatre. Thus, rather than asking why Early Modern women wrote plays, perhaps we should ask why they have been neglected for so long, why they still provoke a certain amount of disbelief and hostility, and primarily why they are still being neglected by professional theatre companies. While the commentaries and essays in this book offer scholarly, challenging and discriminating answers to these questions, it is essential to recognise that a single critical anthology can be only a beginning. Nevertheless, it is the hope and belief of the editors and contributors to this book that, by adding to the growing body of editorial, critical and production work, *Readings in Renaissance Women's Drama* will forward the recognition, acceptance and reinstatement of the Early Modern woman dramatist and her plays.

January 1998

Part I

EARLY COMMENTARIES

INTRODUCTION

The passages included in Part I represent the way in which the critical history of the Renaissance woman dramatist has developed. Until very recently it was often assumed that English women did not write plays in the Early Modern period, and alongside this primary lack of information ran a concurrent unawareness which suggested that there were no corresponding critical works either. However, in the last decade of the twentieth century it has become increasingly apparent that Renaissance women did write plays and that these works had interest and value as both literary and performance texts. Consequently, this sense of 'discovery' generated an assumption that these works had faded into obscurity soon after they were written, and since some of the plays exist only in manuscript form, the apparent lack of critical commentary seemed wholly plausible. This was not the case. The selection of material included here demonstrates that Renaissance women's plays were known about, and often commended, from the sixteenth to the twentieth century. From the panegyrics of their own day, through the historical commentaries of the eighteenth and nineteenth centuries, to the modern editions and growing recognition of women writers in the twentieth century, it must be concluded that the Renaissance woman dramatist has received sustained, and sustainable, critical attention. The following selection of commentaries has been chosen to demonstrate this continuity of interest. As such, the Early Commentaries section of this book provides not only a critical framework for the plays themselves, but also a historicising context for the more recent critical essays contained in Parts II and III.

1

MARY SIDNEY IS PRAISED TO ELIZABETH I

Thomas Churchyard presented this poem to Elizabeth I during the New Year's Day celebrations of 1594; he describes Mary Sidney as a poet in her own right as well as a renowned patroness. Text from John Nichols (1823), *The Progresses and Public Processions of Queen Elizabeth*, London: John Nichols, p. 236.

Pembroke's a pearl, that orient is of kind,
A *Sidney* right shall not in silence sit;
A gem more worth than all the gold of Ind,
For she enjoys the wise Minerva's wit,
And sets to school our poets everywhere,
That do presume the laurel crown to wear.
The Muses nine and all the Graces three,
In *Pembroke's* books and verses shall you see.

2

SAMUEL DANIEL TO MARY SIDNEY

Daniel's closet drama, *The Tragedy of Cleopatra*, was intended as a companion piece to Mary Sidney's *The Tragedy of Antonie*, and in his dedicatory poem Daniel praises Sidney's poetic skill. Text from Samuel Daniel (1594), *Delia and Rosamond Augmented. Cleopatra*, London, no pag.

'To the Right Honourable, the Lady Mary, Countess of Pembroke'

Lo, here the work the which she did impose,
Who only doth predominate my Muse,
The star of wonder which my labours chose
To guide their way in all the course I use.
She, whose clear brightness doth alone infuse
Strength to my thoughts, and makes me what I am,
Called up my spirits from out their low repose,
To sing of state, and tragic notes to frame.

I, who contented with a humble song,
Made music to myself that pleased me best,
And only told of Delia and her wrong,
And praised her eyes and 'plained my own unrest
(A text from whence my Muse had not digressed),
Madam, had not thy well graced *Anthony*
(Who all alone having remained long),
Required his *Cleopatra's* company.

Who if she here do so appear in act,
That for his Queen and Love he scarce will know her,
Finding how much she of herself hath lacked
And missed that glory wherein I should show her,
In majesty debased, in courage lower;
Yet lightening thou by thy sweet favouring eyes
My dark deflects which from her spirit detract,
He yet may guess it's she, which will suffice.

And I hereafter in another kind
More fitting to the nature of my vein,
May, peradventure, better please thy mind
And higher notes in sweeter music strain;
Seeing that thou so graciously dost deign
To countenance my song and cherish me,
I must so work posterity may find
How much I did contend to honour thee.

Now when so many pens, like spears, are charged
To chase away this tyrant of the north,
Gross Barbarism, whose power grown far enlarged
Was lately by thy valiant brother's worth
First found, encountered, and provoked forth;
Whose onset made the rest audacious,
Whereby they likewise have so well discharged
Upon that hideous Beast encroaching thus.

And now I must with that poor strength I have,
Resist so foul a foe in what I may;
And arm against oblivion and the grave,
That else in darkness carries all away,
And makes of all our honours but a prey.
So that if by my pen procure I shall
But to defend me and my name to save,
Then though I die, I cannot yet die all;

But still the better part of me will live,
Decked and adorned with thy scared name,
Although thyself dost far more glory give
Unto thyself, than I can by the same.
Who dost with thine own hand a bulwark frame
Against these Monsters (enemies of honour),
Which evermore shall so defend thy Fame,
That Time nor they, shall never prey upon her.

Those *Hymns* which thou dost consecrate to heaven,
Which *Israel's* singer to his God did frame,
Unto thy voice eternity hath given,
And makes thee dear to him from whence they came.
In them must rest thy ever reverend name,
So long as *Syon's* God remaineth honoured;
And till confusion hath all zeal bereaven,
And murdered Faith and temples ruined.

By this, Great Lady, thou must then be known,
When *Wilton* lies low levelled with the ground,
And this is that which thou may'st call thy own,
Which sacrilegious time cannot confound;
Here thou surviv'st thyself, here thou art found
Of late succeeding eyes, fresh in fame;
This monument cannot be over-thrown,
Where in eternal brass remained thy name.

3

JOHN DAVIES OF HEREFORD COMMENDS MARY SIDNEY AND ELIZABETH CARY

John Davies praises the writing of both Mary Sidney and Elizabeth Cary in the dedication of his own work. Text from John Davies of Hereford (1612), *The Muses Sacrifice, or Divine Meditations*, London, no pag.

'To the Most Noble, and no less deservedly-renowned ladies, as well darlings, as patronesses, of the Muses; Lucy, Countess of Bedford, Mary, Countess Dowager of Pembroke, and Elizabeth, Lady Cary (wife of Sir Henry Cary). Glories of women.'

Pembroke (a paragon of princely parts,
And, of that part that most commends the Muse,
Great mistress of her greatness, and the arts)
Phoebus and Fate make great and glorious!

A work of art and grace (from head and heart
that makes a work of wonder) thou hast done;
Where art seems nature, nature seemeth art,
and grace in both makes all outshine the sun . . . .

My hand once sought that glorious work to grace,
and writ in gold what thou in ink had'st writ;
But gold and highest art are both too base
to character the glory of thy wit!

And did'st thou thirst for fame (as all men do),
thou would'st by all means let it come to light;
But though thou cloud it, as doth Envy too,
yet through both clouds it shines it is so bright! . . .

Cary (of whom Minerva stands in fear,
lest she, from her, should get Art's regency)
Of Art so moves the great-all-moving sphere,
that every orb of science moves thereby.

Thou mak'st Melpomen proud, and my heart great
of such a pupil, who, in buskin fine,
With feet of state, dost make thy Muse to meet
the scenes of Syracuse and Palestine.

Art, Language, yea, abstruse and holy tongues,
  they wit and grace acquired thy fame to raise;
And still to fill thy own and others' songs;
  thine with thy parts, and others' with thy praise.

Such nervy limbs of art and strains of wit,
  time past ne'er knew the weaker sex to have;
And times to come will hardly credit it,
  if thus thou give thy works both birth and grave.

4

WILLIAM SHEARES TO ELIZABETH CARY

The publisher William Sheares dedicated the works of the playwright, John Marston, to Elizabeth Cary because she herself was a writer. Text from William Sheares (1633), *The Works of John Marston, Being Tragedies and Comedies, Collected into one Volume*, London, fol. A4r–A4v.

'To The Right Honourable, The Lady Elizabeth Cary, Viscountess Faulkland'

In his [Marston's] absence, Noble Lady, I have been emboldened to present these works unto your Honours view, and the rather, because your Honour is well acquainted with the Muses; In brief, Fame has given out, that your Honour is the mirror of her sex, the admiration, not only of this island, but of all adjacent countries and dominions, which are all acquainted with your rare virtues and endowments.

5

JONSON AND WROTH

Ben Jonson wrote a number of poems praising the Sidney family and his sonnet to Mary Wroth may be seen as part of a general pattern eulogising their cultural activities. However, the specific references to Venus and Cupid suggest a knowledge of her drama in which the two mythological figures play an important part. Text from: Ben Jonson (1640), *The Under-wood* xxviii, in *Ben Jonson*, ed. C. H. Herford and Percy Simpson, Oxford: Clarendon Press, 1947, vol. VIII, p. 182.

A Sonnet, to the noble Lady, the Lady MARY WROTH

I that have beene a lover, and could shew it,
   Though not in these, in rithmes not wholly dumbe,
   Since I exscribe your Sonnets, am become
A better lover, and much better Poet.
Nor is my Muse, or I asham'd to owe it
   To those true numerous Graces; whereof some,
   But charme the Senses, others over-come
Both braines and hearts; and mine now best doe know it:
For in your verse all *Cupids* Armorie,
   His flames, his shafts, his Quiver, and his Bow,
   His very eyes are yours to overthrow.
But then his Mothers sweets you so apply,
Her joyes, her smiles, her loves, as readers take
For *Venus Ceston*, every line you make.

6

ELIZABETH CARY'S BIOGRAPHY

Two of Cary's daughters became nuns, following their mother in her dedication to Catholicism, and one of them (probably Anne (Dame Clementia)) wrote a biography of her which includes some brief references to her dramatic writings. The biography was written sometime in the 1640s, but was not published until the nineteenth century. Text from Richard Simpson, ed. (1861), *The Lady Falkland: Her Life. From a MS. in the Imperial Archives at Lille*, London: Catholic Publishing and Bookselling Co. Ltd., pp. 9 and 54.

From this time she writ many things for her private recreation, on several subjects and occasions, all in verse (out of which she scarce ever writ anything that was not translations): one of them was after stolen out of that sister-in-law's (her friend's) chamber, and printed, but by her own procurement was called in. Of all she then writ, that which was said to be the best was the 'Life of Tamberlaine' in verse. . . .

After her lord's death she never went to masques nor plays, not so much as at the court, though she loved them very much, especially the last extremely; nor to any other such public thing.

7

CELEBRATING SEVERAL LADIES

One of the earliest commentaries upon Early Modern women writers was compiled by George Ballard in 1752. His short biographies cover four of the women referred to in this collection (Joanna Lumley, Mary Sidney, Elizabeth Brackley and Margaret Cavendish) although not all the material is relevant to their dramatic work. Ballard is a mine of information and fascinating not least because he includes female authors whose works have not yet been rediscovered. Text from George Ballard (1752), *Memoirs of Several Ladies of Great Britain*, Oxford: W. Jackson, pp. 121–2 and 301.

On Joanna Lumley

She translated from Greek into English the Iphigenia of Euripides. At the beginning of the argument of the play are these words, *After that the Captain of the Grecian* – . The manuscript of this performance is likewise in the aforementioned library, 15.A.9 [the Royal Library at Westminster]. What other things this learned lady may have translated, or wrote of her own composition, or when she died, I know not.

On Margaret Cavendish

Upon which, the Marquis, after sixteen years banishment, made immediate preparation for his return to his native country; leaving his lady behind him to dispatch his affairs there; who having managed them to general satisfaction, she soon followed her consort into England, where she spent much of the remaining part of her life in composing and writing letters, plays, poems, philosophical discourses, and orations. Mr. Giles Jacob says, she was the most voluminous dramatic writer of our female poets; that she had a great deal of wit, and a more than ordinary propensity to dramatic poetry. [*Lives of the Poets*, vol. 1, p. 190] And Mr. Longbain tells us, that all the language and plots of her plays were her own; which is a commendation preferable to fame built on other people's foundation, and will very well atone for some faults in her numerous productions.

8

THE CAVALIER'S LADY AND HER PLAYS

One of the earliest collections of the works of Margaret Cavendish and her husband, William Cavendish, the first Duke of Newcastle, was collected and edited by Edward Jenkins, who hoped to redeem the Duchess's reputation as a 'Honourable and Virtuous' woman. While he praises her poetry, his criticism of her plays adopted, what was to become, the predictable dismissive tone. Text from Edward Jenkins, ed. (1872), *The Cavalier and His Lady. Selections from the Works of the First Duke and Duchess of Newcastle,* London: Macmillan and Co., pp. 27–8.

Two folios of plays written by the Duchess only serve to show how incapable she was of good dramatic writing. She had neither tenderness, passion, nor heart; therefore she could not appreciate, much less present, the finer parts of human nature, the delicate shades of sensibility, the purer and more hidden depths of feeling, or even those superb passions which the dramatic poet fills into his canvas with vivid and masterful delineation. Her cold, conversational, pedantic dialogues are to true dramatic works as a Chinese landscape is to a Cuyp or a Turner.

9

THE FIRST SCHOLARLY EDITION OF MARY SIDNEY'S *ANTONIE*

Alice Luce was the first editor to publish an edition of a play by an Early Modern woman dramatist, and it is interesting to note the difference in tone between her introductory comments and those of male commentators, for example T. S. Eliot (pp. 21–2 in this collection). Text from Alice Luce (1897), *The Countess of Pembroke's Antonie*, Weimar: Verlag Von Emil Felber, p. 39.

The sister of Sir Philip Sidney could hardly fail to be a lover of plays 'full of stately speeches and well sounding Phrases, clyming to the height of Seneca his stile and full of a notable morality.' Her Antonie is the first of that series of pure Senecan plays which appeared in the last decade of Elizabeth's reign, and which indicates the continuous revolt in higher literary circles against the overwhelming progress of the English romantic drama. We shall see that it afterwards became the model of the only two plays in the literature which are written wholly in the style of French Seneca drama.

10

LUMLEY'S PLAY FIRST PUBLISHED

Joanna Lumley's translation was not available in printed form until this early-twentieth-century edition. Text from Harold H. Child, ed. (1909), *Iphigenia at Aulis Translated by Lady Lumley*, Malone Society Reprints, pp. v–vii.

The play now for the first time printed is the earliest attempt to render into English a work of one of the Greek dramatists. The translator was Jane, daughter of Henry Fitzalan, twelfth Earl of Arundel, and wife of John, first Baron Lumley of the second creation. It is a pity that the natural companion of the present piece, Princess Elizabeth's translation, also a tragedy of Euripides, is not forthcoming . . . It seems probable that husband and wife pursued their classical studies concurrently, and that the present play was translated at no long period subsequent to their marriage.

11

THE FIRST MODERN EDITION OF *MARIAM*

Dunstan's edition of Elizabeth Cary's *The Tragedy of Mariam* was the first attempt to contextualise the play for a modern readership; while basic in its annotation the edition proved a pathbreaking endeavour in the scholarship on Early Modern women's drama. Text from A. C. Dunstan (1914), *The Tragedy of Mariam 1613*, Malone Society Reprints, pp. xiii and xv–xvi.

Josephus gives us two versions of the story of Mariam, one in the *Wars of the Jews*, the other in the *Antiquities*, Lady Cary uses the latter version. She follows Josephus fairly closely, but makes several alterations, sometimes compressing, sometimes amplifying, frequently transposing events, occasionally inventing scenes, to simplify the story and to observe the unities . . .

There is some internal evidence for attributing the drama to Sir Henry Cary's (Viscount Falkland's) wife. After Lady Falkland's death a biography of her was written by one or more of her daughters and revised by one of her sons *(The Lady Falkland: her life*, &c., ed. R. S. 1861). The editor discusses the authorship of this biography in the introduction to his edition.

We know from this book that Lady Falkland was a great reader, that she herself wrote, and that she loved plays very much. There are some passages in the *Life* which are reflected in the drama. We read on p. 16 'she did always much disapprove the practice of satisfying oneself with their conscience being free from fault, not forbearing all that might have the least show or suspicion of uncomeliness or unfitness' and that she had 'Be and Seem' inscribed in her daughter's wedding ring. This maxim we find in the Chorus to Act III. Her letter to the king (p. 150) shows the attitude which the Lady Falkland thought it right for a woman to adopt towards her husband. This is reflected in this chorus and in ll. 1833–40, whilst the villain of the piece (Salome) holds quite opposite views. In the play we read (ll. 1795–6):

My head waies downwards: therefore will I goe To try if I can sleepe away my woe.

On p. 17 of the *Life* we learn that Lady Falkland was frequently depressed, that she could sleep at will, and was in the habit of sleeping to cure depression. Less striking is a correspondence between p. 22 of the *Life,* where we are told that Lady Falkland would confess to 'finding much more delight in obliging than in being obliged', and ll. 657–8 of the play.

12

EARLY CRITICAL RECOGNITION OF ELIZABETH CARY AND MARGARET CAVENDISH

Myra Reynolds was one of a group of female critics and historians who, at the start of the twentieth century, located and analysed the works of early women writers. Text from Myra Reynolds (1920), *The Learned Lady in England 1650–1700*, Boston, MA: Houghton Mifflin Co., pp. 33–4 and 127–8.

Her [Elizabeth Cary's] work as an author began early, for her first play was written about the time of her marriage. It was dedicated to her husband. A second play, *The Tragedy of Mariam the Faire Queene of Jewry*, was written when she was eighteen or nineteen; though not printed till 1613. She was early recognised as one of the most intellectual women of her time.

The Duchess of Newcastle wrote numerous plays. Twenty-one were published in 1662, and in 1668 five more appeared. They are described as hardly more than allegorical dialogues arranged in successive scenes, but without plot, and showing no power of dramatic portrayal. The Duchess herself is evidently the original of several of the characters. In her plays as in her scientific studies the particular boast of the Duchess is that whatever she writes is spun out of her own fancy:

But noble readers, do not think my plays
Are such as have been writ in former days;
As Johnson, Shakespeare, Beaumont, Fletcher writ,
Mine want their learning, reading, language, wit.

It goes without saying that these plays were not suited for stage presentation, and, in point of fact, very few of them were ever put into rehearsal. One of the plays that did appear drew a great crowd, but the motive was curiosity to see the Duchess rather than any interest in the play.

13

WOOLF ON MARGARET CAVENDISH

Margaret Cavendish was one of the women writers rediscovered by Virginia Woolf and this early essay discussing her life and work was to lead to the more polemical focus on Early Modern women dramatists in *A Room of One's Own* (see pp. 23–4). Text from Virginia Woolf (1925), 'The Duchess of Newcastle', *The Common Reader. First Series*, London: Hogarth Press, pp. 106–7.

Worse still, without an atom of dramatic power, she turned to play-writing. It was a simple process. The unwieldy thoughts which turned and tumbled within her were christened Sir Golden Riches, Moll Meanbred, Sir Puppy Dogman, and the rest, and sent revolving in tedious debate upon the parts of the soul, or whether virtue is better than riches, round a wise and learned lady who answered their questions and corrected their fallacies at considerable length in tones which we seem to have heard before.

14

T. S. ELIOT ON SENECAN DRAMA

T. S. Eliot's comments upon Mary Sidney's 'shy recluses' dominated criticism of Early Modern closet drama and Sidney's own contribution to the dramatic genre for over sixty years. Text from T. S. Eliot (1927) 'Seneca in Elizabethan Translation', rpt. T. S. Eliot (1932) *Selected Essays*, London: Harcourt Brace Jovanovich, pp. 76–9.

It is improper to pass from the questions of Seneca's influence upon the Tragedy of Blood and upon the language of the Elizabethans without mentioning the group of 'Senecal' plays, largely produced under the aegis of the Countess of Pembroke. . . .

It was after Sidney's death that his sister, the Countess of Pembroke, tried to assemble a body of wits to compose drama in the proper Senecan style, to make head against the popular melodrama of the time. Great poetry should be both an art and a diversion; in a large and cultivated public like the Athenian it can be both; the shy recluses of Lady Pembroke's circle were bound to fail. But we must not draw too sharp a line of separation between the careful workman who laboured to create a classical drama in England and the hurried purveyors of playhouse successes: the two worlds were not without communication, and the work of the earlier Senecals was not without fruit. . . .

Now, in comparison with the supposed influence of Seneca on the barbarity of Elizabethan tragedy, and his supposed bad influence upon the language, what do we find in the plays of those who took him as their model in their attack upon the popular stage, in that attack in which Daniel, in his dedication *Of Cleopatra* to the Countess of Pembroke, declared himself the foe of 'Gross Barbarism'? Deaths there are, of course, but there is none of these tragedies that is not far more restrained, far more discreet and sober, not only than the Tragedy of Blood, but than Seneca himself. Characters die so decently, so remote from the stage, and the report of their deaths is wrapped up in such long speeches by messengers stuffed with so many moral maxims, that we may read on unaware that any one concerned in the play has died at all. Where the popular playwrights travestied Seneca's melodrama and his fury, the Senecals travesty his reserve and his decorum. And as for the language, that, too, is a different interpretation of Seneca. How vague are our notions of bombast and rhetoric when they must include styles and vocabularies so different as those of Kyd and Daniel! It is by opposite excesses that Senecals and popular dramatists attract the same reproach. The language of Daniel is pure and restrained; the vocabulary choice, the expression clear; there is nothing far-fetched, conceited, or perverse.

CLEOPATRA.

What, hath my face yet power to win a Lover?
Can this torne remnant serve to grace me so,
That it can Caesar's secret plots discover,
What he intends with me and mine to do?
Why then, poor beauty, thou hast done thy last,
And best good service thou could-'st do unto me;
For now the time of death reveal'd thou hast,
Which in my life did'st serve but to undo me.

The first two lines are admirable; the rest are good serviceable lines; almost any passage from *Cleopatra* is as good, and some are far better. The whole thing is in excellent taste. Yet we may ponder the fact that it would not have made the slightest difference, to the formation of our Augustan poetry, if Daniel and his friends had never written a line; that Dryden and Pope are nearer allied to Cowley; and that they owe more to Marlowe than to the purest taste of the sixteenth century. Daniel and Greville are good poets, and there is something to be learned from them; but they, and Sir John Davies who somewhat resembles them, had no influence. The only one of Lady Pembroke's heroes who had influence is Edmund Spenser.

15

VIRGINIA WOOLF ON 'JUDITH SHAKESPEARE'

In her seminal work on women writers, *A Room of One's Own*, Virginia Woolf addressed the question as to why there were no women playwrights in the English Renaissance, which was, after all, a golden age for drama. The passage quoted below has, since the late 1980s, become an important element in the criticism of Early Modern women dramatists and as such it is essential to include it here. Text from Virginia Woolf (1929), *A Room of One's Own*, London: Hogarth Press, pp. 69–75.

Be that as it may, I could not help thinking, as I looked at the works of Shakespeare on the shelf, that the bishop was right at least in this; it would have been impossible, completely and entirely, for any woman to have written the plays of Shakespeare in the age of Shakespeare. Let me imagine, since facts are so hard to come by, what would have happened had Shakespeare had a wonderfully gifted sister, called Judith, let us say. Shakespeare himself went, very probably, – his mother was an heiress – to the grammar school, where he may have learnt Latin – Ovid, Virgil and Horace – and the elements of grammar and logic. He was, it is well known, a wild boy who poached rabbits, perhaps shot a deer, and had, rather sooner than he should have done, to marry a woman in the neighbourhood, who bore him a child rather quicker than was right. That escapade sent him to seek his fortune in London. He had, it seemed, a taste for the theatre; he began by holding horses at the stage door. Very soon he got work in the theatre, became a successful actor, and lived at the hub of the universe, meeting everybody, knowing everybody, practising his art on the boards, exercising his wits in the streets, and even getting access to the palace of the queen. Meanwhile his extraordinarily gifted sister, let us suppose, remained at home. She was as adventurous, as imaginative, as agog to see the world as he was. But she was not sent to school. She had no chance of learning grammar and logic, let alone of reading Horace and Virgil. She picked up a book now and then, one of her brother's perhaps, and read a few pages. But then her parents came and told her to mend the stockings or mind the stew and not moon about with books and papers. They would have spoken sharply but kindly, for they were substantial people who knew the conditions of life for a woman and loved their daughter – indeed, more likely than not she was the apple of her father's eye. Perhaps she scribbled some pages up in an apple loft on the sly, but was careful to hide them or set fire to them. Soon, however, she was out of her teens, she was to be betrothed to the son of a neighbouring wool-stapler. She cried out that marriage was hateful to her, and for that she was severely beaten by her father. Then he ceased to scold her. He begged her instead not to hurt him, not to shame him in this matter of her marriage. He would give her a chain of beads or a fine petticoat, he said; and there were tears in his eyes. How could she disobey him? How could she break his heart? The force of her own gift alone drove her to it. She made up a small parcel of her belongings, let herself down by a rope one summer's night and took the road to London. She was not seventeen. The birds that sang in the hedge were not more musical than she was. She had the quickest fancy, a gift like her brother's, for the tune of words. Like him, she had a taste for the theatre. She stood at the stage door; she wanted to act, she said. Men laughed in her face. The manager – a fat, loose-lipped man – guffawed. He bellowed something about poodles dancing and women acting – no woman, he said, could possibly be an actress. He hinted – you can imagine what. She could get no training in her craft. Could she even seek her dinner in a tavern or roam the streets at midnight? Yet her genius was for fiction and lusted to feed abundantly upon the lives of men and women and the study of their ways. At last – for she was very young, oddly like Shakespeare the poet in her face, with the same grey eyes and rounded brows – at last Nick Greene the actor-manager took pity on her; she found herself with child by that gentleman and so – who shall measure the heat and violence of the poet's heart when caught and tangled in a woman's body? – killed herself one winter's night and lies buried at some crossroads where the omnibuses now stop outside the Elephant and Castle.

16

THE FIRST EDITION OF *THE CONCEALED FANCIES*

While Starr's editorial material is often somewhat condescending towards Jane Cavendish and Elizabeth Brackley, this was an important work since it contributed to the growing awareness of the Cavendish women's involvement in the production of drama. Text from Nathan Comfort Starr (1931), '*The Concealed Fansyes*: A Play by Lady Jane Cavendish and Lady Elizabeth Brackley', *Proceedings of The Modern Language Association* 46, pp. 803–5 and 837.

But to return to the young ladies at Welbeck. In August 1644, Welbeck Abbey surrendered to the Parliamentary forces at the demand of the Earl of Manchester. Extracts from the Earl's letter to the Committee of both kingdoms give an interesting account of the capture.

> . . . I was further moved by the Committee and gentlemen of Nottingham for the reducing of the garrison of Welbeck to the obedience of the Parliament, because it was a great annoyance to those parts . . . Upon my coming near Welbeck, I sent a summons to the place, and they with great civility sent to parley with me. The next day, Friday, they rendered the house to me upon composition.

After mentioning his generous terms, the strength of the garrison and the equipment found there, he continues:

> The house I preserved entire, and put a garrison into it of Notts' men . . . The place is very regularly fortified, and the Marquis of Newcastle's daughters, and the rest of his children and family are in it, unto whom I have engaged myself for their quiet abode there . . .

So here we have Newcastle's daughters brought into direct contact with the unpleasant realities of warfare. Bolsover Castle in Derbyshire surrendered on about August 16 to Major-General Crawford of the Parliamentary forces, and the young ladies were deprived of their other estate. So willy-nilly they had to stay at Welbeck, under the care of Colonel Thornhaugh, the commander of the garrison. Lord Fairfax must have exercised himself in their behalf, for in April, 1645, we find the Ladies Jane and Frances Cavendish writing him an interesting letter.

> For his Excellence the Lord Fairfax, these humbly present. May it please your Lordship, Your favors are so continued us, that they are not only to be acknowledged, but repeated as comforts, since your lordship's care of us we may justly confess is much beyond our merit. Now give us leave to present our humble thanks to your lordship for your noble favors, which oblige us as long as we live to owe your excellence a faithful acknowledgment. Colonel Bright hath been lately at Bolsover, and is to give your lordship some account of that garrison. We linger our remove from thence till we have some certainty of that business, hoping, that if he concur with the committee of Derby and some others for disgarrison of that place, to have the favour to be admitted to that house, which we the more desire by reason that town is assigned to us for maintenance, which will yield very little, I fear, if it continue still a garrison. However, whatsoever your excellence's pleasure, it shall be most welcome to Your lordship's most humble and obliged servants,
> Jane Cavendysshe
> Fra. Cavendysshe
>
> April 17th, 1645
> My sister Brackley presents her most humble service to your lordship, and gives your excellence many thanks for the favour of your lordship's protection.

But Welbeck was not yet lost for King Charles. In July, the former governor of the manor, Colonel Fretchville, and a Frenchman, Major Jammot, recaptured the Abbey in a brisk little engagement. Newcastle's daughters were almost certainly there at the time. And three weeks later the King himself stopped off there during his northern campaigning. However, in November, 1645, the Abbey seems again to have been in the hands of the Parliamentarians. As to the whereabouts of the ladies after this we have only the scantiest evidence. Certain it seems that both Welbeck and Bolsover were disgarrisoned by the Roundheads on November 13, 1645. But apparently troops were again quartered in the Derbyshire seat, for on September 5, 1645, an order was issued providing for the withdrawal of the troops, and the demolition of the castle. That Newcastle's daughters would have stayed at Bolsover seems unlikely. In the absence of evidence to the contrary one might assume that Welbeck was left in their charge. However, another possibility may be suggested. They all may have gone to Ashridge, the Hertfordshire seat of Lord Brackley. On the whole, this seems the more plausible theory, for the Ladies Jane and Frances certainly could not have relished staying alone at Welbeck. Lady Brackley, naturally, would have returned to her husband. And the play must certainly have been written by the two sisters in direct collaboration . . .

As a literary production, *The Concealed Fansyes* is practically without value. Its conformity to the Jonsonian comedy of humors, and its specific indebtedness to Jonson are sufficiently obvious without Detailed comment, nor is it necessary to dwell upon the resemblance between the brothers in the play and those of *Comus.* The chief interest of the work lies in the artless revelation of the activities of seventeenth century ladies of fashion, living in the country. As might be expected, the authors did not hesitate to use material based on the circumstances of their own family. With our knowledge of the historical background against which the ladies Cavendish were placed, we may even undertake to identify more or less certainly the characters in the play.

In the first place, it is well to remember that Jane Cavendish and Elizabeth Brackley had never met their famous step-mother (née Margaret Lucas) at the time *The Concealed Fansyes* was written. Doubtless they had heard of her from her brother Sir Charles Lucas, an officer in Newcastle's army, even before the Duke married her in Paris, during his exile. But that they were genuinely loyal to the memory of their own mother we can scarcely doubt. And probably they regarded Margaret Lucas as a clever schemer; an irresponsible upstart thirsting for advancement. It is certain that friends tried to prevent the impending match; for just what reason it is not quite clear. Even Queen Henrietta Maria attempted to dissuade her lady-in-waiting from the alliance. Rumors of these difficulties must certainly have reached England. Lady Tranquillity in the play probably is meant to be a thinly veiled representation of Margaret Lucas. When she first makes her appearance, she is pictured as vain and idle, scheming cleverly to win Mons. Calsindow's affections, through the aid of his daughters. But they will have nothing to do with her.

17

CARY AND 'A WOMAN'S DUTY'

In an interesting piece on 'Mariam' plays Valency commends Elizabeth Cary's *The Tragedy of Mariam* but depicts her as attacking her own sex. Text from Maurice J. Valency (1940), *The Tragedies of Herod and Mariamne*, New York: Columbia University Press, pp. 87–8 and 90–1.

However this may be, the *Tragedie of Mariam* is certainly not to be numbered among the outstanding Mariamne tragedies. It is noteworthy for a certain regularity; it adheres resolutely to the unities and is full of excellent maxims and long tirades; what action it has is handled with extreme decorum. Indeed, but a single action is represented, and that – a duel between Constabarus and Sillaeus – is hardly relevant to the main plot. With the exception of this romantic tidbit, all the action is messengered.

The plot is a curious jumble of material from Josephus, classical only in its superficial form, and very different from the pathetic tragedies of the French which served as models for this kind of drama. The play is episodic in structure, and makes a somewhat staccato effect . . .

True, E.C. goes somewhat beyond Josephus; she has a low opinion of women in general. None of her female characters are praiseworthy, and the entire sex is apostrophized bitterly in the farewell remarks of Constabarus:

> You creatures made to be the human curse,
> You Tygers, Lyonesses, hungry Beares,
> Teare massacring Hienas, nay far worse
>
> You are the least of goods, the worst of euils,
> Your best are worse than men.. your worst then divels.

Whether E.C.'s attitude toward her sex is to be construed as a tribute to her husband, or as a rebuke to the late queen and, by implication, a compliment to the reigning king, or whether this represents her honest opinion of womanhood, we cannot of course tell. The age had in general no exalted opinion of women; even the *Faerie Queene* occasionally evidences this, and Lady Falkland seems to have been utterly convinced of the truth of this estimate. Dunstan mentions the fact that she had the words *Bee and Seem* inscribed on her daughter's wedding ring, a maxim which is reflected in the chorus to Act Three of *Mariam*. If the play then has a general moral, it seems to be that even a tyrant is entitled to a humble, patient, and loving wife; in any case, it is a woman's duty to preserve appearances.

18

MARY SIDNEY, PHILIP'S SISTER

Even in the mid-twentieth century Mary Sidney's work was still being identified as dependent upon her brother's. Text from Virginia Walcott Beauchamp (1957), 'Sidney's Sister as Translator of Garnier', *Renaissance News* 10, pp. 12–13.

It is not therefore surprising that after Sidney's early death his beloved sister, Mary Herbert, Countess of Pembroke, setting herself the task of preserving his memory and of justifying his views, should look not to England or to Italy but to France for the drama that best exemplified his theories. In the *Marc Antoine* of Robert Gamier she was to find a perfect model for Sidney's picture of a good tragedy and an antithesis of the English type. If, in addition, a more closely personal motivation for her selection is to be allowed, it would lie, not in her own feministic predilections, but in the circumstance that Garnier's *Antoine* was largely based on the French Plutarch so strongly admired by her brother.

Her translation in 1590 of Garnier's *Antoine* became the prototype by means of which she hoped, in Sidney's honor, to reform the English theatre. That she failed, that the stage tradition she set out to destroy was in the next two decades to produce some of the great drama of all time, does not diminish her sincerity of purpose nor the nobility of her personal loyalty to Sidney. And, at any rate, the blend of Senecan manner and of Plutarchan materials, so distinctive a mark of her *Antoine,* established a precedent for most of the other plays produced by members of her coterie and constituted her particular obeisance to the memory and the critical precepts of her brother.

Part II

CONTEXTS AND ISSUES

INTRODUCTION

While most critical essays on women's involvement with drama in the Early Modern period focus upon specific authors or texts, there are several key areas which cut across individual authorship. The pieces in Part II all focus upon an issue which is important to our understanding of the way in which Renaissance women negotiated a route which allowed them to participate in the dramatic discourses of their day. The initial essay included here, Nancy Cotton's commentary on Renaissance noblewomen, was the first contemporary critical work undertaken on Early Modern women dramatists, and as such, it provides us with an important and essential starting point. Thus, the social group from which the Renaissance women dramatists arose was clearly identified as courtly by Cotton. The following two essays, by Barroll and Wynne-Davies, pursue this idea of the social context, while adding a sense of location: Leeds Barroll looks at the role of the court in allowing, and policing, women's dramatic activity, and Marion Wynne-Davies analyses the way in which the English country house served as an alternative arena for women's dramatic output. The next three essays all examine the way in which women gained access to drama through ancillary, but nevertheless important, activities. David M. Bergeron was the first contemporary critic to investigate the way in which women influenced theatre with their patronage. Jean E. Howard excavates the role of women as spectators and 'paying customers' in the Early Modern theatre. Finally, S. P. Cerasano has uncovered important evidence showing that women actually part-owned theatres in the English Renaissance. The last essay, by Gweno Williams, turns away from the history of the women dramatists, instead focusing upon the way in which their plays may be successfully produced today. Thus, the Contexts and Issues part of this book provides the reader with several possible channels of investigation, from social history to contemporary performance.

1

WOMEN PLAYWRIGHTS IN ENGLAND

Renaissance noblewomen

Nancy Cotton

Nancy Cotton published her pathbreaking book, *Women Playwrights in England, c.1363–1750*, in 1980 and in so doing changed the way in which English Renaissance drama was perceived. From that point on it was no longer possible to assume that Early Modern women dramatists did not exist, and a process of establishing them alongside their male counterparts gradually commenced. Cotton refers to all the women dramatists included here, with the exception of Mary Wroth, commenting upon their social context as well as upon specific texts, and thus provides a fundamental introduction to the material collected in this book.

The first recorded woman playwright in England was Katherine of Sutton, abbess of Barking nunnery in the fourteenth century. Between 1363 and 1376 the abbess rewrote the Easter dramatic offices because the people attending the paschal services were becoming increasingly cool in their devotions ('*deuocione frigessere*'). Wishing to excite devotion at such a crowded, important festival ('*desiderans . . . fidelium deuocionem ad tam celebrem celebracionem magis excitare*'), Lady Katherine produced unusually lively adaptations of the traditional liturgical plays.[1] Particularly interesting is her *elevatio crucis*, one of the few surviving liturgical plays that contains a representation of the harrowing of hell. In the *visitatio sepulchri* that follows, the three Marys are acted not by male clerics, which was customary, but by nuns.[2] The Barking plays are not unique, however, in showing the participation of nuns. In religious houses on the continent women sometimes acted in church dramas, and Hrotsvitha of Gandersheim and Hildegard of Bingen wrote Latin religious plays. Although the destruction of liturgical texts in England at the Reformation makes certainty impossible, it is likely, in view of the uniformity of medieval European culture and the considerable authority of women who headed the medieval nunneries, that other English abbesses contributed to the slow, anonymous, communal growth of the medieval religious drama.

Katherine of Sutton was a baroness in her own right by virtue of her position as abbess of Barking.[3] Only women of similar rank wrote drama in England until the Restoration. Virginia Woolf in her fable of Shakespeare's sister in *A Room of One's Own* (New York, 1929) was of course right in her statement that no middle-class woman, however talented, could have written for the Elizabethan public theaters. But Renaissance noblewomen, although they shared some of the disabilities of middle-class women, nonetheless wrote closet dramas, masques, and pastoral entertainments.

The English Renaissance fostered rigorous classical training for ladies, who, like male humanists, translated the ancients. The earliest extant English translation of a Greek play was the work of Lady Jane Fitzalan Lumley (*c.*1537–77), who made a free and abridged prose version of Euripides' *Iphigeneia in Aulis.*[4] Lady Lumley probably translated Euripides shortly after her marriage at the age of 12. This precocious marvel worked directly from the Greek at a time when secondhand translation from Latin was much more usual. The Latin tragedies of Seneca of course found many translators. Even Queen Elizabeth, during the early years of her reign, sometime around 1561, translated the chorus of Act II of *Hercules Oetaeus.*[5]

Imitations of Senecan tragedy were popular in aristocratic and academic circles. An influential figure in this tradition was Mary Sidney Herbert, Countess of Pembroke (1561–1621).[6] Mary Sidney studied at home with private tutors and attained proficiency in French, Italian, probably Latin, and perhaps Hebrew. At the queen's request, she lived for a time at court, which served her as a finishing school. When she was 16, her parents married her to Henry Herbert, Earl of Pembroke, a match economically and politically advantageous, even though the earl was nearly thirty years older than Mary. After her marriage Mary Herbert lived at Wilton House, the earl's home in Wiltshire, where she had four children, collected a notable library, and became famous as a translator, patron of literature, and editor of the *Arcadia.* The countess's dramatic activity grew out of her close relationship with her brother, Sir Philip Sidney (1554–86). In his *Defence of Poesie* Philip attacked English romantic drama, advocating instead the classical drama of Seneca. He admired a play 'full of stately speeches, and wel sounding phrases, clyming to the height of Seneca his style, and as full of notable morallitie, which it dooth most delightfully teach'.[7]

After Philip's death Mary translated the *Marc-Antoine* of Robert Garnier (1534–90), the most assured French Senecan dramatist, whose eight tragedies were notable for their vigorous but polished style. Written in 1590, the countess's *Antonie* transforms rhymed French alexandrines into pedestrian blank verse. Rather better are the choral lyrics, written in a variety of meters and rhymes. Here, for example, is the opening of the chorus to Act III:

> Alas, with what tormenting fire
> Us martireth this blinde desire
>   To staie our life from flieng!
> How ceaslеslie our minds doth rack,
> How heavie lies upon our back
>   This dastard feare of dieng!
> *Death* rather healthfull succor gives,
> *Death* rather all mishapps relieves
>   That life upon us throweth:
> And ever to us doth unclose
> The doore, wherby from curelesse woes
>   Our wearie soule out goeth.[8]

The Countess of Pembroke had *Antonie* printed in 1592 and thus became the first woman in England to publish a play. *Antonie* was reprinted in 1595, 1600, 1606, and 1607;[9] although unacted, it was widely influential. Swayed by example, or coerced by friendship or patronage, members of the countess's circle turned out numerous Senecan imitations.

Among the earliest, oddly enough, was a translation of Garnier's *Cornelie* made in 1594 by Thomas Kyd, who, as author of *The Spanish Tragedy* (1587), was the chief exponent at the time of the blood-and-thunder action drama. Presumably hoping for patronage, Kyd promised a translation of *Porcie*, but this never appeared. Samuel Daniel, long a protégé of the countess, wrote *Cleopatra* (1593) and *Philotas* (1604), the best of the plays on the Pembroke model. Samuel Brandon in 1598 published *The Virtuous Octavia*. Fulke Greville, Lord Brooke, Philip Sidney's friend and later biographer, wrote *Mustapha* and *Alaham* in the late 1590s, and in the next decade William Alexander, Earl of Stirling, published *Darius*, *Croesus*, and *The Alexandraean Tragedy*.

The countess also published a dramatic dialogue, which she wrote for the royal entertainment about 1592, when she was expecting a visit from the queen. A pastoral containing ten six-line stanzas, *Thenot and Piers in Praise of Astraea* was published in 1602 in the anthology *A Poetical Rhapsody*, which went through four editions by 1621. In each of the ten stanzas, Thenot's praise of Astraea (goddess of justice, a poetical name for Queen Elizabeth) is criticized by his fellow shepherd Piers. The last stanza, in a graceful turn of compliment, discloses why Piers is dissatisfied at praise of the queen:

Thenot. Then Piers, of friendship tell me why,
My meaning true, my words should ly,
And strive in vaine to raise her.
Piers. Words from conceit do only rise,
Above conceit her honour flies;
But silence, nought can praise her.[10]

This is the first original dramatic verse written by a woman to appear in print.

Before the Countess of Pembroke died, and probably because of her example, an Englishwoman for the first time wrote and published a full-length original play. This was Elizabeth Tanfield Cary, later Viscountess Falkland (1586–1639). More is known about Elizabeth Cary than about most figures of the period because one of her daughters wrote a detailed biography of her mother.[11] Lady Falkland was the only child and heiress of a wealthy Oxford lawyer, Lawrence Tanfield, later Sir Lawrence and Lord Chief Baron of the Exchequer. She was startlingly precocious, teaching herself French, Spanish, Italian, Latin, Hebrew, and 'Transylvanian' (*Life*, p. 5). She loved to read so much that she sat up all night. When her parents refused her candles, she bribed the maids to smuggle them in; by the age of 12 she had run up a debt to them of a hundred pounds 'with two hundred more for the like bargains and promises' (*Life*, p. 7), a considerable sum in those days even for an heiress. As a child she made translations from Latin and French and at 12 found internal contradictions in Calvin's *Institutes of Religion* – upsetting behavior for a child of good Protestants.

About the age of 15 or 16 Elizabeth Tanfield was married to a knight's son named Henry Cary. After the marriage had secured the Tanfield fortune, Henry followed the custom of the times and left his bride with her parents while he finished his military service abroad. During this period, sometime between 1602 and 1605, Elizabeth Cary, who, according to her daughter, loved plays 'extremely' (*Life*, p. 54), wrote two closet dramas. Cary's first play was set in Sicily and dedicated to her husband; the title is unknown and the play is lost. Her second play, dedicated to her sister-in-law, was *Mariam, the Fair Queen of Jewry*.

A Senecan tragedy based on Josephus's *Antiquities*, *Mariam* is carefully researched and constructed. The play is attentive to historical details but also is sensitive to dramatic effectiveness. As the play opens, rumor has just reached Jerusalem that Caesar has executed Herod at Rome. The first half of the play shows the effects of this news. Queen Mariam is torn between grief for her husband and joy. She rejoices at Herod's death because he had killed her brother and grandfather and because he had left orders for her own death in case he did not return. Pheroras, now happily freed from his brother's authority, immediately makes a love marriage with his maid Graphina. Herod's cast-off first wife Doris now hopes to unseat Mariam's children as heirs and install her own son Antipater on the throne. Only Salome regrets the loss of Herod, but her sorrow is self-interested. She wishes to marry her Arabian lover Silleus. If Herod were alive, she could accuse her husband Constabarus of treason for protecting the two sons of Baba. Salome also hates Mariam, but sees no way to remove her haughty sister-in-law. While these events are underway, constant pointers remind us that the characters believe the rumor of Herod's death because they wish to.

The reversal comes in 3.2 with the news that Herod is alive and will arrive immediately. Herod's delight as he returns in Act 4 is short-lived. Salome now has the upper hand and her machinations lead to the catastrophe. She offers to protect Pheroras and his bride if he will accuse Constabarus of treason. She tricks Herod into believing that Mariam has been unfaithful in his absence. Herod, a man of impulse, orders the executions of Constabarus, Baba's sons, and his own beloved queen. In Act 5 a nuntius recounts to Herod the noble death of Mariam. He also reports that Salome's agent in the plot against Mariam has confessed and committed suicide. Herod now realizes the magnitude of his loss and becomes frantic with grief.

The play is a sophisticated performance for a largely self-educated person of 17. Cary is careful with details, and the absence of anachronisms is unusual in the period. Stylistically and dramaturgically, the play is competently though conventionally Senecan. Action is discussed rather than dramatized, and the gory details of the execution are properly left to a nuntius. Cary uses literarily varied prosody instead of the dramatically supple blank verse of her theatrical contemporaries. *Mariam* is written in rhymed quatrains, with occasional couplets and sonnets inserted. Cary has, however, infused this dramatically awkward mixture of verse forms with emotional intensity at key points.

Salome, for example, is most convincing when she meditates an unorthodox method of removing Constabarus so that she can marry Silleus:

> He loves, I love; what then can be the cause,
> Keepes me f[rom] being the Arabians wife?
> It is the principles of Moses lawes,
> For Con[s]tabarus still remaines in life,
> If he to me did beare as Earnest hate,
> As I to him, for him there were an ease,
> A separating bill might free his fate:
> From such a yoke that did so much displease.
> Why should such priviledge to man be given?
> Or given to them, why bard from women then?
> Are men then we in greater grace with Heaven?
> Or cannot women hate as well as men?
> Ile be the custome-breaker: an beginne
> To shew my Sexe the way to freedomes doore.
> (sig. B3^r)

In the Renaissance this was of course villainess talk, but villainess or not, Salome was ahead of her time in her attitude toward equitable divorce laws.

The active and lustful Salome makes a provocative contrast with the passive and chaste Mariam, who initiates no action whatever, not even to save her own life. As she is facing death, she decides that her fault was a sullenness of temper that prevented her from defending herself. She feels guilty because she had placed her full reliance on her chastity of body without giving her husband her chastity of spirit; she had, then, been guilty of a certain infidelity of mind. This seems a harsh self-accusation for a woman whose husband had murdered two of her close relatives, but her conclusion is nonetheless reinforced by the chorus's strong statement of the duties of wives:

> When to their Husbands they themselves doe bind,
> Doe they not wholy give themselves away?
> Or give they but their body not their mind,
> Reserving that though best, for others pray?
> No sure, their thoughts no more can be their owne,
> And therefore should to none but one be knowne.
>
> Then she usurpes upon anothers right,
> That seekes to be by publike language grac't:
> And though her thoughts reflect with purest light,
> Her mind if not peculiar is not chast.
> For in a wife it is no worse to finde,
> A common body, then a common minde.
>
> (sig. E4[r])

These are hard beliefs for a woman who wished to be a writer.

The vividness of Cary's treatment of Mariam and Salome suggests that she had the range of emotional experience and the imaginative power to appreciate both attitudes toward experience. Cary apparently entered marriage with an impossible idealization of wifely behavior, which she expresses through Mariam, and with an even more impossible ideal of an independent, even rebellious, intellectual life, embodied in Salome. These deeply ambivalent attitudes shaped the remainder of her life. An intellectual heiress of Catholic leanings joined with a careerist courtier in a Protestant court, Cary lived with her husband twenty years, during which she bore eleven children and was nearly always either pregnant or nursing. Her intellectual and artistic talents found their only outlet in religion. During her marriage she continued to read theology and discussed religious doctrines with distinguished prelates. At the same time, she acted out her ideals of wifely behavior. She taught her children to love their father better than their mother. She acceded to her husband's wishes that she become a fashionable dresser and an accomplished horsewoman, despite her indifference to clothes and terror of horses. She mortgaged her jointure to advance her husband's career, whereupon her father disinherited her in favor of her oldest son, Lucius Cary, who also inherited his mother's literary talent. It is not surprising that she had periods of depression severe to the point of mental illness. Meanwhile, Henry Cary achieved a seat on the Privy Council, the rank of viscount, and the Lord Chief Deputyship of Ireland.

In 1626 Lady Falkland rebelled. She converted to Catholicism, nearly ruining her husband's career. He repaid her by abandoning her, taking custody of her children, and stripping her house of the bare necessities of life. Lady Falkland's poverty and suffering were severe; for long periods she lived in semistarvation. She appealed to the court for help (Queen Henrietta Maria was a French Catholic) and finally in 1627 the Privy Council ordered Lord Falkland to support his wife, although seven months later he still had not complied with the order. Lady Falkland turned again to writing, producing a life of Edward II, poems to the Virgin, and lives of saints. She translated Catholic polemics; her translation of Cardinal Perron's reply to King James was publicly burned. Lady Falkland kept her rebellious spirit to the end. In her last years she kidnapped two of her sons and, defying the Star Chamber, smuggled them to the continent to become Catholics.

Given the outward docility of Elizabeth Cary's married life until 1626, it is strange that *Mariam* was ever published. None of her other creative works were printed, and *Mariam* was not entered for publication until 1612, ten years after it was written, and did not actually appear until 1613. Her daughter claims, 'She writ many things for her private recreation . . . one of them was after stolen out of that sister-in-law's (her friend's) chamber, and printed, but by her own procurement was called in' (*Life*, p. 9). This explanation is suspect for a number of reasons, not the least of which is that the Stationers' Register shows that there was nothing surreptitious about the publication of the play.[12] Moreover, Lady Falkland's daughter makes the standard excuse of the period for an aristocrat who stoops to publication. Cary herself scorns such excuses in the introduction to her translation of Cardinal Perron: 'I will not make use of that worn form of saying I printed it against my will, moved by the importunity of friends.'[13]

A more likely explanation is that the publication of *Mariam* was inspired by the Countess of Pembroke. Both Mary Herbert and Elizabeth Cary were well acquainted with John Davies of Hereford, the famous master of calligraphy. Davies was a protégé and intimate of the Pembroke circle; he made a beautiful manuscript of Philip Sidney and Mary Herbert's translation of the psalms. He was also Elizabeth Cary's writing master. Davies must have spoken to his brilliant young pupil about his distinguished patroness and her activities. Indeed, the immediate cause that prompted Cary to publish her play may have been a poem by Davies. In 1612 he prefaced his 'Muse's Sacrifice, or Divine Meditations' with a poetical dedicatory letter to the Countess of Pembroke, the Countess of Bedford, and Elizabeth Cary. Davies compliments the Countess of Pembroke for her psalms and then praises 'Cary, of whom Minerva stands in feare':

> Thou mak'st Melpomen proud, and my Heart great
>   of such a Pupill, who, in Buskin fine,
> With Feete of State, dost make thy Muse to mete
>   the scenes of Syracuse and Palestine.
> . . .
> Such nervy Limbes of Art, and Straines of Wit
>   Times past ne'er knew the weaker Sexe to have;
> And Times to come, will hardly credit it,
>   if thus thou give thy Workes both Birth and Grave.[14]

Davies then chides all three ladies because they 'presse the Presse with little' they have written. Could the woman who wrote Salome's speech resist the appeal for publication on behalf of her sex's honor? *Mariam* was entered for publication in December of the same year as the appearance of Davies's poem. However *Mariam* came to be printed, and so preserved, it was never intended for acting. Neither the Countess of Pembroke nor Viscountess Falkland wrote their plays for the stage; *Antonie* and *Mariam* were written as closet drama. To write for the public stage was déclassé. It was a queen who broke down this barrier of caste and helped break down also the barriers against actresses.

Queen Henrietta Maria (1609–69) arrived in England at the age of 16 as the bride of Charles I.[15] In 1626, during her first year in her new country, the young queen acted at court in a pastoral play and masque that she herself wrote and directed. The play, which has been lost, was written in French and performed by the French ladies who attended the queen. Letters of Englishmen commenting on the occasion show the dismay produced even in an audience carefully handpicked:

> On Shrovetuisday the Quene and her women had a maske or pastorall play at Somerset House, wherin herself acted a part, and some of the rest were disguised like men with beards. I have knowne the time when this wold have seemed a straunge sight, to see a Quene act in a play but *tempora mutantur et nos.*

'I heare not much honor of the Quene's maske, for, if they were not all, soome were in men's apparell.' Ambassadors from continental courts were more sophisticated. The Venetian ambassador admired the 'rich scenery and dresses' and the 'remarkable acting' of the queen. 'The king and court enjoyed it, those present being picked and selected, but it did not give complete satisfaction, because the English objected to the first part being declaimed by the queen.' The ambassador from Florence was equally complimentary:

> She acted in a beautiful pastoral of her own composition, assisted by twelve of her ladies whom she had trained since Christmas. The pastoral succeeded admirably; not only in the decorations and changes of scenery, but also in the acting and recitation of the ladies – Her Majesty surpassing all the others. The performance was conducted as privately as possible, inasmuch as it is an unusual thing in this country to see the Queen upon a stage; the audience consequently was limited to a few of the nobility, expressly invited, no others being admitted.[16]

The English disapproval of the queen's performing a role on stage must have come as a surprise to Henrietta Maria. She had been reared in a court where nobility and even royalty acted in masques and plays. Her brother Louis XIII as a child led his brothers and sisters in amateur theatricals.

Although she has been suggested as the author of the anonymous lost pastoral *Florimene*, presented by the queen's ladies at court in December 1635, Henrietta Maria apparently wrote no more plays, but her incorrigible love of acting liberalized aristocratic attitudes towards actresses. After the disapproval of her 1626 court performance, she continued to have amateur theatricals in her private apartments and to dance in court masques. In 1633 she took the chief part in another play, *The Shepherd's Paradise*, written by the courtier Walter Montague for her and her ladies. Again there was a furor. Puritan William Prynne had the bad luck to publish *Histriomastix*, his attack on the stage, within a few days of the queen's performance. Prynne inopportunely denounced 'Women-Actors, notorious whores': 'And dare then any Christian woman be so more then whorishly impudent, as to act, to speak publicly on a Stage (perchance in man's apparel, and cut hair, here proved sinful and abominable) in the presence of sundry men and women?'[17] Prynne was condemned to have his ears cut off, the queen continued to act, amateur theatricals became common in polite circles, and by 1660 the profession of acting on the public stage was open to women. The admission of actresses to the stage was important for women playwrights because as actresses women for the first time obtained practical theatrical apprenticeship. By the eighteenth century there would be a number of actress-playwrights.

Henrietta Maria helped transform aristocratic attitudes not only toward actresses but also toward the commercial stage. She was the first English queen to attend plays at public theaters. Her considerable power over her husband caused Charles I to do what no English king had done before – he looked over scripts and even suggested plots for several plays written by others. The queen introduced from France the cults of *préciosité* and Platonic love and persuaded courtiers like Cartwright and Carlell to write plays illustrating her pet theories; thus the gentleman playwright came into existence. By the Restoration persons of the highest social rank in England were writing for the public stage.

This upper-class interest in playwrighting is seen in Lady Jane Cavendish (1621–69) and her sister Lady Elizabeth Brackley (*c.*1623–63).[18] The Cavendish sisters, daughters of William Cavendish, Duke of Newcastle, were, by both upbringing and marriage, part of the world of aristocratic theatricals. Before the war their father was a patron of the playwrights Brome, Shirley, and Jonson. In 1633 and 1634 Jonson wrote entertainments for the king's visits to the Newcastle estates; perhaps Jane and Elizabeth were present. About 1640 *The Country Captain*, publicly attributed to Newcastle but largely written by James Shirley, was performed at the Blackfriars Theatre. Lord Brackley, Elizabeth's future husband, in 1634 appeared with the king in Thomas Carew's masque *Coelum Britannicum*. The same year Brackley acted in Milton's *Comus* at Ludlow Castle; his sister and brother were also principal performers, their parents the chief spectators. With this background, it is not surprising that the Cavendish sisters should themselves write plays. Sometime between 1644 and 1646, the young women, both in their early twenties, collaborated on two plays. *A Pastoral* remains in manuscript, but *The Concealed Fansyes* was published in 1931. The authors here had promising raw material but were unable to construct a coherent plot. The story line, clumsily handled, shows a sound and simple comedic pattern: two sisters, Lucenay and Tattiney, are wooed by Courtly and Presumption. The men plan to tame their wives after marriage, but the women turn the tables and tame their husbands. The dialogue reflects the concerns of the authors as heiresses. Lucenay and Tattiney repeatedly and bluntly discuss marriage as the buying and selling of heiresses for dowries and estates. Lucenay dreads marriage: 'My distruction is that when I marry Courtly I shall bee condemn'd to looke upon my Nose, whenever I walke and when I sitt at meate confin'd by his grave winke to looke upon the Salt, and if it bee but the paireing of his Nales to admire him' (p. 815). After her marriage she describes how she escaped this servility. By refusing to keep her place, she throws her husband into a

> conflict, betwixt Anger and mallencholly not knoweinge whether my behaivour proceeded from neglect or ignorance, then hee declared himselfe by allygory and praysed a Lady, obedyent ffoole in towne, and swore hir Husband was the happyest man in the world. I replyed shee was a Very good Lady, and I accounted him happy that was hir Husband, that hee could content hinmselfe with such a Meachanick wife. I wishe sayd hee shee might bee your Example, and you have noe reason to sleight hir, for shee is of a noble family. I knowe that sayd I, and doe the more

> admire why shee will contract hir family, Noblenes and Birth, to the servitude of hir husband, as if hee had bought hir his slave, and I'm sure hir Father bought him for hir, for hee gave a good Portion, and now in sense who should obey?
>
> (pp. 834–5)

The conversational patterns are convincing; the use of indirect conversation suggests a writing skill born of epistolary, rather than dramatic, cultivation.

After collaborating with her sister in *The Concealed Fansyes*, Lady Jane Cavendish was present during the military action when the Parliamentarians captured and recaptured her home, Welbeck Abbey. She saved the art treasures of Bolsover Castle, another of the Newcastle estates. She raised money for her exiled father by selling her jewels and plate and sent him a thousand pounds of her private fortune. She refused to marry until the age of 33 because she refused anyone but a royalist, and at the time most royalists were in exile. After her marriage, she bore three children and continued to write, producing several volumes of verse. Nothing further is known of Lady Brackley.

The Cavendish sisters' young stepmother, Margaret Cavendish, Duchess of Newcastle (1623–73), was the first woman in England to publish collections of plays and England's first feminist playwright.[19] Her career as a prolific writer is surprising in view of her secluded upbringing and poor education. She was born Margaret Lucas, youngest of the eight children of a wealthy country gentleman who died before she was 2, leaving the family affairs in the strong hands of his wife. The family was exceptionally close-knit and exclusive, drawing the sons- and daughters-in-law into the family orbit. Margaret, as the youngest, grew up painfully shy of strangers. As a child she was indulged in her habit of wearing clothes of her own flamboyant design, one of the trademarks of the 'eccentricity' for which she was later notorious among her contemporaries. Her education was undisciplined. After the death of Queen Elizabeth, a reaction had set in against rigorous studies for gentlewomen. Margaret describes an education almost negative:

> As for tutors, although we had for all sorts of virtues, as singing, dancing, playing on music, reading, writing, working, and the like, yet we were not kept strictly thereto, they were rather for formality than benefit; for my mother cared not so much for our dancing and fiddling, singing and prating of several languages, as that we should be bred virtuously, modestly, civilly, honorably, and on honest principles.[20]

Her lack of education marred all her writing; she never absorbed some elementary principles of grammar, and the idea of revision was unknown to her. Later in life, Margaret felt keenly her lack of learning and spoke strongly for education for women.

At the age of 20, the bashful Margaret Lucas astonished her family (and her biographers) by attending the distressed Queen Henrietta Maria as a maid of honor and then following the queen into exile in France. The explanation of her puzzling behavior is that Margaret was a female cavalier, whose romantic gesture for a lost cause was in the spirit of the age. In France she met and married the exiled Marquis, later Duke, of Newcastle, thirty years her senior, whom she adored with fervent hero worship. Her marriage was an ideal one for a seventeenth-century woman writer. William Cavendish was himself an amateur poet and playwright, and a generous patron of writers, philosophers, and artists. He encouraged and assisted his young, beautiful, childless wife in her writing, her 'chiefest delight and greatest pastime' (*Plays Never Before Printed*, 1668). She describes their relationship in a letter to the duke in her *Philosophical and Physical Opinions* (1663):

> Though I am as Industrious and Carefull to serve Your Lordship in such imployments, which belong to a Wife, as Household affairs, as ever I can . . . yet I cannot for my Life be so good a Huswife, as to quit Writing . . . . you are pleased to Peruse my Works, and Approve of them so well, as to give me Leave to Publish them, which is a Favour, few Husbands would grant their Wives; But Your Lordship is an Extraordinary Husband, which is the Happiness of Your Lordships Honest Wife and Humble Servent Margaret Newcastle.

After her marriage, she began, out of ambition, to write with a view to publication: 'I am very ambitious, yet 'tis neither for beauty, wit, titles, wealth, or power, but as they are steps to raise me to Fame's tower, which is to live by remembrance in afterages.'[21] This desire for fame is the key to her personality.[22] She saw literature as the only avenue to renown for a woman:

> I confess my Ambition is restless, and not ordinary; because it would have an extraordinary fame: And since all heroick Actions, publick Imployments, powerfull Governments, and eloquent Pleadings are denyed our Sex in this age, or at least would be condemned for want of custome, is the cause I write so much.
>
> (An Epistle to my Readers, *Natures Pictures*, 1656)

The first Englishwoman to publish extensively, the duchess produced a dozen books, including poetry, fiction, scientific and philosophical speculations, letters, and declamations. She was the first woman in England to publish her autobiography, the first to publish a biography of her husband, the first to write about science.

In 1662 the duchess published *Plays*, a collection of closet dramas written while she was abroad. The volume includes fourteen plays, several in two parts. In 1668 she brought out a smaller collection, *Plays Never Before Printed*, which includes five plays and various dramatic fragments. In these volumes are some of the most ardently feminist plays ever written. In Part II of *Loves Adventures*, for example, Lady Orphan, disguised as the page Affectionata, wins great fame as a soldier; the Venetian States make her Lieutenant-General of the army and a member of the Council of War. The Pope invites Affectionata to Rome and offers to make her a cardinal.

Another military woman, Lady Victoria, appears in *Bell in Campo*. Refusing to be left at home when her husband goes to war, Lady Victoria raises a female army and accompanies the men to battle. Victoria points out to her troops that masculine contempt for female ability ultimately rests on the physical weakness of women, but urges that right education could make women good soldiers, 'for Time and Custome is the Father and Mother of Strength and Knowledge' (*Plays*, p. 588). She urges:

> Now or never is the time to prove the courage of our Sex, to get liberty and freedome from the Female Slavery, and to make our selves equal with men: for shall Men only sit in Honours chair, and the Women stand as waiters by? shall only Men in Triumphant Chariots ride, and Women run as Captives by? shall only men be

> Conquerors, and women Slaves? shall only men live by Fame, and women dy in Oblivion?
>
> (*Plays*, p. 609)

Encouraged by Victoria, the woman army achieves heroic exploits, rescuing the men from military disaster. They are rewarded after the war with special privileges. Lady Victoria herself is given a public triumph, a suit of gold armor, and a sword with a diamond hilt; her statue is set up in the center of the city.

In *Youth's Glory and Death's Banquet* Sir Thomas Father Love, over the objections of Lady Mother Love, is rearing their daughter, Lady Sanspareille, with an education masculine and intellectual:

> *Mother Love.* What? would you have women bred up to swear, swagger, gaming, drinking, whoring, as most men are?
>
> *Father Love.* No, Wife, I would have them bred in learned Schools, to noble Arts and Sciences, as wise men are.
>
> *Mother Love.* What Arts? to ride Horses, and fight Dewels.
>
> *Father Love.* Yes, if it be to defend their Honour, Countrey, Religion; For noble Arts makes not base Vices, nor is the cause of lewd actions, nor is unseemly for any Sex.
>
> (*Plays*, p. 124)

Lady Sanspareille is melancholy because of her desire for fame, which she describes in words like those that Margaret used about herself:

> Know it is fame I covet, for which were the ambitions of Alexander and Caesar joyned into one mind, mine doth exceed them . . . my mind being restless to get to the highest place in Fames high Tower; and I had rather fall in the adventure, than never try to climb.

She despairs that she may not have 'a sufficient stock of merit, or if I had, yet no waies to advance it' (*Plays*, p. 130). She resolves, with her father's consent, never to marry, but to devote herself to poetry:

> for that time which will be lost in a married condition, I will study and work with my own thoughts, and what new inventions they can find out, or what probabilityes they conceive, or phancies they create, I will publish to the world in print . . . but if I marry, although I should have time for my thoughts and contemplations, yet perchance my Husband will not approve of my works, were they never so worthy, and by no perswasion, or reason allow of there publishing; as if it were unlawfull, or against nature, for Women to have wit. . . . some men are so inconsiderately wise, gravely foolish and lowly base, as they had rather be thought Cuckolds, than their wives should be thought wits, for fear the world should think their wife the wiser of the two.
>
> (*Plays*, p. 131)

In Part II Lady Sanspareille fulfills her ambitions, addressing assemblies of amazed savants on learned and literary topics. After her untimely death, her memory is preserved by statues set up in all the colleges and public places in the city.[23]

While interesting for their early feminist heroines, the Duchess of Newcastle's plays are the poorest of her works. Her plays, like those of her stepdaughters, are structurally incoherent. She produces original and arresting raw materials for plots that are never constructed; actions are discussed rather than dramatized. Her usual method of organization is to take three unrelated story lines and alternate scenes among them mechanically. Often the individual scenes have no beginning, middle, or end; one scene simply stops abruptly and an unrelated scene follows. The most common type of scene is a dialogue or trialogue in which one character orates, harangues, or lectures to the other(s). Occasionally there is a real conversation, but generally there is no interaction among characters. The characters are personified abstractions, such as The Lord Fatherly, The Lord Singularity, The Lady Ignorant; and development of such characters rarely occurs.

The duchess was aware of these obvious flaws: 'Some of my Scenes have no acquaintance or relation to the rest of the Scenes; although in one and the same Play, which is the reason so many of my Playes will not end as other Playes do' (To the Reader, *Plays*). She offered this poem as 'A General Prologue to all my Playes':

> But Noble Readers, do not think my Playes,
> Are such as have been writ in former daies;
> As Johnson, Shakespear, Beaumont, Fletcher writ;
> Mine want their Learning, Reading, Language, wit:
> The Latin phrases I could never tell,
> But Johnson could, which made him write so well,
> Greek, Latin Poets, I could never read,
> Nor their Historians, but our English Speed;
> I could not steal their Wit, nor Plots out take;
> All my Playes Plots, my own poor brain did make
> From Plutarchs story I ne'r took a Plot,
> Nor from Romances, nor from Don Quixot,
> As others have, for to assist their Wit,
> But I upon my own Foundation writ.

There is another reason for the peculiar structure of her plays. In the 1662 collection she says that she wrote her plays from her husband's example, and, indeed, the duchess's plays follow the pattern of the duke's unaided efforts. An example of his unretouched work survives, *A Pleasante & Merrye Humor of A Roge*,[24] an unstructured dramatic sketch. Professional playwrights like Dryden, Shirley, and Shadwell turned the duke's sketches into professional plays which were then performed in the London theaters. The duchess, looking up to her husband, assumed that this was the way plays were written: 'I have heard that such Poets that write Playes, seldome or never join or sow the several Scenes together; they are two several Professions.' She explains that, as her plays were written while she was in exile, she was 'forced to do all my self . . . without any help or direction' (To the Readers, *Plays*).

Structurally incoherent as they are, the plays of the Duchess of Newcastle are historically significant as early feminist statements. They made a statement to her contemporaries partly by their physical appearance. The two volumes of plays, like all the duchess's works, were large, handsome books with sumptuous engravings of the author's portrait. Her title pages carried the resounding ascription 'Written by the Thrice Noble, Illustrious, and Excellent Princess, the Duchess of Newcastle.' With princely arrogance, she sent copies to friends, protégés, and even to the libraries of the universities. And no matter how much she was ridiculed, she was too rich and powerful to be ignored. Her books, although often empty of artistic worth, existed, and the medium – handsome folios written by a woman – was the message.

Contrary to general contemporary belief, none of her plays was performed. Pepys, on 30 March 1667, recorded, 'Did by coach go to see the silly play of my Lady Newcastle's called "The Humourous Lovers".' A month later Pepys was still unaware that the play was a professional version of one of the duke's sketches. In April he wrote that the duchess 'was the other day at her own play, *The Humourous Lovers*.'[25] The same play was attributed to the duchess by others. In May 1667, Gervase Jaquis wrote to the Earl of Huntington, 'Upon monday last the Duchess of Newcastls play was Acted in the theater in Lincolns Inne field the King and the Grandees of the Court being present and soe was her grace and the Duke her husband.'[26]

Notes

1 Katherine of Sutton's plays are preserved in the Barking ordinarium. Sibille Felton, abbess of Barking from 1394 to 1419, caused this to be written and presented it to the convent in 1404. Karl Young was the first to publish the Barking plays, in 'The Harrowing of Hell in Liturgical Drama,' *Transactions of the Wisconsin Academy of Sciences, Arts, and Letters* 16 (1910): 888–947. Young later included the plays in his *Drama of the Medieval Church*, 2 vols (Oxford: Clarendon Press, 1933), 1: 164–6, 381–4. Meanwhile, the entire ordinale had been edited by J. B. L. Tolhurst and printed in two volumes of the Henry Bradshaw Society Publications in 1927–8. The Latin quotations are from Young, *Drama*, 1: 165.

2 Although English women did not act on the public stage until almost exactly three hundred years later, they participated more widely in English medieval drama than is generally realized. Women belonged to religious gilds responsible for plays – for example, the York Pater Noster Gild and the Norwich St Luke's Gild – and participated to some extent in the trade gilds. See Karl Young, 'The Records of the York Play of the *Pater Noster*,' *Speculum* 7 (1932): 544; Lucy Toulmin Smith (ed.) *York Plays* (Oxford: Clarendon Press, 1885), pp. xxviii–xxxix; Harold C. Gardiner, *Mysteries' End*, Yale Studies in English, 103 (New Haven, CT: Yale University Press, 1946), p. 42; Eileen Power, *Medieval Women* (Cambridge: Cambridge University Press, 1975), pp. 55–69. At Chester the 'wurshipffull wyffys' of the town bound themselves to bring forth the pageant of the Assumption of the Virgin. This pageant was a regular part of the Chester cycle until it was excised at the Reformation. The wives acted their play separately in 1488 before Lord Strange and again in 1515. See W. W. Greg (ed.) *The Trial and Flagellation with Other Studies in the Chester Cycle*, Malone Society Studies (Oxford: Oxford University Press, 1935), pp. 137, 170–1; F. M. Salter, *Mediaeval Drama in Chester* (Toronto: University of Toronto Press, 1955), pp. 50, 70–1. Women also participated in church *ludi*. There are records of an Abbess of Fools or Girl Abbess elected from the novices on Holy Innocents' Day at the nunneries of Godstow and Barking in the thirteenth century. See Eileen Power, *Medieval English Nunneries c. 1275–1535* (Cambridge: Cambridge University Press, 1922), p. 312.

3 Barking was an abbey holding of the king in chief; as tenant in chief, Katherine of Sutton was a baroness in her own right. She was almost certainly a noblewoman by birth also. In the later Middle Ages Barking accepted novitiates only from the aristocracy and the wealthiest bourgeois class; moreover, the nun of highest social rank usually became abbess. See Power, *Medieval English Nunneries*, pp. 4–13, 42.

4 Information about Lady Lumley is taken from the introduction to *Iphigeneia at Aulis*, edited

by Harold H. Child for the Malone Society Reprints (London: Chiswick Press, 1909). Myra Reynolds, *The Learned Lady in England 1650–1760* (Boston, MA: Houghton Mifflin, 1920), pp. 13–14, also discusses Lady Lumley.

5 In *The Poems of Elizabeth I*, ed. Leicester Bradner (Providence, RI: Brown University Press, 1964).

6 Biographical information is taken from Frances Berkeley Young, *Mary Sidney Countess of Pembroke* (London: David Nutt, 1912) and Mona Wilson, *Sir Philip Sidney* (London: Duckworth, 1931). *Antonie* has been edited by Alice Luce (Weimer: E. Felber, 1897) and by Geoffrey Bullough in *Narrative and Dramatic Sources of Shakespeare*, 8 vols. (New York: Columbia University Press, 1957–75), 5: 358–406. The translation of the psalms by the Countess of Pembroke and Sir Philip Sidney has been edited by J. C. A. Rathmell (Garden City, NY: Doubleday, 1963). This volume is supplemented by G. F. Waller, *'The Triumph of Death' and Other Unpublished Poems by Mary Sidney, Countess of Pembroke* (Salzburg: Institut für Englische Sprache und Literatur, 1977). The Pembroke circle of Senecan writers is discussed by John W. Cunliffe, *The Influence of Seneca on Elizabethan Tragedy* (London: Macmillan, 1893); Joan Rees, *Samuel Daniel* (Liverpool: Liverpool University Press, 1964); Cecil Seronsy, *Samuel Daniel* (New York: Twayne, 1967). T. S. Eliot discusses the influence of the Pembroke circle in 'Apology for the Countess of Pembroke,' *The Use of Poetry and the Use of Criticism* (London: Faber and Faber, 1933). Mary Herbert is memorialized beautifully but stereotypically in 'On the Countesse Dowager of Pembroke,' long ascribed to Ben Jonson but written by William Browne of Tavistock, in *Ben Jonson*, ed. C. H. Herford and Percy and Evelyn Simpson (Oxford: Clarendon Press, 1925–52), 8: 433.

7 *The Complete Works of Sir Philip Sidney*, ed. Albert Feuillerat (Cambridge: Cambridge University Press, 1912–26), 3: 38.

8 *The Countess of Pembroke's 'Antonie'*, ed. Luce, p. 97.

9 A. W. Pollard and G. R. Redgrave, *A Short-Title Catalogue of Books Printed in England, Scotland, and Ireland 1475–1640* (London: The Bibliographical Society, 1926), pp. 255, 412.

10 *A Poetical Rhapsody*, ed. Hyder Rollins (Cambridge, MA: Harvard University Press, 1931), 1: 17.

11 This was edited and published in 1861 by Richard Simpson as *The Lady Falkland: Her Life* (London: Catholic Publishing Company). In-text citations refer to this volume. Two biographies based on the *Life* are Lady Georgiana Fullerton, *The Life of Elisabeth Lady Falkland* (London: Burns and Oates, 1883) and Kenneth B. Murdock, *The Sun at Noon* (New York: Macmillan, 1939), pp. 6–38. Both are concerned with Cary as a Catholic convert; neither is aware of her unique position in the history of English drama. *Mariam* was edited for the Malone Society Reprints by A. C. Dunstan and W. W. Greg (Oxford: Oxford University Press, 1914). In-text citations refer to this edition; I have modernized the u/v and i/j conventions and discarded nonfunctional italics. *Mariam* is discussed at length by A. C. Dunstan in *Examination of Two English Dramas* (Königsberg: Hartungsche Buchdruckerei, 1908). Dunstan also discusses Cary's use of source material in the introduction to the Malone Society edition of the play. *Mariam* is briefly discussed by Alexander Witherspoon, *The Influence of Robert Garnier on Elizabethan Drama* (New Haven, CT: Yale University Press, 1924), pp. 150–5, and Maurice J. Valency, *The Tragedies of Herod and Mariamne* (New York: Columbia University Press, 1940), pp. 87–91. Valency points out that Cary's *Mariam* is the first of many English plays written about Herod and Mariamne. Donald A. Stauffer, 'A Deep and Sad Passion,' *The Parrott Presentation Volume*, ed. Hardin Craig (1935; reprinted, New York: Russell and Russell, 1967), pp. 289–314, shows that Elizabeth Cary wrote *The History of Edward II*, formerly ascribed to Henry Cary.

12 Introduction to the Malone Society edition, p. ix.

13 Quoted by Fullerton, *Life of Lady Falkland*, p. 120.

14 *The Complete Works of John Davies of Hereford*, ed. Alexander Grosart (Edinburgh: Edinburgh University Press, 1878), 2: 4–5.

15 Biographical information is taken from Carola Oman, *Henrietta Maria* (London: Hodder and Stoughton, 1936). Henrietta Maria's pervasive influence on theatrical history is discussed in detail by Alfred Harbage, *Cavalier Drama* (1936; reprinted, New York: Russell and

Russell, 1964), which suggests the queen as the author of *Florimene*; and by Kathleen M. Lynch, *The Social Mode of Restoration Comedy* (New York: Macmillan, 1926).

16 Quotations are from Gerald Eades Bentley, *The Jacobean and Caroline Stage* (Oxford: Clarendon Press, 1941–68), 4: 548–9.

17 Quoted by Harbage, *Cavalier Drama*, pp. 14–15.

18 Except for my inferences about the effect of Newcastle's dramatic activities on his daughters, biographical information on the Cavendish sisters is taken from the DNB and from Nathan Comfort Starr's introduction to his edition of *The Concealed Fansyes* in *Proceedings of the Modern Languages Association* 46 (1931): 802–38. Page references in the text refer to Starr's edition. Harbage, *Cavalier Drama*, pp. 228–9, describes the plays of the Cavendish sisters.

19 I have drawn on a number of sources for biographical information. Standard and useful are Douglas Grant, *Margaret the First* (Toronto: University of Toronto Press, 1957) and Henry Ten Eyck Perry, *The First Duchess of Newcastle and Her Husband as Figures in Literary History* (Boston, MA: Ginn, 1918). Of the numerous biographical essays, the finest is Virginia Woolf's in *The Common Reader* (New York: Harcourt, Brace, 1925), pp. 101–12. The best source of biographical material is the duchess herself, particularly in the introductions, dedications, and letters in her various works. Her autobiography, 'A True Relation of my Birth, Breeding, and Life,' originally the last section of *Natures Pictures* (1656), is included by C. H. Firth in his edition of the duchess's *Life of William Cavendish, Duke of Newcastle* (London: John C. Nimmo, 1886). These two works of the duchess are available in several editions. Firth also prints the duchess's letter 'To the Two Most Famous Universities of England,' a moving appeal for education for women.

20 'A True Relation,' ed. Firth, pp. 157–8.

21 Ibid., p. 177.

22 My interpretation draws upon Jean Gagen, 'Honor and Fame in the Works of the Duchess of Newcastle,' *Studies in Philology* 56 (1959): 519–38.

23 Jean Gagen focuses on this type of character, which she calls 'the oratorical lady,' in her excellent discussion of the duchess's plays in 'A Champion of the Learned Lady,' ch. 2 in *The New Women: Her Emergence in English Drama 1600–1730* (New York: Twayne, 1954). Gagen's discussion led me to examine the pervasive feminism in the duchess's plays.

24 Francis Needham (ed.) *Welbeck Miscellany*, 1 (1933) from a fair copy in the duke's handwriting.

25 *Pepys on the Restoration Stage*, ed. Helen McAfee (New Haven, CT: Yale University Press, 1916), pp. 171–2.

26 *The London Stage, 1600–1700*, ed. William Van Lennep (Carbondale, IL: Southern Illinois University Press, 1965), p. 108. Harbage, *Cavalier Drama*, pp. 232–3, suggests that the duchess wrote at least the first draft of *Lady Alimony*, performed at the Cockpit in 1659. While the play is structurally odd and schematic enough to be hers, its anonymity is conclusive proof against her authorship.

2

THE ARTS AT THE ENGLISH COURT OF ANNA OF DENMARK

Leeds Barroll

In this new essay Leeds Barroll challenges the conventional view of Anna of Denmark as subservient to her husband, James I, in matters of patronage, and consequently lacking any input into the cultural milieu of her period. Instead, Barroll uncovers a female monarch who was at the very centre of Early Modern artistic production and whose influence was equally as powerful as that of the king. This essay therefore demands a rereading of the role of women in the Jacobean court and clearly demonstrates that the court itself was a strong basis for female involvement in the dramatic arts.

Feminist criticism since the mid-1970s has contributed substantially to our understanding of female authorship and artistic production in Early Modern England, and thus to a critical reconfiguration of Shakespeare's cultural milieu. The emphasis in much of this criticism, however, has been on the emergence of voices in non-aristocratic settings – on the experiences of those women who collectively represent a large segment of the English population. This essay samples different voices by considering the influence of Queen Anna of Denmark, Consort to James I, and her court on the production of Early Modern high culture.[1] These voices may add usefully to the chorus both as a necessary complement to the important feminist work just described, and as a corrective to the traditional (and mostly male-authored) view of Anna herself as an insignificant cultural force.

Further, the complex, politically based networks of court patronage in Shakespeare's time do form an essential component in the cultural picture that we are trying to develop for the Early Modern period. Many of those recently identified women artists who are now reformulating the literary canons of the period were themselves inevitably connected to, and influenced by, aristocracy-based systems of patronage. Yet the critical assumption that in the Jacobean court these systems were male-dominated has, I believe, greatly distorted the evidence for how these cultural networkings fashioned themselves, and thereby shrouded our understanding not only of the artistic production of the court, but consequently of the larger society lying outside of it. This problem of misperception may, I suggest, be usefully addressed through a revisionist account of Anna's court that focusses not only on what art may be associated with it, but also – and just as importantly – on who made this association possible. The evidence for Anna's centrality in the high culture of the Jacobean period is to be found, literally, all around her – in the group of people she personally assembled to showcase her own importance as consort through the agency of art. This all began – her court was partially configured – in the speed with which James, after he was proclaimed king in March 1603, travelled to England with his entourage but without the queen. The English noblewomen that Anna of Denmark would naturally require to constitute her own new train would not be immediately available since they awaited the funeral in London of Queen Elizabeth on 28 April. Deciding that his queen could meet the majority of the English female nobility when she approached London in July, James ordered the English Privy Council on 15 April to send 'some of the ladies of all degrees who were about the [old] Queen, as soon as the funerals be past – or some others whom you shall think meetest and most willing to abide travel.'[2] Robert Cecil and the Privy Council complied, choosing noblewomen according to their own political criteria which resulted, as one contemporary put it, in the selection of 'two countesses, two baronesses, two ladies, and two maids of honor' to ride north 'with an escort of two hundred horse.'[3]

A brief glance at the two countesses selected by Cecil and the Privy Council suggests the political nature of this privileged female group. One countess was the wife of Edward Somerset 4th Earl of Worcester (a member of the Privy Council), who had become Queen Elizabeth's Master of the Horse after Essex lost that position.[4] The Countess of Worcester, born Elizabeth Hastings, had long attended Queen Elizabeth.[5] The other countess was Frances Howard, Countess of Kildare, whose father, the Lord Admiral, Charles Howard Earl of Nottingham (also a member of the Privy Council) had been the only baron created earl by Queen Elizabeth during the last twenty years of her reign. First married to Henry Fitzgerald [Irish] Earl of Kildare, who died in 1597, Frances was now the wife of Henry Brooke 11th Lord Cobham, who held the crucial position of Warden of the Cinque Portes.[6] Lady Kildare had also been one of Queen Elizabeth's ladies, close enough to the monarch to have reputedly attempted to prejudice her against the wife of Sir Walter Ralegh.[7]

This arrangement for surrounding the new queen with Elizabeth's former attendants was, however, circumvented. As Howes, in his continuation of the Stow chronicles, respectfully put it long after Anna of Denmark's new court was a *fait accompli*: 'Before the departure of these personages aforesaid [the official group], diverse ladies of honor went voluntarily into Scotland, to attend her Majesty in her journey into England.'[8] This second group, led by Lucy Russell, Countess of Bedford,[9] moved quickly north, presumably before Anna arrived in Berwick-on-Tweed, and captured the new queen. For the Countess of Bedford was speedily appointed to the highest position in the court of Anna of Denmark, that of her only English Lady of the Bed Chamber.[10]

Bedford's appointment has significant implications for the nature of the new queen's English court and its artistic connections because, through kinship, marriage, and friendships, she was part of a circle that included the most significant patrons of literature, drama, painting, and music in England.[11] The Countess of Bedford's father, Sir John Harington of Exton, was first cousin to Sir Philip Sidney and, of course, his two surviving siblings, Mary (née Sidney) Countess of Pembroke and Sir Robert Sidney. Mary Sidney's sons were the young Earl of Pembroke and his brother the future Earl of Montgomery, both to be dedicatees of the Shakespeare First Folio. But the appointment of the Countess of Bedford as Anna of Denmark's first Lady also brought the Essex group into Anna's purview because the Earl of Essex had married Sir Philip Sidney's widow Frances Walsingham. Lady Walsingham's daughter by Sir Philip married Essex's life-long friend, Roger Manners, Earl of Rutland, and both Essex and Rutland were close to the Earl of Bedford (Lucy Bedford's husband). Rutland and Bedford, in fact, along with the Earl of Southampton, rode with Essex in his London uprising of 1601. At the same time, Lucy Bedford was close to both of the Earl of Essex's sisters, Penelope Rich and Dorothy, Countess of Northumberland (one of whose daughters was named Lucy[12]).

The coherence of this group and its potential for the cultural configuration of the new queen's court through the influence of the Countess of Bedford, are suggested long before James's accession. A supper at Essex House on 14 February 1598 included 'my Ladies Leicester, Northumberland, Bedford, Essex, Rich: and my Lords of Essex, Rutland, Mountjoy, and others. They had two plays which kept them up till 1 o'clock after midnight.'[13] Four years later, in late 1602, three months prior to James's accession, the Countess of Bedford's father, Sir John Harington, had guests for the holidays: 'the Earls of Rutland and Bedford, Sir John Gray and Sir Henry Carey with their ladies, the Earl of Pembroke, Sir Robert Sidney [uncle to Pembroke and to the Countess of Rutland] and many more gallants.'[14] All were spending the last Christmas of Elizabeth's reign as guests of the father of that countess who would become Anna of Denmark's most influential lady.[15]

Undoubtedly the 28-year-old Countess of Bedford was immediately attractive to the 29-year-old Anna of Denmark at their first meeting in 1603. As early as 15 June, Lady Anne Clifford, who, at age 14, must, to some extent, have been echoing the sentiments of her mother, the Countess of Cumberland, and of her aunt, the Countess of Warwick, observed that 'my Lady of Bedford' was already 'so great a woman with the Queen' that everybody much respected her – 'she having attended the Queen from out of Scotland.'[16] And on 25 June, when the queen's progress reached Althorp in Northamptonshire, Bedford was still the only countess appointed to Anna's most prestigious Bed Chamber. Significantly, the only other lady mentioned as in favor with the new queen – one from the official group sent north by the Privy Council – was Penelope Rich, a member, as noted, of the social group that included Lucy Bedford.[17]

Official appointments to Anna's court (except that of the Countess of Bedford) did not surface, however, until months later – 2 February 1604 – when the Earl of Worcester, now James's Master of the Horse, described three groupings of women around the new queen. These were described, as if in descending degrees of status, as ladies belonging to the 'Bed Chamber,' the 'Drawing Chamber,' and the 'Private Chamber.'[18] Here is Worcester's list of names, in his order.

'Bed-Chamber':	The Countess of Bedford The Countess of Hertford
'Drawing-Chamber':	The Countess of Derby The Countess of Suffolk Penelope Lady Rich The Countess of Nottingham Susan de Vere [Audrey] Lady Walsingham [Elizabeth] Lady Southwell
'Private Chamber':	'All the rest.'

'Maids of Honor': Cary
Middlemore
Woodhouse[19]
Gargrave
Roper

(Lodge, 3.88–9)[20]

Those appointed to the 'Drawing-Chamber,' although not as prestigiously positioned as Bedford and Hertford,[21] nevertheless clearly comprised an inner circle. That this circle was replete with patrons of the arts is emphasized by the presence of Penelope Rich to whom the queen had shown favor during the previous summer. Rich's own intellectual gifts seem to have been considerable. When Bartholomew Young, for example, translated the *Diana* of George Montemayor in 1598, he dedicated the translation to her, writing of 'that singular desire, knowledge, and delight wherewith your ladyship embraceth and affecteth honest endeavors, learned languages' (STC 18044). In this regard he recalled to Rich a time when he had given an oration in French, she being in the audience, and said he had especially feared her censure because 'of your ladyship's perfect knowledge of the same.' 'Now once again,' he continued, 'in this translation out of Spanish (which language also with the present matter being so well known to your ladyship),' he submitted himself to her censure. Penelope Rich, for this or other reasons, was also one of the nobles to whom John Florio dedicated his translation of Montaigne's essays and she seems to have been significant to poets, painters, and composers. Aside from her well-known importance in Sir Philip Sidney's *Astrophel and Stella*, Rich appeared in a number of dedications in works of various media. She was praised by the composers John Dowland and William Byrd, Henry Constable wrote a number of sonnets to her, while the painter Nicholas Hilliard named his daughter after Penelope.[22]

In Anna of Denmark's inner circle was also a noblewoman designated as 'The Countess of Derby.' Always present in the lists of those ladies featured in the queen's masques, she has often been misidentified as Alice Spencer Stanley, *Dowager* Countess of Derby whose second husband was Sir Thomas Egerton, Lord Privy Seal. The dramatic interests of the dowager countess, together with her former court activities under Queen Elizabeth, indeed might argue eloquently for her presence among Anna's ladies. Thus, because a 'Countess of Derby' was named (as usual) among the list of noble dancers in Anna's *Masque of Beauty* in 1608, it has seemed highly relevant that Antimo Galli, a young Italian who saw the masque, identified one dancer as 'Alicia Darbi,' thereby suggesting to future scholars that Alice Dowager Countess of Derby was indeed one of Anna's ladies.[23] But there was another, younger, Countess of Derby who was actually the 'Derby' in Anna's circle. The Dowager Countess Alice had been married to Ferdinando Stanley 5th Earl of Derby, who had died without an heir in 1594. Consequently, his brother, William Stanley, became 6th Earl; when William married, his own wife became known as the 'Countess of Derby,' and Alice became Dowager Countess – even though this distinguishing terminology was seldom insisted upon in contemporary parlance except in the most formal ritual. Nonetheless it was the present Earl of Derby's countess who was specifically identified by Worcester in 1604 for he referred to her as 'my Lady Derby, the younger,' presumably to distinguish her from the dowager countess.[24]

Born Elizabeth de Vere, this Countess of Derby, virtually ignored in accounts of Anna's milieu, was born in 1575, a daughter of Edward de Vere, 17th Earl of Oxford, and his wife, the former Anne Cecil, sister to Robert Cecil (who was thus Elizabeth de Vere's uncle).[25] Something more of a courtier than the Dowager Countess of Derby, Elizabeth (born in 1575) had, in fact, come to court as a Maid of Honor at age 13 after her mother had died in 1588. The young woman was brought up there by her grandfather, Queen Elizabeth's chief minister, Lord Burghley, whose own wife died just a year after Elizabeth's arrival. But Elizabeth remained at the palace until her marriage in 1595 and thus from an early age had a rather extensive experience with the workings of Queen Elizabeth's court.[26] More to the present point, the Countess of Derby's own cultural associations are not without interest as they touched on the public drama of the time. Her father, Edward de Vere, Earl of Oxford, had, of course, been patron of an acting company from 1580 to 1602 and John Lyly had been in his employ.[27] Elizabeth's husband, William Earl of Derby, was also interested in drama, sponsoring the Earl of Derby's Servants, and described in 1599 as 'busy penning comedies for the common players.'[28] There is also a record in 1601 of Elizabeth Derby's intercession (at Derby's urging) with her uncle, Robert Cecil, to help avert a ban on playing directed against her husband.[29] Elizabeth was 28 at the time of James's accession, and thus in the age-group of the ladies Queen Anna seems to have held most closely (Bedford and Hertford). Moreover, as it turned out, not only was Elizabeth a member of Anna's court until the queen's death, but at the time of the queen's funeral she was also designated Chief Mourner.[30]

Perhaps at Derby's intervention her younger sister, Susan de Vere, also became one of Queen Anna's ladies in this favored second group. Turned 16 in May 1603, the young Susan seems then to have become a great favorite of the new queen, and through the marriage that she soon made may even have strengthened the social ties of Anna's court both to the Sidney circle and to the king's Bed Chamber. For less than a year after the appearance of the above list of ladies, Susan married the Earl of Pembroke's younger brother, Philip (soon to become Earl of Montgomery, and along with his brother, a great favorite of King James), in what was called a wedding of two favorites – the court event of Christmas 1604.[31] Thus, through most of Anna's reign, Susan would be allied to the Herbert circle – to her mother-in-law the Countess of Pembroke, to her brother-in-law, the Earl of Pembroke, master of the great house Wilton, and also to her husband's uncle, Mary Sidney's brother, Sir Robert Sidney.

As the Countess of Montgomery, Susan was a very active patron of the arts. George Chapman, for example, inserted a dedicatory leaf to her in the 1609 edition of his translation of the *Iliad*, and she was the subject of Ben Jonson's *Epigram* 104. Montgomery also patronized John Donne: in 1619 he preached a sermon at The Cockpit, a group of apartments adjacent to Whitehall occupied by the Earl and Countess of Montgomery, and the countess asked him for a copy of his text which he sent her.[32] Significantly, later in the reign, she would be the dedicatee of Lady Mary Wroth's *Urania*, written by the daughter of Robert Sidney.

But it is, of course, the broadly ranging cultural activity of Lucy Bedford, Anna's Lady of the Bed Chamber, which would seem to be of the greatest importance to the cultural configuration of the new queen's court.[33] Many of Bedford's acts of patronage are well known to scholars, but her continued energy in this respect is succinctly and forcefully indicated by a letter she would write to her good friend Lady Jane Cornwallis in November 1624 (about five years after Queen Anna's death). Lady Jane's father-in-law, Sir Nicholas Bacon, a great collector of paintings, was at this time on the point of death, and the Countess of Bedford wrote Lady Jane because she had learned that Sir Nicholas 'had some pieces of painting of Holbein's which I am sure, as soon as [the Earl of] Arundel hears, he will try all means to get.' Bedford implored Lady Jane, if the paintings were indeed to be sold, that she use her influence with her husband to save them (the letter refers to them as 'pieces') for Bedford. 'For I am a very diligent gatherer of all I can get of Holbein's or any other excellent master's hand; I do not care at what rate I have them for price.' She also asked Lady Jane to commission her husband, whose judgment Bedford apparently admired, to procure her any other paintings 'if he know any such thereabouts' and 'upon any conditions.' Some of the paintings that she herself owned, Bedford continued, 'I found in obscure places, and gentlemen's houses, that, because they were old, made no reckoning of them; and that makes me think it likely that there may yet be in divers places many excellent unknown pieces for which I lay wait with all my friends.' 'Dear Madam,' she concluded,

> Let me hear by this bearer whether I have not been misinformed concerning these pictures, and if I have not, make them sure either for me or nobody. And be not curious to think I may pay too much, for I had rather have them than jewels.[34]

The interests of Lady Bedford were not, of course, confined to painting. Before James's accession, in 1600, for example, the English composer John Dowland had dedicated his *Second Book of Airs* to her. Her influence on letters, however, was more extensive. In the realm of translation alone, her patronage was significant. George Chapman wrote a sonnet to her in the preface to the earliest (1598) edition of his translation of the *Iliad*. Earlier in the 1590s, John Florio had dedicated his first publication, an Italian dictionary, to Bedford after she was married, and later he finished his famous translation of the *Essaies* of Montaigne as a resident in her house, observing that the countess had introduced him to the scholarly Theodore Diodati and Matthew Gwynne, his collaborators in the project. She was patron, too, of Philemon Holland, who dedicated his 1606 translation of Suetonius's *History of the Twelve Caesars* to her.

Poets also received Bedford's support. Michael Drayton had begun dedicating work to her when she was 13,[35] and in the years before Queen Elizabeth's death, Ben Jonson presented Bedford a printed copy of *Cynthia's Revels* in which was inserted a leaf containing a set of verses to her.[36] Samuel Daniel, through the countess's influence, wrote the first masque (*The Vision of the Twelve Goddesses*) that Anna of Denmark presented. Moreover, Bedford stood as godmother to the poet John Donne's second daughter.

The most intriguing aspect of Bedford's history, in light of her close relationship to Anna of Denmark, is her possible intersection with the career of William Shakespeare. We recall that Bedford's circle before the Essex uprising included the Earl of Southampton (dedicatee of *Venus and Adonis* and *Lucrece*) who was close to her husband, to Rutland, and to Essex, all of whom rode together against Elizabeth. But the countess can be connected even more directly to matters Shakespearian, if not to Shakespeare himself, through a 1595 Christmas at Burleigh-on-the-Hill, the opulent residence of her father, Sir John Harington. According to Jacques Petit, tutor to the Countess of Bedford's younger brother, John Harington, and servant to Anthony Bacon (secretary to the Earl of Essex and a good friend of Penelope Rich), this holiday naturally featured the presence of Harington's daughter who showed great liberality.[37] And at New Year, Petit reported, professional actors from London performed *Titus Andronicus*, a play probably owned by Shakespeare's company, the Lord Chamberlain's Servants.[38]

Thus the relationship of others in Bedford's (and thus Queen Anna's) circle to the biography of Shakespeare is an intriguing subject. It cannot be fully explored here, but several instances are suggestive. In one such, the Christmas of 1604–5 (James being briefly absent from London), the Earl of Southampton entertained Queen Anna at his house in the city, using Shakespeare's company, the King's Servants, for the occasion, on which they were scheduled to present their play, *Love's Labour's Lost.*[39] In another instance, it was for the Earl of Rutland's brother that Richard Burbage and William Shakespeare together would execute an Accession Day Tilt *impressa* in 1613.[40]

Finally, one male noble appointed to Anna's household himself did nothing to detract from the cultural ambience of the new queen's official circle. The court of the Queen Consort was considered separate from the king's, at least socially and, to a certain extent, financially. It had its own subsidy and officials who, in many respects, were often counterparts of officials in the court of the monarch.[41] Such a one was the Lord Chamberlain – not of the king's but of the queen's household. The *King's* Lord Chamberlain officially regulated access to the sovereign and was responsible for all matters pertaining to his household, duties offering opportunity for much political power; the Earl of Suffolk (James's Lord Chamberlain) was, in fact, a close political advisor. For her own Lord Chamberlain Anna controverted the king's choice for her and selected instead a noble close to the Countess of Bedford and her network. This was Sir Robert Sidney, brother of the Countess of Pembroke and of Sir Philip Sidney, and thus uncle of the young Earl of Pembroke and of his brother, the Earl of Montgomery.

Queen Anna's Lord Chamberlain is best known to cultural historians for his great house, Penshurst, celebrated by Ben Jonson for its hospitality to the arts and artists, but Sir Robert was himself a writer of poetry surviving in an autograph manuscript of thirty-five sonnets and twenty-four other poems. He was also quite fond of music. In 1598 the Earl of Southampton procured songs for him in Paris from the music-seller Léon Cavellat, and John Dowland, whose godfather Robert Sidney was, presented to him in 1610 *A Musical Banquet*, noting in the dedication 'the love you bear to all excellency and good learning (which seemeth hereditary above others to the noble family of the Sidneys,) and especially to the excellent science of music.'[42] And, to offer a final example, Sidney was one of the nobles who helped Thomas Bodley establish his now-famous library at Oxford, donating £100.[43]

Robert Sidney may even have had a certain relevance to Shakespeare's activities by virtue of his official position. It is important to recall that one of the officers reporting to the king's Lord Chamberlain (the Earl of Suffolk) was the Master of the Revels who controlled all London actors and theatres, summoning them for performances at court before the king every year. The queen's Lord Chamberlain may have had similar, if far less extensive, responsibilities for plays paid for by and presented to the separate court of the Queen Consort. This now seems clear from fragmentary documents that show Sir Robert signing warrants of payment to professional acting companies (specifically Shakespeare's) in 1615.[44]

An equally interesting result of Sidney's appointment to the court of the queen was the introduction of his daughter, Lady Mary Wroth, to the queen's circle.[45] The title of Wroth's well-known work is, of course, *The Countess of Montgomery's Urania*; indeed, Susan de Vere (the Countess of Montgomery), one of Anna's ladies, seems herself to have had an extensive interest in the early forms of the novel we call 'romances,' the form to which Lady Wroth was so attracted. In 1619, for example, when Anthony Munday, who had been translating *Amadis de Gaul* through several editions since the 1590s, dedicated his work to the Earl of Montgomery, he noted the *countess's* activity. Speaking of how he finished his work at 'the urgent importunities of that worthy lady by whom I have thus boldly presumed,' he also mentioned that the labor of gathering various editions of the *Amadis* was lightened by the countess, for 'by the help of that worthy lady I have had such books as were of the best editions.'[46]

Finally, when viewing the arts patronage emanating from the court of Anna of Denmark, it would be a great mistake to ignore the queen herself. She has been most commonly associated with the opulent masques that she introduced to the Stuart court, and these are indeed central to her cultural significance in the Jacobean reign, yet all but one of these spectacles were designed for Christmas court revels. Moreover, a masque endured only for the space of one night (not counting its rehearsals) in the annual activities of a queen busy with ceremonies. Indeed, such masques did not even occur in every year of her reign. Anna presented and danced in only seven such spectacles between 1603 and 1612, dancing in no others for the remainder of her life (she died in 1619 at age 45). Thus although in conventional literary history Anna of Denmark has been exclusively associated with works scripted by Samuel Daniel or Ben Jonson and designed by Inigo Jones, this body of art in no way encompasses the wide range of the queen's cultural interests.

Like the Countess of Bedford, Anna's patronage did favor letters. For example, she sponsored John Florio, from whom she learned to speak Italian with great fluency, appointing him as 'Reader of the Italian' and Groom of her Privy Chamber.[47] Samuel Daniel, probably England's most respected lyric poet at that time, was another Groom of her Privy Chamber, writing for the queen not only his two masques, but also two pastorals. But the queen seems to have been most inclined to music and the visual arts. Graham Parry has noted (p. 149) that she provided Inigo Jones with his first full-scale monumental commission, while the great garden-designer Salomon de Caus (who later dedicated his *Institution Harmonique* [1615] to the queen) was called upon to decorate her gardens at Somerset House and Greenwich. Under Anna's influence too the Royal Collection of paintings began once more to expand.[48] Patronizing artists such as Isaac Oliver, in 1617 she also drew into her service Paul van Somer, the most advanced painter in England before the coming of Mytens and Van Dyke, while Constantino de'Servi (as reported by the Florentine ambassador Ottaviano Lotti) stood in high favor with the queen 'who takes pleasure in the portraits from life he has painted for her.'[49]

Finally, Anna of Denmark's great interest in music – shared by her son Henry Prince of Wales – is adumbrated by John Chamberlain's observation that she kept at her court 'more than a good many' French musicians (Chamberlain, vol. 2, p. 56). Further, the queen was conversant enough with lute music so that when, in 1606, John Dowland was dismissed from his position with her brother King Christian of Denmark, she wrote Lady Arabella Stuart asking her to allow that lady's own lutanist, Thomas Cutting, to go to the Danish court in Dowland's place (Poulton, p. 399). Indeed, Dowland's own experience in England is highly suggestive of how hospitable the climate of Anna's court was to artists of his profession. Described by musicologists as the best lutanist of his time – as well as the most gifted composer – John Dowland, serving, as noted above, at the court of Christian IV, sent to his wife in England (1600) the manuscript of his *Second Book of Airs*, dedicated to Lucy Countess of Bedford (see p. 52). Surely it was because of this contact that in 1603, after the accession of James and Anna, Bedford now being Anna's chief lady-in-waiting, Dowland crossed over to England. The royal couple, avoiding the severe plague conditions then current, were never in one place very long that summer, but, in autumn, the court was temporarily established at Winchester, to which the composer made his way. That he actually enjoyed an audience with the new queen is apparent in a later dedication when he reminds Anna that he 'had access' to her in Winchester. One result of this connection (which has never been mentioned) was that when, in the following spring, Dowland published his famous *Lachrimae* (S.R. 2 April 1604), a series of seven pavannes written for five viols and lute, he inscribed them to Anna, who was thus the dedicatee of one of the most famous music collections produced in Europe at that time.[50]

Feminist studies have rewritten the history of letters and the fine arts in the Early Modern period by focusing on women who produced poetry, prose, painting, and music, unearthing lives and *opera* buried under a plethora of texts produced by men. But few scholars would claim that Early Modern women inevitably discovered or revealed their potentialities through the practices of art alone. When offered advantages rivalling those granted men – or even when deprived of these advantages – women of talent found other outlets. Thus, though events cannot rediscover Anna of Denmark as poet, musician, painter, or even dancer, they nevertheless shape her as an appropriate subject for the history of Early Modern artistic production. Her behavior as Queen Consort led her to create for the arts in the early Stuart court a rich and hospitable climate – a climate, ironically, which historians have subsequently credited to King James. But if future assessments of figures such as William Shakespeare, John Donne, and even Ben Jonson seek to anchor them in the contexts of their chronological period, it might well be said that while they may have lived at the time of King James, they flourished in a milieu of high culture centered around Anna of Denmark.

Notes

1 The Queen's first name, for obvious reasons, seldom appears in the correspondence of others to whom she was simply 'the Queen', but at least five instances indicate that she considered the Danish 'Anna' her name. She so signs it in a holograph letter (1603) to James ('so kissing your hands/I rest/yours/Anna R[egina]'). Similarly, her oath of office, when she was invested as Queen of Scotland, began in a Scottish account of 1590: 'The Queen's Majesty's Oath: "I Anna, by the grace of God, Queen of Scotland".' See *Papers Relative to the Marriage of King James the Sixth of Scotland* (Edinburgh, 1828), pp. v, xviii. A doggerel poem by John Burel of the same year, describing the 'form and manner' of the Queen's Scottish coronation, has one stanza beginning: 'Anna, our well-beloved Queen' (see *Papers*). John Dowland's *Lachrimae* (London, 1604) is dedicated to 'the most sacred and gracious princess Anna Queen of England', while John Florio, a gentleman of the Queen's Privy Chamber and her Italian teacher, offered his second rendering of his well-known Italian dictionary, *Queen Anna's New World of Words* (London, 1611), to 'the Imperial Majesty of the highest-born Princess, Anna of Denmark'.

2 Such a meeting had, in fact, already been arranged for the vicinity of Windsor on 2 July. For these matters see John Stow, *Annals [as continued by Edmond Howes]* (London, 1615), sig. 3Z5 (p. 826). Hereafter cited as Stow. See also *Calendar of the MSS of the Marquess of Salisbury Preserved at Hatfield House*, edited by M. S. Giuseppi, 23 vols (London: Historical Manuscripts Commission, 1883–1976), 15:52. Hereafter cited as *Salisbury MSS*. James's order was issued 15 April (see *Salisbury MSS*, 15:52–53). For the date of Anna's departure from Edinburgh, see David Calderwood, *History of the Kirk of Scotland* (Edinburgh: Woodrow Society, 1845), 6.232.

3 See *Original Letters [First Series]*, ed. Henry Ellis (London, 1824), 3.70; John Nichols, *The Progresses . . . of James the First* (London, 1828), 1:190. Hereafter cited as Nichols, *James*. See also *Calendar of State Papers and Manuscripts Relating to English Affairs, Existing in the Archives and Collections of Venice and in Other Libraries of North Italy*, ed. R. Brown *et al.* 35 vols (London: Historical Manuscripts Commission, 1864–), 10:27. Hereafter cited as *SPV*.

4 A member of the Privy Council, the earl had been Queen Elizabeth's special envoy to Edinburgh to bear England's congratulations on the occasion of James's marriage to Queen Anna in 1592. See E. C. Williams, *Anne of Denmark* (London, 1970), p. 160. In 1602 he

was prestigious enough to increase to three the number of acting companies allowed in London, when his troupe began playing at the Boar's Head – see E. K. Chambers, *The Elizabethan Stage* (Oxford, 1923), 2:225–6. Hereafter cited as Chambers, *ES*.

5 There is an allusion by the earl to his wife's 'service' to the queen (*Salisbury MSS*, 12:43). The countess was also included among the ladies awarded prizes by Sir Thomas Egerton and his wife at the Harefield entertainment of Queen Elizabeth the previous summer. The countess's age is not known, but she had been married to Worcester since 1571 and if, as was true of many of her peers, she had married as young as 15, she was at least 47 in 1603. See *Complete Peerage*, ed. H. A. Doubleday *et al.* (London, 1910–59), 12.2:856. Hereafter cited as *Peerage*.

6 See *Peerage*, 7:240 for one date of remarriage – 1601 – but she was already remarried by 23 August 1600: *Manuscripts of the Lord de L'Isle and Dudley Preserved at Penshurst Place*, ed. C. L. Kingsford and William A. Shaw, 6 vols, (London: Historical Manuscripts Commission, 1936), 2.479. Hereafter cited as *L'Isle*. Kildare married Frances Howard in 1590 but died in 1597 fighting in Ireland in the wars against Tyrone: see *Peerage*, 7:240. After her remarriage to Cobham, who was of lower degree, Lady Kildare retained her former title, as was customary (e.g., the Dowager Countess of Derby married to Sir Thomas Egerton remained 'the Countess of Derby [*sic*]).'

7 Her presence at the Harefield Entertainment with the Countess of Worcester also suggests her inclusion among Elizabeth's circle of ladies (*Salisbury MSS*, 13:84). Kildare's influence would be attested to by what happened after her husband, Lord Cobham, was attainted in 1603 and put in the Tower for life. Although the lands of an attainted noble were ordinarily confiscated by the Crown, Frances, on 13 May 1604, was granted Cobham Hall along with Cobham's other lands for the rest of her life, the reversion of Cobham Hall only then being granted to the Duke of Lennox: see *Peerage*, 3:349 *n.* g.

8 See Stow, sig. 3Z3^{v} (p. 823).

9 With the countess were two women who themselves are of some significance. They were her mother, Ann Kelway Harington, who with her husband would later be entrusted with the guardianship of Princess Elizabeth (the future Elizabeth of Bohemia), and also 'Lady Hatton.' This second noblewoman was niece of Sir Robert Cecil, her father being Cecil's older brother Thomas Lord Burghley, son and heir to Queen Elizabeth's great servant. Elizabeth Burghley had married William Hatton, nephew and heir of Sir Christopher Hatton, Queen Elizabeth's late Lord Chancellor. Upon her husband's death in 1597, Elizabeth Hatton surprised observers by declining the optimal marriages she might then have made as a result of her dead husband's fortune and her own Cecil lineage. She married, instead, Sir Edward Coke, future Lord Chancellor of England.

10 The queen had one Scottish Lady of the Bed Chamber who continued to serve her in this capacity. (see note 21). Of course the male officials appointed by the Crown to oversee the consort's moneys and properties were powerful in the kingdom and thus probably 'high officials' at Anna's court. The present discussion, however, is centered on those whose opinions may have influenced the queen herself – and her actions.

11 Relevant here is Essex's own systematic cultural patronage in the appointment of personal secretaries such as Edward Reynoldes: see Paul E. J. Hammer, 'The Uses of Scholarship: the Secretariat of Robert Devereux, Second Earl of Essex, c.1585–1601,' *English Historical Review* 109 (1994), 26–51, who also notes the links between this group surrounding Essex and the circle around Prince Henry (p. 50 *n.* 5).

12 See Sir John Chamberlain, *Letters*, ed. N. E. McClure, 2 vols (Philadelphia, PA: American Philosophical Society, 1939), 2:85. Hereafter cited as Chamberlain. The Countess of Bedford was also friendly with Barbara Gamage Sidney, Sir Robert Sidney's wife.

13 'Leicester' was Lettice (or Laetitia), Countess of Leicester, mother of the executed Earl of Essex and of his sisters, Penelope (Devereux) Rich and Dorothy (Devereux), Countess of Northumberland. Leicester was now married to Mountjoy's kinsman, Sir Christopher Blount, one of the five or six persons connected with the special performance of Shakespeare's *Richard II* before the Essex rebellion and one of the few persons executed for the conspiracy. See Barroll, 'A New History for Shakespeare and his Time,' *Shakespeare Quarterly*, 39 (1988): 441–64.

14 For these two passages, see *L'Isle*, 2:322; Chamberlain, 1:179.

15 For Bedford's friendship with the Earl of Pembroke, see Michael Brennan, *Literary Patronage in the English Renaissance* (London: Routledge, 1988), p. 156. Unfortunately, when Pembroke married on 4 November 1604, his spouse, Mary Talbot, one of the three (known) daughters of the 7th Earl of Shrewsbury, though apparently willing to join the queen's group, and positioned advantageously through her husband to do so at an early stage in Anna's reign, does not seem to have made a good courtier: see Edmund Lodge, *Illustrations of British History* (London, 1838), 3:151–2, 161–2. Hereafter cited as Lodge. This is in interesting contrast to Mary's sister, Althea, who, after she married the young Earl of Arundel on 30 September 1606, seems to have gained quick access to the queen.

16 See *The Diaries of Lady Anne Clifford*, ed. D. J. H. Clifford (Wolfeboro Falls, NH, 1991), p. 23. Hereafter cited as *Clifford*.

17 Anne Clifford remarked that, late in June, the queen 'showed no favor to the elderly ladies, but to Lady Rich and such like company.' In July, this sentiment was reaffirmed elsewhere by the remark that 'the ladies Bedford, Rich, and Essex' were especially in favor with the new queen. See *Clifford*, p. 23; *Dudley Carleton to John Chamberlain*, ed. Maurice Lee, Jr (New Brunswick, NJ: Rutgers University Press, 1972), p. 35. Hereafter cited as *Carleton*. Identification of 'Lady Essex' in July 1603 is problematic because Frances Walsingham, widow of Sir Philip Sidney and then of the Earl of Essex, would have by then married the (Irish) Earl of Clanricard (by 12 April 1603: Chamberlain, 1:193). I assume that the Irish earldom could not claim the (English) precedence of the Essex name and that, consequently, the Countess of Clanricard, as Essex's widow, was still known as the Countess of Essex. Clifford's 'Lady Essex' was almost certainly not Laetitia, widow of the 1st Earl of Essex and then widow of the Earl of Leicester, and again widow of the conspirator Christopher Blount, unless she used her Essex rather than her Leicester name. I have not found an instance of Laetitia doing so.

18 See Lodge, 3:88. Although Worcester (probably with more authority than most) described Bedford as being of the 'Bed Chamber,' Dudley Carleton described her as having been sworn to the 'Privy Chamber.' See Nichols, *James*, 1:190. For a general discussion of the Privy Chamber, see Chambers, *ES*, 1.42; Pam Wright, 'A Change in Direction: The Ramifications of a Female Household, 1558–1603', in *The English Court*, ed. David Starkey *et al.* (London, 1987), pp. 147–82 for the Chamber under Queen Elizabeth; and Neil Cuddy, 'The Revival of the Entourage: the Bedchamber of James I, 1603–1625' in Starkey, ibid., pp. 173–225, for the Chamber under James.

19 She was either Anne Woodhouse, wife of Sir Julius Caesar, or Mary Woodhouse, wife of Sir Robert Killigrew. See R. C. Bald, *John Donne: A Life* (Oxford: Oxford University Press, 1970), pp. 441–2, 454.

20 See Lodge, 3:88. A list of Anna's 'servants,' compiled before 18 March 1606, is calendared in *Salisbury MSS*, 24:65–7.

21 Although Worcester makes no reference to Scottish ladies or nobility, a Lady of the Bed Chamber missing from this list and worthy of mention because she had served as Anna's Lady of the Bed Chamber in Scotland and had accompanied the queen to England was Jean Drummond, daughter of Patrick, 3rd Lord Drummond. Indeed, eleven years later, in 1614, the Countess of Bedford would attest to Drummond's elevated status when, writing to her close friend Lady Jane Cornwallis, Bedford observed that her plans to visit Cornwallis were on hold because of Lady Drummond's illness. Bedford was expected to fill in for Drummond who became ill during a period when she was scheduled to serve her waiting-time as Lady of the Bed Chamber. Later that year Anna sponsored an elaborate wedding for Drummond, with a masque by Samuel Daniel, when she married Robert Kerr of Cessford, 1st Lord Roxborough. For the details of the occasion see Samuel Daniel, *Hymen's Triumph*, ed. for The Malone Society by John Pitcher (Oxford: Oxford University Press, 1994): Introduction and Chapter 5. For Cornwallis, see *The Private Correspondence of Jane Lady Cornwallis* (London, 1842), p. 30. Hereafter cited as *Cornwallis*.

22 See M. S. Rawson, *Penelope Rich and her Circle* (London, 1911), for Rich's patronage of Hilliard.

23 See John Orrell, 'Antimo Galli's Description of *The Masque of Beauty*, *Huntington Library Quarterly*, 43 (1979), 13–23. See also French R. Fogle, 'Such a Rural Queen', in *Patronage*

in Late Renaissance England, (Los Angeles: Clark Memorial Library, 1983), pp. 3–29. Antimo Galli, *Rime* (London, 1609), sig. 12[v]. Galli has the correct first names of all the other women in the masque.

24 Anne Clifford's account of events in June 1603 also refers to this younger Derby. According to Clifford, when Anna met a number of English noblewomen at Dingley's: 'Hither also came my Lady of Suffolk, my young Lady Derby and Lady Walsingham, which three ladies were the great favorites of Sir Robert Cecil.' See *Clifford*, p. 23. Fourteen years later this Countess of Derby was still in an influential position at the queen's court. Clifford, attempting to move the king about her inheritance in January 1617 (p. 45) regarded 'Lady Derby, my Lady Bedford, My Lady Montgomery' as a group (p. 44). Lady Walsingham was probably Audrey Shelton Walsingham.

25 Elizabeth had two younger sisters: Bridget, born in 1584, married Francis Norris (Norreys) Lord Norris, the future Earl of Berkshire. Susan, born in 1587, would marry the Earl of Pembroke's younger brother, Philip Herbert, Earl of Montgomery (see also note 32).

26 Elizabeth is interestingly described in the west panel of the Burghley Memorial in Westminster Abbey as 14 years old in 1589 and grieving bitterly 'for the loss of her grandmother and mother, but she feels happier because her most gracious Majesty has taken her into service as a Maid of Honor' – tr. from the Latin by B. M. Ward, *The Seventeenth Earl of Oxford 1550–1640* (London: John Murray, 1928), p. 262.

27 The Earl of Oxford, as is well known, was reputed to have written plays, being mentioned by Francis Meres as 'the best for comedy amongst us,' but he probably did not influence her tastes, except negatively, since he was separated from her mother and saw his daughters rarely. For Oxford, see E. K. Chambers, *William Shakespeare: A Study of Facts and Problems* (Oxford: Clarendon Press, 1930), 2.193–4.

28 For William Earl of Derby's other patronage, see Virgil B. Heltzel, 'English Literary Patronage 1550–1630' (unpublished typescript: Folger Shakespeare Library, Washington, DC), 'Stanley', and Thomas Heywood, 'The Earls of Derby and the Verse Writers and Poets of the Sixteenth and Seventeenth Centuries' in *Remains . . . of Lancaster and Chester* (London: Chetham Society, 1853), 29. See also *Salisbury MSS*, 13.609 and Chambers, *ES*, 2:194.

29 For documentation of these points see Chambers, *ES*, 2:127. Elizabeth's own attitude towards the theatre is nonetheless ambiguous. Her letter to her uncle concludes 'I could desire that your furtherance might be a mean to uphold them [the players], for that my lord, taking delight in them, it will keep him from more prodigal courses.'

30 The countess appears to have been highly competent – for example, she assumed responsibility for the administration of the Isle of Man, part of her husband's domain. Her son referred to her as 'wise' and noted that after her death her husband grew 'infirm and disconsolate and willing to repose himself from the troubles of the world.' See J. J. Bagley, *The Earls of Derby* (London: Sidgwick and Jackson, 1985), pp. 68 ff. and Barry Coward, *The Stanleys* (Manchester: Chetham Society, 1983), pp. 60–1.

31 See *Carleton*, pp. 66–7.

32 See Bald, *John Donne*, p. 341. John Donne, *Letters to Several Persons of Honor* (London, 1651), sigs D4[v]–E[v], wrote the countess in 1619. For Susan de Vere, see also Graham Parry, *The Golden Age Restor'd* (Manchester: Manchester University Press, 1981), pp. 108–11.

33 See Florence Humphreys Morgan, 'A Biography of Lucy Countess of Bedford, the Last Great Literary Patroness', doctoral dissertation, University of Southern California: January 1956, pp. 52–157; B. H. Newdigate, *Michael Drayton and his Circle*, corrected edition (Oxford: Oxford University Press, 1961), Ch. 5; Barbara J. Lewalski, 'Lucy, Countess of Bedford: Images of a Jacobean Courtier and Patroness', in Kevin Sharpe and Stephen Zwicker (eds) *The Politics of Discourse* (Los Angeles: University of California Press, 1987), pp. 52–77.

34 See *Cornwallis*, pp. 50–1.

35 For Lucy Bedford's age, see Newdigate, *Michael Drayton*, ch. 5.

36 Jonson also mentioned the countess in an ode which was his contribution to 'The Phoenix and the Turtle. See Newdigate, *Michael Drayton*, p. 64 *n*. 1.

37 For Bacon's friendship with Rich, see the letter from her to Bacon quoted by Sylvia Freedman, *Poor Penelope* (Windsor: Kensal House, 1983), p. 117.

38 See Gustav Ungerer, 'An Unrecorded Elizabethan Performance of *Titus Andronicus*,' *Shakespeare Survey* 14 (1970), 102–9.
39 For the complications, see Barroll, *Politics, Plague, and Shakespeare's Theater* (Ithaca, NY: Cornell University Press, 1991), pp. 126–7.
40 See Chambers, *William Shakespeare*; 2.153. There is often confusion concerning the identity of the Rutlands. Francis Manners 6th Earl of Rutland (made a Knight of the Bath at the creation of Prince Charles as Duke of York in 1605 [see *Carleton*, p. 67]) was not the son but the younger brother of the childless 5th Earl of Rutland who died 26 June 1612 (*Peerage*, 11:259–62).
41 The following were the officers of the queen's household, appointed, for the most part, in July 1603: Sir Robert Cecil, *Lord High Steward*; Sir Robert Sidney, *Lord High Chamberlain and Surveyor General*; Sir George Carew, *Vice Chamberlain and Receiver*; Sir Thomas Mounson, *Chancellor*; The Earl of Southampton, *Master of the Game*; Thomas Somerset, *Master of the Horse*; Mr. William Fowler, *Secretary and Master of Requests*: see Lodge, 3.65.
42 See Robert Sidney, *Poems*, ed. P. J. Croft (Oxford: Clarendon Press, 1984), p. 52 and Diana Poulton, *John Dowland* (Berkeley, CA: University of California Press, 1982), p. 315.
43 For Penshurst activities see J. C. A. Rathmell, 'Jonson, Lord L'Isle and Penshurst,' *English Literary Renaissance* I (1971), 251. For Sidney's poetry, see Hilton Kelliher and Katherine Duncan-Jones, 'A Manuscript of Poems by Robert Sidney: Some Early Impressions,' *British Library Journal* 1 (1975), 107–44; and Katherine Duncan-Jones, '"Rosis and Lyso": Selections from the Poems of Sir Robert Sidney,' *English Literary Renaissance* 9 (1979), 240–63. For Robert Sidney and music, see his *Poems*, ed. Croft, pp. 48–54. For Sidney and the Bodleian, see Millicent V. Hay, *The Life of Robert Sidney* (Washington, DC: Folger Books, 1984), p. 207, and Margaret P. Hannay, *Philip's Phoenix* (New York: Oxford University Press, 1990), p. 278 *n.* 19. George Chapman dedicated the 1609 edition of his translation of Homer's *Iliad* to Sidney.
44 See *Malone Society Collections* 6, ed. David Cook and F. P. Wilson (Oxford: Oxford University Press, 1961), Appendix B.
45 See *L'Isle* 3.412, 421; 4.45, 276, 282.
46 See *Amadis of Gaule*, tr. Anthony Munday (London, 1619), sig. A4^{v}. See Brennan, *Literary Patronage*, p. 157 for the Countess of Montgomery's interest in *Amadis de Gaule*.
47 See also F. A. Yates, *John Florio* (Cambridge: Cambridge University Press, 1934), p. 246. In Scotland Anna's Secretary had been a literary figure: the poet and scholar William Fowler who, significantly, became her Secretary and Master of Requests in England (see *n.* 41). For his other activities, see *DNB* and William Fowler, *Works* (Edinburgh: Scottish Text Society, 1914–40), ed. H. W. Meikle, James Craigie, and John Purves, vol. 3; see also James K. Cameron, 'Some Continental Visitors to Scotland in the Late Sixteenth and Early Seventeenth Centuries', in *Scotland and Europe*, ed. T. C. Smout (Edinburgh: John Donald, 1986), pp. 45–61. He regularly entertained intellectuals visiting Scotland, including the nephew of Tycho Brahe in 1602. See also Edward J. Cowan 'The Darker Vision of the Scottish Renaissance' in *The Renaissance and Reformation in Scotland*, ed. Ian B. Cowan and Duncan Shaw (Edinburgh: Scottish Academic Presses, 1983), p. 138.
48 See Oliver Millar, *The Tudor, Stuart and Early Georgian Pictures in the Collection of H. M. the Queen* (London, 1977), and for a general description of Anna's activities in fine arts patronage, see Roy Strong, *Henry Prince of Wales and England's Lost Renaissance* (London: Thames and Hudson, 1986) p. 249, *n.*5.
49 See Strong, pp. 91–2, 106.
50 For the reputation of *Lachrimae*, see Poulton, *John Dowland*, pp. 60–1.

3

'MY SEELED CHAMBER AND DARK PARLOUR ROOM'

The English country house and Renaissance women dramatists

Marion Wynne-Davies

The fundamental role of the English country house in facilitating female authorship during the Early Modern period is becoming increasingly apparent, and Marion Wynne-Davies's examination of this locational context sheds important light on the way in which Renaissance women used the seclusion and security of such environments to produce dramatic texts. This new essay also demonstrates the importance of familial writing in the period with specific reference to the Sidney/Herbert/Wroth group and to the Cavendish family.

Virginia Woolf's well-known concept of a 'room of one's own' is not totally inappropriate for the Early Modern period.[1] However, rather than the individual rooms envisaged by the early-twentieth-century reader, the secure spaces which enabled Renaissance women to nurture their creative talents were located for the most part in the large castles and houses scattered across the British Isles. It is important to remember, however, that such environments were accessible only to rich and/or noble women and, in addition, that these possible 'havens' were mostly controlled by men. Indeed, it was precisely this combination of a secure space, wealth and male complicity that allowed a few Renaissance women dramatists to evade the lonely suicides visualised by Woolf, and to experience an environment suited to literary productivity. In this essay I intend to focus on two specific locations which served as sites for women's dramatic writing: Penshurst Place and Welbeck Abbey. Penshurst was the family home of the Sidneys, while Welbeck was the main residence of the Cavendishes, and both houses functioned not only as a secure situation for female authorship, but also as projected 'sets' for the plays themselves. This particular combination of a protected space and an imaginative arena is clearly evident in Mary Wroth/Sidney's pastoral comedy and in the plays of the two Cavendish sisters, Jane and Elizabeth Brackley. As such, it is through their works that I intend to explore how the English country house proved to be a benign inspiration for Early Modern women dramatists.

A seemingly perfect example of the secure conditions outlined at the start of this essay may be seen in the various houses of the Sidney family: for example, Philip's ideal knighthood, Robert's careful Neoplatonism, Mary Sidney's pious scholasticism, Mary Wroth's innovative independence and William Herbert's worldly statecraft are set off perfectly by the lauded pastoralism of Penshurst, the learned 'academy' of Wilton, and the clandestine passages of Baynard's Castle. Here the social standing, wealth and cultural position of the family combine with the beautiful, gracious and protected houses, simultaneously propagating a discourse which enabled both male and female creativity to flourish. Indeed, the Sidneys and Herberts used their houses both to entertain professional writers, safeguarding their endeavours within the cloak of patronage, as well as a personal refuge from the outside world where mutual creativity wove an even stronger protective fabric about those encased.[2] There are well-known examples of this usage, as in Ben Jonson's panegyric 'To Penshurst' where he praises the Sidneian patronage,

> But what can this (more than express their love)
>   Add to thy free provisions, far above
> The need of such? whose liberal board doth flow
>   With all that hospitality doth know!
> Where comes no guest but is allowed to eat
>   Without his fear, and of thy lord's own meat.[3]

A parallel usage, this time by a family member, may be seen in Philip Sidney's self-imposed retreat to his sister's house, Wilton, where he composed his *Arcadia* in her presence.[4]

The central site of the initial part of this inquiry will, however, be Penshurst, and its starting point will be August 1617, when Lady Anne Clifford made several visits to the Sidney family and recorded them in her diary. On the first of the month she visited 'Lady Wroth' and was joined there by 'Lady Rich', on the 12th and 13th she 'spent most of the time in playing Glecko & hearing Moll Neville reading the *Arcadia*', and then on the 19th,

> I went to Penshurst on Horseback to my Lord Lisle where I found Lady Dorothy Sidney, my Lady Manners, with whom I had much talk, & my Lord Norris, she and I being very kind.
>
> There was Lady Worth who told me a great deal of news from beyond the sea, so we came home at night, my Coz. Barbara Sidney bringing me a good part of the way.[5]

The women described visiting one another during this brief period were all part of the same familial grouping, either through direct descendancy or via marriage.[6] Of course, the political factions of the country as a whole are represented in and by this network, the Essex faction (both generations) being an important binding force, the more sustainable familial ties was also functioning as an important factor in deciding who was present, but there is yet another important element present in the gathering at Penshurst, that of gender.

Penshurst, like all familial houses functioned as a place where noble women could find pleasure in one another's company without the darker and more dangerous intrigues of the early-seventeenth-century court. The picture drawn by Clifford toys with the idea of a female 'academy'; it is an image decorated with the embellishments of literary texts and toned to the liking of a companionate body of female wits, it is then an environment particularly and exclusively for women, a 'feminine' safe house. One of the women present at this gathering was Lady Mary Wroth, who is described as bringing important information 'from beyond the sea', which in 1617 would have signified the continued conflicts in the Netherlands. Wroth's contribution to the gathering would, no doubt, have been considered interesting, for she was not only a member of the family group, but also an accomplished author in her own right; it is highly likely that she would have been working on a project in 1617, which corresponds with the period between the death of her husband (Robert Wroth died in 1614) and the aborted publication of the first part of her prose romance, *Urania* in 1621. Moreover, Wroth was at the same time engaged in an adulterous affair with yet another Sidney, her cousin William Herbert, and had two illegitimate children by him during this same period, possibly giving birth at Penshurst. She would have been considered a woman of notoriety and, at first, it is easy to imagine her as a marginal figure amongst her secure and sedate companions. But, surprisingly, her inclusion only compounded the network of difficulties faced by the women present at Penshurst. Anne Clifford for example, was involved, with the strong support of her mother, in a lengthy battle to confute her father's will and win her rightful inheritance over the appointed male relative and, despite the antagonisms of her husband and the king, she consistently refused to yield, finally triumphing in default when she inherited the titles in 1643. Indeed, almost all the other women present had, or were soon to encounter, similar difficulties, and as a consequence, were, had been or would be, excluded from the court world and were thus compelled to use Penshurst as a 'safe' house in a very real way.[7] For them the refuge offered was not merely a country retreat from which they could emerge refreshed, but an absolute necessity without which they would have been ostracised and disgraced. As such, the congregation at Penshurst, with its secret alliances and clandestine affairs, offered a brief moment of security for its female participants.

Wroth's play, *Love's Victory*, presents a similar group of women, here allegorised as shepherdesses gathered together in sisterly companionship to recount their experiences of love. Dalina, one of the shepherdesses, initiates the series of narratives:

> Now we're alone let everyone confess
> Truly to other what our lucks have been,
> How often liked and loved, and so express
> Our passions past; shall we this sport begin?
> None can accuse us, none can us betray,
> Unless ourselves, our own selves will bewray.
> (III. ii. 21–6)[8]

Of course, what the speaker, Dalina, means when she claims that they are 'alone' is that no men are present. The women are thus able to reveal their histories to one another without the threat of patriarchal censure; their 'luck' in love and the number of men they have 'liked' may be openly recounted instead of concealed within a code of social expectation which allowed only for arranged marriages and a single emotional commitment from women. As with the real women, the shepherdesses have various tales of woe to recount: Dalina herself has spurned four suitable wooers and now regrets her fickleness, 'the next that comes I'll have' (III.ii.51); Simeana confesses that she has been constant though disregarded by the man she loves; Phillis is similarly steadfast in her affections, but has been rejected in a kindly fashion; while Climeana, who is Simeana's rival, has forsaken one man for another only to discover that her new love disdains her. Further, Musella, who is the central female protagonist of the play, must marry a buffoon to satisfy her father's will (perhaps recalling Anne Clifford's circumstances), although she is in love with the noble Philisses. Altogether, the panoply of romantic difficulties encountered by the shepherdesses is not far from those faced by the women in Penshurst, with their records of illicit affairs, sexual and economic. Thus, Wroth recreated in her drama the female assemblies in which she participated, for undoubtedly the one recounted by Clifford in her diary was a single example of a common occurrence, thereby affirming, not only the importance of the safe house, but also of the female community within its walls.

However, Wroth's feelings about her own sojourn at Penshurst must have been somewhat ambivalent, for while the Sidney/Herbert protective residences shielded her from the displeasure of king and court, William Herbert, her cousin and lover, had no need for such 'protection'. While she was banished from the hub of courtly activity and had only the country house in which to exercise her glittering wit and sparkling intellect, Herbert was one of the most powerful nobles in the land and in the year previous to this gathering at Penshurst, 1616, had become Lord Chamberlain. The gender difference is reinforced by an interesting parallel to the seclusion of Mary Wroth within the safety of Penshurst and the careful closeting of her affair and two bastard children, for in 1601 William Herbert had entered into an affair with a court lady, Mary Fitton, but had refused to marry her when she became pregnant; consequently Herbert was imprisoned in the Fleet then, after the baby died at birth, was banished from court by Queen Elizabeth I, and was forced to retreat to the family home, Wilton.[9] From the safety of this stately house Herbert fired off volleys of letters demanding freedom and a return to the court, since,

> I endure a very grievous imprisonment. For do you account him a free man that is restrained from coming where he most desires to be [that is, the court].[10]

William Herbert certainly did not feel protected by Wilton, but imprisoned by it. In contrast, Wroth, in one of her many autobiographical narratives, describes the fate of *Lindamira* (a partial anagramatised version of Ladi Mari) who is likewise banished from court at the displeasure of a queen, and whose 'honour' is 'cast downe, and laid open to all mens tongues and eares, to be used as they pleased'.[11] Neither Wroth nor Herbert picture themselves as happy to be exiled from the court, but the man is more concerned with his freedom and his self-determination, whereas the woman agonises over the manner in which her reputation has suffered and from the way in which her actions have allowed her to be categorised as unchaste, that is, 'laid open to all men'. As such, Wilton confines Herbert, preventing him from being a 'free man', whereas Penshurst shields Wroth from the common usage of 'tongues and eares'. More galling surely for Wroth was that when Herbert's indiscretion led to further illegitimate children, this time her own, the gender balance of the court had swayed even more in his favour, the misogynistic James promoting his noblemen regardless of sexual infidelities, and punishing the women instead. Admittedly, Elizabeth I's regular use of banishment as a form of controlling her young male courtiers revealed more about her own self-centred system of loyalties than any supposed 'feminism', but there can be no question that women's standing at court diminished rapidly and consistently throughout James I's reign. For Wroth, therefore, the secure environment of Penshurst Place had ambiguous connotations: it may have enabled her to write *Love's Victory*, both through its supportive familial structure and through its literary resources, but at the same time that combination of material and imaginative surroundings served to contain and imprison her. Although the 'chamber' was Wroth's 'own', at the same time it was 'seeled' shut.

The quotation at the beginning of this essay, 'my seeled chamber and dark parlour room', is taken from Jane Cavendish and Elizabeth Brackley's play *The Concealed Fancies*, and refers to the dismay and isolation experienced by the two sisters Luceny and Tattiney when their male relatives depart to fight in the Civil War.[12] The play's characters and their experiences draw considerably upon the lives of the Cavendish family themselves, while their family home, Welbeck Abbey, is represented in the drama by Ballamo. Moreover, it was the siege and capture of Welbeck which seems to have driven the two Cavendish sisters into writing plays, which they intended to be performed by their family and friends, when the battles were over, the king restored to the throne, and their pre-war existence resumed. Thus, like Wroth, the two Cavendish sisters were trapped within their country house, although in this instance the incarceration was necessitated by warfare rather than court propriety, and like Wroth too, this ambiguous situation proved a catalyst to their literary productivity. But, while earlier families such as the Sidneys and Herberts remained comparatively secure within their economic and locational stations, for the Cavendish family the disorder and lack of stability experienced during the Civil War was never to be overcome, and the security of the Renaissance English country house was ultimately dismantled.

The houses which had been deemed 'safe' during the late sixteenth and early seventeenth centuries became, during the period of the Civil War and the Interregnum, sites of conflict and destruction. The Cavendish family is here representative of the widespread disruption experienced by many Royalist households; Welbeck and Bolsover, the two houses supervised by Jane Cavendish in the absence of William Cavendish her father, were respectively commandeered and plundered by the Puritan troops during the Northern campaign, while St John's Abbey, the childhood home of Margaret Cavendish, William's second wife (and a dramatist in her own right), was utterly destroyed during the siege of Colchester.[13] Moreover, although their status was never in question, all three women suffered from economic hardship in relation to their previous expectations; Jane records how she managed to take two pairs of sheets with her from Welbeck, while Margaret's account of her life with her penniless husband in Antwerp recorded in *The Life of William Cavendish* can leave little doubt as to the precarious nature of their budget.[14] On the other hand, it must be acknowledged that none of the Cavendish family suffered the hardships experienced by the majority of the British populace during the same period; for example, Jane was able to raise £1000 to send to her father, and Margaret always kept her own maid, Elizabeth Chaplain, although the new duchess did ask her servant to pawn the gifts given to her in more prosperous times. Within their own premises, however, Jane, Elizabeth and Margaret Cavendish, together with William Cavendish, all confronted an overwhelming reversal in their fortunes which not only undermined their material security, financial and locational alike, but also challenged the very ideological foundations of their lives. What is, perhaps, most remarkable, is that these adverse conditions provided the environment necessary for literary productivity; Jane and Elizabeth wrote two dramatic entertainments while besieged in Welbeck and Margaret began 'to conceive' her extensive canon while in the chilly exile of the Rubenhuis in the Netherlands.

One of Margaret Cavendish's works, 'A Dialogue between a Bountiful Knight and a Castle Ruined in War', provides an example of this sharp contrast between the Cavendish country houses before and after the Civil War. The poem records a conversation between the knight, Charles Cavendish (William's brother) and Bolsover Castle, which is personified as a distressed lady referring to a pre-war pastoral ideal:

And on this pleasant hill he [Cavendish] set me high,
To view the vales below, as they do lie,
Where like a garden is each field and close,
Where fresh green grass, and yellow cowslip grows;
There did I see fat sheep in pastures go,
And hear the cows, whose bags were full, to low.[15]

This self-pastoralization invokes the country-house idealism epitomised in Ben Jonson's 'To Penshurst' (already quoted in relation to the idealisation of the Sidney family), and although Jonson's poem might initially appear a far distant antecedent to Margaret Cavendish's verse, the allusion becomes more apt when considered alongside Jonson's two country-house masques written for William Cavendish to celebrate visits paid by Charles I: 'The King's Entertainment at Welbeck' (1633) and 'Love's Welcome. The King and Queenes Entertainment at Bolsover' (1634).[16] In the former a pastoral vision, similar to the nostalgic vision of the post-Civil War poem, is presented:

The joy of plants, the spirit of flowers,
The smell, and verdure of the bowers,
The waters murmure; with the showers
Distilling on the new-fresh howers.
(10–14)[17]

Margaret Cavendish was, of course, familiar with Jonson's work for her husband even though the entertainments took place twenty years before they met, and she cites both the author and the cost of the events in her *Life of the Duke of Newcastle*: '*Ben Johnson* he employed in fitting such Scenes and Speeches as he could best devise . . . [and made] This Entertainment at *Bolsover*-Castle in Derbyshire, some five miles distant from *Welbeck* . . . it cost him in all between Fourteen and Fifteen thousand pounds'.[18] Cavendish's presentation of Bolsover as a pre-war pastoral retreat is therefore perfectly commensurate with the location's prior literary identity and she might well have drawn upon Jonson's actual text or her husband's account of it. What is doubtful given the date of 1651 is that she could easily refer to other pastoral visions of the Cavendish houses, ones which were also influenced by Jonson but which were written while the family still resided in their ancestral home. Sometime between Jonson's 1634 masque and 1637 (the following text in the MS is dated 'Christmas Day 1637') William Cavendish wrote 'a country masque, a Christmas toy' specifically for his daughters, who were subsequently, between 1644 and 1645, to use similar material in their own *A Pastorall,* which is contained in the same manuscript book as *The Concealed Fancies.*[19] Jane Cavendish and Elizabeth Brackley's pastoral play evokes the same setting as Jonson's work, but the lamentations of its shepherds and shepherdesses are a prelude to the complaint of Margaret's personified Bolsover, for the country has already been divided by war and many royalists were by then exiled in France. The three shepherdesses, representing Jane, Elizabeth and their sister Frances, sing of their sadness now 'He', their father William Cavendish, is no longer with them:

His absence makes a Chaos sure of me,
And when each one doth looking look to see
They speaking say, That I'm not I,
Alas do not name me for I desire to die.[20]

These sentiments are not far removed from the Knight's address to the castle in Margaret's 'A Dialogue' where he begins, 'Alas, poor Castle, how great is thy change . . . To me thou dost seem strange' (1–2), and where the Castle concludes by wishing for death, 'or let me die by your most noble hand' (35–6).

Yet, the pastoral bounty of Margaret Cavendish's poem, which is suggested by the Castle's nostalgic vision of 'fat sheep' and 'cows, whose bags were full' (15–16), has already vanished in the conflicts of the Civil War, for in Jane and Elizabeth's comic antemasque two countrymen bewail their losses:

> *Hen:* I have lost my melch cow.
> *Pratt:* And I have lost my sow.
> *Hen:* And for my corn I cannot keep,
> *Pratt:* Neither can I my pretty sheep.
> *Hen:* And I have lost four dozen of eggs.
> *Pratt:* My pigs are gone and all their heads.[21]

The drama affords the possibility of laughter in a way which the poem clearly eschews. There are several possible explanations for this apart from the difference in personal style between the three authors. First, the dramatic form is able to offer sufficient time for a variation in tone and the hybrid structure of comedy/masque allows for a shift between the romantic shepherds and shepherdesses (the nobility) and the humorous rustic characters (the lower classes). Indeed, the Cavendish sisters employ a similar variation of tempo through class in their more formal play *The Concealed Fancies.* Second, although Margaret Cavendish might have had access to the texts of Jonson's masques, she did not see them being performed; on the other hand it is highly likely that Jane and perhaps Elizabeth (they would have been 11 and 6 in 1633 and 12 and 7 in 1634, the years of the two Jonson entertainments) would have been present to see the low comedy of the antemasques where at Welbeck a '*May Lady* . . . and Sixe Maids . . . drest after the cleanliest Countrey guise' appeared and at Bolsover there is a whole procession of '*Mechanickes*'.[22] Finally, the earlier work is set at that precise moment of change when it is impossible to know whether or not the pastoral ideal will once more be realisable, as such, the Knight in Margaret's poem can offer very little hope, 'Alas, poor Castle, I small help can bring' (37), whereas in Jane and Elizabeth's drama a character aptly entitled 'Freedom' calls for the last dance 'Come Music, lets now have a round,/ To prove my country wenches rightly sound'.[23] However, the most striking change occurs in the sexual references, for in the earlier work the women may remain chaste, refusing the advances of their swains since,

> Our vow will admit no such toy,
> For absent friends give us no joy,[24]

the allusion being to the exile of their father and brothers in France, whereas in the later poem the Castle presents her conquest in terms of a rape, describing how her 'rights [have been] o'erpowered', how her 'Beauty and innocency are devoured' and how the penetration of her walls, earlier described as a 'girdle' by the male garrison with their 'guns . . . pistols . . . [and] bullets' have 'made passages' and left her 'destroyed'. Although these two works are separated by only seven years the Civil War discourse has for the Cavendish women shifted from a melancholy linked with hope to a bleak and desolate vision. The castles of Welbeck and Bolsover which serve as sites for this ideological shift move from the ideal pastoralism of Jonson and William Cavendish in the 1630s, through the besieged threats experienced by Jane and Elizabeth in the 1640s, to the plunder and destruction that Margaret witnessed in 1651. As the Knight so aptly comments 'how great is thy change'.

The Cavendish sisters clearly recognised that their own imprisonment within the confines of Welbeck Abbey reflected the destabilisation of the whole Royalist hierarchy, upon which their noble identity and the security of their country house had depended. Since both *A Pastorall* and *The Concealed Fancies* were finished before the end of the Civil War and the final denouement of the Cavalier cause, both plays end on a hopeful note with families being reunited. Yet, both texts simultaneously betray the fear which had penetrated the political discourses of the period. Welbeck Abbey, and to a lesser extent Bolsover Castle, had become tomb-like in their restriction and imprisonment of Jane and Elizabeth; hence the images of the 'seeled chamber' and 'dark parlour room'. Moreover, the only form of escape available was an imaginative projection into a post-war world, which the two sisters erroneously believed would restore their former way of life. As such, their plays evoke a world which resides inescapably in their family home, Welbeck Abbey, the very place which constituted their immediate gaol. Thus, the distinct ambivalence evident in Wroth's writings, in which Penshurst provided a secure base for her literary endeavours but also isolated her from the hub of her cultural subjectivity, the court, is echoed in the plays of the two Cavendish sisters, who likewise were both repressed and enabled by their situation. Perhaps it was the severe form of this repression, in Wroth's banishment from court and the Cavendishes' imprisonment, that enabled these women dramatists to transform the material aspects of their internment into the clear theatrical visions evident in the text.

Unlike other Early Modern women dramatists, Wroth, Brackley and Cavendish all include sufficient stage directions and internal narrative evidence to prove that the plays were written with performance envisaged, if not intended. The desire to recreate the lost world beyond the boundaries of their 'seeled chamber[s]' served as a powerful catalyst in the inscribing of a dramatic process, which might not activate that world, but which could at least 'act' it out in the imagination. There is no evidence that these plays were performed at the time, although twentieth-century productions have proved that plays by Early Modern women are performable, and successfully so at that.[25] Thus, in a final swing of the prison door, the voices of Wroth, Brackley and Cavendish are liberated into the dramatic arena, their plays escaping the boundaries which enclosed the playwrights, enabling the Early Modern woman dramatist finally to lay claim to a full and open recognition beyond the graceful facade of her English country house.

Notes

1 Virginia Woolf, *A Room of One's Own* (1929; St Albans: Triad Paperbacks, 1977).
2 Michael Brennan, *Literary Patronage in the English Renaissance: The Pembroke Family* (London: Routledge, 1988).
3 Ben Jonson: *Ben Jonson. The Complete Poems*, ed. George Parfitt (Harmondsworth: Penguin Books, 1975), pp. 96–7; 'To Penshurst', ll. 57–62.
4 Margaret P. Hannay, *Philip's Phoenix: Mary Sidney, Countess of Pembroke* (Oxford: Oxford University Press, 1990), pp. 47–50.
5 *The Diaries of Lady Anne Clifford*, ed. D. J. H. Clifford (Stroud: Alan Sutton, 1990), pp. 60–1.

6 Full details of the familial connections of the women present are given in Marion Wynne-Davies, '"For *Worth,* Not Weakness, Makes in Use But One": Literary Dialogues in an English Renaissance Family', *The Double Voice: Gendered Writing in the Early Modern Period*, ed. Elizabeth Clarke and Danielle Clark (London: Macmillan, 1998), and are the focus of a chapter on the Sidney family in my forthcoming book, *Safe Houses: Familial Discourses in the English Renaissance.*

7 In the younger generation, Dorothy Percy Sidney had been married clandestinely the previous year, and Isabella was to be secretly married the following year. Of the older women, Bridget had frequently lived apart from her husband (who was soon to commit suicide with a cross-bow), and even Barbara Gamage Sidney, the 'noble, fruitful [and] chaste' lady of Jonson's celebrated poem, had arranged a match against the Queen's wishes with the now irreproachable Lord de L'Isle.

8 Mary Wroth, *Love's Victory*, in S. P. Cerasano and Marion Wynne-Davies (eds) *Renaissance Drama by Women: Texts and Contexts* (London: Routledge, 1996); all future references to this text will be made parenthetically.

9 For biographical details of Wroth and Herbert see Gary Waller, *The Sidney Family Romance: Mary Wroth, William Herbert, and The Early Modern Construction of Gender* (Detroit, MI: Wayne State University Press, 1993).

10 Ibid., p. 79.

11 Josephine A. Roberts (ed.) *The Poems of Lady Mary Wroth* (Baton Rouge, LA: Louisiana State University Press, 1983), p. 31.

12 Jane Cavendish and Elizabeth Brackley, *The Concealed Fancies*, in S. P. Cerasano and M. Wynne-Davies, *op.cit.*

13 Margaret Cavendish, *The Life of . . . William Cavendish* (London: A. Maxwell, 1667); Geoffrey Trease, *Portrait of a Cavalier: William Cavendish, First Duke of Newcastle* (London: Macmillan, 1979), pp. 114–43; and Kathleen Jones, *A Glorious Fame: The Life of Margaret Cavendish, Duchess of Newcastle, 1623–1678* (London: Bloomsbury, 1988), p. 68.

14 Jones, *op.cit.*, pp. 53–129.

15 Margaret Cavendish, 'A Dialogue Between a Bountiful Knight and a Castle Ruined in War' in Alastair Fowler, *The Country House Poem: A Cabinet of Seventeenth-Century Estate Poems and Related Items* (Edinburgh: Edinburgh University Press, 1994), pp. 315–16.

16 Ben Jonson, *Ben Jonson*, ed. C. H. Herford and Percy Simpson (Oxford: Clarendon Press, 1937), VII, pp. 787–814.

17 Ibid., VII, p. 792.

18 Margaret Cavendish, *The Life of the Duke of Newcastle*, *op.cit.*, p. 139.

19 Trease, *op.cit.*, p. 73 and Bodleian MS Rawlinson Poet 16.

20 Jane Cavendish and Elizabeth Brackley, Bodleian MS Rawlinson Poet 16; I have standardised and modernised all spelling and punctuation.

21 Ibid.

22 Ben Jonson, *Ben Jonson*, *op. cit.*, VII, pp. 799–800 and 809.

23 Cavendish and Brackley, *op.cit.*, Bodleian MS Rawlinson Poet 16.

24 Ibid.

25 For details of performances of plays by Early Modern women dramatists see Gweno Williams's essay in this collection (pp. 95–107).

4

WOMEN AS PATRONS OF ENGLISH RENAISSANCE DRAMA

David M. Bergeron

David M. Bergeron's essay was the first interrogation of the influence of women patrons on English Renaissance drama which focused upon their cultural influence rather than upon the basic economic support offered. This rereading of patronage as an active involvement with the literacy product was an important critical evaluation of 1980s historicism, and is here specifically used to uncover the impact women had on the public theatre. Bergeron's essay remains one of the key works on women's patronage of Renaissance drama.

In the attempts to reassess the position of English women in the society of late Tudor and early Stuart times no one, to my knowledge, has looked very closely at their relationship to one of the most popular endeavors: namely, the theatre. We know, of course, that women were not allowed as actors on the regular stage; and yet they performed frequently in other dramatic entertainments, principally masques. Several writers have detected a decline in the status of women after the death of Elizabeth and the advent of the anti-feminist Jacobean court, but I do not think that the issue is that simple.[1] Indeed, two recent essays find evidence of 'modern feminism' and the development of 'women's rights movements' in the literature.[2]

Somewhere between these two opposing arguments lies the truth. Clearly James did not care much for women, but women maintained positions of prominence at court and in the arts nevertheless. And curiously, one of the movements that contributed to the supposed emergent feminism was, of all things, Puritanism – an argument that has been convincingly advanced by Juliet Dusinbere.[3] As Dusinbere observes, 'The drama from 1590 to 1625 is feminist in sympathy' (p. 5), and this is true not only of Shakespeare but also of almost all his contemporaries. No appreciable diminution in the status of women occurs with the death of Elizabeth; I would argue, in fact, that a significant index of the importance of women exists for the drama, not as characters in plays – for that is another subject – but rather as sponsors and patrons of theatrical activity.[4]

Women impinge on English drama of the Renaissance in several obvious ways. Clearly they constituted a large part of the audience, whether in the public theatres or at private performances, and from one there is an eyewitness account of theatrical events. The Lady Anne Clifford kept a diary, revealing much about her intellectual life – her reading of

Montaigne, Chaucer, Spenser, the *Arcadia*, Ovid, Augustine – and her social life, including her attendance at dramatic performances.[5] She was present for several masques, saw Fletcher's *The Mad Lover* in 1617, and noted the burning of the Banqueting House at Whitehall in January 1619.

Women could also sponsor theatrical events. When Queen Elizabeth was on progress in 1592, the Dowager Lady Russell, widow of Francis Russell, second Earl of Bedford, acted as hostess for Elizabeth's stop at Bisham in August. She provided dramatic entertainment of a typical sort, common to many progress shows for the queen.[6] Pastoral figures, such as Pan and Ceres, welcoming and praising the sovereign, dominated the brief pageant entertainment. As one scholar has noted: 'Lady Russell had invited all the wit, the talent, and distinction, which she could convene, for the entertainment of her royal mistress, who prolonged her stay at Bisham several days.'[7]

Even women dramatists appeared, though we have no evidence that their plays were performed or were intended to be performed. Mary Herbert, Philip Sidney's sister and a translator and writer of some skill, produced a brief pastoral dialogue, *Thenot and Piers in Praise of Astraea* (1592), and *Antonie* (1592), a translation of Robert Garnier's French play. *Mariam, the Fair Queen of Jewry* (1613 text, written 1602–5) by Elizabeth Cary (wife of Henry Cary, Viscount Falkland) has the distinction of being the only extant play written by a woman in this era that was not a translation. Proficient in several languages, Elizabeth Cary did a number of translations, primarily of religious writings, but also of the epistles of Seneca.[8]

Though they never performed on the public theatre stage, women did appear regularly in private performances of masques, not only joining in the final dances but also impersonating some of the symbolic and mythological figures in the masque proper. The list of masque 'actresses' is as impressive as it is long – some forty-six in Jonson's masques alone, starting with Queen Anne and later Queen Henrietta Maria and including Lady Anne Clifford and others.[9] A perplexing comment in Jonson's *Conversations* suggests that perhaps he was planning to use women in a pastoral play of some sort:

> he heth a Pastorall jntitled the May Lord, his own name is Alkin Ethra the Countess of Bedfoords Mogibell overberry, the old Countesse of Suffolk ane jnchanteress other names are given to somersets Lady, Pemb[r]ook the Countess of Rutland, Lady Wroth.[10]

Henrietta Maria provoked controversy because of her theatrical activities. She encouraged plays and masques at court, and she often performed in the masques. In February 1626, she and her ladies performed a French pastoral at court, 'at which there was some murmuring.'[11] The pastoral was Racan's *Artenice*, and it was 'Queen Henrietta's speaking like a common player in the first part of her performance and the masculine dress of some of the ladies which raised the eyebrows.'[12] In January 1633, after months of preparation and rehearsal, the queen performed in Walter Montagu's pastoral, *The Shepherd's Paradise*.[13] This was enough to stir William Prynne's blood and pen, leading to his *Histrio-Mastix* and thus to his prosecution. Tradition and the Puritans notwithstanding, one could have seen women performing in dramatic shows.

During the period from the accession of Elizabeth to the closing of the theatres, patronage of the drama took several forms, beginning with the crucially important sponsorship of the court itself. The court remained the single most significant institution for the support of drama, including within its bureaucracy a Master of the Revels, and ultimately, in the reign of King James, placing all the principal acting companies under royal patronage. City governments and trade guilds were also active, producing and financing civic pageants, such as royal entries and Lord Mayor's shows. The Inns of Court made their contribution by sponsoring drama and preparing masques for special occasions. With the advent of public theatre buildings in the latter part of the sixteenth century a new group of patrons emerged: namely, the paying, theatregoing audience. What this meant to the flourishing of drama is simply incalculable: it created a class of professional dramatists and actors, able to earn their living exclusively from theatrical endeavors. The final major group of theatre-patrons was a diverse and wide-ranging collection of noblemen and courtiers, including women, who served, like Leicester and the Lord Chamberlain, as sponsors of acting companies or caused certain dramatic shows to take place. Though they lost some of their prominence when James took over the companies, such noblemen nevertheless remained important in both direct and indirect ways by their continued patronage of drama.

Recent scholarship has come a long way toward understanding the functioning of the early English theatre. Discarded is the misleading and naive view of W. J. Lawrence, who once claimed: 'In those days all writing done for pay was looked upon as soiled in the process, and unworthy of patronage.'[14] Such a simplistic approach was countered more than half a century ago by Virgil Heltzel in his essay, 'The Dedication of Tudor and Stuart Plays.'[15] But Heltzel had his own excesses, as when he claimed that 'during the entire reign of Queen Elizabeth and for some years after, the ordinary stage play was not thought worthy of patronal favor and none was dedicated' (p. 74). Heltzel thought 1613 a kind of turning point, after which dedications of regular drama increased. But before then Jonson had dedicated *Volpone* (1607) to the universities, *Catiline* (1611) to William Herbert, *The Alchemist* (1612) to Mary Wroth, and special issues of *Cynthia's Revels* (1601) to Camden and the Countess of Bedford, while Chapman had dedicated the *Tragedy of Byron* (1608) to Walsingham and *The Widow's Tears* (1612) to John Reed, to cite the most obvious examples. And neither Lawrence nor Heltzel called attention to the number of women who were dedicatees of the dramatic texts. By a study of such dedications we can gain some understanding of the nature of women's significance as patrons.[16]

Why did some dramatists dedicate their plays to women? The answers are seldom certain. If we expect in each case to pinpoint some deed, some beneficence, that led the dramatist in gratitude to dedicate his play to a particular woman, we shall be both frustrated and disappointed. One thing, however, is clear: writing a play and dedicating it to a patroness in hope of some immediate financial reward does not seem to have ranked very high on the list of purposes. Several other themes run through the dedications. In some instances the dramatist wished to become known to the woman, with the implied expectation of some benefit. But many dramatists simply sought recognition, hoping that the patroness's name would lend a kind of luster to their effort. Some writers acknowledged previous benefits from the patroness. Others used the dramatic text as the occasion to celebrate an event or to celebrate and honor the woman. In those cases where the woman was herself a writer, the dedication became a means of tribute to a fellow writer also serving the muses. And some dedications seem to exist in order to provide the writer, either the dramatist or the publisher, the opportunity to defend drama, either in the particular or in the abstract. These ideas and purposes will become apparent as we turn to a study of the women singled out as patronesses of drama.

The fourteen women that I have identified as patrons of drama – that is, as recipients of dramatic dedications – range from the well known to the relatively obscure. The most vexing problem is to determine the circumstances that might have led to the dedication or the context for it. Four of the women share a dedicatory statement with someone else. The 1591 revision by Robert Wilmot of *Tancred and Gismund*, for example, praises Mary, Lady Petre (wife of John, Baron Peter) and Anne, Lady Gray (wife of Baron Gray of Groby) for their rare virtues as noted by many people '(which are not a fewe in Essex).'[17] Wilmot wishes to be known to them and has 'deuised this waie . . . to procure the same.' He says: 'I shall humblie desire ye to bestow a fauourable countenance vpon this little labor, which when ye haue graced it withall, I must & will acknowledge my selfe greatly indebted vnto your Ladyships.' Calling them a 'worthy pair,' Middleton dedicates his *The World Tossed at Tennis* (1620) to Mary Howard and her husband Charles, Baron of Effingham. Obviously these are Middleton's friends, and he offers this drama to them to celebrate their wedding: 'Being then an entertainment for the best – / Your noble nuptials comes to celebrate.'[18] John Ford hopes that Mary and John Wyrley will look with favor on *The Lady's Trial* (1639), which he offers 'to the mercy of your *Iudgements*: and shall rate *It* at a higher value . . . if you onely allow *It* the favour of *Adoption*.'[19] In these brief examples one observes three different motivations for the dedications: to become known to the patroness, to honor a special event, and to have the play received favorably.

Bridget Radcliffe, Countess of Sussex, receives Thomas Kyd's adulation in the dedication to his translation of Garnier's *Cornelia* (1594), in what seems a rather blatant appeal for reward. Though Kyd first modestly refers to his work as 'rough, vnpollished,' he warms to the task and finally declares: 'A fitter present for a Patronesse . . . I could not finde.'[20] He is aware of the countess's 'noble and heroick dispositions' and her 'honourable fauours past (though neyther making needles glozes of the one, nor spoyling paper with the others Pharisaical embroiderie)'; and he thus presumes upon her 'true conceit and entertainement of these small endeuours, that thus I purposed to make known my memory of you and them to be immortal.' Whether the countess rewarded Kyd is uncertain, but she was also the dedicatee of other literary works, including Greene's *Philomela*.[21]

Philip Massinger cites the precedent of Italy, where women have granted patronage and protection to writers (though he need not have looked across the waters), as justification for sending his play *The Duke of Milan* (1623) to Katherine Stanhope (wife of Philip Lord Stanhope, eventually Earl of Chesterfield). He leaves these 'weake, and imperfect labours, at the altar of your fauour' because 'there is no other meanes left mee (my misfortunes hauing cast me on this course)' than to let the world know 'that I am ever your Ladyships creature.'[22] Lady Katherine was also the dedicatee of a few other works, primarily religious writings, all after Massinger's desperate plea for assistance.

Though we know little of Samuel Brandon, the author of *Virtuous Octavia* (1598), he seems to have been acquainted with Lady Lucy Audley (Audelay), wife of George, first Earl of Castlehaven, to whom he dedicated this play. He proclaims her 'Rare Phoenix' and 'Rich treasurer, of heauens best treasuries.'[23] And he closes: 'These lines, wherein, if ought be free from blame,/ Your noble *Genius* taught my Pen the same.'

Certainly Ben Jonson knew Mary Wroth, to whom he addressed three poems, *Epigrammes* ciii and cv and *Underwood* xxx, and his play *The Alchemist* (1612). Mary Wroth, a niece of Philip Sidney and wife of Sir Robert Wroth, was characterized by Jonson to Drummond as 'unworthily married on a jealous husband.'[24] Praised by a number of writers, including Chapman in his translation of the *Iliad*, she also performed in Jonson's *Masque of Blackness*. Not surprisingly, then, Jonson dedicates one of his finest dramas to her, praising her value, uncommon 'in these times.'[25] And Jonson's relatively brief statement provides him the occasion to glance at those who indulge in fulsome praise: 'But this, safe in your iudgement (which is a SIDNEYS) is forbidden to speake more; least it talke, or looke like one of the ambitious Faces of the time: who, the more they paint, are the lesse themselues.' Intentionally or not, Jonson draws a link between the dedication and the play proper, whose character *Face* is essential in the grand con game of alchemy and who takes on many guises, each one making him less himself. Jonson's satiric bent, which has full rein in the play, surfaces in the dedication to the patroness. It is also interesting to note that *Epigramme* ciii emphasizes Mary Wroth's Sidney connection and *Epigramme* cv finds in her 'all treasure lost of th'age before,' both themes in *The Alchemist* statement, suggesting that they may all have been written about the same time.

In the final decade before the theatres close, Joseph Rutter, who according to Bentley became a disciple of Jonson in his old age, celebrates the virtues of Lady Theophilia Cooke (Coke) in the translation of the second part of *The Cid* (1640). He recalls a conversation and wishes that the French author of the play (Corneille) had her wisdom; he offers the play to her patronage 'lest I be thought indiscreet in placing it else-where, or unmindfull of what I owe you, though this be the least part of that returne which is meant to you.'[26] In 1635 three other works were dedicated to Lady Theophilia. Reflecting apparent long experience with the Willoughby family, William Sampson selects Ann to be patroness for his *The Vow Breaker* (1636): 'it properly prostrates it selfe to you, for a patronesse.'[27] He praises her 'Candor, beauty, goodnes, and vertues: against those foule mouthd detractors, who . . . sought to villifie an unblaunchd Laune, a vestall puritie, a truth like Innocence.' In part Sampson is responding to his critics, 'ignorant Censurers (those Critticall Momes that have no language but satirrick Calumnie).' But he closes with a wish for Ann Willoughby: 'continue ever in that noble pedigree of vertues, . . . heaven keepe you from faunning parasites, and busie gossips, and send you a Husband, and a good one.' (She was eventually married to Thomas Aston.)

A personal relationship in these cases makes the woman a natural choice for patroness of the drama. The dramatist James Shirley more explicitly than others confronts the issue of selecting a woman for patroness instead of a man. In the dedication of *Changes, or Love in a Maze* (1632) to Dorothy Shirley (no relation) he acknowledges 'custom, that to men/ Such poems are presented; but my pen/ Is not engag'd, nor can allow too far/ A Salic law in poetry, to bar/ Ladies th'inheritance of wit.'[28] But, as the evidence shows, by 1632 singling out women as dedicatees of drama, if not commonplace, was not uncommon.

Elizabeth Cary, referred to above as a dramatist, received the dedication for *The Workes of Mr. Iohn Marston* (1633); she was cited for recognition by the publisher of the volume, William Sheares. He uses the dedication as a means of defending drama and touting the virtues of the plays contained in the collection. He does not understand why plays 'should appeare so vile and abominable, that they should bee so vehemently inveighed against.'[29] Perhaps it is because they are 'plays': 'The name it seemes somewhat offends them, whereas if they were styled Workes, they might haue their Approbation also' (sig. A3^{v}). Hoping to have 'pacified that precise Sect,' Sheares has styled the collection *The Works of Mr. IOHN MARSTON.* He next praises Marston, 'equall unto the best Poets of our times,' whose work is 'free from all obscene speeches' and who is 'himselfe an enemie to all such as stuffe their Scenes with ribaldry, and lard their lines with scurrilous taunts and jests' (sigs. A3^{v}, A4). This defense makes one wonder if Sheares has read the plays carefully and observed the language of, for instance, *The Dutch Courtesan.* Because Elizabeth Cary is herself a writer 'well acquainted with the Muses,' Sheares is 'imboldened to present these Workes unto your Honours view' (sig. A4). Indeed, the report is that Lady Elizabeth is 'the Mirror of your sex, the admiration, not onely of this Iland, but of all adjacent Countries and Dominions, which are acquainted with your rare Vertues, and Endowments' (sig. $A4^v$). Sheares does not seem to speak from personal knowledge of the woman; and can we suppose that he knew that she had become a Catholic? It is difficult to see how such a dedicatee would quieten the 'precise Sect.' In any event, he obviously thought her reputation sufficient to enhance his publishing venture. She had, after all, been the dedicatee of several other works, beginning with Drayton's *Englands Heroicall Epistles* (1597).

The final two women patrons of drama are the best known: the Countess of Bedford and the Countess of Pembroke. Lucy Russell, wife of Edward, third Earl of Bedford, received more dedications than any other woman associated with the drama; these dedications, coming from such writers as Daniel, Davies, Drayton, Florio, Chapman, and Jonson, range over a forty-four year period, 1583 to 1627, suggesting her continuing prominence and importance for writers. The fortunes of John Donne were also closely involved with the countess.[30] Hers is an explicit case of reward and support to a number of writers. With regard to the drama, she has importance particularly for Jonson and Daniel.

Because of her prominence at court and her influence with Queen Anne, the countess doubtless paved the way for Jonson's masques. She herself performed in *The Masque of Blackness*, *Masque of Beauty*, *Hymenaei*, and *The Masque of Queens*; 'she organized *Lovers Made Men* for Lord Hay in 1617.'[31] In a special issue of *Cynthia's Revels* (1601), Jonson included an address praising the countess. Because it is brief and not often reprinted, I quote the entire dedication, entitled 'Author *ad Librum*,' found in the copy in the William Andrews Clark Library, Los Angeles:

> Goe little Booke, Goe little *Fable*
> vnto the bright, and amiable
> LVCY of BEDFORD; she, that Bounty
> appropriates still vnto that *County*:
> Tell her, his *Muse* that did inuent thee
> to CYNTHIAS fayrest *Nymph* hath sent thee,
> And sworne, that he will quite discard thee
> if any way she do rewarde thee
> But with a *Kisse*, (if thou canst dare it)
> of her white Hand; or she can spare it.

One can be reasonably sure that Jonson hoped for and indeed received more than a simple kiss for his dramatic text. *Epigrammes* lxxvi, lxxxiv, and xciv also celebrate Lucy Russell.

When Jonson was in jail for his part in *Eastward Ho*, he apparently wrote a letter to the countess, or at least that is the conjecture of his modern editors Herford and Simpson. He begs for help: 'if it be not a sinne to prophane yor free hand with prison polluted Paper, I wolde intreate some little of your Ayde, to the defence of my Innocence.'[32] Jonson marvels that he is in jail: 'our offence a Play, so mistaken, so misconstrued, so misapplied, as I do wonder whether their Ignorance, or Impudence be most, who are our adversaries.' He closes with the implied request for help: 'What our sute is, the worthy employde soliciter, and equall Adorer of youre vertues, can best enforme you' (I, 198). Whether the addressee was indeed the Countess of Bedford, which seems most plausible, and whether she assisted, we do not know; but Jonson was freed from prison, and surely such influential friends as the countess could only help his case. We may have here, in fact, an unusually effective instance of patronage, in which the patroness aids the cause of drama by helping gain the release of the dramatist from prison. But then, implicit in the role of patron is the task of protector.

The Countess of Bedford offered considerable help to Samuel Daniel. She, 'who had charge of the Queen's masque for the first Christmas of the new reign, recommended Daniel to the Queen';[33] the result was Daniel's *The Vision of the Twelve Goddesses*, performed on 8 January 1604 at Hampton Court and dedicated to the countess. Daniel's pastoral *The Queen's Arcadia* was presented before the queen and the countess at Christ Church, Oxford in August 1605. 'He long continued to profit by Lady Bedford's introduction to the Queen, for she appointed him together with John Florio, to be a Groom of her Privy Chamber.'[34]

In the authorized text of the masque Daniel provides a 210-line statement, certainly the longest dedication of a dramatic text. He provides a lengthy account of 'the intent and scope of the project,' describing all the mythological figures, their iconography, and their function, and thereby greatly enhancing the understanding of the masque. Rather than get involved in the complex and sometimes contradictory iconological interpretation of figures, Daniel says that 'we took their aptest representations that lay best and easiest for us.'[35] He provides this extended account because he does not want the experience to slip into oblivion, for '(by the unpartial opinion of all the beholders, strangers and others) it was not inferior to the best that ever was presented in Christendom' (p. 30). And equally important, the dedication offers the means whereby Daniel 'might clear the reckoning of any imputation that might be laid upon your [the countess's] judgment for preferring such a one to her Majesty in this employment' (p. 30). Not only did the countess make it possible for Daniel to write the masque, but also she performed the role of Vesta in the entertainment.

The literary and dramatic fortunes of Daniel involve also the patronage of Mary Herbert, Countess of Pembroke, renowned for her support of writers. Pearl Hogrefe sums up Mary Herbert's contribution to literature:

> She gave practical help and encouragement to many writers when she became the Countess of Pembroke and lived at Wilton House; she influenced the writing of her brother, Philip, during his brief life; she edited and published all his prose and his poetry after his death; she published her own translations from French and Italian and had an outstanding part in turning the Psalms into Elizabethan lyrics.'[36]

Understandably she receives a number of dedications of literary works from such writers as Daniel, Spenser, Davies, Breton, Morley, and Fraunce.

The drama contains several acknowledgments of her as patroness. Abraham Fraunce dedicates *Amyntas Pastoral* (1591) to the countess, saying, 'If *Amyntas* found fauour in your gracious eyes, let *Phillis* bee accepted for *Amyntas* sake.'[37] Fraunce for the most part discusses and defends poetic form. If we may strain the point slightly and allow Sidney's *Arcadia* (1598 edition) as partially a dramatic text because it includes *The Lady of May*, a progress entertainment of 1578, then Sidney's dedication of the romance to his sister may be included. His moving statement credits her with being the inspiration for his work:

> For my part, . . . I could well find in my heart, to cast out in some desert of forgetfulnes this child, which I am loth to father. But you desired me to do it, and

> your desire, to my heart is an absolute commandement. Now, it is done onely for you, onely to you.'[38]

Most of it, he says, was written in her presence. The chief protection for his work, Sidney writes, will be 'bearing the liuerie of your name' (sig. ¶ 3^{v}). In the most personal statement in any of the dedications examined here, Sidney closes: 'And so . . . you will continue to loue the writer, who doth exceedingly loue you, and moste heartilie praies you may long liue, to be a principall ornament to the family of the *Sidneis*,' which is exactly what Mary Herbert did. She, of course, is no ordinary or conventional patroness for her brother's work: she inspired it and brought it to light by editing and publishing it.

More typical is William Gager's address to the countess in his *Ulysses Redux* (1592). He does not know her personally: 'Nimis inverecunde facio, illustrissima Domina, qui tibi, ne de facie, vix de nomine, cognitus, literis tamen meis Celsitudinem tua[m] interpello' (I am perhaps acting audaciously, most illustrious lady, who am known to you if not by appearance then at least by name, thus to intrude upon your ladyship with my writings).[39] But he is encouraged to be audacious, has heard much about her, and has admired her brother and the whole family, 'totam etiam Sidneiorum gentem.' Because of her extraordinary spirit and candor, he has sought some means to be known to her, 'vt aliqua tibi honesta ratione innotescerem'; and nothing could be more honest than literature, 'ac praesertim poetica.' Gager also recalls the indebtedness of many poets to her ('debent Poete nostri' [sig. A2]) and makes a valuable observation about patronage: it aids the giver as well as the recipient by providing glory. The dedication closes with Gager's wish that she will favorably receive his *Ulysses* and with confidence that she will: 'Quare peto a te, Nobilisima Comitissa, vt Vlysi, non in Ithacam, sed in scenam iam primum venienti, tanquam altera Penelope, saltem manum tuam exosculandam porrigere digneris. Quod te prestituram, plane confido.' (Therefore, most noble Countess, I ask you to be another Penelope and deign at least to extend your hand to be kissed by Ulysses as he comes, not to Ithaca, but now for the first time onto the stage. And I have full confidence that you will do so [sigs. A2^{v}–A3]). Her expected act of favor Gager describes as 'humanitate.'[40]

At the time that Gager was writing his academic dramas, the countess was leading a whole group of writers, including Kyd and Daniel, in translating Garnier's tragedies. Why Mary Herbert should have wished to make these French classical plays available in English remains unclear, but one can reasonably speculate that this program of translation and these particular dramas fit the ideas found in Philip Sidney's *Apologie*.[41] At any rate, the true course of English drama passed them by; theirs, as it turned out, was a program of the past, not the future charted by Marlowe and Shakespeare.

Having already dedicated *Delia* and *Rosamond* to the countess, Daniel seemed a prime candidate for carrying the English Garnier banner and hewing to classical principles of dramatic construction. By 1594, Daniel was 'deeply immersed in the Wilton atmosphere and *Cleopatra* is Pembroke work in a much fuller sense than *Delia* and *Rosamond* are. Daniel is keenly aware that this verse drama marks a new and probably decisive stage in his literary career.'[42] The play is an excellent example of what the 'Pembroke school' aimed at: 'a shapely and complete artefact that could be fingered piece by piece and admired for its skill and polish.'[43] How many other literary figures of this era self-consciously set out to shape the direction of dramatic form with a clear-set system of principles? The Countess of Pembroke is a patron of extraordinary quality, even if theatre history may in retrospect see the effort as a failure.

In the dedicatory statement prefaced to *Cleopatra* (1594), Daniel touches on several issues as he directs his thanks and praise to the countess. He begins with an acknowledgment of the countess's involvement with – and inspiration for – his translation:

Loe heere the worke which she did impose,
Who onely doth predominate my Muse:
The starre of wonder, which my labours chose
To guide their way in all the course I vse.
Shee, whose cleere brightnes doth alone infuse
Strength to my thoughts, and makes mee what I am;
Call'd vp my spirits from out their low repose,
To sing of state, and tragick notes to frame.[44]

He admits that his drama is a direct response to the countess's own *Antonie*: 'thy well grac'd *Anthony/* . . . Requir'd his *Cleopatras* company' (14, 16). And he acknowledges her support: 'thou so graciously doost daine,/ To countenaunce my song and cherish mee' (29–30). Thus he must labor to be worthy of this investment: 'I must so worke posterity may finde/ How much I did contend to honour thee' (31–2). As Daniel closes this extended statement, he voices what must have been a common idea for those who sought in patronage, if not financial reward, at least recognition:

But, (Madam,) this doth animate my mind,
That fauored by the Worthyes of our Land,
My lynes are lik'd; the which may make me grow,
In time to take a greater taske in hand.
(109–12)

But Daniel also provides an apology for the Pembroke endeavor on both aesthetic and moral grounds. Their cause is no less than 'To chace away this tyrant of the North:/ *Gross Barbarism*' (34–5), first encountered and done battle with by Philip Sidney, thereby emboldening others to wrest 'that hidious Beast incroching thus'(40). The references to 'darkness,' 'foe,' and 'Monsters' assure a stridently moral tone to the effort of poetry: this is no ordinary defense of drama as seen, for example, in the comment by William Sheares affixed to the Marston edition. In a nationalistic vein Daniel defends their style against the disregard of their European counterparts, 'That they might know how far *Thames* doth out-go/ The musique of Declyned Italie' (77–8). He wishes that the work of Sidney and Spenser were better known, enchanting the world 'with such a sweet delight' (91), thus demonstrating 'what great ELIZAS raigne hath bred./ What musique in the kingdome of her peace' (93–4).

Clearly Daniel needs the patronage of the countess far more than she needs him: 'Although thy selfe dost farre more glory giue/ Vnto thy selfe, then I can by the same' (51–2). He praises her translation of the Psalms, 'In them must rest thy euer reuerent name' (61). By such artistic efforts and by, one supposes, her acts of patronage the countess has achieved a fame that will be known 'When *Wilton* lyes low leuell'd with the ground' (66). And, in words reminding us of Shakespeare's *Sonnets*, Daniel says: 'This Monument cannot be ouer-throwne,/ Where, in eternall Brasse remaines thy Name' (71–2).

Later editions of *Cleopatra* provide an interesting insight into the waxing and waning of patronage. As Joan Rees points out, the verse dedication was omitted in the editions of 1605 and 1607; but by the 1611 text the dedication, slightly revised, reappeared, suggesting that the countess had resumed her patronage of Daniel.[45] Though he covers much of the same ground, some changes occur, as one would expect in a statement written nearly twenty years later. He acknowledges their renewed relationship: 'And glad I am I haue renewed to you/ The vowes I owe your worth, although thereby/ There can no glory vnto you accrew.'[46] The dedication begins by calling attention to the obvious fact that the countess is a woman, a point not emphasized in the 1594 verses:

> Behold the work which once thou didst impose
> Great sister of the Muses glorious starre
> Of femall worth, who didst at first disclose
> Vnto our times, what noble powers there are
> In womens harts, and sent example farre
> To call vp others to like studious thoughts . . .
> (sig. E3)

Why Daniel should make this point in 1611 is uncertain; perhaps in the era of the male-dominated court it seemed worth noting the remarkable accomplishments of women and of the countess in particular.

This study of women patrons of the drama may be seen as a verification of Daniel's comment that there are noble powers in women's hearts, powers that led to the creation and active support of the drama, that inspired some dramatists to do their work, that provided financial support, that offered the much-desired but sometimes elusive quality of favorable recognition. Assessing the contribution of women to the flourishing of drama during the Renaissance becomes not simply a matter of tallying monies expended, but rather of taking into account reputations secured, possibilities gained, doors opened, and the more intangible qualities of guiding and supporting spirits. Without understanding the role of women as patrons we possess a partial and incomplete picture of theatrical activity in this its richest period.

Notes

1 For support of this research I am indebted to a grant-in-aid from the American Council of Learned Societies and the General Research Fund of the University of Kansas.
The argument of Jean Gagen in *The New Woman: Her Emergence in the English Drama 1600–1730* (New York, 1954), p. 16, and in Pearl Hogrefe, *Tudor Women: Commoners and Queens* (Ames, IA, 1975), p. 142.

2 Catherine M. Dunne, 'The Changing Image of Woman in Renaissance Society and Literature,' in *What Manner of Woman: Essays on English and American Life and Literature*, ed. Marlene Springer (New York, 1977), pp. 15–38; David J. Latt, 'Praising Virtuous Ladies: The Literary Image and Historical Reality of Women in Seventeenth-Century England,' in *What Manner of Woman*, ed. Springer, pp. 39–64. Apparently neither writer had a chance to consult Professor Hogrefe's book.

3 Juliet Dusinbere, *Shakespeare and the Nature of Women* (London, 1975), p. 5.

4 Other studies that are of some interest: Gamaliel Bradford, *Elizabethan Women* (Cambridge, MA, 1936); Carroll Camden, *The Elizabethan Woman* (Houston, TX, 1952); Ruth Kelso, *Doctrine for the Lady of the Renaissance* (Urbana, IL, 1956); Mary R. Mahl and Helene Koon (eds) *The Female Spectator: English Women Writers before 1800* (Bloomington, IN, and London, 1977); M. Philips and W. S. Tomkinson, *English Women in Life and Letters* (Oxford,

1926); Roger Thompson, *Women in Stuart England and America: A Comparative Study* (London and Boston, MA, 1974).

5 V. Sackville-West, *The Diary of the Lady Anne Clifford* (London, 1923). G. E. Bentley in *Jacobean and Caroline Stage* (Oxford, 1956) has cited most, but not all, of Lady Anne's theatrical references. See also George C. Williamson, *Lady Anne Clifford . . . Her Life, Letters, and Work* (Kendal, 1922).

6 For brief discussion see David M. Bergeron, *English Civic Pageantry 1558–1642* (London and Columbia, SC, 1971), p. 62. For the text of the entertainment see John Nichols, *Progresses of Elizabeth* (London, 1823), III, pp. 130–6.

7 J. H. Wiffen, *Historical Memoirs of the House of Russell* (London, 1833), II, p. 14.

8 Hogrefe, *Tudor Women*, pp. 133–4.

9 For a list see C.H. Herford and P. Simpson (eds) *Ben Jonson* (Oxford, 1950), X, pp. 440–5.

10 Herford and Simpson, *Jonson*, I, pp. 143. The speculation that the play was *The Sad Shepherd* is inconclusive.

11 Bentley, *Jacobean and Caroline Stage*, III, p. 453.

12 Bentley, *Jacobean and Caroline Stage*, IV, p. 549.

13 Bentley, *Jacobean and Caroline Stage*, IV, pp. 917–20.

14 W. J. Lawrence, 'The Dedication of Early English Plays,' *Life and Letters*, 3(1929), 31.

15 V. Heltzel, in *Studies in English Language and Literature Presented to Professor Dr. Karl Brunner*, ed. Siegfried Korninger, *Wiener Beiträge zur Englischen Philologie*, 65(1957), 74–86.

16 In a brief note Franklin B. Williams calls attention to the prominence of women as patronesses of all forms of writing. He finds that 733 women had books dedicated to them in the STC period ('The Literary Patronesses of Renaissance England,' *Notes and Queries*, 207[1962], 365).

17 Robert Wilmot, *Tancred and Gismund* (London, 1591), sig. * 2^{v}.

18 *The Works of Thomas Middleton*, ed. A. H. Bullen (London, 1886), VII, p. 141.

19 *The Lady's Trial* (London, 1639), sig. A3^{v}.

20 Kyd, *Cornelia*, in *The Works of Thomas Kyd*, ed. F. S. Boas (Oxford, 1955), p. 102.

21 References come from Franklin B. Williams, *Index of Dedications and Commendatory Verses in English Books before 1641* (London, 1962). Arthur Freeman explores Kyd's relationship to the Radcliffe family, suggesting that Henry, 4th Earl of Sussex might have been a patron of Kyd; see *Thomas Kyd: Facts and Problems* (Oxford, 1967), pp. 34–7.

22 *The Duke of Milan* (London, 1623), sig. A3. As the editors of Massinger point out, Katherine Stanhope was the 'sister of Fletcher's patron, the Earl of Huntingdon, and his relationship is surely the reason for Massinger's approaching her' (*The Plays and Poems of Philip Massinger*, ed. Philip Edwards and Colin Gibson [Oxford, 1976], I, xxxiii).

23 Brandon, *The Virtuous Octavia* (London, 1598), sig. A2.

24 Herford and Simpson, *Jonson*, X, 50.

25 *The Alchemist* (London, 1612), sig. A2^{v}.

26 *2 The Cid* (London, 1612), sig. A4.

27 *The Vow Breaker* (London, 1636), sig. A3.

28 *The Dramatic Works and Poems of James Shirley*, ed. Alexander Dyce (1833; rpt New York, 1966), II, 272.

29 *The Workes of Mr. Iohn Marston* (London, 1633), sig. A3. Elizabeth's husband, Henry Cary, was the subject of Jonson's *Epigramme* lxvi.

30 See Patricia Thomson, 'The Patronage of Letters under Elizabeth and James I,' *English*, 7(1949), 278–82. See also her essay, 'The Literature of Patronage, 1580–1630,' *Essays in Criticism*, 2(1952), 267–84.

31 Herford and Simpson, *Jonson*, X, 440.

32 Herford and Simpson, *Jonson*, X, 197.

33 Joan Rees, *Samuel Daniel: A Critical and Biographical Study* (Liverpool, 1964), p. 90.

34 John Buxton, *Sir Philip Sidney and the English Renaissance* (London, 1954), p. 229.

35 'The Vision of the Twelve Goddesses,' ed. Joan Rees in *A Book of Masques in Honour of Allardyce Nicoll* (Cambridge, 1967), p. 26.

36 Hogrefe, *Tudor Women*, p. 124. In her dissertation Mary Ellen Lamb suggests that the

importance and extent of the countess's patronage has been exaggerated: 'her husband's wealth, her brother's fame, and her own reputation for generosity were probably responsible for the many single works dedicated to her by authors who do not seem to have been acquainted with her' ('The Countess of Pembroke's Patronage,' PhD dissertation, Columbia University, 1976, p. 255). The facts are that some thirty texts were dedicated to her, the second highest number of books dedicated to a woman other than royalty (the first being the Countess of Bedford with thirty-eight) – see Williams, 'The Literary Patronesses of Renaissance England,' p. 366. Ms Lamb further claims that: 'A patron's influence cannot be assumed for every author who dedicated a work; it must be indicated in some other way besides a dedication or the possible use of a literary model' (p. 241). But such a view creates more problems than it solves. The simple act of dedicating a text does indicate influence, whatever it may prove precisely about an act of patronage.

37 *Countess of Pembrokes Ivychurch* (London, 1591), sig. A2.
38 *The Countess of Pembrokes Arcadia* (London, 1598), sig. ¶3.
39 William Gager, *Ulysses Redux* (Oxford, 1592), sig. A2.
40 One might also include Christopher Marlowe in the list of dramatists who wrote dedications to the countess, though Marlowe's statement is prefixed to *Amintae Gaudia Authore Thoma Watsono* (1592). The dedication, signed by 'C. M.' and in Latin, sounds several familiar themes. Marlowe promises that 'in the foremost page of every poem' he will 'invoke thee Mistress of the Muses to my aid' (Mark Eccles's translation in *The Complete Works of Christopher Marlowe*, ed. Fredson Bowers [Cambridge, 1973], II, 539). Marlowe's exact relationship to the countess is indeterminate.
41 See, for example, Alexander M. Witherspoon, *The Influence of Robert Garnier on Elizabethan Drama*, Yale Studies in English, 65 (New Haven, CT, 1924), p. 67, and *passim*.
42 Rees, *Samuel Daniel*, p. 43.
43 Rees, *Samuel Daniel*, p. 48.
44 Samuel Daniel, *Cleopatra* (London, 1594), sig. H5, lines 1–8.
45 Rees, *Samuel Daniel*, p. 149.
46 Samuel Daniel, *Certaine Small Workes* (London, 1611), sig. E4.

5

WOMEN AS SPECTATORS, SPECTACLES, AND PAYING CUSTOMERS

Jean E. Howard

Jean E. Howard's continuing work on the role of women as spectators of Renaissance drama has proved a watershed for the way in which we reconstruct the dynamics of public performance in the Early Modern period. Using contemporary documentary material Howard analyses the way in which women were perceived both as audience and as object, both as innocents to be protected and threats to the dominant patriarchy. The questions which arise from her investigations remain important starting points for further textual explorations.

In the 'Documents of Control' section of *The Elizabethan Stage*, E. K. Chambers records a 1574 Act of the Common Council of London which represents an attempt to restrain and regulate public playing within the Liberties.[1] The reasons cited for such restraint are numerous and familiar: the gathering together of playgoers in inns and yards spreads the plague; it creates opportunities for illicit sexual encounters; and it provides the occasion for the dissemination, from the stage, of 'unchaste, uncomelye, and unshamefaste speeches and doynges.'[2] The document is long, and it contains little that would surprise anyone familiar with Renaissance polemic against the public stage or with the numerous petitions sent by the City to the queen and her council urging the restraint of playing during the next thirty years. What particularly interested me, however, was the way the document concludes, which is thus:

> this Act (otherwise than towchinge the publishinge of unchaste, sedycious, and unmete matters:) shall not extend to anie plaies, Enterludes, Comodies, Tragidies, or shewes to be played or shewed in the pryvate hous, dwellinge, or lodginge of anie nobleman, Citizen, or gentleman, which shall or will then have the same thear so played or shewed in his presence for the festyvitie of anie marriage, Assemblye of ffrendes, or otherlyke cawse withowte publique or Commen Collection of money of the Auditorie or behoulders theareof, reservinge alwaie to the Lorde Maior and Aldermen for the tyme beinge the Judgement and construction Accordinge to equitie what shalbe Counted suche a playenge or shewing in a pryvate place, anie things in this Acte to the Contrarie notwithstanding.
>
> (p. 276)

What is striking to me here is the absolutely clear demarcation between the dangers of public playing, involving the 'Commen Collection of money of the Auditorie,' and the acceptability of playing within a 'pryvate hous, dwellinge, or lodginge' where presumably no money was collected and where the audience had therefore not been transformed by a commercial transaction from guests to customers. As was to be true in a number of anti-theatrical tracts and petitions from the City, what is specified here as objectionable about certain kinds of theatrical activity is less the matter or content of plays *per se*, and more the practices surrounding public playing: specifically, the removal of the scene of playing from the controlled space of the nobleman's house to a public venue; the dailiness of public playing versus its occasional use, for example, as part of a wedding festivity; the transformation of those who attend the play from guests or clients of a great man or wealthy citizen to paying customers; and, implicitly, the transformation of dramatists from straightforward servants of the nobility to something more akin to artisan entrepreneurs. In short, in this document public playing is presented as altering social relations by the emergent material practices attendant upon play production and attendance, quite apart from any consideration of the ideological import of the fictions enacted on the stage.

Another document written a few years later, when amphitheater playhouses were an established fact, underscores a similar point. In *The Schoole of Abuse* (1579), Stephen Gosson, drawing on Ovid and classical attacks on the theater, rehearses a number of objections to the public theater that were to become standard tropes of English anti-theatrical polemic: theater teaches immorality; it allures the senses rather than improves the mind; it encourages flouting of the sumptuary laws; it serves as a meeting place for whores and their customers.[3] While Gosson certainly raises objections to the *content* of plays, he too is keenly alert to the disruptive potential embedded in the very activity of going to a play. It provides occasion, for example, for the conspicuous display of ornate attire and for the promiscuous mixing together of social groups. The money that allowed an upstart crow to ape the clothes of his betters and to display them at the theater also allowed him to purchase a seat in the galleries. While the public theaters were hierarchically designed to reflect older status categories (common men in the pit; gentlemen in the galleries; lords on the very top), in actuality one's place at the public theater was determined less by one's rank than by one's ability or willingness to pay for choice or less choice places. Money thus stratified the audience in ways at least potentially at odds with older modes of stratification, a fact with which Ben Jonson was still ruefully coming to terms several decades later when in the preface to *Bartholomew Fair* he satirically enjoins various members of the audience at the Hope Theatre to offer criticism of his play strictly in proportion to the amount of money they had laid out at the theater door.

> It is further agreed that every person here have his or their freewill of censure, to like or dislike at their own charge, the author having now departed with his right: it shall be lawful for any man to judge his six pen'orth, his twelve pen'orth, so to his eighteen pence, two shillings, half a crown, to the value of his place; provided always his place get not above his wit. And if he pay for half a dozen, he may censure for all them too, so that he will undertake that they shall be silent. He shall put in for censures here as they do for lots at the lottery; marry, if he drop but sixpence at the door, and will censure a crown's worth, it is thought there is no conscience or justice in that.[4]
>
> (Induction, 76–86)

At court, as Jonson's epilogue to the same play suggests, he can count on a spectator, the king, whose judgements are absolute and whose position is fixed, unaffected by the fluidity of market relations. In the public theater things are different. Much to Jonson's dismay, his art has become rather too much like a Bartholomew Fair commodity liable to judgment by those who can and will pay to see it, whatever their rank, education, and taste.

I wish to suggest that in such a context the ideological consequences of playgoing might be quite different for different social groups. Gosson indirectly broaches this issue in what is for me the most interesting part of his tract, namely, the concluding epistle, which is addressed to 'the Gentlewomen, Citizens of London,' a category of playgoer apparently significant enough to warrant Gosson's specific attention.[5] From Andrew Gurr's important study, *Playgoing in Shakespeare's London*, we now know that women were in the public theater in significant numbers and that the women who attended the theater were neither simply courtesans nor aristocratic ladies; many seem to have been citizens' wives, part of that emergent group, 'the middling sort,' whom Gosson most explicitly addresses.[6] The presence of such women at the theater clearly worries Gosson, and he voices his worries in a typically paternalistic form: i.e., as a concern for women's safety and good reputation. What Gosson argues is that the safest place for women to be is at home, busy with household management, with neighborhood gossips, and, for recreation, with books. As he says, 'The best councel I can give you, is to keepe home, and shun all occasion of ill speech.'[7] The dangerous place for women to be is the theater. The interesting question is why.

Ostensibly, the threat is to women's sexual purity. In the body of his tract Gosson argues that the theater is a place for sexual assignations; it is a 'market of bawdrie.'[8] Various wantons and paramours, knaves and queens 'Cheapen the merchandise in that place, which they pay for elsewhere as they can agree.'[9] Presumably, any woman – and not just a prostitute could fall prey to passion if inflamed by the allegedly lewd behavior of the actors or by the amorous addresses of her male companions at the theater. Yet in his concluding epistle, Gosson dwells less on the possibility that the gentlewoman citizen may go off to sleep with a fellow playgoer and more on the danger posed to her by being gazed at by many men in the public space of the theater. As Gosson says:

> Thought is free; you can forbidd no man, that vieweth you, to noute you and that noateth you, to judge you, for entring to places of suspition.[10]

The threat is not so much to a woman's bodily purity, as to her reputation. In Gosson's account the female playgoer is symbolically whored by the gaze of many men, each woman a potential Cressida in the camp of the Greeks, vulnerable, alone, and open to whatever imputations men might cast upon her. She becomes what we might call the object of promiscuous gazing. Gosson presents the situation entirely paternalistically. For the 'good' of women he warns them to stay at home, to shut themselves away from all dangers, and to find pleasure in reading or in the gossip of other women.

Yet who is endangered, really, by women's theatergoing? The intensity of Gosson's scrutiny of the woman playgoer indicates to me that her presence in the theater may have been felt to threaten more than her own purity, that in some way it put her 'into circulation' in the public world of Elizabethan England in ways threatening to the larger patriarchal economy within which her circulation was in theory a highly structured process involving her passage from the house and surveillance of the father to the house and surveillance of the husband. This process was more complicated and class specific than I am indicating here, and it is also true that men, at least in the elite classes, often had their marriage choices determined by the father and were in no absolute sense free agents. But it was as the privileged sex that men circulated through the structures of Elizabethan society, and it was they to whom women were by and large accountable, and not vice versa. The threat the theater seems to hold for Gosson in regard to ordinary gentlewomen is that in that public space such women have become unanchored from the structures of surveillance and control 'normal' to the culture and useful in securing the boundary between 'good women' and 'whores.' Not literally passed, like Cressida, from hand to hand, lip to lip, the female spectator passes instead from eye to eye, her value as the exclusive possession of one man cheapened, put at risk, by the gazing of many eyes. To whom, in such a context, does a woman belong? Are her meaning and value fixed, or fluctuating? How does one classify a woman who is not literally a whore and yet who is not, as good women were supposed to be, at home? To handle the ambiguity, the potential blurring of ideological categories, Gosson would send the gentlewoman citizen out of the theater and back to her house, husband, father, books, and gossips, where such questions admit of easier answers.

Yet I suspect the threat to the patriarchal order is even more complex than I have so far indicated. By drawing on the Cressida analogy, I have seemed to assent to Gosson's most fundamental premise, namely, that women in the theater were simply objects of scrutiny and desire, and that in that position they were in danger of being read as whores or otherwise becoming commodities outside the control of one man. But what if one reads the situation less within the horizons of masculinist ideology and asks whether women might have been empowered, and not simply victimized, by their novel position within the theater? In the theatrical economy of gazes, could men have done all the looking, held all the power? Joel Steinberg could not bear the thought that Hedda Nussbaum was looking at him, and he beat her eyes until artificial tear ducts had to be inserted in one of them.[11] Is it possible that in the theater women were licensed to look – and in a larger sense to judge what they saw and to exercise autonomy – in ways that problematized women's status as object within patriarchy? I have no definitive answer to my own question yet, but what I tentatively suggest is that Gosson's prescriptive rhetoric may be a response, not only to a fear *for* woman, but also to a fear *of* woman, as she takes up a place in an institution which, as Steven Mullaney has argued, existed at least symbolically on the margins of authorized culture, opening space for the transformation, as much as the simple reproduction, of that culture.[12] At the theater door, money changed hands in a way which enabled women access to the pleasure and privilege of gazing, certainly at the stage, and probably at the audience as well. They were therefore, as Jonson ruefully acknowledges, among those authorized to exercise their sixpence worth, or their penny's worth, of judgement. Whether or not they were accompanied by husbands or fathers, women at the theater were not 'at home,' but in public, where they could become objects of desire, certainly, but also desiring subjects, stimulated to want what was on display at the theater, which must have been, not just sexual opportunity, but all the trappings of a commodifying culture worn upon the very backs of those attending the theater and making it increasingly difficult to discern 'who one really was' in terms of the categories of a status system based on fixed and unchanging social hierarchies. As Jean-Christophe Agnew has argued, the Renaissance stage made the liquidity of social relations in a commercializing culture its theme.[13] I would simply argue that the practice of playgoing may have embodied that liquidity, not simply thematized it. For Gosson good wives who took up a place at the public theater were dangerously out of their true and appropriate place, and he clearly meant to return them to that proper place by threatening those who remained in the place of danger with the name of whore. The question is, when is a person out of her place *in* danger and when is she *a* danger to those whom, by her new placement, she is displacing?

I am suggesting that in the public theater, where men and women alike were both spectacles and spectators, desired and desiring, I doubt that only women's chastity or women's reputations were at risk, despite Gosson's polemic to that effect. Even when this theater, through its fictions, invited women to take up the subordinate positions masculine ideology defined as proper for them, the very practice of playgoing put women in positions potentially unsettling to patriarchal control. To be part of urban public life as spectator, consumer, and judge moved the gentlewoman citizen outside of that domestic enclosure to which Gosson would return her. While it does no good to exaggerate the powers of women in such a situation, I think the anti-theatrical polemicists were right to worry about female theatergoing, though not only for the reasons they were able to articulate. Reading Gosson, I wonder about the unsaid of his text. Focusing on the danger *to* women, did he not also feel endangered *by* them? In short, was Gosson's unspoken fear that the practice of female theatergoing, the entry of the middle-class woman into the house of Proteus, was part of a larger process of cultural change altering social relations within urban London and putting pressure on the gender positions and definitions upon which masculine dominance rested?

Notes

1 Two longer versions of this essay have been published elsewhere. 'Scripts and/versus Playhouses: Ideological Production and the Renaissance Public Stage' appeared in *Renaissance Drama* 20(1989), 31–49, and a second version appears as Chapter 4 ('The Materiality of Ideology: Women as Spectators, Spectacles, and Paying Customers in the English Public Theater') in Jean Howard, *The Stage and Social Struggle* (London: Routledge, 1994), pp. 73–92.

2 E. K. Chambers, *The Elizabethan Stage*, 4 vols (Oxford: Clarendon Press, 1923), IV, pp. 273–4.

3 Stephen Gosson, *The Schoole of Abuse* (1579; rpt New York: Garland, 1973).

4 Ben Jonson, *Bartholomew Fair*, ed. Eugene M. Waith (New Haven, CT: Yale University Press, 1963), pp. 30–1.

5 S. P. Zitner, in 'Gosson, Ovid, and the Elizabethan Audience,' *Shakespeare Quarterly* 9(1958), 206–8, explores the extent to which Gosson's account of the Elizabethan playgoing audience in the body of *The Schoole of Abuse* draws upon passages in Ovid's *Art of Love*. He concludes that Gosson's descriptions should not be taken as an unmediated eyewitness report of Elizabethan theatergoing. Gosson's debt to Ovid, as well as his polemical intentions, must be taken into account before one accepts his treatise as description of objective fact. In this essay I am more interested in the concluding epistle to the gentlewomen of London than in the body of the tract. More importantly, however, I assume that all of Gosson's tract is ideological and interested, rather than dispassionately objective. I am concerned with why Gosson and his fellow anti-theatricalists circulated certain narratives (whatever their source) about women at the theater; and I wish to offer a counter-account of what the middle-class woman's presence in that cultural space may have signified in terms of changing social relations in Early Modern England.

6 Andrew Gurr, *Playgoing in Shakespeare's London* (Cambridge: Cambridge University Press, 1987), esp. 56–60.

7 Stephen Gosson, *The Schoole of Abuse*, Sig. F4.

8 *Ibid.*, Sig. C2.

9 *Ibid.*, Sig. C2.

10 *Ibid.*, Sig. F2.

11 On November 1, 1987, Hedda Nussbaum called the police who came and removed 6-year-old

Lisa and 16-month-old Mitchell Steinberg from the apartment Nussbaum shared with Steinberg. Both Lisa and Nussbaum had been severely beaten, and Lisa died four days later. In treating Nussbaum for her many injuries, doctors had to insert silicon tubes to allow one of her eyes to drain properly. Her exact words of explanation were that Steinberg had 'a fear of being stared at and repeatedly poked her in the eyes for this offense' (*New York Times*, December 1, 1988).

12 Steven Mullaney, *The Place of the Stage: License, Play, and Power in Renaissance England* (Chicago: University of Chicago Press, 1988), esp. pp. 26–59.

13 Jean-Christophe Agnew, *Worlds Apart: The Market and the Theater in Anglo-American Thought, 1550–1750* (Cambridge: Cambridge University Press, 1986), esp. pp. 111–14.

6

WOMEN AS THEATRICAL INVESTORS

Three shareholders and the second Fortune Playhouse

S. P. Cerasano

In this new essay S. P. Cerasano demonstrates that women not only were involved in the public theatre through patronage or spectatorship, but also had strong economic interests in the playhouses themselves. By uncovering the evidence of female ownership Cerasano radically opens out a further area of female influence in Renaissance drama. At the same time she paints a lively picture of the realities of women's actual expectations of their role in Early Modern theatre.

Although women were notably absent from the English Renaissance stage they were involved in theatrical economics in a variety of different ways – as spectators, patrons, and as gatherers of entrance fees at the playhouse doors. But even more surprisingly, perhaps, they held economic interests in several playhouses. When James Burbage built the Theatre in 1576 he relied on his brother-in-law, John Brayne, for financial backing. At Brayne's death, ten years later, part of this loan was still outstanding, and so Brayne's widow, Margaret, became an investor somewhat by default. In attempting to recover her husband's assets she was ultimately forced into a lawsuit against Burbage claiming that she held an assignment of the moiety of the lease by inheritance. The court upheld that an earlier arbitrament should be honored, but when Widow Brayne sent a collector to the Theatre to stand at the galleries and gather half of the fees for her, he was refused entrance. Finally, Burbage's refusals led to a confrontation during which James Burbage and his wife called Margaret a whore and threatened that at any subsequent fray she and her supporters would be met with pistols 'charged with powder and hempseed to shoot them in the legs.' At her death in 1593 the conflict had not been settled.[1] Yet Margaret Brayne's situation was not as unusual as it would seem. Several other women of the period, also widows, either inherited theatrical investments or sought them out.

One of the most conspicuous examples of female shareholders occurs in the 1620s in connection with the second Fortune Playhouse. On 9 December 1621 the Fortune Playhouse burned down. Edward Alleyn, the actor who had once performed Doctor Faustus on the Fortune stage and who had originally owned the playhouse, noted only that 'this night att 12 of ye clock ye Fortune was burnt.'[2] Perhaps this account seems brief, even dispassionate for one who was so intimately connected with the playhouse for so many years, both as a performer and as a manager and proprietor; but as a seasoned entrepreneur Alleyn viewed the playhouse as a business investment, a piece of property that could easily be bought and sold, and just as easily destroyed by fire. John Chamberlain, London's chief chronicler and gossip, recorded the extent of the damage in a much more sensational account:

> On Sonday night here was a great fire at the Fortune in Golden-Lane, the fayrest play-house in this towne. It was quite burnt downe in two howres, & all their apparrell & play-bookes lost, whereby those poore companions are quite undone.[3]

The 'poore companions' to whom Chamberlain referred were doubtless the Lord Palsgrave's Men, who performed at the playhouse and who would have owned the playbooks, props, and costumes that were stored in the tiring house at the Fortune. This formed a sizeable investment for any playing company, and what it represented for the players can only be imagined. Yet Alleyn would have sustained as great, or a greater loss, having invested a minimum of £1320 initially on the playhouse and its surrounding property, plus eighteen years' worth of maintenance costs.[4]

Not to be defeated by this loss, Alleyn went immediately to work making arrangements to build a new playhouse, in brick. The financial arrangements for the construction of the playhouse also differed. This time he decided to form a syndicate and lease to it the site at a rent of £128 6s., under an obligation to fund the construction of the new playhouse at a cost of £1000.[5] When the first Fortune had originally been constructed in 1600 it had been funded by Alleyn and his father-in-law, Philip Henslowe. They assumed the financial burden of renting and maintaining both the grounds and the playhouse, in addition to the taphouse and other buildings on the property. In return for the use of the playhouse the acting company who resided there paid rent and a portion of their profits. In 1618, however, the playhouse was showing the effects of age, and Alleyn's circumstances had changed. Henslowe had passed on in 1616, so Alleyn was managing their many investments by himself. Alleyn himself was no longer an active performer, and many of the players with whom he had built his career were no longer performing. As a result of these factors, and perhaps in order to recoup part of his initial investment, Alleyn decided that the players should take on more financial responsibility; they should, in fact, become housekeepers, as the King's Men were for the Globe. This seems to have been an extension of earlier decisions. Under revised arrangements, initiated in 1618, ten leading members of the Palsgrave's Men had signed leases for the Fortune, its taphouse, and garden. They were to pay Alleyn an annual rent of £200, plus a rundlette of sack and another each Christmas.[6] Three years later, as a result of the fire as reported by Chamberlain, they had essentially invested £600 to use a theatre that no longer existed.

Despite the vulnerability of the playhouse and the magnitude of the investment required to build a new playhouse, Alleyn was able to find ten persons (not all were players) who were willing to become shareholders in the new Fortune. That the investors were not all players is indicative of the changes in the economic and professional climate of the time, for traditionally those who shared the profits of a playhouse, such as the Globe, were those who performed on its stage, or those who, like Philip Henslowe, had close ties to the theatrical world and had financed the building of the playhouse. As the 1620s approached, however, many of the players of Shakespeare's and Alleyn's generation had either died or retired. Increasingly their shares, treated like property, were bequeathed to others. In this transitional climate and perhaps even as a result of it, women – probably for the first time – made a showing in the financial sector of the public playhouses.[7]

Not surprisingly, given these circumstances, the shareholders in the second Fortune Playhouse were mostly non-players. In addition to Charles Massey and Richard Price (two players and longstanding colleagues of Alleyn's), the group included Thomas Wigpitt, bricklayer, and Anthony Jarman, carpenter, both of whom had potentially been involved in the actual construction of the theatre. The group also included Thomas Sparks, merchant taylor, William Gwalter, innholder, John Fisher, barber surgeon, and Adam Islip, stationer. Not all of these men paid for whole shares; some purchased half shares. Consequently, when the agreement was settled in the presence of Henry Underwood and Mathias Alleyn (Alleyn's nephew), a much enlarged group was named; and as some sharers dropped out over the years they were replaced by others, also non-players.

Amongst the original group of shareholders who purchased one half share for 51 years on 20 May 1622 was Frances Juby, a widow. On 1 August 1623 Margaret Grey purchased a half share for 50 years, and on 24 March 1623/4 Mary Bryan purchased a whole share for 49½ years.[8] Consequently, within the first two years of the life of the new Fortune three women held significant investments therein. It was an unprecedented situation; but at least in the case of Mistresses Juby and Bryan, they had prior connections to the theatrical community.

Frances Juby was the widow of actor Edward Juby, who had performed with companies at the Rose and Fortune playhouses from 1594 until his death in 1618, and who filled prominent roles within the history of the companies with which he performed. Juby seems to have been a colleague of Alleyn's from the very beginning, from the time when both were young actors in the early 1590s. Like Alleyn, Juby must have participated in the repertory that included Marlowe's *Doctor Faustus*, *Tamburlaine the Great*, and *The Jew of Malta*. According to the annotations on several dramatic plots he performed roles in several of the grand displays for which the company was known: the King in *Frederick and Basilea* (1597), Calcipius Bassa and Avero in *The Battle of Alcazar* (*c.*1600–1), Pitho and a Moor in *I Tamar Cam* (1602).[9]

Juby appears frequently throughout Henslowe's *Diary* witnessing various transactions, authorizing payments on behalf of the company, and acknowledging company debts.[10] Following the accession of King James, Alleyn's company received a patent from Prince Henry. After the first New Year's performance before the prince, in January 1604, 'Edward Alleyn and Edward Jubie' were the acknowledged payees for the troupe, receiving £6 12s. 4d. On 24 November Juby received the company's payment by himself for 'a play before the Queen,' and he was named in the Lord Chamberlain's accounts as the sole company payee up to 1615.[11]

Although Juby served as the business manager of the company he was also a prominent 'servant' to the crown in his capacity as a player. He was listed in the coronation list of 15 March 1604; he was named fourth in the formal patent for the Prince's Men (1606); and he appears in the household list of 1610. After the prince died in November 1612, Juby was named third in the subsequent patent for Palsgrave's Men. (The Elector Palatine took up the patronage of the Prince's Men.) In a letter from Charles Massey to Alleyn, Massey requested a loan of £50 on his share in the company, offering repayment from his daily wages according to a schedule that he claimed that Juby would execute:

> I wolde get m^{r} Jube to reseve my gallery mony, and my qua[r]ter of the house mony for a yeare to pay it in wth all, and if in [six] months I sawe the gallerye mony would not dow [then in] the othe[r] six monthes he should reseve [my whole] share, only reservinge a marke a wek[e to furnish] my house with all.[12]

Additionally, there is evidence that the Jubys and the Alleyns were close personal friends. In the years up to 1606, when Alleyn lived near the Rose Playhouse in the parish of St Saviour's Southwark, Juby and his wife lived nearby. Alleyn noted in his diary that on 13 September 1618, Juby and his wife dined with him at Hall Place in Dulwich, unexpectedly ('unlookt for').[13] And Juby was one of the original lessees of the Fortune in October, one month later. Barely two months after the Jubys had supped with the Alleyns the register at St Saviour's notes: 'Edward Jubye a man [was] buried in the church.'

Clearly, when Frances Juby invested in a share of the second Fortune she had, in some sense, inherited the share that had belonged to her husband. Thus, like Margaret Brayne, Frances Juby's financial interest was inherited. Edward Juby might well have lacked sufficient time to draw up a standard will. A noncupative will – a brief statement taken after his death and witnessed by several persons – states only that his wife should be his executrix 'willing her to bury him decently & pay his debt*es*.'[14] However, it is significant to remember that Alleyn had to agree to *grant* her a share of the playhouse. One wonders whether a discussion of the terms of the agreement might have constituted some of the substance of the meeting when, on 28 April, one month before the signing of the lease, Mistress Juby dined with others at Alleyn's house. Nevertheless, because there is evidence that the Jubys and the Alleyns enjoyed a lengthy personal and professional friendship, there is no reason as to why Alleyn would have hesitated essentially to extend Edward Juby's share to his wife. He obviously felt some loyalty to his deceased friend and colleague, and Mistress Juby must have possessed the necessary means to undertake the investment. Owning a share in a playhouse did not only deliver profit. Like the other investors Frances Juby agreed to participate in funding the construction of the playhouse, later 'covenanting to bear a proportionate part of all repairs.' She would also have contributed to the normal ongoing maintenance of the taphouse and grounds, and to any expenses related to sewer repairs or other, extraordinary damages. For this privilege, Frances agreed to pay a substantial annual rent of £10. 13s. 10d.[15]

By contrast with Mistress Juby, little is known of Margaret Grey who took up a half share in the playhouse for 50 years over a year later, on 1 August 1623, and who shortly thereafter, on 29 January 1623/4, expanded this to a whole share. Like Frances Juby, Margaret Grey was identified as a 'widow'; however, whatever other connection she had to Alleyn or to the company is unclear. Amongst the names of the virtually several hundred actors, dramatists, and investors connected with the theatrical community of the period none of them seems to have been surnamed 'Grey.' The likeliest possibilities are that she was known to the Henslowe-Alleyn family, perhaps a distant relation or someone within their acquaintance. (There are several female members of the extended Henslowe-Alleyn family – sisters-in-law – and cousins named 'Margaret'.)[16] The fact that Margaret Grey was able to upgrade her holdings from a half to a full share would suggest that she was solvent at the time of the 1623/4 agreement. Nevertheless, by 1637 her ability to retain her share was challenged by Mathias Alleyn, who had become master of Dulwich College. In a suit entered in the Court of Chancery, Alleyn and other college officials alleged non-payment of rent on the part of Margaret Grey and two others who had purchased shares upon the deaths of some of the original shareholders. The defendants argued that they had paid their rents until Christmas, 1635, when plague restrictions had forced the closure of the playhouses. 'And soe, acteing of playes being the way to rayse the rent (and forbiden), the defendants have not ever since bene able, nor are chargeable as they conceive, to pay rents.'[17]

More is known about Mary Bryan than about the other female shareholders, in part because she was wealthy enough to write an impressive will. In his early days, her husband, George Bryan, was an actor, touring in Denmark and Germany (1586–7), and then seems to have returned by 1590–1 when he performed in *The Seven Deadly Sins* with Strange's Men.[18] With John Heminges, Bryan is identified as a payee at court for the Chamberlain's Men in December 1596, but his association with that company is not traceable at any later date.[19] His name appeared in 1603, and in 1611–3, amongst the Chamber accounts as an ordinary Groom of the Chamber. Bryan's association with Strange's Men in the early 1590s would have brought him into contact with Alleyn who was periodically associated with that company at the same time; and Bryan's court appointment would have brought him into association with Philip Henslowe, who was a Groom of the Chamber and later a Gentleman Pensioner. That his acting career was brief seems to have had little effect upon Heminges and Condell, who named him in the list of actors in the First Folio of Shakespeare's plays. But by 1623, the date of the Folio's publication, Bryan seems no longer to have been living.

George Bryan's success was significant enough to enable his wife to purchase the largest portion possible of the new Fortune, one whole share. The designation of Bryan as 'Mr' ('Master') in the plot of *The Seven Deadly Sins* (he was one of three actors so designated) would indicate that he was a shareholder in Strange's Men.[20] In all likelihood Bryan sold whatever shares or theatrical properties he owned when he left playing for a position at court. But interestingly, his widow financed a share in the new Fortune, a share that she enjoyed for only eighteen months prior to her own death in January 1625/6.[21]

Mary Bryan made out her will in December 1625, and it was proved in late January, three weeks following her burial. The document suggests that she was fairly well off at the time of her death and therefore could well afford to purchase a share of the Fortune. In addition to the traditional bequests to the poor of the parish Bryan lists ten specific persons to whom she left bequests. These include two 'cousins', a 'kinsman', a former servant who became a haberdasher, a handful of friends, and Richard Buckley, servant to the Earl of Sussex. (Interestingly, the Earls of Sussex were patrons to a company of players, with various associations to Marlowe and Henslowe, from the early part of the sixteenth century. A company under the Sussex name is recorded as performing occasionally in the provinces, to 1618.) Bryan's will is also distinguished by the mention of silver beer bowls, gold bracelets, and a petticoat with gold lace, as well as a 'bedstead, bedding, and furniture . . . on which she now lies,' and 'one little featherbed.'[22] The remainder of her unspecified possessions went to her kinsman, Joseph Coningham, citizen and haberdasher of London, her sole executor. This bequest presumably included the Fortune share which fourteen years later was reassigned to Tobias Lisle.[23]

During the life of the second Fortune Playhouse many of the sharers continued to be players associated with the companies who performed within its walls; and of the non-players, most had a tenuous connection with playing or none that is easily traceable. Anthony Jarman, carpenter, and Thomas Wigpitt, bricklayer, seem to have been joint contractors who supervised the construction of the second Fortune. Both of them dined with Alleyn and some of the Fortune shareholders at his home in Dulwich on 18 August 1622, and the playhouse seems still to have been under construction partway into the next spring.[24] Edward Jackson of London, gentleman, and John Fisher of London, barber surgeon, had no professional link to the theatre world of the time. William Gwalter, an innholder, might perhaps have had an interest in the taphouse adjoining the playhouse, but was not otherwise involved in theatrical investments. Adam Islip was only marginally involved with the theatre, being a prominent stationer and one of the wardens of the Stationers Company in the early 1630s. It was he who took the fees and granted permission for several plays to be printed, such as Ben Jonson's *Staple of News* and Philip Massinger's *The Maid of Honour*.

Alleyn's decision to sell shares of the second Fortune to Frances Juby, Margaret Grey, and Mary Bryan must have been complex as well as unprecedented. But as suggested in the opening of this essay, his decisions would have resided chiefly in the fact that Alleyn was a businessman. By 1618 – probably because he wished to disburden himself of much of the responsibility for the theatre – he made a move to lease out the first Fortune to the players. At this time Alleyn was getting on in years, and in 1619 he drew up the foundation deed for Dulwich College, a combination orphanage and pensioners' home that was to absorb most of his interest and capital. It was also to be his most important legacy as he had no children by either of his wives. By 1621 when the first Fortune was destroyed, it would seem, Alleyn wanted to maintain this middle position. Yet he was probably also interested in maintaining his investment on a more limited scale. Alleyn's deep-seated loyalty to the Fortune's players, some of whom were life-long friends, doubtless played into his decision as well; and as Frances Juby and Mary Bryan were financially solvent *and* deeply involved with Alleyn's professional past it would seem that he judged them a good risk to be shareholders. Margaret Grey remains a more mysterious presence, her ties to Alleyn obscured by the passage of time. Still, given Alleyn's tendency to play the businessman before all other roles, he doubtless judged her to be someone who could be trusted to make regular payments.

There is no indication of how great a return the investors enjoyed on their investments. Traditionally, historians have held that the Fortune never fully recovered from the fire that, as Chamberlain reported, caused all of the 'apparrell & play-bookes' to be 'lost.' Alleyn's only surviving account book stops in 1622, just before the second Fortune opened. He died in November 1626. Any profit became part of his estate and would have been paid to Dulwich College. But the Fortune's success or lack thereof is debatable. Perhaps more than encouraging a successful enterprise, by allowing shares to be sold to women Alleyn was participating in a more generalized trend of the early 1620s – that of allowing shares to pass to non-players.[25]

Nor was this a trend unique to Alleyn's enterprise, or a trend that would end with the shares held by Margaret Grey, Frances Juby, and Mary Bryan. By the early 1620s the players who had served as the founders of the playhouses in the last decades of the sixteenth century had mostly retired or they had died; and throughout the course of their professional lives the concept of what a share represented had changed significantly. Shares had evolved into property, in the way any house or piece of land was considered property at that time. Consequently, it could be sold back to the company or, alternately, passed on to heirs. Increasingly the latter became the dominant trend, and so increasingly shares were held by non-players, many of them widows. In 1604 Robert Browne, actor and owner of the Boar's Head Playhouse, died leaving all of his possessions to his wife Susan. The Widow Browne subsequently remarried, this time the famous actor-comedian Thomas Greene, who died and left her his estate. She then married James Baskervile. In 1634 her son from her first marriage, William Browne, an actor with Queen Anne's Men and Prince Charles's Men, died. In his will he bequeathed:

> unto my dearly beloved mother Susan Greene alias Baskervile, all such summe and summes of money debts dueties claymes chalenges and demaundes what-

> soever, as either is, ought, or shalbe due owinge or belonginge unto me forth out of and from the Redd Bull Playhouse . . . whereof I am a member and fellow sharer.

William Browne's wife, Anne, also received a portion of his estate, 'all other my goodes chattells cattell plaite readye moneys debts and whatsoever else of mine' remaining after his other bequests and debts had been paid.[26] She remained single for only a short time and thereafter married John Rhodes, possibly another actor. (There were several of the same name connected with the theatre in London, but in different capacities.) Then, perfectly in keeping with other trends, she and her new husband invested in a theatrical venture, and so did her former mother-in-law, Susan Baskervile. There is a document trail, starting in 1637, surrounding the Chancery suit in which it was alleged that Margaret Grey was negligent in paying her rent upon her lease of the Fortune Playhouse. This trail leads eventually to an answer filed as the suit continued, eleven years later, in 1648. Here, it is clear that John Rhodes and Susan Baskervile both owned shares in the second Fortune Playhouse,[27] a business with which Baskervile, at least, seems to have had no personal or professional connection; nor did any of her husbands. For her, it was simply an investment, one of the ways in which women gained an entree into the world of the public theatres, although, as many of these examples suggest, the opportunities for women to exert a financial influence seem to have been the result both of accident and intention.

Notes

1 E. K. Chambers, *The Elizabethan Stage* (Oxford: Clarendon Press, 1923), II, 387–93. Hereafter cited as Chambers, *ES*.
2 George F. Warner, *Catalogue of the Manuscripts and Muniments of Alleyn's College of God's Gift at Dulwich* (London: Spottiswoode, 1881), p. 191. Hereafter cited as *Warner*.
3 Chambers, *ES*, II, 442.
4 J. Payne Collier, *The Alleyn Papers* (London: Shakespeare Society, 1843), p. xiv ('What the Fortune cost me, Novemb., 1599'), and *Warner*, p. 339 (Alleyn's expenditures on the Fortune, 1602–8).
5 W. W. Greg (ed.) *Henslowe Papers* (London: A. H. Bullen, 1907), pp. 28–30. Hereafter cited as *HP*.
6 *HP*, pp. 27–8.
7 S. P. Cerasano, 'The "Business" of Shareholding, the Fortune Playhouses, and Francis Grace's Will,' *Medieval and Renaissance Drama in England*, 2(1985), 231–51.
8 *Warner*, p. 30.
9 *Warner*, pp. 135–42, 144–8.
10 R. A. Foakes and R. T. Rickert, *Henslowe's Diary* (Cambridge: Cambridge University Press, 1968).
11 Mary Susan Steele, *Plays and Masques at Court* (New York: Russell & Russell, 1926), pp. 136, 139, *passim*.
12 Edwin Nungezer, *A Dictionary of Actors* (New Haven, CT: Yale University Press, 1927), pp. 213–14 offers much information on Juby. His letter to Massey is transcribed in *Warner*, pp. 64–5.
13 Nungezer, *Dictionary*, p. 214.
14 E. A. J. Honigmann and Susan Brock (eds), *Playhouse Wills, 1558–1642* (Manchester: Manchester University Press, 1993), p. 113.
15 *Warner*, pp. 29–30.
16 S. P. Cerasano, 'Revising Philip Henslowe's Biography,' *Notes and Queries*, ns 32(1985), 66–72, and 'Edward Alleyn's Early Years: His Life and Family,' *Notes and Queries*, ns 34(1987), 237–43.
17 *Warner*, pp. 54–7; this quotation from Manuscript I, no. 115, p. 54.

18 Chambers, *ES*, II, 304, and *Warner*, pp. 129–32.
19 Steele, *Plays*, p. 110.
20 *Warner*, p. 130, and Chambers, *ES*, II, 304.
21 The original muniment for Bryan's share has disappeared, but it is recorded in a Chancery dispute (1646) involving arrears of rent due on leases of the Fortune (*Warner*, pp. 245–7).
22 PRO/PROB10/431, extracted in Honigmann and Brock, *Playhouse Wills*, pp. 149–50.
23 *Warner*, pp. 54–5, 247.
24 G.E. Bentley, *The Jacobean and Caroline Stage* (Oxford: Clarendon Press, 1941–68), 7 vols (*JCS*), VI, 154–7.
25 For a more comprehensive discussion of the changes in shareholding arrangements, see S. P. Cerasano, 'The "Business" of Shareholding, the Fortune Playhouses, and Francis Grace's Will,' *Medieval and Renaissance Drama in England*, 2(1985), 231–51.
26 Chambers, *ES*, II, 304, 320; Bentley, *JCS*, II, 391–2, 451; Honigmann and Brock, 90–2, 179–80, 229. See also, Herbert Berry, *The Boar's Head Playhouse* (Washington, DC: Folger Books, 1986), p. 209, n. 18.
27 *Warner*, pp. 54–6, 341.

7

'WHY MAY NOT A LADY WRITE A GOOD PLAY?'[1]

Plays by Early Modern women reassessed as performance texts.[2]

Gweno Williams

In this innovative new essay Gweno Williams discusses the performability of the plays written by Renaissance women writers, drawing upon her own experience of producing Margaret Cavendish's *The Convent of Pleasure.* She also draws upon the experimental work undertaken by the Women and Dramatic Production Project, to confirm unquestionably that the texts considered in Part III of this book may be successfully staged before a late-twentieth-century audience. By focusing upon the performance aspect of the plays, Williams not only revises our understanding of the dramas' contemporary production values, but also makes us reconsider the theatrical awareness of the Renaissance women playwrights who wrote them.

Prologue

Since approximately 1970 a rich and varied range of writing by Early Modern women has been rediscovered by both feminist critics and Renaissance scholars and has become widely available for study and discussion. Texts in genres such as poetry, drama, romance, autobiography, conduct books, spiritual testimony, and biography have been reassessed as critically interesting and important and have been published in modern editions or anthologised, some for the first time since their original date of publication, others, which previously existed only in manuscript, for the very first time.[3]

This essay concentrates on drama, the approximately thirty plays written by eight Early Modern women writers between 1550 and 1668, and goes against the current critical consensus by controversially viewing and discussing these plays primarily as performance texts. I argue that the continuing and increasingly undeserved question mark over the issue of the performability of these plays has led to the maintenance of a critical blind-spot, a repeated and sustained ambivalence about their significance and full status as theatrical texts and their unique and important place in the complex history of English drama. By extension this question mark has also been applied to the literary competence, critical judgement, theatrical imagination and dramatic understanding of the writers themselves.

The plays referred to here are *Iphigenia at Aulis* (*c*.1550) by Jane Lumley; *The Tragedie of Antonie* (1595) by Mary Sidney; *The Tragedy of Mariam* (1613) by Elizabeth Cary; *Love's Victory* (*c*.1621) by Mary Wroth; *The Concealed Fancies* (*c*.1645) and *A Pastorall* by Elizabeth Brackley and Jane Cavendish; the approximately twenty plays collected in *Playes* (1662) and *Plays Never Before Printed* (1668) by Margaret Cavendish; *Pompey* (1663) and *Horace* (1668) by Katherine Philips.[4] This list covers a wide range of dramatic genres including tragedy, classical history, comedy and pastoral. Contemporary records of performance exist only for *Pompey* and *Horace*, however, and this has proved to be a serious stumbling block for literary critics and theatre historians alike, demonstrated in particular by a marked critical reluctance to describe or define any of these women writers (including Katherine Philips) as dramatists.

The scale and scope of the above list may well suggest that there is no longer any need to argue the case that Early Modern women were active in the 'Golden Age' of English drama. These plays have been recovered, reclaimed, and are currently being reassessed and repositioned as part of the cultural history of English dramatic writing, as the present volume demonstrates. Indeed, a new comparative perspective on the drama of the sixteenth- and seventeenth-century period may slowly be emerging.[5] Yet the status of these plays and their authors remains significantly contested and problematic. In discussing writers working up to a century apart it is inevitably difficult not to fall into generalisations but I hope to demonstrate that there are a number of crucial common factors relating to the reception of these texts.

There is no doubt that, before about 1663, a combination of prevailing cultural and political attitudes and established theatre practices and traditions made it extremely difficult, if not impossible for a woman dramatist to have a play staged in the public theatre. Ellen Donkin has defined this as 'cultural and economic resistance to women *creating* meaning by becoming playwrights'.[6] Merry Wiesner makes a stronger statement about all aspects of women's achievements in the period between 1500 and 1750:

> Restrictions on women's ability to participate in the creation of culture varied across time and from one geographic area to another, and varied even more sharply from one artistic or literary genre and one scientific field to another, but at no time or place was women's access to cultural institutions the same as men's and at no time was the gender of the creator not a factor in how the work was judged.[7]

Margaret Cavendish wittily dramatises the self-defeating difficulties faced by Early Modern women playwrights in the Introduction to her first volume of plays, in a style reminiscent of earlier playwrights such as Ben Jonson (*Bartholomew Fair*) or John Marston (*The Malcontent*).

> *2 Gentleman*: A woman write a Play! Out upon it, out upon it, for it cannot be good, besides you say she is a Lady, which is the likelyer to make the Play worse, a woman and a Lady to write a Play; fye, fye.
> *3 Gentleman*: Why may not a Lady write a good Play?
> *2 Gentleman*: No, for a womans wit is too weak and too conceited to write a play.
> *1 Gentleman*: But if a woman hath wit, or can write a good Play, what will you say then.
> *2 Gentleman*: Why, I will say no body will believe it, for if it be good, they will

> think she did not write it . . . besides the very being a woman condemnes it, were it never so excellent and rare, for men will not allow women to have wit, or . . . we shall lose our prehemency.[8]

For social, economic, and even moral reasons women writers in England did not have the same privileged professional access to the commercial theatre as men. Nancy Cotton describes the Early Modern period as one when 'theatrical apprenticeship, money and [professional] contacts were virtually impossible for women to obtain'.[9] My thesis is that these particular historical circumstances rather than the quality of their dramatic writing explains why no plays by women were produced on the public stage before 1662.

This argument is interestingly substantiated by the fact that the first public production of a play by a woman, Katherine Philips's *Pompey,* took place in Ireland rather than England and solely as a result of the intervention of her powerful male patron, the Earl of Orrery. Similarly, no unequivocal evidence of private or domestic performances of plays by women in the period has been found, however strong or suggestive the internal textual indications.[10]

Traditionally, however, critics have explained the plays' lack of performance history by their assumed or perceived lack of dramatic merit, a view in which past history is conflated with potential, so that unperformed plays are automatically regarded as unperformable, and demoted to the status of less important and successful texts, whilst the writers are regarded as incompetent, unskilled, or dramatists *manqué.* For drama by Early Modern women still remains significantly overlooked in the male-dominated field of Renaissance drama studies. Indeed, a critical strategy has evolved whereby texts which their authors titled, formally structured and published as plays have until now, almost without exception, been redefined as 'not-plays' by mainstream critics and marginalised because of their lack of recorded performance history. A striking example is the influential theatre historian Alfred Harbage's reclassification of Margaret Cavendish's first volume of plays as 'dialogues' and her second as 'dramatic sketches'.[11] The extent of Harbage's influence can be seen in the fact that even Nancy Cotton follows him and calls both volumes 'dramatic sketches' in her chronology. Such dramatic critical attention as these plays have received often continues to be disparaging or equivocal, labelling them as so-called 'closet drama', an imprecise term which is actually taken to mean 'not intended for performance' or unsuccessful drama. Indeed the term deserves very special scrutiny. It has been called 'a contradiction in terms'[12] and certainly has no equivalent in other performance genres; there is no comparable musical term, for example, for: 'Who would claim music is best left on the page?'[13] It is not a term frequently deployed by writers themselves, arguably no Early Modern woman ever sat down with the intention of writing a 'closet drama', but an often gendered term imposed by later critics. Even critics interested in these plays have readily invoked this blanket term to allow for the possibility of a limited or subsidiary form of production or reading aloud, thereby fudging the larger and crucial question of performability.[14] Admittedly some critics may be responding here to the numerous apologetic and self-deprecating prefaces by women writers. Wiesner however has usefully raised important general questions about the status and meaning of this Early Modern rhetorical convention and its relationship to gender.[15] In some cases a writer's failure to publish her plays has been taken erroneously to indicate their subsidiary status.[16]

My aim in this essay is to interrogate these assumptions and to redress the balance by arguing for the hitherto unrecognised status of all the plays written in English by Early

Modern women as potential performance texts. Nancy Cotton argues that with hindsight the 1660s were a historical moment when 'the time was ripe for women to attempt professional playwrighting'.[17] I want to argue that there is clear evidence of women's ability to write successful and performable drama for at least a full century before this. Only the external social and cultural dynamics and circumstances changed some time after 1660, perhaps in ways that further research will need to determine.

Undoubtedly, ongoing research continues to uncover important information about women's varied and extensive contributions to the world of theatre culture in the period: as performers, patrons, theatre shareholders, printers and audience members. However this is no substitute for serious and detailed consideration of women's achievements as dramatists. Indeed, when the contribution of women to the development of theatre before 1670 is discussed, either attention drifts towards the emergence of women as performers rather than as writers, or actresses and writers are readily elided and their contribution to Early Modern theatre culture and history conflated.[18] Even feminist theatre historians appear to have accepted the critical orthodoxy that no woman wrote successfully for the English stage before Aphra Behn.[19] That this perception overlooks the rapturous reception given to Katherine Philips's *Pompey* in Dublin and London in 1663 and to *Horace* premiered at the English court in 1668 appears to have struck relatively few critics, except Cotton.[20] Arguably current critical perspectives are effectively replicating the past in the overlooking of Early Modern women's achievements as writers of drama. Interestingly, Stephen Orgel has suggested that: 'unwillingness to interrogate the most basic information is characteristic of theatre history as a whole'.[21]

In 1977 the socialist-feminist playwright Michèlene Wandor writing about the process of making contemporary theatre suggested that in the late twentieth century there continues a 'deep-rooted, often not articulated prejudice against the subject matter of plays about women or seen from women's point of view'.[22] This prejudice, identified by Wandor as 'uneasy pre-censorship' which, she argues, continues to prevent plays by women from being staged, appears to have been retrospectively extended to critical perspectives on the plays of the Early Modern women dramatists discussed here.[23]

Thus it is very important to recognise that the rediscovery of the Early Modern plays under discussion has partly been influenced by, and also contributes to, the ongoing broad feminist critical project, inspired and energised by contemporary feminist theatre, of searching for and uncovering 'a "lost" female tradition' of women dramatists.[24] The particular impetus for this is political, and argues for the strong continuity of past and present:

> If the patriarchal canon of literary and theatrical 'greats' is to be centrally deconstructed, then women's work from the past has to come out of the margins of oblivion in order to secure a future for the creative work of women in theatre.[25]

Without this research initiative, 'women's plays will remain invisible, minor, or at best "separate but equal"'.[26] Elaine Aston argues that as 'a result of looking for and concentrating on women playwrights, feminist theatre scholarship has plotted a very different historico-theatrical map to that established by traditional canonical criticism'. [27] This international '"lost" female tradition' begins with Hroswitha of Gandersheim (*c.*935–73), and might include, for example, Aphra Behn (1640–89), Sor Juana Inez de la Cruz (1651–95), Susanna Centlivre (1666–1723), Mercy Otis Warren (1728–1814) and Susan Glaspell (1876–1948).[28] On the other hand, it is baffling to recognise that the most striking omissions from this roll call of theatrical fore-mothers are the dramatists I refer to in this essay. So powerful has been the traditional dismissal of their plays as drama that they have remained almost invisible in the recovered field of feminist theatre history. In this context, it is much more difficult to cite lack of recorded performance history as a reason for exclusion, in view of the widespread inclusion of Mercy Otis Warren, whose plays remain unperformed.

My general objections to the current critical status quo and my reasons for foregrounding the issue of performability in these plays are fourfold. First, a careful, attentive and unprejudiced reading of these texts as performable rather than unperformable reveals considerable exciting evidence in the form of internal stage directions, detailed and precise references to contemporary theatre practices, metatheatrical devices and references, calls for integral stage action, sometimes without supporting dialogue, a frequent emphasis on physicality and on visual effects and specific references to the presence of an audience, particularly in calls for applause.

Second, the Early Modern period was an age with a high level of shared theatrical consciousness as demonstrated by the proliferation of dramatic texts, a strong theatre culture, considerable public debate about the conventions and influence of theatre upon society and a shared understanding and extensive usage of theatrical metaphors in all types of writing. Interest appears to have continued unabated even through the periodic closure of the theatres.[29] It therefore seems extraordinary to argue that these exceptionally literate women writers were immune to or uninfluenced by the pervasive theatre culture of the age. Every single one of the writers listed can be shown to have had access to libraries well stocked with plays, which she read, as both the style and chosen genre of her writing demonstrate. Furthermore, the reading of plays obviously underpins the translations produced by three of these dramatists. Autobiographical and biographical material reveals that these women also went to the public theatres in the periods when they were open, and to a variety of court entertainments.

Third, however, the crucial issue must be to interrogate on the definition of a good play. One important and basic definition of 'good' as far as a play is concerned must include performable. Where a play lacks any performance history, for specific historical or cultural reasons, the evidence to define it conclusively as 'not good' is surely not available. Milhous and Hume argue that: ' A playscript . . . is . . . a vehicle to be completed in performance'[30] whilst the eminent theatre critic John Russell Brown argues that an audience's experience is a central concern: 'a piece of dramatic writing . . . is a mechanism for catching and controlling an audience's attention'.[31] 'An audience must be held. Its interest has to be caught and its expectation aroused and . . . occasionally disappointed.'[32] *The Oxford Companion to the Theatre* defines the word 'play' as

> a generic term applied to any work written to be acted . . . the one essential is that it should be entirely or mainly spoken . . . at certain points in the history of the theatre there may be conflict between the text and its interpreters. A good play may fail in its own day and only be appreciated in revival.[33]

Finally, in 1994 the interdisciplinary research project Women and Dramatic Production was set up by Gweno Williams, Alison Findlay and Stephanie Hodgson-Wright in order to explore and realise empirically these performance potentialities by 'reading with a directorial eye'.[34] So far the project has mounted very successful world premiere productions of

Iphigenia at Aulis, *The Tragedy of Mariam*, *The Concealed Fancies*, and the central section of *The Convent of Pleasure*.[35]

In order to illustrate and support the above points, I will devote the remainder of this essay to a case-study of the play which comprised my individual contribution to the Women and Dramatic Production project: *The Convent of Pleasure* (1668) by Margaret Cavendish.The first recorded performance of the central section of this play took place in 1995, and has since been repeatedly rescreened on video to different international audiences.

The Convent of Pleasure in performance

The recent flood of critical interest in the varied writings of the prolific seventeenth-century author Margaret Cavendish, Duchess of Newcastle (1623–73), has not necessarily extended to her unperformed plays published in folio in 1662 and 1668. They have remained relatively critically unfashionable and problematic, perhaps as a result of the strong historical legacy of extremely negative critical comments on her plays. Three examples among many might be: 'in her plays she is seen almost at her worst';[36] 'unperformed and unperformable';[37] 'structurally [her plays] are incoherent and virtually unperformable'.[38] It is important to note that these judgements may well have been prompted in part by Cavendish's evasive and peculiarly contradictory remarks about the possible performance of her plays in the multiple prefaces to the 1662 volume. It is my contention however that *The Convent of Pleasure* is a highly performable play with a precise and carefully judged dramatic structure which generates audience engagement and involvement. It is entertaining, enjoyable, thought-provoking, fast-moving and theatrically sophisticated in its use of dramatic devices and effects. Polyphonic effects are created by the reiteration of the same material and ideas in different dramatic modes. The dialogue is witty, the play exploits genre conventions in a sophisticated way and creates erotically charged romantic and sexual comedy. Cavendish's plays are particularly interesting for their strong female protagonists, revolutionary sexual politics and highly provocative and challenging perspectives on gender relations. This is a protofeminist play in which women take centre stage in every sense. The main characters are female, they speak the majority of the dialogue, and their actions initiate and drive the plot. In my view *The Convent of Pleasure* stands as a deliberate and witty revision of male-authored plays such as Shakespeare's *Richard II* which allow minimal roles and dialogue to female characters. Demonstrably production can enhance, illuminate, inform and enjoyably complicate this text.

My individual contribution to the Women and Dramatic Production project was a production of the central section of the play from Act 2 scene iv to Act 4 scene i, as a very serious attempt to challenge the negative judgements summarised above. Regrettably, financial constraints (a total production budget of £50 or $80!) precluded staging the whole play. I invited my colleague Bill Pinner, an experienced professional designer and director whose work I particularly admire for its strong grounding in the physical logic of the dramatic text, to direct the play. As a director he would rigorously, even sceptically test out the performance potential of a text which was completely new to him. The actors were second year undergraduates studying drama. There was an agreed commitment to keep the text intact in performance, without any cuts. The whole production was created in a very intensive two week period, from first read-through to the live, world premiere performance. The actors had a significant input to the production through ensemble working, improvisation, decisions about casting, and costume design. They decided, for example, that the women's costumes should be made of paper to emphasise the artificiality and also the ultimately temporary and fragile nature and existence of the Convent of Pleasure. I had wanted rainbow-coloured costumes for the women, to emphasise pleasure and variety; the students opted for white to emphasise the convent setting and sexual naivety or innocence. The men wore ironic parodies of historically inspired real world costumes, and an interesting and subtle detail of this particular production was the gendering of footwear. Women were barefoot, to signal freedom, flexibility and even erotic sensitivity, whilst the men clumped, thumped and blundered around in heavy shoes. These and other insights were generated directly by the actors' responses to the experience of working on the text in performance, others came from the production itself.

The play depicts an idyllic contained separatist all-female community founded by the rich heiress Lady Happy as an alternative to heterosexual marriage for women. The Convent is not an explicitly lesbian community – there is a repeated and significant emphasis on moderation and the word 'innocent' in Lady Happy's manifestos and regulations – but it is certainly an intriguing private interior space for interactive female pleasure of all kinds: 'for retiredness bars the life from nothing else but Men' (1.ii). This convent surely lies on contemporary American feminist Adrienne Rich's 'lesbian continuum'.[39] The Convent of Pleasure offers its inmates life-long variety of sensual pleasure and entertainment together with complete freedom from the burden and dangers of reproductive labour. In other words, the erotic and dramatic economy of the play appears to offer or allow the possibility of a seventeenth-century version of safe sex for women, as Lady Happy's double-entendre suggests:

> Thus will in Pleasure's Convent I
> Live with delight, and with it die.
> (1.ii)

The Convent is not, in my view, Utopian; it is clearly located in the real world of seventeenth-century values, as the scenes set outside the Convent demonstrate. In production, the Convent wall, which both excludes and delimits, encloses and protects, as well as representing the boundary between the real and the ideal, male and female, becomes visible and crucially significant, featuring as barrier or backdrop as appropriate.

One of the most intriguing and enjoyable aspects of *The Convent of Pleasure* is the cross-dressed courtship between the Princess and Lady Happy and its centrality to the erotic and dramatic economy of the play. As a character says in Cavendish's play *The Presence*: 'Lovers scenes are most pleasing to the spectators, and are the best part in a Play.'[40] *The Convent of Pleasure* shifts constantly between apparently foregrounding sexual innocence and implying erotic possibility; a particularly important point in the characterisation of Lady Happy upon whom the convent's existence depends. The play's double investment of acting as 'Recreation' to mean both pastime and also an imaginative and creative reworking of demonstrably unsatisfactory real world heterosexual relationships is a sophisticated way of exploring the possibility and advantages of same sex love in these scenes. The ambiguities centre on the new entrant to the convent around whom the plot revolves, the great foreign Princess, a 'Princely brave woman truly, of a Masculine presence' (2.iii) and her/his developing relationship with and seduction of Lady Happy. I want to argue that the staging of a series of complex erotic encounters between these two protagonists contributes significantly to audience pleasure.

Working backwards from the denouement of the play, our student actors made a clear and unequivocal decision to cast a man as the Princess, something which is by no means critically agreed.[41] He enters the convent independently and alone, as the clumsy men outside could not, and perhaps he is a different kind of man, aligned with play, pleasure and femininity, rather than trouble, obstruction and masculinity. He soon appears disguised (or uncovered) in male costume as part of one of the usual Recreations/**R**ecreations in the Convent of Pleasure, heightening the erotic tempo of the play. I read the Princess as an informed and wittily devised reverse breeches part here. When s/he is undone from her/his artificial female costume, what is discovered underneath is a male body, with the possibility or promise of another variety of sexual pleasure. The uncovered Princess represents a much more sensitive and successful enactment of the other suitors' comic bawdy preoccupations with 'shifts' and the multiple meanings of that word. Our production logically symbolised this by the fact that he was the only man in the play to appear barefoot. Conventional gender categories are also undone through the sustained sexual and linguistic ambiguities surrounding the Princess who not only represents the fluidity of gender construction but also inhabits the liminal space evoked by her/his word play, linguistic indeterminacy and creation of multiple meanings. This is evinced by his fluid and equivocal usage of the term 'Mistress' and by his gender-bending lines at the high point of the seduction as he persuades Lady Happy to kiss,

> These my Embraces though of Female kind,
> May be as fervent as a Masculine mind.
>
> (4.i)

This issue is complicated by the audience's recognition of the Princess's masculinity which in production produces delighted laughter. Lady Happy's complete failure to see beneath his disguise is comic and I believe also draws on Margaret Cavendish's experience of pre-Civil War theatre. She knows it is possible for a male actor to pass as a woman, because she and her contemporaries have been used to seeing it done within living memory. In this play she stages male characters discussing what acting a woman entails and how difficult it is to do well (2.iv). The scene reveals a practical understanding of the acting strategies required with reference to voice, costume, gesture, expression in a manner reminiscent of the Lord's instructions to his page on how to 'usurp the grace, voice, gait, and action of a gentlewoman' in *The Taming of the Shrew* (Induction, 129–30).

The play is astonishingly explicit about the drawbacks of marriage for women suggesting and vividly illustrating why:

> Marriage is a Curse we find,
> Especially to Womenkind:
>
> (4.x)

The multiple reasons are particularly succinctly dramatised in the ten fast-paced scenes of the first play within a play in Act 3, which is set at the precise centre of the play, and underlies the heart of the action and the argument. This careful positioning underscores Cavendish's skilful and effective handling of dramatic structure. It is a detailed and violent catalogue of the horrors that women of all classes and ages suffer at the hands of men in the outside heterosexual world. This inner play marks the first of a series of generic shifts and changes of pace, in a sudden and decisive move away from the dominant mood of comedy, to a rapid series of shocking, graphic and noisy scenes enacting the trouble and pain of Early Modern women's lives, particularly the dangers of pregnancy and childbirth.

Yet Irene G. Dash (in an account of teaching *The Convent of Pleasure*) calls this first play-within-a-play 'one of the most difficult sections of the play' and confusing because of its dramatic structure.[42] She suggests that difficulties of understanding arise 'probably *because* it was a closet drama and not publicly acted' (my emphasis). In production difficulties are not apparent, and the knowing theatre audience can enjoy the complexities created by the visible discomfort of the cross-dressed Princess sitting amongst the complacent onstage audience. Furthermore these scenes of domestic and economic distress contain both pathos and bathos, and are, I contend, open to being played in different ways in different productions. The wailing, screaming women are a fearful sight, yet the very excess of their responses can also be deployed to create comedy. The extended and realistic dramatisation of pregnancy almost to the moment of delivery in this play-within-the-play offers particularly interesting and challenging production opportunities and choices. Alternate scenes depict a single female character in increasingly advanced stages of a pregnancy which apparently ends in the death of both mother and child. This character could be played by a single actor to create the sense of pregnancy as Everywoman's terrifying burden, or by a series of different actors to create the impression of a world crowded with and dominated by the physical and mental distress caused by pregnancy. Again the play's larger premise is enhanced, underscored and complicated by these scenes being played to women who are 'resolv'd to live a single life' free from men who are 'the only troublers of women'(1.ii), something which the horrific speeded-up pregnancy plot economically and graphically illustrates. Medical histories of the period indicate that these scenes under- rather than over state the risks and rigours of childbirth in the Early Modern period.[43] Margaret Cavendish is sensationally dramatising the realities of Early Modern women's lives, and deaths, which are very far removed from a 'paradise of women'.[44] It is also important to note that this is a revolutionary moment in English dramatic writing. In her illuminating and wide-ranging exploration of the concept of bodily shame in Early Modern writing, Gail Kern Paster states that 'Childbirth is especially invisible in dramatic representation, where the act of giving birth has been an offstage event, as unstageable as the other forms of bodily evacuation it so embarrassingly resembles.'[45]

The Convent of Pleasure is characterised by the skilful and confident deployment of different and distinctive theatrical genres and varied and contrasting dramatic modes, such as masque, pastoral, city comedy and epilogue. The colloquial style and realistic circumstantial detail of the first play-within-a-play draws on the conventions of city comedy, whilst the pastoral in Act 4 scene i moves effectively from lyrical abstraction into rural music-making and popular dance. As these metatheatrical interludes multiply, the audience watch the protagonists move from being passive spectators to becoming increasingly central actors, a direct reflection of the growing intensity of their courtship. This dynamic interplay is particularly important in the final play-within-a-play, the visually rich and elaborate Neptune masque, with its disturbing textual insistence upon male and princely power and authority. Cavendish's skilful deployment of the metatheatrical device of multiple plays-within-a-play in distinctly different genres suggests a dramatist who is confident, theatrically sophisticated, and has an informed dramatic imagination. She engages her audience's attention to the full. I contend that the theatre audience watching the reactions of an onstage audience which includes a would-be male wooer in a female disguise which only the audience have seen through, experience a *mise-en-abîme* every bit as subtle, complex, ironic, satisfying, and self-reflexive as The Mousetrap in *Hamlet* or the Masque and Antimasque at the end of *The Revenger's Tragedy.*

Audience pleasure in this play is particularly generated through comedy. Some of the most humorous scenes in the play concern the futile efforts of the male would-be suitors on the outside, including the significantly named Monsieur Take-Pleasure, to penetrate the convent and gain access to the highly marriageable heiresses inside. In the text, these suitors always appear as a group, slow-witted, incompetent, lacking in ingenuity, and often drunk. The actors playing these scenes developed the insight that the play is structured to imply that these ineffectual male efforts to enter the convent constitute habitual repeated actions, taking place on a regular basis. A strong dramatic opposition is therefore set up between the ingenious and creative women on the inside, enjoying endless varieties of play and pleasure, and the unimaginative and ineffectual men trapped in futile repetitive action on the outside. It is also important to stress, however, that the comedy of these scenes does not obscure the fact that they also form part of the rape shadow-plot, the sinister underpinning of the action of the play. The end of Act 4 scene x demonstrates the comic potential of the play, and the way in which the text demands to be reinforced with physical action. The male suitors on the outside explore the possibility of disguising themselves as women in order to enter the convent. Whilst reluctantly recognising the incompetence which would lead them to 'discover' and betray themselves, they revealed a hilarious bawdy obsession with women's undergarments and what lies beneath them. On one hand this is a wonderful opportunity for drunken and blundering physical comedy directly comparable with the dance of the 'Muscovites' in *Love's Labour's Lost* (Act 5 scene ii). On the other hand these scenes exploit bawdy humour to the full through wordplay on 'will(ing)', 'shift' as in women's undergarments, and on convent walls 'a Yard-thick', where 'yard' is synonymous with erect penis.[46] This bawdy dialogue provokes laughter, but also enacts the play's careful distinction between male heterosexual desire which is depicted as crude, insistent and dangerous to women, and the subtle, ingenious and varied 'pleasures' devised by the female convent inmates, with their hints of narcissism and same sex love. The fullest realisation of this gender difference is in *The Convent of Pleasure*'s repeated restagings of the threat of rape. The play's physical setting represents this, with the women voluntarily enclosed, whilst the men endeavour to penetrate their private space in any way they can 'to get Wives' (3.x). The first play-within-the-play concludes its graphic exposition of the horrors of heterosexual relations with the sinister threat of rape (3.x). The only escape is to a nunnery, a deliberately and effectively meta-theatrical and witty invocation and validation of the larger work's premise, a reprise in miniature of the plot. For the marriage which concludes *The Convent of Pleasure* itself carries problematic resonances of rape, when the unmasked Princess asks the Councillors of State leave to 'marry this Lady; otherwise, tell them I will have her by force of Arms' (5.i).

The play's conservative ending looks back to the tradition of Shakespearian romantic comedy with the Princess revealed as a man, Lady Happy married, subsumed and silenced, and the convent dissolved. Lady Happy's final silence is further evidence of the play's intrinsic performability. It is what Philip McGuire has defined as an 'open silence': 'one whose precise meanings and effects, because they cannot be determined by analysis of the words of the playtext, must be established by nonverbal, extratextual features of the play that emerge only in perfomance.' 'Such silences grant to those who produce and perform . . . plays the power to give them shape and coherence, thus ensuring that [they] will vary from production to production'.[47] After all that has gone before, this return to the heterosexual world may disappoint an audience. However, at least temporarily, they have viewed a safe and dedicated space where women could re-create the world in a version which allowed for female play, pleasure, variety and gender ambiguity.

The experience of production confirms my perception that Margaret Cavendish wrote drama in a deliberate, informed and intelligent manner. Her *Sociable Letters* demonstrate that she had read Shakespeare's plays and had a discriminating understanding of his dramatic achievement; her Prefaces also refer to other male dramatists she has read and admired, including Ben Jonson and Beaumont and Fletcher.[48] She was of course throughout her writing life also in close contact with a dramatist with an active interest and involvement in theatre whose plays were staged and revived in London, her husband William Cavendish. In 1661 the poet Shadwell composed a prologue for a revival of William Cavendish's play *The Country Captain*. It offers an appropriate comment on the performance potential of Margaret Cavendish's plays.

> A good play cannot properly be said
> To be revived, because it ne'er was dead:
> Though it seem buried, like the fruitful grain,
> It always rises with increase again.[49]

Epilogue

Evidence for performability may vary from play to play, but it is my contention that each of the plays by Early Modern women mentioned in this essay has performance potential yet to be discovered. I contend that women and ladies could and did write good plays and that this is a significantly under-explored area. To reread these plays as performable opens up new insights into the texts themselves, their relationship with other dramatic works, and the position of women in the period. If these plays are performable then critical attention will need to move from their perceived shortcomings to a much fuller consideration of who and what was excluded from the Early Modern theatre in its 'Golden Age' and why. Their voices ventriloquised, their bodies usurped and their potential as dramatists denied, Early Modern women need to be specifically recovered in the field of drama. A major reassessment of the role women played in dramatic production in the period is required. The early history of women dramatists in England needs to be reassessed and rewritten, so that Aphra Behn, for example, no longer features as a spontaneous beginning, but as the final breakthrough. Finally, there is now an urgent need for more productions to unlock and realise the dramatic potential of these plays. The new insights provided will lead, I believe, to a radical and necessary reconfiguring of the relationship between gender and theatre in the Early Modern period.

Notes

1 Margaret Cavendish, 'An Introduction', in *Playes* (London, 1662), sig. B, p. 2. All quotations from the plays of Margaret Cavendish are taken from the University of Leeds Brotherton Library Special Collection's copies of Margaret Cavendish, *Playes* (London, 1662) and *Plays, Never Before Printed* (London, 1668).

2 I would like to acknowledge the help and support of the following people: Alison Findlay, Stephanie Hodgson-Wright, Bill Pinner, Marion Wynne-Davies, Andrew Gordon, Judy Giles,

Louis Purver, Oliver Pickering and the staff of the Brotherton Library Special Collection, the staff of York Minster Library. Special thanks are due to the actors who realised *The Convent of Pleasure* in its first production: Steph Boyd, Sarah Davies, Claire Donaldson, Vicki Elsdon, Joanne Eyre, Paul Giddings, Debi Haworth, Sarah Hill, Esther Jones, John Matthews, Stuart Ratcliffe, Vivien Routledge, Sarah Salholm, Melissa Shorten, Claire Summerfield, David Tucker, Claire Wiggins.

3 See for example Cerasano, S. P. and Wynne-Davies, M. (eds) *Renaissance Drama by Women: Texts and Documents* (London: Routledge, 1996); Graham, E., Hinds, H., Hobby, E., and Wilcox, H. (eds) *Her Own Life* (London: Routledge, 1989); Greer, G., Medoff, J., Sansone, M. and Hastings, S. (eds) *Kissing the Rod* (London: Virago, 1988); Travitsky, B., *The Paradise of Women* (New York: Columbia University Press, 1989).

4 Jane Lumley, *Iphigenia at Aulis* (Oxford: Malone Society, 1909); Mary Sidney, *The Tragedie of Antonie*, Elizabeth Cary, *The Tragedy of Mariam*, Mary Wroth, *Love's Victory*, Elizabeth Brackley and Jane Cavendish, *The Concealed Fancies*, all in Cerasano and Wynne-Davies (eds), op. cit.; Elizabeth Brackley and Jane Cavendish, *A Pastorall*, Bod. Rawl. MS Poet 16; Margaret Cavendish, *Playes* (London, 1662) and *Plays, Never Before Printed* (London, 1668); Katherine Philips, *Pompey* and *Horace*, in Greer, G. and Little, R. (eds) *The Collected Works of Katherine Philips*, vol. III (Stump Cross: Stump Cross Books, 1993).

5 See for example 'Teaching Judith Shakespeare', *Shakespeare Quarterly* 47 (4), 1996. See also Roberts, J. A., 'Convents, Conventions and Contraventions: *Love's Labor's Lost* and *The Convent of Pleasure*', in Collins, M. J. (ed.) *Shakespeare's Sweet Thunder: Essays on the Early Comedies* (Newark, DE: University of Delaware Press, 1997).

6 Donkin, E., *Getting into the Act: Women Playwrights in London, 1776–1829* (London: Routledge, 1995).

7 Wiesner, M., *Women and Gender in Early Modern Europe* (Cambridge: Cambridge University Press, 1993), p. 148.

8 Margaret Cavendish, *Playes*, op. cit.

9 Cotton, N., *Women Playwrights in England 1363–1750* (London: Associated University Presses, 1980), p. 9.

10 Findlay, A., 'Playing the "Scene Self": Power and Performance in *The Concealed Fancies*', in Russell, A. and Comensoli, V. (eds) *Enacting Gender on the English Renaissance Stage* (Urbana, IL: University of Illinois Press, 1998).

11 Harbage, A., *Annals of English Drama 975–1700* (London: Methuen, 1964), pp. 153, 162.

12 Thomson, P. and Salgado, G., *The Everyman Companion to the Theatre* (London: J. M. Dent, 1985), p. 83.

13 Milhous, J. and Hume, R. D., *Producible Interpretation: Eight English Plays 1675–1707* (Carbondale, IL: Southern Illinois University Press, 1985), p. 32.

14 Hobby, E., *Virtue of Necessity* (London: Virago, 1988), p. 105; Randall, D., *Winter Fruit: English Drama 1642–1660* (Lexington, KY: University Press of Kentucky, 1995), p. 329.

15 Wiesner, op. cit. p. 160.

16 Butler, M., *Theatre and Crisis 1632–1642* (Cambridge: Cambridge University Press, 1984), pp. 105–6.

17 Cotton, op. cit. p. 53.

18 Donkin, op. cit. p. 1.

19 Aston, E., *An Introduction to Feminism and Theatre* (London: Routledge, 1995), chapter 2; Case, S. E., *Feminism and Theatre* (London: Macmillan, 1988), chapter 2.

20 Cotton, op. cit. p. 49.

21 Orgel, S., *Impersonations: The Performance of Gender in Shakespeare's England* (Cambridge: Cambridge University Press, 1996), p. 4.

22 Wandor, M., 'Methods of work – or who lays the first egg?' in 'How Theatre is Made', *Y*, 2, 1997, Arts Magazine of the University of York, p. 7.

23 Ibid.

24 Aston, op. cit. p. 23.

25 Ibid. p. 25.

26 Case, S. E., 'Re-viewing Hrotsvit', *Theatre Journal*, 35, 1983, p. 535.

27 Aston, op. cit. p. 23.

28 See individual entries in Buck, C. (ed.) *Bloomsbury Guide to Women's Literature* (London: Bloomsbury Publishing, 1992).
29 Butler, op. cit.; Randall, op. cit.
30 Milhous and Hume, op. cit., p. ix.
31 Brown, J. R., *Effective Theatre* (London, Heinemann, 1969), p. 28.
32 Ibid. p.9.
33 *Oxford Companion to the Theatre* (Oxford: Oxford University Press, 1983).
34 Milhous and Hume, op. cit., p.10.
35 *Iphigenia at Aulis*, directed by Stephanie Wright, was performed at the University of Sunderland in January 1997; *The Tragedy of Mariam*, directed by Stephanie Wright, was performed by Tinderbox Theatre Company in the Alhambra Studio, Bradford in October 1994; *The Concealed Fancies*, directed by Alison Findlay and Jane Milling, was staged at Bretton Hall in December 1994; *The Convent of Pleasure*, originated and devised by Gweno Williams and directed by Bill Pinner, was staged at the University College of Ripon and York St John in March 1995. For detailed discussion of these productions see Findlay, A., Williams, G. and Wright, S. '"The Play is ready to be Acted": Women and Dramatic Production 1570–1670' in *Women's Writing* (forthcoming).
36 *Dictionary of National Biography*, 1887.
37 Dinesen, B., *Rediscovery: 300 Years of Stories by and about Women* (London: Women's Press, 1981).
38 Shattock, J., *The Oxford Guide to British Women Writers* (Oxford: Oxford University Press, 1993).
39 Rich, A., 'Compulsory Heterosexuality and Lesbian Existence', *Signs*, 5, 1980, pp. 631–60.
40 Margaret Cavendish, *The Presence,* Act 1, Scene 1, p. 3, 1668.
41 Tomlinson, S. '"My Brain the Stage": Margaret Cavendish and the fantasy of female performance' in Brant, C. and Purkiss, D. (eds) *Women, Texts and Histories 1575–1760* (London: Routledge, 1992); Wiseman, S., 'Gender and status in dramatic discourse: Margaret Cavendish, Duchess of Newcastle' in Grundy, I. and Wiseman, S. (eds) *Women, Writing, History 1640–1740* (London: Batsford, 1992).
42 Dash, I. G., 'Single-Sex Retreats in Two Early Modern Dramas: *Love's Labor's Lost* and *The Convent of Pleasure*', *Shakespeare Quarterly*, op. cit., pp. 389, 392.
43 See Eccles, A., *Obstetrics and Gynaecology in Tudor and Stuart England* (London: 1982); Shorter, E., *A History of Women's Bodies* (Harmondsworth: Penguin, 1984).
44 Travitsky, op. cit.
45 Paster, G. K., *The Body Embarrassed: Drama and the Disciplines of Shame in Early Modern England* (Ithaca, NY: Cornell University Press, 1993) p. 163.
46 Partridge, E., *Shakespeare's Bawdy* (London: Routledge and Kegan Paul, 1947), pp. 224–5.
47 McGuire, P., *Speechless Dialect* (Berkeley, CA: University of California Press, 1985), pp. xv, xxi.
48 Margaret Cavendish, *Sociable Letters*, Letter 123, 1664.
49 Shadwell quoted in Grant, D., *Margaret the First* (London: Rupert Hart-Davies, 1957), p. 224.

Part III

EARLY MODERN WOMEN DRAMATISTS

INTRODUCTION

The essays in Part III all focus upon a specific English woman dramatist from the Early Modern period and are ordered according to the chronological position of the female playwrights and their oeuvres. Thus, Elizabeth I and Jane/Joanna Lumley, who both translated plays as young women, come first, and are followed by Mary Sidney, another 'Elizabethan' author, but one whose translation of a drama occurred when she was already a wife and mother. The next two women writers, Elizabeth Cary and Mary Wroth, may be characterised by a closer identification with the Jacobean period, and show a key development in that, rather than translate, they both authored original plays, the first tragedy and comedy (respectively) written in English by a woman. The final three women dramatists represented in this collection all belong to the Cavendish family, Jane and Elizabeth being the daughters of William Cavendish, while Margaret was his second wife. Their plays were written either during or after the English Civil War, and similarly denote an alteration in the way in which women participated in dramatic production, since their witty comedies and emphasis upon female performance mark the shift towards the professional women dramatists and actresses of the Restoration. Thus, this section traces one of the most important periods in the development of the English woman dramatist, from the initial forays into translation, through the composition of the first original texts, to a freedom of action and speech which reached its final culmination in the fully independent female playwrights of the present day.

In conjunction with this sense of a developmental process in the primary texts it is also possible to perceive a series of changes in the critical writings represented here. A number of the extracts and essays included in this section were pioneering explorations of Early Modern women's writing: the contributions by Elaine V. Beilin, Tina Krontiris and Barbara Kiefer Lewalski are all taken from full-length studies of the period which pushed forward our overall understanding of the field. Similarly, a number of essays represent the first key analysis of a particular author: Margaret Hannay on Mary Sidney, Margaret Anne McLaren on Mary Wroth and Margaret J. M. Ezell on the Cavendish sisters are clear examples of these important individualising analyses. However, as research on Early Modern women dramatists increased in volume and depth it became possible to take for granted their reputation, and this liberated a more complex set of separate analyses: Stephanie Hodgson-Wright on Jane Lumley, Margaret W. Ferguson on Elizabeth Cary, Gary Waller on Mary Wroth, Alison Findlay on the Cavendish sisters, and Sophie Tomlinson and Julie Sanders on Margaret Cavendish all concur with this more questioning approach. Thus, criticism on the Early Modern female playwrights collected here has moved from path-breaking commentaries to revisionist readings, and these in turn have thrown up questions and ambiguities which are still under consideration. Finally, therefore, this part offers a thorough and comprehensive account of criticism to date on the Renaissance woman dramatist, while simultaneously establishing a series of issues which will remain of interest in the future.

1

'WE PRINCES, I TELL YOU, ARE SET ON STAGES'

Elizabeth I and dramatic self-representation[1]

Carole Levin

Carole Levin's new essay on Elizabeth I looks primarily at the way in which Elizabeth used her speeches as a form of self-dramatisation, presenting herself simultaneously as author, text and actor. Levin then compares this self-fashioning with Elizabeth's translation of a speech from Seneca's *Hercules Oetaeus*, discovering in the process that the queen relied upon the same political discourses in the play as she did in her speeches. As such, Levin presents us with a female monarch who was as adept at the manipulation of dramatic language as any woman dramatist of her age.

Elizabeth I was very aware from the beginning of her reign how critical it was to her success that she control her self-presentation. Elizabeth early recognized how important it was to show herself to the court and to the English people, and she often used deliberately dramatic moments to gain the support of her councilors and her people. Her religious ceremonies while queen, such as touching for the king's evil and washing the feet of the poor on Maundy Thursday, were public ones.[2] When she was under attack she wanted to be seen, not hidden away. This was a strategy she developed very early. We see this in the letter she wrote to Edward Seymour, Duke of Somerset, in the crisis after Thomas Seymour's arrest in 1549, and it echoed in the way she handled herself in her sister Mary I's reign after the Wyatt rebellion. Once queen, she regularly went throughout the kingdom on progresses, and in 1588 accepted the Earl of Leicester's invitation to come to Tilbury despite councilors who wished her to stay safe at court. Yet we also have to take care as we discuss how Elizabeth presented herself dramatically as we do not always know how much of this presentation was actually Elizabeth's and how much was the way sixteenth-century commentators, also well aware of the metaphors of stage and rule, in turn presented their queen; present-day historians are also quick to use this metaphor. Yet even if Holinshed and Foxe and other sixteenth-century authors, for example, made Elizabeth sound more dramatic at certain key moments than may have factually been the case, that is also significant as a view of the importance of drama to effectively rule at this time.[3]

Though Elizabeth was not herself a playwright, she did have a strong interest in drama that is reflected in the ways she spoke and the strategies she used as queen. We know that she translated Seneca and cared about watching dramatic performances. Plays were frequently performed at her court.[4] But drama was more than pleasure for Elizabeth. It also worked as part of her style of rule, and as means for her to rule successfully. As Steven Mullaney points out, many of the English perceived the Renaissance monarch as an actor on stage, with the 'theatrical apprehension of sovereign power.' Anne Righter (Barton) further argues, 'Moving about his realm in the midst of a continual drama, the ruler bears a superficial resemblance to the actor.' Fritz Levy suggests that role playing was the essence of being a courtier, 'the great courtiers often resembled actors on a stage,' but Elizabeth forced 'her courtiers into roles of her devising, whether or not they approved.'[5]

There are strong interconnections between Elizabeth's court and the drama of her time. This is even more evident when we consider how some of the plays were staged when played at court. Sometimes the queen's seat was itself placed on the stage, so that, in the words of Stephen Orgel, 'there were, properly speaking, two audiences and two spectacles. . . . At these performances what the rest of the spectators watched was not the play but the queen at a play.'[6] Earlier in the century, Sir Thomas More had described politics as a 'king's games: as it were stage plays, and for the most part played upon scaffolds.' On the last point, More was all too correct. Elizabeth often felt 'on stage' as she went about the process of ruling, though this did not necessarily fill her with pleasure. She commented in 1586 with some discomfort, 'We princes, I tell you, are set on stages, in sight and view of all the world.'[7]

The idea of play, presentation, and performance as the essence of public life and sense of self has been carefully articulated by Stephen Greenblatt, who presents this self-consciousness, or self-fashioning, as especially acute in the English Renaissance. Elizabeth as the highest in the realm had not only the most exacting part to play, but in fact many different parts that she herself created. Even in her most casual, seemingly spontaneous remarks, Elizabeth was playing a role, aware of how her audience – whether foreign ambassadors, Parliament, her council, or her people – would respond. Patricia Fumerton suggests that, 'Each of her gestures toward sincere self-revelation is self-concealing, cloaked in the artifice of politics.' While it is possible that Elizabeth had some genuinely open, unpolished and uncensored conversations with her intimates, what we have recorded as evidence of Elizabeth's speech shows the queen in control, masking what she may be thinking, never telling us completely who she is. There are very few recorded utterances that appear utterly spontaneous and without calculation. As Wallace MacCaffrey points out, 'the inner woman remains locked away from us.' Beryl Hughes argues of Elizabeth that 'no other English monarch had such an obsession with her own stage management.'[8]

Elizabeth knew that how she acted could in fact have everything to do with not only her success but with her life, and these were lessons she learned very early, before she even became queen. Renaissance drama often involved family relationships, and some of the most difficult moments of Elizabeth's life also involved her most intimate family relationships open to public inspection. This essay particularly looks at Elizabeth at a number of moments in her life and reign: the incident with Thomas Seymour when she was in her teens, her position in her sister Mary's reign in the aftermath of the Wyatt rebellion, her speech at Tilbury at the time of the Spanish Armada, and her 1601 speech to Parliament at the end of her reign. Some of these moments were especially fraught for Elizabeth, sometimes due to family trials or moments of crisis. At certain key moments in her life Elizabeth used drama and staging as a means to self-protection and to gain prestige and success within her realm, and we see how early Elizabeth developed this strategy.

From the time Elizabeth was very young, she would have felt both the need to learn how to survive in the dangerous vulnerability of the Tudor court and the necessity to develop the skills to do so. She was, after all, the daughter not only of Henry VIII but also of Anne Boleyn, the wife he accused of adultery and had executed. For Elizabeth, both the skill to survive and the vulnerability to attack continued once she was queen.

One of the first crises that Elizabeth had to overcome was the charge that she had behaved inappropriately with Thomas Seymour, when she lived with her stepmother Katherine Parr after Henry VIII's death.[9] As John Foxe later remarked, 'It was no small injury that she suffered in the lord protector's days, by certain venomous vipers.'[10]

When Henry died in January 1547 Elizabeth, then aged 13, went to live in Katherine Parr's household. After what many saw as an indecently short period of widowhood, Parr secretly married Thomas Seymour, the youngest of the new boy king's maternal uncles, in April or early May. Seymour took his nephew, Edward VI, into his confidence and gained his support for the marriage. Though his older brother Edward Seymour, Duke of Somerset and Lord Protector, was furious, nothing could be done when the marriage was made public, and Seymour moved into the Queen Dowager's household at Chelsea. Seymour's relationship with the young Elizabeth became more and more familiar; he would come into her bed chamber in the mornings and tease and sometimes tickle her, sometimes slapping her on the bottom. The presence of Elizabeth's governess Katherine Ashley kept the situation from getting completely out of control, and though Elizabeth seems to have enjoyed bantering with the Lord Admiral, she soon began to rise earlier so she was dressed and at her studies when he appeared. At first Katherine Parr dealt with the situation that developed between her husband and stepdaughter by joining in on the teasing, but after she became pregnant and unwell, Parr began to be concerned. Early in 1548, perhaps after walking in on Elizabeth in Seymour's arms, she suggested that Elizabeth leave her household and set up her own at Cheshunt, which she did with Sir Anthony Denny and his wife. Though Elizabeth at first may have been upset by this exile, she soon realized the wisdom of the Queen Dowager's decision; Elizabeth's relations with Katherine and Seymour remained cordial and she corresponded with them.[11]

The situation became more tragic as well as more dangerous to Elizabeth, however, when Parr died of complications due to childbirth in September 1548. Seymour began to think about marrying the young Elizabeth, a plan that Katherine Ashley unwisely encouraged. If it could be proved that Elizabeth was either Seymour's mistress or had planned to marry him without the council's consent, not only her place in the succession was jeopardized, but possibly also her freedom of movement and even her life were endangered. In the fall of 1548, Thomas Seymour engaged in a number of other unwise and illegal activities, including piracy, coining false money, and eventually an attempt to kidnap his nephew Edward. In January 1549 he was arrested on the charge of high treason and lodged in the Tower. Elizabeth's governess, Katherine Ashley, and her cofferer, Thomas Parry, were also arrested and examined, and in their terror told all about the rompings at Chelsea.

The council sent Sir Robert Tyrwhitt to examine the 15-year-old Elizabeth to find out her role in Seymour's various plots. Though Tyrwhitt wrote to Somerset, 'Yet I do se yt in her Face that she ys guylte,' Elizabeth refused to incriminate herself or her servants.[12] Perhaps to mortify her so that she would confess any transgressions, Tyrwhitt informed Elizabeth that rumors were circulating that she was pregnant. Even at 15, Elizabeth recognized that the court of Edward VI was the important public stage for her to demonstrate her innocence. She wrote to the Lord Protector at the end of a rather long letter explaining the innocence of her relationship with Thomas Seymour:

> I wolde not for al earthely Thinges offende in any Thinge; for I knowe I have a Soule to save, as wele as other Fokes have . . . . Master Tirwit and others have tolde me that ther goeth rumers Abrode, whiche be greatly bothe agenste my Honor, and Honestie (wiche above al other thinkes I estime) wiche be these; that I am in the Tower; and with Childe by my Lord Admiral. My Lord these ar shameful schandlers, for whiche, besides the great Desire I have to see the King's Majestie, I shall most hartely desire your Lordship that I may come to the Court after your first Determination; that I may shewe my selfe there as I am.[13]

Though Somerset did not allow Elizabeth to come to court at this time, Elizabeth saw the need to do so, and to publicly protest her innocence – to show herself *as she was*, to allow people to see that she was neither pregnant nor ashamed of herself. She recognized very early that she not only needed to extricate herself from the crisis and protect her servants, Ashley and Parry, but also needed a public arena so that others would know that she was innocent. Elizabeth repeated the request to Edward himself when she sent him her picture in May 1550.

> I shall most humbly beseech your Majesty, that when you shall look on my picture, you will vouchsafe to think, that as you have but the outward shadow of the body affore you, so my inward mind wisheth that the body itself were oftener in your presence; howbeit, because both my so being I think could do your Majesty little pleasure, though myself great good.[14]

After the Seymour affair Elizabeth dressed with ostentatious simplicity, and did later in Edward's reign, in March 1551 and again in October of that year, manage to come to court and show herself – very consciously self-fashioned – as the ideal modest Protestant young woman. This behavior, MacCaffrey argues, 'suggests her determination to present an image of maidenly modesty and decorum.' John Foxe, in some ways ironic, given Elizabeth's dress once she became queen, lauded her while she was princess for her 'little pride of stomach,' her 'little delight . . . in gay apparel, rich attire, and precious jewels.'[15]

After Edward's death in July 1553 Elizabeth managed to avoid the entanglement of John Dudley, Duke of Northumberland's unsuccessful plot to overturn Henry VIII's will, and Mary welcomed Elizabeth to court. Elizabeth rode behind Mary in the procession when the new queen entered London. This cordiality was, however, short-lived. That Elizabeth, again very conscious of keeping the support of Protestants, was at best half-hearted in her conversion to Catholicism, angered Mary enough that Elizabeth left court By January 1554, the time of Thomas Wyatt's rebellion against the queen's coming marriage to Philip of Spain, Mary was convinced that Elizabeth had known and approved of the plot against her, and on 29 January demanded that Elizabeth return to court to answer questions about that involvement. Simon Renard, the Spanish Ambassador, and Stephen Gardiner, Bishop of Winchester, wanted Elizabeth sent directly to the Tower, but there were a number of members of Mary's council who opposed this plan.

Elizabeth responded to this demand that she was too ill to travel, but this did not satisfy Mary. On 12 February the queen sent three members of her council, Lord William

Howard, Sir Edward Hastings and Sir Thomas Cornwallis, to her residence Ashridge to bring Elizabeth to St James. They were accompanied by two doctors, Thomas Wendy and George Owen, who were to determine just how ill the princess was. If travel would not actually endanger her life, Mary stated, Elizabeth must come to court. While the doctors admitted Elizabeth was not well, they determined that travel would not be life-threatening. Elizabeth, hearing of her cousin Jane Grey's recent execution on 12 February, the same day members of the council had come for her, was not so sure.

They traveled in slow stages since Elizabeth was ill; they took five days to travel 33 miles. Crowds gathered to see her as she passed through London. Simon Renard complained that Elizabeth, dressed in white, a color probably carefully chosen to signify her innocence and virtue, drew back the curtains of the litter so that she might show herself to the people.

> The Lady Elizabeth arrived yesterday, dressed all in white and followed by a great company of the Queen's people and her own. She had her litter opened to show herself to the people, and her pale face kept a proud, haughty expression in order to mask her vexation. The Queen would not see her and had her lodged in part of her house out of which neither she nor any of her suite can pass without crossing the guard, whilst only two gentlemen, six ladies and four servants were permitted to stay with her, the rest being quartered in the city of London.[16]

Elizabeth was held for nearly a month in her rooms in Whitehall while Mary and her council argued over what to do with her. No one was willing to guard Elizabeth under house arrest and Mary decided to send her to the Tower. The Earl of Sussex and one of his colleagues – the records are not clear who this second man was – were sent to take Elizabeth to the Tower by barge, as Mary and her council feared there might be attempts to rescue her if they took her through the streets of London. Elizabeth was extremely distraught by this order and asked that she might see her sister Mary before such an order was carried out. When this request was refused she begged for paper and pen so that she might at least write to Mary. Sussex overrode his colleague and allowed Elizabeth the time to write to her sister. MacCaffrey points out that writing this letter 'was a measure of her desperation but also her personal shrewdness.'[17] Elizabeth's letter beseeched her sister to allow her to see her before being imprisoned in the Tower, where she was afraid she would never emerge. Elizabeth, at this moment of crisis, recognized not only the need to be able to see and talk with her sister, but also how to carefully craft such a request. Going back to that earlier crisis of her life, Elizabeth beseeched Mary:

> I humbly beseech your Majesty to let me answer afore yourself, and not suffer me to trust your councilors . . . I have heard in my time of many cast away for want of coming to the presence of their Prince; and in late days I heard my Lord of Somerset say that if his brother had been suffered to speak with him, he had never suffered . . . . Therefore once again kneeling with the humbleness of my heart, because I am not suffered to bow the knees of my body, I humbly crave to speak with your Highness, which I would not be so bold to desire if I knew not myself most clear, as I know myself most true.[18]

Elizabeth hoped that if she could actually see and talk with her sister, her professions of innocence as she dramatically kneeled before her might save her. The letter, however, gained Elizabeth only one day before she was sent to the Tower. Elizabeth's letter writing meant they missed the tide, and Sussex was concerned that taking the barge at midnight was too dangerous – in the dark Elizabeth might escape. Mary was furious with Sussex that he allowed her sister to write, and she refused Elizabeth's fervent plea to see her. While Simon Renard was convinced that the letter writing was a deliberate plan to waste time so that she could delay going to the Tower, it seems likely that Elizabeth truly believed that were she able to see and *speak with* Mary, she might avert this catastrophe.

The next morning, Palm Sunday, 17 March 1554, when people in London were at mass so they would not be there to either rescue Elizabeth or demonstrate against her imprisonment, she was conveyed to the Tower. It was raining. Elizabeth landed at the gate later known as 'Traitor's Gate' but then called 'the watergate.' At her landing there was a great multitude of servants and warders standing at attention. According to Foxe, Elizabeth took advantage of this audience to proclaim her innocence before her entrance to the Tower, 'Here landeth as true a subject, being prisoner, as ever landed at these stairs; and before thee, O God! I speak it, having no other friends but thee alone.' Her self-presentation then shifted. Elizabeth paused for a moment outside the gate and sat on a stone, even though it was damp with rain. The Lieutenant of the Tower, Sir John Bridges, asked her to come in: 'Madame, you were best come out of the rain, for you sit unwholesomely.' Elizabeth responded: 'It is better sitting here than in a worse place, for God knoweth, I know not whither you will bring me.' Seeing and hearing Elizabeth thus, one of her gentlemen ushers began to weep. Elizabeth scolded him that she did not find his weeping comforting to her; besides no one need weep for her for she was innocent.[19] Whether the young princess actually had the presence of mind to say all this, and whether years later, Foxe actually got her words exactly right, Elizabeth's subjects would have had this dramatic moment firmly placed in their minds, as Foxe's *Acts and Monuments* was one of the most popular books of its age, and not only by order of the upper house of convocation at Canterbury in 1571 in every cathedral church and every household of the church hierarchy,[20] but also in 'countless gentle, clerical and middle-class houses, even in those where other books seldom intruded.'[21]

Despite Elizabeth's very realistic fears, she did survive her sojourn in the Tower to become queen at Mary's death in November 1558. Though Elizabeth claimed nearly thirty years later that she had never been trained to be queen: 'I was not simply trained up, nor in my youth spent my time altogether idly; and yet, when I came to the crown, then entered I first into the schol of experience,' in fact the experiences she had in how to present herself in the reigns of her brother and sister were highly useful to her from the beginning of her reign. MacCaffrey points out that 'she had already, before mounting the throne, acquired a public persona which shaped most of her intercourse with other human beings.'[22]

We can see this from the very beginning of the reign, in the processions the day before her coronation, Elizabeth attempted to carefully fashion the way people perceived her and to present herself to her people so they would accept her as their king as well as queen. To promote this ideology she, in a dramatic fashion, used male analogies with which to compare herself. As Elizabeth moved through London, the entire city, according to the contemporary tract that described it, became 'a stage wherein was shewed the wonderfull spectacle, of a noble hearted princesse toward her most loving people, & the peoples exceding comfort in beholding so worthy a soveraign.' A child from St Paul's school delivered an oration in Latin comparing Elizabeth to Plato's philosopher-king. And Elizabeth herself continued this male identification as a dramatically effective means to convey her power. *Holinshed's Chronicle* reports that during her coronation procession she stopped to pray at the Tower, where she had lately been a prisoner. In her prayer she compared herself to Daniel, rather than using a female biblical reference.

> I acknowledge that thou hast delt as woonderfullie and as mercifullie with me as Thou diddest with thy true and faithfull servant, Daniell thy prophet; whome thou deliveredst out of the den from the crueltie of the greedie and raging lions: even so was I overwhelmed and only by thee delivered. [23]

John King suggests that Elizabeth's active participation in these ceremonies 'was intended to break down any division between the real world and symbolic ideals.'[24]

Thirty years later, at one of the key crises of her reign, the time of the Spanish Armada, this doubling of vision of king and of queen, and this keen dramatic sense, were also very important. Towards the end of July 1588 Robert Dudley, Earl of Leicester, invited Elizabeth to come and inspect her troops at Tilbury, promising her that her soldiers were goodly, loyal and able. While some of Elizabeth's councilors were concerned about what might happen if she paraded herself before a crowd such as this, Elizabeth wanted to come and Leicester promised to guarantee her safety.

On 8 August Elizabeth traveled to Tilbury by river and spent the night at Edward Ritche's nearby house, Saffron Garden. The next morning she reviewed her troops. The feared Spanish invasion was one of the most significant crises of Elizabeth's reign. When she went to Tilbury to rouse the troops, there are descriptions, though we do not know how reliable, of her dressed in breast-plate mounted on a charger with Leicester on one side and the Earl of Ormond, carrying the sword of state, on the other. Her page followed her carrying her helmet.[25] According to eyewitness James Aske, Elizabeth, a 'sacred Generall,' 'marched King-like' as she surveyed the ranks of her soldiers. Camden's account of Elizabeth looking over the troops at Tilbury is more complicated in using both genders simultaneously. He described her 'riding about through the Ranks of Armed men . . . with a Leader's Truncheon in her Hand, sometimes with a martial Pace, another while gently like a Woman, incredible it is how much she encouraged the Hearts of her . . . Souldiers by her Presence and Speech to them.' We see the same doubling of genders in Thomas Deloney's ballad, 'The Queenes visiting of the Campe at Tilsburie with her entertainment there,' registered on 9 August, the day after the event. Deloney referred to Elizabeth's greatness as coming from the fact that she was 'King Henryes royall daughter.' He also described her 'Princely eyes,' and how 'came the Queene on pranceing steede/atired like an Angell bright.' Elizabeth's description of herself at this moment of national crisis also demonstrates the double image she had of herself as both woman and king.

> My loving people . . . I have always so behaved myself that, under God, I have placed my chiefest strength and safeguard in the loyal hearts and good will of my subjects; and therefore I am come amongst you, as you see, at this time . . . being resolved, in the midst and heat of battle, to lay down for my God, and my kingdom, and for my people, my honour and my blood, even in the dust. I know I have the body of a weak and feeble woman, but I have the heart and stomach of a king, and of a king of England too, and think foul scorn that Parma or Spain, or any prince of Europe should dare invade the borders of my realm; to which, rather than any Dishonour shall grow by me, I myself will take up Arms, I myself will be your General.[26]

While being a woman might make her 'weak and feeble' at least in body, Elizabeth claimed, there was nothing weak or feeble about the person of Elizabeth as *seen* at that moment by her troops. Just as male actors played women's parts on stage, Elizabeth as a woman also played the part of a king. Aske described how Elizabeth called her 'Seriant Maior' and 'did will him do this message from her mouth.'[27] This speech was apparently read and reread aloud the next day by officers and by Leonel Sharp, chaplain, to all the soldiers who had not been able to hear Elizabeth, so her speech about having a female body and the spirit of a king was repeated in a male voice. Here is a woman's speech, calling herself a king, read aloud in a male voice, further complicating the response to the issue of gender and power and the way Elizabeth presented herself dramatically.

We might see this as a parallel of Elizabeth as dramatist with a male colleague as actor to other public events. Early in her reign, Elizabeth's speeches to Parliament were read by the speaker. In 1566 after the speaker had read her prepared, formal speech, the queen herself stood up to speak as well. She would be her own actor and this would be a speech by a woman in her own queenly, rather than in another – and male – voice.

Whatever the speech at Tilbury, and how people heard it, the very presence of Elizabeth was a powerful one. Leicester wrote to the Earl of Shrewsbury in a private letter a few days later that, 'our gracious Majesty hath been here with me to see her camp and people, which so inflamed the hearts of her good subjects, as I think the weakest person amongst them is able to match the proudest Spaniard that dares land in England.'[28]

In one of her last public speeches, her 'Golden Speech' to Parliament in November 1601, Elizabeth deftly combined the qualities of the traditional male and female characteristics to provide a view of monarchy that extends gender definitions and shows how even at the end of her life Elizabeth was aware of how to carefully craft how she presented herself and use whatever dramatic gestures were at hand.

> To be a King and wear a crown is a thing more glorious to them that see it, than it is pleasant to them that bear it. For myself, I was never so entice with the glorious name of a King or royal authority of a Queen, as delighted that God hath made me His instrument to maintain His truth and glory, and to defend this Kingdom (as I said) from peril, dishonour, and tyranny and oppression.

Elizabeth wanted Parliament to be well aware that her people perceive her as ruler, as a king wearing a crown, but what she also thought was important for them to recognize about her was her sense of duty and commitment. She was not their queen because she delighted in the glamorous aspects of ruling; she was queen so that she could do God's work of protecting her people from danger and oppression. Elizabeth ended her speech with a statement that sounds overwhelmingly female in gender expectation, presenting herself as one whose great strength came in the love, such as an all-loving mother, she had for her subjects. 'And though you have had, and may have, many mightier and wiser princes in this seat, yet you never had, nor shall have any, that will love you better.' The mutual love between queen and subjects, Elizabeth implied, guaranteed the stability and order of the realm.[29]

Dramatically demonstrating that love was a key element to how Elizabeth, despite serious problems and some failures, managed to well maintain her rule for forty-four years. From the moment she became queen at the age of 25 she stepped onto a stage where she had the leading role in a drama in which she was not only actor but also author. She trained for this role by having already survived serious incidents in the reigns of both Edward and Mary, and having learned a great deal about self-presentation from both these crises. Elizabeth carefully negotiated the difficulties of her rule as an unmarried female by her complex, multilayered manner of dramatic self-presentation. Her contemporaries, in describing Elizabeth, were aware of how she presented herself, and may well have further shaped these moments in their histories, helping to create an Elizabeth I who was both dramatist and dramatic text.

Appendix: Elizabeth I's translation of drama

As the essay described, Elizabeth in her teens had to overcome the scandal of her relationship with Thomas Seymour. At the same time, Elizabeth was also developing her fine intellectual abilities. Elizabeth was 15 when she began to work with Roger Ascham as her tutor. An important part of Ascham's theory of education was his emphasis on literary and rhetorical studies. In her teens Elizabeth became an accomplished linguist. She was fluent in Italian, French, and Latin, and had a working knowledge of Greek. Ascham had developed a method of double translation, where his pupil would translate the Latin piece into English and then back into Latin. Ascham was so impressed with Elizabeth that he said that after six months of doing this daily, her translations were so beautiful 'that some in seven years in grammar schools, yea, and some in the university too, cannot do half so well.'[30]

Every morning Elizabeth worked with Ascham on Greek and in the afternoon they worked on Latin. They read from the Greek New Testament, from the tragedies of Sophocles, and orations by Isocrates and Demosthenes. After dinner Elizabeth worked on Cicero. Her hard work on the classics during her teens gave her an enthusiasm for Greek and Latin and a love of translation that was to last all her life. Ascham reported that Elizabeth not only had a great knowledge of Latin, but also through her translations had developed an eloquent prose style of her own. Ascham was with Elizabeth when she left Katherine Parr's household under a cloud, and during the very difficult time after Katherine's death and when Elizabeth was examined about her relationship with Seymour. In January 1550, however, he left her service, though it is not clear whether it was his choice or hers. When Elizabeth became queen, Ascham returned to her service as her Latin secretary. She insisted that they regularly set aside time from state affairs so that they could read their favorite authors together.

We have a translation from Seneca's play, *Hercules Oetaeus*, attributed to Elizabeth while she was queen.[31] As we know, Elizabeth enjoyed drama, and thought about the issues that drama brought up. This fragment, apparently done purely as a private exercise, raised interesting issues on how to rule effectively. The fragment is a chorus spoken by the Aetolian women to Hercules' wife, Deianira. It emphasized the importance of fidelity, a highly important quality to Elizabeth.

The passage ends by mentioning Daedalus and his son Icarus. Daedalus had invented wings, but Icarus's use of them had tragic results. Icarus borrowed 'his father's feathered wings,' flew too near the sun, and fell to his death into the sea. In a letter that Robert Devereux, 2nd Earl of Essex, once wrote Elizabeth, he described her as the sun that could destroy him if he did not behave as he ought. 'When your Majesty thinks that heaven too good for me, I will not fall like a star, but be consumed like a vapour by the same sun that drew me up to such a height.'[32] Essex has been characterized as an Elizabethan Icarus, and by not having fidelity to Elizabeth, and trying for the crown, flying too near the sun, in 1601 he earned the death of a traitor. But for Elizabeth herself, the image of Icarus is an intriguing one, as she learned very early in her life, certainly from the time of the Seymour scandal when she was 15, that she had to take great care when she 'flew' not to go too near the sun. Rather, she had to make certain that she took a careful course so that she could safely land and plan to fly again as a highly successful queen.

Notes

1 I would like to thank Jo Eldridge Carney, Elaine Kruse, and Lena Cowen Orlin for their help in thinking through the issues of this essay and Jean Akers for her research assistance. I am most grateful to the New Paltz Foundation and the Folger Shakespeare Library for their support of this project. For further reading on many of the issues raised in this essay, see Carole Levin, *The Heart and Stomach of a King: Elizabeth I and the Politics of Sex and Power* (Philadelphia, PA: University of Pennsylvania Press, 1994). Other significant studies that consider Elizabeth's self-representation include Susan Frye, *Elizabeth I: The Competition for Representation* (New York: Oxford University Press, 1993); John N. King, 'Queen Elizabeth I: Representations of the Virgin Queen,' *Renaissance Quarterly*, 43 (spring, 1990), 30–74 and 'The Royal Image, 1535–1603,' in Dale Hoak (ed.) *Tudor Political Culture* (Cambridge: Cambridge University Press, 1995), 104–32; Leah Marcus, 'Shakespeare's Comic Heroines, Elizabeth I, and the Uses of Androgyny,' in Mary Beth Rose (ed.) *Medieval and Renaissance Women: Literary and Historical Perspectives* (Syracuse, NY: Syracuse University Press, 1986), 135–53; Louis Montrose, 'Shaping Fantasies: Figurations of Gender and Power in Elizabethan Culture,' *Representations*, I, 2 (1983), 61–94; Wallace MacCaffrey, 'Politics in an Age of Reformation, 1485–1585,' in John Morrill (ed.) *The Oxford Illustrated History of Tudor and Stuart Britain* (Oxford: Oxford University Press, 1996), 310–29, see especially p. 329.

2 For more on these ceremonies, see Levin, *Heart and Stomach of a King*, ch. 2.

3 For example, Wallace MacCaffrey describes Elizabeth as an infant as 'already playing a part on the political stage.' And during her sister's reign, 'Fate had cast her in two conflicting roles': *Elizabeth I* (London: Edward Arnold, 1993), 4, 24.

4 See Elizabeth I, 'Hercules Oetaeus,' in S. P. Cerasano and Marion Wynne-Davies (eds) *Renaissance Drama by Women: Texts and Documents* (London and New York: Routledge, 1996), 17–21. We know one very specific response to a play at court quite early in her reign. In 1567 the Spanish ambassador Guzman de Silva wrote to Philip II that 'the hatred this Queen has of marriage is most strange. They presented a comedy before her last night until nearly one in the morning, which ended in a marriage, and the Queen, as she told me herself, expressed her dislike of the woman's part.' *Calendar of the Letters and State Papers Relating to English Affairs Preserved in, or originally Belonging to, the Archives of Simancas*, ed. Martin Hume (London: Her Majesty's Stationery Office, 1896–9) 4 vols, I, 367–8.

5 Steven Mullaney, *The Place of the Stage: Licence, Play, and Power in Renaissance England* (Chicago and London: University of Chicago Press, 1988), 105; Anne Righter, *Shakespeare and the Idea of the Play* (London: Chatto and Windus, 1962), 114; Fritz Levy, 'The Theatre and the Court in the 1590s,' in John Guy, *The Reign of Elizabeth I: Court and Culture in the Last Decade* (Cambridge: Cambridge University Press, published in association with the Folger Institute, Washington, DC, 1995), 275.

6 Stephen Orgel, *The Illusion of Power: Political Theater in the English Renaissance* (Berkeley, CA: University of California Press, 1975), 9.

7 John Guy, 'Tudor Monarchy and Political Culture,' in John Morrill (ed.) *The Oxford Illustrated History of Tudor and Stuart Britain* (Oxford and New York: Oxford University Press, 1996), 225; John Neale, *Elizabeth I and her Parliaments, 1584–1601* (London: Jonathan Cape, 1957), 119; *Holinshed's Chronicles*, IV, 933–5. While still King of Scotland, James VI expressed a similar view. In *Basilikon Doron* James wrote: 'It is a trew old saying, that a King is as one set on a stage, whose smallest actions and gestures, all the people gazingly doe behold', Charles Howard McIlwain (ed.) *The Political Works of James I* (New York: Russell and Russell, 1965), 43; Dudley Carleton echoed this idea when James became King of England: 'The next day the king was actor himself, sat out the whole service, went the procession, and dined in public with his fellow knights, at which sight every man was well pleased' (letter to John

Chamberlain July 4, 1603), Maurice Lee, Jr (ed.) *Dudley Carleton to John Chamberlain, 1603–1624: Jacobean Letters* (New Brunswick, NJ: Rutgers University Press, 1972), 35–6.

8 Stephen Greenblatt, *Renaissance Self-Fashioning: From More to Shakespeare* (Chicago: University of Chicago Press, 1980); Patricia Fumerton, '"Secret" Arts: Elizabethan Miniatures and Sonnets,' in Stephen Greenblatt (ed.) *Representing the English Renaissance* (Los Angeles and Berkeley: University of California Press, 1988), 94; MacCaffrey, *Elizabeth I*, 7; Beryl Hughes, 'Success in a Man's World: The Reign of Elizabeth I of England,' *Women's Studies Journal* I (April, 1985), 39.

9 For more on this incident, see Sheila Cavanagh, 'The Bad Seed: Princess Elizabeth and the Seymour Incident,' in Julia Walker (ed.) *Dissing Elizabeth: Negative Representations of Gloriana* (Durham, NC: Duke University Press, 1998), 9–29. I appreciate Professor Cavanagh sharing her essay with me in manuscript.

10 John Foxe, *Acts and Monuments*, ed. Stephen Reed Cattley (London: R. B. Seeley and W. Burnside, 1838), VIII, 605.

11 For descriptions of what went on between Elizabeth and Thomas Seymour, see the confessions of Katherine Ashley and Thomas Parry in William Murdin and Samuel Haynes (eds) *A Collection of State Papers Relating to Affairs in the Reign of Queen Elizabeth from 1542 to 1596 left by William Cecil, Lord Burghley* (London: William Bowyer, 1740–59), I, 95–101.

12 Murdin and Haynes (eds) *Collection of State Papers*, I, 70.

13 Murdin and Haynes (eds) *Collection of State Papers*, I, 90.

14 Frank A. Mumby (ed.) *The Girlhood of Queen Elizabeth I* (London: Constable, 1909) 73.

15 MacCaffrey, *Elizabeth I*, 11; Foxe, *Acts and Monuments*, VIII, 603.

16 Calendar of State Papers, Spain, XII, ed. Royall Tyler (London: HMSO, 1949), 125.

17 MacCaffrey, *Elizabeth I*, 18.

18 Mumby, *Girlhood of Queen Elizabeth*, 116–17.

19 Foxe, *Acts and Monuments*, VIII, 609.

20 D. M. Loades, *The Oxford Martyrs* (New York: Stein and Day, 1964), 30.

21 A. G. Dickens, *The English Reformation* (New York: Schocken, 1964), 305.

22 Neale, *Elizabeth I and her Parliaments, 1584–1601*, 128; MacCaffrey, *Elizabeth I*, 28.

23 James Osborne, *The Quenes Maiesties Passage through the Citie of London to Westminster the Day before her Coronation* (New Haven, CT: published for the Elizabethan Club by Yale University Press, 1960), 11, 28; *Holinshed's Chronicles*, ed. Henry Ellis (London: J. Johnson, 1807–8), IV, 159, 176.

24 King, 'The Royal Image, 1535–1603,' 121.

25 James Aske, *Elizabetha Triumphans: Conteyning the Damned practizes, that the diuelish Popes of Rome have used ever sithence her Highnesse first comming to the Crowne, by mouing her wicked and traiterous subiects to Rebellion and conspiracies, thereby to bereaue her Maiestie both of her lawfull seate, and happy life* (London: printed by Thomas Orwin for Thomas Gubbin, and Thomas Newman, 1588), 19; William Camden, *The History of . . . Princess Elizabeth, late Queen of England containing all the most important and remarkable passages of state, both at home and abroad (so far as they were linked with English affairs) during her long and prosperous reign*, 4th edn (London: Flesher, 1688), 416. We do not, however, have clear evidence that this is how she dressed. Winfried Schleiner states 'I cannot determine what Elizabeth wore that August day . . . . Curiously enough, the writers' descriptions became more and more precise as the Tilbury event receded into the past.' '*Divina virago*: Queen Elizabeth as an Amazon,' *Studies in Philology* 75 (1987), 174, 175. See also, Miller Christy, 'Queen Elizabeth's Visit to Tilbury in 1588,' *English Historical Review* 34 (1919), 52; Felix Barker, 'If Parma Had Landed,' *History Today* 38 (May 1988), 34–41.

26 *Reasons for War Against Spain*, 2nd edn (London: J. Wilford, 1738), 38–40. Of course, there is some dispute about the actual words of Elizabeth's speech at Tilbury. What is generally accepted as her speech was not so accepted until the seventeenth century. It originally comes from Leonel Sharp's letter to the Duke of Buckingham written sometime before 1631. *Cabala, Mysteries of State and Government: in Letters of Illustrious Persons and Great Ministers of State* (London: G. Beddell and T. Collins, 1663), 372–4. His report of her speech is on p. 373. Felix Barker, 'If Parma Had Landed,' *History Today* 38 (May, 1988), 38. Frances Teague suggests 'a tentative acceptance of the speech is warranted' (77n14). John Neale argues 'I see

no serious reason for rejecting the speech,' *Essays in Elizabethan History* (London: Jonathan Cape, 1958), 105, and gives the background to the publication of the speech in a letter from Sharp that was published in *Cabala*. Susan Frye presents an intriguing case for a different speech at Tilbury , published in 1612, from a 1601 sermon by William Leigh. 'The Myth of Elizabeth at Tilbury,' *Sixteenth Century Journal* 23/1 (1992), 95–114; William Leigh, *Queene Elizabeth, Paraleld in Her Princely Vertues, with David, Iosua, and Hezekia* (London: printed by T. C. for Arthur Johnson, 1612), 94. James Aske's version is also quite different, though he admits he was simply giving 'in effect . . . her royall Speech.' Aske, *Elizabetha Triumphans*, 25.

27 Barker, 'If Parma Had Landed,' 38; Aske, *Elizabetha Triumphans*, 26.

28 Edmund Lodge, *Illustrations of British History*, 2nd edn (London: John Chidley, 1838), II, 345.

29 The speech is quoted in full in Neale, *Elizabeth I and her Parliaments*, II, 388–91. See Frances Teague for a discussion of the different versions of this speech and how they reflect different audiences – whether to Parliament or later printed for all the people. 'Queen Elizabeth in Her Speeches,' in S. P. Cerasano and Marion Wynne-Davies (eds) *Gloriana's Face* (Brighton: Harvester, 1991), 75. For a valuable analysis of this speech, see David Harris Sacks, 'The Countervailing of Benefits: Monopoly, Liberty, and Benevolence in Elizabethan England,' in Dale Hoak (ed.) *Tudor Political Culture* (Cambridge: Cambridge University Press, 1995), 272–91.

30 Quoted in Lawrence V. Ryan, *Roger Ascham* (Stanford. CA: Stanford University Press, 1963), 105.

31 For more on the debate over whether or not this is by Elizabeth, and for the complete text, see '[Hercules Oetaeus (Hercules of Mount Oeta)]' in S. P. Cerasano and Marion Wynne-Davies (eds) *Renaissance Drama by Women: Texts and Documents* (London and New York: Routledge, 1996), 7–12.

32 18 October 1591, Walter Bouchier Devereux, *Lives and Letters of the Devereux, Earls of Essex, in the Reigns of Elizabeth, James I, and Charles I: 1540–1646*, 2 vols (London: John Murray, 1853), I, 250. For the characterization of Essex as Icarus, see for example, Robert Lacey, *Robert, Earl of Essex: an Elizabethan Icarus* (London: Weidenfeld and Nicolson, 1971).

2

JOANNA LUMLEY (1537?-1576/7)

Elaine V. Beilin

When Elaine V. Beilin wrote *Redeeming Eve: Women Writers of the English Renaissance* (1987) there was very little information available on any of the women writers she chose to focus upon, and as such, her book stands as the first systematic and detailed analysis of many of the female dramatists included in this volume. We have chosen to represent her pioneering work with two essays, this one on Lumley and another on Elizabeth Cary (see pp. 167–81). The one on Lumley is particularly important since it remains one of the few pieces written about her, and it establishes at the start that Lumley's translation of *Iphigenia at Aulis* was not merely a classroom exercise but a complex negotiation of the topics of gender, rulership and faith.

Joanna Lumley's teenage years were a humanist's delight, for a holograph manuscript includes her Latin versions of five orations by Isocrates, two Latin letters to her father, the Earl of Arundel, and 'The Tragedie of Euripides called Iphigeneia translated out of Greake into Englisshe.'[1] In one of the letters to her father she noted that following the recommendation of Cicero, she was devoting herself to Greek literature and that she derived 'incredibilem voluptatem' (wonderful pleasure) from reading 'Evagoras,' Isocrates' fourth oration to Nicocles.[2] Herself the owner of at least fifteen books, Lumley was fortunate to have a father who collected a large library and to marry John, Lord Lumley, who possessed 'probably the largest private library in Elizabethan England,' having inherited both his father-in-law's library and that of Thomas Cranmer.[3] Sharing his wife's interest in learning, in 1550, John Lumley translated Erasmus's *Institutio Principis Christiani* as *The Education of a Christian Prince*, dedicating the work to his father-in-law. At about the same time, using Erasmus's Latin translation, Joanna Lumley was translating *Iphigenia*, raising the possibility that the two works were companion pieces.

Married shortly after John Lumley's matriculation at Cambridge in 1549, Lord and Lady Lumley remained Catholic, and were prominent at Queen Mary's coronation. However, they also survived the Protestant reigns before and after hers, despite John Lumley's spending at least a year and a half in prison under suspicion of complicity in plots involving Mary, Queen of Scots. Camden memorializes him as a 'person of entire virtue, integrity, and innocence, and in his old age a complete pattern of true nobility.'[4] Little else is known of Joanna Lumley, except that in 1575–6, Sir Nicholas Bacon, Lord Keeper of the Great Seal, sent 'at her desire' an illuminated manuscript of the classical *sententiae* which decorated the long gallery at Gorhambury.[5] Besides indicating Lumley's continuing interest in the classics and something of her taste for moral statement, the gift suggests a possible acquaintance between her and Sir Nicholas's learned wife, Anne Cooke Bacon.

Joanna Lumley's principal work, the translation of *Iphigenia*, is illuminated by her particular circumstances and by consideration of the genre she chose. She seems to be not only the first woman, but also the first person, to translate a Greek drama into English. Perhaps the Lumleys shared a scholarly interest in translation and so each chose to prepare a work by Erasmus. But what drew Joanna Lumley to *Iphigenia* in particular? It may be that using Erasmus's Latin, as copy text or as aid, assured an entirely 'safe,' impersonal voice for a play about female heroism. Drama, especially a translated drama, might indeed have interested a young woman because of its very impersonality. Built on conflict, a play may present several sides to a question, so that seeking the playwright in one character or opinion becomes difficult or impossible. As a mask, it is highly satisfactory because it even precludes the need for a persona; thus, Joanna Lumley appears not as the creator of the play, but as an English voice for Euripides.[6]

The action of *Iphigenia at Aulis* evolves from Agamemnon's terrible dilemma between patriotism and paternal love, for he must decide whether to sacrifice his daughter Iphigenia to Diana to ensure the Greek forces' safe passage to Troy. But it is Iphigenia herself who finally assumes the burden of decision – and a hero's stature – for after overcoming her initial fear and horror, she decides to sacrifice herself for the benefit of her country:

> I wolde counsell you therfore to suffer this troble paciently, for I muste nedes die, and will suffer it willingelye. Consider I praie you mother, for what a lawfull cause I shalbe slaine . . . if this wicked enterprise of the Trojans be not revenged, than truly the grecians shall not kepe neither their children, nor yet their wives in peace: And I shall not onlie remedie all thes thinges withe my deathe: but also get a glorious renowne to the grecians for ever. Suerlie mother we can not speake againste this, for do you not thinke it to be better that I shulde die, then so many noble men to be let of their journye for one womans sake? for one noble man is better than a thousande women. Besides this seinge my deathe is determined amongste the goddes, trulie no mortall man oughte to withstande it. Wherfore I will offer my selfe willingly to deathe, for my countrie.
>
> (fol. 91^{v}–92^{v})[7]

Significantly, the theme here, subordination of the self for the good of one's country, echoes a central theme of the work John Lumley completed in 1550, Erasmus's *Education of a Christian Prince.* The fundamental assumption of Erasmus's work is that it is morally, ethically, and spiritually 'the duty of a good prince to consider the welfare of his people, even at the cost of his own life if need be. But that prince does not really die who loses his life in such a cause.'[8] The prince must imitate Christ's humility, so that Erasmus advises, 'if you cannot look out for the possessions of your subjects without danger to your own life, set the safety of the people before your very life!' (154–5). Erasmus advises the prince's instructor to create the picture of a perfect ruler for the prince to emulate:

> a sort of celestial creature, more like to a divine being than a mortal: complete in all the virtues; born for the common good; yea, sent by the God above to help the affairs of mortals by looking out and caring for everyone and everything.
>
> (162)

In response to John Lumley's interest in such teaching, Joanna Lumley produced a text featuring a noble princess, a female version of the selfless prince. Just as Erasmus's *Education* continually insists on the prince's need of Christianity ('He should be taught that the teachings of Christ apply to no one more than to the prince': 148), his Latin *Iphigenia* suggested to Joanna Lumley that Iphigenia was a crypto-Christian imbued with the spirit, if not the knowledge and grace, of a Christian. When Erasmus renders the Greek with implicitly Christian diction, Lumley provides English parallels. In the renunciation speech to her mother quoted above, numerous phrases resonate with Christian connotations: 'I wolde counsell you therfore to suffer this troble paciently, for I muste nedes die, and will suffer it willingelye . . . . And I shall not onlie remedie all thes thinges withe my deathe . . . . I shall not only leave a perpetuall memorie of my deathe.' The chorus at once responds, 'Suerlie you are happie O Iphigeneya, that you can suffer so pacientlye all this troble.' To Achilles who offers to help her to live, Iphigenia says, 'suffer me rather to save all grece withe my deathe,' and to her grieving mother, 'Be of good comforte mother I praie you' (fol. 93). Iphigenia believes that 'with my deathe I shall purchase unto them a glorious victorie' (fol. 94^{v}). After her miraculous assumption by Diana, the Nuncius tells Clitemnestra, 'this daie your daughter hath bene bothe alive and deade,' and the chorus remarks that she is indeed 'taken into heaven' (fol. 96^{v}), so recalling the words of St John in Revelation 1: 17–18, 'I am the first and the last: I am he that lives and was dead; and behold I am alive for evermore.' By choosing a Greek play about a heroic woman and by selecting those passages from Erasmus with Christian resonance, Lumley composed a version of the play which would pay tribute to a woman's Christian spirit, courage, and eventual sanctification.[9]

Notes

1 *Iphigenia at Aulis Translated by Lady Lumley*, ed. Harold H. Child (Oxford: Malone Society, 1909), p. v. This essay is taken from Elaine V. Beilin, 'The Making of a Female Hero: Joanna Lumley and Elizabeth Cary', in *Redeeming Eve: Women Writers of the English Renaissance* (Princeton, NJ: Princeton University Press, 1987), pp. 153–7 and 313–14.

2 J. G. Nichols quotes the letter in *The Gentlemen's Magazine* 154 (1833), pt 2, p. 495, but see 'Lady Lumley and Greek Tragedy,' *Classical Journal*, 36 (1941), 537–47, in which David H. Greene shows that Lumley used Erasmus's Latin translation of the play, probably in the 1524 edition which contained the Greek text.

3 Sears Jayne, *Library Catalogues of the English Renaissance* (Berkeley, CA: University of California Press, 1956), p. 45.

4 'John Lumley,' *DNB*, 12: 272–4.

5 *Sir Nicholas Bacon's Great House Sententiae*, trans. and intr. Elizabeth McCutcheon, *English Literary Renaissance* Supplements, 3 (1977), p. 66.

6 Greene suggests Lumley read the play in Greek and briefly praises her efforts before condemning her 'total lack of taste and critical ability' (p. 542). Frank D. Crane, in 'Euripides, Erasmus, and Lady Lumley,' *Classical Journal*, 39(1944), 223–8, judges that Lumley 'shows no knowledge of Greek, and none of poetry in any language' (p. 228). Such harshness probably derives from Lumley's failure to produce an accurate, complete, poetic account of the play; however, if her interest was mainly in Iphigenia's character, she may not have cared to do so.

7 The Greek claims that a noble man is better than 10,000 women, while Erasmus's Latin says one man is worthier than many thousands of women, indicating either that Lumley confused her numbers, or thought the comparison excessive. Desiderius Erasmus, *Opera Omnia*, 1703, rpt Georg Ohms Verlagsbuchhandlung (Hildesheim, 1961), 1, 1181.

8 *The Education of a Christian Prince by Desiderius Erasmus*, trans. Lester K. Born (New York: Columbia University Press, 1936), p. 149.

9 So consistent are the echoes that they are surely intentional. For instance, the line that echoes Revelation translates from Greek as 'For this day saw your child dead and beholding (the light of the sun),' but from Erasmus as 'this one day has seen your daughter both dead and alive': 'hic unus filiam mulier tuam/ Et mortuam conspexit et vivam dies' (1186); compare to the Vulgate: 'ego sum primus et novissimus, et vivus, et fui mortuus, et ecce sum vivens in saecula saeculorum.' Earlier, Lumley's 'remedie all thes thinges withe my deathe,' with its Christian diction, derives from Erasmus, 'Haec profecto cuncta redimam morte (si cadam) mea' (1181), 'If I die, I shall truly redeem this whole state of affairs with my death.' The Greek says, 'By dying I shall protect all these things.' Professor Nancy Zumwalt of the Classics Department, University of Massachusetts, Boston, kindly translated and annotated these Greek passages.

3

JANE LUMLEY'S *IPHIGENIA AT AULIS*

Multum in parvo, or, less is more[1]

Stephanie Hodgson-Wright

In this new essay on Jane/Joanna Lumley, Stephanie Hodgson-Wright calls upon her experience as the director of the first production of Lumley's translated drama, *Iphigenia at Aulis*. Consequently, Hodgson-Wright demonstrates authoritatively that, while Lumley translated the Greek and Latin sources into English, her translation is so free it both opens the text out to performance, and reveals an acute awareness of gender politics. Together with Beilin's shorter piece, Hodgson-Wright's essay proves that Lumley's play is worthy of production and analysis.

Iphigenia at Aulis, 'translated out of Greek into English' by Jane Lumley,[2] has come to light in recent years as the earliest surviving English dramatic text by a woman. Despite pioneering work in the 1980s by Nancy Cotton and Elaine Beilin,[3] which drew attention to its existence, the text has been discussed rather briefly by subsequent literary critics and is yet to receive sustained attention. The exact nature and status of the text has proved difficult to determine. It survives in manuscript in a volume,[4] which Harold H. Child suggests 'appears to have served as a commonplace book or rough copy book.'[5] The volume also contains Jane Lumley's Latin translations of Isocrates' *Orations*, which she dedicated to her father, Henry Fitzalan, twelfth Earl of Arundel, and it is probable that *Iphigenia at Aulis* was also intended for him. In attempting to date Lumley's play, Child opts for the earliest terminal date of 1549/50,[6] some time soon after her marriage to John, Baron Lumley. He is careful to remind us that the play, along with her other translations,[7] 'were nevertheless in all probability, still exercises of childhood',[8] and that the text 'is by no means either literal or complete'.[9]

David Greene suggests that, rather than translating the text directly from the Greek, Lumley used Erasmus's Latin translation as an aid.[10] Whilst Greene valorises Lumley's efforts in translation he also condemns the literary worth of the text because of its omissions:

> Her avoidance of the choral odes may be explained on the grounds that they were difficult for her to translate and that *they constituted no part of the action of the play*. . . . The realisation on her part that the chorus was supposed to reflect and utter gems of wisdom would indicate *that she could translate the odes well enough to realise*

> *their function*. . . . Her omissions are restricted to the choral odes and the long speeches of the principal characters. The mythological material she *reduced to its barest fundamentals probably because of its lack of connection with the action*.[11]

Greene, like Child, assumes Lumley was about 13 when she composed the text and, whilst he might not be impressed with the final result, pays due respect to her efforts. Frank D. Crane's reply to this article is a blistering attack upon both Greene's and Lumley's scholarship. His motivation seems to come from Lumley's age and sex, for, given the lamentable state of Greek scholarship in the sixteenth century, he says it is 'very difficult to believe . . . that an English girl of fourteen was able to translate the Iphigenia directly from the Greek in any manner whatever.'[12] In his anxiety to show what a poor effort Lumley's text is, he makes a vitriolic comment which also contains a (doubtless unintentional) compliment: 'The translation is a childish performance, derived directly and carelessly from the Latin, *when the text is followed at all*' (my italics).[13] Despite their differing attitudes towards Lumley's text, both articles conspire to demonstrate that it is culled from more than one source and is not a particularly literal translation of either. Whilst to the Classical scholar this may be an unforgivable fault, to the scholar of English drama this can mean only one thing: that Jane Lumley attempted to create her own version of the play. Her use of both the Latin and Greek versions also helps to date the play. The printed text of *Iphigenia at Aulis* owned by Arundel, which contains the play in Greek and Latin translation, originally belonged to Thomas Cranmer.[14] Jane Lumley could, therefore, not have had access to it until after the accession of Mary I in 1553, when Cranmer was arrested and Arundel gained possession of his library.[15] If we assume that this is the volume which Lumley used as a source, she must have been at least 16 when she wrote her version of the play. Therefore, her *Iphigenia at Aulis* can neither be devalued as merely a poor translation, nor be condemned as a childish exercise.

Jane Lumley's text displays all the characteristics of a workable piece of drama. The verse of her sources is rendered into simple, yet highly speakable prose;[16] the energy of the text became unquestionably obvious during a recent production of the play.[17] The text is shaped and crafted with the greatest emphasis being placed upon the interaction between the characters and the development of the plot, rather than upon highly wrought dramatic orations. None of the vital ingredients of Euripides' original story are missing: Agamemnon's self-torment which gives way to cowardly self-preservation, Menelaus' indignation, Clytemnestra's angry despair and Iphigenia's guileless simplicity are all present, spoken in the everyday prose of the sixteenth-century English nobility. The omissions, as Greene has noted, amount to the removal of most of the Classical references, and the part of the play which is most reduced is the Chorus. Yet Jane Lumley obviously recognised their crucial function in the play, and retained them to provide exit and entrance lines and to speak the occasional piece of moral commentary. Indeed, their first line is Lumley's own addition: 'What is this? Methinks I see Menelaus striving with Agamemnon's servant' (fol. 70^{v}). This not only serves to cue the entrance of Menelaus and Senex, but also makes clear the change of scene from the Prologue, in which the conversation between Agamemnon and Senex has detailed the events leading up to the opening of the play. This re-formed Chorus gives the greatest single clue to what Lumley was trying to do with the play. She styles them, 'a company of women' (fol. 65^{v}) origin unspecified, although both Euripides and Erasmus indicate that they are from Calchis. It is hard to believe that the translation of their nationality was beyond her capabilities, and so we must assume that the omission is deliberate. Lumley's 'company of women' are, potentially, sixteenth-century English women commenting upon a moral dilemma which could, equally potentially, touch upon the religious, political, and dynastic concerns of sixteenth-century England.

The rather bare prose, with its lack of literary adornment, serves to focus the audience upon the moral debate inherent in the play. The conflicting demands of family and country are explored; without sophisticated political rhetoric, the demands of family achieve moral victory. Our sympathies for Agamemnon are engaged whilst he is determined to save Iphigenia, but his cowardly reversal once she has arrived in Aulis is almost comically repulsive. He will not save her because he is scared of his own army. His inability to justify himself after the impassioned pleas of Clytemnestra and Iphigenia testify to the weakness of his position. Achilles, who has become unwittingly allied to Clytemnestra's cause, demonstrates the difficulty of choosing between family and country:

> My mind is troubled more and more, for I am wonderfully moved with your piteous complaint. Wherefore, seeing you have required help at my hand, I will promise you to deliver both you and your daughter from this misery, if by any means I may withstand the cruel pretence of Agamemnon and his brother. For this matter pertaineth unto me also, because that if she being sent for in my name should be slain, then truly it would turn to no small dishonour to me.
>
> (fol. 84^{v})

Ultimately, Achilles puts himself in danger to undertake the action which properly belongs to Agamemnon, emphasising the latter's self-interested abandonment of his daughter as morally reprehensible.

The conflict is resolved by Iphigenia's decision to die, and the play refocuses its attention upon her: by accepting her fate, Iphigenia becomes the controlling dramatic force behind most of the remaining action. The moment at which Iphigenia changes her mind is when the Greek army has divided, with Clytemnestra and Achilles allied on one side, determined to save Iphigenia, and Ulysses leading the other, determined to kill her. Iphigenia's calm voice breaks the moment of tension as Clytemnestra, on Achilles' advice, is standing ready to protect her daughter and Achilles himself is preparing for the arrival of Ulysses and the Greek army:

> *Clytemnestra*: But if he go about to take my daughter away with strong power, what shall I do then?
>
> *Achilles*: You were best to keep her by you, for the matter shall be driven to that point.
>
> *Iphigenia*: Hearken, O mother, I pray you unto my words, for I perceive you are angry with your husband, which you may not do, for you cannot obtain your purpose by that means. And you ought rather to have thanked Achilles, because he so gently hath promised you his help, which may happen to bring him into a great mischief.
>
> (fol. 91^{v})

Faced with being the cause of Clytemnestra opposing Agamemnon, and Greeks opposing Greeks – a double civil war of domestic and national proportions – Iphigenia forgets her desire to live, so earnestly expressed to Agamemnon only a short time before, and decides she 'must needs die and will suffer it willingly' (fol. 92). Yet her resignation is turned into triumphant appropriation, for in offering herself 'for the commodity of my country' (fol. 92), Iphigenia claims sole responsibility for the ensuing victory of the Greeks over the Trojans, thereby awarding herself not just the military honours hitherto reserved for men, but also the everlasting fame of the true hero: 'Wherefore, I will offer myself willingly to death for my country. For by this means I shall not only leave a perpetual memory of my death, but I shall cause also the Grecians to rule over the barbarians' (fol. 92^{v}). Iphigenia also presents herself as an alternative female Christ, saying that she will 'save all Greece with my death' (fol. 93) and asking that Agamemnon should not be hated for his role in her demise (fol. 94).[18]

Iphigenia's attempt to reconcile her mother to her decision is written with a genuinely touching simplicity, which acquires considerable intensity in performance. As the moment of separation comes, Iphigenia's main concern is that her mother should not disgrace herself in her grief, which is underscored by Clytemnestra's increasing desperation:

Iphigenia:	Who is this that will carry me hence so soon?
Clytemnestra:	I will go with you, O daughter.
Iphigenia:	Take heed, I pray you, lest you happen to do that which shall not become you. Wherefore, O mother, I pray you, follow my counsel and tarry here still. For I must needs go to be sacrificed unto the goddess Diana.
Clytemnestra:	And will you go away, O daughter, leaving me, your mother, here?
Iphigenia:	Yea, surely mother, I must go from you unto such a place from whence I shall never come again, although I have not deserved it.
Clytemnestra:	I pray you daughter tarry, and do not forsake me now!

(fols 94–94^{v})

The ripping of the bond between mother and daughter is given primary importance in Lumley's text. Unsurprisingly, after such a traumatic separation, Clytemnestra is doubtful when she hears the Nuntio's tale of Iphigenia's miraculous disappearance from the altar. Agamemnon's final appearance, to give a smug and coldly formal farewell to his wife, emphasises his undeserved good fortune:

> Truly wife, we are happy for our daughter's sake, for surely she is placed in heaven. But now I think it best that you go home, seeing that we shall take our journey so shortly unto Troy. Wherefore now fare you well, and of this matter I will commune more at my return. And in the mean season I pray god send you well to do and your heart's desire.
>
> (fol. 96^{v})

Despite its verbal simplicity, the play deals with a complex debate which offers many opportunities for the subversion of ideological norms. The central conflict of the play, between duty to family and duty to country, undermines the authority of the patriarch within both contexts. Duty to family is presented as the morally superior position, from which Agamemnon increasingly distances himself throughout the play. Ultimately, the familial bond becomes reconstructed as the exclusive bond between mother and child, a productive, life-giving and mutually preserving bond. Moreover, whilst Agamemnon perceives his role as father to include the right to consent to Iphigenia's death, the reason behind his consent is presented as nothing other than political self-preservation. He lacks the higher motivation which Iphigenia later expresses, and thus is eventually characterised as a tyrant, exploiting the weak to retain his power. As Clytemnestra reminds him: 'you were chosen the captain over the Grecians to execute justice to all men, and not to do both me and also your children such an injury' (fol. 88^{v}). Iphigenia's decision to die is expressed in terms which effectively erase Agamemnon from the scenario. Her motivation reconciles the hitherto conflicting duties to family and country, as it clearly comes from a concern that many others, but especially her mother and Achilles, will face danger and death if she does not go to the altar. Iphigenia does not, however, construct herself as a passive object finally submitting to her father's will. Rather, she constructs herself as the full subject of a nation which has called upon her to make the final sacrifice. It is a fact often overlooked that Iphigenia, in offering her life for her country, makes an offer roughly equivalent to that made by the soldiers in the Greek camp, and countless other soldiers before and since. What the play dramatises is not whether this sacrifice is right or wrong, but who has the right to demand it of whom. Lumley's text quite unequivocally demonstrates that it is *not* the father's right to impose it upon his child, but that only the subject has the right to demand it of her- or himself. Ros Ballaster argues that '*Iphigenia* dramatically identifies the importance of the exchange of women in the masculine sphere of military glory and state politics and the struggle of the daughter to acquire a voice in that exchange culture.'[19] Conversely, one could argue that rather than struggling to acquire a voice, Iphigenia possesses one which has considerable moral authority and dramatic power. Indeed, it is perhaps the very success of the feminine voice in the play which led Jane Lumley to emphasise its status as a translation, thereby distancing herself from the content.[20]

When read against the political events of 1553/4, in which Jane Grey, manipulated by her father and father-in-law (the Dukes of Suffolk and Northumberland), ended her short life on the scaffold, the contemporary resonances of Jane Lumley's text become even more apparent. Jane Lumley was, by virtue of her birth, very close to the main political players in the fate of Jane Grey. The highly duplicitous activities of Lumley's father, Arundel, are detailed in the *DNB*:

> On the death of the king, 6 July 1553, Arundel entered with apparent ardour into the designs of the duke. But on the very same evening, while the council were still discussing the measures necessary to be adopted before they proclaimed the Lady Jane, he contrived to forward a letter to Mary, in which he informed her of her brother's death; assured her that Northumberland's motive in conceding it was 'to entrap her before she know of it'; and concluded by urging her to retire to a position of safety. Mary followed his advice; while Arundel continued during more than ten days to concur in Northumberland's schemes with a view to his betrayal. He attended the meetings of the council, he signed the letter to Mary denouncing her as illegitimate, and asserted the title of her rival; he accompanied Northumberland and others when they informed Jane of her accession to the crown, and attended her on the progress from Sion house to the Tower, preparatory to her coronation. Arundel and the other secret partisans of Mary persuaded Northumberland to take the command in person of the force raised to attack Mary, and assured him of their sympathy when he started.[21]

It was Arundel who arrested Northumberland on Mary's behalf, once her position was secure. Henceforth he became one of her closest advisors and was also probably one of those who persuaded Mary to consent to Jane Grey's execution after Thomas Wyatt's rebellion in 1554. As a direct result of Arundel's actions, Jane Grey, his daughter's cousin,[22] was confined to the Tower, tried for treason and finally executed.

The striking connection between the subject matter of Jane Lumley's play and the fate of her cousin has not gone unnoticed.[23] However, the similarities between the cousins make the connection even more unsettling: Jane Lumley and Jane Grey shared a Christian name, were virtually the same age and had received a very similar education. That Arundel's niece, whom he helped send to her death, should have so much in common with his daughter cannot have escaped Jane Lumley's notice. It is not very surprising that whilst looking through those books which her father had acquired as an indirect result of betraying Jane Grey, Lumley's attention should be drawn to a play which is disturbingly reminiscent of the death of her cousin, whose surname, when rendered into Latin, also means 'Greek'.[24] For example, the topography of the play is very similar to that of Jane Grey's last days. Jane Grey arrived at the Tower by boat, just as Iphigenia journeyed to Aulis:

> The weather was warm and sunny as she entered the State barge and went downstream to the broad steps of the Tower of London, where she landed at three o'clock in the afternoon. She wore a white coif with jewels in her hair and a green dress stamped with gold, with hanging sleeves. . . . She walked in procession beneath a canopy to the great hall. The Duchess of Suffolk carried her daughter's train.[25]

The arrival in Aulis of Clytemnestra and Iphigenia 'adorned with all nobles' (fol. 78), and prepared for a great occasion, suitably parallels this. For Jane Grey, the Tower was to change its significance, from palace to prison to place of execution; similarly for Iphigenia, Aulis changes from a place of joy and celebration to a site of terror and destruction. Iphigenia arrives at Aulis expecting a wedding, whereas Jane Grey was already married when she arrived at the Tower, yet the connection between marriage and death is equally strong in each case. Alison Plowden's description of Jane Grey's wedding to Guildford Dudley, whose father intended to make him king via her succession, is notable for its image of Jane 'her hair braided with pearls, being led, literally, as a sacrifice to the altar'.[26] The fact that a marriage match, albeit a feigned one in the play, is instrumental in bringing both Jane and Iphigenia to their deaths is a significant similarity which cannot have escaped the notice of Lumley or her readership. Indeed, Lumley's prose serves to increase the focus upon marriage as a deadly device; the consequence of the feigned match is referred to in the starkest terms on several occasions. For example, Senex, in condemnation of Agamemnon's actions, says 'Thou has prepared grievous things, O king, for thou hast determined to sacrifice thy own child under the colour of marriage' (fol. 69^{v}).

Although there is a very clear parallel between Jane Grey and Iphigenia, the other characters are less obviously equated with the political players of 1553/4. Apart from the occasion of their arrival at the Tower, the Duchess of Suffolk is hardly represented by Clytemnestra. Once Mary I was proclaimed, Jane Grey's mother was more interested in preserving herself and her other two daughters and successfully sought a place at Mary's court. Clytemnestra represents a type of idealised mother figure, who functions within the wider debate of the play as a supporter of the primacy of duty to family over duty to country. Indeed, her attack on Agamemnon is the play's most powerfully emotive speech, in a register less obviously utilised by the women involved in the historical events.[27] Whilst

Achilles might be seen as an implausibly heroized Guildford Dudley, his action in the play bears most relation to the actions of Sir Thomas Wyatt, for it is his act of raising an army which finally sends Iphigenia to her death. Agamemnon can be seen as a composite of Arundel, Suffolk and Northumberland, all of whom bore some responsibility for Jane Grey's death. However, at the last, his likeness to Suffolk is the most striking. Once Mary's accession had been accepted by the Privy Council, Suffolk went to the Tower to tell his daughter what had happened and then left her there to await her fate,[28] which his own ill-judged reaction to Mary's proposed marriage to Philip of Spain helped to secure. Indeed, John Foxe records that Jane Grey saw her father as ultimately to blame:

> Father, although it hath pleased God to hasten my death by you, by whom my life should rather have been lengthened; yet can I so patiently take it as I yield God more hearty thanks for shortening my woful days.[29]

Both Iphigenia and Jane Grey remember their sisters in the short time before their deaths. Iphigenia instructs her mother to ask her sisters not to mourn for her death; Jane Grey wrote a farewell letter to her sister, which said 'as touching my death, rejoice as I do, good sister, that I shall, for losing of a mortal life, win an immortal life'.[30] Iphigenia's concern to tell the Greeks that she has come willingly and therefore wishes to die at the appointed time on the altar has parallels with the report of Jane Grey's death:

> O father, I am come hither to offer my body willingly for the wealth of my country. Wherefore seeing that I shall be sacrificed for the commodity of all Greece. I do desire you that none of the Grecians may slay me privily for I will make no resistance against you.
>
> (fol. 95[v])

Foxe reports that Jane Grey asks the executioner to dispatch her quickly, but as she knelt down to the block asked 'Will you take it off, before I lay me down?' to which the executioner replied that he would not.[31] Both women demonstrate heroic determination to await death on their respective scaffolds, to meet it bravely on their terms rather than have it sprung upon them.

The Chorus, with their relatively silent, constant and yet often unacknowledged presence could, arguably, represent the women of Arundel's household, including Jane herself, during the events of 1553–4. As has already been indicated, the creation of Lumley's Chorus necessarily involved a process of silencing, in order to remove as much of the Classical context as possible. The Chorus's role in the play underlines this process of marginalisation, occupying that liminal yet vital place between the audience and the action, functioning as both moral commentator and stage manager. In this first function, the male characters, to whom they address their comments in the first part of the play, repeatedly ignore them. During the argument between Menelaus and Agamemnon, in which the Chorus feature particularly prominently, their words are totally ignored by the feuding brothers, despite the fact that on more than one occasion the Chorus address the men directly, e.g. 'We also lament your chance, so much as it becometh women to lament the misery of princes' (fol. 76[v]). Nevertheless, the men are clearly aware that the women are present. Having heard the news of Iphigenia's arrival, Agamemnon has decided that he must conceal the truth from her mother, Clytemnestra, until the deed is done and instructs the Chorus to keep quiet about everything they have heard: 'And I pray you also, O ye women, not to open this matter' (fol. 78). The Chorus's relationship with the women characters is markedly different. On seeing the arrival of Iphigenia and Clytemnestra, they determine to make them welcome and comfortable, despite having to keep the dreadful truth from them. Clytemnestra graciously acknowledges the Chorus's rank and status: 'This truly is a token of good luck, that so many noble women meet us' (fol. 78ᵛ). The Chorus is given strength and power by the arrival of Clytemnestra and Iphigenia, and once the struggle begins to save Iphigenia's life, they round on Agamemnon: 'It is meet, O Agamemnon, that you should follow your wife's counsel. For it is not lawful that a father should destroy his child' (fol. 88ᵛ). Once Iphigenia has resigned herself to death, they mark her exit with a song,[32] which offers a simple yet all the more effective enumeration of private injustice and public benefit:

> Behold! Yonder goeth the virgin, to be sacrificed, with a great company of soldiers after her, whose beautiful face and fair body anon shall be defiled with her own blood. Yet happy art thou, O Iphigenia, that with thy death thou shalt purchase, unto the Grecians a quiet passage, which I pray god may not only happen fortunately unto them, but also that they may return again prosperously with a glorious victory.
>
> (fol. 95)

However, once the Nuntio enters with news of Iphigenia's miraculous assumption, the Chorus are willing to believe the story, and point the doubting Clytemnestra to Agamemnon's arrival onstage, for he 'can tell the truth of all this matter' (fol. 96ᵛ). Whilst Iphigenia and Clytemnestra, as exceptional royal women, can offer a drama of resistance to patriarchal power, the Chorus in themselves can offer only a drama of silence and necessary complicity with that power. They have a moment of liberation through their alliance with Clytemnestra and Iphigenia, but unlike these two, are not strong enough to challenge Agamemnon in their own right. Their structural function within the drama demands that they finally accept his version of the truth, in order to utter the lines which end the play: 'O happy Agamemnon, the gods grant thee a fortunate journey unto Troy, and a most prosperous return again' (fol. 97). The conclusion of the play requires their ultimate complicity, just as the events of 1553/4 required the complicity of Jane Lumley.[33]

The extent to which Jane Lumley's complicity was forced, and the extent to which it was given willingly, is not known. Whilst some of the evidence from history and from the play might lead us to infer a sympathy for Jane Grey, the fact that Jane Lumley was a Catholic and part of a dynasty whose fortunes rose with the accession of Mary I might suggest otherwise. However, if the goddess Diana in the play is read as a representation of Mary I, this renders the text highly orthodox in its comments on Mary and her accession, without compromising its subversion of patriarchal authority. Two distinctly gendered economies of truth operate within the play. The demand for Iphigenia's death is fashioned exclusively by men. The priest Calchas (whose words and actions are reported by other characters) interprets the wishes of the goddess Diana as requiring the sacrifice of Iphigenia. Agamemnon, Menelaus and Ulysses agree to it, and the threat of Ulysses coming to take Iphigenia by force is always in the background, although the character never actually appears in the play. Until Iphigenia herself agrees to die, the female characters totally and unequivocally oppose the sacrifice. The reported miracle of Iphigenia's bodily assumption into heaven frustrates the male character's truth-claims, for it demonstrates that Calchas's interpretation of

Diana's wishes, and therefore the subsequent actions of the men, are totally erroneous. As the Nuntio says to Clytemnestra 'she would not have her altar defiled with the blood of your daughter' (fol. 96).[34] The text gives ultimate credence to the female truth economy, and the assumption of Iphigenia places Diana firmly within it. If Diana is read as Mary I, then miraculous assumption of Iphigenia can be interpreted as an attempt to foreground her unwillingness to send Jane Grey to the scaffold, and to obscure Mary's ultimate responsibility for her death, as Iphigenia is removed from the site of political conflict in a cathartically bloodless fashion. Furthermore, with its clear reference to the assumption of the Virgin Mary, the manner of this removal also puts a politically proper Catholic gloss upon the death of the Protestant Jane Grey.

The Chorus's spoken assent to the story of Iphigenia's assumption is of paramount importance, for they are responsible not only for ending the play but also for enacting Jane Lumley's support for Mary I. This politically charged example of the Chorus's vital function as stage managers who help to shape the drama, stands as evidence that Lumley's text did not merely exist as a text to be read privately, but as a text for reading aloud, or private performance, whereby the sensitive and difficult political decisions of the recent months could be considered, and perhaps put to rest. Evidence of an actual performance of Jane Lumley's play has not yet been uncovered and, given the sensitivity of the subject matter, any performance may have been quite discreet.[35] Whilst my own practical investigations have demonstrated that the play is certainly performable, it is still important to consider the evidence available, which points to the likelihood of an envisaged performance in the sixteenth century. Frederick S. Boas's point, that whilst Classical plays were studied principally for scholarly reasons, 'Tudor England, with its inborn passion for acting could never have been content with merely reading the plays of antiquity, even if other countries had not already set them the example', might just as feasibly be applied to a highly educated and cultured household, as to the Oxford and Cambridge colleges to which he refers.[36] And indeed, the domestic setting was an ideal place for some kinds of drama, as Bruce R. Smith notes:

> Just as early sixteenth-century scholars perceived no temporal, philosophical distance between themselves and the ancient scripts, so early sixteenth-century audiences felt no physical, psychological distance between themselves and the actors speaking a few feet away. The organic space of medieval great halls was a perfect setting for the play-as-rhetorical-event.[37]

With its sharply focused and all too relevant debate, a performance of Jane Lumley's play would have constituted just such an event. Furthermore, Jane Lumley's use of Erasmus points to her conscious decision to create a performance text. Erasmus had advocated the performance of plays as a way of developing oratorial skills in schools and universities, and his translations of *Hecuba* and *Iphigenia at Aulis* became key texts in the curriculum. *Iphigenia at Aulis* was the inspiration for two of the more significant academic dramas, John Christopherson's *Jepthah*, completed 1544, possibly performed at Cambridge in 1554–5,[38] and George Buchanan's *Jephthes* (1542/3).[39]

Whilst Jane herself might have been denied the opportunity to take part in university theatricals, her brother, Henry Maltravers, and her husband-to-be, John Lumley, attended Queens' College Cambridge at the very time when classically inspired dramas such as these were being performed. Alan H. Nelson notes that on 9 October 1546, Queens' College mandated the annual public performance of comedies or tragedies and that 'it was conceivably this mandate which set off a flurry of new construction [of theatres] over the next three years'.[40] It is certainly likely that when Jane Lumley wrote her play, she would have known about the theatrical activities at Cambridge from John and Henry, which could have alerted her to the theatrical possibilities of her own text. In addition, she herself would have been no stranger to visual art forms, for her father, as well as ensuring that all his children received a good education,[41] was patron of all kinds of literary and visual art including theatre.[42] Bearing in mind that Lumley's play was probably intended for her father, information supplied by the Earl of Arundel's biographer would support the case that this text was at least read out, for Arundel preferred to hear, speak and communicate in English. His librarian, Humphrey Llhuyd, 'complains that his place of residence had debarred him from any opportunity of either speaking or writing Latin, – another confirmation, perhaps, of the Earl's dislike of any language but his own.'[43] The Earl of Arundel also preferred to speak his own language abroad, defending himself thus: 'I love to speake in that language in which I can best utter my mind and not mistake.'[44] Lumley might have dedicated *written* texts in the Classical languages to her father, but given the Earl's preference for spoken English, *Iphigenia at Aulis* may well have been prepared for the Earl to hear rather than read.

One final piece of evidence is a quarto manuscript commissioned by Jane Lumley.[45] This fourteen-leaf decorated vellum manuscript is a transcription of the sententiae painted on the wall of the Long Gallery at Gorhambury, home of Sir Nicholas Bacon,[46] and was probably prepared in 1575 or 1576.[47] It is not unreasonable to assume that such a request provides particular evidence of Lumley's artistic tastes and sensibilities. Arguably, her admiration of the Gorhambury sententiae demonstrated her appreciation of the interface between the verbal and the visual. Elizabeth McCutcheon tells us that the Long Gallery at Gorhambury 'lent itself to entertainment and recreation of all sorts: games, walks, music, conversation, reading, mumming',[48] and consequently argues that the sententiae, when painted upon the walls of such a place, acquire new dimensions of signification:

> Sir Nicholas Bacon's inscriptions seemingly constitute a complete memory-theatre of a verbal sort. Not only the sententiae themselves, but also what is much less usual . . . the commonplace headings categorising them are painted on the walls of a room intended for reflection and leisure. He thereby created a personal, verbal memory-theatre, an external mirror of and for his conscience and consciousness, complemented by the images in the beautiful glass windows.[49]

McCutcheon's study of the manuscript is also revealing in its comments about the educated Renaissance mind: 'The sententia embodies the Renaissance love of multum in parvo',[50] and she points to Sir Nicholas' particular fondness for using 'pithy prose'.[51] This last phrase might also be applied to Jane Lumley's translation and far from being a cause for criticism, it is precisely this quality which gives the play its dramatic energy. Much of the lyrical material may have gone, but in practice this means that the expressions of received wisdom, the moral dilemma and the relationships between the characters are not only drawn in sharper focus, but also more easily read in terms of contemporary issues. When the play is read against the general backdrop of sixteenth-century gender politics, or the more specific backdrop of Jane Grey's execution, the many and complex resonances of the text shine through. In the case of Jane Lumley's play less text means more interpretation: *multum in parvo* indeed.

Notes

1 Part of this essay first appeared as a paper given at the 1997 Rocky Mountain Medieval and Renaissance Association Conference. I would like to acknowledge the financial assistance from the British Academy and the University of Sunderland, which made it possible for me to give this paper.
2 MS Royal 15 A ix, fol. 63. All quotations from the play will be silently modernised, though reference will be to the original manuscript.
3 Nancy Cotton, *Women Playwrights in England* c. 1363–1750 (Lewisburg, PA: Bucknell University Press, 1980), p. 28; Elaine V. Beilin, *Redeeming Eve: Women Writers of the English Renaissance* (Princeton, NJ: Princeton University Press, 1987) pp. 153–7.
4 'The doinge of my Lady Lumley, dowghter of my L. Therle of Arundell' appears on fol. 1 of the volume.
5 Harold H. Child (ed.) *Iphigenia at Aulis translated by Lady Lumley* (Oxford: Malone Society, 1909), p. vi. Child also notes that the fair copy of 'Oratio Isocratis que Archidamus inscribatur', Royal MS 15 A i, 'is certainly a presentation copy to Lord Arundel'.
6 Jane married John, Baron Lumley (1534–1609) after his matriculation from Queens' College, Cambridge in 1549, but before John made his translation of 'Erasmus his Institution of a Christian Prince', British Library shelfmark Royal 17A xlix. The inscription at the end reads: 'Your lordeshippes obedient sone I. Lumley 1550'. Since Lumley's own father was dead, the dedicatee must be his father-in-law, Arundel.
7 These are housed in the British Library, together with the work of Lumley's sister, Mary, her brother, Henry Maltravers, their step-brother Sir John Ratcliffe, shelfmarks Royal MS A xii 16; 7 D ix; 12 A i-iv; 15 A i; 15 A ii.
8 Child, p. vi.
9 Child, p. vii.
10 David H. Greene, 'Lady Lumley and Greek Tragedy', *Classical Journal* 36 (1941) pp. 536–47, p. 537.
11 Greene, pp. 542–4, italics added.
12 Frank D. Crane, 'Euripides, Erasmus and Lady Lumley', *Classical Journal* 39 (1944), pp. 223–8, p. 224.
13 Crane, p. 228.
14 Sears Jayne and Francis R. Johnson (eds.) *The Lumley Library: The Catalogue of 1609* (London: British Museum, 1956), p. 205. British Library shelfmark 999.d.1.
15 Jayne and Johnson, p. 3 suggest that he was 'probably given at least first refusal of the Cranmer library when it fell into Mary's hands'.
16 Jane Lumley's text is not the only example of a sixteenth-century prose play. F. S. Boas, *University Drama in the Tudor Age* (Oxford: Clarendon Press, 1914), p. 366, notes that Ralph Worsley's *Synedrium Animalum* (1554/5) exists in both a verse and prose form.
17 I directed a cast of final year students from the University of Sunderland. The production was staged in January 1997, at Clifton Hall Studio, Sunderland, with original music by Chris Smith.
18 Beilin, p. 157, identifies a reference to Revelation 1:17–18 'I am the first and the last: I am he that lives and was dead; and behold I am alive for evermore' in the Nuntio's report of Iphigenia's miraculous assumption 'this day your daughter hath been both alive and dead' (fol. 96^{v}).
19 Ros Ballaster, 'The first female dramatists', in Wilcox (ed.) pp. 267–94, p. 270.
20 Beilin, pp. 154–5, suggests that the style 'translation' was a mask used by Jane Lumley as protection for her work and that 'using Erasmus's Latin, as copy text or as aid, assured an entirely "safe" impersonal voice for a play about female heroism'.
21 G. Goodwin, 'Henry Fitzalan, 12th Earl of Arundel (1511–1580)', *DNB* (1889).
22 Jane Lumley's mother Catherine was sister to Jane Grey's father, Henry Grey. Furthermore, Henry Grey himself had been allied in marriage to the Arundel family, Katherine, sister of Jane Lumley's father, Henry Fitzalan. However, Grey managed to disentangle himself from this match in order to make a politically more advantageous match with Frances Brandon, daughter and heir of Charles Brandon, Duke of Suffolk (a title which Henry Grey later

received in his wife's right) and Mary, sister of Henry VIII and widow of Louis XII of France. Jane Grey, along with her two sisters, Mary and Catherine, resulted from the union of Frances Brandon and Henry Grey.

23 Barry Weller and Margaret W. Ferguson (eds.) *The Tragedy of Mariam, The Fair Queen of Jewry with the Lady Falkland: Her Life* (London: University of California Press, 1994) p. 27:

> Jane Lumley may well have chosen Iphigeneia's story not only to paint a portrait of female virtue, but also to explore a situation of familial conflict that bore striking resemblance to dilemmas in her own aristocratic patriarchal family. Jane's father, Henry Fitzalen [*sic*], twelfth Earl of Arundel, was a leader of the Catholic nobility who . . . betrayed his wife's niece, Lady Jane Grey, in a way that helped bring about her execution.

24 Josiah Pratt (ed.) *The Acts and Monuments of John Foxe* (London: Religious Tract Society, n.d., 1877?), p. 425. Hereafter cited as Foxe.

25 David Mathew, *Lady Jane Grey: The Setting of the Reign* (London: Eyre Methuen, 1972), p. 140.

26 Alison Plowden, *Lady Jane Grey and House of Suffolk* (London: Sidgwick and Jackson, 1985), p. 87.

27 In Buchanan's *Jephthes*, the equivalent character is named Storge, which I. D. McFarlane, *Buchanan* (London: Duckworth, 1981), p. 191 interprets as the Greek word for love between parents and children.

28 Mathew, p. 150.

29 Foxe, p. 417.

30 Foxe, p. 422.

31 Foxe, p. 424.

32 Despite being written in prose, this passage proved relatively easy to set to music. Chris Smith's arrangement complemented the increasing proportion of stressed syllables throughout the piece, to emphasise the swelling of emotion as Iphigenia is carried offstage and away from her mother.

33 Gordon Goodwin, 'John, Baron Lumley 1534?–1609', *DNB*, (1893) says: 'On 29 Sept. 1553 he was created K.K. Two days afterwards he attended at the coronation of Queen Mary, and his wife, dressed in crimson velvet, sat in the third chariot of state.' J. G. Nichols, 'Life of the last Fitz-Alan, Earl of Arundel', *The Gentleman's Magazine* 154:2 (1833) pp. 490–500, p. 493, relates that the Earl of Arundel's wife was one of the four ladies on horseback, clad in crimson velvet, who also took a prominent place in the coronation procession of Mary I.

34 Clytemnestra's doubt, albeit misplaced in the larger context of the Iphigenia story, constitutes her own, independent challenge to the masculine version of the truth with which she is presented, and is clearly motivated by Agamemnon's earlier duplicity.

35 If the events of 1553/4 inspired Jane to translate the play, then perhaps Mary's proclamation of August 18 1553 also caused her to be discreet about its existence. Foxe, p. 391, reprints the text, in which she forbade her subjects:

> to interpret or teach any Scriptures, or any manner points of doctrine concerning religion; neither also to print any books, matter, ballet, rhyme, interlude, process, or treatise, nor to play any interlude (except they have her grace's special license in writing for the same), upon pain to incur her highness's indication and displeasure.

36 Boas, p. 15.

37 Bruce R. Smith, *Ancient Scripts and Modern Experience on the English Stage 1500–1700*, (Princeton, NJ: Princeton University Press, 1988), p. 65.

38 For discussions of Christopherson's play, see Boas, pp. 49–60 and Howard B. Norland, *Drama in Early Tudor Britain 1485–1558* (Lincoln, NB: University of Nebraska Press, 1995) pp. 307–18.

39 Boas, p. 19, claims that this was performed at the College of Guienne in Bordeaux before 1545. P. Sharrat and P. G. Walsh (eds) *George Buchanan: Tragedies*, (Edinburgh: Scottish

Academic Press, 1983), pp. 4–10 dispute the certainty of this. Interestingly, they also claim that 'Buchanan's two original plays [*Jephthes* and *Baptistes*] were clearly directed against hypocrisy and idolatry in religious people, and also against tyranny', p. 10. The theological aspcct of *Jephthes* is discussed by McFarlane, pp. 195–201.

40 Alan H. Nelson, *Early Cambridge Theatres: College, University and Town Stages 1464–1720* (Cambridge: Cambridge University Press, 1994), p. 33.

41 See notes above for the shelfmarks of translations by Mary Fitzalan (who married Thomas Howard, Duke of Norfolk 1552–4), Henry Maltravers and John Lumley. It would appear that John Lumley joined Arundel's coterie after his marriage to Jane. According to Jayne and Johnson, p. 5, Jane 'lived most of her married life in her father's house and continued to use his library; not only her translations and exercises (now Royal MSS 15 A i, ii and ix), but also her own books were kept in the main Arundel collection.'

42 Norland, p. xix, names him as one of the Earls of Arundel who, from 1477–1544 sponsored a troupe of actors. Lionel Cust, 'The Lumley Inventories', *The Walpole Society* 6 (1917–18), pp. 15–35, details the huge collection of artefacts belonging ultimately to John Lumley, and gives a full transcription of the inventory made in 1590, which includes no less than 127 musical instruments of 13 different types. Mary F. S. Hervey, 'A Lumley Inventory of 1609', *The Walpole Society* 6 (1917–18), pp. 36–50, reproduces the later inventory, made after John Lumley's death. She makes the important point (p. 37) that Arundel left his entire collection to John Lumley, and that although the two men shared a love of the literary and visual arts, Lumley 'can never have had the means to do so to the extent practised by Lord Arundel', which indicates that the majority of the items listed in both inventories belonged first to Arundel.

43 Nichols, p. 491.

44 Nichols, p. 492.

45 British Library shelfmark MS Royal 17 A xxiii.

46 He was married to Anne Cooke, daughter of Sir Anthony Cooke, tutor to Edward VI. Like Jane and her sister Mary, Anne and her sisters were also highly educated.

47 Elizabeth McCutcheon, *Sir Nicholas Bacon's Great House Sententiae*, English Literary Renaissance Supplements, 3 (1977), p. 17.

48 McCutcheon, p.16.

49 McCutcheon, pp. 20–1.

50 McCutcheon, p. 1.

51 McCutcheon, p. 4.

4

'PATRONESSE OF THE MUSES'

Margaret P. Hannay

This essay is taken from Margaret P. Hannay's comprehensive and intuitive literary biography of Mary Sidney, *Philip's Phoenix: Countess of Pembroke* (1990), the publication of which proved a watershed in Sidney studies. Before Hannay presented her thorough researches it was assumed that Mary Sidney had remained perpetually in her brother's shadow, her literary work offering mere echoes of his greater genius; it is now clear that this is far from the truth. The extract here is taken from Hannay's analysis of Mary Sidney's translation, *The Tragedy of Antonie*, and demonstrates the way in which the play influenced the whole development of politicised drama on the English stage.

By translating Robert Garnier's *Marc Antoine* and sponsoring Samuel Daniel's continuation in *Cleopatra*, the countess helped to naturalize Continental historical tragedy in England. A dozen works followed the closet drama form of Garnier, but far more significant was the use of historical drama as a privileged genre for political content, the use of 'times past' to comment on current affairs. Far from being a retrograde movement against the vibrancy of the popular stage, Garnier's dramas were at the forefront of the contemporary movement in Continental historical tragedy, the avant-garde of the theater.[1]

Like her *Psalmes*, Mary Sidney's drama was based on Continental models in both form and content; form, however, has dominated critical discussions of *Antonius*. Since the mid-nineteenth century, Mary Sidney has been portrayed as the inept leader of a conspiracy against the popular stage. She and her circle of 'shy recluses,' as T. S. Eliot called them, were 'bound to fail' in their campaign against the native dramatic tradition.[2] They were motivated, we are told, by a noble but rather mindless devotion to her brother's dictates in *A Defence of Poetry*. . . . The countess's strategy was supposedly to root out the literary barbarism of Shakespeare and others by fostering insipidly correct dramas based on the model of Robert Garnier. Alexander Witherspoon's condescension is typical of these critics: the countess was the 'leader of the movement against the popular drama' because she vowed to 'undertake that Reformation of English tragedy which her brother had so desired.'[3] She was 'the eccentric leader of this light brigade' who held 'a grudge against the popular tragedy,' a 'bluestocking' who could not handle 'the tragedies . . . of the popular stage,' which 'were of masculine inception and for masculine consumption, strong meat for strong stomachs' (p. 71). Witherspoon's presuppositions become even clearer when he declares that Mary Sidney wrote in 'an age of female ascendancy' when 'the vices and virtues of the day were no longer of the sterner sort. It became an age of poison and innuendo. . . . There was probably never an age in which women held a greater sway physically and intellectually' (pp. 68–9). Witherspoon's final chapter is significantly titled 'The Failure of Lady Pembroke's Movement.' This 'myth of the Countess of Pembroke's dramatic circle,' as Mary Ellen Lamb terms it, went virtually unchallenged until Lamb exposed 'the unlikelihood' that 'the dramatic circle' of the countess existed at all.[4]

Although the countess did not head a conspiracy against the popular stage, her work did have a salutary effect on English drama, an effect that is blurred if we look at only the closet form of *Antonius*. The formal aims of this Continental drama were essentially different from those of later English dramatists, such as Shakespeare. *Marc Antoine* is a drama of character, not of action; Garnier was not interested in events themselves, but in the refraction of events through different viewpoints, giving the perspectives of both the noble protagonists and their subjects. Such drama was eminently suitable for reading aloud on an evening at Wilton, when no professional entertainment was available. As Russell A. Leavenworth notes, Daniel was deliberately writing closet drama in his *Cleopatra*, even in various revisions; like Thomas Kyd in his *Cornelia*, he sought to produce 'a readable dramatic poem,' not a 'stageable drama.'[5] A stageable drama would have taxed the resources of the Wilton household. For this social group, closet drama was an appropriate genre, and apparently others found the works appealing as well. Within five years of publication, Mary Sidney's *Antonius* went through two editions and Daniel's *Cleopatra*, six editions; they were hardly the failures that Witherspoon labeled them.[6]

Nor were they an attempt to supplant the works of Shakespeare. Dates alone should be enough to dispel the idea that by translating *Marc Antoine*, Mary Sidney was trying to strike a blow against Shakespeare, who had barely begun to achieve recognition. *Antonius* is precisely dated 'At Ramsburie. 26 November 1590.' By then, young Shakespeare may have completed *The Two Gentlemen of Verona* and *The Taming of the Shrew*, not yet an oeuvre to challenge the reputation of Garnier, who had been extravagantly praised by Pierre de Ronsard and others of the Pléiade.[7] By importing the Continental model, the countess was consistent with her other translations – of Mornay's *Excellent discovrs de la Vie et de la Mort*, of Petrarch's 'Triumph of Death,' and of the Psalms, based primarily on Huguenot models in both form and content.

By importing this Continental model, the countess was also combating the formal weakness of the early English drama, as her brother advised in *A Defence of Poetry*. More importantly, she demonstrated her conviction that drama could be used for political statement. Her choice of Garnier's play indicates that she shared her family's taste for political drama. *Gorboduc*, the one English drama praised in Sidney's *Defence of Poetry*, was first presented at the Inner Temple in the year of Mary Sidney's birth; her uncle Robert Dudley was Master of the Revels and later used *Gorboduc* as a model for 'political' entertainments, such as those at Kenilworth.[8] Sidney praised *Gorboduc* not only for its style, its 'stately speeches and well-sounding phrases,' but also for its 'notable morality, which it doth most delightfully teach, and so obtain the very end of poesy.'[9] What *Gorboduc* teaches is the danger to the state of the ruler's private passions, the theme also of *Antonius*; like *Antonius*, *Gorboduc* focuses on civil war and ends with the extinction of the princely line.

This political emphasis is evident in Daniel's dedication of *Cleopatra* to Mary Sidney. Written as a companion to her *Antonius*, *Cleopatra* was 'the worke the which she did impose' to call him to a higher form of poetry than his *Delia* and *Rosamond*, poetry that would participate in a campaign against literary barbarism:[10]

Now when so many pennes (like Speares) are charg'd,
To chace away this tyrant of the North:
Gross Barbarism, whose powre grown far inlarg'd,
Was lately by thy valiant Brothers worth,
First found, encountred, and prouoked forth:
Whose onset made the rest audacious,
Whereby they likewise haue so well discharg'd,
Vpon that hidious Beast incroching thus.[11]

Daniel enlists in the campaign against this barbarism:

And now must I with that poore strength I haue,
Resist so foule a foe in what I may:
And arme against obliuion and the graue.
(sig. H6)

In this campaign, he will follow 'great Sydney and our Spencer might,' who are worthy to be equaled with 'those *Po*-singers [the great Italian poets]' (sig. H7). In another reference to Sidney's sonnets two years earlier, Daniel had established Mary Sidney's pivotal role in this campaign. She is the person 'whome the fortune of our time hath made the happie and iudicall Patronesse of the Muses . . . to preserue them from those hidious Beasts, Oblivion and Barbarisme,' a statement that clearly refers to poetry in general, not only to the drama.[12] Similarly, Thomas Watson praised her for combating barbarism and ignorance, thereby aiding the cause of literature.[13] Daniel does see himself as part of a group effort to reform English literature, a movement that Sidney began not simply by making prescriptions for the drama in his *Defence*, but also by writing *Astrophel and Stella* and the *Arcadia*.

Nothing in these dedications justifies the modern assumption that the attack on literary barbarism is an attack on Shakespearean drama; indeed, in the *Cleopatra* dedication, Daniel may well be making a compliment to Shakespeare – a pun on his name in the 'pennes (like Speares)' that are raised to combat barbarism, paralleling Jonson's puns on the first part of his name: 'shake a stage' or, more pertinently, 'shake a lance' at ignorance.[14] By 1594, Daniel could well have believed that Shakespeare was using his pen as a spear against barbarism, for Shakespeare in those four years had written two important poems, 'Lucrece' and 'Venus and Adonis,' and had begun his political comedies and his history plays: Parts 1, 2, and 3 of *Henry VI*, *Titus Andronicus*, *Richard III*, *The Comedy of Errors*, *Love's Labour's Lost*, and possibly even *A Midsummer Night's Dream* and *Romeo and Juliet*.[15]

The countess was far more likely to sponsor than to impede such Shakespearian drama. The most intriguing – and the most doubtful – direct evidence for Mary Sidney's association with Shakespeare is the well-known letter from William Cory, Greek tutor to young George, Earl of Pembroke, who writes from Wilton House on 5 August 1865:

> The house (Lady Herbert said) is full of interest . . . we have a letter, never printed, from Lady Pembroke [Mary Sidney] to her son, telling him to bring James I from Salisbury to see *As You Like It*; 'we have the man Shakespeare with us.' She wanted to cajole the king in Raleigh's behalf – he came.[16]

This letter, known only by Cory's late printed reference, is accurate, and helps to establish that Mary Sidney was far more likely to have been Shakespeare's patron than to have 'set out to destroy' the English 'stage tradition.' The letter reported by Cory, 'if it ever existed,' may be a 'nineteenth century forgery,' as D. Nichol Smith says, but, if so, it was an extremely clever hoax, for it fits the facts in every known detail.[17] (Note that I argue here for the accuracy, not the authenticity, of this letter; its authenticity could be completely established only by the rediscovery of the holograph original.)

First of all, the dates and places fit. King James I, prevented from entering London because of the plague, spent much of the first autumn of his reign holding court at Wilton. In August, he progressed the two miles from the Bishop's Palace to Wilton, stayed there for two days, and eventually returned to Wilton for most of September and October.[18] In November, the court was in Winchester (where Ralegh was tried), and then the king and his entourage returned to Wilton. Although there is no record of the play they presented, Shakespeare's company, the King's Men, was paid 30 pounds to perform before the king at Wilton on 2 December 1603, during the period between Ralegh's trial on 17 November and the date set for his execution, 13 December.[19] If *As You Like It* was performed on this occasion, there would have been considerable irony in the gentle mockery of pastoral retreat being staged at Wilton, where Sir Philip had been rusticated and had written the *Arcadia* for his sister, where more recently William Herbert had been rusticated for getting Mary Fitton pregnant, and where the court of King James lingered in this sheep country, banished from London by the plague.

Second, the countess was indeed trying to save Ralegh and had reason to believe that her son would have the necessary influence with the new king. Philip, 19 years old, was already one of James's favorite young men; in the first months of his reign, the king appointed him a Gentleman of the Privy Chamber and Knight of the Bath. Writing to John Chamberlain on 27 November 1603, Dudley Carleton said,

> I do call to mind a pretty secret that the lady of Pembroke hath written to her son Philip and charged him of all her blessing to employ his own credit and his friends and all he can do for Raleigh's pardon; and though she does little good, yet she is to be commended for doing her best in showing *veteris vestigia flammae*.[20]

(Carleton, quoting Dido's words about Aeneas, '[I recognize] the traces of my old passion,' seems to imply that the countess had once loved Ralegh.) The King's Men performed at Wilton just one week after this letter was written, and perhaps the countess did some good after all; Ralegh was not executed that month, as scheduled.

Her motives for helping Ralegh would have been both personal and political. Ralegh was closely connected to the Pembrokes: cousin to Robert Sidney's wife, Barbara Gamage; half-brother to Adrian Gilbert, a member of the household at Wilton; and husband to Bess Throckmorton, the daughter of Sir Nicholas Throckmorton, who was related to the Herberts and had been Leicester's ally in the Protestant cause. Even apart from these family connections, Mary Sidney and her sons would have had reason to support Ralegh in their constant opposition to a Spanish alliance. Ralegh had been accused of conspiring with the Spanish to put Arbella Stuart on the throne – a preposterous charge against one whose vehement anti-Spanish sentiments kept him in trouble with James I from his presentation of a pamphlet, *A Discourse Touching a War with Spain and the Protecting of the Netherlands*, in May 1603 to the final confrontation at San Thomé, which eventually led to his execution.[21] Sir Philip, of course, had died fighting the Spanish in the Netherlands. That the Herberts continued their anti-Spanish policy under the Stuart reign may be deduced from the numerous anti-Catholic, anti-Spanish works dedicated to Pembroke, including the inflammatory works of Thomas Scott.[22] When Ralegh was finally released from the Tower to go on his circumscribed quest for Spanish gold in Guiana in 1616, Pembroke helped finance the voyage. As late as 1623, Pembroke 'was not well settled in the king's opinion, as he was against the Spanish match.'[23]

Since Cory's letter is accurate in all those details that can be verified – Mary Sidney did ask her son to use his influence with King James to save Ralegh, the king did go from Salisbury to Wilton, and Shakespeare's company did perform before the king just after Ralegh's trial – we may wish to look again at Mary Sidney's connection with drama.

Her family's longstanding patronage of stageable drama made her far more likely to sponsor drama than to undertake a campaign against the popular stage. Her uncles Leicester and Warwick sponsored companies of players, beginning before her birth in 1561, so that she would have associated patronage of the drama with the other patronage duties of her family.[24] During Mary's childhood, the Ludlow accounts include listings for 'the chylderne which did play in the Castell' (1577) .[25] We have already noted that her childhood entertainment also included actors performing the exploits of Robin Hood, singers for May Day, and minstrels.[26] Some players were obviously known to the Sidneys, since Sir Philip later stood as godfather to the son of Richard Tarlton, an actor in Leicester's company.[27]

When Mary Sidney's husband became Lord President of the Council of the Marches of Wales, he continued to sponsor companies of players. There was a cluster of performances at Ludlow in the early 1590s, the primary period of Mary Sidney's own writing and patronage: the Queen's Men, in June 1590 and August 1596; Lord Strange's Men, with which Shakespeare was associated, in August 1593; Worcester's Men, in 1595 and 1596; and Essex's Men, in 1596. The marked increase of dramatic performances at Shrewsbury, another of the standard meeting places for the council, may have also been encouraged by Pembroke as Lord President. Shrewsbury was not on the usual circuit for provincial tours, but during that period ten companies performed, some of them repeatedly, including Lord Strange's Men (many of whose members left the company in 1594 to form the Chamberlain's Men) and, of course, Pembroke's own players.[28]

Although Pembroke's Men was a small company that did not prosper and later became absorbed by the Admiral's Men, Pembroke at least lent these players the protection of his name and encouraged their performance near his various homes during the period when his wife was translating and encouraging closet drama.[29] Furthermore, the actor Simon Jewell's will demonstrates that the countess had some personal responsibility for the players. Jewell's final provision is that 'my share of such money as shalbe givenn by my ladie Pembrooke or by her meanes I will shalbe distributed and paide towardes my buriall and other charges.'[30] The company was short-lived, making the dates of its activity more significant: Pembroke's Men were probably active only in 1592 and 1593, while the London theatres were closed because of the plague, and in 1597, when the theatres were restricted for political reasons. Far from attacking the popular stage, Mary Sidney and her husband provided alternative employment for players and playwrights during these troubled years. All four dramas dedicated to Mary Sidney and her husband were published during these years: Daniel's *Cleopatra*; Abraham Fraunce's *The Lamentations of Amyntas*; and two Latin academic dramas by William Gager, who dedicated *Meleager* to Pembroke and *Ulysses Redux* to the countess.[31]

As we shall see, Mary Sidney's son William assumed her patronage duties when he assumed the other duties of his position as Earl of Pembroke in 1603. Although he served increasingly as patron of sermons and political works, the greatest dramas of the age were dedicated to him, *Works of Benjamin Jonson* (1616) and Shakespeare's First Folio (1623). The dedication of the First Folio to Mary Sidney's sons reads as though they had been well acquainted with Shakespeare for many years: 'since your lordships have been pleased to think these trifles something heretofore, and have prosecuted both them and their author, living, with so much favour, we hope that . . . you will use the like indulgence toward them you have done unto their parent.' Furthermore, the plays have been acted before them: 'for so much were your lordships' likings of the several parts when they were acted as, before they were published, the volume asked to be yours.' [32] Pembroke mourned the death of his 'old acquaintance [Richard] Burbage,' the star of the King's Men, making his personal association with Shakespeare even more likely.[33] Furthermore, as Lord Chamberlain, he had control over the King's Men (the former Chamberlain's Men, Shakespeare's own company, which had changed its name on receiving a royal patent in 1603, soon after the accession of James I). None of this proves Mary Sidney's own patronage of Shakespeare, of course, but the cumulative effect of her family's patronage of drama in general and of Shakespeare in particular makes it likely that Shakespeare did, as Alice Luce suggested, 'come within the circle of her patronage.'[34]

Once we have dismissed the conspiracy theory, we can reformulate the terms of the discussion, looking not at the form of the dramas the countess did translate to commission, but at their political content. As Alexander Witherspoon remarks, what is most notable about Garnier's dramas is their emphasis on the themes of 'love of country, praise of freedom, and emulation of the stern virtues of the ancient Romans.'[35] Whereas Seneca focused on familial disputes, emphasizing the lurid and sensational, Garnier focused on national issues. Michael Brennan also asserts that the countess and her followers discovered 'the relevance of continental dramatic techniques to their urgent desire to comment upon English politics.'[36]

Insofar as Mary Sidney did sponsor drama, it was a drama that focused on political themes, particularly on the duties of the monarch.[37] Both her translation of *Marc Antoine* and Daniel's sequel in *Cleopatra* focus on the conflict between private and public issues, which is also the theme of the other English dramas modeled on Garnier, including Thomas Kyd's translation of Garnier's *Cornelie* (1594), and of Fulke Greville's tragedies, *Alaham* and *Mustapha*, which he intended to dedicate to Sir Philip.[38] Greville's *Antony and Cleopatra* was 'sacrificed in the fire' because of its emphasis on their 'irregular passions in foresaking empire to follow sensuality,' which were 'apt enough to be construed or strained to a personating of vices in the present governors and government.' That play may have alluded to Elizabeth's dalliance with Essex, for Greville's next topic is the fall of his kinsman Essex, which 'stirred up the author's second thoughts to be careful.'[39] William Alexander, who probably knew the countess, wrote his four *Monarchicke Tragedies* in the beginning of James's reign (1603–7), serving as 'a *ragout* of sundry maxims . . . enclosed in a crust of narrative,' as Leavenworth notes. The last play in this group of closet dramas is *The Tragedie of Miriam*, published by Elizabeth Carey in 1613 but probably written at least ten years earlier, a play that used Jewish history to speak of the destruction of the state by familial sins.[40]

By the 1590s, the Sidneys had earned a reputation for speaking boldly on matters of state, particularly in defense of the Protestant cause. After Sir Philip had been rusticated for making many of the same objections to the Alençon match that cost the Puritan John

Stubbs his hand, the family substituted the use of privileged genres for direct discourse with the queen: Philip, 'under the pretty tales of wolves and sheep,' considered 'wrong-doing,' and Mary used admonitory flattery in dedicating her Psalter to Elizabeth.[41] The Sidneys also apparently learned that 'the play's the thing/ Wherein I'll catch the conscience of the King,' as may be demonstrated not only by their use of Shakespearian drama to help Ralegh, but also by their connection with works that invited political censorship.[42] *The Isle of Dogs*, which led to the restriction of players in 1597, was apparently performed by Pembroke's Men.[43] At the beginning of James's reign, the new Earl of Pembroke, William Herbert, became the patron of Ben Jonson. Jonson's *Sejanus*, which had caused him to be summoned before the Privy Council in 1603, was dedicated to young Pembroke when it was published in 1605.[44] Pembroke also intervened on behalf of the players imprisoned for having performed Thomas Middleton's anti-Spanish play, *A Game of Chess*.[45] Even gentle Samuel Daniel, who had lived at Wilton in the early 1590s, became more openly political. His play *Philotas* (1605) caused him much trouble because of its apparent allusions to Essex, as when he says that 'the fall of such a weighty Peere/ Doth shake the State.'[46] His pointed dedication of *Philotas* 'To the Prince' makes the contemporary political applications as clear as did Garnier's own dedication of *Marc Antoine*:

> These ancient representments of times past;
> Tell vs that men haue, doe, and alwayes runne
> The selfe same line of action, and doe cast
> Their course alike . . . .
>   This benefit, most noble Prince, doth yeeld
> The sure recordes of Bookes, in which we finde
> The tenure of our state.
>
> (sig. A4^{v})

His term as licenser of the Queen's Revels was turbulent, since he staged his own *Philotas*, John Marston's *The Dutch Courtesan*, and Jonson's *Eastward Ho!* Not surprisingly, the company forfeited the queen's patronage.[47] Daniel continued to 'Sing of State,' as the countess had requested; he followed *Cleopatra* not only with *Philotas*, but also with his monumental study, *The Civile Wares betweene the Howses of Lancaster and Yorke*, begun at Wilton by early 1594 and eventually dedicated to Mary Sidney in 1609.[48]

When Mary Sidney made her decision to translate a work by Robert Garnier, a magistrate who used his drama to criticize the state, she was making a political statement. As Gillian Jondorf demonstrates, Garnier's tragedies were viewed as political statements by his French contemporaries, such as Etienne Gasteuil, Pierre Amy, and Jacques Liger.[49] More importantly, Garnier himself stresses the relevance of his works to the French civil wars. Of his seven tragedies, six focus on war or rebellion, *Porcie*, published by Robert Estienne in 1568, has the subtitle *tragedie françoise, représentant la cruelle et sanglante saison des guerres civiles de Rome: propre et convenable pour y voir depeincte la calamité de ce temps.*[50] The dedication of *Cornelie* (1574) describes the work as a 'poeme à mon regret trop propre aux malheurs de nostre siècle.' The dedication of *Marc Antoine* (1578) itself speaks of 'les représentations Tragiques des guerres civiles de Rome,' and of '[vous] qui avez en telle horreur nos dissentions domestiques et les malheureux troubles de ce Royaume aujourd'huy despouillé de son ancienne splendeur et de la reverable majesté de nos Rois, prophanee par tumultueuses rebellions.' Such parallels may have drawn Mary Sidney to the Antony and Cleopatra tale, popular on the continent but not yet celebrated in English drama.[51] Her work was thus near the outset of the dramatic movement to comment on contemporary affairs by means of Roman historic allusions, parallel to the use of the Psalms as a privileged genre for political statement.

Although Garnier himself was a Catholic and for one brief period near the end of his life advocated the ultra-Catholic League,[52] his plays stress the dangers of civil war, a topic that would be particularly relevant in the turbulent 1590s, when England feared both civil strife and foreign invasion, a time 'not so well secur'd of the future,' as Daniel wrote.[53] Garnier's works also show a sympathy for the poor, which is unusual among Renaissance magistrates, a sympathy shared by the Sidneys. The 'Argument' of Mary Sidney's *Antonius*, not a direct translation from Garnier, likewise stresses the duties of the ruler to protect the people. 'After the ouerthrowe of *Brutus* and *Cassius*, the libertie of *Rome* being now vtterly oppressed' under '*Octauius Caesar* and *Marcus Antonius*,' Antonius returned to Cleopatra, 'againe falling to his former loues, without any regarde of his vertuous wife *Octauia*, by whom neuertheles he had excellent Children.'[54] Lust and its destruction of the family and the state are to be the focus of the play.[55]

In the most lyric and successful poetry of *Antonius*, the chorus ('first Egiptians, and after Romane Souldiors') gives the comments of the people on the actions of their rulers (sig. F1^{v}). In Act I, the Egyptians say that the passion of Antonius and Cleopatra brings to the people 'Warre and warres bitter cheare' (sig. F1). Philostratus underscores the irony of Cupid's wars:

> Loue, playing loue, which men say kindles not
> But in soft harts, hath ashes made our townes
> And his sweet shafts, with whose shot none are kill'd
> Which vlcer not, with deaths our lands haue full'd.
> (sig. G2^{v})

After Cleopatra accepts responsibility for Antonius's overthrow – 'I am sole cause: I did it, only I' – Charmion begs her to save from Caesar's wrath 'both your Realme and you' (sig. H4). The poignant chorus at the end of Act II praises Egypt, 'O swete fertile land,' even as the Nile is enslaved by the Tiber (sig. I2^{v}). As Cleopatra must accept her failure as a monarch, so Antonius must accept responsibility for his failure as a commander, admitting that while his 'idle armes faire wrought with spiders worke,' his 'scattred men without their ensignes strai'd' (sig. L1^{v}). Antonius has begun by blaming fortune and then pleasure, 'The plague of this our life,' which has made him 'carles of vertue, carles of all praise' (sig. L1). Lest we miss the moral, Lucilius, too, discourses on the poison of pleasure, which takes 'the Roiall scepters' from the hands of kings and gives them to 'some straunger'; while the king plays, the people are 'charg'd with heauy loades' by the king's flatterers. In *Antonius*, a prince's pleasure leads directly to tyranny, to 'mutinous Rebellion,' and to subjection by foreign powers. In this drama, Mary Sidney constantly stresses the duties of the monarch to the common people, whose voice is heard in the choruses. The final chorus, at the end of Act IV, is given to the Roman soldiers, whose case is little better than that of the Egyptians:

> Shall euer ciuile bate
> gnaw and deuour our state?
> Shall neuer we this blade,

Our bloud hath bloudie made
Lay downe? . . .
But as from age to age,
So passe from rage to rage?
(sig. N2)

Cleopatra herself moves from self-pity, to remorse for Antonius, to the realization that she has destroyed Egypt. In Act V, she cries out:

Las! je suis le poison et la peste des miens,
Je pers de mes ayeux les sceptres anciens,
J'asservis ce Royaume à des loix estrangers,
Et privé mes enfants des biens hereditaires.
(Garnier, p. 160)

A passage that Mary Sidney translates:

Alas! of mine the plague and poison I
The crowne haue lost my ancestors me left,
This Realme I haue to straungers subiect made,
And robd my children of their heritage.
(sig. N3^{v})

Daniel's continuation in *Cleopatra* emphasizes the same themes, for his 'Argument' ends with the moral: 'and so heereby, came the race of the Ptolomies to be wholly extinct, and the florishing ritch Kingdome of Egypt vtterly ouerthrowne and subdued' (sig. I1). Once again, Cleopatra is forced to recognize the consequences of her actions for her people: 'My unforeseeing weaknesse must intoome/ My Countries fame and glory with my fall.' As in Mary Sidney's *Antonius*, the chorus of Egyptians reflects on the cost of Antonius and Cleopatra's passion, 'Why by their doing ill,/ Haue wrought the worlds unrest.' Cleopatra now must see 'the dangerous way/ Shee tooke' which led to her own 'decay' (sig. I6^{v}). More importantly for the chorus,

[She] likewise makes vs pay
For her disordred lust,
The int'rest of our blood:
Or liue a seruile pray,
Vnder a hand vniust,
As others shall thinke good.
This hath her riot wonne:
And thus shee hath her state, her selfe and vs vndunne.
(sig. I6^{v})

Cleopatra ends with a final chorus on the dangers to the state of sensuality and luxury, with a bitter appeal to the Nile, now subject to the Tiber, to leave Egypt a desert so that there will be 'nought but dust' to recompense that 'Victors greedy lust' (sig. N7^{v}). The folly of the monarch has brought destruction to the state.

The members of the Dudley/Sidney/Herbert Protestant alliance read drama as they read Psalms, with a Protestant eye. Their analogical reading of drama is evident in the recently discovered *marginalia* of Philip Herbert, Mary Sidney's younger son, in his quarto of George Chapman's French tragedy, *The Conspiracie and Trageody of Charles Dvke of Byron* (1625). Herbert noted parallels with the English court, including references to his own relatives Northumberland and Leicester, and to such current events as the journeys of James Stuart, fourth Duke of Lennox, to Scotland with King Charles I in the 1630s.[56] In the 1630s, Philip Herbert's political stance was essentially unchanged from that of his godfather, Philip Sidney, in the 1580s. Herbert's notations evidence his alliance with the anti-Spanish party and his support of military intervention on behalf of Continental Protestants, the Count Palatine in this case. As Tricomi notes, Herbert's *marginalia* 'give us more reason than ever to speak of a *tradition* of reformist political drama' (p. 345; his italics).

This tradition was initiated, in part, by Mary Sidney. Like Shakespeare's later Roman and English history plays, including *Antony and Cleopatra*, the two dramas translated and sponsored by Mary Sidney emphasize political themes.[57] Written during the 1590s, when the alliance saw Elizabeth's dalliance with Essex as a threat to military intervention for the Protestant cause on the Continent, *Antonius* and *Cleopatra* stress the dangers of privileging private passion over public duty and warn of civil tumult. Rather than portraying the countess as the leader of a campaign to destroy the native dramatic tradition, we can characterize her as among the first to bring the Continental genre of historical tragedy to England, making her a precursor, certainly not an antagonist, of 'the man Shakespeare' and of Jacobean political drama.

Notes

1 Robert Garnier, *Two Tragedies: Hippolyte and Marc Antoine*, ed. Christine M. Hill and Mary G. Morrison (London: Athlone Press, 1975), 4–10.

2 T. S. Eliot, 'Seneca in Elizabethan Translation,' in *Selected Essays: New Edition* (New York: Harcourt, Brace, 1950), 77.

3 Alexander Maclaren Witherspoon, *The Influence of Robert Garnier on Elizabethan Drama* (New Haven, CT: Yale University Press, 1924; reprint, Hamden, CT: Archon, 1968), 67–8. For unquestioning acceptance of this position, see Janette Lewis Seaton, '"The Subject of All Verse": An Introduction to the Life and Work of Mary Sidney Herbert, Countess of Pembroke' (PhD dissertation, University of California, Los Angeles, 1976), 31–6; Sallye Jeannet Sheppeard, 'The Forbidden Muse: Mary Sidney Herbert and Renaissance Poetic Theory and Practice' (PhD dissertation, Texas Women's University, 1980), 61; and the extensive list of critics cited in Mary Ellen Lamb, 'The Myth of the Countess of Pembroke: The Dramatic Circle,' *Yearbook of English Studies* 11(1981), n. 195. Russell E. Leavenworth does challenge Witherspoon somewhat, although he agrees about her 'fastidious taste' and probable disapproval of popular drama: *Daniel's Cleopatra: A Critical Study* Elizabethan and Renaissance Studies (Salzburg: University of Salzburg, 1974).

4 Lamb, 'Myth of the Countess of Pembroke,' pp. 194–202, and 'The Countess of Pembroke's Patronage' (PhD dissertation, Columbia University, 1976), ch. 4. Michael G. Brennan follows Lamb in discounting the conspiracy theory: 'The Literary Patronage of the Herbert Family, Earls of Pembroke, 1550–1640' (PhD dissertation, Brasenose College, Oxford University, 1982), ch. 7. I am grateful to Dr Brennan for allowing me to see his restricted dissertation.

Witherspoon traces Mary Sidney's work to a reaction against the Senecan dramas of the Inner Temple (*Influence of Robert Garnier*, 72–5); Brennan sees her inspiration for translating Garnier in the translations of dramatists of university and Inns of Court, particularly those of Jasper Heywood, George Buchanan, and William Gager ('Literary Patronage of the Herbert Family,' 164).

5 Leavenworth, *Daniel's Cleopatra*, 3.

6 *Antonius* was published in 1592 and 1595 by William Ponsonby. On the various editions of *Cleopatra*, see John Pitcher, 'Editing Daniel,' *The 1985 Forum of Renaissance Text Society* (Papers presented at the annual meeting of the Modern Language Association, 1985), 10.

7 Brian O'Farrell, 'Politician, Patron, Poet: William Herbert, Third Earl of Pembroke, 1580–1630' (PhD dissertation, University of California, Los Angeles, 1966), 268. Mary Sidney probably saw an early performance of *The Taming of the Shrew* by Pembroke's Men and may well have met Shakespeare by this time.

8 David C. Price, *Patrons and Musicians of the English Renaissance* (Cambridge: Cambridge University Press), 29.

9 Sir Philip Sidney, *A Defence of Poetry*, in *Miscellaneous Prose of Sir Philip Sidney*, ed. Katherine Duncan-Jones and Jan Van Dorsten (Oxford: Clarendon Press, 1973), 113.

10 On their 'literary crusade' against the wave of barbaric drama, see Joan Rees, *Samuel Daniel: A Critical and Biographical Study* (Liverpool: Liverpool University Press, 1964), 46. See also Eliot, 'Seneca in Elizabethan Translation,' 78.

11 Daniel, 'To the Right Honourable, the Lady Marie, Countess of Pembroke,' in *Delia and Rosamund Augmented*, sig. H6.

12 Samuel Daniel, 'To the Right Honourable, the Lady Mary, Countesse of Pembroke,' in *Delia*, sig. A2. This prose dedication of 1592 was replaced by the poetic dedication in 1594.

13 Watson, *Amintae Gavdia* (London: William Ponsonby, 1592), sig. A2.

14 Ben Jonson, 'To the Memory of my Beloved, the Author Mr. William Shakespeare: and What He Hath Left Us,' in *Ben Jonson: The Complete Poems*, ed. George Parfitt (New Haven, CT: Yale University Press, 1982), 263.

15 Dates from *William Shakespeare: The Complete Works*, ed. Stanley Wells and Gary Taylor (Oxford: Oxford University Press, 1986), listed under individual plays.

Some critics, such as John Buxton, were fairer, noting that although the countess had 'little interest . . . in the London stage,' she could not have predicted what Shakespeare would write: *Sir Philip Sidney and the English Renaissance* (London: Macmillan, 1954), 199–201. See also T. S. Eliot, 'Apology for the Countess of Pembroke,' in *The Use of Poetry and the Use of Criticism* (London: Faber and Faber, 1933), 37–52, which is actually a defense of Sir Philip's strictures against drama of his day in *A Defence of Poetry*.

16 *Extracts from the Letters and Journals of William Cory*, ed. Francis Warre Cornish (Oxford: printed for the subscribers, 1897), 168. A pleasantly eccentric theory, based on this letter and the conviction that such plays as *Antony and Cleopatra* 'showed feminine rather than masculine intuition,' is that Mary Sidney wrote some of the plays of Shakespeare: Gilbert Slater, *Seven Shakespeares: A Discussion of the Evidence for Various Theories with Regard to Shakespeare Identity* (London: Cecil Palmer, 1931), 217. Slater calls Rosalind 'a self-portrait of the authoress,' Mary Sidney, and finds the seven ages speech 'a particularly feminine passage' (219). Slater also believes that she wrote most of Sidney's 'The Lady of May' (227) and became the literary executor for Edward de Vere, Earl of Oxford, devoting the rest of her life to 'completing his unfinished work and adding to it' (236). (The Earl of Oxford, of course, wrote the majority of Shakespeare's plays, according to Slater.)

17 D. Nichol Smith, 'Authors and Patrons,' in *Shakespeare's England: An Account of the Life and Manners of his Age* (Oxford: Clarendon Press, 1916), 2:202.

18 John Nichols, *The Progresses, Processions and Magnificent Festivities, of King James the First* (London: J. B. Nichols, 1828), 1:250.

19 On the political pastoral of *As You Like It*, see David Bevington, *Tudor Drama and Politics: A Critical Approach to Topical Meaning* (Cambridge, MA: Harvard University Press, 1968), 297–8.

Nichols records that the court was at Salisbury from 26 to 28 August, and at Wilton on 29 and 30 August; from mid-September through October, there is extensive official correspondence dated 'From the court at Wilton,' although there was a brief sojourn in Winchester between 18 and 25 October. On 25 October, the court was again at Wilton. Most of November was spent in Winchester. The king returned to Wilton at the beginning of December, was at Whitehall on 17 December for the creation of knights, spent Christmas hunting at Roydon, and returned to Whitehall for Philip Herbert's marriage to Susan de Vere on St John's Day (Nichols, *Progresses of King James the First* 1: 250–90, 313, 470). See also the list of letters and royal proclamations dated 'from Wilton' in *Calendar of State Papers, Domestic Series, . . . James I*, ed. Mary Anne Everett Green (London: Longman, 1872), 6: 47–59, and the report of Piero Duodo and Nicholo Molin, Venetian ambassadors, on 1 December 1603: *Calendar of Letters and State Papers Relating to English Affairs, preserved in the archives and collections of Venice and in other libraries of northern Italy*, ed. Rawdon Brown, G. Cavendish Bentinck, and Horatio F. Brown (London: Her Majesty's Stationery Office, 1897), 10: 116–17.

On this performance by the King's Men, see John Tucker Murray, *English Dramatic Companies, 1558–1642* (London: Constable, 1910), 1: 147–50, and E. K. Chambers, *The Elizabethan Stage* (Oxford: Clarendon Press, 1923), 4: 168.

20 Dudley Carleton to John Chamberlain, 27 November 1603, *Dudley Carleton to John Chamberlain, 1603–1624: Jacobean Letters*, ed. Maurice Lee (New Brunswick, NJ: Rutgers University Press, 1972), 44–5. Carleton is quoting *Aeneidos*, 4: 23.

21 On that final débâcle, see Stephen J. Greenblatt, *Sir Walter Ralegh* (New Haven, CT: Yale University Press, 1973), ch. 6; Robert Lacey, *Sir Walter Ralegh* (New York: Athenaeum, 1974), ch. 45.

22 O'Farrell lists works dedicated to Pembroke ('Politician, Patron, Poet,' Appendixes II and III). Brennan presents a 'Chronological Table of Texts dedicated to the Herbert Family, 1550–1640' ('Literary Patronage of the Herbert Family,' Appendix 3).

On Pembroke's anti-Spanish activities, see Annabel M. Patterson, *Censorship and Interpretation: The Conditions of Writing and Reading in Early Modern England* (Madison, WI: University of Wisconsin Press, 1984), 74.

23 Sir John Oglander, *A Royalist's Notebook*, ed. F. Bamford (London: Constable, 1936), 6.

24 See, for example, the 1574 request of Leicester's Men to wear his livery for added protection (Dudley Papers III, f. 125, Longleat). Leicester was also connected with the Children of the Chapel Royal and the children's company at St Paul's. His players went to the Low Countries, probably to perform for his inauguration as governor: Eleanor Rosenberg, *Leicester: Patron of Letters* (New York: Columbia University Press, 1955; reprint, New York: Octagon, 1976), 301–8.

25 Murray, *English Dramatic Companies*, 2: 324–35.

26 De L'Isle MS U1475, 56(2), 1574.

27 *The Poems of Sir Philip Sidney*, ed. William A. Ringler, Jr (Oxford: Clarendon Press, 1962), 362.

28 On the schedule of tours, see Ludlow and Shrewsbury accounts in Murray, *English Dramatic Companies* 2: 324–5, 389–93. See also Gerald Eades Bentley, *The Profession of Player in Shakespeare's Time, 1590–1642* (Princeton, NJ: Princeton University Press, 1984), ch. 7.

E. K. Chambers had followed J. O. Halliwell-Phillips in suggesting that Shakespeare was in Pembroke's Men (*The Elizabethan Stage* 2:130), a theory disproved by the work of David George, 'Shakespeare and Pembroke's Men,' *Shakespeare Quarterly* 32(1981), 305–23. On Pembroke's Men, see also Brennan, 'Literary Patronage of the Herbert Family,' 248–57.

29 *Henslowe's Diary*, ed. R. A. Foakes and R. T. Rickert (Cambridge: Cambridge University Press, 1961), 72–3, 164–5.

30 Will of Simon Jewell, proven 23 August 1592, in Mary Edmond, 'Pembroke's Men,' *Review of English Studies*, n.s. 25(1974): 130. Karl P. Wentersdorf argues that she was merely paying for a performance at Wilton: 'The Origins and Personnel of the Pembroke Company,' *Theater Research International* 5 (1979–80): 45–68.

31 *Meleager* had been performed before Leicester, Pembroke, and Philip Sidney in 1584. When it was printed by the Oxford Press, founded by Leicester, it had a formal dedication to Essex, with a prologue and epilogue addressed to Pembroke. Three of the four extant copies of *Ulysses* are dedicated to Lord Buckhurst; only the fourth has the special dedication to Mary Sidney: William Gager, *Meleager* (1592), *Ulysses Redux* (1592), *Panniculus Hippolyto Assutus* (1591), ed. J. W. Binns (New York: Georg Olms Verlag, 1981), 7, 10.

32 *William Shakespeare: Complete Works*, xlii.

33 Gerald Eades Bentley, *The Jacobean and Caroline Stage; Dramatic Companies and Players* (Oxford: Clarendon Press, 1941), 6, citing Egerton MS 2592, f. 81, British Library.

34 Mary Sidney, *Countess of Pembroke's Antonie*, 11.

35 Witherspoon, *Influence of Robert Garnier*, 3.

36 Brennan, 'Literary Patronage of the Herbert Family,' 179. Brennan and I reached this conclusion independently; his restricted dissertation reached me after the original version of this paper was submitted for the Thirty-Third Meeting of the Renaissance Society of America, Tempe, Arizona, 14 March 1987.

37 Here I disagree with Lamb, who argues that plays with female heroes were dedicated to female patrons, and plays with political themes to male political figures ('The Countess of Pembroke's Patronage,' 239).

Lamb has suggested that these dramas appealed to Mary Sidney because of their emphasis on dying well, one form of heroism traditionally available to women. While Lamb is obviously correct, the countess also found through these dramas a less traditional form of female heroism – writing and sponsoring political works: 'The Countess of Pembroke and the Art of Dying,' in *Women in the Middle Ages and the Renaissance: Literary and Historical Perspectives*, ed. Mary Beth Rose (Syracuse, NY: Syracuse University Press, 1986), 207–26.

38 See *The Prose Works of Fulke Greville, Lord Brooke*, ed. John Gouws (Oxford: Clarendon Press, 1986), xiii. Although Buxton has accused Mary Sidney of turning Thomas Kyd from his true vocation as dramatist (*Sidney and the English Renaissance*, 200), we should note that this closet drama – dedicated not to her but to the Countess of Sussex – was written during 1593, when the theaters were closed because of the plague.

39 Greville, 'Dedication to Sir Philip Sidney,' in *Prose Works*, 93.

40 Sandra K. Fischer, 'Elizabeth Cary and Tyranny, Domestic and Religious,' in *Silent but for the Word: Tudor Women as Patrons, Translators, and Writers of Religious Works*, ed. Margaret P. Hannay (Kent, OH: Kent State University Press, 1985), 225–37; Elaine Beilin, *Redeeming Eve: Women Writers of the English Renaissance* (Princeton, NJ: Princeton University Press, 1987), 157–76.

41 Sidney, *A Defence of Poetry*, 95. On the connection between these protests and the 'Statute of Silence,' see Patterson, *Censorship and Interpretation*, 25–6.

42 *Hamlet* III, i:605–6, in *William Shakespeare: Complete Works*, 753.

43 On Pembroke's Men, see *English Dramatic Companies* 1:59–72. Charles William Wallace argues that the Swan Theatre was the home of Pembroke's Men in 1597 when *The Isle of Dogs* was performed: 'The Swan Theatre and the Earl of Pembroke's Servants,' *Englische Studien* 43 (1910–11): 365. Pembroke's players were revived in 1625 to 1627, under the protection of William Herbert, 3rd Earl of Pembroke.

44 O'Farrell, 'Politician, Patron, Poet,' 270–1. On *Sejanus*, see Patterson, *Censorship and Interpretation*, 49–58. On Pembroke and Jonson, see also David Norbrook, *Poetry and Politics in the English Renaissance* (London: Routledge and Kegan Paul, 1984), 178–92 *passim*.

45 Margot Heinemann, *Puritanism and Theatre: Thomas Middleton and Opposition Drama under the Early Stuarts* (Cambridge: Cambridge University Press, 1980), 264–83.

46 Samuel Daniel, *Certaine Small Poems lately printed: with the tragedie of Philotas* (London: Simon Waterson, 1605), sig. F2.

47 Rees, *Samuel Daniel*, 97. Patterson puts *King Lear* in this context (*Censorship and Interpretation*, 58–73).

48 The first part of *The Civile Wares betweene the Howses of Lancaster and Yorke* was entered on the Stationer's Register in October 1594. On Daniel's 'Letter from Octavia,' dedicated to the Countess of Cumberland, and early editions of *The Civile Wares*, dedicated to Mountjoy, see Rees, *Samuel Daniel*, 62–88.

49 Gillian Jondorf, *Robert Garnier and the Themes of Political Tragedy in the Sixteenth Century* (Cambridge: Cambridge University Press, 1969), 26–7. Jondorf, dismissing most topical allusions, does argue that there may be a parallel between *Marc Antoine* and Henri III, who was popularly perceived as a war hero who had degenerated into sensuality, and that the play contains allusions to the Netherlands campaign of Alençon which was envisioned in 1577 as a means to prevent civil war by engaging in foreign war (36).

50 His plays were published between 1568 and 1583; the wars of religion lasted from 1559 to 1598.

51 For the history of Cleopatra in continental literature, see Marilyn L. Williamson, who lists ten

dramas in four languages written between 1543 and 1607 based on Plutarch's account of Cleopatra: 'Antony and Cleopatra in the Late Middle Ages and Early Renaissance,' *Michigan Academician* 5(1972): 145–51; Leavenworth, *Daniel's Cleopatra*, 101; Marlene Consuela Browne, 'Shakespeare's Lady Macbeth and Cleopatra: Women in a Political Context' (PhD dissertation, Brown University, 1976), 150; Marilyn L. Williamson, *Infinite Variety: Antony and Cleopatra in Renaissance Drama and Earlier Tradition* (Mystic, CT: Lawrence Verry, 1974); J. Max Patrick, 'The Cleopatra Theme in World Literature Up to 1700,' in *The Undoing of Babel: Watson Kirkconnell, the Man and his Work*, ed. James Russell Conway Perkin (Toronto: McClelland and Stewart, 1975), 64–76.

52 Jondorf, *Robert Garnier*, 44.

53 Daniel, *Civile Wares*, sig. A2.

54 Mary Sidney, *Discovrse of Life and Death. Written in French by Ph. Mornay. Antonius, A Tragedie Written also in French by Ro. Garnier. Both done in English by the Covntesse of Pembroke* (London: William Ponsonby, 1592), sig. F1.

55 Mary Sidney adds the line 'the stage supposed Alexandria,' which does not imply that the play was written to be acted – nor was Daniel's *Cleopatra*. In fact, when Daniel wrote *Philotas*, he made a point that he had been forced to write for the stage (sig. A5^{v}).

56 A. H. Tricomi, 'Philip, Earl of Pembroke, and the Analogical Way of Reading Political tragedy,' *Journal of English and Germanic Philology* 85(1986): 332–45. Herbert's copy is at the British Library: George Chapman, *The Conspiracie and Trageody of Charles Dvke of Byron, Marshall of France* (London: Thomas Thorp, 1625). See, for example, 'Ihon of . . . Northum . . . 'on signature O2, a clear reference to his great-grandfather Northumberland, despite the cropped pages.

57 On political themes in Shakespeare's *Antony and Cleopatra*, see Robert P. Kalmey, 'Shakespeare's Octavius and Elizabethan Roman History,' *Studies in English Literature* 18(1978): 275–87; Paul Lawrence Rose, 'The Politics of *Antony and Cleopatra*,' *Shakespeare Quarterly* 20(1969): 379–89; Marilyn L. Williamson, 'The Political Context in *Antony and Cleopatra*,' *Shakespeare Quarterly* 21(1970): 241–51, and *Infinite Variety*, 238–44; Helen Morris, 'Queen Elizabeth I "Shadowed" in Cleopatra,' *Huntington Library Quarterly* 32(1969): 271–8; Keith Rinehart, 'Shakespeare's Cleopatra and England's Elizabeth,' *Shakespeare Quarterly* 23(1972): 81–6. For a New Historicist reading of the play, see Leonard Tennenhouse, *Power on Display: The Politics of Shakespeare's Genres* (New York: Methuen, 1986), 142–6. See also the Marxist reading in Paul N. Siegel, *Shakespeare's English and Roman History Plays: A Marxist Approach* (Rutherford, NJ: Fairleigh Dickinson University Press, 1986).

Although a detailed study of diction is beyond the scope of this discussion, Shakespeare's *Antony and Cleopatra* does seem indebted both to Mary Sydney's *Antonius* and to Samuel Daniel's *Cleopatra*. See Ernest Schanzer, 'Daniel's Revision of his *Cleopatra*,' *Review of English Studies* 8(1975): 375–81; Geoffrey Bullough, *Narrative and Dramatic Sources of Shakspeare* (New York: Columbia University Press, 1966), 5: 229–31; Ernest Schanzer, '*Antony and Cleopatra* and the Countess of Pembroke's *Antonius*,' *Notes and Queries* 201(1956): 152–4.

5

MARY HERBERT

Englishing a purified Cleopatra

Tina Krontiris

Tina Krontiris's book, *Oppositional Voices: Women as Writers and Translators of Literature in the English Renaissance* (1992), was the first critical text which brought together the key women writers of the Early Modern period and analysed them in terms of theme and genre. The essay here is taken from a longer piece which compares Mary Sidney with Elizabeth Cary, and contrasts the way they portray the female characters in their plays. In her analysis of Mary Sidney's *The Tragedy of Antonie*, Krontiris positions Sidney at a junction between conformity and radicalism, and stresses the importance of her role as an example to later women writers.

In 1575, when she was 15, Mary Sidney entered an arranged marriage with the 50-year-old William Herbert, Earl of Pembroke. He was a humanist, patron of the arts, and one of the wealthiest aristocrats in England.[1] Her marriage apparently offered her a fair degree of freedom. Various references to her husband suggest that she may even have been the dominant one in the pair.[2] Two years after the wedding, young Mary followed her husband to the Pembroke residence at Wilton, the 'little court in the depths of the country.' From this post Mary Herbert played a prominent role in the cultural life of England for nearly a quarter of a century. Under her direction, Wilton became a literary centre, comparable to continental literary salons. Friends, literary acquaintances, and prospective protégés visited and sometimes stayed at Wilton to present their work, circulate manuscripts, partake in discussions, and even to watch theatrical performances.[3] The milieu included well-known authors like Daniel, Spenser, Ralegh, Jonson, and John Davies of Hereford, but also minor writers like Abraham Fraunce, Nicholas Breton, Gervase Babington, and Samuel Brandon. Lady Herbert patronized these and other men, though the number of authors to whom she paid more than a token fee has been exaggerated. After the death of her brother, Sir Philip Sidney, she devoted much time to editing and publishing their work. Her own literary accomplishments include several translations – Mornay's treatise *Discourse of Life and Death*, Garnier's play *Antonie*, Petrarch's *Triumph of Death*; a versification of the Psalms, to which her brother Philip had also contributed; and a few original poems – 'A Dialogue between two shepheards,' 'The Dolefull Lay of Clorinda,' 'To the Angel spirit,' and 'Even now that Care.'[4]

As this activity shows, Mary Herbert was a woman of literary ambition. But the forms she used to express this ambition clearly suggest an indirect, self-effacing strategy. Her case tells an interesting story about the interplay between personal ambition and compliance with culturally constructed feminine roles. Extremely reluctant to display her talents, she usually worked from behind curtains, using men as protective shields. Significant men in her life became surrogate figures, public substitutes of her own creative self.

Her brother Philip was apparently one of these substitutes. Understandably, his premature death caused her a great deal of pain, especially as there had been a strong bond between them, made stronger still by common intellectual interests. But this tragic event was apparently also the catalyst for much creative energy, as nearly all of her works date from after his death (she was 25 when he died). She became preoccupied with editing and publishing the work he had left in manuscript form, and she tried to popularize his ideas. In her choice of subjects for translation she went to sources he had favoured. Even when she published some of her own work, she declared that she did it to honour her brother. This devotion was an expression of her love for him as well as a shield of protection from seeming to seek fame – a strictly unfeminine endeavour in her culture. A woman that published in her own name could be suspected of self-display. The sister of Sir Philip Sidney, the admired 'shepherd poet' of Elizabeth's court, could also be suspected of trying to compete with her famous brother, to show that she was better. Public self-effacement becomes a way out of this bind. In the dedication of the Psalms to her brother, she apologizes for the inferiority of her own part of the translation. But in view of the many changes she introduced to improve her brother's phrasing in the part he versified,[5] her apologies stand in contrast to a privately expressed confidence in her own poetic ability, and point to a split between private and public expression.

Sometimes she hired male writers to do what sometimes she could have done better than they. Such members of her circle as Samuel Daniel, Nicholas Breton, and Abraham Fraunce were particularly instrumental in expressing her wishes and ideas. While she acted as a generous patron to these and other men, there was an unusual interdependence between herself and the authors she commissioned. The system of patronage, of course, by its very nature fostered such an interdependence. In seeking financial support and protection, an author often had to make compromises in what he wrote. But the countess seems to have had an especially binding relationship with the authors she patronized. This is evident above all by the fact that she usually assigned works to her protégés.[6] The case of Samuel Daniel, under her patronage for many years, illustrates this relationship. Next to her brother, Daniel seems to have been the most important surrogate figure. Most of the works he dedicated to her were her assignments. His *Cleopatra* certainly and his 'Letter from Octavia' very probably were written as sequels to her translation of *Antonie*. Even his *Civil Wars* was a direct response to her wishes. The most suggestive evidence of the strong demands made by the countess on Daniel is contained in his 'Funerall Poeme' which he wrote for his later patron, Charles Blount, Lord Mountjoy: 'Nor was it [Mountjoy's patronage] such, as could lay on me/ As t'inforce m'observance, beyond thee,/ Or make my conscience differ from my tongue.'[7] Daniel's need to articulate this point and the fact that he was impressed by Mountjoy's laxity probably suggest that under his previous patron he lacked complete freedom in writing.

While patronage offered Mary Herbert a way of channelling authorial creativity, it also became a kind of cultural trap for her, pushing her further into a conventional role. Prospective protégés fashioned her public image. Breton painted her portrait as a reflection of the Duchess of Urbino in Casteglione's *Courtier*: 'who hath redde of the Duchesse of

Urbino, may saie, the Italians wrote well: but who knows the Countess of Pembroke, I think hath cause to write better.'[8] Many authors reinforced this image by commenting on her intellectual endowments, her generosity, the inspiration she imparted, and her noble task of making her brother's work known. Some even attributed a specific morality to her. In translating Tasso's *Aminta*, for example, Abraham Fraunce changed a love scene in a pastoral dialogue to conform to what he thought would be a tribute to the countess. Unlike Tasso's heroine, Fraunce's Phillis refuses to let Aminta kiss her because without marriage this kind of love is not 'Discreate and sober.'[9] Likewise, Thomas Moffet, the physician and entomologist of the Pembroke circle, wrote a long poem of female silkworm moths as symbols of chastity, hoping to appeal to what he perceived to be the countess's notions of sexual modesty.[10] These and other authors who sought the countess's favours praised not only qualities that they saw in her but also those they thought she would wish to have. (Breton's vision of the countess as a spiritual being who rejects all earthly things in his *Countesse of Pembrokes Love* is an excellent example of this.) In so doing, such authors contributed to constructing the countess's identity as a pious and learned woman, at the same time as they reflected their culture's notions of respectable female conduct. This explains their emphasis on her role as patron rather than as author, despite her talent. Mary Herbert seems to have acquiesced in the construction of this identity, as Queen Elizabeth I accepted and reinforced the image of Gloriana, the Virgin Queen. But as in Queen Elizabeth's case, the constructed identity also became a kind of trap. The image of the pious, learned, and generous patroness inspired respect and raised her status but it also restricted her development as an author.

Remaining within this frame meant, among other things, very little direct writing and publishing. Indicatively, Mary Herbert worked almost exclusively in the area of translation. When she translated secular literature she stuck closely to the original text.[11] This shows how hesitant she was to appear assertive. To translate freely is to risk one's own interpretation. To translate literally is to seek protection in the idea of conveying the author's meaning exactly.

Antonie

Of Mary Herbert's several translations, the one that stands out as particularly interesting is that of Garnier's play *Antonie*, published in 1592. Literary critics have so far seen this play mainly in relation to Shakespeare's *Antony and Cleopatra* or to the countess's attempt (or supposed attempt) to reform the English stage according to Sir Philip Sidney's dramatic precepts, expressed in his *Apology for Poetry*. Mary Herbert's devotion to her brother's ideals and Daniel's statement about chasing away 'Grosse Barbarisme' in his dedication of *Cleopatra* (*Antonie*'s sequel) have been cited as evidence that the play was intended as an attack on, or answer to, popular drama. Mary Ellen Lamb has contested this view, arguing that the Countess of Pembroke never thought of waging a battle against popular theatre and that her translation of Garnier's play sprang quite simply from her interest in *ars moriendi*, or the art of dying well.[12] My purpose here is not to engage in this debate but to focus on the translator's identity as a woman publishing a secular play in the sixteenth century.

Mary Herbert's choice of play for translation seems to indicate that while her forms of authorial expression may have been conservative, her ideas were not. Written in the French neo-Senecan tradition for an elite audience and intended for private reading rather than stage production, *Antonie* is characterized by its refined language and moral tone.[13] But whereas its form is thus restrained, and therefore suitable for a female translator like the countess, its ideas and attitudes are bold and at times subversive in the context of sixteenth-century ideology and culture. The play interrogates conventional definitions of masculine and feminine virtue, opposes the established association of overt female sexuality with loose morals, and reveals the psychological and sexual complexes of those holding political power.

Antonie offers a sympathetic view of the adulterous lovers, and especially of Cleopatra, the woman who up to that time had been presented to the English public as a seductress.[14] Following a number of French and Italian contemporary versions, rather than Plutarch or the Roman authors, the play idealizes and conventionalizes its heroine according to sixteenth-century standards. First, it purifies her by purging her love from political motives and thus dissociates her from the image of the political conniver found in Plutarch and other sources. Unwavering in her loyalty to her lover, the heroine of *Antonie* never contemplates alliance with Caesar. Upon Antony's fall, the pragmatic Charmion, Cleopatra's woman, suggests:

> You see him ruin'd, so as your support
> No more henceforth can him with comfort raise.
> With-draw you from the storme: persist not still
> To loose your selfe: this royall diademe
> Regaine of Caesar.
>
> (11. 529–33)[15]

Charmion's advice, however, only serves to highlight Cleopatra's idealism:

> *Cl.* Sooner shining light
> Shall leave the day, and darknes leave the night:
> Sooner moist currents of tempestuous seas
> Shall wave in heaven, and the nightly troopes
> Of starres shall shine within the foming waves,
> Then I thee, Antony, leave in deepe distres.
>
> (11. 533–8)

In other sources the Egyptian queen's decision to commit suicide in the end is linked to various motives. Daniel's Cleopatra, for example, fears humiliation as a queen in the streets of Rome and as a woman in the eyes of Octavia.[16] In contrast, Garnier's heroine tries to prove, almost single-mindedly, her loyalty to her lover:

> Die Cleopatra then, no longer stay
> From Antony, who thee at Styx attends:
> Go joyne thy Ghost with his, and sob no more
> Without his love within these tombes enclos'd.
>
> (11. 1905–8)

Second, the play legitimizes Cleopatra's relationship with Antony by appropriating conventional marriage terminology and gender roles. The adulterous love affair is referred to as a 'holy marriage'; Cleopatra is not the concubine but the 'wife-kindhearted'; Antony is her 'deare husband,' and their children 'our deare babes.' In this way the play also inadvertently annuls the marriage between Antony and Octavia and sets up the love relationship as the more authentic of the two. This is not to say, of course, that the play condones Antony's treatment of his wife Octavia, for it does not. Antony is made to regret, among other things, his lack of respect for 'Thy wife Octavia and her tender babes' (1. 122). The translator, too, is sympathetic towards Octavia and critical of Antony. In the play's Argument (her own original composition) Mary Herbert states that Antony fell to 'his former loves, without any regarde of his vertuous wife Octavia, by whom nevertheles he had excellent children.' But the sympathetic references to Octavia do not convince us that Antony should go back to his legal wife; they are hardly enough to cancel any of the play's positive attitudes towards the principal characters. The sympathy towards Octavia, who in most sources had been presented as an example of female gentleness and fidelity, serves as a safeguard against any obvious rejection of the institutionalized marriage. It also enables a woman like Mary Herbert to publish the play without running the risk of appearing to endorse the abandonment of wives in favour of romantic lovers. The Octavia–Antony marriage which is being undermined in the play was the prevalent type among the aristocracy in England and exemplified, ironically, by the countess's own to the Earl of Pembroke.

In addition to deploying conventional marriage and marital language, the play also deploys motherhood as a means of gathering support for Cleopatra. Unlike most other analogues, *Antonie* makes dramatic use of Cleopatra's children. Her parting from them is described in very moving terms:

Farwell, my babes, farwell my heart is clos'd,
With pittie and paine, my selfe with death enclos'd,
My breath doth faile. Farwell for evermore,
Your Sire and me you shall see never more.
Farwell sweet care, farwell.

(11. 1865–9)

This motherly quality further helps to erase the image of the seductress and to establish Cleopatra as a legitimate spouse: the mother of illegitimate children is, after all, still a mother. But while the play seems to capitalize on Cleopatra's role as a mother, it does not at the same time support conventional ideas on motherhood. It shows, on the contrary, that the lover's instinct is stronger than the mother's. This is clearly brought out in a stichomythia between Cleopatra and Charmion:

Ch. Live for your sonnes. *Cl.* Nay for their father die.
Ch. Hardhearted mother! *Cl.* Wife, kindhearted, I.
Ch. Then will you them deprive of royall right?
Cl. Do I deprive them? no, it's dest'nies might.

(11. 555–8)

In the conflict between maternal and romantic love, Cleopatra chooses the latter. Here and throughout the play she is made to affirm her identity as a faithful lover. Antony's love is to her 'More deare then Scepter, children, freedome, light' (1. 410). In the context of her idealism, her choice does not invite blame. Meanwhile, in the process of these dialectics, the play celebrates sexual love and undermines motherhood.

While conventionalizing Cleopatra with reference to the seductress figure, the play dismantles Antony's identity as the great warrior/hero. In his defeat, Antony is shown to be anything but the great warrior. His plaintive tone, his self-pity ('poore Antony,' he keeps saying to himself), his bitterness, and his jealousy reveal him to be very weak, or what, by sixteenth-century conventional standards would be considered 'woman-like.' As several critics have pointed out, Cleopatra is the stronger one in the pair; she is less vacillating and more self-possessed. Yet, significantly, Antony's weakness seems to stem not from his position as an adulterous man (he is hardly blamed for loving Cleopatra) but from his dependence on martial glory as a source of strength. In revealing this weakness of Antony, the play throws into question traditional notions of masculinity and the basis of its strength, while at the same time it claims our sympathy for Antony the confused and self-deluded lover rather than Antony the debased man. It is interesting in this respect that Garnier's *Antonie* is the only play in the French and Italian non-Senecan group which shows sympathy for, rather than disappointment in, the 'weak' behaviour of the fallen Antony.[17]

The play then does not condemn the lovers on moral grounds. Whatever blame is laid is bound up with matters of politics, precisely because the private identities of Antony and Cleopatra are not independent from their political identities. When Antony says that Cleopatra has 'triumphed' over him and that she alone shall 'command' him, his language keeps reminding us of the connection between the sexual and the political. Although this connection is not as interestingly explored in Garnier as it is, say, in Shakespeare (Garnier's characters are much less complex), the subject of realpolitik is very directly, although briefly, dealt with and so is the relation of political rulers to the people they govern.

Despite references to Destiny and Fortune, *Antonie* ultimately reveals that historical events are the products of power relations among rulers and that these relations are informed by sexual and political insecurities. Two prime examples of this are Cleopatra's decision to join Antony in battle lest once away he might return to Octavia, and Antony's fear during the battle that she was fleeing to side with Caesar. The play further explores the idea of fear as a determining element in the character of powerful rulers such as Antony and Caesar. Antony's main complaint in his fall, so he tells us, is not that he has lost his political power (empire), but that he has been defeated by a man whom he considers to be woman-like:

> A man, a woman both in might and minde,
> In Mars his schole who never lesson learn'd,
> Should me repulse, chase, overthrow, destroy,
> Me of such fame, bring to so low an ebbe?
> (11. 1060–4)

In other words, Caesar has deprived Antony not only of his power as a ruler but also of his masculine virtue, for in Antony's mind manhood is directly related to martial performance. Apparently Antony associates his combat in war and politics with an opportunity to exhibit virility. Hence to be defeated by a stronger man is itself a kind of victory:

> Yet if to bring my glory to the ground,
> Fortune had made me overthrowne by one
> Of greater force, of better skill then I:
> One of those Captaines feared so of olde,

. . .
The lesse her wrong, the lesse should be my woe:
Nor she should paine, nor I complaine me so.
(11. 1080–93)

But Antony's comments about Caesar's weakness reflect his own insecurity and fear. His constant suspicion of and even adamant belief in Cleopatra's betrayal, despite his friends' protestations to the contrary, is evidence of this. Furthermore, his pronouncement of Caesar's womanish weakness is a striking piece of irony, for it is he who has been displaying weak and 'unmanly' behaviour. Antony's conventional notions of masculinity cannot be taken at face value.

The ruler's struggle to maintain political power is the subject explored in relation to Caesar and his intended treatment of Antony. In the seventeenth chapter of his *The Prince*, Machiavelli states:

> Upon this a question arises: whether it be better to be loved than feared or feared than loved? It maybe answered that one should wish to be both, but, because it is difficult to unite them in one person, it is much safer to be feared than loved, when, of the two, either must be dispensed with.[18]

This is also Caesar's opinion in an argument he holds with Agrippa on the same subject in the fourth act of the play:

Caes. Then to the end none . . .
We must with bloud marke this our victory,
For just example to all memorie
Murther we must, until not one we leave,
Which may hereafter us of rest berave.
Ag. Marke it with murthers? Who of that can like?
Caes. Murthers must use, who doth assurance seeke.
. . .
Ag. What ease to him that feared is of all?
Caes. Feared to be, and see his foes to fall.
Ag. Commonly feare doth brede and nourish hate.
Caes. Hate without pow'r comes commonly too late.
Ag. A feared Prince hath oft his death desir'd.
Caes. A Prince not fear'd hath oft his wrong conspir'd.
Ag. No guard so sure, no forte so strong doth prove,
No such defence, as is the peoples love.
(11. 1495–1514)

Like Machiavelli's prince, Caesar places political expediency above consanguinity or loyalty to past alliance. 'Bloud and alliance nothing do prevaile,' says Antony referring to Caesar (1. 1010). According to Caesar, execution, not clemency, is the best treatment for his opponents. He must kill those who pose a threat to his power, hoping that the fear of such a severe punishment will act as a deterrent to active political opposition: 'For just example to all memorie' (1. 1498).

Antonie does not endorse or reject these political ideas. It simply shows the way they work. The play's position is less equivocal, however, with regard to the relationship between rulers and common people. The latter are shown to be unfortunately dependent on the former. This theme, present also in Shakespeare, is a very central one in Garnier. The latter is very clearly sympathetic towards the people who suffer as a result of shifts in power at the top ranks of the political hierarchy.

Although direct blame of Antony and Cleopatra specifically is avoided, criticism of those in power is expressed in several terms by the chorus and by powerless but creditable characters like Diomid, Philostratus, and Lucilius.

The chorus serves as a critical voice through its structural positioning in the play and its elegiac theme and tone. At the end of each act the choral passage forms a lamentation song on man's sufferings in general and on those of the Egyptians in particular. The juxtaposition of these passages forces the reader to consider the actors and the victims of the situation. Diomid, Philostratus, and Lucilius are more direct in their criticism. One of the main issues they address is the obligation of the rulers towards the people they govern. To what extent should a ruler's actions and personal life be guided by the interests of the governed? Diomid, Cleopatra's secretary, goes so far as to say that the ruler should sacrifice his/her individual concept of virtue and should deploy personal assets in the interest of the state. His recommendation for Cleopatra is not basically different from what Machiavelli advocated and Elizabeth I practised:

> Alas! It's our ill hap, for if hir teares
> She would convert into her loving charmes,
> To make a conquest of the conquerer,
> (As well she might, would she hir force imploie)
> She should us safetie from these ills procure,
> Hir crowne to hir, and to hir race assure.
> (11. 735–40)

This course of action, which amounts to a form of prostitution, sounds unreasonably demanding on the 'pure' Cleopatra, until we are reminded (by Lucilius and Philostratus, especially) that it was she and Antony who created the disastrous situation in the first place. In this way the play exposes to criticism the queen's treatment of her affair with Antony as a purely domestic matter. Cleopatra's concern is how to be loyal to her lover and her children – not how to save the Egyptians from the disaster she has brought upon them. Philostratus, the philosopher, is in fact the only one who shows concern for the fate of the people. He addresses the chorus of Egyptians feelingly ('come you poore people') and from outside the palace walls comments on the situation created by those inside. He sees that the Egyptians are faced with captivity or death and hopes for the lesser of the two evils. The message is clear: the rulers have made a mess and the people must pay for it. This is the realist part of the play, which portrays governors according to the way they function in actuality. The idealist part shows the lovers attempting to abide by a form of behaviour which transcends reality.

The idealist and the realist aspects come into conflict. The play's sympathy for the woman (the lover) clashes with its criticism of Cleopatra the ruler. This conflict is not reconciled, or even clearly focused. But it is important that the play generates unorthodox questions with respect to sexuality and political power.

Was the translator aware of the play's oppositional potential? There is little evidence either way, but she cannot have been altogether unaware of the fact that she was introducing the English audience to a favourable view of Cleopatra. Daniel's play *Cleopatra*, written to accompany the countess's, 'well-grac'd Antony,' is based on the same favourable view.[19] The translator must also have been aware of Garnier's association with liberal ideas. Author of several neo-classical plays named after women and husband to an authoress, Garnier was very much preoccupied with the theme of political corruption and women's role as agents of justice. His heroines are far from the submissive wives of sixteenth-century conduct books. Porcie and Antigonie are admired for their fidelity to family and country, but such fidelity, though presented as pious, requires insubordination to tyrannical rule. His women are applauded for taking political action rather than condemned for interfering with men's politics. They are encouraged to be independent-minded, though apparently they are still expected to conform to society's rules regarding virtuous behaviour. But sexuality does not become a major criterion in their condemnation or approval. Although politically Garnier was not a radical, he was critical of authority. Looking mainly to the past for solutions, he sought reforms within the existing social and political structure. A republican sentiment runs through several of his plays, including *Antonie*.[20]

But consciously or not, Mary Herbert contributed to undermining certain dominant ideas in her culture. The woman's role as mother was considered one of the strongholds of the nuclear family and was elaborated in many guides.[21] The language of motherhood which the play deploys in the depiction of its heroine suggests that she is to be seen in this role. Yet Cleopatra rejects it to remain faithful to her lover – and she is not condemned. Indeed, sexual love receives a kind of glorification in the play as it becomes legitimized through marital language and at the same time idealized as worthy of sacrifice. In the sphere of politics, the play contributes to a demystification of the ruler's identity and power. Like many other Renaissance plays,[22] *Antonie* offers at least a glimpse into the actual mechanisms of state power. Perhaps Mary Herbert did not see this, but others around her may have. (One might call to mind Daniel's *Philotas* and its connection with the Essex affair.)[23]

Mary Herbert also contributed to establishing a female literary heritage, leaving a useful legacy to women writers who came later. As a socially accepted type of a female intellectual model, she held the potential of being appropriated by conservative men to inhibit assertively creative women.[24] But she could equally be appropriated by women writers in various constructive ways. Mary Wroth profited later from the metrical forms the Countess of Pembroke introduced in her translations, and Elizabeth Cary published a closet drama not unlike *Antonie*. As the first woman to publish a secular play in English,[25] Mary Herbert chose to translate the work of an author who might be called 'feminine' in his approach: Garnier presents female figures that women can identify with, and in his presentation he uses strategies which could be employed also by women writers. Moreover, the countess's reputation among male authors as a competent versifier and serious supporter of literature helped to a recognition, even among literary circles, of women's artistic abilities. Daniel's remark in his dedication of *Cleopatra* that the countess 'opened mens eyes' to women's talents is not merely praise; it is also a revealing statement which suggests that their eyes had been closed. When a woman writer achieves a certain reputation among her male colleagues she makes the atmosphere a little easier for other women who come after. In this respect Lady Pembroke's aristocratic status was very important because it lent validity to a model. A woman like Isabella Whitney who wrote more original poetry a couple of decades earlier could not have served as a model because she lacked high social standing.

Notes

1 Her parents viewed the match as an opportunity for social advancement, as we can gather from the letter of Sir Henry Sidney to the Earl of Leicester – see Frances Young, *Mary Sidney, Countess of Pembroke* (London: David Nutt, 1912), pp. 28–9. But we have no evidence of young Mary's feelings on the matter.

2 Nicholas Breton says that Mary Herbert's husband was in 'no meane commaund.' A certain codicil that survives from the earl's will points to some sort of breach between them, but it is impossible to determine the source or nature of the problem, which was apparently resolved before the earl's death. (See Frances Young, op. cit., pp. 81–2.)

3 For evidence of Mary Herbert's theatrical activity see Josephine Roberts, 'Part II: Mary Sidney, Countess of Pembroke,' *English Literary Renaissance*, 14.3(1984), p. 426; and Mary Edmond, 'Pembroke's Men,' *Review of English Studies*, 25(1974), pp. 130–1. In *The Herberts of Wilton* (1967), Sir Tresham Lever mentions that Shakespeare's *As You Like It* was performed at Wilton in 1603.

4 Of these, only the *Discourse* and *Antonie* were published (together in 1592) by Lady Herbert. A couple of her occasional poems appeared in collections by Spenser and Francis Davison. The rest of her work remained unpublished until long after her death. See Gary Waller's edition, *The 'Triumph of Death' and other Unpublished and Uncollected Poems by Mary Sidney, Countess of Pembroke (1561–1621)* (Salzburg: Institut für Englische Sprache und Literatur, 1977), and his study, *Mary Sidney, Countess of Pembroke: A Critical Study of her Writings and Literary Milieu* (Salzburg: Institut für Englische Sprache und Literatur, 1979).

5 Gary Waller examines these changes in *Mary Sidney*, op. cit. In a carefully researched essay, Beth Wynne Fisken also examines the revisions of the Psalms and finds that Mary Herbert's constant reworking of image, syntax, and form led to the 'development of a style independent of her brother's influence, reflecting her own ideas, tastes, and experiences.' (See 'Mary Sidney's Psalmes: education and wisdom,' in M. Hannay (ed.) *Silent But for the Word* (Kent, OH: Kent State University Press, 1986), p. 169.)

6 Mary Ellen Lamb, 'The Countess of Pembroke's patronage,' *English Literary Renaissance*, 12.2(1982), pp. 167–73.

7 Ibid., p. 168.

8 Quoted by Waller in *Mary Sidney*, op. cit. pp. 41–2.

9 Lamb, op. cit., p. 170.

10 Ibid., pp. 175–6.

11 Alice Luce, the first modern editor of *Antonie*, made a useful comparison between Garnier's original text and the countess's translation and found that Lady Herbert stuck to the original even at the occasional expense of awkward rendering – see *The Countess of Pembroke's Antonie* (Literarhistorische Forschungen, 1987). This is apparently not the case with her translations of more solemn subjects. Diane Bornstein analyses the countess's Englishing of Mornay's *Discourse of Life and Death* and concludes that the English text is a faithful but skilful and idiomatic rendering of the original: 'The style of the Countess of Pembroke's translation of Philippe de Mornay's *Discours de la vie et de la mort*,' in M. Hannay (ed.) *Silent But for the Word*, p. 134.

12 Mary Ellen Lamb, 'The myth of the Countess of Pembroke: the dramatic circle,' *Yearbook of English Studies*, 11(1981), pp. 195–202.

13 For the difference between Senecan and neo-Senecan traditions in France, Italy, and England see T. S. Eliot, 'Seneca in Elizabethan translation,' in *Selected Essays* (London: Faber and Faber, 1932), esp. p. 83; and 'Senecan tradition in England, ' in *The Political Works of Sir William Alexander*, vol. I, ed. L. E. Kastner and H. B. Charlton (London: Blackwood, 1921), esp. pp. 163–85.

14 See Mary Morrison, 'Some aspects of the treatment of the theme of Antony and Cleopatra in tragedies of the sixteenth century,' *Journal of European Studies*, 4(1974), pp. 113–25; and Max Patrick, 'The Cleopatra theme in world literature up to 1700,' in J. R. C. Perkin (ed.) *The Undoing of Babel* (Toronto: McClelland and Stewart, 1975), pp. 64–76.

15 Textual citations here and throughout refer to Geoffrey Bullough's edition of *Antonie* in

Narrative and Dramatic Sources of Shakespeare, vol. 5 (Princeton, NJ: Princeton University Press, 1981).

16 *The Tragedy of Cleopatra*, Act I, ll. 67–70.

17 Morrison, op. cit., p. 120.

18 *The Prince*, trans. W. K. Marriott (London and Toronto: Dent and Dutton, 1908), p. 134.

19 For Daniel's Cleopatra, motherly feeling comes last, despite the fact that her children figure dramatically in the play.

20 Alexander Witherspoon, *The Influence of Robert Garnier* (New York: Archon, 1924, rpt 1968), pp. 8–9.

21 Betty Travitsky (ed.) *The Paradise of Women* (Westport, CT: Greenwood Press, 1981), p. 9.

22 See Jonathan Dollimore, *Radical Tragedy: Religion, Ideology and Power in the Drama of Shakespeare and His Contemporaries* (Brighton: Harvester, 1984).

23 Daniel was suspected of involvement in the Essex rebellion on account of his *Philotas*. He vehemently denied any connection, but the fact is that his play was interpreted differently by Elizabeth's censoring authorities.

24 See, for instance, the Denny-Wroth case, described in ch. 4 of *Oppositional Voices: Women as Writers and Translators of Literature in the English Renaissance* (London: Routledge, 1992), the book from which this essay is taken.

25 Lady Joanna Lumley had translated Euripides' play *Iphigenia at Aulis* around 1550, when she was a young teenager. But she never published her work, which appears to have been a classroom exercise. It was edited by Harold Child and printed for the Malone Society, Oxford, in 1909.

6

ELIZABETH CARY (1585–1639)

Elaine V. Beilin

Elizabeth Cary is one of the most prominent of all the women dramatists referred to in this collection, with several editions of her plays readily available and the associated critical approaches developing quickly. Given this precocity it is important to remember that in 1987 when Elaine V. Beilin published her hugely influential *Redeeming Eve: Women Writers of the English Renaissance* Cary was still relatively unknown and that Beilin's part-essay on her (the remainder is on Joanna Lumley, which is also included here; see pp. 125–8) represented new research. Indeed, Beilin's analysis of Cary's *The Tragedy of Mariam* made a significant impression on future Cary criticism and still stands as one of the most incisive accounts of her work.

In 1641, Clarendon remarked that Elizabeth Cary was 'a lady of a most masculine understanding, allayed with the passions and infirmities of her own sex.' In 1962, Douglas Bush wrote that 'Lucius Cary was the son of . . . a devoutly Catholic mother of literary, masculine, and eccentric character.'[1] The attribution of masculinity that has haunted Elizabeth Cary's intellectual achievements may explain why women so carefully guarded or apologized for their abilities. For many reasons, Cary – a scholar, dramatist, poet, religious polemicist, wife, and mother – encountered difficulties in practically every aspect of her life; a source of continual conflict was her attempt to live the 'masculine' life of the mind while devotedly carrying out the role and duties of a woman.

The full-length biography of Elizabeth Tanfield Cary, Viscountess Falkland, written by one of her daughters, enriches interpretation of her work, because there are clear parallels between her experiences as a woman and wife and the content of her play, *The Tragedie of Mariam, The Faire Queene of Jewry*. In this respect, *Mariam* seems atypical, if not unique, among Elizabethan and Jacobean closet dramas, and suggests that a woman writer actually modified conventional forms to express her particular subject. As the study of Aemilia Lanyer's treatment of poetic praise and Mary Wroth's use of romance and sonnet sequence also suggests, late Renaissance women writers may indeed have been striving to create their own distinctive literature from existing traditions.

Written by one of her four daughters, all of whom became nuns at Cambrai, *The Lady Falkland: Her Life* (*c.*1655) is complicated by the author's reverence for her mother and by her own piety. The daughter's central interest is her mother's conversion to Catholicism, and so the biography becomes a spiritual history verging on hagiography of Lady Falkland, who withstood persecution from her husband and her society for decades. Nevertheless, the account of Elizabeth Cary's early years seems relatively free from bias and accurate when compared to other sources, and if the biographer sympathized strongly with her mother, by no means does she cast her father as a villain.[2] What the biographer does consistently reveal is that all her life, Elizabeth Cary struggled with established authority, whether it was that of her parents, the Protestant church, her mother-in-law, or her husband. She wrote *Mariam* sometime during the first decade of her marriage, when she was beginning to live under her husband's authority; juxtaposed to *The Lady Falkland: Her Life*, *The Tragedie of Mariam* seems to be closely related to the life of its author as a young married woman.[3]

Mariam is also unique as a drama in two other respects: it is the first English play about the private lives of King Herod the Great and Queen Mariam, and it is the only early play on the subject in which the drama centers on Mariam's tragedy.[4] Cary drew her material from Lodge's 1602 translation of Josephus's *Jewish Antiquities*, which provides a detailed account of Herod's career. But Cary's protagonist is Mariam, around whom she designs a drama relevant to Cary's own time and indeed to her own life. With countless other writers of the sixteenth and seventeenth centuries, Cary treats the question of obedience to authority, and in particular, the obedience of a wife to the authority of a husband. Through the characters and choruses, she presents both the orthodox view of wifely obedience and a challenge to that tradition. In the end, this conflict gives way to a Christian allegory, by which the drama is resolved.

Elizabeth Cary's unwillingness merely to endorse accepted attitudes is startling, considering how social theory, law, religion, and custom upheld a husband's authority. In Renaissance England, the authority of a husband over his wife was a principle constantly uttered in pulpit and press. Indeed, a wife's obedience was as strongly urged as the subject's obedience to the monarch or the Christian's to the church. The Elizabethan additions to the *Homilies* included one 'Of the state of matrimony' advocating wifely obedience, and in *Basilikon Doron*, James I instructed his son in the authority of a husband as in the authority of a king.[5] In the early seventeenth century, the two famous divines, Dr William Gouge and William Whately, preached and later published their advice on marriage which centered on the wife's duty to obey.[6] St Paul was everywhere quoted as the authority for domestic arrangement: 'Wives, submit yourselves unto your husbands, as unto the Lord.' In the face of such strictures, Elizabeth Cary's independent spirit seems all the more extraordinary, and her conflicts all the more understandable.

Elizabeth Cary was brilliant, pious, energetic, and talented. If her biographer is correct, she was one of the most prolific literary women of her time. Before she was 17, she translated Ortelius, and later wrote two plays and a life of Tamburlaine, translated Cardinal du Perron, and composed verse lives of St Mary Magdalen, St Agnes Martyr, and St Elizabeth of Portugal, as well as many lesser verses. She is also the possible author of a history of the reign of Edward II.[7] At the same time, she led the life of a daughter of the upper gentry: she married the man chosen by her parents and had eleven children. If it were not for her daughter's biography, Cary's image would be that of the well-born, well-educated Renaissance woman who was a wife and mother, and author of classical or pious works as well – a 'learned and virtuous' woman like Margaret More Roper, Anne Cooke Bacon, or Mary Sidney Herbert. But the *Life* is a disturbing document that details the many conflicts and emotional crises that Elizabeth Cary experienced during much of her life. Many of her troubles came from her early attraction and final conversion to Catholicism, an act that caused spiritual, familial, and political struggles. Some of the biographer's information suggests that certain of Cary's problems also stemmed from the continual, internal clash between her desire for intellectual independence and achievement and the requirements of her position as daughter, wife, and mother.

She was the only child of Sir Laurence and Lady Elizabeth Tanfield of Burford Priory, Oxford. Her stern parents bore a reputation in the country for hardness and arrogance. Lady Tanfield in particular was disliked by the inhabitants of Great Tew, who complained that 'she saith that we are more worthy to be ground to powder than to have any favour showed to us.' [8] Whether Elizabeth Cary's mother was harsh at home, the biographer does not say; but Cary seems to have been an isolated child who without teachers learned French, Spanish, Italian, Hebrew, and Latin, and who 'was skilful and curious in [needle] working, never having been helped by anybody' (*Life*, p. 5). Elizabeth, without siblings 'nor other companion of her age, spent her whole time in reading, to which she gave herself so much that she frequently read all night' (*Life*, p. 6). In an attempt to discipline this intellectual thirst, her mother forbade the servants to give her candles, but Elizabeth bribed her attendants to bring her the necessary light. Her father was totally devoted to his work as a judge, and is mentioned in other contexts in the *Life* only when he gave Calvin's *Institutes* to the 12-year-old Elizabeth (the biographer claims she found Calvin wanting) and when he married her to Sir Henry Cary. Although the biographer's glimpse of Elizabeth Cary's childhood is brief, she describes a solitary, precocious, independent spirit who would circumvent or even challenge authority when her quest for knowledge demanded it.[9]

The Tanfields contracted the alliance with Sir Henry Cary in June 1602, the marriage took place in the autumn, and the 17-year-old bride continued to live at home for the first year or more, perhaps until the autumn or Christmas of 1603. The biographer claims that 'about that time' Henry Cary went to Holland 'leaving her still with her own friends.' It was the conventional arranged marriage, for the *Life* records that Henry Cary married Elizabeth 'only for being an heir, for he had no acquaintance with her (she scarce even having spoken to him) and she was nothing handsome, though then very fair' (p. 7). The biographer does not directly reveal Lady Cary's attitude except to note that while living at home and separated from Sir Henry, her letters to her husband were written by others under her mother's orders. In view of Cary's precocious ability, it is possible that her mother did not approve of what she would send to Sir Henry, or that the new wife was not inclined to write.

Sometime in the second year of the marriage, Sir Henry's mother insisted that Elizabeth come to live with her. The young bride did not get along well with her mother-in-law and Lady Katherine Cary, vested with her own power of a parent, treated her daughter-in-law strictly. Lady Katherine was

> one that loved much to be humoured, and finding her not to apply herself to it, used her very hardly so far as at last to confine her to her chamber, which seeing she little cared for, but entertained herself with reading, the mother-in-law took away all her books, with command to have no more brought her.
>
> (*Life*, p. 8)

Those books, catalogued near the end of the *Life*, reveal Cary's prodigious appetite for learning:

> She had read very exceeding much; poetry of all kinds, ancient and modern, in

> several languages, all that ever she could meet; history very universally, especially all ancient Greek and Roman historians; all chroniclers whatsoever in her own country, and the French histories very thoroughly; of most other countries something, though not so universally; of the ecclesiastical history very much, most especially concerning its chief pastors. Of books treating of moral virtue or wisdom (such as Seneca, Plutarch's Morals, and natural knowledge, as Pliny, and of late ones, such as French, Mountaine, and English, Bacon), she had read very many when she was young, not without making her profit of them all.
>
> (*Life*, p. 113)

So habitual and dedicated a reader would find peculiar frustration in the removal of her books, and at this point the *Life* notes that Cary 'set herself to make verses' (p. 8).

Again, she appears as an isolated figure, persecuted by her mother-in-law, and visited only in secret by one of her husband's sisters and a waiting gentlewoman. But Sir Henry's return ended her captivity and 'from this time she writ many things for her private recreation, on several subjects and occasions, all in verse.' (*Life*, p. 9). Life with Sir Henry was difficult, however. Later, summing up her parents' relationship, the biographer depicts her father as a stern figure whom her mother was able to please only through the exercise of enormous self-discipline. Like many other young women of her time, Elizabeth Cary, joined to a man she did not know, had to curtail her independent impulses to suit his wishes:

> He was very absolute; and though she had a strong will, she had learned to make it obey his. The desire to please him had power to make her do that, that others could have scarce believed possible for her; as taking care of the house in all things (to which she could have no inclination but what his will gave her), the applying herself to use and love work.
>
> (*Life*, p. 14)

For his sake, although she feared horses, she rode; she dressed well, although 'dressing was all her life a torture to her' and in fact, she went only so far as to let others tend her 'while she writ or read.'

Nevertheless, Cary continued to follow her own interests. Most notably, the biographer records that 'when she was about twenty years old, through reading, she grew into much doubt of her religion' (p. 9). The biographer thought that reading Hooker in particular caused her to question her Protestant faith, but for personal or political reasons, Cary waited another twenty years before breaking openly with her husband, church, and state.

Elizabeth Cary's conflict arose because she was both an independent intellectual and also very much a woman of her time, with a strong sense of duty as a wife and later as the mother of eleven children. The biographer emphasizes her strict principles:

> she did always much disapprove the practice of satisfying oneself with their conscience being free from fault, not forbearing all that might have the least show or suspicion of uncomeliness or unfitness; what she thought to be required in this she expressed in this motto (which she caused to be inscribed in her daughter's wedding-ring): *Be and seem.*
>
> (*Life*, p. 16)

This insistence on the conformity of appearance and reality may help to explain how, despite her intellectual cravings and religious troubles, Cary could be a diligent housekeeper and teacher of her children – but not, apparently, without inner conflict and considerable psychic cost.

Symptoms of mental stress did not appear at once, but in later years they would include long bouts of sleeping to escape depression. Sleeping was 'her greatest sign of sadness.' This 'she was used to say she could do when she would, and then had most will to when she had occasion to have sad thoughts waking.'[10] When she was pregnant with her second and fourth children (Lucius, 1609–19; Lorenzo, 1612), she 'had some occasion of trouble' and became subject to such melancholy 'that she lost the perfect use of her reason' (*Life*, p. 16). The biographer suggests that 'it is like she at first gave the more way to it at those times, thinking her husband would then be most sensible of her trouble, knowing he was extraordinarily careful of her when she was with child or gave suck, as being a most tenderly loving father' (*Life*, p. 17). That Elizabeth Cary used her pregnancies to attract her husband's attention to her 'trouble' suggests a pathetic call for affection. But they were an ill-matched pair: he was a soldier and courtier, an active, worldly man of severe and stubborn temperament; she was an introspective, unworldly woman of deeply religious bent. Their relationship deteriorated with time, and much later in 1625, a final rift was caused by Lady Falkland's open conversion to Catholicism. At this point, Henry Falkland cut off her allowance, removed everything he could from the house, and took away her children and all but one servant. Hasty judgment and some vindictiveness, rather than religious indignation, characterized his actions, and only a Privy Council order restored to Lady Falkland a subsistence maintenance.[11]

In *The Tragedie of Mariam*, Cary seems to have used the figures of the drama to represent some of the problems and contradictions which were surfacing in her early married life, and to place her struggles in a wider context. The play may be seen as a psychomachia, one that Elizabeth Cary resolved by extending the limits of her personal conflict.

No contemporary notice of *Mariam* survives. While early criticism tended to belittle Cary's subject matter and poetic skills, more recently, critics have given closer attention to what Cary actually achieved. Leonora Brodwin noted that 'however inferior her poetic and dramatic talents may be, Cary's treatment of Herod does show a remarkable perception of one of the most complex psychological types.' Nancy Cotton Pearse has suggested that the 'sentiments expressed in the play are autobiographical,' and that Cary's ambivalence about her life is reflected in the contrasting characters of Mariam and Salome. Sandra Fischer thinks *Mariam*, based on Cary's own experience, reveals 'how a woman handles tyranny and maintains her own integrity.'[12] What is indeed remarkable about this play is the unusual prominence given to a virtuous woman's psychological conflicts, the carefully balanced polemic on the question of woman's place, and the extraordinary fifth act in which the female protagonist becomes a type of Christ. If not a great work, if not poetically brilliant, *The Tragedie of Mariam* is created from a strong conflict intelligently understood and sometimes eloquently expressed.

Mariam is based on material in Chapters 15 and 16 of Lodge's translation of Josephus's *Jewish Antiquities*. Strictly maintaining the unity of time, Cary collapses years of Josephus's account into the events of a day. While Herod, King of the Jews, is making peace with Octavius Caesar after Actium, his prolonged absence provokes a rumor of his death. In the first three acts, the main characters respond to the news: Herod's brother, Pheroras, thinking he is now free of the king's prohibition, plans to marry the low-born Graphina; Salome,

Herod's sister, decides to divorce her husband, Constabarus, in favor of her lover, Sylleus; Constabarus in turn frees the sons of Baba whom he has been hiding from Herod for twelve years. Queen Mariam, at first mourning Herod, recalls that he had ordered her death in the event of his own, and this knowledge, together with his previous execution of her grandfather and brother, initiates her own rebellion. In Act 4 Herod returns to find treason everywhere and his wife cold and accusatory. Salome, Mariam's inveterate enemy, convinces Herod that the queen had plotted with her guardian Sohemus to poison him, and also betrays Constabarus and the sons of Baba. Herod orders the execution of all his enemies, including his wife. Mariam dies nobly, leaving Herod to bitter regret and 'Frantike passion for her death.'[13]

The historical context is vital to Cary's characterization. Josephus's narrative covers 29–28 BC, and if the imminence of the Christian era were not already obvious, the margins in Lodge's 1602 translation note the number of years remaining until the birth of Christ.[14] Cary would thus be continually reminded as she read the *Antiquities* that these were the last years of the old dispensation, and she would surely recall Herod the Great as an archetypal villain of the old law and a common symbol of envy, wrath, cruelty, and murder, chiefly remembered for the Slaughter of the Innocents.[15] Believing a new era to be at hand to replace the laws of Herod's kingdom, Cary reinterpreted Josephus's history, and through the workings of Christian allegory, Mariam's defiance of Herod takes on an entirely different aspect. In one sense, she is rebelling against order, but in another, she is heralding the new law.

The most crucial differences between *Mariam* and its source are in Cary's Christian perspective and in her understanding of Mariam's character. Josephus thinks that 'nothing more grieved Mariam' in her relationship with Herod 'but that she had not any hope to live after him, if so be he should happen to die, especially for the order he had left as concerning her' (*Josephus*, p. 396). Josephus's Mariam is a schemer who bribes Sohemus to reveal Herod's order with 'pretty presents and feminine flatteries'; and Josephus finds all of Mariam's 'incredible and apparent hatred' for Herod to have its source in her anger at this order (*Josephus*, p. 397). And while he finds her

> chaste and faithfull unto him; yet had she a certaine womanly imperfection and naturall frowardnesse, which was the cause that she presumed too much upon the intire affection wherewith her husband was intangled; so that without regard of his person, who had power and authoritie over others, she entertained him oftentimes very outrageously.
>
> (*Josephus*, p. 397)

Josephus consistently disapproves of Mariam's outspokenness, even when she complains of her father's and brother's deaths, for from Herod 'she received nothing that might discontent her,' yet 'she presumed upon a great and intemperate libertie in her discourse' (*Josephus*, p. 399).

By contrast, Cary's Mariam is psychologically more complex: from the first scene, her Mariam thinks less about Herod's order for her death than about the conflicting passions in her heart; she thinks about Herod's jealousy destroying her love, but also about her own early love for him. Cary's Sohemus is 'mov'd to pitie by Mariam's distrest estate,' for her Mariam is incapable of using feminine wiles in any situation and is, if anything, naive about her powers. In other words, the one character flaw that explains Mariam for Josephus is insufficient for Elizabeth Cary, who creates new problems of private and public behavior for her protagonist and probes more deeply into her character.

Indeed, Cary structures the play to make Mariam's conflict between obedience to and rebellion against Herod's authority the central concern. Since Herod does not appear until Act 4, the first three acts mainly elucidate Mariam's position through soliloquy and through the other characters' acting out her psychomachia. We find that Mariam gradually turns away from the influence of Herod's rule, a rule of passion and irrationality, but that her way is beset with inner turmoil and outer conflict. She begins the play torn by her emotions, identifying herself primarily as a woman in love. Eventually, however, she finds she must conquer passion with reason, and learns that she must defy Herod's authority whatever the consequences.

Marriage is the battlefield of the play. Virtue and vice collide through Mariam's and Salome's opposing views on marriage; two minor characters, Graphina and Herod's ex-wife, Doris, provide still other perspectives on wedded life. At the same time, Salome and Graphina dramatically represent the opposing sides of Mariam's dilemma. A philosophical commentary is provided by the choruses – particularly the chorus to Act 3 which considers a wife's duties – and by Constabarus's long last speech on womankind.

Both Mariam and Salome state their positions in Act 1. Mariam is as chaste, loyal, and naive as Salome is promiscuous, inconstant, and scheming. Mariam's heart is 'too chaste a Scholler . . . To learn to love another than my Lord,' while Salome lusts after a new husband as soon as she tires of the old. This time, Salome's means are wholly unorthodox, as she plans to use divorce, a right given only to Hebrew men, to rid herself of Constabarus:

> Why should such priviledge to men be given?
> Or given to them, why bard from women then?
> Are men then we in greater grace with heaven?
> Or cannot women hate as well as men?
> Il'e be the custome-breaker: and beginne
> To shew my Sexe the way to freedomes doore,
> And with an offring will I purge my sinne,
> The law was made for none but who are poore.[16]
> (B3)

Salome's seizure of male prerogative, accompanied by so cynical a view of law, shakes the proper order of things, for Cary does not allow such female rebellion to go unanswered. Imaging the ancient world in terms of traditional medieval and Renaissance order, Constabarus articulates the orthodox response to impending disorder:

> Are Hebrew women now transform'd to men?
> Why do you not as well our battels fight,
> And weare our armour? suffer this, and then
> Let all the world be topsie turved quite.
> Let fishes graze, beastes, [swine], and birdes descend,
> Let fire burne downewards whilst the earth aspires:
> Let Winters heat and Summers cold offend,
> Let Thistels growe on Vines, and Grapes on Briers,

Set us to Spinne or Sowe, or at the best
Make us Wood-hewers, Waters-bearing wights.
(B4^{v}–C)

In a deeply offended tone, underlined by anaphora and oxymoron, Constabarus raises the specter of the 'mannish woman' and the 'womanish man,' both signs of divinely arranged order turned upside down. He reacts both to Salome's vociferousness and to her sexual aggression, the reverse of traditional feminine silence and chastity.[17] Cary writes most vividly here, perhaps an indication of the importance she attached to this war between the sexes. That she should have created a dialectic between husband and wife is interesting, but it is even more noteworthy that she does not allow the conventional pro-husband response to dominate in either poetic form or content. At the same time, authorial approval cannot easily be assigned to Salome, the villain, and Constabarus's argument bears all the weight of tradition. Tensely, the two sides balance, partly because the even match between Salome and Constabarus foreshadows the difficult situation soon to face Mariam, and partly because Cary may have been unwilling to resolve the conflict.[18]

Salome expresses Mariam's rebellious tendencies, although Mariam herself is no villain. The slave, Graphina, represents Mariam's purity at the very time when the queen intends to disobey her husband. As Salome's opposite, Graphina is the epitome of traditional female virtue: she is chaste, obedient, and silent. In the scene Cary invents between Graphina and her lover, Pheroras, Graphina is modestly silent, speaking only when addressed and then with humility and gratitude for Pheroras's having chosen her. She promises 'steadfast love/ And fast obedience.' The word 'silence' is associated with Graphina five times in less than thirty lines, making her a significant foil to the vociferous Salome and even to Mariam's 'unbridled speech.' Compared to Salome, Graphina is feeble and lackluster, but literary virtue often appears less interesting and lively than vice, and requires the reader to distinguish the truth. Cary may have given Salome better lines because dramatic villains customarily reflected the attractiveness of vice; or it may be that she enjoyed articulating Salome's impudence much more than Graphina's pious orthodoxy.

More important, Cary here represents the dilemma which continually faced women writers themselves: in a culture that associated silence with feminine virtue, the articulate woman, whether her message was Salome's or Mariam's, risked all the opprobrium reserved for 'lewde, idle, froward, and unconstant women.'[19] The writer's problem, like Mariam's, was to prove that her utterance did not make her an unnatural woman nor preclude her virtue.

The extremes that Salome and Graphina physically embody also exist in Mariam's mind. By the middle of Act 3, Mariam, though chaste and virtuous, finds that she must disobey Herod. Discovering that he is, after all, alive, Mariam feels the prison walls closing around her again. Her love turns to hatred, and rather than fear Herod, she now rejects their old relationship:

I know I could inchaine him with a smile:
And lead him captive with a gentle word,
I scorne my looke should ever man beguile,
Or other speech, then meaning to afford.
(E2^{v}-E3)

The once-submissive Mariam determines to stand against her husband, identifying herself with the forces of innocence and good against those of evil. Abjuring the temptations of power and position and having sworn 'solemn vowes' to forsake Herod's bed, she staunchly concludes, 'Let my distressed state unpittied bee,/ Mine innocence is hope enough for mee' (E3). It is not enough for Elizabeth Cary, however; against this ringing declaration, she sternly casts a Third Chorus which ponderously recites the code of laws for Judea's wives:

> Tis not enough for one that is a wife
> To keepe her spotles from an act of ill:
> But from suspition she should free her life,
> And bare her selfe of power as well as will.
>
> (E3ᵛ)

Wives belong to their husbands body and soul, so much so that even 'their thoughts no more can be their owne' (E4ᵛ). Not only total loyalty to her husband, but total lack of desire for public recognition must govern the true wife's actions. In the judgment of such authority, Mariam stands guilty both because of her confidential talks with Sohemus and because of her rebellion against Herod. In the dramatic structure of the play, the Third Chorus ensures that there is a complete separation between Mariam and established authority.

The extent of Mariam's isolation is marked by her final, brief confrontation with Herod, late in the play. Quietly defying her husband, Mariam returns his passionate declarations with sober accusations that he has killed her relatives. Her stance is like that of an early Christian martyr – an analogy that may well have been in Cary's mind.[20] While Josephus's unequivocal moral is that disobedience means death, even for the otherwise virtuous Mariam, Cary goes on to create an elaborate mechanism by which Mariam can be both rebel and virtuous woman. She begins by making the very voice of order, Constabarus, into Mariam's eulogist.

Constabarus, also betrayed by Salome, goes to his execution cursing all womankind except Mariam. According to Constabarus, the world that destroys Mariam is thoroughly evil, peopled by women who are 'Tygers, Lyonesses, hungry Beares,' the fallen Angels, the scourge of mankind, the second flood, destroyers of order and laws: 'Your best are foolish, froward, wanton, vaine,/ Your worst adulterous, murderous, cunning, proud' (G). Evil entered the world with women and is maintained by them, particularly those who deny their proper place and take upon themselves men's roles. This vituperation, reminiscent of many literary attacks on women, should theoretically apply to Mariam herself. But Cary uses it here to effect Mariam's complete separation from her environment by making her 'alone of all her sex,' the virtuous exception. While Constabarus claims women caused the first fall, Mariam with whom he associates 'grace,' is gradually being established as the atoner for that fall. After this assertion of Mariam's uniqueness, her death cannot be an execution, but a sacrifice.

In her last soliloquy, Mariam praises humility, implying her own abandonment of worldly pride. The Third Chorus detailed her breach of fealty to Herod, the old law; Constabarus distinguished her from all other women; and her final speech separates her from the world: 'And therefore can they but my life destroy,/ My Soule is free from adversaries power' (G4). Although Salome and Herod are responsible for Mariam's death, ironically they free her from themselves, from malice, passion, wrath, and pride.

At the climax of the play is the transfiguration of Mariam: her death is an allegory of the Crucifixion, for she foreshadows redemption from the old law, typified by Herod's kingdom. By transcending his earthly authority, she points to a higher and final authority.

A Nuntio describes Mariam's death to Herod in a speech filled with analogies to the death of Christ. In the second line of Act 5, the Nuntio already refers to Mariam as 'your heavenly selfe,' and he reports on going

> To see the last of her that was the best:
> To see if death had hart to make her stoop,
> To see the Sunne admiring *Phoenix* nest.
> (H2)

The resurrection of the phoenix traditionally symbolized the resurrection of Christ, and the death of Mariam mirrors that event.[21] She was calm and mild, her look keeping 'the world in awe.' But her mother, Alexandra, turned on her to 'loudly raile' and revile her, recalling the multitude reviling Christ. Even Herod is shocked at this treatment of the 'worlds delight.' But Mariam 'came unmov'd with pleasant grace,/ As if to triumph her arrival were.' Herod asks, 'But what sweet tune did this faire dying Swan/ Afford thine eare: tell all, omit no letter' (H2^{v}). To the Christian ear, Herod's metaphor recalls the bird who sings joyfully at its imminent death, for it knows that death leads to eternal life. Mariam's last words to the Nuntio allude to the resurrection: 'By three daies hence if wishes could revive,/ i knowe himselfe would make me oft alive' (H3). Finally, the Nuntio records that she prayed silently, 'And thus to heav'n her heav'nly soule is fled.' In his darkness, Herod indeed wishes for Mariam's resurrection, but cannot understand how this might occur, other than to hope for some sort of magic trick.

In a clear allusion to the suicide of Judas Iscariot, the Nuntio then reports that he found the butler who betrayed Mariam hanging himself on a tree.[22] Realizing Mariam's innocence, Herod knows 'She was my gracefull moytie, me accurst,/ To slay my better halfe and save my worst' (H3^{v}). The Nuntio in fact identifies Mariam with Abel, a traditional type of Christ: 'If sainted *Abel* yet deceased bee,/ Tis certaine *Mariam* is as dead as hee' (H3^{v}). Herod himself intensifies the allusion by representing himself as worse than Cain. As Mariam's light surpasses Herod's darkness, like Christ, she surpasses all classical comparisons. More beautiful than Venus, more clever than Mercury, chaster than Cynthia, Mariam is the reality next to which 'the/ *Greekes* but dreame.' They are but the shadow, she the real substance.

By raising Mariam to spiritual heroism at the end of the play, Cary removes her protagonist from the earthly problems that beset her to a transcendent state. The idealization of Mariam changes her from a disobedient wife and subject to a prophet of Christianity. With Mariam's death, the play becomes a triumph of the spirit over the flesh, of patience over passion. This reading of Mariam emphasizes concerns that appear to have their spiritual roots in Elizabeth Cary's own life. While Cary seems to have accepted the tradition of male authority, her own experience living under its rule was difficult and often painful. Her biographer claims that her mother consciously made Sir Henry the arbiter of her actions, even though her own instincts directed her elsewhere. Whether Salome speaks for Cary's rebelliousness or Graphina articulates her ideas on obedience is unclear; significantly, the first four acts of the play consider both duty and individual need and reveal Cary's concern with the difficulties of obedience in an authoritarian marriage, especially in matters of individual conscience.

While viewing a play through the playwright's life is often problematic, to do so in this case allows insights not possible from a simple dramatic analysis. For instance, the play may indeed echo something of Herod's medieval heritage, or of Salome's similarity to popular stage villains; using Graphina and Salome to represent Mariam's two sides may recall the medieval Virtue and Vice, the Good and Bad Angels of *Dr Faustus* or even Desdemona and Iago in *Othello*. But more crucial to the play is the character of Mariam, who is an unusual balance of virtue and error, of chastity and pride, crowned by final sanctification. No stereotyped Castiza or Castabella, nor yet possessing the dramatic power of a Webster heroine, Mariam serves Cary's purpose by undergoing her own conflicts and then becoming a divine symbol. Current dramatic conventions, with which Cary was certainly familiar, may account somewhat for the shape of the play, but give little help in understanding Mariam's character or the ending.

Certainly, the coincidental parallels between the lives of Mariam and Elizabeth Cary are striking: an isolated woman, an ill-matched marriage, an authoritarian husband who dominates even from afar, a cold and unsympathetic family. These analogies alone may have drawn Cary to choose her subject from Josephus. But if the play began with the author's attraction to a historical figure, it developed into a discussion of woman's place, of marriage, and the strong identification of a female character with the Christian ethic. Mariam's heroic martyrdom may also have been Cary's attempt to justify the way she chose to live her own life.

In this respect, the fifth act assumes considerable interest. While the idealization of Mariam as a spiritual hero certainly seems to evolve from a historical context in which Mariam represents the new religious dispensation, her glorification may also have psychological roots. The playwright's double perspective on Mariam, which results from sympathizing with her problems and yet knowing she defies proper authority, is simplified by redesigning her death. Cary makes Mariam a purely symbolic figure who does not appear at all in Act 5. The emotional crises evaporate and we are left with a repentant Herod and a final chorus seeking a 'warning to posteritie' in the play's events.

To Elizabeth Cary, problems, whether in art or in life, could be solved by glorifying the specifically Christian virtues of patience, fortitude, and unselfishness. Certainly in the early stages of her marriage, she attempted to live by this creed, suppressing self-interest and patiently guiding herself to submit. The biographer cites her mother's rule, 'that wherever conscience and reason would permit her, she should prefer the will of another before her own' (*Life*, p. 13). Similarly, her play, after four acts of rampant self-assertion by the characters, ends with heroic self-abnegation, making the protagonist a precursor of Christ's self-sacrifice. Perhaps Cary's own religious longings prompted her to give a female character such a role. Her attraction to Catholicism included particular devotion to the Virgin Mary; the biographer recalls that she

> bore a great and high reverence to our blessed Lady, to whom, being with child of her last daughter (and still a Protestant), she offered up that child, promising, if it were a girl, it should in devotion to her bear her name, and that as much as was in her power, she would endeavour to have it be a nun.
>
> (*Life*, p. 18)

Earlier, while still struggling with the form of her faith, Cary drew the Mariam of Act 5, perhaps to create a model of the divinely inspired woman, an ideal of patience in adversity, of fortitude under oppression.

Mariam may have meant even more to Cary, because she also dramatizes the problems of the woman writer struggling between the private sphere of silent feminine virtue and the public world of masculine discourse. When Mariam speaks to someone besides her husband, she breaks the rules governing feminine utterance; when she reasons and argues with Herod, she compounds her disobedience by expressing it eloquently. Cary specifically shows how Mariam's 'unbridled speech' precipitates her condemnation. But even if she speaks publicly, as the virtuous exception in Constabarus's misogynist attack, Mariam also resembles the learned and virtuous Renaissance woman, the atoner who devoted herself to redeeming her sex from Eve's guilt. On one hand, Mariam's death punishes her outspokenness, so warning women to be silent; on the other hand, it makes her a martyr. Mariam's Christian triumph may well reflect Cary's optimism for her own art by detaching her surrogate from earthly oppression. By affirming Christian values, Cary modified the challenge her writing posed to traditional feminine boundaries. And significantly, she designated woman's Christian heroism as an important subject for the woman writer.

Cary's intense religious devotion offered her a way to understand her position and to live her life, but not without intellectual conflict and mental anguish. In her play, however, she could create a fictional resolution for her dilemmas and a triumph for her highest ideals. Cary deliberately ends the play with Mariam calm, dignified, and victorious, while Herod is half mad with grief and despair. Not only do they appropriately represent the new law and the old, but Elizabeth Cary may also have fulfilled her own wishes in the triumph of Mariam over Herod. The end of the play, where history, allegory, and psychodrama merge, certainly alters the perspective of Josephus's narrative, and perhaps also the nature of authority itself. In the end, Herod's authority as husband and king is supplanted by the power of Mariam, to whom Cary gives the higher authority of Christian doctrine.

It is tempting to suggest that the identification of a female protagonist with the Christian ethic is Cary's way of superseding male authority, which she otherwise seems to support. In her own life, she always deferred to Henry Cary, and taught her children to revere him, although her Catholicism and their incompatibility brought about a bitter separation lasting from 1625 to just before his death in 1633. In her account of her parents' marriage, the author of the *Life* clearly wished her mother to be remembered not as a rebel, but as a pious woman who recognized a hierarchy of duty: her first priority was God, and she sacrificed to her faith not only physical comfort and material needs, but also a conventional marriage and family life.

As a writer, Cary dramatized the dilemmas of a virtuous woman whom she developed as a Christian hero. Like other women writers, she introduced a feminine type, an allegorical figure like the wise virgins or brides of Christ to emphasize the transcendent power of feminine spirituality; but for the first time, evidence exists that this allegory actually emanated from the writer's perception of her own life as well as from her literary and religious education. If feminine images and symbols were important in the works of earlier writers, here they seem to be inextricably linked to the complex process of becoming a writer.

Notes

1 *The History of the Rebellion and Civil Wars in England, begun in the year 1641 by Edward, Earl of Clarendon*, ed. W. Dunn Macray (Oxford, 1888), 3:180; Douglas Bush, *English Literature in the Earlier Seventeenth Century* (Oxford: Clarendon Press, 1966), p. 343.

2 *The Lady Falkland: Her Life*, ed. R. S. from a manuscript in the Imperial Archives at Lille (London: Catholic Publishing and Bookselling, 1861). In his biography of Lucius Cary, Kurt

Weber suggests that a 'proper discount' should be made on the biography because it was written under 'pious influences' as a religious duty. Still, Weber himself makes substantial use of the *Life*. *Lucius Cary*, Columbia Studies in English 147 (New York, 1940), pp. 11–12. Donald Stauffer praises the biography, calling it 'a notable piece of individualization.' He continues, 'its subtle appraisals and almost brazen analyses of motives are written with a certain dry intelligence that puts to shame the effusive contemporary masculine biographers.' After criticizing the style, Stauffer concludes, 'as a whole the life is distinctive and original, and succeeds in the highest aim of biography: the reconstruction of a personality in thought and actions.' *English Biography before 1700* (Cambridge, MA: Harvard University Press, 1930), pp. 148–50.

3 The play was written between 1602 and 1612, probably in the earlier part of the period. See Beilin, 'Elizabeth Cary and *The Tragedie of Mariam*,' *Papers in Language and Literature* 16(1980), n. 6.

4 In *The True Tragedy of Herod and Antipater: With the Death of faire Marriam* (1622), Gervase Markham and William Sampson focus on the father and son; in Massinger's *The Duke of Milan* (1623), the central character is the Herod figure.

5 The Homilie reads, 'Now as concerning the wives duety, what shall become her? Shall she abuse the gentlenesse and humanity of her husband and, at her pleasure, turne all things upside downe? No surely. For that is far repugnant against Gods commandement, for thus doeth *Saint Peter* preach to them, Yee wives, be ye in subjection to obey your owne husbands.' *Certaine Sermones of Homilies, appointed to be read in Churches, in the time of Queene Elizabeth I*, Scholars Facsimile (Gainesville, FL, 1968), p. 242. In *Basilikon Doron*, James writes, 'Ye are the heade, she is your body: It is your office to command, and hers to obey, but yet with suche a sweete harmonie, as she should be as readie to obey as ye to command; as willing to follow, as ye to go before: your love beeing whollie knit unto her, and all her affections lovingly bent to followe your will.' *The Basilikon Doron of King James VI*, ed. James Craigie (Edinburgh and London: Blackwood & Sons, 1944), pp. 133–5.

6 In *A Bride-Bush: or, A Direction for Married Persons* (London, 1619), William Whately does enjoin mutual aid and benevolence, but instructs the husband to keep and use his authority, because it is ultimately God's (chs 8, 9). In William Gouge's *Of Domesticall Duties: Eight Treatises* (London, 1622), subjection is the main topic of the third treatise on the 'particular Duties of Wives': 'And good reason it is that she who first drew man into sin should be now subject to him, lest by womanish weaknesse she fall againe' (p. 269).

7 Cary dedicated 'The mirror of the Worlde translated out of French' to her great-uncle, Sir Henry Lee. The manuscript is in the church at Burford, Oxfordshire. See Kenneth Murdock, 'Passion and Infirmities: The Pilgrimage of Elizabeth Cary, Viscountess Falkland, 1585?–1639,' *The Sun at Noon: Three Biographical Sketches* (New York: Macmillan, 1939), pp. 10–11. A play set in Sicily, mentioned by John Davies in his dedication to Cary of *The Muses Sacrifice*, seems to be lost. So does the 'Life of Tamburlaine' in verse, mentioned in the *Life* as 'that which was said to be the best' of all that she had by then written (p. 9). In the late 1620s, the *Life* also records that 'she began her translation of Cardinal Perron's works, of which she translated the reply to the king's answer in thirty days . . . some time after she procured it to be printed, dedicating it to her Majesty; but Dr. Abbots, then lord of Canterbury, seized on it coming into England, and burnt it; but some few copies came to her hands . . . . She likewise here began the rest of his works, which she finished long after, but was never able to print it' (pp. 38–9).

In *The Reply of the Cardinall of Perron, to the Answeare of the Most Excellent King of Great Britaine*, translated into English (Douay, 1630), the author tells the reader, 'I will not make use of that worne-out forme of saying, I printed it against my will, mooved by the importunitie of Friends: I was mooved to it by my beleefe, that it might make those English that understand not French . . . reade *Perron*.' Calling the author 'a most noble heroine,' a prefatory poem makes much of her speed and skill in translation: 'One woman, in one Month, so large a Booke,/ In such a full emphatik stile to turne.'

The *Life* also attributes to this period the composition of the versified saints' lives 'and both before and after, many verses to our blessed Lady . . . and of many other saints' (p. 39), all now apparently lost.

A work entitled *The History of the Life, Reign, and Death of Edward II*, signed 'E. F.' and dated 1627 was found among Henry Falkland's papers and 'Printed verbatim from the Original' in 1680. In his study of the influence of drama on historical biography, Donald A. Stauffer speculated that the author was not Henry Falkland, as was long supposed, but Elizabeth Falkland. His evidence included the initials, Elizabeth's interest in drama, and the aptness to her life of the 'deep and sad passion' professed by 'E. F.' in the preface. If the last point signifies at all, it must be because of Elizabeth Falkland's own experiences, not, as Stauffer suggests, because she was the mother of the passionate and sensitive Lucius Cary. Stauffer detects similarities between *Edward II* and *Mariam*: 'fatal uniformity of technique, thoughts circumscribed in two verses, almost invariably end-stopped lines, and lengthy philosophical disquisitions.' 'A Deep and Sad Passion,' *Essays in Dramatic Literature: the Parrott Presentation Volume*, ed. Hardin Craig (New York: Russell and Russell, 1935), p. 314. This description could, however, apply to many other plays, and there are numerous differences between the two works. In a note, Stauffer indicates that 'E. F.' is identified as Edward Fannant in the British Museum copy, and he does conclude conditionally by saying, 'If this work be hers.' In *The Paradise of Women*, Betty Travitsky appears to refer to Stauffer when she asserts that *Edward II* 'has been shown to have been written by Lady Falkland,' but she introduces no new evidence (London: Greenwood, 1981), p. 210. In her review of Travitsky, Muriel Bradbrook accepts the attribution, adding that the work 'was surely meant as mirror for the subjection of the reigning king to his favorite Buckingham. It is more courageous, and more seditious, than it is recognized.' *Tulsa Studies in Women's Literature* 1(spring 1982), 93. The best evidence is the initials. Perhaps significant is E. F.'s admission, 'nor fear I Censure, since at the worst, 'twas but one Month mis-spended,' the same claim that Elizabeth Falkland made for the Perron translation.

8 'Sir Laurence Tanfield,' *DNB*, 19:357.

9 The biographer also tells a story of how her mother as a child of 10 cleverly brought justice to her father's court by seeing through the intimidation of the defendant. If the story is apocryphal, Elizabeth Cary may still have had the wit and fearlessness to prompt such an anecdote.

10 In Act 4 of *Mariam*, Herod, believing Mariam to be false, goes off 'To try if I can sleepe away my woe.'

11 The biographer's credibility increases when other sources corroborate the main drift of her characterizations, particularly that of her father. *DNB* relays the character of Lord Falkland as Lord Deputy of Ireland after 1622: 'In office he showed himself both bigoted in his opinions and timid in carrying out a policy which continually dallied with extremes; though conscientious, he was easily offended, and he lamentably failed to conduct himself with credit when confronted with an unusual difficulties.' 'Henry Cary,' 3:1150.

12 A. C. Dunstan, *Examination of two English Dramas: 'The Tragedy of Mariam' by Elizabeth Carew; and 'The True Tragedy of Herod and Antipater: with the Death of Faire Mariam,' by Gervase Markham, and William Sampson* (Königsberg, 1908), p. 49; A. M. Witherspoon, *The Influence of Robert Garnier on Elizabethan Drama*, Yale Studies in English 65 (New Haven, CT, 1924), 154; Bush, *English Literature in the Earlier Seventeenth Century*, p. 23; Brodwin, *Elizabethan Love Tragedy 1587–1625* (New York: New York University Press, 1971, and London: University of London, 1972), p. 389, n. 2; Pearse, 'Elizabeth Cary, Renaissance Playwright,' *Texas Studies in Language and Literature* 18 (Winter 1977), 605, and also Nancy Cotton, *Women Playwrights in England c. 1363–1750* (Lewisburg, PA: Bucknell University Press, 1980), pp. 31–7; Fischer, 'Elizabeth Cary and Tyranny, Domestic and Religious,' in *Silent But for the Word: Tudor Women as Patrons, Translators and Writers of Religious Works*, ed. Margaret Hannay (Kent, OH: Kent State University Press, 1985), p. 227.

13 *The Tragedie of Mariam, The Faire Queene of Jewry* (London, 1613), The Argument. Hereafter cited in the text.

14 *The Famous and Memorable Workes of Josephus, a Man of Much Honour and Learning Among the Jewes, Faithfully translated out of the Latine, and French, by Tho. Lodge, Doctor in Physicke* (London, 1602). Hereafter cited in the text.

15 In the Wakefield cycle *Herod the Great*, Herod is so characterized. Many Renaissance works of art depict the Slaughter of the Innocents, usually showing Herod giving the command for the massacre to begin.

16 Josephus's description of Salome's actions is Cary's source, although she gives Salome all her dramatic life. Josephus says, 'Not long after it happened, that *Salome* fell at debate with *Constabarus* for which cause she sent a libell of divorse to her husband, notwithstanding it were against the lawes and ordinary customes of the Jewes. For according to our ordinances, it is onely lawfull for the husband to do the same . . . . But *Salome* without respect of the lawes of the countrey, grounding her selfe too much upon her owne authoritie, forsooke her husband.' (p. 400).

17 In Chapter 7 of *Women and the English Renaissance* (Urbana IL: University of Illinois Press, 1984), Linda Woodbridge argues that in the late sixteenth and early seventeenth centuries, the appearance on London streets of women dressed as men influenced a series of literary counterparts: 'All through these years, literature maintained a steady interest in female man-nishness, male effeminacy, and the whole question of the "nature" of men and women, often suggesting that traditional sex roles were undergoing pronounced mutation in the modern world' (p. 153). While Salome could easily have evolved from a long literary tradition of women attempting to dominate men (Eve, Deianira, Cleopatra), perhaps Cary was influenced by contemporary concern, particularly through her great interest in the drama. See Lisa Jardine's discussion of strong women and the 'female bogey' on stage in Chapter 3 of *Still Harping on Daughters* (Totowa, NJ: Barnes and Noble, 1983).

18 The battle for sovereignty between husband and wife is a common dramatic theme, although most treatments are comic, intended to satirize the uxorious husband and the folly of female rule. See *Johan Johan the Husband* (1533) and Jonson's *Epicoene* (1609). Also comically handled is the popular theme of the rebellious woman returned to her proper place; see Marston's *The Courtesan* (1604), Fletcher's *The Sea Voyage* (1622) and *Rule a Wife and Have a Wife* (1624), and Massinger's *The City Madam* (1632). In tragedy, the fatal dangers of wife ruling husband are suggested in Lady Macbeth and Goneril, and in Beaumont and Fletcher's *The Maid's Tragedy* (1610). *Mariam* resembles *Othello* in opposing two married couples, as well as in the parallel characters of Othello and Herod, Desdemona and Mariam. Both plays raise the issue of female sexuality: Desdemona's passion for Othello and Emilia's lusty com-mentary suggest women are men's equals in 'affections,/ Desires for sport, and frailty.' Unlike the inevitable tragedy of passion in *Othello*, however, the outcome of *Mariam* depends partly on history and partly on Cary's profound interest in redeeming Mariam. Once Salome has fulfilled her functions of propounding feminine power and endangering Mariam, she fades from the play, and Mariam becomes increasingly spiritual.

19 *The Araignment of Lewde, idle, froward and unconstant women* (1615) is Joseph Swetnam's virulent attack on women.

20 Cary clearly alters the explicitly sexual rebellion she found in her source: 'When as about midday the king had withdrawne himself into his chamber to take his rest, he called *Mariamme* unto him to sport with her, being incited thereunto by the great affection that he bare unto her. Upon this his commaund she came in unto him; yet would she not lie with him, nor entertaine his courtings with friendly acceptance, but upbraided him bitterly with her fathers and brothers death' (*Josephus*, p. 398).

21 Florence McCulloch notes that 'all versions of Physiologus agree that the phoenix symbolizes Christ, who had the power to come back to life.' *Medieval Latin and French Bestiaries* (Chapel Hill NC: University of North Carolina Press, 1960), p. 158.

22 See Matthew 27:5. There is no such reference to the butler's end in Josephus.

7

THE SPECTRE OF RESISTANCE

The Tragedy of Mariam (1613)

Margaret W. Ferguson

Margaret W. Ferguson's essay was originally published in 1991, yet it remains at the forefront of Cary scholarship in that it argues emphatically and with much justification that Elizabeth Cary was the most radical as well as the most skilful woman playwright of her day. Moreover, after a close reading of the gender implications of the play and an analysis of the female characters, Ferguson is able to stress that *The Tragedy of Mariam* is, in its depiction of the female subject, as relevant in the 1990s as when it was first written.

She was the only child of a rich lawyer; she was precociously bright but not beautiful; she was married at 15 to an aristocrat who wanted an heiress's dowry. He was Protestant, as were her parents; she converted secretly to Catholicism in the early years of what proved a stormy marriage. Most of what we know about this female contemporary of Shakespeare (she was born around 1585 and died in 1639) comes from a biography written (anonymously) by one of her daughters who became a Catholic nun in France. This daughter does not however mention the fact about her mother that contributes most to her claim on the attention of modern literary critics, namely that she was evidently the first of her sex in England to write an original published play. Her name was Elizabeth Cary and her play, printed in London in 1613, was entitled *The Tragedie of Mariam, The Faire Queene of Jewry*. Mary Sidney Countess of Pembroke had translated Robert Garnier's *Marc Antoine* in 1592, and Cary's play is clearly indebted to that aristocratic experiment in Senecan closet drama.[1] But Cary's interest in the drama and in women's relation to that genre goes far beyond that of any female English writer we know before Aphra Behn. According to her daughter, Cary loved plays 'extremely,'[2] and for a time at least managed to go occasionally to the London theater. Her authorship of *Mariam*, along with an early play now lost, makes her the first woman in England to attempt substantial original work in the drama, a genre socially coded as off-bounds to women, authors and actresses alike.[3]

Cary's play was never performed on stage, and whether or not it was published with her permission, much less at her active request, is a question I wish I or anyone could answer.[4] Having that information would make it considerably easier than it is now to accomplish one of my chief aims in this essay, which is to prepare the ground for assessing the political significance of this play, both in its own time and in ours. Access to more empirical information about the circumstances of the play's publication would be useful because the question of a woman's right to assume a 'public' voice is both central to the drama and unanswered within it. That unanswered question, which is, moreover, central not only to the play but also to Renaissance debates about the nature and proper behavior of womankind, underlies the lack of consensus among the play's readers about its ideological statement. *Mariam* seems at times to mount a radical attack on the Renaissance concept of the wife as the 'property' of her husband; but the play also seems – or has seemed to some of its readers, both feminist and anti-feminist – to justify, even to advocate, a highly conservative doctrine of female obedience to male authority.[5] I don't intend to make a case for or against either of these interpretations. I hope, rather, to show how, and to begin to show why, the play's ideological statement is so mixed, so contradictory.

The Tragedie of Mariam tells the story of the marriage between King Herod and his second wife, the royal-blooded Jewish maiden Mariam. Like many other Renaissance dramas about this ill-fated match, *Mariam* is based on a narrative in Josephus's *Jewish Antiquities* (*c.* AD 93), which was published in an English translation by Thomas Lodge in 1602.[6] Evidently following Lodge's Josephus quite closely, the author nonetheless revises her source significantly. She compresses, amplifies, and transposes material in order to observe the dramatic unities, and she alters the characterization of the heroine and other female figures, as well as the portrait of the troubled marriage between Mariam and Herod, in ideologically charged ways.[7]

The play opens at the moment in Josephus's narrative when Herod has been summoned to Rome by Caesar to answer for his earlier political association with Mark Antony, who had helped him acquire Judea. Having overthrown Antony, Caesar is likely to punish Herod, and indeed a rumor of his execution reaches Jerusalem, bringing joy to many who had suffered under his tyranny and bringing relief mixed with sorrow to his wife. Her ambivalent reactions to the news of Herod's death become even more complex when she learns from Sohemus, the man charged by Herod to guard her during his absence, that orders had been given that she should be killed in the event of Herod's death. Outraged by Sohemus's revelation of her husband's jealous possessiveness, and grieving still for the brother and grandfather Herod had murdered in order to secure his claim to the Judean throne (as Mariam's mother Alexandra continually reminds her), Mariam is unable to rejoice when Herod does unexpectedly return from Rome at the beginning of Act 4. His sister Salome, who hates being placed in a subordinate position both by Mariam and by the Jewish marriage laws which prevent women from suing for divorce, schemes to get rid of her husband Constabarus and Mariam too. Fanning Herod's anger at his unresponsive wife by 'proving' that Mariam is engaging in adultery with Sohemus and is at the same time plotting to poison Herod, Salome convinces the still-infatuated king to order Mariam's death by beheading. After the execution, which is described by a messenger, Herod spends most of the final act regretting, as Othello does, the loss of his 'jewell.'[8] Unlike Othello, however, this jealous husband created by a female playwright laments not only his innocent wife's death but, specifically, the loss of her too lately valued powers of speech.[9]

At the beginning of the play, Mariam is torn between the demands of wifely duty, which coincide at least intermittently with her feelings of love for Herod, and the demands of her conscience, which are initially defined in terms of family loyalty and voiced through the figure of Mariam's mother Alexandra. The nature of Mariam's dilemma shifts, however, as the play progresses, partly because her long soliloquies, like Hamlet's, work to dissolve binary oppositions. Also like *Hamlet* Cary's play gives us, at the level of character, dramatic foils who mirror certain aspects, and unrealizable potentials, of the central figure. At first glance, Cary's two major foils seem to come from a medieval morality play: on the one hand there is Salome, who works, Vice-like, to plot Mariam's death; on the other, there is Graphina, a slave girl loved by Herod's younger brother Pheroras. Virtuous, humble, obedient, she seems to embody the ideal of womanhood prescribed in Renaissance conduct books.[10]

The ethical opposition symbolized by these two characters, an opposition which emerges, specifically, as one of different modes of speech, is however also shot through with complexities. Salome's structural resemblance to the morality Vice figure is partly occluded when she is made to speak crudely but eloquently against the injustice of Jewish law which gives (rich) men but not women the right to divorce (1.4); and Graphina – the only character whose name is not found in Josephus's text or in Lodge's translation of it – becomes more opaque the more one studies her brief appearance in Cary's text (2.1).[11] She is strongly associated with the feminine virtue of modest silence, but the dramatic presentation prevents us from conceiving of that virtue as a simple alternative to the 'vice' of female speech, either Salome's or Mariam's. Pheroras tells Graphina that he prefers her to the bride Herod had designated for him because that 'baby' has an 'infant tongue' which can scarcely distinguish her name 'to another's ear' (2.1.17–18); the 'silent' Graphina evidently has won her lover's admiration for her powers of speech: 'Move thy tongue,' he says, 'For silence is a sign of discontent' (2.1.41–2). She obeys. The strange little scene queries the logic of the 'chaste, silent, and obedient' topos first by suggesting that womanly 'silence' may function just as erotically as speech in a non-marital relation (the conduct books never consider this possibility); and second, by suggesting that a certain kind of speech signifies the same thing that 'silence' does in the discourse of wifely duty, that is, compliance with the man's wishes: Graphina tells her lover only what he wants to hear, when he wants to hear it. She may therefore be said to figure a mode of 'safe' speech, private speech that neither aims at nor produces offense. Cary's invented name for this character might, on this line of interpretation, be significant: the name evidently plays on the Greek verb *graphein*, 'to write.'

If the figure of Graphina represents for Cary both the possibility of a non-transgressive mode of discourse (like private writing?) and the possibility of a mutually satisfying love relation, neither of those possibilities is available to the play's heroine. The first words Mariam speaks, which are also the play's first words, epitomize the problem:

> How oft have I with public voice run on
> To censure Rome's last hero for deceit:
> Because he wept when Pompey's life was gone,
> Yet when he liv'd, he thought his name too great.

These lines, which are spoken in soliloquy and initiate a complex parallel between Mariam's situation and that of Julius Caesar,[12] link the theme of female public voice immediately with the idea of transgression ('run on') and the idea of 'censure.' In the original edition, the first line ends with a question mark. This seems at first merely an oddity of seventeenth-century 'rhetorical' punctuation, but the question itself, voiced at the play's threshold moment by a female character whose 'unbridled speech' eventually plays a major role in her husband's decision to censor her voice definitively, is not by any means simply rhetorical. It is, we might say, complexly rhetorical – for several reasons. First, to make it the kind of question that obviously requires the affirmative answer 'very often,' the reader must 'run on' over the line's end and its punctuation. The structure of the verse creates for the reader a slight but significant tension between pausing – to respect the seemingly self-contained formal and semantic unit of the first line – and proceeding, according to the dictates of the syntactic logic which retrospectively reveals the first line to have been part of a larger unit. The verse thereby works to fashion a counterpoint between formal and semantic strains. We pause on the theme of 'running on,' we run on to encounter the theme of censure (as 'censorship' and 'critical judgment' both). The lines work not only to anticipate the drama to come (deploying the strategy of the 'pregnant' opening most famously used in *Hamlet),* but also to mark the play, for Cary herself and perhaps for her first 'private' readers, with something we might call the woman author's *signature.*

That signature consists not of a name but of a Chinese box set of questions about the logic of the Pauline injunction against female public speech and the cultural rule of chastity that injunction ostensibly supported. Like a lawyer presenting ambiguous fact situations to a judge, Cary invites us to consider whether the play text itself is 'covered' by the law: Is *writing* a form of 'public voice'? Is a *drama* not necessarily intended for performance on the public stage a legitimate form of female verbal production? Is a *soliloquy* – by theatrical convention, a 'private' speech overheard (overread?) by an audience – legitimate? In short, the play opens in a way that seems designed to test, but not overtly to disobey, the rule proscribing 'public voice' for women. Here we have a written representation of a female character soliloquizing, as if in private, about a prior event of (ambiguously) culpable public speech – ambiguously culpable because the comparison with Caesar's speech 'degenders' Mariam's prior speech act, although the issue of gender, and a potential male audience's response to the speaker's gender, is clearly on the heroine's (and the author's) mind. Mariam goes on to transform the figure of Caesar from an (imperfect) model for a speaker to an authoritative model for an audience or judge. She suddenly apostrophizes the 'Roman lord' with an aggressively defensive apology for exhibiting a fault (rash judgment) commonly ascribed to the daughters of Eve, but also characteristic of many male rulers including Caesar (who died when he failed to heed Portia's dream-inspired warnings against a public appearance):

> But now I do recant, and, Roman lord,
> Excuse too rash a judgement in a woman:
> My sex pleads pardon, pardon then afford,
> Mistaking is with us but too too common.
> (1.1.5–8)

Mariam's opening lines arguably address a problem that has to do not only with female speech in general but also with the play's own mode of material existence, indeed, its *right* to exist in the world. The act of writing, for oneself or for an audience of family and friends, would seem – like the dramatic form of the soliloquy – to occupy a shady territory between private and public verbal production. Because of the ambiguous status of writing, Cary could in one sense have applied Mariam's opening question to herself and answered it with a decorum the fictional character lacks. 'How oft have I with public voice run on?' 'Never.' But that answer would not have satisfied the culturally constructed censoring power that the play text ascribes chiefly to the figure of the tyrant-husband but also to the Chorus, and, at certain moments, to the heroine herself, speaking, evidently, for an aspect of the author's own conscience or superego.[13]

According to her daughter, Cary

> did always much disapprove the practice of satisfying oneself with their conscience being free from fault, not forbearing all that might have the least show or suspicion of uncomeliness or unfitness; what she thought to be required in this she expressed in this motto (which she caused to be inscribed in her daughter's wedding ring): *Be and seem.*
>
> (*Life*, in *Mariam*, p. 195)

This passage, which attributes to Cary a rule of spiritual and social conduct as fraught with problems as the rules Hamlet formulates for himself, might be paraphrased as follows: never be satisfied that you really are as virtuous as you may seem to yourself – but always be what you seem. The difficulty of putting such a principle into practice is dramatized, in Cary's play, by the fact that the Chorus formulates one version of this rule in order to condemn Mariam for following (and articulating) another version of it.

At the end of Act 3, just after Mariam learns, through her guardian Sohemus, that Herod is still alive, she swears that she will never disguise her true feelings through hypocritical speech (3.3.1168–9) and she vows also to abandon her husband's bed (3.3.1136). Interestingly, Sohemus chastises her, after she has left the stage, for her verbal intransigence but not for her refusal to pay her sexual 'marriage debt':

> Poor guiltless queen! Oh, that my wish might place
> A little temper now about thy heart:
> Unbridled speech is Mariam's worst disgrace,
> And will endanger her without desert.
>
> (3.3.181–4)

His lines anticipate the Chorus's criticism of her in a long speech which virtually equates female speech – and the *will* to utterance – with unbridled sexual behavior:

> 'Tis not enough for one that is a wife
> To keep her spotless from an act of ill:
> But from suspicion she should free her life,
> And bare her self of power as well as will.
> 'Tis not so glorious for her to be free,
> As by her proper self restrain'd to be.
>
> When she hath spacious ground to walk upon,
> Why on the ridge should she desire to go?
> It is no glory to forbear alone
> Those things that may her honour overthrow.
> But 'tis thankworthy if she will not take
> All lawful liberties for honour's sake.
>
> That wife her hand against her fame doth rear,
> That more than to her lord alone will give
> A private word to any second ear,
> And though she may with reputation live,
> Yet though most chaste, she doth her glory blot,
> And wounds her honour, though she kills it not.

When to their husbands they themselves do bind,
Do they not wholly give themselves away?
Or give they but their body, not their mind,
Reserving that, though best, for others' prey?
No sure, their thoughts no more can be their own,
And therefore should to none but one be known.

Then she usurps upon another's right,
That seekes to be by public language grac'd:
And though her thoughts reflect with purest light,
Her mind if not peculiar is not chaste.
For in a wife it is no worse to find,
A common body, than a common minde.

And every mind, though free from thought of ill,
That out of glory seekes a worth to show,
When any's ears but one therewith they fill,
Doth in a sort her pureness overthrow.
Now Mariam had, (but that to this she bent)
Been free from fear, as well as innocent.

(3.3.215–50)

In this remarkable speech, Cary's Chorus offers contradictory statements about the precise nature of the error Mariam has committed. According to the second stanza, the error involves indulging in, rather than refraining from, something that is characterized as 'lawful' liberty. When the Chorus goes on to specify the error as a fault of *speech*, however, its 'lawful' status seems to disappear. By stanza five, the error is the distinctly illegitimate political one of 'usurping upon another's right.' And there is a corresponding contradiction in the Chorus's views of the 'virtue' it is advocating. In the third stanza, which stresses the duty of relinquishing desires for speech and fame, the virtue being advocated is quite distinct from the possession of physical chastity: the woman may be 'most chaste' even if she does grant a 'private word' to someone other than her husband. By stanza five, however, chastity has evidently been redefined as a figurative property pertaining to the mind, which is 'not chaste' if it's 'not peculiar' (in the old sense of 'private property' given by the OED). Which formulation are we to take as authoritative?

Interpreting the Chorus's speech becomes even more difficult when we try to read it in its dramatic context, as an ethical prescription for this particular heroine. The final lines seem to suggest that Mariam's tragic fate could have been averted had she refrained from speaking her mind to anyone other than her husband. But the play's subsequent development makes this notion absurd: it is precisely because Mariam speaks her mind not only to others but also, and above all, to her husband that she loses her life. Transgressive speech, defined as non-hypocritical speech, when Mariam says 'I cannot frame disguise, nor never taught / My face a look dissenting from my thought' (4.3.145–6), is, however, not the whole problem: Mariam also contributes to her downfall by refusing to sleep with Herod. She censors the wrong thing: his phallus rather than her tongue.[14]

The problem of her sexual withholding is addressed by the Chorus only obliquely, in the form of the (apparently) rhetorical question, 'When to their husbands they themselves do bind, / Do they not wholly give themselves away?' By the end of its speech, the Chorus has evidently suppressed altogether the crucial issue of Mariam's denial of Herod's property rights to her body. The strange logic of the speech anticipates that of Herod's later accusation of Mariam: 'she's unchaste, / her mouth will ope to ev'ry stranger's ear' (4.7.434–5). The equation of physical unchastity with verbal license, expressed through the provocative image of the woman's mouth opening to a man's ear, alludes, perhaps, not only to the common Renaissance trope of the female tongue as a substitute penis but also to anti-Catholic propaganda against Jesuit priests as Satanic corrupters of women and of the institution of the confession, where male 'strangers' received women's secrets. The image of a female mouth promiscuously opening to a male ear rewrites Mariam's fault as one of double excess or 'openness,' whereas what the play actually shows is that Mariam's verbal openness is a sign of sexual closure. Her behavior entails a property crime in certain ways more threatening than adultery is to the dominant ideological conception of marriage: this crime takes to a logical extreme, and deploys against the husband, the paradoxical ideal of wifely chastity elaborated by so many (mostly Protestant) Renaissance writers.

Neither the Chorus nor any other character in the play can clearly articulate this central problem in Mariam's behavior. The Chorus concludes by asserting that Mariam would have been 'free from fear, as well as innocent' if only she had been willing to forbear filling 'any's ears but one' with her words. The pronoun *one* evidently refers here, as it does in the earlier phrase 'none but one,' to the husband. Since the play makes it hard to give a simple 'yes' to the Chorus's question about whether women should give themselves 'wholly' away in marriage, however, we need to ask whether the shifter *one* might alternatively refer to God or, as Catherine Belsey suggests, to the wife herself.[15] Mariam is after all in danger because she speaks to her husband, and perhaps Cary's point, if not the Chorus's, is that if a wife has such thoughts she 'would be wiser to keep them to herself, precisely because in marriage they are no longer her own' (Belsey, pp. 173–4). Salome, who successfully manipulates her husband and brother and other male characters by *never* telling them what she really thinks, offers an intriguing counterpoint to Mariam in the sphere of female verbal politics. Indeed, as Martha Slowe has cogently argued, 'while Mariam who is chaste arouses suspicions by her open speech, Salome, who takes sexual and discursive liberties, preserves her reputation by guarding her speech and appearing to confine it to patriarchal limits.'[16] Moreover, the play seems obliquely to ratify Salome's tactics of feigning by leaving her unpunished at the end; as Betty Travitsky has observed, the play confounds conventional moral and generic expectations by failing to expose Salome's villainy, for she is guilty of numerous crimes including that of husband murder – the felony which Renaissance jurists called petty treason and regarded as much more heinous than wife murder, since the former unlike the latter involved an offense against the very concept of 'degree.'[17]

The very real possibility that Mariam should have followed Salome's stark model of 'private vice, public virtue' rather than the Chorus's more conventional (but very confused) prescriptions is countered, however, by the fact that verbal hypocrisy, had she adopted it, would *not* have worked to save her (married) life unless it were accompanied by sexual surrender of a kind Salome is never required to undergo. In any event, the Chorus's ethical precepts begin to look at best incoherent, at worst cynically similar to Salome's dark twisting of the 'be and seem' motto into a rationalization for wives to seem as others think that they should be.

This Chorus is the moment in the drama where Cary most directly interrogates her play's own right to exist. However we construe the injunction that wives should reveal their thoughts to 'none but one,' it is clear that the Chorus draws around the wife a circle of privacy so small that she would err by *circulating* a manuscript, much less by publishing it. Had Cary obeyed the rule of privacy set forth by her Chorus, she might have written a play, but we would not be reading it. The play offers, however – in addition to the fascinating example of Salome's powerfully amoral and apparently successful verbal exploits – an equally problematic but more theologically sanctioned model for female disobedience to masculine authority. Behind the figure of the non-compliant Mariam lies, I would suggest, a cultural discursive construction that we might label 'minority religious dissent' and trace in both Catholic and Protestant writings on the Christian subject's and/or wife's right to disobey a prince, magistrate or husband on those occasions when his commands conflicted with the dictates of Christian conscience.[18] Protestant discussions of this (limited) right of dissent are well known, but Catholic teachings, which of course often portray an individual conscience disobeying ungodly authority on the advice of a Jesuit priest, are less frequently cited by modern students of English Renaissance literature.[19] If, however, historians are right in finding a distinct gender asymmetry in English recusant culture (more women than men adhered to the pre-Reformation dogmas and rituals), a passage like the following, from the Jesuit Henry Garnet's *Treatise on Christian Renunciation* (158?), would seem an important subtext for Cary's play (and her life too, as reported by her daughter): 'your husbands over your soul have no authority,' the treatise advises its female readers, 'and over your bodies but limited power.'[20]

The language Mariam uses to justify her resistance to a husband who is also a king clearly belongs to this discursive tradition of minority religious dissent, a tradition that drove a wedge into the apparently hegemonic social rule linking female chastity with silence and obedience: they can 'but my life destroy, / My soul is free from adversaries' power' (4.8.569–70), Mariam says after Herod has accepted Salome's false charge of adultery and proclaimed his intention to kill his wife.[21] Although the Chorus continues to argue that Mariam should have submitted to Herod's authority, thereby paying her marital 'debt' and winning, through submission, the 'long famous life' denied her as an object of writerly ambition (4.8.664), Elaine Beilin rightly argues that the play's final act reconceives, and simplifies, the ideological conflict between the Chorus's perspective on wifely duty and Mariam's by presenting her death as an allegorical version of Christ's crucifixion.[22] Josephus had shown Mariam meeting her death with noble fortitude, but Cary adds numerous details that give Mariam a specifically Christological aura: the butler of Cary's play, for instance, suborned by Salome to accuse Mariam of seeking to poison Herod, hangs himself from a tree, as Judas does, in remorse for his betrayal; in Josephus, there is no mention of the butler's death.

Cary further revives her source by specifying the mode of Mariam's death; Josephus simply says that Herod ordered her executed, whereas in Cary's play, there is considerable emphasis on the 'fact' that she is beheaded. This detail, unremarked by Cary's critics so far as I know, seems an overdetermined and historically volatile allusion: it conjures up the ghost of Mary Queen of Scots, whose son ruled England when Cary wrote her play and who was in the eyes of many English Catholics a victim of Protestant tyranny; it also links Mariam with the figure of Christ's harbinger John the Baptist, beheaded by Herod's servants at Salome's request. Finally, the detail implies a possible similarity between Mariam and Anne Boleyn, killed by a royal husband who had broken with the Catholic church to divorce his first wife and who was explicitly likened to the tyrant Herod by some of his disapproving subjects.[23] Infused with rich but obscurely coded theological and political meanings, Cary's play surrounds Mariam's death with an aura of sanctification altogether absent from Josephus's narrative.

There is however a price for such sanctification, with its uncannily proleptic justification of the rebellious path Cary herself would follow when she converted publically to Catholicism in the mid-1620s, enraging and embarrassing both her father and her husband, who was then Lord Deputy of Ireland. In the play's final act, Mariam is not only absent from the stage but also represented, through the messenger's account of her last moments, as a woman who has somehow learned to bridle her tongue. On the way to her scaffold, she is cruelly taunted by her mother, who, after having urged Mariam throughout the play to despise Herod, now suddenly and cravenly condemns Mariam for 'wronging' princely authority (5.1.1968). Enraged at this report of Alexandra's behavior, Herod asks Mariam's response and learns, from the messenger, that 'she made no answere' (5.1.1992); she died, he adds, after saying 'some silent prayer' and 'as if she were content' (2026–7). The wickedness associated with the female tongue and with women in general (according to Constabarus's misogynist tirade against Salome's sex [4.6.1578–1619]), is here symbolically transferred from Mariam to her mother, who takes Mariam's place as the object of Herod's censoring wrath: 'Why stopt you not her mouth? where had she words / to darke that, that Heaven made so brighte?' (5.1.1979–80), he asks the messenger, and we remember that Herod has just exercised his power to stop Mariam's mouth. Once he has done so, in what seems the play's most complex and ambivalent irony, he suddenly starts to value Mariam's words with passionate desire: 'But what sweet tune did this faire dying Swan / Afford thine eare: tell all, omit no letter,' he exclaims (5.1.2008–9); and again, in an exchange that seems designed to effect wishful revenge on the tyrannical censorious husband, he asks for the 'food' of her words, nourishment he all too belatedly craves.

Cary imagines Herod coming to value Mariam's voice at the moment when the disputed property of her body is absent both from the stage and from the narrative 'present': 'Her body is divided from her head,' the messenger announces, and the graphic image of the dead and sundered woman (which appears nowhere in Josephus's account) allows us further to gauge the price Mariam must pay for her freedom of conscience. The price includes not only a symbolic acceptance of a lesson of female silence, now, however, seen as a virtue enjoined by God rather than by social authority; the price also includes the female saint's earthly body. To assess what that loss figured as a sacrifice might mean for the symbolic and real economies of Cary's upper-class culture, insofar as we can infer them, or for our own critical and erotic economies (but who is this 'we' I'm hypostasizing?) would be a task as intriguing as it is beyond the scope of the present essay. I shall conclude, however, by simply stating my strong suspicion that intellectuals in modern western societies have by no means shrugged off the burdensome ideological legacy of Cary's play, in which a female subject's desires for spoken, written, or printed words are seen as somehow inimical to her desires for life, much less for bodily pleasure.

Notes

1 First published as *Antonius* for William Ponsonby in 1592, the work was reprinted by Ponsonby in 1595 as *The Tragedie of Antonie Done into English by the Countess of Pembroke*. STC 11623. Reel no. 243. Rpt *The Countess of Pembroke's 'Antonie'*, ed. Alice Luce in *Literarhistorische Forschungen*, 3 (Weimar: Emil Felber, 1897). For useful comments on Mary Sidney's translation and its influence on various dramatists including Cary, see Betty Travitsky (ed.)

The Paradise of Women: Writings by Englishwomen of the Renaissance (1981, rpt New York: Columbia University Press, 1989), pp. 116, 216.

For invaluable help in the preparation of this essay I would like to thank Elaine Beilin, David Kastan, Mary Nyquist, Mary Poovey, and David Simpson. I would also, and above all, like to thank my mother Mary Anne Ferguson, in whose honor this essay was originally written, in a longer version published in *Tradition and the Talents of Women*, ed. Florence Howe (Champagne-Urbana, IL: University of Illinois Press, 1991).

2 Cited from *The Lady Falkland: Her Life*, first published in 1861 and reprinted in *The Tragedy of Mariam, Fair Queen of Jewry*, ed. Barry Weller and Margaret Ferguson (Berkeley and London: University of California Press, 1994); the quotation is from p. 224. The *Life*, by one of the four of Cary's daughters who became nuns, exists in a single manuscript found in the English Benedictine convent in Cambray and now in the archives of the Department of the North, at Lille. Subsequent references to this work will be given in the body of the essay and are all from the Weller/Ferguson edition.

3 For useful discussions of Cary's life, writings (many of which are evidently lost), and status as the first Englishwoman to publish an original play, see Nancy Cotton Pearse, 'Elizabeth Cary, Renaissance Playwright,' *Texas Studies in Language and Literature* 18(1977), 601–8; Sandra K. Fischer, 'Elizabeth Cary and Tyranny, Domestic and Religious,' in *Silent But for the Word: Women as Patrons, Translators, and Writers of Religious Works*, ed. Margaret P. Hannay (Kent, OH: Kent State University Press, 1985), pp. 225–37; Elaine Beilin, 'Elizabeth Cary and *The Tragedy of Mariam*,' *Papers on Language and Literature* 16 (winter 1980), 45–64, rpt in *Redeeming Eve: Women Writers of the English Renaissance* (Princeton, NJ: Princeton University Press, 1987); and Betty Travitsky, 'The *Feme Covert* in Elizabeth Cary's *Mariam* in *Ambiguous Realities: Women in the Middle Ages and Renaissance*, ed. Carole Levin and Jeanie Watson (Detroit, MI: Wayne State University Press, 1987), pp. 184–96. See also the introductory material to the selections from Cary's work in *The Paradise of Women*, ed. Betty Travitsky, pp. 209–12; in *The Female Spectator*, ed. Mary R. Mahl and Helene Koon (Bloomington, IN: Indiana University Press, 1977), pp. 99–102; and in *Kissing the Rod: An Anthology of Seventeenth-Century Women's Verse*, ed. Germaine Greer *et al.* (New York: Farrar, Straus, Giroux, 1988), pp. 54–5. In a paper entitled 'To Seem, to Be, Elizabeth Tanfield Cary: A Woman's Self-Fashioning' and circulated to members of the seminar on 'Renaissance Women as Readers and Writers' at the 1990 Shakespeare Association of America meeting, Donald W. Foster offers a cogent analysis of Cary's entire writing life.

4 The fact that the play was entered in the Stationers' Register (Dec. 1612) and licensed by the Master of the Revels leads A. C. Dunstan to surmise that it 'can hardly have been printed without the author's knowledge and at least acquiescence': *The Tragedie of Mariam*, 1613; Malone Society Reprints (Oxford: Horace Hart for the University Press, 1914), p. ix.

5 Angeline Goreau, who takes Cary's Chorus as unequivocally representing the author's opinions, sees the play as an ideologically conservative text in 'Two English women in the seventeenth century: notes for an anatomy of feminine desire,' in *Western Sexuality: Practice and Precept in Past and Present Times*, ed. Philippe Aries and André Bejin, trans. Anthony Foster (Oxford: Blackwell, 1985), pp. 104–5; and in her introduction to *The Whole Duty of a Woman: Female Writers in Seventeenth-Century England* (Garden City, NY: Doubleday, 1985), p. 13. In *The Tragedies of Herod and Mariamne* (New York: Columbia University Press, 1940), p. 90, Maurice Valency states that 'the author sides throughout with Herod,' having 'a low opinion of women in general.'

6 For persuasive evidence of Cary's reliance on Lodge, whose conversion to Catholicism in the late 1590s may have sparked Cary's interest in his work, see A. C. Dunstan's introduction to *Mariam*, pp. v–ix. See Valency, *Tragedies*, and also Gordon Braden, *Renaissance Tragedy and the Senecan Tradition* (New Haven, CT: Yale University Press, 1985), for information about other versions of the Herod and Mariam story on the Renaissance stage.

7 To study Cary's revisions of Josephus, which are more complex than this essay can indicate, I have used both the Loeb Classical Library bilingual edition of the *Antiquities of the Jews*: Book 15 is in vol. 8 of the Loeb *Josephus*, trans. Ralph Marcus, ed. and completed by Allen Wikgren (Cambridge, MA: Harvard University Press, 1963) and Thomas Lodge, *The Famous*

and Memorable Works of Josephus (London: Peter Short, 1602; copy in the Beinecke Library, Yale University).

8 See *Mariam*, Act 5, scene 1, line 119. All quotations of *Mariam* are from the edition of Weller and Ferguson cited in note 2.

9 For discussions of the verbal and structural parallels between *Mariam* and *Othello* see Margaret W. Ferguson, 'A Room Not Their Own: Renaissance Women as Readers and Writers,' in *The Comparative Perspective on Literature*, ed. Clayton Koelb and Susan Noakes (Ithaca, NY: Cornell University Press, 1988), pp. 93–116; the Introduction to *The Tragedy of Mariam*, ed. Weller and Ferguson, pp. 41–3; and Gordon Braden, *Renaissance Tragedy*, pp. 167 and 128, note 11. The long history, and cultural significance, of metaphorically equating a wife with private property, a valuable 'treasure,' or jewel in need of strict guarding, is discussed by Patricia Parker, *Literary Fat Ladies* (London: Routledge, 1987), pp. 126–54.

10 For discussions of the ideals of female behavior prescribed by conduct books, educational treatises, and other Renaissance texts, see Suzanne W. Hull, *Chaste, Silent and Obedient: English Books for Women 1475–1640* (San Marino, CA: Huntington Library, 1984); Angeline Goreau, *The Whole Duty of a Woman*; Peter Stallybrass, 'Patriarchal Territories: the Body Enclosed,' in *Rewriting the Renaissance*, ed. Margaret Ferguson, Maureen Quilligan, and Nancy Vickers (Chicago: University of Chicago Press, 1986), pp. 123–42; and Ann R. Jones, *The Currency of Eros: Women's Love Lyric in Europe, 1540–1621* (Bloomington, IN: Indiana University Press, 1990), pp. 1–18.

11 'With one exception,' as Dunstan notes in his Introduction to *Mariam* (p. xii), 'the names of all the characters are taken from Josephus.' The exception is the name of the slave woman loved by Pheroras. Josephus and Lodge mention a 'Glaphyra,' wife to a certain Alexander, near the part of the narrative in which Pheroras's story appears.

12 As Germaine Greer notes (*Kissing the Rod*, p. 56), Cary alludes here to Plutarch's account of Caesar weeping when he learned of his popular rival Pompey's death. The anecdote, which appears both in the 'Life of Caesar' and in that of Pompey, ironizes Caesar's grief: he had after all ardently desired and indirectly engineered Pompey's murder. Cary's analogy works to imply that Mariam is Herod's political rival and also that her desires somehow *caused* his (supposed) death in Rome, where he has gone, ironically enough, to answer Julius Caesar for using murder as a means to the throne.

13 For evidence of Cary's own husband's conventional views on women's duty as 'private' beings see, for instance, Sir Henry's letter of 20 December 1626, complaining of his 'apostate' wife's 'over-busy nature' and lamenting that she refuses to retire 'quietly' to her mother's country house, State Paper Office, Dublin, quoted in the Introduction to *Mariam*, ed. Weller and Ferguson, p. 55, n. 28. On other Renaissance women who challenged the cultural definition of women as private beings, see Merry E. Wiesner, 'Women's Defense of Their Public Role,' in *Women in the Middle Ages and Renaissance: Literary and Historical Perspectives*, ed. Mary Beth Rose (Syracuse, NY: Syracuse University Press, 1986), pp. 1–27.

14 In *Still Harping on Daughters: Women and Drama in the Age of Shakespeare* (1983; rpt New York: Columbia University Press, 1989), pp. 121–3, Lisa Jardine discusses numerous texts, among them *The Taming of the Shrew* and *Othello*, which bawdily deploy the common Renaissance tropes on the tongue as a women's 'weapon' and as her substitute penis. Cary's plays on female tongues as (illicitly) phallic should be read with reference to the ideologically charged semantic field in which female tongues operate in English Renaissance culture. See, for instance, Catherine Belsey's discussion of the play *Lingua* (1607), in which the heroine is imprisoned in a phallic tower and guarded by thirty watchmen 'to keep her from wagging abroad': *The Subject of Tragedy: Identity and Difference in Renaissance Drama* (London and New York: Methuen, 1985), p. 181.

15 Belsey, *The Subject of Tragedy*, p. 173. There is a fascinating nearly contemporary analogue for Cary's formulation – corroborating readings of either 'God' or 'oneself' for Cary's 'none but one' – in Lady Mary Wroth's *Pamphilia to Amphilanthus*(1621); Sonnet 36 of this sequence suggests that the woman writer-lover's testimony should be hid 'From all save only one': *The Poems of Lady Mary Wroth*, ed. Josephine A. Roberts (Baton Rouge, LA: Louisiana State University Press, 1983). I am indebted to Margreta de Grazia for this reference, discussed in the paper she wrote for the 1990 Shakespeare Association of America seminar on Renaissance

Women and entitled: 'The Body of Lady Mary Wroth's Writing in *Pamphilia to Amphilanthus*.'

16 Slowe, 'Speech Crimes in *The Tragedy of Mariam*,' p. 5; this is also a paper done for the 1990 Shakespeare Association of America seminar on Renaissance Women.

17 See Travitsky, 'Husband Murder and Petty Treason in English Renaissance Tragedy,' *Renaissance Drama*, n.s. 21(1990), 171–98.

18 The notion of a Christian subject's right to 'passive resistance' on the grounds of conscience has a long history but becomes a vexed political issue in the Reformation, as Quentin Skinner has shown: *The Foundations of Modern Political Thought*, vol. 2 (Cambridge: Cambridge University Press, 1978), pp. 12–19, and as Constance Jordan remarks, citing Skinner, in *Renaissance Feminism: Literary Texts and Political Models* (Ithaca, NY: Cornell University Press, 1990), p. 24, note 25. See her discussion of the common analogy between 'the political status of the woman vis à vis the male head of the family and of the subject vis à vis the magistrate' (pp. 23–4) and her more detailed discussion of 'exceptions' to the rule of wifely obedience allowed in some Protestant treatises on marriage (pp. 214–20).

19 Valuable exceptions to this generalization are Sandra K. Fischer's essay on Cary in *Silent But for the Word* (cited in note 3) and Marta Straznicky's paper on Cary in the context of the English Catholic community, 'Rewriting the Source: The Work of Elizabeth Cary and Authoritative Female discourse in the Renaissance,' a paper circulated for the 1990 Shakespeare Association of America seminar on Renaissance Women.

20 The quoted passage, from Henry Garnet, *Treatise on Christian Renunciation*, is cited in Marie Bowlands, 'Recusant Women 1560–1640,' in *Women in English Society 1500–1800*, ed. Mary Prior (London and New York: Methuen, 1985), p. 165. For useful general discussions of the key role of Catholic wives of both Protestant and recusant landowners in maintaining 'a subversive, underground religion' (Straznicky, p. 4), see also John Bossy, *The English Catholic Community 1570–1850* (London: Darton, Longman and Todd, 1975), ch. 7 and Retha M. Warnicke, *Women of the English Renaissance and Reformation* (Westport, CT: Greenwood Press, 1983), pp. 164–85.

21 Compare Mariam's assertion of spiritual freedom with the statement by the Lady in Milton's *A Masque* (1637): 'Thou canst not touch the freedom of my mind/ With all thy charms, although this corporal rind/ Thou hast immanacl'd, while Heav'n sees good'; quoted from John Milton, *The Complete Shorter Poems*, ed. John Cary (London: Longman, 1971), p. 209; and see also the similar proclamation by the heroine of the anonymous play of 1620, *Swetnam the Woman Hater Arraigned by Women*, 2.1.97, in '*Swetnam the Woman Hater': The Controversy and the Play*, ed. Coryl Crandall (Lafayette, IN: Purdue University Press, 1969), p. 73.

22 See Beilin, 'Elizabeth Cary,' pp. 58–60 and also Sandra K. Fischer, 'Elizabeth Cary and Tyranny,' esp. 235–7.

23 I am grateful to Peter Rudnytsky for helping me trace allusions to Henry VIII in Cary's text. The evidence suggests that many English Catholics criticized Henry VIII by figuring him as a type of Herod-the-tyrant, a composite character which, like his morality play predecessor, often conflated the identities of three different biblical Herods – Herod the Great, slaughterer of the innocents; Herod Antipas, who judged Christ and ordered John the Baptist's death; and Herod Agrippa. I'm indebted for this information to Rebecca W. Bushnell's fine summary of scholarship on the medieval Herod figure, and her analyses of various humanist Herod plays, in *Tragedies of Tyrants: Political Thought and Theater in the English Renaissance* (Ithaca, NY: Cornell University Press, 1990), ch. 3.

For a fuller discussion of the complex topical allegory in *Mariam*, and of the play's parallels to George Buchanon's drama *Baptistes, sive Calumnia* (1577), see the Introduction to *The Tragedy of Mariam*, ed. Weller and Ferguson, pp. 30–5.

8

RESISTING TYRANTS

Elizabeth Cary's tragedy

Barbara Kiefer Lewalski

Barbara Kiefer Lewalski' s piece on Elizabeth Cary's *The Tragedy of Mariam* is extracted from her book, *Writing Women in Jacobean England* (1993), which is the first full-length critique of women writers at the beginning of the seventeenth century. Clearly, as the first English woman to write a dramatic tragedy, Elizabeth Cary is central to Lewalski's overall analysis, and the essay highlights in particular Cary's revolutionary treatment of marriage and of free speech for women. In addition, Lewalski's work demonstrates a development in the criticism on women writers of this period in that, since the value of the play is no longer in question, the essay is able to explore more contentious and unresolvable issues in Cary's writing.

Elizabeth (Tanfield) Cary, Viscountess Falkland (1585–1639), was the first Englishwoman to write a tragedy, the Senecan *Tragedie of Mariam* (1613).[1] She was also the first Englishwoman to write a full-scale history, the Tacitean *History of the Life, Reign, and Death of Edward II* (*c.*1627–8).[2] Those works engage issues important in her own life and also in the Jacobean state: the claims of conscience, the analogy of domestic and state tyranny, the powers of kings and husbands, the rights and duties of subjects and wives, the justifications for resistance to tyrants, the role of counselors and favorites, and, most interesting, the possibility and power of nonviolent or passive resistance. Some critics find *Mariam* distressingly (or at its cultural moment necessarily) contradictory, especially in regard to the issue of women's silence; others interpret it from the chorus's vantage point, as denying to wives and subjects any right of resistance (even internal) to their lords.[3] But though the work's contradictions reflect gender anxieties, they find close parallels in contemporary Senecan dramas and histories written in the Tacitean mode – genres often perceived as dangerous by Elizabethan and Jacobean censors precisely because they allow for the clash of ideological positions and for the sympathetic representation of resistance and rebellion. Cary, like Samuel Daniel and Fulke Greville, chose genres and took over generic strategies which allowed her to explore dangerous political issues, focused in her case by the situation of queen-wives subjected at once to domestic and state tyranny.

Most of Cary's other writing does not, apparently, survive. We have her childhood translation of Abraham Ortelius' *Mirroir du Monde*.[4] Also, there is a late epitaph on Buckingham (*c.*1628), and a translation of Cardinal Perron's *Reply* to King James, published at Douay in

1630.[5] Apparently lost, however, are other works mentioned in an anonymous *Life* written by one of her daughters:[6] early translations of Seneca's epistles; a verse 'Life of Tamurlane' (said to be her best early work); a manual of moral precepts for her children written during a life-threatening illness; several hymns and poems to the Virgin; saints' lives in verse (Mary Magdalene, Agnes the Martyr, and Elizabeth of Portugal); translations of all the works of Cardinal Perron (intended as a help for Oxford scholars who knew no French); and translations of other French divines, including the Flemish Benedictine monk Louis de Blois (*Life*, pp. 9, 13, 39, 109). The memoir also mentions an essay 'which was thought the best thing she ever penned'; answering a Protestant controversial tract by her son Lucius (*Life*, p. 114).[7] The most serious loss is another tragedy that both she and her tutor, John Davies of Hereford, refer to as predating *Mariam*; it was apparently set in Sicily and dedicated to her husband.[8]

Cary's tragedy and history may be usefully contextualized with reference to the circumstances of her own life. A major factor was the clash of authorities claiming her obedience, which led her to develop a strong if conflicted sense of self. Throughout her life, parents, family, husband, and the English Church and court establishment urged their various demands, to which Elizabeth opposed her own needs – a powerful attraction to learning and to Roman Catholicism, the latter culminating in her formal conversion in 1626. Constructing Elizabeth Cary's life is complicated by the fact that the major source, a memoir by her daughter written about 1655, is conceived as hagiography and exemplary biography – a providential narrative of conversion, patient endurance of persecution by family and society, and final triumph over oppressors. That unsigned work was probably but not certainly written by her eldest living daughter, Anne, who became a Benedictine nun, Dame Clementina.[9] It was revised by her son Patrick, who, the nineteenth-century editor notes in his preface, 'erased several passages which he considered too feminine, and added a few notes and sentences of his own.' We have to allow for the author's strong sympathy for her mother, for the revising son's interest in deleting or modifying what seemed to him indecorous, for the probable exaggeration of Cary's accomplishments and religious virtues, for the fact that Cary herself must have been the sole source of information about her early life, for the fitting of fact to the hagiographic paradigm, and for the general unreliability of family gossip and anecdote. Fortunately, other contemporary records can supplement and counterbalance this memoir.[10] Read critically, the biography often registers Cary's sense of her own life, albeit through a distorting filter. It also reveals, as Elaine Beilin notes, Cary's reputation as a deviant or disorderly woman, refusing her assigned role and mounting strong resistance to patriarchal control.[11]

All her life Cary seems to have been caught up in conflict between social and ideological pressures to conform and submit and an inner imperative to resist and challenge authority. Her father, Sir Lawrence Tanfield, was an able and highly successful lawyer, judge, and (after 1607) Chief Baron of the Exchequer; her mother, Elizabeth Symondes, was descended from country gentry and may have felt that her marriage to a lawyer involved a descent in the social scale.[12] In their county seat, Burford in Oxfordshire, both were greatly resented for harshness and arrogance, for revoking rights guaranteed to the town under its charter, and later for bribe taking.[13] A precocious only child, Elizabeth Cary grew up at Burford Priory, Oxfordshire (and later Great Tew), reading omnivorously, learning languages, translating, and writing verses. The *Life* underscores her filial reverence – she always addressed the mother 'who was never kind to her' on her knees (*Life*, pp. 21–3) – but it also reveals her independence and resistance to parental authority in intellectual matters. She learned to read very young and often read all night, bribing the servants to supply the candles her mother refused; and at age 12, upon receiving a copy of Calvin's *Institutes* from her father, she regaled him with arguments about the work's inconsistencies (*Life*, p. 7).[14] Stories about her early language learning (obviously originating with her) portray her as an autodidact and proud of it. She reportedly resisted early tuition in French but soon learned it on her own, as well as Spanish, Italian 'very perfectly,' and Latin; she also learned Hebrew 'with very little teaching' and Transylvanian from some native speaker, but forgot this last and also some of her Latin and Hebrew from lack of use (*Life*, pp. 4–5). Despite the disclaimers, she may have had some language tuition from John Davies of Hereford, who refers to her as his 'Pupill.'[15]

In 1602 she married Sir Henry Cary. As Nancy Cotton Pearse observes, the union 'raised Tanfield from the upper middle class into the gentry, and the Tanfield fortune raised Henry Cary from the gentry into the peerage.'[16] Elizabeth was 17 and Henry about 26. The *Life* states bluntly that he married her 'only for being an heir, for he had no acquaintance with her (she scarce even having spoken to him) and she was nothing handsome, though then very fair.'[17] Henry Cary studied at Gray's Inn and Oxford, was knighted by Essex at Dublin Castle in 1599, and went to fight in the Low Countries in 1603; he was captured by the Spanish at Ostend in 1605, and returned in 1606 after paying an exorbitant ransom that greatly damaged his estate.[18] While he was away Elizabeth lived first at home and then with her mother-in-law, Lady Katherine Cary, adopting a stance of solitary independence and quiet resistance to family expectations and authority. Her mother reportedly had her letters to Henry Cary ghost-written by others, leading him to think that the first genuine letters from her were forgeries (*Life*, pp. 8–9). Did she refuse to write? Or were her letters expected to display learning or sentiments Cary would find disturbing? Reportedly also her mother-in-law found her lacking in proper deference and used her 'very hardly,' confining her to her chamber and removing her books, at which point she began writing verses (*Life*, pp. 7–8).

At his return Henry Cary began his successful career as a courtier – Gentleman of the Bed Chamber and Master of the Jewel House, then Knight of the Bath (1608), Comptroller of the Household and Privy Councillor (1618), Viscount Falkland in the Scottish peerage (1620), and Lord Deputy of Ireland (1622). The *Life* portrays Elizabeth as struggling continually to conform her own inclinations and 'strong will' to that of her 'very absolute' husband (p. 14): she learned to ride though she feared horses; she took 'care of her house in all things'; she came to live at court when Cary became Comptroller (p. 19); she dressed well though she found it a 'torture' (allowing others to tend her 'while she writ or read'). She bore eleven children between 1609 and 1624, nursed them all except for Lucius (who was brought up from infancy with his grandfather Tanfield), and took great care of their education, especially in moral and religious matters (pp. 11–12). The observation that she was constantly 'either with child or giving suck' is crossed through in the manuscript, presumably by Patrick.[19] Reportedly, she taught her children to love their father more than herself, and they did so (p. 14).

Yet the *Life* also testifies to an ongoing process of self-definition. Elizabeth read very widely – especially history, poetry, moral philosophy, and the Church Fathers:

> She had read very exceeding much; poetry of all kinds, ancient and modern, in several languages, all that ever she could meet with; history very universally, especially ancient Greek and Roman historians; all chroniclers whatsoever of her own country, and the French histories very thoroughly; of most other countries some-

> thing, though not so universally; of the ecclesiastical history very much, most especially concerning its chief Pastors. Of books treating of moral virtue or wisdom, (such as Seneca, Plutarch's Morals, and natural knowledge, as Pliny, and of late one such as French, Mountaine, and English, Bacon), she had read very many when she was young, not without making her profit of them all. Of the fathers she had read much, particularly the works of St. Justin Martyr, St. Jerome, very much of St. Augustine and of St. Gregory.
>
> (*Life*, p. 113)

She also read 'most that has been written' in religious controversy – Luther and Calvin, Latimer, Jewel, and 'all English writers of name,' especially Thomas More. She continued writing verses 'for her private recreation, on several subjects' (*Life*, p. 9). She also continued her Rome-ward journey, rejecting Hooker's defense of the English church in his *Ecclesiastical Polity* and disputing with various learned clerics.[20] And she began to play a role at court, associating herself with a coterie of Romanizing ladies: Katherine Manners (the future Duchess of Buckingham), the Countess of Arundel, and the Countess of Derby.

Recognition of Cary's intellectual and literary gifts came early, from several would-be clients. Drayton dedicated a pair of poems in his *Englands Heroicall Epistles* (1597) to the very young Elizabeth Tanfield, proclaiming her a fourth Grace and a tenth Muse, adorned by nature and education with 'many rare perfections,' among them her excellent French and Italian, and her precocious 'judgment and reading.'[21] Her one-time tutor Davies of Hereford associates her with Mary, Dowager Countess of Pembroke, and Lucy, Countess of Bedford, as dedicatees of *The Muses Sacrifice* (1612); he proclaims them the three Graces, 'as well Darlings as Patronesses of the Muses' and rulers 'of ARTS whole Monarchie, and WITS Empire.'[22] He describes Elizabeth Cary as a writer of tragedies (one set in Sicily, one in Palestine), as a famous linguist knowledgeable in abstruse tongues (Hebrew is hinted), and as a poet who far surpasses her sex in wit and art:

> CARY (of whom Minerva stands in feare,
> lest she, from her, should get ARTS Regencie)
> Of ART so moves the great-all-moving Spheare,
> that ev'ry Orbe of Science moves thereby.
>
> Thou mak'st Melpomen proud, and my Heart great
> Of such a Pupill, who, in Buskin fine,
> With Feet of State, dost make thy Muse to mete
> the Scenes of Syracuse and Palastine.
>
> Art, Language; yea, abstruse and holy Tones,
> thy Wit and Grace acquir'd thy Fame to raise;
> And still to fill thine owne, and others Songs;
> thine, with thy Parts, and others, with thy praise.
>
> Such nervy Limbes of Art, and Straines of Wit
> Times past ne'er knew the weaker Sexe to have;
> And Times to come, will hardly credit it,
> if thus thou give thy Workes both Birth and Grave.

Davies's tribute, and his comment that these three ladies have regrettably though understandably withheld most of their fine poetry from the debased press,[23] may have prompted Cary to publish *Mariam* shortly thereafter. In the wake of that publication the bookseller Richard More dedicated his new edition of *Englands Helicon* to her as 'Englands happy Muse, / Learnings delight.'[24]

An inner conflict between domestic subservience and intellectual independence offers itself readily enough as an explanation for her periods of depression, manifested in long spells of sleeping and even, during two pregnancies, loss of 'the perfect use of her reason' (*Life*, p. 16). Such conflicts would only be intensified by her reported conviction that innocence of conscience ought always to be manifested in external behavior – avoiding 'all that might have the least show or suspicion of uncomeliness or unfitness' (*Life*, p. 16). The *Life* interprets the motto she had engraved on her daughter's wedding ring, 'Be and Seem,' as a demand for decorous behavior, but it points rather to a higher ideal, relevant both to Cary's drama and to her own life choices: personal integrity. She reportedly advised that daughter, Catherine, married at age 13 to Lord Home, that 'whersoever conscience and reason would permit her, she should prefer the will of another to her own' (*Life*, p. 13). But this apparent proposal of abject wifely submission in fact makes the wife's reason and conscience absolute judge in all cases.

In 1622 Falkland prevailed upon his wife to mortgage her jointure properties to help raise the large sums he needed to take up his appointment in Ireland as Lord Deputy. That imprudence so incensed Tanfield that he disinherited his daughter and left his fortune and estates (Burford and Great Tew) to his grandson Lucius (*Life*, pp. 15–16). Falkland's harshly repressive policies toward the Catholics in Ireland, together with his bigotry, vacillation, political obtuseness, and financial folly, no doubt distressed his wife and certainly irritated the Privy Council. His 1623 and 1624 proclamations banishing Jesuits and other priests made trouble during the negotiations for Prince Charles's Spanish marriage; and his mismanagement, quarrels with the Irish nobles, and illegal seizure of lands led to his recall in 1629.[25]

Elizabeth Cary took her own direction in Ireland. She learned to read Gaelic from a Bible, and she started up ambitious trade school-cum-factories to train Irish children ('more than eight score prentices') in the cloth trades (*Life*, pp. 18–19). That project collapsed after two years, owing in part to her credulity and financial ineptitude but chiefly to a disastrous fire and flood.[26] She also took on the role of literary patron: Richard Belling dedicated his *Sixth Booke to the Countesse of Pembrokes Arcadia* to her with thanks for her favors and encouragement.[27]

During Falkland's tenure in Ireland the marriage foundered. In 1625 he sent Elizabeth to England to be relieved of her uncomfortable presence, embarrassing Romanizing sympathies, and expensive projects. At first he seems also to have hoped she could help him at court by answering his critics. But from the outset his letters disparage his wife and women generally, expressing a barely concealed desire to be rid of her and at the same time to control her actions. His notion was that she and the children accompanying her (the three youngest) should stay with and be supported by her mother at Burford Priory while he was in Ireland; the eldest unmarried daughter, Anne, was at court, a maid of honor to Queen Henrietta Maria, and the rest were with him. Writing to the Secretary of State Sir Edward Conway in January 1626, Falkland takes ungracious note of his wife's efforts on his behalf:

> By all my wives letters I understand . . . that she beginns to conceive hir selfe some able body in courte, by your countenance to doe me courtesies, if she had the wit as

> she hath the wyll. She makes it appeare she hath donn me sum good offices . . . I must thanke hir much for hir carefull paynes in it though it was but an act of duty in hir, to see me righted when she knew me wronged . . . I beseech your Lordship still to continue that favour to us boath . . . giving hir good counsell and good countenance within a niew World and Courte, att such a Distance from hir husband, a poore weake woman stands in the greatest neede of: to despatch hir suits.[28]

On 5 April he disdainfully repudiates her apparently unproductive diplomacy, tries hard to silence her, and urges Conway to effect her return to her mother's house:

> For hir abilitys in agencye of affayres, as I was never taken with opinion of them, soe I was never desirous to imploy them if she had them, for I conceyve woemen to be noe fitt sollicitors of state affaires, for though it sometymes happen that they have good witts, it then commonly falls out that they have over-busye Natures withall: for my part I should take much more comefort to hear that she weare quiettly retyred to hir Mother's into the country, then that she had obtayned a greate suite in the courte . . . If your Lordship will trye your skyll to persuade hir with content to that retraite, I shalbe bound to you for yt . . . Yf not, I must have yt donn an other way.[29]

But Lady Tanfield flatly refused to take on such a charge for a daughter she had never understood or much liked.

When Elizabeth Cary openly professed Roman Catholicism in November 1626, she found herself isolated, attacked, cast off by husband and family, and in acute financial distress. Her daughter attributes her decision to an apparition of the Virgin Mary to her eldest daughter, Catherine, as she was dying in childbirth at age 17 (*Life*, p. 18). A more mundane impetus was the example of Queen Henrietta Maria and the recusant and crypto-Catholic ladies of her court. Roman Catholicism may have afforded these ladies some self-validation through the honors it accorded the Virgin and numerous female saints, and it certainly offered them a heady mix of danger, power, and importance.[30] Undercover priests courted them assiduously as a fifth column which could win back the nation for the true religion; and Laudian bishops such as Dr John Cosin of Durham worked as assiduously to retain them within an Anglo-Catholic community. Elizabeth Cary was urged, and at one point forcibly constrained, to delay her conversion by her good friend Lady Denby (Buckingham's sister), who was also dallying with Rome (*Life*, pp. 27–9).[31] Cary had evidently planned a covert profession, which could have been accommodated in that court without trouble. But when Lady Denby and Buckingham informed King Charles that she had been received into the Roman Church, he ordered a formal inquiry, which made the affair public and scandalous.[32]

The king had Cary confined to her rooms for six weeks while concerted efforts were made to reconvert her (*Life*, pp. 29–30). Falkland immediately stopped her allowance, had her children and all but one of the servants removed, and left her without coal, wine, food, or money to buy provisions, in an effort to starve her into submission; she survived on crusts of bread and tidbits brought by her servant, Bessie Poulter (*Life*, pp. 31–3). Falkland's letters to the king and court officials display the fury of a thwarted patriarch and Protestant zealot. He denounces his 'Apostate' wife and those in the queen's court who subverted her, decries the danger to himself 'to nourish that serpent in my bosom' (alluding injudiciously to the king's similar danger), and demands vehemently that she be sent home to her mother in Burford as the 'onely way for her recovery and Reclamation.'[33] The king so ordered, but the Duchess of Buckingham won a stay for Elizabeth by raising doubts as to whether her mother would receive her.[34] In furious response. Falkland denounced his wife's 'feminine wily pretences . . . assisted by feminine mediation' and refused any support to her until she followed his wishes. He demanded passionately that his orders for his wife be enforced, or else that he be given a legal separation, so as to avoid further dishonor and ruin:

> Surely her residency ought to be according to her husbands election and not her owne. Soe *our* religion teacheth, And if *hir* newe Profession teach contrary points of doctrine in that as abhominable as in other things, let me first obtaine an utter and absolute divorce, That I may be separated from all interest in hir person and wayes, soe that dishonour and confusion of face, with ruine of fortune may not thereby assayle me and overwhelme me; and I shalbe contented then to quitt my clayme of superioritye, and being made free, leave hir free.[35]

His letter of 5 July 1627, accuses her of contriving her mother's refusal with 'serpentyne subtelty . . . conjoined with Roman hypocrisy' so that she might stay with her popish friends, and insistently but implausibly denies any responsibility for the loss of her jointure and her father's inheritance. He also vents his outrage at the notoriety he expects to suffer 'over all the Christian world' owing to 'this defection of his wives and her violent contestation with him, against duty and the Lawe Matrimoniall.'[36]

Some collusion between mother and daughter is possible, given their common interest in preventing Elizabeth's return home. But, in sharp contrast to Anne Clifford's supportive mother, Lady Tanfield seems to have been only too sincere in her harsh denunciation of her daughter's ungodly, unfilial, and unwifely conduct:

> Bes— I parcayve by your last letors . . . that I shall never have hope to have any comfort from you . . . My desiers was . . . to have you to lyve with your husband, and to lyve in that relegeon wherin yow war bred . . . to me, he [Falkland] cannot comand you I will not exsept [accept] of you, and if by any exterordenary devise he cold compell you, you shall fynd the worst of it . . . For my part, you may lyve wher you ples. if in essexe, then shall you have som such pore stuf from London as I can spar, and if you shold live at Cote [Coates, a small family estate in Oxfordshire] ther is yet some stuf, that may sarve your turn . . . bes, all your resons are grounded out of your own will and your fauteses [faults] . . . Now I see with a hevey sowel an utter ruin and over throw of you all, though I shall leve to wryt to you or desiere to heere from you.[37]

Cary's formal conversion was a gesture of opposition and resistance, pitting her private conscience against the massed authority and pressure of family and society. Reduced to extreme want and acute misery, she no doubt found some models in the female saints and martyrs whose lives she versified, but she did not suffer in silence, as her daughter's memoir suggests (*Life*, p. 36). Rather, she kept up a barrage of forceful, sharply worded, and rhetorically effective letters and petitions to King Charles, Coke, Conway, and the Buckingham ladies, seeking to avoid being sent to her mother, and asking that Falkland be required to supply her with food, house rent, apparel, household staff, and a settled allowance. The substance and style of these letters display an assertive self claiming the rights of conscience and common humanity. Her petition to the king on 18 May (sent with a copy of her mother's repudiating letter) vigorously urges the dire consequences of the king's decree and the plausibility of her own plan. She shrewdly presses her legal and moral claims against Falkland without directly blaming him, and graphically portrays her deprivations and sufferings:

> Upon my lords goinge into Ireland, I was drawne, by seeinge his occasions, to offer my joynter into his handes, that he might sell, or morgage it, for his supply, which accordingly was done, and that beinge gone from mee, I have nothinge to trust to, hereafter, but my mothers bounty, at her death, for my father disinherited mee, onely, for resigninge my joynter . . . She vowes, if ever I come to hir, either willingly, or by comand . . . shee will never, neither in her life nor at her death, either give mee any thinge, or take any care for mee. Therefore I must humbly importune your majesty to call back a comand so prejudiciall to mee . . . I heard by a person of quality, that your majesty was pleased to beleeve that I altered my profession of religion upon some court hopes, but I beseech you, how wicked soever you may censure mee, to bee, (as it is no lesse, to make religion a ladder to clime by) yet judge me not so foolish, as to understand so little, the state of this time, as to think promotion, likely, to come that way . . . (If my lord woulde allow mee meanes competent, in any indifferent bodys judgement) I woulde take a little house, in essex, neere a sister of my lords, and a deere frend of mine, the lady Barrett . . . I desire nothynge but a quiet life, and to reobtaine my lords favour, which I have done nothynge to loose, but what I coulde not with a safe conscience, leave undone . . . I beseech your majesty, to comand one of your secretarys, to send for [my lord's] agent, and to comand him . . . [to] supply me weekely with [what is] . . . necessary to support mee for victualls, houserent, and apparell . . . Consider how pressant my wants are, that have not meanes, for one meale.[38]

Adjudicating the matter, a Privy Council commission determined that she should go to Coates (the house her mother agreed to lend her in Oxfordshire) and receive £500 a year from Falkland's estate; also, that her 'great want' should be supplied with 'immediate means.' Falkland, however, delayed payment, and Elizabeth remained in a little house outside London, in dire need and wholly dependent on the charity of friends and the queen (*Life*, pp. 37–8). On 27 August she wrote with wry irony to Conway (who had hesitated to enforce an order attaching Falkland's funds): 'None is lother to have my Lord Deputy, discontented, then I, but alas! where the question is, whither hee shoulde bee displeased, or I sterved, it will admit no dispute.'[39] In October 1627 the Privy Council commission handed down a formal order: Falkland was to provide her a suitable establishment and maintenance at Coates, including 'meat, drink, and all necessaries,' nine servants, furniture and horses 'to take the air,' clothing, and £100 a year for her private expenses, and also to pay her accrued debts of £272. Failing this, he was to pay her £500 a year.[40] Months later, however, the resistant Falkland still had not paid, and she had to keep up constant pressure.[41] In any event she did not go to Coates but stayed in and near London, close to her Catholic friends: in 1632 or thereabouts she was officially listed as a recusant in the county of Middlesex, lodging in Drury Lane.[42] Henrietta Maria seems to have effected some kind of reconciliation between Henry and Elizabeth in 1631, and in 1633 they were together for a few months at Falkland's country estate, Berkhamstead, in Hertfordshire. That year Falkland broke his leg in a fall from a horse, aggravated the wound when he dutifully rose to his feet in the presence of the king, had to have the leg amputated, and subsequently bled to death.[43]

As a widow, Elizabeth Cary was even more dramatically embroiled in struggles with family, civil, and religious authorities as she undertook to convert her many children and to find money to live on.[44] The eldest daughter, Catherine, had died in 1626 in childbirth. The two eldest sons often stayed with her while at Oxford, but they eluded her proselytizing efforts, carried on through dinnertime discussions with priests and other Catholics and through formal religious disputations (*Life*, pp. 52–56). Lucius, the Falkland and Tanfield heir celebrated by Jonson and Clarendon as the embodiment of Cavalier virtues, came under the influence of the erstwhile Catholic-turned-rationalist William Chillingworth, who had disguised his defection from Rome while a tutor in Cary's household.[45] Lorenzo left England in 1634 to take up a military commission in Ireland. By that date the elder daughters, Anne and Elizabeth, were known Catholics: Archbishop Laud complained to King Charles of the 'practice of the Ladye their Mother,' who had failed to send them as directed to live with Lucius at Great Tew; and he proposed to call her before the High Commission.[46] Lucius took the younger children to Tew and, when his mother dismissed the deceiving Chillingworth, brought him there as tutor for Patrick and Henry (*Life*, p. 83).[47] This prompted Elizabeth Cary to mount a daring rescue in 1636 with the connivance of her daughters Mary and Lucy; they spirited the boys away at night, by coach and ship, to be educated in France by the Benedictines.[48] The report of a Privy Council inquiry portrays Elizabeth adopting a shrewd posture of vagueness about the whole affair:

> She saith, that shee did knowe of their cominge awaye from the Lorde Faulklande their brother, and shee did appointe horses to bee sente to them for that purpose, they both havinge beene verie desirous to bee sente for awaye: but shee doth not knowe where they are now, but doth assuredlie beleeve they are well and in saefeteye, for shee hath hearde soe much. Beeinge further demanded whether they are now about London or in Englande, or sente beyonde the seas, shee saith shee knoweth not where they are, nor whether they be in Englande or out of Englande.[49]

Infuriated by these 'uncertaine and illusorie Answers,' the Council of the Star Chamber took order for her continued questioning 'to answer the charge against her for sending over into forraigne parts twoe of her Sonnes, without Lycence, to be educated there . . . in the Romish Religion,' and provided that 'in case she shall in her answer use the like subterfuge & evasion as heretofore . . . she is to stand Committed prisoner to the Tower.'[50] They let the matter drop, however, apparently recognizing the *fait accompli*. The boys became Benedictine monks, though both at length returned to England and renounced Catholicism. Four of Cary's daughters – Anne, Elizabeth, Lucy, and Mary – became and remained nuns in the Benedictine convent of Cambray. The fifth, Victoria, married Sir William Uvedale in Wickham in 1640.[51] Commenting on Lucius's heritage from Elizabeth, the historian Clarendon paid reluctant tribute to her 'most masculine understanding,' though allied as he saw it with the 'passion and infirmities of her own sex.'[52] She died in October 1639 at the age of 54, needy to the last.[53]

Cary's tragedy *Mariam* explored the issue of domestic tyranny long before Cary herself felt the full force of such tyranny as a result of her conversion. Nonetheless, Falkland's arbitrary nature and low opinion of women make it likely that she experienced often enough the married woman's vulnerability to abuses of power. One terminus for the drama's composition is 1602, the publication date for her principal source, Thomas Lodge's translation of Josephus.[54] The other is suggested but not proved by the dedication to her 'worthy Sister, Mistris Elizabeth Carye' – evidently Elizabeth Bland Cary, wife of her husband's brother, Philip, who could not properly have been addressed as 'Mistris' after 1605, when her husband was knighted.[55] References in that dedicatory verse epistle to Henry's absence (like Phoebus' nocturnal sojourn in the Antipodes) point to the period of his military adventures and imprisonment (1602–6). *Mariam* was probably written toward the end of that period, since Elizabeth also claims authorship of an earlier drama set in Sicily and dedicated to her husband.[56] She could of course have revised or even rewritten the drama extensively after Davies's 1612 poem urged its publication. An anecdote in the *Life* about a work pirated from the chamber of her sister-in-law and then published is recognizably a version of the common aristocratic excuse for stooping to publication, but (along with the dedication) it may suggest some collaboration between the two women in having the drama published. The daughter's statement that Cary recalled this pirated work from the press may refer, as Beilin suggests, to the dedicatory poem, which was in fact removed from most copies of the drama.[57]

Cary is not likely to have encountered, and does not seem to be indebted to, earlier Herod and Mariam plays.[58] Rather, her tragedy finds its place in the line of French Senecan tragedies inaugurated in England by the Countess of Pembroke's translation of Robert Garnier's *Marc-Antoine*.[59] In addition to this influential precedent by an aristocratic woman, the closest analogues for *Mariam* are other tragedies written by members of the countess's circle: Samuel Daniel's *Cleopatra* and *Philotas*, and Fulke Greville's *Mustapha*.[60] These classicizing dramas stand apart from the popular stage drama of the period, and also eschew the trappings of Italianate Senecanism – ghosts, stage violence, horrors and atrocities, vendettas, gruesome effects, marvels.[61] But they are not mere academic exercises, as is evident from their authors' fears and the censors' inquiries. Rather, they were a recognized vehicle for the exploration of dangerous political topics – the wickedness of tyranny, the dangers of absolutism, the modes of and justifications for resistance, the folly of princes, the corruption of royal favorites, the responsibilities of counselors.[62] Though these topics pervade English tragedy of the late Elizabethan and Jacobean periods, they received elaborate intellectual analysis in French Senecan drama, as did conflicting theories of monarchy, tyranny, and rebellion. Several generic features promoted such analysis: the primacy of speech over action; long rhetorical monologues; the prominence of women as heroines and villains; and a chorus which speaks from a limited rather than an authorized vantage point. These dramas often make a strong case for aristocrats and magistrates who resist tyranny on the ground of their own rights and responsibilities to the state, recalling positions developed by Calvin, the Jesuit Robert Parsons, and the *Vindiciae Contra Tyrannos*, among others.[63] The dramas do not overtly sanction or encourage rebellion; their perceived danger resides in the complexity and ambiguity with which issues of tyranny and rebellion are treated. We do not know whether Cary read any or all of them in manuscript or print before publishing *Mariam*, but her interests, her reading habits, and her tutor Davies's connections make that plausible.

The Garnier-Countess of Pembroke *Antonie* (1592) shows Antony and Cleopatra and their confidants analyzing issues of fate and guilt, shameful life versus suicide, in the wake of the Actium debacle. The political issue, explored in multiple perspectives, is Caesar's absolutism, given free rein by Antony's defeat. In a debate on the sources of the absolute ruler's strength and resemblance to God, Agrippa locates it in mercy and the people's love, Augustus in severity and the people's fear. A chorus of Roman soldiers finds hope of peace but also intimations of danger in Augustus' absolute rule, while an Egyptian chorus sees that it portends Egypt's slavery to Rome, prepared for by Cleopatra's (and Egypt's) weakness, folly, and licentiousness.

Daniel offered his *Cleopatra* as a companion piece to the countess's *Antonie*, focusing on Cleopatra after Antony's death. In the first (Elizabethan) version (1594) Cleopatra is an aging, weak, indecisive, and passive woman, evoking pity but little admiration – a 'sweet distressed Lady' in the words of her Roman admirer Dolabella, but in the view of the Egyptian chorus a licentious, pleasure-seeking queen who has infected Egypt with vice and servility. Augustus' tyranny is explored, but at some remove: through a pathetic report of the murder he ordered of the boy Cesario (Cleopatra's son by Julius Caesar); and through a debate by Augustus' counselors setting the inhumanity of killing an innocent against the necessities of the state. In the much-revised Jacobean version (1607) – with Essex's rebellion and execution, Ralegh's imprisonment, and James's absolutist claims in the background – the critique of tyranny is much more forceful. Cesario, now a speaking character, takes on himself the duty to return someday to rule Egypt, and just before his murder portrays himself in pathetic and powerful terms as an innocent sacrificed to Augustus' desire for sole power. Cleopatra is now forceful and resolute, her fault not licentiousness but pride. Her dramatized death scene displays her 'great mind' withstanding a barrage of arguments to save herself and staging her death as a triumph over tyranny: 'Witnes my soule parts free to Antony, / And thou prowd tyrant Caesar doe thy Worst' (V.ii).

Between these two versions came Daniel's *Philotas*, staged at Blackfrairs and published in 1605, with a dedication to Prince Henry urging the analogy of past times to present.[64] It brought Daniel before the Star Chamber to answer charges that the work alludes to the Essex affair, shadowing Cecil as the vindictive and manipulative Craterus. His defense was a claim that much of the drama predated the rebellion and that its themes of ambition and envy are universal.[65] The drama invites sympathy for Philotas, an attractive, valiant, bountiful young general beloved by the people and presumably loyal to Alexander, but imprudent in scorning the king's powerful counselors and in openly disputing Alexander's claims to divine descent and powers. Craterus, suborning witnesses by terror and playing on the king's fears, has Philotas falsely accused of treasonous plots and horribly tortured. He maintains his innocence long and stoically, seeming to speak for the rights of Englishmen at risk from monarchical absolutism, Star Chamber courts, and exaggerated claims of divine right.[66] At length he confesses to conspiring to overthrow Alexander, but the Nuntius who reports the scene questions whether that confession was simply the product of torture. The chorus of three Greeks and one Persian debate their forms of government, the Persian plausibly terming them both tyrannies, since Grecian laws are merely a stalking horse for the monarch to do what he will. Daniel affixed an 'Argument' and an 'Apology' to the published work, as a sop to the censors with Essex and Cecil on their minds; they are patently at odds with the drama's general tenor, and thereby underscore the interpretive openness and danger of these Senecan dramas. In a transparent gesture to Cecil, the 'Apology' declares that Philotas' guilt was 'providentially discerned' by Craterus, 'one of the most honest men that ever followed Alexander,' who thereby prevented the 'imbroyling' of the state, or its transformation into 'a monstrous body with many heads.'[67]

Fulke Greville's *Mustapha* is an even more complex exploration of responses to tyranny.[68] An Elizabethan version written in the mid-1590s highlights the dangers of factions warring over the succession; the Jacobean versions (a 1609 truncated edition, and another written around 1607–10) highlight the monarch's tyrannical suspicions of his subjects, the danger of rule by favorites, and the destruction of the state caused by political evils – a not so covert warning, as Ronald Rebholz notes, of incipient tyranny in England.[69] In all the versions Mustapha is the worthy, honorable, and universally beloved son of the aging Soliman the Magnificent, who envies his popularity (as James envied Prince Henry) and fears him as a possible usurper. Soliman's second wife, Rossa, is a type of the ambitious courtier who manipulates and dominates the monarch, at length persuading him that security and public order require Mustapha's death, on the mere suspicion of treason. Other positions represented include a chorus of Bashas, court sycophants who promote tyranny by flattering kings, subverting laws, and undermining people's rights; Camena, daughter to Rossa and Soliman, who argues for and acts upon the higher claims of reason and natural law and for that is executed by her own mother; a chorus of priests, who argue various theological positions (humble obedience to tyrants, self-preservation as a mandate of divine law, and even the use of force against oppressive tyrants); and a chorus of Tartars, who speak for nature and reason against theological mystification. The hero, Mustapha, speaks for and enacts absolute obedience to kings – 'Our gods they are, their God remaines above. / To thinke against annoynted Power is death' (IV.iv) – but his portrayal as a Christ-like martyr positions this response to tyranny above nature.

Achmat, the good counselor, is in some degree normative: he recognizes a duty to his Prince's honor rather than his humors, and also a higher duty – 'I first am Natures subject, then my Princes / . . . My God is not the God of subtill murther' (II.i). He first thinks to support the popular uprising provoked by Mustapha's death, as justified by the people's 'old equalities of Nature' and the establishment of kings 'for the good of all'; but at length he determines to quell it on the pragmatic ground that the state's 'prosperity' is better preserved by tyranny than anarchy, which destroys all order, power, and right (V.iii). Yet his decision and justification are put in question since they leave Rossa in absolute control, promising to rule with unfettered cruelty. At the end, the famous 'Chorus Sacerdotum' descants on humankind's bondage to the contradictory laws of nature and religion, with the latter itself contradicted by conscience: 'Yet, when each of us, in his owne heart lookes, / He findes the God there, farre unlike his bookes.'

In Cary's *Mariam* political and domestic tyranny are fused in Herod the Great, a ruthless Idumaean usurper of Israel's throne; his name also evokes the various biblical Herods associated with the Massacre of the Innocents, the trial of Jesus, and the martyrdoms of John the Baptist and various apostles.[70] Issues of obedience and resistance in both the state and the family are explored with the genre's typical complexity and ambiguity. The drama is conspicuously well made: the first half (to the turning point at Act III, scene ii) presents the gains in liberty, happiness, and moral good brought about by the presumed death of the tyrant; the last half portrays the manifold evils unleashed at his return. Observing the unity of time, Cary condenses events and incorporates materials from other parts of the Herod story to heighten the dramatic tension around Herod's supposed death and return, and also to provide apt foils for and conflicting perspectives on Mariam.

Early soliloquies and dialogues bring the pressure of antecedent events to bear on present action. With the aid of Rome, Herod has supplanted Hircanus, the hereditary king and priest in Israel, divorced his Idumaean first wife, Doris, disinherited their son Antipater, and married Hircanus' granddaughter, the singularly beautiful Mariam, whom he loves with fierce intensity and jealous passion. To secure his throne – to which his only legitimate claim comes through Mariam's line – he had old Hircanus murdered, and arranged a drowning accident to remove the new high priest, Mariam's brother Aristabolus. Called to Rome to answer murder charges leveled by Alexandra (mother to Mariam and Aristabolus and daughter to Hircanus), he left orders with his sister Salome's husband, Josephus, to kill Mariam in the event of his death so no other man could possess her. Reinstated as king, he had Josephus killed for telling Mariam about the decree for her death, taking that as evidence supporting Salome's false charge that they were lovers. Just before the play begins, Herod is again called to Rome and is in grave danger of death as a partisan of the defeated and recently deceased Antony; he leaves another order for Mariam's death with his officer Sohemus, who again reveals it to her.

Cary's drama opens with reports of the tyrant's death, which produce general relief, liberation, and a sense of new beginnings. Mariam is torn between grief and joy – grief for the ardent husband she once loved, joy that the tyrant who murdered her kin, imprisoned her out of jealousy, and twice decreed her death will not return. Her mother, Alexandra, rejoices in the death of the usurper – '*Esaus* Issue, heyre of hell' – who killed her father and son (I.ii). Mariam's son ascends the throne, and in his minority Mariam and Alexandra wield power. Herod's brother Pheroras, forced by Herod to agree to a dynastic marriage with his infant niece, rejoices that he may now marry his beloved but lowborn Graphina: 'This blessed houre, till now implored in vaine, / Which hath my wished libertie restor'd, / And made my subject selfe my owne againe' (II, i). Salome's second husband, Constabarus, has for twelve years at great personal peril concealed the two sons of Babus (who were under decree of death from Herod as kin of Hircanus); now neither he nor they are any longer at risk, and they joyfully embrace their liberty, planning to serve the state with merit and valor.[71] Sohemus no longer need fear the tyrant's wrath for disobeying and revealing his order to kill Mariam. Even those who regret Herod's death inadvertently benefit from it. Salome had planned to provoke Herod to execute Constabarus by telling him about Babus' sons, but now she intends to clear her way to a new marriage by divorcing her husband – a scandalously illegal act for a woman in Israel but hardly as wicked as murder. And Herod's rejected wife, Doris, will no longer be able to indulge her groundless hopes that Herod might return to her or at least make Antipater his heir – so she will likely give over her murderous plots to forward that cause.

At Herod's return (IV, i) all the hopeful new beginnings, launched under female rule, are crushed. Pheroras, suborned by Salome with a promise to help preserve his marriage to Graphina, reveals the story of Constabarus and Babus' sons – and they are all led off to death. Sohemus is executed for presumed adultery with Mariam and the revelation of Herod's decree. Mariam refuses Herod's sexual advances and berates him for decreeing her death and killing her kin, reinforcing his jealous conviction that she has been unfaithful with Sohemus. Salome bribes Mariam's servant to offer (as if from Mariam) a cup of poison to Herod, after which the servant hangs himself in remorse for his treachery. Salome extorts a decree for the death of Mariam from the desperate, vacillating Herod. Mariam's mother, Alexandra, denounces her daughter, en route to execution, for wronging 'noble Herod' – a blatantly hypocritical and in the event fruitless effort to placate him. A messenger recounts the details of Mariam's noble death, and Herod runs mad with grief and remorse, persuaded at last of her innocence and inestimable worth.

In the political realm Salome plays the role of evil courtier and counselor, encouraging the tyrant's passions and wickedness so as to advance her own interests and desires. The power of tyranny to corrupt is made manifest in the treachery of Pheroras and Mariam's servant, and in Alexandra's hypocrisy. Gestures of political resistance are limited: Alexandra's initial denunciation of Herod's crimes to Rome; Constabarus' valiant efforts to save Babus' sons; the principled disobedience of the 'good counselor' Sohemus. At the end of Act II the Chorus points out the 'weake uncertaine ground' for the report of Herod's death, so eagerly believed by most because it sorts with their desires. The Chorus's stated moral warns against self-deception and credulity, but the inference may be drawn that wishes and chance are hardly enough to destroy a tyrant.

Like the other English Senecan dramas, Cary's *Mariam* intertwines the spheres of public life and private desire, but here issues of love and domestic tyranny are central. Mariam's tragic choice – to reject Herod's love and bed as a gesture of conscientious resistance and personal integrity – is read from a number of perspectives, as the dramatic structure sets Mariam against several foils. First there is Graphina, whose true love for Pheroras reprises Mariam's earlier love for Herod, while her silence and humility seem to embody stereotypical feminine ideals.[72] Those ideals are problematized, however, by the class disparity between Graphina and Mariam: they suit with Graphina's lowly station, whereas the highborn Mariam (whose family are the legitimate kings and priests of Israel) has some right to exhibit family pride and self-regard. The Graphina–Pheroras love match evokes sympathy, but we also know that because of it Pheroras betrays Constabarus and Babus' sons. Another foil is Mariam's mother, Alexandra, whose single-minded hatred of Herod contrasts with the complexity of Mariam's feelings, even as her later hypocrisy in disguising that hatred contrasts with Mariam's integrity. There is also Doris, Herod's divorced wife, who responds to her marital wrongs in a manner very different from Mariam – by cursing her rival's children and devising poison plots against them.

Salome is the chief foil. She repeatedly and maliciously slanders the innocent Mariam for marital infidelity while she herself flaunts her illicit affairs and has two husbands killed when she is ready to replace them. Thoroughly wicked, she will do anything to compass her own will: 'I meane not to be led by president, / My will shall be to me in stead of Law' (I.vi). Most readers of the age would share Constabarus' view that his wife's 'private conference' with her new lover Silleus is shameful, and that her proposal to divorce her husband is shocking – a gender confusion that threatens order in nature and society:

> Are Hebrew women now transform'd to men?
> Why do you not as well our battels fight,
> And wear our armour? suffer this, and then
> Let all the world be topsie turved quite.
> Let fishes graze, beastes, swime, and birds descend,
> Let fire burne downewards whilst the earth aspires;
> Let Winters heat and Summers cold offend,
> Let Thistels growe on Vines, and Grapes on Briers,
> Set us to Spinne or Sowe, or at the best
> Make us Wood-hewers, Waters-bearing wights:

You are the first, and will I hope be last,
That ever sought her husband to divorce.
(I.vi)

Yet for all that, her argument for women's right to divorce is given full and forceful airing, as it proposes a kind of evenhanded justice for unhappy wives:

If he [Constabarus] to me did beare as Earnest hate,
As I to him, for him there were an ease,
A separating bill might free his fate:
From such a yoke that did so much displease.
Why should such priviledge to man be given?
Or given to them, why bard from women then?
Are men then we in greater grace with Heaven?
Or cannot women hate as well as men?
Ile be the custome-breaker: and beginne
To shew my Sexe the way to freedomes doore.
And with an offring will I purge my sinne,
The lawe was made for none but who are poore.
(I.iii)

Mariam's claims to personal integrity set her apart from all these women, and her assertion of rights within marriage contrast sharply with Salome's move from radical social disruption to murder.

The drama offers several formulations of the tragic flaw that precipitates Mariam's tragedy. The Chorus, a company of Jews, construes it variously in their several odes, judging Mariam according to their very conservative notion of a wife's duty. They claim that Mariam seeks to be free of Herod 'for expectation of variety'; that she has invited suspicion by her too free conversation with others; that she seeks public glory; and that she exhibits an ignoble vengefulness of mind (I.vi; III.iii; IV.viii). But these positions are undermined by the drama as a whole. We soon realize that Mariam seeks no other lover, that she loved Herod devotedly until his wrongdoing destroyed that love, and that the qualities the chorus ascribes to her pertain rather to Salome, Alexandra, and Doris. Obviously the Chorus sees women as interchangeable entities. The drama especially problematizes the Chorus's notion that Mariam's 'public' speech has undone her, for, as Margaret Ferguson observes, Mariam's trouble stems rather from the one kind of speech they allow – private speech to her own husband.[73]

Mariam clearly does not fulfill the standard the Chorus sets for proper wifely behavior – the entire subjection of mind as well as body to her husband:

Do they not wholy give themselves away?
Or give they but their body not their mind,
Reserving that though best, for others pray?
  No sure, their thoghts no more can be their owne,
  And therefore should to none but one be knowne.
(III.iii)

In this genre, however, the Chorus is expected to speak from a partial, not an authoritative, vantage point. Their standard does not square with the principle Cary herself enunciated and tried to live by, since it makes no provision for 'reason and conscience' in dealing with evil. It also ignores the distinction, so important to this genre and to the age, between rightful authority and tyrannical power. The Chorus appeals to a higher and more universal Stoic standard at the end of Act IV, concluding that Mariam was swayed by 'sullen passion' to refuse Herod, when she should have been led by a virtuous pride to rise above her injuries and to pay him the due marital debt.[74] But their final definition of Stoic virtue – 'To scorne a freeborne heart slave-like to binde' – intimates that subjection to Herod's loathed bed might well amount to spiritual slavery for a freeborn queen (IV.viii).

Sohemus identifies Mariam's tragic flaw more reliably, as imprudent speech: 'Unbridled speech is *Mariam*'s worst disgrace, / And will indanger her without desart' (III.iii). She exhibits this trait when she enrages Salome by referring to her base birth, and infuriates Herod by casting up to him all the old wrongs and flatly refusing his love and his bed. This characterization derives from Josephus, whose Mariam is a woman of unparalleled courage, nobility, beauty, and chastity, marred only by a 'natural frowardness' and 'a great and intemperate libertie in her discourse' with Herod and others.[75] Sohemus, ready to die for disobeying Herod and preserving Mariam's life, praises her pure heart and 'grave majestie,' which elicit admiration even as they prohibit love (III.iii). The Nuntius who describes to Herod her noble, courageous death laments that with her die 'beautie, chastitie and wit' (V.i). Herod, who in life doted on her beauty and understood nothing of her mind or her feelings, celebrates her after death for all these qualities: the beauty of Venus, the chastity of Diana, the wit of Mercury (V.i). And now that he has silenced her forever, he ironically values her every word, demanding of the messenger, 'Oh say, what said she more? each word she sed / Shall be the food whereon my heart is fed' (V.i).[76]

As she goes to her death, Mariam herself attributes her plight to imprudence, pride, and the presumption that her innocence and Herod's love would protect her. Throughout, however, she insists on preserving the integrity of her own thoughts and feelings, and this insistence subverts conventional formulations of wifely duty and male idealization. The motif begins in her opening soliloquy as she admits the complexity of her feelings: grief for the death of the husband she once loved; relief that his jealous tyranny is past. Upon hearing of Herod's return, she at once explains to Sohemus the impossibility of pretending love in the face of such wrongs: unable 'to live with him I so profoundly hate,' she has, she declares, 'with solemne vowes . . . forsworne his Bed' (III.iii). She recognizes her sexual power over him but scorns hypocritical pretense in the interests of prudent self-preservation:

> I Know I could inchaine him with a smile:
> And lead him captive with a gentle word,
> I Scorne my looke should ever man beguile,
> Or other speech, then meaning to afford.
> (III.iii)

She looks to her innocence as a shield, not so much from outward danger as from 'the pangs of inward griefe,' and refuses to sully her spirit 'to be commandresse of the triple earth' (III.iii). To Herod, who calls constantly for her, urges her to love him, promises her ever more gifts and power, and insists that she accept his explanations for the death of her kin, she maintains her right to her own judgments and feelings: 'My Lord, I suit my garment to my minde, / And there no cheerfull colours can I finde'; 'No, had you wisht the wretched *Mariam* glad, / . . . My brother nor my Grandsyre had not dide'; 'I cannot frame disguise, nor never taught / My face a looke dissenting from my thought' (IV.iii). When Salome puts her plot in place – the poison cup and the suggestion that Mariam and Sohemus are lovers – Mariam is almost speechless with amazement: 'Is this a dream?' At length she manages a dignified denial – 'they can tell / That say I lov'd him. *Mariam* saies not so' – but finds it useless (IV.iv).

At the end, Mariam recognizes that prudent humility would have saved her, and admits that the conjunction of chastity and humility is the feminine ideal. But she shows little chagrin over her lack of humility, and certainly no new accession of it, as she projects her triumph over earthly tyrants and imagines an appropriately female heavenly reward – not in Abraham's bosom but in Sarah's lap:

> And I had singly one, but tis my joy,
> That I was ever innocent, though sower:
> And therefore can they but my life destroy,
> My Soule is free from adversaires power.
> You Princes great in power, and high in birth,
> Be great and high, I envy not your hap:
> Your birth must be from dust: your power on earth,
> In heav'n shall *Mariam* sit in *Saraes* lap.
>
> (IV.viii)

Indeed, the drama goes some distance toward disjoining the triad of virtues that constitute the era's feminine ideal, inviting sympathetic identification with a heroine who is chaste but manifestly neither silent nor obedient. Reinforcing that sympathy, several analogies associate Mariam's innocent, noble, unjust death with Christ's crucifixion: the betraying servant who hangs himself upon a tree; Mariam's prediction that Herod 'three daies hence' will wish to revive her. Moreover, Mariam's resistance to domestic tyranny has as a direct result the potential overthrow of the tyrant's political power. Herod runs mad, and he explicitly admits that rebellion against him would be justified:

> You dwellers in the now deprived land,
> Wherein the matchles *Mariam* was bred:
> Why graspe not each of you a sword in hand,
> To ayme at me your cruell Soveraignes head.
> . . .
> Tis I have overthrowne your royall line.
>
> (V.i)

Historically Herod was not deposed, but Cary's drama ends by holding forth that possibility.

Mariam is the last published in a series of closet Senecan dramas concerned with forms of tyranny, and should perhaps be seen as the first of a series of tragedies (1610–14) that focus on female resistance to tyrants in the domestic sphere – women who seek to control their own sexual choices, challenging the orthodox ideal of submission.[77] Cary's heroine does not rise to the high eloquence of the Duchess of Malfi, and whereas the Duchess acts to realize her own sexual desire, Mariam's sexual self-assertion takes the form of refusing to have her love commanded. Nevertheless, *Mariam*'s challenge to patriarchal control within the institution of marriage is revolutionary, as the heroine claims a wife's right to her own speech – public and private – as well as to the integrity of her own emotional life and her own self-definition. Cary's *Mariam* intimates that such integrity is the foundation for resistance to tyranny in every sphere.

Notes

1 *The Tragedie of Mariam, the Faire Queene of Jewry. Written by that learned, vertuous, and truly noble Ladie, E. C.* (London, 1613; rpt Malone Society, Oxford: Oxford University Press, 1914). I cite the 1613 edition by Act and Scene. One of the three copies in the British Library has a near-contemporary manuscript note on the title page, 'Lady Eliz. Carew only piece [play].' Margaret Ferguson and Barry Weller have edited *Mariam* together with a *Life* of Cary written by her daughter (see note 6), *The Tragedy of Mariam the Fair Queen of Jewry with The Lady Falkland Her Life* (Berkeley, CA: University of California Press, 1994).

2 *The History of the Life, Reign, and Death of Edward II, King of England, and Lord of Ireland. With the Rise and Fall of His Great Favourites, Gaveston and the Spencers. Written by E.[lizabeth] F.[alkland] in the year 1627, and printed verbatim from the Original* (London, 1680). The Author's Preface is dated '20 February 1627 [1628].' The grounds for this attribution are discussed in detail in Barbara K. Lewalski, *Writing Women in Jacobean England* (Cambridge, MA: Harvard University Press, 1993), Appendix A, 317–20.

3 Among those who read the work as espousing total wifely submission are Betty S. Travitsky, 'The *Feme Covert* in Elizabeth Cary's *Mariam*,' in *Ambiguous Realities*, ed. Levin and Watson, 184–96; Maurice J. Valency, *The Tragedies of Herod & Mariamne* (New York: Columbia University Press, 1940) 88–91; Nancy Cotton Pearse, 'Elizabeth Cary, Elizabethan Playwright,' *Texas Studies in Literature and Language*, 18 (1976–7), 601–8, and Cotton, *Women Playwrights in England, c. 1363–1750* (Lewisburg: Bucknell University Press, 1980), 31–9. Catherine Belsey's reading emphasizes contradictions in the text which at once affirm and deny subjectivity to Mariam, *The Subject of Tragedy: Identity and Difference in Renaissance Drama* (New York and London: Methuen, 1985), 164–75. Readings closer to my own in recognizing some subversive elements in the work are Sandra K. Fischer, 'Elizabeth Cary and Tyranny, Domestic and Religious,' in *Silent but for the Word: Tudor Women as Patrons, Translators, and Writers of Religious Works*, ed. Margaret P. Hannay (Kent, OH: Kent State University Press, 1985), 225–37; and especially Margaret W. Ferguson, 'Running On with Almost Public Voice: The Case of "E.C.",' in *Tradition and the Talent of Women*, ed. Florence Howe (Urbana, IL: University of Illinois Press, 1991), 37–67. Elaine Beilin reads Mariam as attaining to the role of Christ-like martyr-heroine in *Redeeming Eve: Women Writers of the English Renaissance* (Princeton, NJ: Princeton University Press, 1987), 157–76.

4 The MS is at the vicarage, Burford, Oxfordshire; based on the abridged edition of Ortelius (Amsterdam, 1598), it is without maps. The hand is very different from Elizabeth's later cursive writing: it is evidently a schoolgirl exercise in careful printing as well as in translation. The dedication (to her uncle Sir Henry Lee) is signed E. Tanfelde.

5 The witty, tonally-ambivalent epitaph is BL, Egerton MS 2725, f. 60, headed 'An Epitaph upon the death of the Duke of Buckingham by the Countesse of Faukland.' The speaker is Buckingham:

> Reader stand still and see, loe, here I am
> Who was of late the mighty Buckingham;
> God gave to me my being, and my breath;
> Two kings their favourers, and a slave my death;
> Now for my Fame I challenge, and not crave
> That thou beleeve two kings before one slave.

The Perron translation (always attributed to Elizabeth Cary) is *The Reply of the Most Illustrious Cardinall of Perron, to the Answeare of the Most Excellent King of Great Britaine* (Douay, 1630).

6 *The Lady Falkland, Her Life*, ed. R.[ichard] S.[impson], from a manuscript in the Imperial Archives at Lille (London: Catholic Publishing, 1861); cited as *Life*, with page number. The work is noted in Donald Stauffer, *English Biography before 1700* (Cambridge, MA: Harvard University Press, 1930), 148–50. Georgiana Fullerton's biography *The Life of Elizabeth, Lady Falkland*, Quarterly Series, 43 (London, 1872), follows the daughter's account very closely.

7 The *Life* reports that Lucius Cary had answered a *Defence of the Church of Rome*, by Elizabeth's friend, Mr. Montague; Lucius charged Catholics with the divisions occasioned in families by conversions. Her essay answered his.

8 See p. 183.

9 The work is usually ascribed to Anne, the eldest surviving daughter and the one with widest experience: she was a maid of honor at court and led a group of nuns to Paris to establish a community. But Lucy, also a Benedictine, is another possibility, given that the text characterizes her more fully than the other children.

10 They include personal and public letters in the State Papers Domestic, State Papers (Ireland), and Carew Manuscripts (Lambeth Palace); BL, Additional MSS 11,033 and 3827, and BL, Harleian MSS 1581 and 2305; and contemporary dedications and praises from clients or would-be clients. See also T. Langueville, *Falklands* (London, 1897), 1–94; Kenneth B. Murdock, *The Sun at Noon: Three Biographical Sketches* (New York: Macmillan, 1939), 6–40; Kurt Weber, *Lucius Cary, Second Viscount Falkland* (New York: Columbia University Press, 1940).

11 Although the *Life* emphasizes Elizabeth's humility, it also portrays her 'heedlessness' and lack of social decorum, testifying to a deep-rooted indifference to conformity and custom. She often forgot where she was and whom she was with or whom she had met; she neglected her dress and social expectations; she would kneel down in public to ask a blessing of priests. Her carelessness about money is writ large – notably her disposition to give largess when she had no notion of her own financial resources. Beilin argued a similar case in a paper at the Modern Language Association, Washington, DC, December 28, 1989.

12 Her attitudes are discussed in Ferguson, 'Running On,' 41, 62–3, n. 21.

13 Weber, *Lucius Cary*, 8–10. Lady Tanfield seems to have been especially resented.

14 She was said to owe the servants £100 for candles, and £200 more, probably for books and writing materials. One (perhaps apocryphal) anecdote in the *Life* tells of the 10-year-old Elizabeth visiting her father's court and saving a woman accused of witchcraft, who had confessed (after interrogation and torture) to causing sickness and death to many persons. Elizabeth reportedly whispered to her father to ask the woman if she had bewitched her uncle (present in court and obviously healthy); when the woman said yes, her confession was seen to be the result of fear, and was dismissed. *Life*, p. 5–6.

15 John Davies of Hereford, *The Muses Sacrifice* (London, 1612), sig. ***3v.

16 Pearse, 'Elizabeth Cary,' 602.

17 *Life*, p. 7. She was elsewhere described as rather short and fat. On June 27, 1602, Chamberlain wrote to Carleton the precise sums involved: 'Sir Henry Carey [is to marry] Mr. Tanfeild's daughter with $2{,}000^{li}$ presently, $2{,}000^{li}$ at two years, and $3{,}000^{li}$ at his death, yf he chaunce to have more children, otherwise to be his heir.' John Chamberlain, *Letters*, ed. N.E. McClure (Philadelphia, PA: American Philosophical Society, 1939) 3 vols, I, 153. As this letter reveals, the *Life* is mistaken in dating the marriage two years earlier, in 1600.

18 *DNB*, 'Henry Cary,' III, 1149–50; Weber, *Lucius Cary*, 15–16; *The Scots Peerage*, ed. James Balfour (Edinburgh, 1906), III, 609–12.

19 *Life*, p. 15. Her eleven children born alive were Catherine, b. 1609, m. Lord Home 1622, d. 1626 (in childbirth); Lucius, b. 1610, d. 1643 (in the Battle of Newbury); Lorenzo, b. 1613, d. 1642 (in battle in Ireland); Anne, b. 1614, professed as Dame Clementina 1639, d. (?); Edward, b. (?), d. 1616; Elizabeth, b. 1617, professed as Sister Augustina 1638, d. 1683; Lucy, b. 1619, professed as Sister Magdalena 1638, d. (?); Victoria, b. 1620, m. Sir William Uvedale 1640, d. (?); Mary, b. 1622, professed as Sister Maria 1638, d. 1693; Patrick. b.

1624 in Ireland, d. 1656; Henry, b. 1625 (?), professed as Father Placid, d. 1656. See Balfour, *Scots Peerage*, 609–12, and Weber, *Lucius Cary*, *passim*.

20 She met with clerics frequenting the house of Richard Neale, Bishop of Durham and later Archbishop of York, and was persuaded by them that she might safely remain in the English Church at present. *Life*, p. 9–10.

21 Michael Drayton, *Englands Heroicall Epistles* (London, 1597); rpt 1598, 1599, 1600, 1602; with *The Barrons Warres*, 1603; also in *Poemes Lyrick and Pastorall* (London, 1605 and 1623). The epistles for the young Elizabeth – an exchange between William de la Pole, Duke of Suffolk, and Queen Margaret – fittingly portray Petrarchan devotion and admiring friendship rather than amorous passion. Drayton adopts a Petrarchan stance himself, claiming that Petrarch's praises of Laura have not evoked in him such admiration of women as has his own observation of Elizabeth.

22 John Davies of Hereford, *The Muses Sacrifice or Divine Meditations* (London, 1612), sig. ***2, identifies Elizabeth Cary as 'Wife of Sr. Henry Cary,' suggesting her relative obscurity compared to the others, but also the need to distinguish her from several other Elizabeth Carys with whom she might be (and has been) confused: Elizabeth Bland Cary, her sister-in-law and the dedicatee of *Mariam*; Elizabeth Spencer Cary, second Lady Hunsdon; and Elizabeth, wife of Sir George Carey, who was the guardian of Prince Charles.

23 Ibid., sigs. ***3v, A–Av. Ferguson, 'Running On,' 44–5, unpacks the contradictory messages in Davies's poem, which on the one hand urges the noble ladies to publish, but on the other reinforces the cultural construct of publication as a debasement of noble status and a likely indicator of a woman's sexual license.

24 *England's Helicon. Or, The Muses Harmony* (London, 1614).

25 'A Proclamation . . . for Banishing of Jesuits and Priests from Ireland,' in *Catalogue of the Carew MSS (Lambeth) 1603–1624* (London, 1873), 432–3. *DNB*; Weber, *Lucius Cary*, 30–4.

26 *DNB*, 'Elizabeth Cary,' III, 1151. *Life*, p. 19–21. Falkland at first seems to have tolerated the enterprise as possibly good for public relations, though he offered no support or financial assistance and allowed it to collapse entirely after Elizabeth left Ireland.

27 Richard Belling [or Beling], *A Sixth Booke to the Countesse of Pembrokes Arcadia* (Dublin, 1624). Later, the bookseller William Sheares sought her patronage for his edition of Marston, as one 'well acquainted with the Muses.' John Marston, *The Workes* (London, 1633).

28 SP 63 (Ireland) 242/213, Lord Falkland to Lord Conway, January 26, 1626.

29 SP 63 (Ireland) 242/280, Falkland to Conway, April 5, 1626. The *Life*, p. 36, asserts that a servant poisoned Falkland's mind against his wife claiming that she worked to block his affairs at court. Conway's answer, commending Elizabeth's 'good sollicitation' for Falkland, elicits further truculence and blame shifting: 'I rather wishe she weare at home with hir Mother . . . then travayling to procure Court favour for me . . . from whence I have never receyved other [than] . . . diminutions.' SP 63 (Ireland) 242/284.

30 A few years earlier, King James had charged his judges 'to have a special care of the papists, and likewise of their wives; for he said, the women were the nourishers of papistry in this kingdom . . . which our Catholic ladies take very ill.' Sir Thomas Wynne to Sir Dudley Carleton, February 14, 1618–19, Nichols, II, 136. Noted recusant (or crypto-Catholic) women of the Caroline court include Queen Henrietta Maria; Buckingham's mother; Buckingham's wife, Katherine (Manners), who was persuaded to conform outwardly after he married her; Lady Jane Weston; and Lady Jane Clifford.

31 Lady Denby (or Denbigh), to whom Crashaw addressed a famous verse epistle urging her to convert, did not finally make that move and tried hard to restrain Elizabeth from doing so – at one point even locking her in her chambers. Elizabeth escaped, and was promptly received into the Roman Church by one Father Dunstan (Pettinger).

32 Had the conversion remained private – a matter of rumor only – Falkland would have hated it on principle but would not have felt himself shamed and his prospects threatened. Lady Denby probably felt she had to reveal Cary's action lest she be charged with complicity; and the king evidently thought he had to inquire once the affair was public. Cary's letter to her husband, abstracted and enclosed in his letter to Coke on December 29, 1626, claims she is not placing him in jeopardy by entertaining priests illegally and at his expense. She also lays all the unwelcome publicity to the king's charge:

> You chardge me with feedeing Priests and Jesuists; for Jesuists, to my knowledge, I never saw the face of any one in my leif, nor intend not to doe. For Priests, it is true I must have conversed with some, els I could not have bene what for no death I will deny my self to be. For feeding them, it is possible some one man may have sum tymes, dined or supped heere, but yf there weare a bitt the more, or yf I ever appointed any thing, but only satt down to such as they provided, I wilbe subject to your displeasure. *And since it pleased his Majesty, to make me wheather I would or not, declare my self Catholike, which is on Tuesdaye last a Month, there is not one of that function ever entred within this howse.*

SP 63 (Ireland) 243/515. Falkland's cover letter to Coke declares: 'If I cannot prevayle by the assistance of his Majestys just Power, I must Resorte to a separat[i]on *a mensa et thoro*, which I intend for a Last Refudge yf I despayre of her recovery . . . that deales soe treasonablye with me.' SP 63 (Ireland) 243/515.

33 SP 63 (Ireland) 243/503, December 8, 1626, Falkland to the king:

> Howe cann your Throne be long well established, or your sacred Person safe in it, whilest these Locusts of Rome, whose Doctrines are as full of horrid treasons, as many of their lives full of horrible Impieties, be permitted to pass at Liberty . . . Some of these Priests as I am informed, expect to receive speedy preferment in hir Majesty's household . . . for the Apostate hir selfe, since I was not so happie to obtain her Confinement at the first to her Mothers, which possibly might have prevented this falling away; yet I most humbly beseech your Majestie that shee may bee nowe committed thither, with Commandment to her Mother to receive hir, and to keep hir safe and free from anv Communication by word or letter with . . . those Inchanters.

34 Katherine, Duchess of Buckingham, wrote to Conway on Elizabeth's behalf on March 24, 1627, and again on June 20, 1627. SP 16 (Charles I) 58/17, 71/55.

35 SP 63 (Ireland) 244/630, April 4, 1627, Falkland to Conway.

36 SP 63 (Ireland) 245/726, Falkland to Conway (now Viscount Killultagh). He explains his failure to relieve Elizabeth's needs on two grounds:

> First, of an impossibility for my estate to affoord that which the wealth of both the Indiaes cannot supply . . . Next, for that she is and lives, that, there, and as I would not have hir: & will never allow hir penny to be such and thereas and where she is . . . That hir father disinherited hir for hir obedience to mee is much misrepresented by hir; he foresawe in hir that bade condition which she hath since manifested to the world which made him do that he did against hir and me for hir sake. If hir joynture be sould, it is she that hath the benefitt of the sale, and hath spent treble of the valliew of yt out of my purse . . . If hir mother refuse to receyve hir and doe conjure hir stay, it is hir self that hath sued for these rejections, to have the better collor still to remayn wheare she is . . . Lawe Matrimoniall, notwithstanding hir specious pretences, doth require that he [the king] should remove hir, and settle hir with hir Mother, where she shall receyve such allowance from mee as is fitt for hir: but nothinge for hir Popelinges that depends uppon hir.

37 SF 16 (Charles I) 62/62, May 6, 1627.

38 SF 16 (Charles 1) 63/89, May 18, 1627. The cover letter to Conway (ibid., 63/102) enclosed her mother's letter and urges that her petition to the king be presented 'when my lord steward and my lord chamberlaine are by, in whose good wishes, I have much confidence.' She also hopes for the support of Buckingham: 'If you can, I pray you let the duke of Buckingham bee present, for I know, hee will second so just and necessary, a request.' She has most confidence in the Romanizing Buckingham ladies, promising Conway, 'If you second it strongly . . . I dare bee bound, you shall receave extraordinary thankes from all the three great ladyes of my Lord of Buckinghams family.' An earlier letter to Conway on March 24, SP 16 (Charles I) 58/19, vigorously protests the king's order

to command me to my mothers in the nature of a prisoner . . . I have committed no fault that I know of, and though I had, sure I beleeve the kinge would take some other way for my punishment, then so unusuall a one, as to sterve mee to death. My mother hath exprest to mee, that if ever I come downe to her (which she beleeves his majesty will never inforce mee to doe), she will never give mee the least releefe now, or at her death . . . I have nor meat, drinke, nor clothes, nor mony to purchase any of them, and longe, have I bene, in this misery. I ly in a lodgynge, where I have no meanes to pay for it.

39 On August 13 she had appealed to Conway to preserve her from starvation by getting an order to pay her out of money due Falkland from a grant for pipe staves, SP 16 (Charles I) 73/81. Conway responded (ibid., 75/29, August 27) that the grant of the pipe staves was already a matter of much discontentment to Falkland, and to give part of the award to her would further embroil the matter. Her response, quoted in the text, concludes by urging him to find some other means, if not this, to meet her needs (ibid., 75/85, August).

40 On September 8, 1627, Conway reported to Sir Richard Weston, Chancellor of the Exchequer, that the king 'hath been pressed with infinite importunity from the Lady Falkland' and directed him to take some course to provide for her, SP 16 (Charles 1) 77/24. The formal provision, dated October 4, 1627, is reported in a letter to Falkland dated October 31, SP 63 (Ireland) 245/822. The council further provided for changes in attendants or places of residence if necessary, reserving to themselves the right to arbitrate any difficulties.

41 In May 1628 the king directed the Privy Council to subtract from Lord Falkland's salary the allowance for Lady Falkland mandated by their decree of October 4, 1627, SP 63 (Ireland) 246/1021. On June 27, 1628, Falkland proposed in a letter to the king (ibid., 246/1050) to pay £300 rather than the £500 stipulated, claiming straitened circumstances and declaring truculently that it should be enough, though the Indies could not supply her humors. He also begs she be forbidden to come within ten miles of the court or the City of London, to 'silence the scandal and shame' she has brought upon him.

42 SP 16 (Charles I) 229/131. The report is undated; the *Calendar* supplies the date, 1632, but queries it. A deleted sentence in the *Life* indicates Cary's involvement at this time in several unsuccessful suits and projects to get free from debt.

43 *Life*, p. 46; Murdock, *Sun at Noon*, 8.

44 She assigned the small part of her jointure that she still retained to the payment of her debts, and also £100 of the £200 she had from her parents; this left her only £100 for living expenses (*Life*, p. 51). She remained dependent upon the charity of friends and occasional grants from the king and queen. Lucius, now Lord Falkland, was apparently a dutiful son, but he complained with some justice of her imprudence in managing her finances (*Life*, p. 83–4, records her constant outlays for charity and support of priests). Lucius resisted the council's recommendation of December 9, 1636, that he settle an allowance on her, and proposed instead 'not [to] ty my selfe to give her any certaine allowance' but rather to supply her wants as he can. SP 16 (Charles I) 337/40. He claimed not to have known how dire her situation was.

45 Ben Jonson, 'To the Immortal Memory and Friendship of that Noble Pair, Sir Lucius Cary and Sir H. Morison,' *Underwood* no. 70, H&S, VIII, 242–7. Edward Hyde, Earl of Clarendon, *The History of the Rebellion and Civil Wars in England, begun in the year 1641*, ed. W. Dunn Macray, 6 vols (Oxford: Clarendon Press, 1888), III, 178–90. Weber, *Lucius Cary*, 167–70.

46. SP 16 (Charles I) 272/29, July 20, 1634. Laud holds out hope that the daughters may yet be reclaimed: 'But the greatest thinge I feare is that the Mother will still be practisinge, and doe all shee can to hinder.'

47 Anne, the maid of honor, soon returned to her mother and court life, her maintenance provided by the Duchess of Buckingham; Elizabeth also returned. This left Mary and Lucy with Patrick and Henry at Tew. See *Life*, p. 84.

48 On pretense of a holiday trip, the children arose at an early hour and set off together. The boys ran off to a waiting coach, then were taken by boat (in the charge of very drunken boatmen) to London and thence abroad. Weber, *Lucius Cary*, 176–80; Murdock, *Sun at Noon*, 33–7. See SP 16 (Charles I) 337/230 for the testimony of the coachman, Henry Auxley.

49 SP 16 (Charles I) 321/29, May 16, 1636. This report, and that of May 28 (at which she indicated that she thought her sons were in France, probably Paris), are signed by Elizabeth and the Chief Justice, John Bramston.
50 SP 16 (Charles I) 322/6, Star Chamber, Order of Council, May 25, 1636.
51 *Life*, p. 111–12; Weber, *Lucius Cary*, 301–26.
52 Clarendon, *History of the Rebellion*, III, 180.
53 She was buried in the burial ground of Henrietta Maria's private chapel at St James's Palace – now covered by a road.
54 Thomas Lodge, trans., *The Famous and Memorable Works of Josephus* (London, 1602).
55 Philip Cary (Carew) was knighted at Greenwich in 1605. William A. Shaw, *The Knights of England*, 2 vols (London, 1906), II, 137.
56 I cite the Huntington copy of *Mariam* (STC 4613) by act and scene number. The dedicatory poem (present in that copy) reads:

> When cheerfull *Phoebus* his full course hath run,
> His sisters fainter beams our harts doth cheere:
> So your faire Brother is to mee the Sunne,
> And you his Sister as my Moone appeere.
>
> You are my next belov'd, my second Friend,
> For when my *Phoebus* absence makes it Night,
> Whilst to th'*Antipodes* his beames do bend,
> From you my *Phoebe*, shines my second Light.
>
> Hee like to *SOL*, cleare-sighted, constant, free,
> You *Luna*-like, unspotted, chaste, divine:
> Hee shone on *Sicily*, you destin'd bee,
> T'illumine the now obscurde *Palestine*.
> My first was consecrated to *Apollo*,
> My second to *Diana* now shall follow.

57 Cary's play was entered on the Stationers' Register in December 1612, and published the following year. The anecdote specifically mentioning the sister-in-law, along with the warm dedication to her in the drama, points to *Mariam* as the work in question. The dedicatory poem may have been removed because the dedicatee (now Lady Carew) did not want her name associated with the publication, or perhaps because it would identify the author publicly, as the initials alone did not. For Davies's poem alluding to a 'Sicily' tragedy, see p. 183.
58 Valency, *Tragedies of Herod*, 291, lists the following as predating Cary's drama: the Herod mystery plays; Hans Sachs, *Tragedia der Wütrich König Herodes* (MS, 1552); Ludovico Dolce, *Marianna* (1565); L. L. de Argensola, *La Alejandra* (1772), performed c.1585; Alexandre Hardy, *Mariamne* (1625), performed *c.*1600; and two Latin plays at Cambridge University by William Goldingham (1567) and Patrick Adamson (1572).
59 Robert Garnier, *M. Antoine* (Paris 1578). *Discourse of Life and Death written in French by Ph. Mornay. Antonius A Tragedie written also in French by Ro. Garnier. Both done in English by the Countess of Pembroke* (London, 1592); Mary Sidney, Countess of Pembroke, *The Tragedie of Antonie* (London 1595), ed. Alice Luce (Weimar, 1897).
60 Samuel Daniel, *The Tragedie of Cleopatra* (London, 1594; rpt 1599, 1601, 1602, 1605; rev. edn, 1607, 1609, 1611). I cite the 1599 and 1611 versions. Daniel, *Certaine Small Poems Lately Printed: With the Tragedie of Philotas* (London, 1605; rpt 1607, 1611, 1623). I cite by act and scene number in the 1623 edition. Fulke Greville, Lord Brooke, *Mustapha*. MS C, 1594–6; London, 1609; rev., MS W, 1607–10; and in *Certaine Learned and Elegant Workes of the Right Honorable Fulke Lord Brooke* (London, 1633). I cite by act and scene number in the 1633 edition. Other works in the Countess of Pembroke's line of French Senecan tragedies include Thomas Kyd's translation of Garnier's *Cornelia* (London, 1594); Samuel Brandon, *The Tragicomeodi of the Vertuous Octavia* (London, 1598); Fulke Greville, *Alaham* (1599–1604, rev., MS. W, 1607–10), in *Certaine Learned . . . Workes*; Sir William Alexander, *Darius* (1603), *Croesus* (1604), *The Alexandrian* (1607), and *Julius Caesar* (1607). In

Sejanus (1603–4) and *Cataline* (1611), Jonson attempts (unsuccessfully) to revise the genre to make it viable on the stage.

61 For an illuminating discussion of the two strains, Italian and French Senecanism, see H. B. Charlton (ed.) *The Poetical Works of Sir William Alexander*, 2 vols (London, 1921), I, introduction.

62 Responses to the Daniel and Greville plays suggest that contemporary analogues were widely recognized: to Essex and Elizabeth; to the Burleigh faction versus Essex and the Protestant war party; to James I's theories of absolutism, his corrupt court, and notorious favorites; to assassination attempts and rumored conspiracies – Essex's rebellion (1602), Guy Fawkes (1605), Arbella Stuart's royal claims and elopement (1609). Greville also composed an *Antony and Cleopatra* sometime before 1601 and committed it to the fire at the time of Essex's rebellion, claiming that it might be 'construed, or strained to a personating of vices in the present Governers, and government.' *Sir Fulke Greville's Life of Sir Philip Sidney*, ed. Nowell Smith (Oxford: Clarendon Press, 1907), 156. See also notes 64–8.

63 Junius Brutus [Hugh Languet], *Vindiciae Contra Tyrannos, sive, de principis in populum, populique in Primcipem, legitima potestat* (Frankfort, 1608), also attributed to Du Plessis Mornay, whose works were translated by Philip Sidney and his sister. The argument of the tract is that any group of nobles or magistrates (or even one such) in whom is vested some measure of governing authority devolved from the people may resist or overthrow by force a tyrant who threatens ruin to God's Church or to the Commonwealth. R. Doleman [Robert Parsons], *A Conference about the Next Succession to the Crowne of Ingland* (n.p., 1594), questions the notion of automatic succession, and argues the right of those empowered to act for the people to depose a ruler, especially if the Pope sanctions it.

64 The drama was staged on January 3, 1605, by the Children of the Queen's Revels, the company and theater for which Daniel was special licenser and which were becoming a locus for audacious plays. Daniel's troubles seem to have stemmed more from the production than the publication.

65 Daniel's letter to his patron Devonshire (Mountjoy) reiterates his testimony: 'First I tolde the Lordes I had written 3 Acts of this tragedie the Christmas before my L. of Essex troubles, as divers in the cittie could witnes.' Grosart, *Works of Samuel Daniel*, III, xxii–xxiii. His letter to Cecil (Cranbourne) explains the supposed contemporary analogies by the 'universall notions of the affayres of men . . . No tyme but brought forth the like concurrencies, the like inter-striving for place and dignitie, the like supplantations, rysings & overthrows.' He offers, however, 'yf it shall seeme skandalous to any by misconceiveing it,' to withdraw 'the booke & mee to my poore home, pretending some other occasion, so that the suppressing it by authoritie might not make the world to ymagin other matters in it then there is.' Hatfield, Cecil Papers 191/123. No penalty was imposed, but his career was damaged; he had no court commissions until the queen commissioned *Tethys Festival* from him in 1610.

66 The 'Argument' to *Philotas* notes that Alexander's claim of divinity 'withdrew many the hearts of the nobilitie and people from him.'

67 'Apology,' Grosart, *Works of Samuel Daniel*, III, 180–1. The 'Apology' appeared for the first time in the 1623 edition, though it was obviously written much earlier; since Daniel managed to deflect official trouble, he perhaps thought publishing it at the time would simply call attention to the problem. The 'Argument' provided sufficient cover by offering a somewhat similar misreading of the drama (sigs. A6–A6v).

68 After the death of Sidney, Greville's closest literary relationship was with Daniel, whom he probably introduced to the Countess of Pembroke's Wilton circle and to other literary women.

69 Ronald A. Rebholz, *The Life of Fulke Greville, First Lord Brooke* (Oxford: Clarendon Press, 1971), 200–5.

70 Valency, *Tragedies of Herod*, 23. Herod the Great massacred the Innocents; Herod Antipas condemned John the Baptist and interrogated Jesus; Herod Agrippa sat in judgment on Paul and other apostles.

71 This episode occurred much later in Josephus's account of Herod, but Cary incorporates it here to reinforce the motif of liberation and new beginnings.

72 Ferguson, 'Running On,' 47–8, makes the plausible argument that Graphina (the only

character not present in Josephus or in the Lodge translation, though the name is perhaps suggested by Glaphyra, wife to a certain Alexander) is purposively named as a play on *graphesis* (writing). She seems to represent a safe, nontransgressive discourse in compliance with her husband's wishes, which is rewarded with Pheroras' devoted love. It is, however, a love that overpowers his moral sense.

73 Ibid., 52–3.

74 This is substantially the recommendation of Fulke Greville in his *Letter to an Honorable Lady*, in *The Prose Works of Fulke Greville, Lord Brooke*, ed. John Gouws (Oxford: Clarendon Press, 1986), 138–76. Citing the opinions of 'worthie men, borne under Tyrants,' he draws an explicit parallel to the case of a lady matched with a tyrannous husband: 'the comparison holdinge in some affinitie betweene a wives subjection to a husband and a subjects obedience to his soveraign' (154). But Greville, unlike the chorus of *Mariam*, would not imprison the lady in her domestic sphere; instead he comforts her with liberation from that realm to 'newe *Ideas*, larger ends, and nobler wayes,' whereby she may win fame in all the world and finally with God (172). Joan Rees, *Fulke Greville, Lord Brooke, 1554–1628: A Critical Biography* (London, 1971), 173–7, and Mark Caldwell, 'The Prose Works of Fulke Greville, Lord Brooke' (PhD dissertation, Harvard University, 1973), xxiv–xxvi, argue that the letter was probably addressed to Margaret Clifford, Countess of Cumberland.

75 Lodge, *Workes of Josephus*, 398–9.

76 Cf. Ferguson, 'Running On,' 56–7.

77 Shepherd, *Amazons and Warrior Women*, 107–28, points to a group of such plays staged in the years 1610–14: Chapman's *Bussy D'Ambois* (1610–11) and *Second Maiden's Tragedy* (1611); Dekker's *Meet Me in London* (1611–12); Tourneur's *Atheist's Tragedy* (1611); and Webster's *Duchess of Malfi* (1612). Among the circumstances promoting the treatment of such themes, Shepherd cites Arbella Stuart's love match in defiance of James's restrictions and his harsh and arbitrary response, and also James's wrangles with the Parliament of 1610 over his absolutist claims and prerogative.

9

AN UNKNOWN CONTINENT

Lady Mary Wroth's forgotten pastoral drama, 'Loves Victorie'

Margaret Anne McLaren

The title of Margaret Anne McLaren's essay on Mary Wroth's play, *Love's Victory*, was particularly apt since before the publication of her analysis in Anne Haselkorn's and Betty Travitsky's collection, *The Renaissance Englishwoman in Print* (1990) very few people knew of the play's existence. In her pathbreaking work McLaren offers a clear and informative discussion of the play while at the same time warning us not to neglect this first dramatic comedy written by an English woman.

Lady Mary Wroth was a member of the famous Sidney family who set a stamp on Elizabethan and early Jacobean society in the fields of courtesy, literature, and politics. The Sidneys retain an aura of mystique and glamour even (perhaps especially)in the present day in a different, nuclear age. Unlike her uncle Sir Philip Sidney and, later, her aunt the Countess of Pembroke, Lady Wroth remained obscure both as a woman and as a writer, in part because she dared to write fiction that dealt with such matters as love and sex, rather than confining herself like her aunt to religious and moral works and to translation. 'Worke oth' workes leave idle bookes alone / for wise and worthyer women have writte none,' snarled a contemporary satirist of the first and only work by Lady Wroth to appear in print during her lifetime, in 1621.[1]

That book constituted the first part of a prose romance by Lady Mary Wroth, which she dedicated to her best friend Susan Vere (first wife of Philip Herbert, Earl of Montgomery, younger brother to William Herbert, Earl of Pembroke) and entitled *The Countesse of Mountgomeries Urania*, or, *Urania* (1621). The work, however, was suppressed soon after it was published, on the grounds that it was a *roman-à-clef* which caricatured prominent members of the court of James I. Whether Lady Wroth ever intended to have her work published remains in doubt, but there is no question about her seriousness as an author.[2] Apart from the printed first half of *Urania* (1621), four of her holograph manuscripts survive, a sequence, 'Songs and sonnets beginning with poems from Pamphilia to Amphilanthus' (a version of the poems appearing in the published part of *Urania*), a second half of the romance called 'The first and second books of the secound part of the Countess of Mongomerys Urania' ('Urania, Part Two'), and an almost completely unknown pastoral drama called 'Loves Victorie,' which exists in two copies.[3]

Lady Wroth's work, which belonged for so long to what Adrienne Rich calls the 'Great Silence' surrounding women's art and history, is gradually being rescued from oblivion.[4] The present essay focuses attention on the play 'Loves Victorie,' the least known of her productions. Although the following remarks must be partial because access to only one of the manuscript versions is possible at present, study of this text contributes to our understanding of Lady Wroth's oeuvre as a whole and to our appreciation of the particular contribution made by women to the development of English literature.

Lady Wroth's obscurity, like her father's, was due to unflattering comparison of her work with that of Sir Philip Sidney and the Countess of Pembroke, as well as to the lack of significance generally attached to works of art below the first rank. In *Signs Taken for Wonders*, Franco Moretti has highlighted the shortsightedness of such an exclusive view of literature.[5] Taking issue with the Annales school of French literary criticism, Moretti objects to the idea that

> 'normal literature' . . . has no place in criticism. The result is that, at present, our knowledge of literary history closely resembles the maps of Africa of a century and a half ago: the coastal strips are familiar but an entire continent is unknown. Dazzled by the great estuaries of mythical rivers, when it comes to pinpointing the source we still trust too often to bizarre hypotheses or even to legends.[6]

Moretti claims that literary historiography has for too long comprised an '*histoire événementielle*, where the "events" are great works or great individuals.' He argues instead for the study of literary genres as a whole, including 'low' or 'mass literatures,' and an examination of the 'norm' that produces meanings that he believes are far from 'predictable' or 'banal'.[7]

Lady Wroth was exceptional as a Sidney (so she believed) and as a female author who ventured into areas that few of her sex dared to enter, but her work – especially 'Loves Victorie' – is genre bound and owes important debts to both earlier and contemporary models. Examining the play in the light of Moretti's theories offers special rewards when it is studied in relation to the literary and social norms prevailing in Lady Wroth's lifetime. 'Loves Victorie' is predictable in its surface direction, that of conventional Renaissance pastoral. Its theme could be summed up in the words of a courtier-turned-shepherd in 'Urania, Part Two' who complains that he and his fellows 'are forced to serve an other master . . . which is the most tirannicall thing called love, heere wee whine, heere wee cry, sigh, lament, write cruell harsh, and unsufferable complaining, and groaning lamentations' (bk 2, fol. 3bv).

Although both 'Loves Victorie' and 'Urania, Part Two' are constructed along similarly stereotyped ideological lines, the drama notably lacks the irony underlying the mock shepherd's satirical plaint. In 'Loves Victorie,' dislocations that arise from the interaction of writer and milieu are typically expressed in silence.

G. F. Waller in *English Poetry of the Sixteenth Century* emphasizes the significance of ideology in Renaissance literature, a term he glosses as 'the system of images, attitudes, feelings, myths, and gestures which are peculiar to a society, which the members who make up that society habitually take for granted'.[8] The thrust of his analysis is to examine the pressure of history on texts and thus to apply the tools of structuralism and poststructuralism to Renaissance literature in a manner that usefully complements Moretti's ideas. Waller considers the effect of 'oppositional voices,' among different writers on the one hand and within a single text on the other,[9] while Moretti refers to the 'non-univocal' and even 'self-contradictory' text.[10] Moretti does not exclude univocal analyses but talks of the need to approach the text 'not as if it were a vector pointing neatly in one direction, but as if it were a light-source radiating in several directions or a field of forces in relatively stable equilibrium'.[11]

Critics like Moretti and Waller thus provide models to show how a 'normal' work like 'Loves Victorie,' a manuscript that seems totally conventional and one that is almost wholly forgotten by literary history, can be seen as a complex, rich text if we approach it as an intersection of discourses, an example of give and take between literary and social structures, and as a field of tensions, contradictions, and absences. Studied in this manner, 'Loves Victorie' offers a view of the court and its disguises and obsessions from a point of view that has seldom been considered: the view of a woman author whose images usually link with social norms but sometimes betray significant evidence of nonlinkage, whose writing is marked by conspicuous gaps and even by silence.

Terry Eagleton's comments on Pierre Macherey's Marxist notions concerning 'decentred' form are pertinent here:

> For Macherey, a work is tied to ideology not so much by what it says as by what it does not say. It is in the significant *silences* of a text, in its gaps and absences, that the presence of ideology can be most positively felt. It is these silences which the critic must make 'speak'. The text is . . . ideologically forbidden to say certain things; . . . it is always *incomplete.* Far from constituting a rounded, coherent whole, it displays a conflict and contradiction of meanings; and the significance of the work lies in the difference rather than unity between these meanings.[12]

In some ways the self-contradictions (more obvious in the case of the complete 'Urania') that mark Lady Wroth's productions reflect the peculiar dualism of the times in which she lived. As Moretti puts it in a second essay, the Jacobean court was, despite the much celebrated formal decorum of its public demeanor, 'the exemplary site of an unrestrained conflict of private interests'.[13] Waller's theory of the pressure of history on writers insists that the literary text is not a simple reflection of the social text. The social structure interacts with the literary structures as a field of forces we can usefully map. Lady Wroth's particular contribution derives from the pressure that gender exerts on this interaction. The results can be surprisingly unconventional, even in her pastoral drama where she does her best to tailor the social textures of the play to fit literary prototypes.

Drawing on a variety of commentators, Waller makes an observation, which is apt in this connection:

> The text's detours, silences, omissions, absences, faults, and symptomatic dislocations are all part of what we focus on in addition to, and even at times in preference to, its surface. We look for the different languages, literary and social that hover in the vicinity of the text, trying to master and muffle it; in particular we focus on places where the seemingly unified surface of a work is contradicted or undermined, where the text 'momentarily misses a beat, thins out or loses intensity, or makes a false move – where the scars show, in the face of stress.[14]

The aim of the present essay is to examine several different languages that make up 'Loves

Victorie'; the language of the court with its predictable and ideologically conventional use of Petrarchan and Neoplatonic images and philosophy, the language of comedy with its use of anti-Petrarchan elements and satire, and the language of myth and ritual with its references to spring, the gods, and associated rites of love. Less obviously, but no less strikingly, 'Loves Victorie' also makes use of a special language of avoidance, where the author chooses to emphasize the festive and positive aspects of her story in keeping with the public nature of her chosen medium (courtly drama) in preference to the potentially dark and despairing possibilities inherent in the plot and lurking at every twist and turn.

The language of avoidance which mutes the text from time to time can be seen as the device of a Renaissance or, more particularly, a Jacobean woman. It derives from a complex disjunction between the discourse of courtship and the context in which it is used. It serves to stress the frustration and helplessness of women characters caught in the age-old dichotomy between the image of woman in popular mythology – queen, goddess, all-powerful mistress – and her everyday subordination imposed in the name of love. The play, which determinedly avoids the contentious issues more openly addressed in the complete 'Urania,' is a text whose stability is only relative. There is a disturbing vacuum beneath the surface, an absence that amounts to a muffling of the text (quite apart from the fact that the Huntington manuscript is unfinished), that calls for detailed analysis.

Lady Wroth's work, however indirectly in 'Loves Victorie' where the ambiguities and dislocations of her theme of sexual love erupt less obviously than in her prose or lyrics, reflects the increasing powerlessness of women and new limitations affecting them. The changing idea of the lady at the Jacobean court contrasts sharply with that obtaining in Elizabethan times. Humanist values regarding the importance of education for women – upper-class women at least – were giving way to a new emphasis on woman's traditional domestic role. Hence the political overview of the world evident in a Jonson or a Shakespeare is less central to the world of a Lady Wroth who inhabited a milieu only too ready to berate her as a woman meddling in matters beyond her sphere. The device of avoidance serves to limit the scope of the dramatic action in 'Loves Victorie' and to shift the focus from macrocosm to microcosm.

It is a commonplace of literary criticism to point to the tensions and unfulfilled ambitions informing the courtly poetry of writers like Wyatt, Ralegh, or Sir Robert Sidney. The mistress of many a sixteenth-century poem represented Queen Elizabeth: her lover's pleas voiced demands for material favors in the form of perquisites or office at court. In a similar way, Jacobean masque constructed an ideal Platonic realm intended to embody the political claims promulgated by the Stuart monarchy. Lady Wroth's characters, on the other hand, are more likely to reflect homely realities than political concerns. Her themes are highly personal and her work less open to allegorical interpretation than much of the prose and poetry of her male contemporaries. 'Loves Victorie' resembles her other works in picturing not an exterior, outward world, but an interior, inward realm that begins and ends with the experience of human rather than divine love and sifts the ever-shifting quicksands of the relationships between men and women.

The plot of the Huntington version of 'Loves Victorie' can be summarized as follows:

> Somewhere in an unnamed country in the environs of Arcadia twelve shepherds and shepherdesses wander the fields and valleys looking after their sheep. The men are called Philisses, Lissius, Rustick, Lacon, Arcas (or Argas), and Forester. The women are named Musella, Simena, Dalina, Fillis, Climena, and Silvesta. The

> buffoon Rustick, who is richer than the others, looks after cattle as well. Much of the action revolves around the difficulties the characters experience in conveying their feelings of love to the partners of their choice, and the women are faced with a special dilemma because the consensus is that they should not take an active role in courtship. A variety of love relationships is presented, ranging from the comic, one sided and earthy longings of Rustick, to the mutual, passionate, and virtuous feelings of Philisses and Musella, which join love with reason. Another type of love is seen in the relationship between Silvesta and Forester, where the nymph eschews human love and Forester agrees (reluctantly) to commit himself to a sexless compromise in the manner of the courtly or Neoplatonic lover.
>
> Two mythological characters, Venus and Cupid, provide a framework for the play and an internal commentary on the action. When Philisses's best friend Lissius scorns the power of love, Venus, enraged, orders Cupid to wreak havoc among the pastoral troup. Jealousy, suspicion, and gossip infect the lovers. The play comes to a climax when Musella reveals to Philisses that her father has betrothed her to Rustick in his will, and that, although he is dead, her mother feels obliged to fulfill her husband's promise. The play breaks off at the point when Musella and Philisses pledge their undying love and agree to visit the temple to seek an unknown solution.

Following the fashion for tragicomic drama, which reached its apogee in the seventeenth century, Lady Wroth has constructed a five-act play that concludes each of its first four acts (the fifth is incomplete in the Huntington manuscript) with the appearance of the goddess Venus – although at the end of Act 3 the speech heading 'Venus' is followed by a blank page, the speech not having been copied out. In three of her four appearances Venus is accompanied by her son Cupid. Lady Wroth rigorously eschews contemporary allegory, and the two mythological figures function as a structural device not unlike the diversions, played one by one in each of the first four acts, which range from storytelling to the reading of prophetic rhymes and the telling of riddles.[15] In a play that sees little action and whose characters seem at times to resemble the 'talking heads' of modern television drama, these games serve as focus for the psychological drama that constitutes the real heart of 'Loves Victorie.'

Each diversion offers the opportunity for the aims of Venus and Cupid as spelled out at the end of Act 1 to be realized. The mythological figures do not interact with the other characters in the play (except for a reference to a meeting with Venus in one of the shepherds' songs, and some awareness on Dalina's part of what the gods are up to). However, like Andrea and Revenge in *The Spanish Tragedy*, Venus and Cupid act as Chorus, so that when Lissius protests with humor that his friend Philisses has fallen in love – 'this is the humor makes our sheapheards rave / I'le non of this, I'le souner seeke my grave' (LVH. 1v. 19–20) and several of his companions seem less than deeply involved in their love affairs, Venus protests, speaking to Cupid,

> Fy this is nothing, what is this your care
> that among ten the haulf of them you spare
> I would have all to wayle, and all to weepe
> will you att such a time as this goe sleepe
> awake your forces, and make Lissius find
> Cupid can cruell bee as well as kind.
> (LVH, 4v. 33–8)

The following discussion spells out the meaning of the play's title. 'Loves Victorie' is not merely intended to suggest that in the end true love will win out. Very simply the title means power: the power of Venus and Cupid to humble everyone in the play, even those who seem most immune to love. Cupid assures Venus,

> they shall both cry, and waile, and weepe
> and for our mercy shall most humbly creepe
> love hath most glory when as greatest sprites
> hee downward throwse unto his owne delights
> then take noe care loves victory shall shine
> when as your honor shall bee raisd by mine.
> (LVH, 5r. 5–10)

The disturbances just perceptible beneath the surface of the play are embodied in Venus, with her malevolence, her power to wreak havoc, and her association with lust. These are characteristics that Shakespeare was very careful to exclude in *The Tempest* (*c.*1611) by banning 'Mars's hot minion' from the betrothal masque for Miranda and Ferdinand (4.1.91–101). Jonson retains but subdues them when he produces Venus in *The Haddington Masque* (1608) at the side of her husband, Vulcan. Yoking passionate love to matrimony, the goddess vows, 'My lamp shall burn / With pure and chastest fire'.[16] Likewise in Samuel Daniel's *Vision of Twelve Goddesses* (1604), Venus appears with 'mild aspect,' carrying a scarf of amity designed 'T'ingird strange Nations with affections true'.[17]

Classical gods and goddesses have played a part in pastoral poetry and drama from the earliest times, and Venus and Cupid were always favorite motifs in Lady Wroth's work: the first sonnet of *Pamphilia to Amphilanthus* opens with an account of a dream in which both mother and son appear (*Urania* [1621], sig. 4Ar). Lady Wroth would have been familiar with the use made of mythological figures by Tasso in his *Aminta*, by Daniel in his tragicomedy, *Hymen's Triumph* (1614), and by Jonson in a play like *Cynthia's Revels* and masques such as *Love Freed from Ignorance and Folly*, performed in 1611.[18] But the bitter and recurrent despair, which marks her songs and sonnets (in both printed and manuscript versions) and 'Urania, Part Two,' conveys a sense of personal pain in relation to the theme of love which is quite lacking in the complacent depiction by her male contemporaries of Venus *Domestica*.

Of course pastoral is traditionally cast in the comic mode. The despair of the lyrics is largely absent in 'Loves Victorie' where difficulties in love, while not entirely ignored, are (more or less) resolved in keeping with convention. The death of the heart, a major theme in Lady Wroth's other work, is downplayed in the drama. Although the Huntington manuscript breaks off, and although there are oppositional voices affecting the comic discourse, the play points toward closure and foreshadows a 'happy ending.' It can be compared with an episode in 'Urania, Part Two' where ten shepherds and shepherdesses led by a brother and sister appear in a similarly lighthearted situation (bk 2, fols 3av–5bv). Names are duplicated – Arcas, Rustick, Magdalina (Dalina in the dramatic version) – although roles vary somewhat: Musella of 'Loves Victorie' is a more central character than her counterpart who is named in the play as Philisses's sister Simena; the Venus and Cupid of 'Urania, Part Two' appear only in the imagery of courtly love employed by Arcas and Rustick, while the Cupid of 'Loves Victorie' has more in common with the mischievous god of Jonson's *Cynthia's Revels*, whose dual identity as Eros and 'loves enemie' Anteros, causes division and maximum confusion.[19] This is a device that Jonson uses again in 1613 in *A Challenge at Tilt*.[20]

In 'Loves Victorie,' Cupid introduces difficulties into the lives of the rustics in order to demonstrate the overwhelming power of Venus. The portrayal of the troubling goddess herself probably owes most to an earlier entertainment, *The Lady of May*, devised by Lady Wroth's uncle Sir Philip Sidney. This divertissement was written for Robert Dudley, Earl of Leicester, Sidney's uncle, on the occasion of a visit by Queen Elizabeth to his country mansion at Wanstead in 1578 or 1579. Queen Elizabeth, like Lady Wroth's Venus, provides a frame for the playlet. A summary follows:

> The queen is walking in Wanstead gardens when she is addressed by a country-woman who explains that her daughter, the lady of May, is being sought in marriage by two suitors: one a lively and generous (but poor and bad-tempered) forester called Therion, the other a rich and kindly (but quiet and meditative) shepherd called Espilus. The lady appears, pulled this way and that by opposing parties of foresters and shepherds, while a pedantic schoolmaster named Rombus tries unsuccessfully to separate them. The May lady, who affects not to recognize the queen nevertheless bows to her superior beauty and asks her to choose a husband on her behalf. The two rivals engage in a singing competition, and their supporters, the old shepherd Dorcas and the young forester Rixus, continue the argument. Finally, Queen Elizabeth delivers her judgment and chooses the shepherd Espilus. The lady of May concludes with the conceit that she hopes the flourishing of May will long represent the life and reign of the queen.

Like Lady Wroth's Venus, Sidney's Elizabeth is as all-powerful in this spring world as she is elsewhere. The May lady recognizes the queen's intrinsic superiority and quickly yields pre-eminence to her.[21] Spring functions, in both Sidney's and Lady Wroth's plays, as a resonant metaphor opposed to a picture of winter, death, and decay. The effect of Queen Elizabeth's 'gay apparel' covered in flowers either real or embroidered, remarked on by the May lady, is to create a rival Queen of May. So too in 'Loves Victorie,' Venus appears in the guise of Flora – or a May lady – and, like Elizabeth, is described in terms of a *locus amoenus*. The shepherd Lacon sings:

> By a pleasant rivers side
> hart and hopes on pleasures tide
> might I see within a bower
> proudly drest with every floure
> which the spring can to us lend
> Venus, and her loving freind.
> (LVH, 4r, 47–52)

Each lady is the epitome of beauty in her world, and each personifies the idea of love. Lady Wroth's choice of Venus as the presiding genius in her play can be construed as a delicate compliment to the part played by Elizabeth in Sidney's work. Like Elizabeth, who represents the outsider solicited to resolve difficulties within the drama, Venus is part of the story but exists outside it as well: she not only initiates action but also brings it to a successful conclusion.

More strikingly, the goddess Venus serves Lady Wroth as an analogue of female power, whereas for Sidney's generation the strongest feminine symbol was the Virgin Queen (as Spenser's *Faerie Queene* resoundingly testifies). Queen Elizabeth's essential strength derived from her single status which meant that she was not under the power of any man and could keep suitors vying for her favors even when the game had become little more than a sham. Elizabethan writers associated her with the moon goddess Diana (Artemis, Cynthia) who represents married and unmarried chastity but herself remains woman alone, virgin huntress, possessed by no man, although as goddess of childbirth she assists the fruitfulness of others. In Petrarchan terms, the queen represented beauty and a love forever unattainable. 'Thus, by a paradox, sex, having created a problem, itself solved it, and the reign was turned into an idyll, a fine but artificial comedy of young men – and old men – in love.'[22]

By the time Lady Wroth came to write her play about forty years later, there was no compelling living female image on which to focus as representative of the power of the feminine principle such as Elizabeth had provided in the previous era. What power Queen Anne possessed derived solely from her relational position as wife of a monarch and mother of the kingdom's heirs. A reaction had set in concerning the question of women's independence and education. In Lady Wroth's fictional world the kind of supremacy that Elizabeth had wielded over her domain, including the area of personal relationships and marriage, could only be paralleled by a mythological figure with power over love, in whose name, supposedly, women were to subject themselves more stringently to the rule of men.

Clearly virginity no longer conveyed the same sense of vigor and authority in the Jacobean age that it had in the Elizabethan. Sex is important to Lady Wroth as a theme in her work. Nevertheless it is interesting to note that the lover of Venus in 'Loves Victorie' is not named. The name of the goddess of love traditionally signifies diverse meanings – sometimes she is linked to sexual passion and adultery, sometimes to marriage. Lady Wroth's Venus is her own woman, her anonymous lover strictly incidental to the symbol she represents.

This symbol does not go completely unchallenged in 'Loves Victorie.' There are oppositional voices apparent in the drama which provide evidence of the kind of symptomatic dislocation making minor texts as revealing in their way as more important works of the same period. The first woman character to appear in 'Loves Victorie,' apart from Venus in the privately owned copy of the play,[23] is the erstwhile shepherdess Silvesta who, because she has been rejected by Philisses, has become a nymph of Diana and vowed herself to celibacy:

> for thanks to heaven, and to the Gods above
> I have wunn chastity in place of love;
> now love's as farr from mee as never knowne,
> then bacely tied, now freely ame mine owne;
> slavery and bondage with mourning care
> was then my living sighs, and teares my feare,
> butt all these gon now live I joyfully
> free, and untouch'd of thought but chastitye.
> (LVH, 2r. 15–22)

Silvesta functions as an antithesis to Musella who is passionately and deeply in love with Philisses, the same man the nymph once loved herself. Musella's love acts as a contrast to the earthy, possessive, and fickle passions of Rustick and Dalina. Musella's role provides an instance of the intersection of discourses characteristic of Lady Wroth's work. Silvesta's new independence, for instance, suggests an attractive alternative to the suffering that friends like Musella continue to endure. The reiterated stress on the 'freedom' experienced by those no longer in love strikes a plangent note which echoes oddly in the context of a play that promises at several points that the ending will be a happy one *with all the lovers restored to suitable partners.* 'I see thou'rt bound who most have made unfree,' observes Silvesta addressing Musella in Act 3 (LVH, 11r. 30), the line recalling sonnet 14 in the first section of *Pamphilia to Amphilanthus* in which the speaker laments that love 'captive leads me prisoner bound, unfree' (*Urania* [1621], sig. 4A4v). The opposition of love and freedom betrays a sense of the author's despair, which is otherwise largely banished from the text of the play.

Although Silvesta's unorthodox decision about the place of love in her own life is not the dominant view of the play, from a structural point of view her ideas are given prominence. She appears near the start of Acts 1 and 2 where she expresses herself at length. She gives the opening speech in Act 3, and her name is mentioned by Musella in the first line of Act 4. While Silvesta is absent from the fragmentary Act 5 in the Huntington version, Musella's despair at the prospect of losing Philisses (because her parents have betrothed her to Rustick) neatly illustrates the kind of dilemma the nymph is able to side-step as a result of her dedication to virginity and the goddess Diana:

Chastity my pleasure is
folly fled
from hence now I seeke my blis
cross love dead.
(LVH, 11r. 9–12)

Silvesta henceforth avoids the difficulties inherent in human loving, much in the same way that Lady Wroth avoids spelling out the implications of the presence of oppositional voices such as those of Silvesta, Musella, or the fickle Dalina. The note of irony sounded from time to time when Lissius scoffs at love is muted in the overall pattern of the play, which is more commonly marked by a reiteration of the significance of the ideal of heterosexual love. Silvesta nevertheless speaks a language that is very different from that of Musella and Philisses: her experience of love and her conclusions reveal the tension beneath the surface of the work – 'where the scars show, in the face of stress.'

Venus makes a crucial statement at the end of Act 2, written on a quarto leaf appended to the text, possibly a later addition. She directly addresses the audience, almost certainly envisaged by Lady Wroth as a courtly one: 'harts obay to Cupids sway / prinses non of you say nay' (LVH, 10r. 16–17). The goddess warns,

lett your songs bee still of love
write noe satirs which may prove
least offensive to his name.
(LVH, 10r. 22–4)

Her image is not only appropriate to the pastoral setting but in addition strikes a vulnerable note. If her listeners ignore her injunction concerning satires,

> . . . you will butt frame
> words against your selves, and lines
> wher his good, and your ill shines
> like him who doth sett a snare
> for a poore betrayed hart
> and that thing hee best doth love
> lucklesly the snare doth prove.
> (LVH, 10r–v. 25–9, 1–2)

The comparison of the writer who satirizes love with a hunter who accidentally kills the thing he loves best is a telling one by which Lady Wroth reveals a great deal about her own aims as an author. Not for her the satiric portrait that Jonson paints in *The Christmas Masque* (1616) of Venus as a deaf tirewoman, speaking in the manner of a poor old woman from Pudding Lane, while the lord of Misrule is played by 'Tom of Bosoms Inn'.[24] The earthy or risqué element favored by several writers of pastoral dramas and sometimes masques is almost wholly absent from 'Loves Victorie.' With the possible exception of a few remarks by Forester about his difficulties in viewing Silvesta in a wholly platonic light, Lady Wroth avoids the titillating elements that inform the work of her male contemporaries.

She also avoids the extremes of either panegyric or violence characteristic of their productions. For instance, Forester and Silvesta's relationship may owe something to the example set by Clorin in Fletcher's *Faithful Shepherdess* (1608), who dedicates herself to the memory of her dead lover.[25] Clorin is courted in the meantime by the shepherd Thenot, and when she tests his sincerity by offering herself to him, thereby breaking her vows, he rejects her, having built his love on the expectation that she is unobtainable.[26]

The self-protective ambiguity informing Clorin's offer and the roughness of Thenot's repudiation are aspects that Lady Wroth avoids in favor of a gentle and disarming use of humor. She employs instead the anti-Petrarchan imagery used by Sidney in the *Arcadia* to describe the rustic Mopsa in her depiction of Rustick's love for Musella. The buffoon celebrates his beloved as 'whiter then lambs wull'; he says her eyes 'do play / like goats with hay' and that her cheeks are as red 'as okar spred / On a fatted sheeps back'; and, finally, that her breasts 'are found / as aples round' (LVH, 4r. 25, 29–30, 36–7, 39–40). Lady Wroth's nonviolent pastoral images, however much they poke fun at the language of courtly love, bear little relation to the savage irony informing Fletcher's play. In another example from *The Faithful Shepherdess*, the shepherdess Amoret is twice wounded to death by her lover Perigot as the result of a misunderstanding, stuffed down a well and left for dead by a different rustic, the lascivious Sullen Shepherd.[27]

'Loves Victorie' eschews the aggressive sexuality of incidents such as the foregoing or the Sullen Shepherd's expression of regret that he failed to rape Amoret, or Chloe's and Amarillis's frustrated efforts to find themselves sexual partners.[28] Likewise, whatever Lady Wroth may owe to *Hymen's Triumph* (1614),[29] she avoids the frankness shown by Daniel's Silvia. A shepherdess disguised as a boy and stabbed nearly to death by a jealous forester called Montanus who mistakes him (her) for a rival, Silvia tells the audience that the reason for her alias as Clarindo is to avoid premarital sexual relations with her lover.[30]

In 'Loves Victorie' Lady Wroth not only employs the language of avoidance in regard to the cruder physical manifestations of 'love,' but also extends it to the political, social, and courtly dimensions with which in 'Urania, Part Two' she invests a troup of seeming rustics, almost identical with those of the drama. The world of 'Urania, Part Two' is in turmoil; a group of young princes and princesses have been abducted, and the sophy of Persia has put Asia to the sword. Here, the shepherds and shepherdesses described by Arcas as suffering for love are really disguised courtiers awaiting their opportunity to end the enchantment in which the lost princes and princesses are trapped. Arcas himself is the courtier Amicles and Rustick turns out to be a young Morean knight called Folietto.

Whereas the conventional fields and woods of 'Loves Victorie' echo only to the sounds of silence (even Philisses's pipe is hushed), in 'Urania, Part Two' they are resonant with drumbeats from other wider worlds. Much play is made early in the manuscript on Folietto's color – he is black – but the issues this raises and the uncomfortable experiences he undergoes as a raw recruit called to the problematic and frustrating search for the lost princes (bk 1, fol. 11ar–v), which recall Ariel's tormenting of Stephano and Trinculo in *The Tempest*, are entirely omitted in the drama. So too is the notion expounded by Rustick (Folietto) that his and his friends' sufferings for love are largely a fiction designed as a cover for their true mission, a notion which makes the ironies of Lady Wroth's use of pastoral elements in 'Urania, Part Two' explicit.

In 'Loves Victorie' the rustics are real. Their world stops at the edge of field and forest and there is no mention of court or courtiers. The names of major characters like Philisses and Musella may owe their origins to the court, perhaps to specific examples like Philip Sidney who was sometimes nicknamed Philisides, the shepherd knight, and Stella (Penelope Rich), the muse of Sidney's Sonnets. Their language may be couched in the ideologies of courtly and Neoplatonic love. Nevertheless, the connection ends on this surface level. Philisses and Musella are locals fixed, however improbably, in their rural setting. They and their companions (at least in the Huntington manuscript) do not turn out to be the disguised sons and daughters of kings and queens. They are confined by their author to the never-never world of the pastoral.

This world does however include consideration of the proper roles of men and women in courtship. A curious sexist element rears its head in the course of the play which reflects the prejudices of the age and exemplifies the particular reaction of a woman writer to the implications of those prejudices in regard to the relationship between the sexes. In Act 2, Lissius, an avowed enemy of Cupid, cynically describes what he regards as men's characteristic relation to women, who are imaged in terms of animals from the pastoral realm:

> for wee should woemen love butt as our sheepe,
> who beeing kind, and gentle gives us ease,
> butt cross, or strayning, stuborne, or unmeeke
> shun'd as the woulf which most our flocks disease.
>
> (LVH, 6v. 31–4)

The effect of such an attitude on the meaning of the play as a whole is less simple than it seems when we come to such instances as Arcas chiding Dalina a few pages later for being overbold in claiming her turn in the riddling game immediately after Musella. One woman has spoken already, he says. Now a *man* should follow (LVH, 8r. 2). More disturbingly, Lissius rounds on Climena in Act 3 and berates her for making advances toward him; 'fy, I doe blush for you, a woman woo, / the most unfittest , shamfullst thing to doo' (LVH, 14r. 28–9).

Musella, the ideal of pastoral womanhood in the play, is only too well aware of the prohibition on women's assertiveness in love: 'some times I faine would speake then straite forbeare / knowing itt most unfitt; this woe I beare.' Silvesta agrees: 'indeed a woman to make love is ill' (LVH, 11v. 33–6).

The result is that when on Silvesta's advice Musella gets up early to meet Philisses in the woods (where he wanders bewailing his love), she pretends she is there by chance. Moreover, she feels that she cannot act directly to comfort her lover and is constrained to wait until he takes the initiative: 'I faine would comfort him, and yett I know / nott if from mee 't'will comfort bee or noe' (LVH, 15v. 47–8). Careful not to court Philisses overtly, Musella can only respond to his bleak and generalized remarks with the timid suggestion, 'tell mee who 't'is you love, and I will give / my word I'le win her if she may bee wunn' (LVH, 16r. 19–20). The reader senses the pressure of what remains unspoken – Musella's longing to express herself without restraint and of her own free will.

Such muffling of the main issue – the treatment of women as second-class citizens – is not allowed to pass entirely without comment in the play. Dalina, a woman who has chosen her own way (although not entirely happily), makes the point in the middle of the drama that she has never taken love particularly seriously:

> this is the reason men ar growne soe coy
> when they parseave wee make their smiles our joy
> lett them alone, and they will seeke, and sue,
> butt yeeld to them, they will with scorne poursue;
> hold awhile of they'll kneele, nay follow you,
> and vowe, and sweare, yett all their othes untrue.
> (LVH, 13v. 30–5)

Such straight speaking is unusual in 'Loves Victorie.' In the main, the relationship between the sexes is approached obliquely, tentatively; there is a hesitancy on the part of the author to bring the difficulties lying just beneath the surface of her story to open view. Literary and social norms are nevertheless implicitly questioned again and again by allusions to the inadequacy of the received ideologies to account for women's particular experiences and points of view. But this questioning remains implicit in 'Loves Victorie.' Inconstancy, as in the case of Lissius and Simena, is merely a matter for unfounded rumor or the experience of minor and ridiculous characters such as Dalina and Climena. Major roles such as Philisses and Musella are unaffected by character weaknesses like fickleness. The threat to their love is external as in the case of Romeo and Juliet. The contrast to the tragic on-again, off-again relationship of Queen Pamphilia and Emperor Amphilanthus in the complete 'Urania' (the emperor is always susceptible to a pretty face) could hardly be greater.

Whether Lady Wroth's avoidance of issues with which she was preoccupied in her prose fiction and her other poetry constitutes self-restraint or a new direction in her work is debatable. The play *may* have been written in the aftermath of the bitter criticism of the freedom Lady Wroth was alleged to have displayed in describing the private lives of her fellow courtiers in *Urania* (1621). The prospect of public performance may also have had a significant effect on her choice of tone, and certainly the style is more in keeping with the Platonic ideals of the masque than with the darker realities of the rest of her fiction.

Finally, it remains true that the oppositions of love and death and of summer and winter, reiterated throughout 'Loves Victorie,' function as sign posts to the real obsessions characterizing Lady Wroth's work. Musella may present the sun in the parlance of Neoplatonism but she is followed always by her 'shadowe' (Rustick). As the buffoon hastily follows in the shepherdess's wake when she exits at the end of Act 4, Philisses acerbically remarks,

> noe follow; shadowes never absent bee
> when sunn shines, in which blessing you may see
> your shadow'de self, who nothing in truth are
> butt the reflection of her too great care.
> (LVH, 20r. 26–9)

Philisses may not realize it, but in Rustick he sees a copy of the 'shadow'de self' that he, like all of us, reflects. Where love exists, the possibility of 'joy's decay' is also present (LVH, 17v. 19). The image is the last symptomatic dislocation to be referred to here. The Huntington manuscript breaks off on a note of uncertainty. Flying in the face of the wishes of Musella's parents, the shepherdess and Philisses express their undying love for one another. Philisses offers Musella his life and she replies on an ominous note,

> that I will aske, and yours requite with mine
> for mine can nott bee if nott joined to thine,
> goe with mee to the temple, and ther wee
> will bind our lives, or els our lives make free.
> (LVH, 21v. 41–4)

While they agree, finally, not to do away with themselves, the reader's impression is that from beginning to end Lady Wroth continually avoids the more dangerous rift zones of the human heart. Simena, in the last line of the Huntington version, remains unclear as to whether or not the two lovers plan to fulfill a suicide pact: 'butt what will you tow doe / both dy, and mee poure maiden quite undoe' (LVH, 21v. 62–3). The question remains unanswered in the Huntington version. Throughout the play Venus has promised the audience a happy ending. This seems likely to be fulfilled, but love remains 'shadow'de.'

At first sight Lady Wroth's 'Loves Victorie' may seem to follow the mainstream of late-sixteenth-century and seventeenth-century pastoral drama, but a close examination reveals the many different ways in which her imagery and choice of language – especially her silences – reflect the special experience of a woman writing in Jacobean England. Beneath the soothing assurances that all will be well lies a 'labourinth of woe, and care' (LVH, 16r. 23). Lady Wroth's insights, her achievements, and especially her failures in 'Loves Victorie' contribute usefully to our understanding of Renaissance literature in general and to our appreciation of the experience of women in an earlier age in particular, 'Let him not dy,' Silvesta pleads with Musella, speaking on behalf of the despairing Philisses (LVH, 12r. 6). It is important that we as a modern audience do not allow an almost forgotten but unexpectedly revealing manuscript like 'Loves Victorie' to die.

Notes

1 The poem, which Lady Wroth believed was written by Lord Edward Denny, Baron of Waltham, is included with a vituperative correspondence between the two, copies of which are held at the University Library of Nottingham, reference number Cl LM 85/1–4.

Abbreviations

Urania (1621) *The Countesse of Mountgomeries Urania*. London: John Marriott and John Grismand, 1621. *STC*²: 26051

'Urania, Part Two' The first and second books of the secound part of the Countess of Montgomerys Urania. Newberry Library. Chicago. Shelfmark Case MS fY 1565. W 95

LVH *Loves Victorie*. Huntington Library, San Marino, CA. Shelfmark HM 600 (Note: line references include act and speech headings. Punctuation at the end of quotations is silently emended.)

Complete 'Urania' Refers to both the first and second parts of the prose romance (*Urania* [1621] and 'Urania, Part Two')

The following spellings are modernized and regularized in all quotations: w^{t}/with; w^{ch}/ which.

2 Margaret A. Witten-Hannah (now McLaren), 'Lady Wroth's *Urania*: The Work and the Tradition', PhD dissertation, University of Auckland, 1978, pp. 66–107.
3 A second version of 'Loves Victorie' is privately owned and is due to appear shortly in photo-facsimile edited by Michael G. Brenan of the University of Leeds (kindly communicated by him). Thanks are also owing to M. A. Halls, Archivist, King's College Library, Cambridge, for information and to Fiona McLaren for inquiries made on my behalf.
4 Adrienne Rich, *Of Woman Born* (1976, reprint New York: W. W. Norton, 1977).
5 Franco Moretti, 'The Soul and the Harpy', trans. David Forgacs, in *Signs Taken for Wonders* (London: Verso editions New Left Books, 1983).
6 Ibid., p. 15.
7 Ibid., pp. 13, 15.
8 Gary F. Waller, *English Poetry of the Sixteenth Century* (London: Longman, 1986), p. 9.
9 Ibid., p. 10.
10 Moretti, p. 21.
11 Ibid., p. 22.
12 Terry Eagleton, *Marxism and Literary Criticism* (1976, reprint London: Methuen, 1985), pp. 34–5, italics in the original.
13 Franco Moretti, 'The Great Eclipse: Tragic Form as the Deconsecration of Sovereignty', trans. David Miller, in *Signs Taken for Wonders* (London: Verso editions New Left Books, 1983), p. 72.
14 Waller, p. 12.
15 Similar games are played by the courtiers in Jonson's play *Cynthia's Revels* acted in 1600 and published in 1616: C. H. Herford and Percy Simpson (eds) *Ben Jonson* (Oxford: Clarendon Press, 1925–38), 8 vols, IV, p. 110.
16 Stephen Orgel (ed.) *Ben Jonson: The Complete Masques* (New Haven, CT: Yale University Press, 1969), p. 117.
17 Alexander B. Grosart (ed.) *The Complete Works in Verse and Prose of Samuel Daniel* (*c.* 1885, reprint New York: Russell and Russell, 1963), 5 vols, III, p. 200.
18 W. W. Greg, *Pastoral Poetry and Pastoral Drama* (New York: Russell and Russell, 1959), pp. 15, 156; Josephine A. Roberts, *The Poems of Lady Mary Wroth* (Baton Rouge, LA: Louisiana State University Press, 1983), pp. 54–5.
19 Herford and Simpson IV, p. 167.
20 Orgel, pp. 198–9.
21 Katherine Duncan-Jones and Jan van Dorsten, *Miscellaneous Prose of Sir Philip Sidney* (Oxford: Clarendon Press, 1973), p. 24.

22 J. E. Neale, *Queen Elizabeth I* (1934, reprint Harmondsworth: Penguin, 1967), p. 70.
23 Roberts, p. 67.
24 Orgel, pp. 236–7, 240.
25 Fredson Bowers (gen. ed.) *The Dramatic Works in the Beaumont and Fletcher Canon* (Cambridge: Cambridge University Press, 1966), 6 vols, III, pp. 501–2.
26 Ibid., p. 564.
27 Ibid., pp. 542–3, 560.
28 Ibid., pp. 535, 514–15, 540. The motif of rape recurs in Jonson's *Sad Shepherd*, where Lorel is advised by his mother, the witch Maudlin, to rape the nymph Earine (Herford and Simpson VII, p. 30). Jonson's lost pastoral 'The May Lord' (in which Lady Wroth was assigned a part) may also have had an influence on 'Loves Victorie': G. B. Harrison (ed.) Ben Jonson, *Timber, Discoveries* (1614); *Conversations with Drummond of Hawthornden* (1619), (1923, reprint Edinburgh: Edinburgh University Press, 1966), p. 17.
29 The betrothal of Musella has similarities to that of Silvia in *Hymen's Triumph* (Grosart III, p. 388).
30 Grosart III, p. 367.

10

'LIKE ONE IN A GAY MASQUE'

The Sidney cousins in the theaters of court and country

Gary Waller

The previous essay on Mary Wroth's play, *Love's Victory*, in this collection was published in 1990, and it is important to note the speed with which Wroth studies have become established, since this extract by Gary Waller was published three years later as part of his monograph on Wroth's familial writings, *The Sidney Family Romance: Mary Wroth, William Herbert, and the Early Modern Construction of Gender* (1993). Wroth is now regarded as one of the most important writers of her age, and Waller, whose criticism of her work is extensive, here offers a detailed and acute analysis of the gender politics of her play.

As a woman in the Jacobean court, as a lady-in-waiting and occasional dancer, Mary Wroth played an appropriately decorative and silent part in the margins of the spectacle of the court; her primary role was simply to be seen, as a graceful, minor contributor to the dazzling visual display that mirrored for its participants the gloriousness that was a central part of the court's self-image. Like one of her characters in her prose romance, *Urania*, she 'both saw those sports the Court affects, and are necessary follies for that place, as Masques and Dauncings, and was an Actor my selfe amongst them' (*Urania*, p. 457). Her cousin William Herbert, third Earl of Pembroke – who was her lover and fathered two children with her – was likewise a minor participant in the orchestrations of court display, but, as a man, 'naturally' he took on more active roles as a dancer, tilter, and challenger, and in his highly visible public roles as patron and political authority.

One of the roles that Pembroke did not play was that of playwright: of the two cousins, it was Wroth who actually wrote a play, even though it was never published and may not have been acted, even privately. So far as we know, too, she had no direct contact with the public theater, although Naomi Miller has argued that, especially in *Urania*, there are many signs of Wroth's interest in a concept of the dramatic and the theatrical very different from those derived from the masque and the specular theater of the court: many revelations occur in dramatic dialogues that echo the conversations between heroines and confidantes, like Beatrice and Hero, in Shakespeare's comedies. But what Margaret McLaren terms 'the mechanics of seeming' in *Urania* suggests that Wroth was aware that court theatricals displayed what must have been, especially for a woman, an all too familiar metaphor for the gender politics of the court. Several key episodes occur in 'theaters,' which are depicted not merely as sites of dramatic entertainment but of enchantment and self-discovery, as if one of the functions of artifice and role playing were to reveal the origins and destiny of the actors, not merely the roles they play.[1] When Pamphilia asserts that 'an Actor knowes when to speake, when to sigh, when to end: a true feeler is wrapped in distempers, and only can know how to heare' (*Urania*, p. 314), she may be displaying a disdain for feigned emotion, but the sorrowful queen and every other character in the romance are constantly on display, arranging scenes to display themselves as surely as the Jacobean courtiers in their elaborately staged performances, onstage and off. Pamphilia arrives at the House of Love in calculatedly spectacular fashion, in a 'Chariot of Watchet, embroydred with Crimson silke, and purle of silver.' Bacon pointed out that the 'glories' of tournaments are 'chiefly in the Chariots, wherein the Challengers make their entry.'[2] When King Antisius of Romania arrives with his knights to take part in the Accession Day tournament – thus echoing the same event in the court of James – they are referred to, not without some extended irony, as actors (*Urania*, pp. 123, 341). In *Urania* there are a number of scenes in which the male propensity to self-display and self-advertising are satirized. The sly humor, directed even at the matchless Amphilanthus, is both consistent and serious: the pressures and contradictions of the court, whereby men had to constantly struggle for recognition, produced what Greenblatt terms a 'virtually fetishistic emphasis on manner,' and meant that performative and adaptive role playing became a supposedly 'natural' part of the male courtier's identity.[3] Wroth's romance gives us a demystification along gendered lines: it enacts a woman subject's acknowledgement of the power of and yet alienation from the 'naturalness' of male display.

Theatrical metaphors, then, carried a particularly intense ideological weight in the lives and writings of the Sidney cousins, not least in relation to the politics of gender. The very act of being a woman author itself involves playing parts that are, as it were, not found in the accepted scripts for women. Yet to take on the role of a writer, as Heather Weidemann points out (and Wroth's treatment by Lord Denny attests), does not in itself produce a 'happy proliferation of subversion.'[4] If taking on an unfamiliar role, disguising, and trying to play new parts all suggest liberation from assigned gender identities – as they do, at least for a time, in Shakespeare's comedies, most obviously in *As You Like It* – they may equally signify the oppression of never having any owned subject position, which is what Pamphilia complains about when she exclaims 'O afflictions, how many severall ways have you . . . how many maskes, how many false faces can you procure, to delude inocent faith' (*Newberry 1*, fol. 21). The fragility of the theatrical metaphor is never far from the surface in such remarks. The commonplace Renaissance metaphors of the world as the theater of God's glory or the court as a theater of magnificence assert a correspondence between specular surface and underlying reality, where what is acted is part of the natural and providential. But the world of theatricality in *Urania* is fundamentally insecure and untrustworthy. The acceptance of the self as theatricalized never allows a man or, especially, a woman an escape from assigned roles and actions. If a woman wants to attain to even a fantasy of autonomy, she must act within the confines of the roles assigned to her. In one of the many patently autobiographical episodes in *Urania*, Wroth tells the story of Lindamira, in which a court lady has her queen's favors withdrawn. Lindamira's career at court is ruined: 'all her favour was withdrawn as suddenly and directly, as if never had . . . the night pass'd, they are in their old clothes againe, and no appearance of what was.' Instead of abandoning the court, she finds that she can only function by 'remaining like one in a gay Masque' (*Urania*, p. 424).

She has, it seems, no real self, no owned desires, no stable point from which she can assert her desires apart from those assigned to her as a woman in the court.

The story of Lindamira is one indication of how Wroth's awareness of the theater was not confined to being gazed at in the masques. Yet it must have been especially from studying the masques that Wroth realized how she and other women were trapped and, indeed, molested, in a theatrical space of far more moment than that provided by the masque. Before 1632 and the innovations introduced by Queen Henrietta Maria to court entertainment that were so disapproved of not only by the Puritans, but also by courtiers like Dudley Carleton, women took part only as silent dancers.[5] Even that had been, in the first decade of James's reign, regarded somewhat uneasily. In *The Masque of Queenes* (1609), Jonson had introduced court ladies, but men or boy actors still played the female roles in the anti-masque. Bel-Anna, Queen of the Ocean, personifying the queen herself, is described as simply reflecting her husband's masculine virtue, 'humbling, all her worth / To him that gave it.' She is, we are told, 'a spectacle so full of love and grace / Unto your court.' The masques may have shown Wroth how patriarchy's traditional commodification of women's sexuality was blatantly demonstrated in the silent women on display in the processions and dances of masques and court entertainments. They are scripts for entertainment, but also scripts of gender assignment in the wider world. The ideology of sexual hierarchy and gender assignment in the masques is consistent and blatant: in Campion's *The Lord's Masque*, male masquers are 'men fitt for wars,' the female masquers are statues that are eventually transformed into 'women fitt for love.' If the active male body is at the heart of the male fantasy of autonomy, the unmoving female body is meant to be a body on display, and, by implication, available to be touched at will by the males.[6]

For all the modern interest in Jacobean masques, it is curious that there has been little analysis of their gender politics. It may be that the masque is so obviously archaic and of largely antiquarian interest that it seems hardly worth subjecting to rigorous cultural analysis. But the masque was the most prestigious 'literary' form of the age, one in which a vast proportion of the court and therefore the country's wealth was invested, and no less than, say, Disneyland or Madonna today, deserves analysis, at the very least, to reveal the ways by which it formed and articulated its society's dominant ideologies – not least those of gender. Wroth is all the more interesting, therefore, in that she provides the rare occurrence of a critique of the masque and its gender assumptions from a woman's viewpoint – and by someone who took part in masques. Her treatment of the ways that women and women actors are produced by their dramatic contexts is valuable precisely because it is articulated by a product of the system she is attempting to demystify. What Weidemann terms the instability that 'necessarily attends the construction of the female subject' in the period is all the more powerful because of its being spoken by someone who was in the subject-ed position within the system she is critiquing, further who had been marginalized, and, at the time she is writing, was like Lindamira, expelled from it. Is *Urania*, as Lamb suggests, in part motivated by Wroth's anger towards the court that cast her adrift?[7]

Over and over, Wroth's female characters describe the pressures they feel beset by in terms of theater, performance and display. The forsaken Lindamira feels she can regain the queen's favor only by 'remaining like one in a gay masque,' even while 'she was only afflicted' (*Urania*, p. 424), and she ponders her tactics of self-presentation, deciding that her best image is to 'effect silence,' returning to the state of Jonson's and Campion's female statues. Theatricality, like gender assignment itself, is beset by ambivalence. Taking part in a masque, like entering the court itself, offers the illusion of power, even or perhaps especially to the otherwise powerless female subject. But, in fact, it creates her as the product of both a collective gaze and the gazes of individual men. What reactions might a woman have in this situation? I have elsewhere discussed a poem in which Pamphilia was able to, as it were, turn the gaze back on the gazers.[8] But that is a rare note. Usually the situation is one in which the woman is perplexed, even victimized:

Like to the Indians, scorched with the sunne,
The sunn which they doe as theyr God adore
So ame I us'd by love, for ever more
I worship him, less favors have I wunn,

Better are they who thus to blacknes runn
And soe can only whitenes want deplore
Then I who pale, and white ame with griefs store,
Nor can have hope, butt to see hopes undunn;

Beesids theyr sacrifies receavd's in sight
Of theyr chose sainte: Mine hid as worthies rite;
Grant mee to see wer I my offrings give,

Then lett me weare the marke of Cupids might
In hart as they in skin of Phoebus light
Nott ceasing offrings to love while I Live.

(Poems, p. 99)

Whether, as Roberts suggests, line 5 refers to Wroth's memory of having taken part in *Blacknesse*, what Weidemann terms 'theatrical consciousness,' is certainly at the forefront of the poem.[9] Pamphilia describes herself as a masquer, 'receavd' in sight of the court; without the identity afforded by the court and its ritual theatricals she is 'worthless.' Yet to be chosen to play a role in the specular theater of the court is to be disclosed as the court's creation, and so individually exploitable and expendable. At best it may serve to reveal the constructed nature of being a woman – but that may be an unbearable burden for her, since there appears to be so little possibility of changing her state. To discover that one is constructed in ways one did not suspect is a recurring and disillusioning discovery in *Urania*: the work actually opens with a 'masked' woman, a shepherdess who has just learnt to her bewilderment that she is, in fact, high born, and who thus is unable to say who she 'really' is. This opening episode is an ironic reversal of the classic family romance: instead of the pleasurable fantasy of having noble parents, Urania is distressed to find that she is not, as she had supposed, a humble shepherdess. Thereafter, as the work unfolds, the divided desires of the book's title character become characteristic of all the women. In the main group of plots, centered on Pamphilia, despite her insistence on truth and transparent virtue, she continually finds herself regretting that she must play roles in accord with others' desires: 'Pamphilia made some signe of Joye, but a Signe indeed it was for how could joye come where such desperate sorrow did abound, yet the Seeming gave great content to all the beholders (*Newberry 1*, fol. 21). She continually blames herself for appearing to dissemble: 'when did I ever play so foolish a part? justly may I bee condemned for this error, and blamed for so much lightnes' (*Urania*, p. 321).

Yet how can a woman in the court avoid playing parts? Obviously enough, Pamphilia's roles include those of a queen, a friend, a daughter, but also, more deviously, those of a lover, a deceiver of rivals in love, and especially that of a contented friend to her cousin, while at the same time vowing love to him and bewailing his continual infidelities. In the masque presented by the seer Lady Mellisea, as in the Jacobean court, the masquers sing and perform, then pull off their vizards, and dance with the ladies. Wroth presents an image of nostalgic happiness, an idealized picture of 'Emporesses, all the kings, and princes.' Then it is as if such an ideal image is always in danger of disappearing: 'Butt heere we have longe stayd, therfore we must a while leave this Court in all hapines, and content' (*Newberry 1*, fol. 15). That seems to have been, for Wroth, the overwhelming force of the theatrical activities and the theatrical self-presentation of the court: to draw attention to its own ephemeral nature, while never providing the means to construct an alternative. Late in the 1621 edition of *Urania*, the princess Lisia tells of how a lady is suspected of scandal at court, leaves, and then tries to recreate the ideal image of joy and gaiety:

> at last [she] sought company, some she got together, but of what sort? those that were of the age before, who having young minds rumbled up their old carcases, and rubd over their wrinckling faces like old wainscot new varnished: and little sweeter was some of their beauties . . . an noise they also made of mirth, banqueting and inviting company, but all would not serve, the glaringst signe, or greatest bush, drawes not in the best company: no more did they make the Court much the fairer. Dance they did, and all ridiculous things that ancient, but young made women could invent to do . . . Lord how I admird the alteration, and the place, being changd from what it was, as much as from a Court to a Playhouse.
>
> (*Urania*, p. 486)

It is an astonishing demystification of the court, its theatricalities and self-dramatizations projected upon the women interpellated into its self-admiring system. How intriguing, too, that it is the playhouse that is used to represent at once the downfall and disgrace of exile from the court, and yet, by extension, an alternative to it.

Perhaps the most striking example of the theatrical metaphor in *Urania* is the complex episode in the second part which is centered on a masque presented in Pamphilia's honor by her eventual husband, Rodomandro, King of Tartaria. The masque celebrates the triumph of Honor over Cupid; it thus stages the Tartarian king's high-minded virtue by comparison with his rival Amphilanthus, who is identified with Cupid. Rodomandro plays his role so well, conveying his deep and virtuous love for Pamphilia so effectively – if not to the love-torn queen, then certainly to the assembled company – that Amphilanthus reacts with violent jealousy, and confronts Pamphilia with his love. He promises absolute fidelity to her, and together they take public vows of intent – 'performed,' we are told in an ambiguous ceremony, 'butt nott as an absolute marriage though as perfect as that' (*Newberry 1*, fol 14). But their vows are never fully consummated, a lesson underlined by the masque. Cupid is subjected to Honor, just as in her life as a queen Pamphilia must submit to Honor rather than Passion, and Wroth's love for her cousin had to be subordinate to the demands of the family and her role in its aggrandizement.

Reading Wroth's life in relation to *Urania*'s concerns with the theatrical, an intriguing contrast between the two cousins emerges. In his career, as in his poems and letters, Pembroke presents himself as a male wanting to be in control of the events in which he was caught, a man who risked little, keeping his private affairs strictly subordinate to his public roles, never (at least after the Mary Fitton affair) allowing passion to triumph over honor. By contrast, his cousin, as a woman, was far more subject to others' desires, except (and perhaps only briefly) in her writing and her sexuality. As Pamphilia's struggles show, a woman may create a fantasy of control; but generally, to take a part in the specular theater of a male-dominated world is, for a woman, to lack any material agency. Hence it is all the more intriguing that, of the two Sidney cousins, Pembroke remains the relatively aloof patron of the drama, the presider over court entertainments; Wroth – positioned as a woman as part of the spectacle of the court and its theater – wrote a play. Her venture into playwriting, however, is indicative of the limited possibilities afforded to women: where Aphra Behn fifty years later could write plays for the public stage, Wroth's was designed at most for private presentation. Until 1989, when it was first published, it existed only in two manuscripts, one imperfect, and it was probably rarely read for over 450 years.

Love's Victory is a pastoral drama in five acts. It portrays the highly idealized romantic interactions of four couples, whose wooings and boohooings are overseen by Cupid and his mother Venus. It was most likely written about the same time as the continuation of *Urania*, in the early 1620s. Both Josephine Roberts and Barbara Lewalski speculate that it might have been written for private performance, perhaps for Sir Edward Dering (1598–1644). He was a collector of plays and known to present private performances, possibly including women actors. He was also a near neighbor of Wroth's family home in Kent. Dering may have owned the original, unfinished manuscript of the play, now in the Huntington. But there is no evidence for its having been acted at his instigation or at any other time.[10] Lewalski has traced the generic conventions within which it operates: those of the pastoral tragicomedy, which puts into dramatic form the typical atmosphere and themes of the pastoral eclogue. Tasso's *Aminta* (1580) and Guarini's *Il Pastor Fido* (1590) are the best known examples of the form. Sidney had disparaged such works as 'mongrell Tragedicomedie,' but by the early seventeenth century tragicomedy had become a respectable and – if we extend its scope to include related and equally mixed works like Shakespeare's *The Winter's Tale* – dramatic kind. In 1610 Fletcher offered a definition, claiming that 'it wants deaths, which is inough to make it no tragedie, yet brings some neare it, which is inough to make it no comidie.' Lewalski suggests that Wroth probably had only a general awareness of the controversies over the nature and legitimacy of tragicomedy, but in writing *Love's Victory*, she certainly 'looked to the canon of the new kind – Tasso, Guarini, Daniel, Fletcher – to provide . . . the horizon of generic expectations,' which included lyrical songs and choruses, stock characters and a miraculous ending. There are four pairs of lovers. Recent readers of the play have suggested there are various family references in their names and relationships. The most prominent male lover, Philissus (Philip Sidney?), is in love with Musella (Muse + Stella?), but fears, wrongly as it turns out, that she loves his friend Lissius (Matthew Lister, Pembroke's mother's physician who was, it was gossipped, seen as a possible husband for the dowager countess?) who in turn comes to love Philissus's sister Simeana (Mary Sidney, Pembroke's mother herself?). To complicate the action, Silvesta loves Philissus, but renounces her love for him in favor of Musella, and also rejects the love of the unsophisticated Forester, at least until the play's end. The flirtatious Dalina and the boorish Rustick (yet another satiric portrait of Wroth's late husband?) are also united at the end. Other minor characters interact with these four main couples: Arcas, who tries to slander Philissus and Musella, and so is the play's obligatory villain; the outsider Climeana, who courts Lissius far too blatantly; Fillis and Lacon, who are respectively, the rejected suitors of Philissus and Musella.[11]

The most important characters in the play's scheme, however, are the two gods, Venus and Cupid, who preside and quarrel over the activities of the mortals. When Lissius scorns the power of love, Venus is insulted and orders that Cupid's hitherto merely mischievous intentions towards the mortals should become more intensified. She announces at the end of Act 1 that she 'would have all to waile, and all to weepe' (1.387), and then at the end of Act 3 that she is still dissatisfied that some of her victims are 'to slightly wounded' (3.336). Musella reveals to Philissus that her father's will has commanded her to wed Rustick and that she therefore must give him up. Finally, however, Venus intervenes in the lovers' favor, claiming that the miraculous survival and uniting of Philissus and Musella is her own work and giving judgment against the villain Arcas. At the end, like the monarch mingling with the dancers in a masque, the mythological figures appear to and join with the mortals. The play's end can thus be read either as a sentimental celebration of true love winning out or as McLaren argues, something more elevated, a demonstration of the power of Venus and Cupid to humble everyone in the play, even those who seem most immune to love. All the lovers, Cupid assures Venus,

> . . . shall both cry, and sigh, and wayle, and weep,
> And for owr mercy shall most humbly creepe.
> Love hath most glory when as greatest sprites
> Hee downward throwse unto his owne delights.
> (2.405–8)

Love's Victory has an attractive languidness that, if we look at the history of dramatic forms in the period, not only has affinities with the masque, but also anticipates the pastoral plays encouraged by Queen Henrietta Maria in the late 1620s and 1630s. There is no evidence that Wroth returned to court to take part in those pastorals: she would have been, after all, a woman in her forties, with a scandalous past, a reputation for frankness or even slander, in debt and without landed or financial power, a poor relation of a family whose influence on the national scene was waning. But it is intriguing to see how her work anticipates many of the fashions that were the taste of the court in the next decade or more.

The conventional machinery of the plays written for Henrietta Maria is all patently evident in *Love's Victory*: the paraphernalia of Cupid's arrows, love's secrecy, hope, jealousy, impossible chastity, and fortuitous interventions of the deities are all commonplace ingredients of the court entertainments of the 1630s – just as they had been of romance stories, poems and dramas over the previous half century and throughout the long and devious tradition of romance narrative back to the Greek romances. The play's clichés are the familiar ones of the tired Petrarchism typical of much of the court poetry of the time, including Pembroke's: love is 'a paine which yett doth pleasure bring,' (2.94), at once a mystery, a gift from heaven, and a perpetual betrayal. These undemanding paradoxes are dressed up in the equally conventional landscape of the court masque: 'a Landt-shape of Forrest, Hils, Vallies, Cottages, A Castle, A River, Pastures, Heards, Flocks, all full of Countrey simplicity,' as Jonson describes it in *The Sad Shepherd*.'[12] On a much grander scale, what Jonson depicts is also the landscape of *Urania*. In fact, in the continuation of the romance, there is an episode that uses the same material: a group of shepherds and shepherdesses, led by a brother and sister, undergo similar experiences. Names also recur: Arcas, Rustick,

Magdalina. In the *Urania* version, a group of young princes and princesses, some of the 'lost children' around whom some episodes of the continuation of the romance are built, have been kidnaped by the Sophy of Persia, and they gather together to recount their experiences. The episode serves as a metaphor of escape from the violence in the world outside the pastoral, an attitude that is taken to an extreme by Folietto (a shepherd rather like Rustick), who asserts that even the sufferings of love are largely fictional. In Wroth's dramatized version of the situation (we have no way of saying which was a reworking of which), the political context is omitted. Nonetheless, even in the more seemingly escapist world of dramatic pastoral, the complex world of politics does manage to creep in. On the most elementary level, Wroth brings references from her own far from serene life into the pastoral. The most obvious are the probable references to her (presumably, when the play was written, late) husband in the character of Rustick, who is unsophisticated and vulgar, and unaware of the love between Musella and Philissus; and finally both revealing his ignobility and obligingly allowing a wish fulfillment ending to occur by abandoning his claims to Musella and disavowing all the promises she has self-sacrificingly made to fulfill her father's will that she should marry him. His gesture is perhaps a wistful fantasy on Wroth's part as she looks back on the relations between herself and her father, her cousin, and her husband. The scripts of the family romance play out over and over.

What is especially attractive about *Love's Victory* is its humor. Jonson had insisted that comedy was a necessary part of court entertainments, even when they were designed as serious celebrations. *Love's Victory* is permeated not only by humor, but by a crisp irony, which is consistently directed even towards the presiding deities. Their threats are more fustian than serious, and most of the action is lighthearted. Rustick is the continual butt of lighthearted joking: he expresses his love for Musella in terms similar to Sidney's Mopsa in *Arcadia*: she is 'whiter then lambs wull,' her eyes 'play / like Goats with hay,' and her cheeks are red as 'Okar spred / On a fatted sheep's back' (11.337, 341–2, 348–9). In addition to the overt comedy of the play, its treatment of love is also intriguing. Beneath the clichés of 'Love's sweet pleasing paine' (3.372) are some interesting contradictions. As McLaren suggests, much of the action centers on characters' difficulty in communicating, trying to convey their affections and choices to the partner of their desires. Further, she suggests, it is the women who are faced with special difficulties, since they are interpellated into erotically passive roles. The malice of Venus's commands – 'they shall have torment when they think to smile' (1.402) – translates into an anxiety born of their roles as women. It is they who are most disadvantaged in communicating and choosing. The extent of the masochism and paralysis in *Pamphilia to Amphilanthus* and *Urania* never approached, but it is important to note that the one woman character who claims some degree of sexual autonomy, Dalina, is clearly disapproved of. She blatantly asserts:

> This is the reason men ar growne soe coy,
> When they parceave wee make theyr smiles owr joy.
> Lett them alone, and they will seeke, and sue,
> Butt yeeld to them and they'll with scorne pursue.
> Hold a while of, they'll kneele, and follow you,
> And vowe, and sweare, yett all theyr othes untrue.
> Lett them once see you coming then they fly,
> Butt strangly looke, and they'll for pitty cry.
> (3.249–56)

As the play unfolds, such sentiments are clearly set up in order to be silenced. Yet at the same time, *Love's Victory* implies that there are some limited areas of female agency. The dominant ideology of pastoral romance is that life represents a harmonious movement, through misprision and misfortune, to a happy marriage in which individual desires are reconciled with social stability. It is the ideology of a benevolent patriarchy typical of Shakespeare's *As You Like It* or *A Midsummer Night's Dream*. There are forces opposed to or skeptical about such a pattern, but they generally exist to be firmly rejected. In *As You Like It* it is Jaques who opposes such harmony; in *Love's Victory*, significantly, it is a woman, Silvesta, who vows to remain dissociated from men and marriage:

> Butt farewell folly, I with Dian stand
> Against love's changinge and blinde foulerie,
> To hold with hapy and blest chastitie.
> For love is idle, hapines ther's none
> When freedom's lost and chastity is gon
> . . .
> Now love's as farr from mee as never knowne,
> Then bacely tyde, now freely ame mine owne.
> (1.126–30, 157–8)

Where the play's heroine, Musella, is overjoyed to be finally married to her beloved and gives appropriately dutiful thanks to the presiding deities, Silvesta claims that independence is preferable, and her rejection of the ideology of benevolent patriarchal marriage is certainly rendered as a far more attractive alternative than Jaques's rejection of the happinesses of the 'country copulatives' at the end of *As You Like It*. Silvesta believes it is possible to 'make a cleane shift to live without a man' (5.187). The emphasis on 'freedom' and being 'mine own' is not rendered ironically: it is clearly an affirmation that defies, without obviously negative consequences, Venus's warning that unless mortals follow her dictates, they 'will butt frame / Words against your selves.' Women, according to Venus, should accept their parts in the play of love: 'Love the king is of the mind / Please him, and hee wilbe kind' (2.324–5, 330–1). Being 'mine own' may not be a sustainable fantasy, but it does mark a woman's assertion of her right to the kind of individuation that seems natural to men. It is, however, worth pointing out the intriguing contradiction here. Being 'mine owne' would not meet with the approval of the age's moral orthodoxy for men or women, as the figures of Richard III, Iago, or Edmund remind us. Yet such characters, as Shakespearian commentators have long pointed out, are putting into play an emergent sense of the individualized subject, the Cartesian 'I,' that in less than a century will seem as 'natural' as it seemed 'unnatural' around 1600. All the more significant, therefore, that, as I have suggested, being 'mine owne' is at the core of Wroth's gendering of the family romance: for a woman, being like a man involves a degree of autonomy rarely presumed by a woman, and it is significant that it is one of the recurring fantasies of *Love's Victory*.

As is the case in Wroth's other writings, *Love's Victory* also places a strong emphasis on female friendship, as a 'womanspace' not to be ruled by men. The sharing of stories and gossip – something to be benevolently exchanged among both men and woman, though initiated and presided over by the women – is an attractive aspect of the play that connects it with both *Urania* and *Pamphilia to Amphilanthus*. It is, however, worth noting Arbella Stuart's tart remark about the ladies in Queen Anne of Denmark's court (who would have most likely included Mary Wroth herself) and their indulgence in the kind of entertainment favored by Wroth's characters:

> certain childeplayse remembred by the fayre ladies. Viz. I pray my Lo. give me a course in your park. Rise pig and go. One peny follow me. &c. and when I cam to Court they weare as highly in request as ever crackling of nuts was. So I was by the m.^{rs} of the Revelles not onely compelled to play at. I knew not what for till that day I never heard of a play called Fier. but even persuaded by the princely example I saw to play the childe againe.[13]

Trivial though they may have been (though presumably no more than the gossip and boys' games of male courtiers), such activities, especially when exclusively the province of women, may be seen as part of an attempt by the politically powerless to carve out a distinctive space of pleasure and discovery for themselves. In Act 4 of *Love's Victory*, the lovers play at riddles, and Rustick is laughed at for his ignorance – perhaps another jest at Wroth's husband, who, as we can see from Jonson's poem to Sir Robert Wroth, preferred the company of rural friends and animals and may well have been impatient at such courtly pastimes. As Lewalski notes, the satiric portrait of Rustick not only permits Wroth some amusing asides at her late husband's expense, but also allows her to align herself with the emerging ideology of the Stuart court's valorization of the urban pastoral, as opposed to the rustic values of the country, and to stress the dominance of the women, secure in their own discursive space. In Act 3, the game is played only by the women, who share their stories of past loves. Dalina tells stories of what the moral orthodoxy of the time would term her fickleness though another way of describing her activities might be in terms of sexual autonomy and experimentation, activities presumably acceptable for men, but forbidden to women. As in *Urania*, Wroth stresses that voicing such desires may lead only to pain, and thus a woman is well advised to accept her place within a benevolent marriage. Dalina's desire for the security marriage offers, therefore, comes through in her amused but still serious vow to accept the next proposal she receives. Simeana then tells of her constancy and of her secret hopes regarding an unnamed lover. Fillis tells of her unrequited love for Philissus. Climena tells of following a lover who later rejected her and of her present love for Lissius. While there are warnings that each may not necessarily be telling the whole truth, the scenes are a touching and (especially when Simeana and Climena quarrel) amusing revelation of the mixture of subjection, fantasy, and realism of women's roles in trying to find some alternative spaces within a gendered script they did not write.

For we can also see emerging from the scene what Lewalski terms 'an implicit feminist politics' that is unusual in the genre in which Wroth is writing.[14] Not only is Venus rather than Cupid the dominant presiding deity, but more importantly, among the mortals the women's actions are more dominant and forceful. I have argued that the dominant fantasy of the woman's family romance is in effect to occupy the brother's place, to have the possibility of inheriting the father's autonomy and movement.[15] But there is another, perhaps more mature, fantasy in the family romance for women and men alike, one that is often enacted in *Urania* but only hinted at in *Love's Victory* as it was in *Pamphilia to Amphilanthus*. It is the fantasy of a mutual love regardless of gender, an erotopia of mutuality. It is a fantasy of community, not of competitive individualism. Significantly, therefore, where the values of community and human relations are central, it is significant, as Miller puts it, that they are mainly asserted by the women. Musella is a faithful confidant to men and women alike, especially in helping to reunite Lissius and Simeana. Dalina advises Simeana to act cautiously at first, and then, when they hear Lissius's confession of his love, to respond encouragingly. Musella in particular articulates for herself and her companions a clear range of choices and options: while misjudging Philissus's love for her, she does eventually respond to him, and takes Simeana's advice to think through her situation. Musella discovers herself in conflict with her mother's desire that she obey her father's will, and she contemplates:

> . . . my state
> Agreed on by my father's will which bears
> Sway in her brest, and duty in mee. Fate
> Must have her courses, while that wreched I
> Wish butt soe good a fate as now to dy.
> (5.12–15)

Ethical questions arise here that were common to women of Wroth's class and which she herself had been deeply affected by, above all: is Musella bound to marry Rustick because of her father's will? Unlike many women in the Jacobean court, including perhaps Wroth herself, Musella seizes the initiative. It is she who decides that she and Lissius should visit the temple of Venus, where they will either find some mysterious end to their dilemma or die together. In a pastoral romance, as in a daydream, the miraculous wishfulfilment comes true.

Thus at the play's end we can see an interesting contradiction. We could say that the triumph of the lovers is as much a victory for perseverance as for love. The pastoral genre, of course, prepares us for a marvelous ending – the revival of the statue of the dead Hermione in *The Winter's Tale*, the return of Cymbeline's children, the reuniting of Pericles, Thaisa, and Marina – but as with Shakespeare's romances, the miracles at the end of *Love's Victory* are as much decided by human, and specifically female, agency as by supernatural intervention. Philissus and Musella go to the temple; they are about to stab themselves in a last act of mutual devotion when Silvesta offers them a more convenient method, a poison that (seemingly) kills them. Then she and Simeana inform the others what has happened. Rustick disclaims all rights to Musella, at which point the apparently dead lovers revive. This happy ending against all possible odds, including death, must have embodied a common fantasy for Wroth and her circle: that in the opposition between duty and love, reason and passion, if love could be pursued absolutely, it would be rewarded by the gods. Venus claims that Silvesta has been an 'instrument ordain'd,' and 'when Venus wills, men can nott but obay' (5.490, 536). These sentiments reassert the pastoral convention that all events are benevolently controlled by a mysterious providence; they also reassert the equal beneficence of providential patriarchy – yet that conclusion has been made possible by the devotion and cunning of the lovers themselves, especially the women. And at the level of fantasy enactment, something even more intriguing is emerging: the autonomy of men, envied by women, is maybe not finally satisfying, even to men. Enacted even briefly, contained in *Love's Victory* is, once again, a fantasy of mutuality.

Notes

1 Naomi J. Miller, 'Engendering Discourse,' pp. 154–72 in Naomi J. Miller and Gary Waller (eds) *Reading Mary Wroth: Representing Alternatives in Early Modern England* (Knoxville, TN: University of Tennessee Press, 1991; Margaret [Witten-Hannah] McLaren, 'Lady Mary Wroth's *Urania*: The Work and the Tradition,' unpublished doctoral dissertation, University of Auckland, 1978.

2 Sir Francis Bacon, *The Essayes or Counsels, Civill and Morall*, ed. Michael Kiernan (Cambridge, MA: Harvard University Press, 1985), p. 118.

3 Stephen Greenblatt, *Renaissance Self-Fashioning* (Chicago: University of Chicago Press, 1980), p. 162.

4 Heather L. Weidemann, 'Theatricality and Female Identity in Mary Wroth's *Urania*,' in Miller and Waller (eds) *Reading Mary Wroth*, pp. 206–7.

5 Suzanne Gossett, '"Man-maid, begone!" Women in Masques,' *English Literary Renaissance* 18(1988), 96–113.

6 *Ben Jonson*, ed. C. H. Herford and Percy Simpson (Oxford: Clarendon Press, 1937), I, pp. 243, 245.

7 Weidemann, 'Theatricality,' p. 200; Mary Ellen Lamb, *Gender and Authorship in the Sidney Circle* (Madison, WI: University of Wisconsin Press, 1990), p. 25.

8 Gary Waller, *The Sidney Family Romance: Mary Wroth, William Herbert, and the Early Modern Construction of Gender* (Detroit, MI: Wayne State University Press, 1993), ch.6.

9 Weidemann, 'Theatricality,' p. 202.

10 Josephine A. Roberts, 'The Huntington Manuscript of Lady Mary Wroth's Play, *Love's Victory* and the Pastoral Tragicomedy,' in Miller and Waller (eds) *Reading Mary Wroth*, p. 88.

11 Barbara Lewalski, 'Mary Wroth's *Love's Victory* and Pastoral Tragicomedy,' in Miller and Waller (eds) *Reading Mary Wroth*, pp. 88–108.

12 *Jonson*, VII, p. 7.

13 Sara Jayne Steen, 'Fashioning an Acceptable Self: Lady Arbella Stuart,' *English Literary Renaissance*, 18(1988), 84.

14 Lewalski, 'Mary Wroth's *Love's Victory* and Pastoral Tragicomedy,' p. 96.

15 Waller, *Sidney Family Romance*, pp. 37–46.

11

'TO BE YOUR DAUGHTER IN YOUR PEN'

The social functions of literature in the writings of Lady Elizabeth Brackley and Lady Jane Cavendish

Margaret J. M. Ezell

In this pioneering essay on the two Cavendish sisters first published in 1988, Margaret J. M. Ezell drew attention to a manuscript volume which contained two little-known plays, *A Pastorall* and *The Concealed Fancies.* The works had been composed while Jane and Elizabeth were imprisoned in their home during the English Civil War, and Ezell draws upon this historical and social background in her analyses. The resulting critique ensures that, because of the plays written by the Cavendish sisters, we must now revise the accepted notions of public and private drama in the mid-seventeenth century.

The manuscript volume 'Poems, songs, a Pastorall & a Play' by Lady Elizabeth Brackley (1626–63) and Lady Jane Cavendish (1621–69), the daughters of the Duke of Newcastle, interests the literary historian for several reasons. First, the nature and format of the volume itself offers insights into the literary practice of the Civil War years. Second, when viewed overall, the contents of the volume provide a case study of the literary activities of two educated seventeenth-century Englishwomen, a case study whose findings do not agree with the popular image of the intimidated female author fearing to violate 'feminine "modesty"' and producing 'closet' literature; what Angeline Goreau, in a volume which brings into play the whole question of 'closet' versus 'coterie' authors, terms 'entirely private forms of writing not destined for publication and dealing with what limited experience might come within the circumference of a lady's life.'[1] Finally, since the sisters are not significant for any striking originality in their lives, the very conventionality of their writings makes their literary production intriguing as a social document. The unexpectedness of much of its contents exposes our twentieth-century assumptions about literature, authorship, and what women's writings *should* be like.

While the notoriety of their stepmother, Margaret Cavendish, Duchess of Newcastle, has resulted in her receiving steady attention as a woman author from her time to the present day, one must look hard to find traces of the duke's daughters by his first wife, Elizabeth Bassett. Frances, the youngest, is hardly ever mentioned except on genealogical tables. Jane, the eldest, fares slightly better, having been the recipient of a poem by William Davenant on her marriage to Charles Cheyne.[2] She also appears in biographies of the duchess as being in opposition to her father's remarriage, although little concrete evidence is cited.[3] Elizabeth, Lady Brackley, later the countess of Bridgewater, is seldom cited in connection with her father; instead, she has been recorded in the role of the perfect and pious wife of the 2nd Earl of Bridgewater. Even though she married into the family for whom *Comus* was written, with her husband one of its principal actors, the usual references to her are the epitaphs which her grieving husband caused to have carved on their tombstones.[4]

The manuscript itself is a handsomely produced fair copy folio volume of 162 pages.[5] It is neatly and formally designed with title page, page numbers, and a table of contents at the end listing the pieces by title. The title page is decoratively spaced and declares in large letters the volume to be 'Poems Songs a Pastorall and a Play by the Rt Honble Lady Jane Cavendish and Lady Elizabeth Brackley.' Although it is undated, this page shows plainly that 'and a Play' was squeezed in after the initial lettering; the play, the last item in the volume, may thus have been a later addition. There is also a second table of contents on a loose sheet inserted at the beginning. This table of contents is in a sprawling eighteenth-century hand and thriftily utilizes a sheet of paper where an earlier and neater hand started as an essay headed 'Mechanicae Artes' on the skills of 'Bezalell' in the book of Exodus; evidently, later generations of readers found the earlier convention of listing the contents at the end of a volume awkward. The contents break down as follows: pages 1–45, occasional verse; 49–84, a pastoral; and 87–157, a play. The poems are not specifically attributed or signed, but in the pastoral, the author of each scene is designated by the initials 'JC' or 'EB' in the upper left hand corner.

In 1931, Nathan Comfort Starr published part of the manuscript, the play 'The Concealed Fansyes,' with a brief biographical introduction. Since subsequent literary commentators have relied almost exclusively on Starr for their biographical data and critical approach to the text, it is worth rapidly summarizing his opinions. Starr believes the volume was composed between 1642 and 1649, during which time Elizabeth married Brackley and later became the Countess of Bridgewater, and he surmises that the play was written to amuse the elderly Earl of Bridgewater at Ashridge.[6] He does not discuss the poetry of the pastoral, even as possible indicators of the composition date. The content of the play he deems 'practically without value,' dismissing it as conventionally Jonsonian with 'obvious' debts to *Comus*. Its only significance, he feels, is in its 'artless revelation of the activities of seventeenth-century ladies of fashion living in the country' (Starr, p. 837). Although he finds the types Jonsonian, he also declares the material to be largely autobiographical, noting that the female characters 'converse with such freedom and reality that we cannot but feel that it is the authors themselves who are speaking' (Starr, p. 838).

This presentation of the sisters as authors without art or artful intentions, rather clumsily adapting personal experience, is continued in Nancy Cotton's account of them in *Women Playwrights in England* (1980). Of the three paragraphs allotted them, two are biographical; the text concerning the play itself does not discuss the contents of the rest of the volume. Cotton stresses the theme of marriages motivated by economic considerations as being a reflection of the women's personal concerns as heiresses, and concludes like Starr that the authors were 'unable to construct a coherent plot.' She feels, too, that the conversations between the women characters are its high point, but also declares that they represent a 'writing skill born of epistolary, rather than dramatic cultivation.'[7] While Starr concedes the text might possibly have been staged, Cotton does not believe it at all likely.

Thus, previous accounts of this volume and its authors have stressed the strained relationship of Newcastle and his daughters after his marriage and have focused on one section only. The only piece commented on at any length in terms other than biographical is the play, declared to have been designed only for the immediate family, a text not intended for public performance, which is derivative in its overall form and good in part only by artless autobiographical accident. If, however, one steps back and views the contents of the volume as a whole, a different and more intimate picture of the authors is revealed, one showing their literary ambitions and training as well as some specific responses to the state of their society.

The exact nature of the literary activity displayed in this volume has previously been ignored. Superficially, it seems to fit nicely into Virginia Woolf's category of 'those earlier women writers shut up in parks among their folios . . . solitary great ladies who wrote without audience or criticism, for their own delight alone.'[8] The obscurity of the pieces and their authors, especially in contrast with the notoriety of their abrasive stepmother, might seem to confirm a view that they fit in the mold of the 'modest' aristocratic female author, 'emboldened by high social position to write academic plays and translations, like Mary Herbert, Countess of Pembroke.'[9] Unlike Margaret Cavendish, it might easily be concluded, Newcastle's daughters must have kept their places as mere female scribblers who confined themselves to socially acceptable literary limits, 'closet poetesses' as a recent biography of the duchess has dismissed them.[10]

And yet these simple assumptions about early women writers become quite suspect when one looks closely at the actual contents of the volume. The repeated insistence on the 'artlessness' of the 'good' parts of the play sounds rather like that subtler form of critical bias identified by Joanna Russ as 'denial of Agency' or 'she didn't write it; it wrote itself.'[11] Also, if indeed the contents of this volume represent the limits of socially acceptable literary activities for seventeenth-century women in their subject matter and form, a consideration of the whole volume entails widening our twentieth-century notion of what was conventionally available for earlier women writers.

Individual poems might be written for personal pleasure, but what are the intentions behind compiling a formal manuscript volume? Fame and fortune are the typical reasons given for why authors collect their scattered pieces into the permanent form of a handsome, bound book. But, given that no income would be derived from a manuscript volume (even if the authors had desired it), what fame, then, could they find?

The prominent display of the authors' names on the title page indicates that the women had no desire to hide their literary accomplishments. These pieces were not 'closet' poems in the sense that they were hidden or anonymous. On the other hand, few of the pieces are specifically attributed. Since the individual pieces, with the exception of the scenes in the pastoral, were not signed, the volume suggests a collaborative and cooperative effort rather than pieces of individual workmanship. This implies the authors do not seem to have felt much anxiety over being recognized, or not, for individual literary accomplishments. Poetry here is not the unique, original product of a lone artistic soul; with only a few exceptions, the poems do not 'belong' to an individual.

This seemingly casual approach to authorship, infuriating to modern editors, is not necessarily a modest gender characteristic. One need think only of the efforts required to untangle the lyrics of the Sons of Ben or the later Restoration court poets to recognize that a larger issue of attitudes toward authorship and audience is involved. The Cavendish sisters' literary activities do fit quite well into the literary practices of the 'gentleman-amateur' variety recently detailed by Arthur Marotti in connection with Donne's works. Marotti argues that Donne 'designed his poems specifically for a succession of social environments' and that they were 'not composed for a wide literary audience but rather for coterie readers.'[12] This coterie tradition of restricted readership for occasional poems is familiar to scholars of Renaissance literature. It is not a tradition, however, which has been studied in relationship to early women's writings. When Donne writes for a limited readership in a specific environment, it is referred to as 'coterie' writing: when a woman of the period does so, it becomes 'closet' writing, a negative and diminishing adjective, in line with the view of women writers of this period as isolated individuals who did not seek a wide audience because their talents were discouraged and unappreciated.[13]

The volume was designed for a controlled readership, but, given the general pattern of seventeenth-century literary activity, not necessarily an uncritical one. What then was the function of this collection and what was its intended readership: to use current terms, what was the socioliterary environment and how does this volume typify its concerns?

For readership, 'family' is the obvious answer. But in this instance, the cozy domesticity of the term may mislead us concerning the critical sophistication of the audience intended. At the time of the compilation of the volume, the Cavendish sisters were part of two extraordinary and powerful families of wide-ranging intellectual and literary credentials. A survey of the contents reveals poems addressed to an extended network of aunts, uncles, grandparents, relatives by marriage, friends, and royal personages. There are, furthermore, fifteen occasional poems on unnamed 'noble friends,' both male and female, who presumably read the works penned in their praise.

Nor were these readers unsophisticated country squires. Newcastle was called 'our English Maecenas' by Gerard Langbaine for his patronage of drama and poetry. During the years his daughters were growing up, he numbered Jonson, Hobbes, Shirley, Suckling, and Davenant among his literary friends, as well as minor manuscript poets such as William Sampson.[14] Newcastle commissioned Jonson's masque *Love's Welcome at Bolsover* for the king and queen in 1634; its central theme of the circle of platonic love also appears a decade later in his daughter's writings.[15] Whatever modern critics may think of Newcastle's literary judgements, his contemporaries viewed him as an astute, active participant in the literary world of his day.

The marriage of Elizabeth to John Egerton brought an even more impressive set of literary credentials with it. The commitment of the Earls of Bridgewater to the literary arts is most visible in the public performances given at their command of works by Carew, Milton, and Lawes; their family records show that a theatrical wardrobe for actors and actresses was carefully maintained during this period.[16] The Dowager Countess of Derby, who died in 1637 before Elizabeth's marriage, had established a pattern of feminine patronage, with Donne, Spenser, Shakespeare, and Daniel indebted to her; she also left behind an impressive library.[17] Viewed in this context, the Cavendish and Egerton families offer a more substantial and challenging literary environment than our notion of 'family' or closet suggests.

The contents of the volume confirm in tone and subject that it was envisioned as having a public or social dimension. The general intent of these pieces is to praise virtue and lament the conditions brought on by the war. The virtues of the king and queen and the Prince of Wales are applauded as well as those of family members. This praise tends to be of a generic, not a personal, nature; men are praised for courage and constancy, women for wit and sweetness. The terms are so conventional and so general that one is left with a type rather than an individual; the subjects are held up as absolutes, the perfection of the virtues they embody. 'Quintessence' is thus the favorite modifier.

More than anything else, however, these poems are a public proclamation of patterns of behavior. Repeatedly, the subjects are lauded for being 'examples'; both the king and Newcastle are called 'the Great Example,' while Viscount Brackley is the 'Pattern fit to emulate/ By your sex.' Elizabeth Brackley is depicted by her sister as 'The Quintessence of Cordiall' and is furthermore one whose 'nature [is] only fit for Caesar's wife,' the most public of roles. Their mother, likewise, was 'what of women could be perfect lov'd/ But she was that, & the true style of good/ Then in a word she was the quintessence of best.'

The emphasis in this praise is also on the individual as a metaphor or emblem to assist others in reaching this level of perfection. Readers are constantly urged to look at the subject in order to see the physical representation of an abstraction. In 'On a Noble Lady,' the woman becomes the emblem of the virtues praised and the poem a didactic portrait for those unacquainted with her.

> Thy self a sacred Church, so each should look
> On thee, as on the holy Bible book.
> Thy quicker Eye doth say, I can even tell
> The points of all Religions truly well.[18]

By studying these individuals, the reader is 'taught' abstractions and, by patterning him- or herself after the subject, could achieve a similar condition. One of King Charles' most laudable characteristics, therefore, is that 'Thou Great Example art, the very trace/ Of goodness' self, your looks teach piety' (p. 9).

Recognizing this emphasis on establishing living patterns of abstract values is crucial to understanding the nature of the literary endeavor, especially when one considers the probable dates of its composition. Many of these poems were composed during the war years while the sisters were personally involved in the struggle which severely disrupted their former way of life. While Elizabeth Brackley was safely ensconced with her father-in-law, the old Earl of Bridgewater, who managed to avoid much of the Parliamentary zeal, Jane and Frances were present at the siege of Welbeck, which fell to the Parliamentary troops in 1644. Jane apparently was also responsible for much of the art from Newcastle's other lost estate, Bolsover.[19]

The realities of civil war surface throughout the volume. There are numerous direct references to their father's role in specific battles and his subsequent flight to France, giving a note of anxiety to even the lighter verse. There is a poem lamenting 'A False Report of Your Ladyship's Landing' and, even in a poem directed to the 'Heavenly Father,' Newcastle's military activities are mentioned and it concludes, 'Yet I desire he would say to me/ Thy Father's landed safe, hath sent for thee' (p. 41). The war also plays a prominent part in both the pastoral and the play. In the 'Antemasque' by 'JC' the characters are five witches who meet to congratulate each other on the trouble they have caused.

> *Hagg*: This is a brave world for us now for we metamorphoise everybody.
> *Pre*: But I doubt we are but the Fly of the Cart Wheel, for we are but the people that's talked on, to serve other's designs, and our pride to ourselves makes us think we are Actors.

Bell: Thou'rt a fool; hath not our mischief made war, and that a miserable one, to make Brother hate brother?
Hagg: Sister hate Sister.
Bell: Wife hate Husband, and other kindred hate their divisions of hatred.
Hagg: And have not we done brave?

(p. 50)

In the subsequent scenes by 'EB,' country wives meet to discuss how all their livestock has been taken for the tribute by the greedy witches, and the wish that the centaurs might prove less demanding in their spoils. The play, too, features warfare and looting, with a garrison under siege which Starr believes is Welbeck.

One sees in these poems and dramas, composed during what Earl Miner calls the 'Cavalier Winter,' a consistency in tone and intention. There is the emphasis on recognizing the *integer vitae*, the quintessence of the noble life, which survives in spite of the chaos around it. As Miner writes of the male Cavalier poets, praising friends and reaffirmation of friendship are a central defense against the disorienting and destructive currents of war; 'the discrimination of bad from good and the celebration of good is central to poetry of friendship,' suggests Miner, because 'the poetry of friendship sustains and continues the little society of the few, and it demonstrates as well powers of mind and feeling.'[20]

The poems and dramas of these royalist women likewise act as reaffirming bonds between members of a threatened society. In civil war, the enemy is not a faceless foreigner; it could be a kinsman or a former friend. The contents of the volume offer a link between brothers absent at the wars and sisters defending the home, between like-minded friends, and between subjects and monarchs. In this sense, the volume serves as a repository of talismans against the 'metamorphosis' of personality and beliefs brought on by the 'witches' of war.

The idea of the importance of literature as an agent of social cohesion is hardly new. Again, as with the notion of 'coterie' verse, what is new is its application to writings by women. History abounds with accounts of heroic women such as Lady Halkett, Lady Brilliana Harley, and Lady Fanshawe, actively involved on both sides of the conflict, defending their homes from military attacks, enduring sieges, and spying on the enemy. In literary history, however, women have traditionally been depicted as passive and silent; the literary activities of this period are described and defined in masculine terms: 'Stuart England was full of educated men writing to each other in verse,' states Graham Parry, summarizing the view, 'it served to strengthen the ties of kinship, marriage, education and patronage, and to give distinction to the intellectual contact of thoughtful men.'[21] Miner's theory of the social mode of Cavalier verse explains why male friendship was celebrated as superior to male/female love; in his reading of the period, women were excluded from the central concerns of Cavalier verse – *integer vitae*, the *Vita Beata*, and the *Vir Beatus* – because of their lack of classical education and limited public roles. A seventeenth-century poet, by definition a man, would have had 'more in common with a man of his own age and education than a woman perhaps barely more than half his age and perhaps scarcely able to read.'[22]

Even feminist critics support this theory of the socially isolated, undereducated female poet. According to anthologists of women writers, writing supposedly subjected women to 'ridicule and censure'; in this picture of feminine literary history, seventeenth-century women writers 'knew quite well that if one woman signed her work with her own name, she opened herself to moral and social abuse.'[23] Seventeenth-century women either are not supposed to have written at all, or to have written against society, not to have been a sustaining part of it. Those hearty few such as Margaret Cavendish, who published her works rather than circulating them privately, are always depicted as being in an adversarial relationship with their society because of their literary ambitions.

This is a reasonable point of view, if one accepts the conventional depiction of female writers as isolated, intimidated, and secretive. Even though we know that female contemporaries of Jonson such as Lucy, Countess of Bedford, Lady Mary Wroth, and Lady Alice Egerton wrote verse, when one thinks of the seventeenth century one thinks of the Sons of Ben, not the Daughters. We do not associate women with the Cavalier tradition of literature except as the subject of male compliment or complaint.

The Cavendish sisters obviously do not fit this twentieth-century concept of female literary life. Their works are signed, handsomely presented, public in tone, and, as will be discussed later, actively encouraged. Their use of poetry and drama is not for private, 'closet' confession or personal revelations but for the confirmation of social values and standards of a conventionally Cavalier nature. In this context of conventionality, the unexpected notes struck in the verse and drama are particularly interesting.

In the midst of formulaic praise for male and female virtues, one finds a continuous vein of early feminist free-thinking. Cotton believes the attack on marriages based on economic pragmatism in 'The Concealed Fansyes' to have been merely an autobiographical aside, but the constant presence of female voices commenting on love, marriage, and power suggest an interest in the more general issues of women's roles.

The basic plot of the play is a reversal of *The Taming of the Shrew*, where the women modify the men's unsuitable views on matrimonial relationships. The sisters Tattiney and Luceny are pursued by Presumption, Courtly, and Corpolant, while their father M. Calsindow, is being chased by Lady Tranquility, believed by Starr to represent Margaret Lucas. There are also three 'Lady Cozens' trapped in a garrison who are also besieged by lovers. The central issue concerns the balance of power in marriage in comparison with courtship.

Presumption announces his post-marriage scheme to Courtly. 'Fayth but I'le tell you the way I thinke of, as soone as I am marryed I will let hir knoew I am hire Husband . . . . Shee shall neither looke, walke, or speake, but I wilbee hir perpetuall vexation' (p. 818). Courtly, however, doubts the success of such methods for 'Mistris Tattyny lookes as if shee were proepared for ye ridgeness of a Husband'; she would probably just leave him, Courtly argues, since her father raised his daughters and 'his decurse uses not to bee dull, catachryseinge, and they very much with him' (p. 819).

Courtly has a different view of marriage and courtship. For his part, he will attempt 'to possess my sweet Luceny of my sincere affection,' and 'if I can make hir passionately love mee' Luceny 'shall thinke me worthy of my freedome, and soe wee will contynue the conversation and friendship of Lovers without knowing the words, of man and wife' (p. 819). For Courtly, there is no difference between the relationship before and after marriage where friendship is the basis.

The play's sisters, too, have their views on men and power. Tattiney is quite aware of Presumption's plot, but announces happily, 'doe you think Sister, the words sayeinge in the Church shall make mee minde him more, then I doe now[?] he is my Servant for I intend to bee his Mistris' (p. 816). The gentle Luceny does not approve of this attitude, however, and she reminds her sister that 'How often Sister have you read the Bible over and have forgotten man and wife should drawe equally in a yoke[?]' (p. 815). They are however both quite aware of the conventions of courtship and lovers' rhetoric and do not place much stock in them. They are, instead, amused by their male suitors' pretenses to wit: Tattiney remarks that she sees 'noe such marracles in their language,' to which Luceny points out, 'Wye that's because wee have beene brought up in the creation of good languages which will make us ever our selves' (p. 817).

This theme of self-possession, derived in part through the mastery of one's words, is manifested in all the female characters, even the unattractive and presumptuous Lady Tranquility and the outspoken serving maids. The three lady cousins announce at one point that they prefer to be 'a pritty toyeing Shee' to being married. However, at the end of the play, all are wed or are on the way to being so – but on the women's terms. The final speeches underline the theme of mutual respect and friendship as the basis of marriage:

Ta: His Mistris, this you may see is an equall marriage,
and I hate those people that will not understand,
matrymony is to ioyne Lovers.
Lu: But thinkes Husbands are the Rodd of Authority.
Ta: Or a Marriage Clog.

(p. 835)

The ideal of marriage in this drama is a companionate one, with equal respect between parties, neither being the servant or the master of the other. To marry is to confirm a friendship, set a bond, and 'to reioyce.'[24]

Perhaps the most unexpected feature of this volume – given its independent, profemale bias, and given current theories of female authorship – is the persona of Newcastle which is created. Many of the poems are either addressed to 'My Lord my Father' or contain references to him and the effects of his absence. Because of the steady reference to Newcastle throughout this volume, it seems that Starr's conclusion that the Earl of Bridgewater was the recipient of the dedication is unlikely. The forms and concepts used in the poems in this volume which refer to Newcastle are commonplace in seventeenth-century verse by men, Jonson in particular. What is unusual is the application of these forms and conceits to a father–daughter relationship.[25]

The series of 'Passion' poems, if read out of context, would naturally be assumed to refer to a lover. Most concern the writer's distress over the absence of the loved one; even his absence, however, is a potent force. In 'Passion's Invitation,' the speaker begins with an awkward Donne-like order:

For God's sake come away and land
And so my grief will prove a sand;
Then rocks of sadness I shall be no more
In sadly dropping at my Eyelids door.
And, if delay, I know, I then shall be
Despair's Anatomy, for each to see.
Once more I beg this of you; Prithee come
Then joy is my companion's total sum.

(p. 15)

Similarly, in 'Passion's Contemplation (p. 2),' every household item, every event is metamorphosed in the speaker's mind into an emblem of the father's situation: 'The torment I receive is thought of mind/ That nothing can I see but sorrow find' (p. 4). The fire makes her think of battles, her subsequent tears make her think of the sea on which he is sailing, her sighs are tempest which threaten the ship.

The only release from the tension of his absence is in imagining his return. In 'Love's Universe,' which uses an extended metaphor of the speaker's emotions representing a microcosm of natural forces and of the seasons, the writer concludes that her only possibility of summer will be 'Father, Brother for to see.' In 'Hopes Still' the speaker adopts a bantering tone, saying she will happily convert to Catholicism to bring him home – 'In Tear's beads/ Thinking your love merits by good deeds.' This drastic step failing, she then promises, 'Then Puritan I'll be, & with Long prayer pray/ Come into England Lord, & make thy way' (p. 45). The poem concludes, 'So, pray, that for your Daughters you will send/ Which Message, I will call my Heaven of end.'

The pun on the Puritan plea for true religion to return to England also ties in with another common term associated in these poems with Newcastle. He is repeatedly and conventionally referred to as 'My Lord'; but in several poems he also takes on explicitly God-like responsibilities and powers. In these poems, the earthly father takes on the powers of God to create, to sustain, and to save. An early poem in the volume, 'Passion's Letter to My Lord, My Father' sets the framework for this analogy. The speaker directly compares the powers of creation possessed with those of God. She fits their relationship, the despair over his absence, and her own dependence on him into the scheme of Christian belief.

My Lord, it is your absence, makes each see,
Your company creates, and makes me free;
For without you, I am [a] dull piece of earth,
And so continue nothing, till you make my birth;
For want of you I can too truly tell,
The several ways of grief that makes a Hell;
So in the midst of passion's grief 'twas such,
As I did think my life was much, too much;
So went love's resolution to make way,
Quitting sad life, which I call'd Holy day.
But then considering, that alive you be,
I kept my life, which is even lent from thee;
Thus doth my life, both ebb and flow, with you;
And as I hope for happiness, 'tis true.

(p. 1)

The concluding lines of 'Passion's Contemplation (p. 1 passim)' reiterate the theme of father-worship, and again make explicit reference to the similarities of her earthly and spiritual fathers in that their presence or absence determines the difference between Heaven and Hell.

What makes a Hell I'm sure Divines do say
The presence of God's light deprived away.
Our heavenly Father, then our earthly may,
Make Hell on Earth to his Children the same way.
The hell I'm in, since no content can have
Yet I do hope your presence will me save.

(p. 3)

While the imagery and the concept of absence as hell, or the negation of creation, is conventional in religious verse, it is extraordinary as applied here.

Newcastle is represented in his secular roles, as well. His profession as a soldier leaves the poets in constant fear for his safety. However, his skills as a warrior and courtier are repeatedly, and conventionally, praised.

My Lord your Picture speaks you this to be,
A courtier and a soldier each may see.
And so both love & war you can true tell
Having on both sides known the trade full well.
(p. 4)

While the commendations of his soldierly abilities are hardly surprising, the poets' appreciation of his prowess as a ladies' man goes against Starr's impression that they believed their father to be the victim of Margaret Lucas's snares. In 'A Song,' Newcastle is represented as the irresistible lover.

Maid, wife, or widow, which bears the grave style
Newcastle but name him I know then she'll smile
From thence you may follow this track in her face
So read by their Eyes, they will run Cupid's race.
. . .
His General Summons demanding the same
In his true gallantry, sweetness of fame
Which doth our Sex'[s] garrison ever to take
So desirous to yield.
(p. 13)

Finally, and most interestingly, the poets appeal to their father as their literary progenitor, seeking through the mastery of 'good language' to 'be your Daughter in your Pen.' The poems dedicating the pastoral to him are uncharacteristically marked by initials, making them clearly identified and personal. 'EB' writes that, in spite of her sorrow at his absence, 'yet shepherdesses can see to read / And so upon your stock of wit I feed / So beg your blessing to like this.' 'JC', too, places herself as a character in a drama in her longer and more complex petition for approval.

My Lord it is your absence makes each see
For want of you, what I'm reduc'd to be:
. . .
So what becomes me better then
But to be your Daughter in your Pen.
If you're now pleas'd, I care not what
Becomes of me, or what's my lot.
(p. 84)

There seems little question that the final readership for the volume as a whole was 'the English Maecenas' himself, patron of Jonson and amateur of verse. This is not a volume written in defiance of paternal authority or the social definitions of feminine modesty; it is an effort to live up to the intellectual and literary standards through public performance, 'to be your Daughter in your Pen,' in complete and confident possession of the power of writing.

It is also clear that the subject matter and style of the volume were anticipated as pleasing its readership. There is supporting external evidence that the women were encouraged to gain paternal approval through literary means. Even apart from his later championing of Margaret Cavendish's literary efforts, one finds in Newcastle's early correspondence an active encouragement of all his children to excel in the arts. There is a charming exercise addressed to all of his offspring (Charles, Jane, 'Bess,' 'Franke,' and Harry) where Newcastle wrote a couplet to each child, leaving room underneath for the child's verses to him. Young Jane would appear to have been the most enthusiastic:

Sweet Jane
I know you are a rare Inditer
And hath the Pen of a most ready writer.
WN
My Lord
I know you do but jest with me
& So in obedience I right this nothing.
Jane Cavendysshe[26]

Also, in this collection of early correspondence, there is a verse dedicated to his daughters, 'to be writt in my Booke before the maske booke.' From it, one gathers that the daughters had been active participants in their father's literary activities, as instigators of pieces and transcribers of manuscript volumes.

[You] knowe, I was nott nice, or coye,
Butt made a Countrie Masque, or Christmas Toye,
Att your desiers; Butt I did not Looke,
You would recorde my follies in a Booke.
Your loveinge & in this your obedient father
W:N:[27]

Like M. Calsindow in the play, who raised his daughters with good conversation to be independent and to preserve their 'own selves,' Newcastle provided an environment where literary achievement was encouraged equally for his sons and daughters; he also offered in his own writing practices the activity of manuscript circulation as an acceptable intellectual pursuit. There is no sense that he believed certain subjects to be improper for women or the public display of their talents to be immodest, and in this he may be compared, to his advantage, with the assumptions of certain modern critics.

Nor does he appear to be alone in this apparent unconventionality. The volume, with all of its independent, profemale sentiments, has none of the defensive posturings of a work such as the contemporary *The Womens Sharpe Revenge* (1640) by Mary Tattlewell and Ioan Hit-Him-Home, which addresses similar issues concerning male/female power structure. The Cavendish sisters do not seem to be anticipating a hostile response. Apparently such topics were acceptable subjects for the Earls of Bridgewater as well; Lady Alice Egerton, too, wrote verse in addition to performing it, and this volume contains admiring references to her poetic abilities.

Far from their literary efforts being considered eccentric or immodest, great care was taken in both families to preserve these women's writings in a handsomely calligraphed volume. Like Donne and other coterie poets, but unlike the duchess, the Cavendish sisters retained control of their readership. However, by confusing 'public' with 'publication,' we have misinterpreted the manuscript activities of these early women writers. Theirs was indeed a self-limiting readership, but this in no way indicates that this readership was uncritical or unsophisticated or that the authors lacked a 'public' voice and subject matter.

The manuscript volume by the Cavendish sisters thus offers an alternative picture of the literary landscape of the mid-seventeenth-century woman writer. This in turn raises questions about the degree to which these women can be dismissed or classed as untypical, and the degree to which our different expectations for male and female writers have shaped our anticipation of what we should find in their writings. Instead of isolated figures toiling secretly and shyly, we have a collaborative production, designed to please a reasonably extensive audience. Instead of being a defiant or subversive act, these pieces serve as a formal effort to confirm threatened social values and relationships. Even though the tone is profemale in matters of personal relationships, it is nevertheless presented as fitting comfortably into the world of the authors. These authors expected and no doubt gained approval for their independent beliefs as well as their literary efforts. For the Cavendish sisters, literature was a social tool, one to link generations and to continue traditions.

Notes

1 Angeline Goreau, *Reconstructing Aphra: A Social Biography of Aphra Behn* (Oxford, 1980), 149, 153–4.

I wish to thank the following for permission to quote from manuscripts cited in this essay: Bodleian Library, British Library, and the Keeper of Manuscripts, Nottingham University Library.

2 Henry Ten Eyck Perry, *The First Duchess of Newcastle and her Husband as Figures in Literary History* (Boston, MA, 1918), 121.

3 Douglas Grant, *Margaret the First: A Biography of Margaret Cavendish, Duchess of Newcastle 1623–1673* (Toronto, 1957), 73, 82, 230–1.

4 Bernard Falk, *The Bridgewater Millions, A Candid Family History* (London, 1942), 69–70, 75. Ruth Perry's biography of Mary Astell consolidates this treatment of the duchess as an isolated persecuted literary victim in an unsympathetic environment. She fails to mention the duke's daughters at all and reduces Newcastle himself to a man 'harmlessly addicted to horsemanship and swordsmanship.' *The Celebrated Mary Astell: An Early English Feminist* (Chicago, 1986), 114.

5 Bodleian Library, MS Rawl. Poet. 16.

6 Nathan Comfort Starr, 'The Concealed Fansyes: A Play by Lady Jane Cavendish and Lady Elizabeth Brackley,' *Proceedings of the Modern Languages Association*, 46 (1931), 836.

7 Nancy Cotton, *Women Playwrights in England, c. 1363–1750* (Lewisburg, PA, 1980), 40–1.

8 Virginia Woolf, *A Room of One's Own* (New York, 1929), 66.

9 Katherine Rogers (ed.) *Before Their Time: Six Women Writers of the Eighteenth Century* (New York, 1979), vii.

10 Sara Heller Mendelson, *The Mental World of Stuart Women: Three Studies* (Amherst, MA, 1987), 27.

11 Joanna Russ, *How to Suppress Women's Writing* (London, 1983), 20–2.

12 Arthur F. Marotti, *John Donne, Coterie Poet* (Madison, WI, 1986), x, xi.

13 Margaret J. M. Ezell, *The Patriarch's Wife: Literary Evidence and the History of a Family*

(Chapel Hill, NC, 1987), ch. 3. Josephine Roberts's excellent introduction to her edition of Lady Mary Wroth's verse offers a parallel pattern of manuscript circulation by a woman writer of the preceding generation; Roberts does not enter into labeling Lady Mary Wroth's writings as either 'closet' or 'coterie.' *The Poems of Lady Mary Wroth*, ed. Josephine A. Roberts (Baton Rouge, LA, 1983).

14 Perry, *The First Duchess*, 99–100.

15 Graham Parry, *The Golden Age Restor'd: The Culture of the Stuart Court 1603–42* (New York, 1981), 180–1.

16 See the introduction of Lady Alix Egerton's *Milton's Comus: Being the Bridgewater Manuscript with Notes and a Short Family Memoir* (London, 1910).

17 See French R. Fogle's article on the countess in *Patronage in Late Renaissance England*, ed. Louis Knafla (Los Angeles, 1983), 1–29 and 'A Catalogue of my ladies Books at London 1627 & 1631,' Henry E. Huntington Library MS EL 6495. The Huntington also holds the countess's 'Meditation on the Countess of Bridgewater' (*c.*1636), a collection of her devotions, Huntington MS EL 6888.

18 Bodleian MS, Rawl. Poet. 16, p. 6. Subsequent references to this volume will be included in the text. Because the argument of this essay concerns the contents and the historical context of these poems and is not primarily concerned with presenting an edition, spelling has been standardized and omitted endstops silently included.

19 Starr, 'The Concealed Fansyes . . . ,' 803–5.

20 Earl Miner, *The Cavalier Modes from Jonson to Cotton* (Princeton, NJ, 1971), 275.

21 Graham Parry, *Seventeenth-Century Poetry: The Social Context* (London, 1985), 10.

22 Miner, *Cavalier Modes*, 275.

23 *The Norton Anthology of Literature by Women*, ed. Sandra M. Gilbert and Susan Gubar (New York, 1985), 50–6; Louise Bernikow (ed.) *The World Split Open: Women Poets 1552–1950* (London, 1979), 20. See also Antonia Fraser, *The Weaker Vessel* (London, 1984), 335–6 for a summary of this view.

24 These views correspond closely with those expressed by Lady Brackley in her devotional writings, preserved after her death in another handsome manuscript volume. 'Some account of Marriage as an unhappy life, by reason there is an obedience must belong from the wife to the Husband,' she observes. But this 'obedience' is not servility but 'to have an affection; and love him to him, as a friend, and so to speake their mind, and opinion freely to him, yet not value him ye lesse' (British Library MS Eg. 607, ff. 150, 152–3). True marriage, she insists, is a 'companions way' and 'where both these parties do not perfectly agree, with passionate and sincere affection, but 'tis the happyest condition, a friendship never to broke, as ye words of Matrimony say, till death them part' (f. 160).

25 Obviously this volume, in addition to its importance for literary historians, provides very interesting materials for social historians tracing the history of the family. The issue of the existence of affectionate family relationships and the bonding between parents and children is outside the scope of this essay; but it is noteworthy that in this supposedly rigidly patriarchal era, with fathers cast as the dominant forces in family life, there are numerous examples of women poets celebrating the virtues of their husbands, children, and female friends but rarely are fathers the subject of poetic devotion. See Ezell, *Patriarch's Wife*, ch. 4.

26 University of Nottingham Library MS, Portland Papers Pw 25, ff. 18–19.

27 Ibid., ff. 16–17.

12

'SHE GAVE YOU THE CIVILITY OF THE HOUSE'

Household performance in *The Concealed Fancies*

Alison Findlay

In her new essay on Elizabeth Brackley's and Jane Cavendish's play, *The Concealed Fancies*, Alison Findlay builds upon the initial descriptions in the previous essays collected here and undertakes a complex and thorough analysis of the individual text. Focusing upon the house and its family as a background to the play, Findlay explores a number of issues, including the gender politics of familial relationships and household space, and the significance of costuming in such an intimate dramatic portrayal. As such, Findlay's essay signifies the recognition of the Cavendish sisters as vital playwrights whose work may be clearly envisaged in performance.

The Cavendish household, as both a physical space and a group of people, contributed vitally to the composition and performance dynamic of *The Concealed Fancies* by Jane Cavendish (1621–69) and her younger sister Elizabeth Brackley (1626–63). At the head of the household, William Cavendish provided an example of literary and theatrical creativity which he encouraged his children to follow. He recognised that Jane had 'the pen of a most ready writer' and urged Elizabeth 'Bess, you must write too, write but what you think / Now you're a girl, dissemble when you link.'[1] His comments to Elizabeth suggest that the family home was a privileged haven for uncensored self-expression. Here she could write openly 'what you think', whereas in the 'link' or bond of marriage she would be obliged to 'dissemble'. Jane and Elizabeth freely acknowledge their debt to their father. The handsome folio of 'Poems, Songs, a Pastorall and a Play' which they prepared for him often shows admiration akin to idolatry. The first poem addresses William Cavendish as 'The Great Example', while in the second, Jane describes him as the god-like source of her life and writing: 'Your company creates, and makes me free, / For without you, I am dull peece of earth / And soe contynues nothinge, till you make my birth.'[2] Luceny, the elder sister in *The Concealed Fancies*, echoes these sentiments, declaring her father 'shall be my alpha and omega of government' (2.3.32).[3]

William can be seen as a source of theatrical as well as literary inspiration for his daughters. Besides patronising the work of professional dramatists and composing plays for the commercial stage, he staged productions in the family homes. Jane and Elizabeth would probably have seen Ben Jonson's *The King's Entertainment at Welbeck* (1633), and *Love's Welcome to Bolsover* (1634), a celebration for Charles I and Henrietta Maria.[4] These lavishly mounted entertainments, and Cavendish's own 'country masque', apparently a 'Christmas Toy' for his daughters, would have established the idea of household performance for Jane and Elizabeth.[5] It is even possible that costumes from Jonson's shows may have remained at Welbeck and Bolsover, tangible reminders of the festivities and a resource for the sisters' own productions. No evidence of a Cavendish performance of *The Concealed Fancies* has yet been discovered, but since household theatre leaves little documentary evidence in comparison to professional or court drama, this cannot be taken as incontrovertible proof that the play was not staged by the authors. As I have argued elsewhere, Jane and Elizabeth certainly wrote with three-dimensional performance in mind, composing *The Concealed Fancies* for a specific coterie audience.[6]

The creative community of the Cavendish household, with William at its head, obliges us to rethink ideas of female authorship as an isolated, closeted activity, as Margaret Ezell has pointed out.[7] Nevertheless, to read *The Concealed Fancies* as part of 'The Cavendish Phenomenon', can also unjustly diminish its significance by subsuming it into the canon of male-authored drama. Dale Randall notes that neither Jane nor Elizabeth could be expected to share their father's experience in professional theatre and judges their own effort 'not a bad game for a couple of beleaguered young women to play.'[8] On one level, this judgement is valid. *The Concealed Fancies* is primarily a 'family' entertainment designed for a very specialised, non-commercial 'playing' arena, completely unlike the world of professional theatre. There is serious purpose behind such 'play', however. I wish to argue that Jane and Elizabeth deliberately employ that context in order to question women's positions in the family. Excluded from the public stage, they write a play for and about the household, a piece which 'doth become a woman's wit the very way' (Prologue 8) in its manipulation of that restricted, conventionally feminine, space.

The household is a curious, ambiguous location in *The Concealed Fancies*, representing freedom and captivity, paternal absence and control. Not even the settings of the play are straightforward. The main plot and sub-plot seem to take place in two different houses: the first occupied by Luceny and Tattiney, their suitors and servants, the second presenting Ballamo, a Royalist castle in which three female cousins are besieged. Nevertheless, Lord Calsindow is the head of each house, since Caution, a servant of the cousins, names him as his master and their father (4.6.9–15). The overlap of characters and settings can be explained in the light of the semi-autobiographical nature of *The Concealed Fancies*. William Cavendish, like Lord Calsindow in the play, held two family seats at Welbeck Abbey and Bolsover Castle. Jane and Elizabeth use two dramatic settings, equivalents of their homes, to recreate different aspects of their experiences in the Civil War: grief at their father's exile, and their involvement in military attacks from the Parliamentary forces. In the characters of Luceny and Tattiney and the cousins, Sh., Cicelly and Is. (whose names are never given in fuller form in the manuscript), Jane and Elizabeth represent fragmented images of themselves within a dramatic framework over which they have control as authors. The roles were clearly written to be performed by Jane (Luceny and Sh.), Elizabeth (Tattiney and Cicelly) and their younger sister Frances (Is.). The identities of authors, actors and characters are often deliberately elided in metatheatrical references to acting 'your scene[s]' (1.4.3), but the roles were not simply continuations of the sisters' off-stage personalities. Within the fictional households they construct, Jane and Elizabeth enjoy the freedom to play out 'fancies' or aspects of their identities, desires, fantasies, which were usually concealed.

This is apparent in the main plot, whose action centres on the absence and triumphal return of the controlling father figure. Lord Calsindow's exile gives Luceny and Tattiney the opportunity to manage the courtship process themselves, to negotiate equal partnerships with Courtley and Presumption. Their resistance to these suitors, whom they mock mercilessly, is not based on a determination to refuse them, but to educate them as suitable marriage partners. Luceny and Tattiney conceal their 'fancies', or affections, in a quest to remain mistresses of themselves even after marriage. Richard Braithwait describes the use of subterfuge in wooing in *The English Gentlewoman* (1631):

> There is a pretty pleasing kinde of wooing drawne from a conceived but concealed *Fancy*; which, in my opinion, suits well with these amorous younglins: they could wish with all their hearts to be ever in the presence of those they love, so they might not be seene by those they love. Might they chuse, they would converse with them freely, consort with them friendly, and impart their truest thoughts fully, yet would they not have their bashfull loves find discovery. They would be seene, yet seeme obscured; love, but not disclos it; see whom they love but not bee eyed.[9]

Luceny and Tattiney do not adopt literal disguises but their performances as scornful mistresses effectively mask any attraction they may have to the men. Far from being a means to declare their love, the 'scene' (or seen) selves (1.1.3) they present to Courtley and Presumption are designed to educate them on the subject of gender roles. Luceny and Tattiney are free to openly criticise their lovers, inducting them into a more liberal attitude to women's place in the family, like that which seemed to operate in the Cavendish household. In this sense, the heroines' 'concealed fancies' are not just their attraction to Courtley and Presumption but their wish to establish relationships in which each may 'continue [her] own' (2.3.108), rather than being subsumed in marriage by a husbandly 'rod of authority' (Epilogue.88).

In the context of a domestic performance, with the authors and members of their household as actors, levels of role play become more complex. *The Concealed Fancies* may have been a means for Jane and Elizabeth to establish their own identities in relation to husbands and suitors. In 1644–5 Elizabeth was already married to John Egerton, Viscount Brackley, but was apparently still living with her family, so Tattiney's transition from mistress to wife would have been directly relevant to her situation.[10] The authors make deliberate use of the household playing arena to further their political points. In a private theatrical, Welbeck Abbey (or Bolsover Castle), becomes a stage on which actors perform in a fictional space. But as the Cavendish homes, these venues are simultaneously social spaces in which authors and actors lived. Through its constant use of metatheatrical effects, *The Concealed Fancies* ingeniously blurs the lines between role play on and off-stage, both of which happen in the same place. The self-conscious performances of the fictional characters, who frequently comment on each other's ability to stage a scene, makes the behaviour expected of men and women in the household look just as theatrical. Confined to domestic production, Jane and Elizabeth make a virtue of necessity and use the house to demonstrate that gender roles are themselves performative.[11]

Luceny and Tattiney's resistance to their suitors is combined with a deep sense of grief at the absence of their father. Instead of looking outside the household for husbands, they withdraw more firmly into it. In Act 3 scene 2, Tattiney personifies long-suffering sadness while Luceny is dedicated to passionate grief and determines to 'put unquiet life quite out'

(3.2.8), or commit suicide. She gives dramatic expression to Jane's extreme sentiments, or 'madness' (3.2.13), found in many of the poems. In 'Passions Letre [Letter] to My Lord my Father', she protests:

Soe in the middle of passions griefe twas such,
As I did thinke my life was much too much;
Soe went loves resolution to make way
Quitinge sad life, which I call'd Holyday.[12]

Suicide was, of course, illegal in the eyes of the law and damnable in the eyes of God, but within the fantasy of the play Jane can pursue it as writer and actor. The outlawed 'gallant action' (3.2.3) of suicide gives her the chance to play out dangerous extremes of emotion, including an obsessive and exclusive love for her father which comes disturbingly close to incestuous desire in some poems. The scene is dramatically exciting since Tattiney is unable to stop Luceny and her suicide is prevented only by the intervention of an angel, a prelude to the equally miraculous reappearance of Lord Calsindow at the end of the play.

The sisters' decision to retire to a nunnery reaffirms their commitment to their father's cause rather than their suitors' entreaties of love, although it is not clear whether they are motivated by a renewed bout of grief or a desire to escape the suitors and reform Presumption's misogynist attitudes. Having laid out a rigidly patriarchal model of husbandly government, Presumption receives a letter informing him of the sisters' withdrawal and remarks 'I doubt I never shall enjoy my dear / For she my rigid thoughts certain did hear' (3.3.112). In a household performance, Elizabeth, in costume, probably would have overheard his plans for Tattiney from offstage. Retreat to the nunnery represents a wish to remain in the family home with a father who is 'an understanding gentleman' (3.3.53) and whose discourse, unlike Presumption's, 'uses not to be dull catechising' (3.3.54). Jane and Elizabeth dramatise their own reluctance to leave the sanctuary of the Cavendish family circle in which women are given space to 'write but what [they] think'.

In the nunnery scenes, the authors deliberately play on the name of their home, Welbeck Abbey, and its former life as a religious house, to further the image of themselves cloistered with grief. Before its dissolution, Welbeck had been the largest of the white canon order of Premonstratensian monasteries in the country.[13] In his *Antiquities of Nottinghamshire* (1677) Dr Robert Thoroton described the priests 'with Candles burning, and *Stoles* hung at their necks', remarking that 'the religious performances of the Monks in the Quire of the great Church of St *James*' had been superseded by the entertainments of William Cavendish's riding school at Welbeck.[14] In a production by Jane and Elizabeth, the monks' 'religious performances' would have been recreated – and regendered – in the music, costumes and ritual of the nunnery scenes. Luceny and Tattiney appropriate a previously male space to share a communion of loss and hope with poor 'innocent souls' (4.1.1) who suffer 'melancholy of the mind' (3.5.24). Tattiney promises to mix their griefs on some kind of a 'holy stone' or altar (4.1.21), so perhaps the authors even made use of the house chapel for this scene. As Suzanne Westfall remarks, any space could become a stage, and promenade-style was a characteristic feature of household theatricals.[15] Tattiney's description of herself praying in a sheet of 'white innocence' (5.2.13) implies that the nuns' habits would have been white, linking them back to the monks and simultaneously declaring the sisters' loyalty to William Cavendish since white coats were the uniform of his troops in the Civil War.[16]

Jane and Elizabeth's direct engagement with the military realities of the Civil War is explored in the Ballamo plot of *The Concealed Fancies.* The fate of the three imprisoned cousins is based on the situation of the Cavendish sisters, whose homes were overtaken by the Parliamentary forces. When the Earl of Manchester captured Welbeck on 2 August 1644, he reported that 'Newcastle's daughters, and the rest of his children and family are in it, unto whom I have engaged myself for their quiet abode there'.[17] Ten days later, Bolsover Castle also surrendered to the Parliamentary troops.[18] It seems probable that the sisters remained in Welbeck, writing *The Concealed Fancies* in late 1644 or early 1645, although they did make attempts to recover Bolsover Castle. On 17 April 1645, Jane and Frances Cavendish wrote to Lord Fairfax from there, appealing for it to be disgarrisoned and 'to have the favour to be admitted to that house'. Their request was unsuccessful and even though Welbeck was briefly recaptured by the Royalists in July 1645, it was under Parliamentary control again by November.[19]

In keeping with the authors' experiences, the ownership, appropriation and invasion of space is a recurrent feature in *The Concealed Fancies.* Since their mother's death in April 1643, Jane and Elizabeth were left in control of their father's estates while he was absent in battle or exile, just as Luceny, Tattiney and the cousins are made mistresses of Lord Calsindow's houses. Luceny has the power to offer Corpolant 'the civility of the house' (2.1.41) in the place of her father. At the same time, as Royalists, the heroines are besieged and become captives in their own homes. Through scenes of imprisonment and invasion, Cavendish and Brackley explore the sympathies and differences between Royalist men and women.[20]

The cousins' plight is paralleled by that of Action and Moderate, whose names identify their responses to imprisonment. The soldiers, while not of the aristocracy, are certainly 'of our party' (3.6.11) and are presented sympathetically, demonstrating a cross-gender bond between Royalist victims. Margaret Ezell has pointed out that by composing Royalist plays and poems, Jane and Elizabeth style themselves as part of a male literary coterie.[21] In *The Concealed Fancies*, the stewards, prisoners, male and female aristocrats of Lord Calsindow's households identify with a common cause, regardless of gender or class difference. Action's anger probably gives voice to the sense of frustration experienced by the Cavendish sisters. He comments bitterly 'I walk daily in the garden and, when I see the rogues go by me in scorn, will not put off my hat!' (3.6.31). No doubt Jane and Elizabeth felt equally resentful, walking in their own garden under the gaze of the occupying soldiers. The need to constantly censure their behaviour towards their enemies is represented by Moderate, who advises 'I . . . . desire you not to be so liberal of your tongue. It may do you hurt and our party no good' (3.6.12). Jane and Frances's scrupulously polite letter to 'his Excellence the Lord Fairfax' suggests they followed such counsel themselves, whatever their true feelings about the 'company of rascally knaves' (3.6.10).[22]

Differences between Royalist men and women emerge in the images of reappropriation or invasion of the household. The cousins' situation is relieved as the Elder and Younger Stellow break in to Ballamo to rescue them, but this happy resolution is achieved only at a price for Sh., Cicelly and Is. The freedom they had inside the house, in Lord Calsindow's absence, expands to a mere ten lines of 'liberty' (5.1.3) from thoughts of duty or marriage before Ballamo is repossessed on behalf of men. Once the Parliamentary soldiers are removed, the Stellows' triumphal entrance reasserts patriarchal control over the house. Other male invasions are presented less positively. When Courtley and Presumption intrude on the private grief of the nunnery, Luceny and Tattiney are justly outraged, especially since the suitors' ungallant action involves deception. The stage direction 'Courtley's discovery

& Presumption', suggests that they have made their way in by disguising themselves as suppliants.[23] While the 'Two Poor Women' echo Luceny and Tattiney's love for friends 'in a far country' (4.1.13) and suffering by military 'plunder' (4.1.19), the 'Poor Men's' loves and losses follow the selfish desires of the suitors:

> FIRST POOR MAN [Courtley]:
> One that I loved as my soul rejected me.
> LUCENY:
> Take this, and be assured, you shall grow wiser or have your mistress love you . . . .
> SECOND POOR MAN [Presumption]:
> And my grief is I loved a woman and she would not marry me.
> LUCENY:
> Take this as a scourge to whip your folly away.
>
> (4.1.6)

Luceny's responses reiterate the heroines' earlier stance. It is not surprising that Courtley and Presumption's 'discovery', or removal of their disguises to burst into triumphant love songs, does not achieve the desired effect. Luceny and Tattiney are only likely to be converted to marriage by a miracle, so Courtley and Presumption are obliged to stage one.

They appear disguised as gods, to bring Lord Calsindow home in a spectacular climax celebrating the restoration of the father in the Royalist tradition of the court masque. If costumes from the Jonson entertainments were still in the Cavendish houses, Jane and Elizabeth may have imagined Courtley and Presumption disguised as the two Cupids of *Love's Welcome at Bolsover*, who descend 'from the Cloudes'.[24] In *The Concealed Fancies*, the heroes enter with a song 'sung by 2 Gods coming downe out of the skye' to usher in Lord Calsindow as a symbol of paternal authority:[25] a father who gives away his daughters in marriage, a king who commands his subjects in the little commonwealth of the household. Luceny and Tattiney's roles as domineering mistresses seem to be eclipsed by the appearance of these divine commanders. They dutifully take off their nuns' robes and put on the 'garments' brought by the gods. Although the nature of the new clothes is not specified, it is clear that they are intended to symbolise a shift from withdrawal to betrothal, and the heroines voice no objections when their father gives them away to Courtley and Presumption.

The supreme position of the husband or father is brought into question by the highly ambiguous nature of the sequence, however. While the authors seem to be imitating the court masque with nostalgia for the conservative traditions it celebrates, the audience (and probably the heroines), are fully aware that the 'gods' are just Courtley and Presumption, dressed up in a last-ditch attempt to win their mistresses' loves. There is at least a hint of parody when Luceny and Tattiney ask 'Are you god-cheaters? / Or are we not ourselves?' (5.2.9). The 'gods' are very obviously theatrical 'cheats' whose power is only a construct of performance. The self-assured Luceny and Tattiney are able to see this clearly enough, and use of the Cupids' costumes would have heightened the effect. The role of dominant husband as divinely-appointed head of the family is as artificial as Courtley and Presumption's disguises, a shadow of authority.

Domestic performance conditions are ideally suited to capturing the ambiguity of the scene. Jane and Elizabeth may have wished to create a magnificent spectacle like those staged for the king and queen's visits, but even if they had access to the costumes for these previous entertainments, they certainly did not have an equivalent budget. Aware that they would have had to draw on the resources immediately available to them, they may have made use of this apparent deficiency to further their witty questioning of male dominance. The overambitious attempt to stage a divine spectacle within the household is perhaps just what Jane and Elizabeth were dramatising: parodically destabilising patriarchal authority whilst seeming to celebrate it. Certainly, in the play's Epilogue, Luceny and Tattiney are still free to determine their own place in the household. Tattiney describes hers as 'an equal marriage' (Epilogue.85), while Luceny reports that her persistently witty self-assertion eventually forced her husband to leave the room 'with a forced kind of mirth' (Epilogue.50).

Within the seemingly conservative framework of the plots then, the heroines retain a playfully subversive quality. This is evident not only in their attitudes to suitors, but to the household itself. Their conduct as mistresses in Lord Calsindow's absence is far from what was expected of a dutiful housewife. Thomas Becon's conduct book, *The Book of Matrimony* (1564) set forward the typical idea of a woman's place:

> It is the duty of an honest and godly wife diligently to look unto those things which are within her house and by no means to suffer anything to perish or to be unfruitfully and wastefully spent. For as the man is bound to make provision for his family and to bring it home, so is it the part of an honest and wise woman to provide that all things be safely kept and spent in good order, as we be taught by the very fowls of the air . . . . yea, and that she being at home, be not idle or spend her time playing dice or cards, and in such like vain and unfruitful pastimes, but that she spend her time in fruitful and necessary occupations, profitable to her husband, to herself, to her family, and to the commonweal.[26]

Duty and pleasure are diametrically opposed in Becon's guidelines. The wife or daughter of the house must dedicate herself to careful supervision: regulating the consumption of supplies and ensuring the maintenance of all items of property on her husband or father's estate. While the control of resources seems to empower her, her high-status position is illusory since her time is spent in work designed, primarily, to be 'profitable to her husband'. In most cases, the household finally belonged to a man. Feminist historians have been eager to discover 'the existence of a subculture, in which women were able to express themselves through the ownership and the use of material goods that surrounded them in their households', but Lorna Weatherill argues that the overbearing pressure on women to see themselves 'as part of a family' whose interests must be served before their own, makes this doubtful.[27]

The Concealed Fancies provides contrary evidence. In both the main plot and the subplot, the heroines deliberately flaunt the role of dutiful housewife in the pursuit of pleasurable 'rarer recreation' (3.4.79). The play explores the unconventional nature of their behaviour through their relationships with a network of servants, the living fabric of the household. The servants are caricatures whose dominant features may well represent the personalities of staff in the Cavendish houses. Jane's poem 'The Caracter' includes cameo portraits of Cavendish's 'servants', which could be the starting point for the roles of Mr Proper, Mr Friendly, Discretion, Pert, Toy, Care and Pretty. The poem concludes with a self-referential picture of 'the Ladies' who 'sitt / All day to give their Caracters of witt', as though Jane and Elizabeth are caught in the act of writing *The Concealed Fancies*.[28] In a coterie performance, with household servants in role, private jokes about the actors' idiosyncrasies could be shared by an audience of 'insiders'.

The servants' names – 'Proper', 'Gravity', 'Discretion', 'Sage' and 'Grave' – signify the proper attitudes of their mistresses towards their positions of responsibility, but Luceny, Tattiney and the cousins pointedly ignore the promptings of these characters. Far from spending their time in Becon's 'fruitful or necessary occupations' about the house, Luceny and Tattiney are still in bed, according to Mistress Sage (1.3.7). Gravity complains 'Fie, fie, as I am an honest man those wits will ne'er be housewives, and nothing angers me more, but they'll neither chide nor commend' (1.3.8). Their complete indifference to his work as a cook seems symptomatic of a failure to take on the supervisory role of mistress. With a pointed reference to the authors, Gravity comments that poetry is far more interesting to them than what is left in the pantry for dinner (1.3.42–4). The sisters spend their time indulging in Becon's 'vain and unfruitful pastimes': improvising witty ripostes to their suitors, in the form of speech or song, or even making bets with each other, behaviour which Becon would no doubt classify with 'playing at dice or cards'. When performed in a household, the subversive qualities of these actions take on extra resonance.

Through the characters, Jane and Elizabeth make a good-humoured commentary on their own literary endeavours, acknowledging the unconventional nature of their preoccupation with words rather than household affairs, yet maintaining the value of composing plays, poems and lyrics. In *The Concealed Fancies*, linguistic skill is valued above the more traditionally feminine activities of needlework, cookery or gardening as a means of self-expression in the home. Luceny points out 'we have been brought up in the creation of good languages which will make us ever our selves' (2.3.142). William Cavendish's encouragement to 'write but what you think' gives them licence to rewrite their positions in the household as leisured authors rather than domestic managers. Such a move is perceived as distinctly subversive by Presumption. His method for teaching Tattiney the 'fashion to obey' (3.3.44) is to put her in charge of the household accounts: 'I would have her take the week books which is the only way to make her incapable of discourse or entertainment' (3.3.37). In Presumption's fears, Cavendish and Brackley draw attention to the political power of their own 'discourse or entertainment'. *The Concealed Fancies* constitutes a critique of the traditional domestic role both in its sympathetic presentation of the heroines and in the very conditions of its own composition: the act of writing and perhaps producing the play on the part of the authors. Although Jane made attempts to protect the family property and to raise money to send to her father, the play demonstrates that the role of housewife is inadequate as the sole definition of female identity within the home.[29]

The cousins in the sub-plot are no better than Luceny and Tattiney. In fact, Sh. flatly refuses to look at the account books sent to her by the steward Caution, even though she has not seen them for a fortnight. She impatiently dismisses Sage with the words:

> Go formality and tell his formalityship I have other business than to stupefy my brain with how many quarters of malt is bought, and in that how much I am cozened, neither care I how many scores of sheep have been plundered from me.
> (4.3.15)

A more blatant rejection of Becon's model of domestic duty can hardly be imagined. Sh.'s excuse is that this is a plot on Caution's part to test whether she trusts him or not, but Caution later claims he knows of no such plot (4.6.4–10), which makes her determination not to see the books for a whole month seem even more outrageous. The shock effect of such lines would have been heightened if they were spoken in the walls of Welbeck or

Bolsover, as Jane and Elizabeth surely envisaged. Sh. and her cousins are dedicated to seeking out pleasure in their father's absence. Bored with the fruitful occupation of learning French, they determine to break into their father's cabinets, a neat inversion of the male invasions of space elsewhere in the play. In Lord Calsindow's box of cordials they discover fruits much more attractive:

> SH.:
> Take one of these cakes, and you cousin, they're very good ones.
> CICELLY:
> We never saw these before, come we'll put them up.
> SH.:
> No, take another, he'll never want them.
> IS.:
> Truly, if he knew he would wonder how we durst offer to look of them.
> SH.:
> I wish he saw us in a prospective.
>
> (3.4.39)

Stealing the father's fruit in the form of cakes, cordials, 'preserved nutmegs' and 'morabollans' or plums (3.4.56) has obvious connections with the story of Eden, where Eve's consumption of the fruit of knowledge transforms her from an obedient daughter into an active consuming subject. Sh.'s allusion to Lord Calsindow watching them 'in a prospective' or through a telescope, grants him the omniscient viewpoint of God, overseeing their transgressions. In metatheatrical terms, it also refers to William Cavendish as the most significant reader or audience for the piece, whose approval the actors seek so earnestly in a special Prologue and Epilogue. The radical nature of breaking into the father's property is clear in the comment 'he would wonder how we durst offer to look of [at] them', but Sh.'s wish to be seen satisfying her appetite registers a need for women's desires and pleasures to be openly acknowledged.

Confections, preserved fruits and cordials are part of a particularly feminine world of creativity and pleasure.[30] Indeed, one of Jane's poems in the folio manuscript addresses her sister as 'the quintessence of Cordiall', telling her 'your presence is Balsam to my braine'.[31] The cousins refer to 'our friends cordials' (3.4.29), Elizabeth Grey's recipes for such restoratives, which the Cavendish sisters may have seen in manuscript since she was a relative.[32] Lord Calsindow has locked up Elizabeth Grey's cordials in a box, as though to contain the power they represent, but in his absence the cousins bring them out into the open, along with the open expression of their own enjoyment in eating, drinking and exploring.

The picture of feminine leisure and sensory pleasures is expanded in scenes showing Lady Tranquillity, another character who uses 'cordials' (1.2.44). Lady Tranquillity's name signals her fondness for relaxation rather than work. She vows to keep to her bed in order to 'plump up my face' (1.2.10) and looks forward to preparing her costume and make-up for 'Five hours without interruption!' (2.1.39). The detailed attention she gives to clothes and cosmetics, 'the best dress for the face' (1.2.40), seems highly suspicious from a feminist point of view until we remember that all her preparation is primarily for a female audience: Luceny and Tattiney. In a comment rich with metatheatrical resonance, Lady Tranquillity notes that these two women 'can give such characters as to make a lady appear, or not appear' (1.2.13). Behind the idea that Luceny and Tattiney will represent Lady Tranquillity to their father, lies an awareness of Jane and Elizabeth who construct the aspiring mother-in-law to appear in their play.

The possibility that Lady Tranquillity could be based on reports of Margaret Lucas, who was to marry William Cavendish in December 1645, makes the character portrayal curiously prophetic. Lady Tranquillity's world of sensory delights in which women are both actors and spectators looks forward to Margaret Cavendish's play *The Convent of Pleasure*, where Lady Happy founds a house devoted to women's 'Ease and Conveniency' and 'Pleasure and Delight'. The furniture includes 'a great Looking-Glass in each Chamber, that we may view our selves and take pleasure in our own Beauties whilst they are fresh and young'.[33] Lady Tranquillity is a comic figure in *The Concealed Fancies* but through her exaggerated character, Jane and Elizabeth signal the possibility of transforming the house into a space dedicated to women's pleasure. There are hints of exclusively female delight even in the nunnery where Luceny and Tattiney cocoon themselves as spirits. Tattiney remarks that 'ghosts do love to have their own delights' (4.3.15)[34] and Luceny refers to her 'seeled chamber' as a 'fine delitive [delightful] tomb' (4.1.21–2). The threat posed by this secretive, private world of feminine rapture is swiftly swept aside by the suitors' appearance as gods, the key moment in returning the house to its male owners.

Even more than cordials or cosmetics, clothes are powerful tools of resistance for Luceny and Tattiney. This seems surprising since, costumed as they are in the low-cut, laced dresses of Caroline court fashion, they are inevitably caught up in the structures of femininity which further their subjection. As Christopher Breward points out, women's fashions of the Early Modern period did not take the female body or its comfort as the starting point for their designs but 'responded instead to the dictates of portraiture and constant display'.[35] Act 4 scene 4 of *The Concealed Fancies* shows that Jane Cavendish and Elizabeth Brackley were acutely conscious of the pressures on women to model themselves as objects of the male gaze. Courtley's song as a vendor highlights the complex gender politics surrounding women as consumers of luxury goods, while Courtley and Presumption's speeches to their mistresses' pictures highlight their interest in Luceny and Tattiney as beautiful objects for display: framed and silent rather than active and desiring.

Although they are trapped in these material 'frames' of femininity, Luceny and Tattiney's choice of garments accords them a sense of agency which they use to the full. Luceny reports that she dressed 'in a slight way of carelessness which becomes as well, if not better, than a set dress' (1.4.6). She deliberately chooses such attire in contrast to the formal dress and artificial postures of love adopted by Courtley, criticising both as superficial by mocking his 'new suit' (1.4.48). Luceny's decision not to wear 'set dress' broadcasts her rejection of conventional courtship rituals; Courtley's failure to recognise the message condemns him to a humiliating process of unmasking as Luceny pre-empts or ridicules each of his poses as courtly lover (1.4.50–109).

Freedom, self-determination and costume are intimately linked for both the heroines. Their vows to continue mistresses of themselves after marriage are fulfilled as they remain mistresses of their wardrobes. Tattiney wittily assures Luceny

> I protest, Presumption shall never see me out of order when I am married – but in a morning, and at night, in my several satin petticoats and waistcoats, and always in my careless garb.
>
> (2.3.145)

The desires of the suitors for a 'mechanical wife' (Epilogue.40), modelled rigidly on conventional ideas of wifely deference, are obviously going to be frustrated by such behaviour. Both recognise the importance of dress as a manifestation of inward sobriety and obedience, as outlined in conduct books. Presumption determines to subjugate Tattiney, and 'let her know I am her husband' (3.3.7), by controlling her wardrobe: undermining her faith in her own taste, and, once a year, bringing her a fashionable gown from London 'which with long continuing in the country, she shall not know how to put on' (3.3.31). By these means, he triumphantly asserts, 'I'll see in what garb I can bring her to' (3.3.85).

Far from conforming to either their husband's wishes, or moral prescriptions on modest dress, Luceny and Tattiney are more like Richard Braithwait's example of a shrew who 'wears her clothes negligently, of purpose to move her husband to tax her for her sluttishness, whose reproof she retorts with hail shot and pellets him with words as disgraceful as she is fulsome.'[36] In the Epilogue, Luceny tells how she outwitted her husband by paying lip-service to the idea of obedience:

> I looked soberly, as if I would strictly observe him, yet dressed myself contrary to his instruction, and my behaviour was according to my dress, so much as he said, sweet heart, do you go abroad today? . . . methinks you are very fine.
>
> (Epilogue.14)

Luceny's fine dress disturbs Courtley precisely because it telegraphs that she is a free woman who will travel abroad rather than a *feme coverte*. William Vaughan's conduct book, *The Golden Grove* (1608), pointed out that a wife 'must not be too sumptuous and superfluous in her attire, as: decked with frizzled hair, embroidery, precious stones, gaudy raiments and gold put about, for they are the forerunners of adultery.'[37] Luceny is not promiscuous; she promises that Courtley will find her 'a true piece of virtue' as a wife (2.3.135). By means of dress, however, both she and Tattiney assert ownership of their bodies and their own sexuality, refusing to become commodities in their husbands' houses. Tattiney reports that after marriage 'I was myself, and held my petulent garb' (Epilogue.78).

In a domestic performance, clothes take on additional layers of meaning since many of the costumes would belong to members of the household. Peter Stallybrass has argued that garments, as material objects, become fetishized on stage, acquiring an identity of their own drawn from their original wearers or functions which gives them a 'curious precedence over the actor'. In public theatres 'the costume hovers between a fetishized identity from the past' and 'its new possibilities once it has been appropriated'.[38] In a private theatrical, such as a Cavendish production of *The Concealed Fancies*, the fetishization effect would be all the more pronounced, since the costumes would be worn in the same place, and possibly by the same people, as in their previous life as ordinary clothes. The use of Jane, Elizabeth and Frances's wardrobe to dress Luceny, Tattiney and the cousins would literally embody the possibility that these witty, self-assertive heroines are aspects of the Cavendish sisters. As well as signalling subversive 'new possibilities' of behaviour on the part of the authors, clothes may have contributed to the more conservative fantasy of family reunion in the play. Given the fetishization effect, perhaps even absent friends could have been 'presented' through their garments. If Jane and Elizabeth costumed the actors playing Lord Calsindow and the Stellow Brothers in their father and brothers' clothes, the tantalising possibility of those loved ones returning home might have been brought one 'stage' nearer.

The play's persistent references to clothes and their significance are part of Jane and

Elizabeth's wider project of rewriting the household according to their 'fancies'. Through an extremely clever manipulation of domestic artefacts, conventions, and space, *The Concealed Fancies* projects the ultimate fantasy of its authors: to forge independent personalities for themselves in their writing and in their marriages, whilst remaining daughters of the house.

Notes

1 A. S. Turberville, *A History of Welbeck Abbey and its Owners, Volume 1: 1539–1755* (London: Faber and Faber, 1938), pp. 45–6.
2 The manuscript is Bodleian Rawlinson MS Poet 16. The poems are on p. 1.
3 *The Concealed Fancies* is found on pages 87–157 of the manuscript. Nathan Comfort Starr published a transcript, 'The Concealed Fancies: A Play by Lady Jane Cavendish and Lady Elizabeth Brackley,' *Proceedings of the Modern Languages Association* 46 (1931), 802–38. A modernized-spelling edition of the play is included in S. P. Cerasano and Marion Wynne-Davies, eds., *Renaissance Drama by Women: Texts and Documents* (London and New York: Routledge, 1996). All quotations are taken from this edition.
4 Ben Jonson, *Ben Jonson*, ed. C. H. Herford and Percy and Evelyn Simpson (Oxford: Clarendon Press, 1925–52), 7, 787–814. The entertainments are discussed with reference to their household settings by Cedric C. Brown, 'Courtesies of Place and Arts of Diplomacy in Ben Jonson's Last Two Entertainments for Royalty', *The Seventeenth Century*, 9 (1994), 147–71.
5 Geoffrey Trease, *Portrait of A Cavalier: William Cavendish, First Duke of Newcastle* (London: Macmillan, 1979), p. 37. Margaret Cavendish also mentions another entertainment at Welbeck in her *Life of William Cavendish, Duke of Newcastle to which is added the True Relation of My Birth, Breeding and Life*, ed. C. H. Firth, 2nd edn (London: Routledge and Sons, no date), p. 104.
6 Alison Findlay, Stephanie Hodgson-Wright and Gweno Williams, '"The Play is Ready to be Acted": Women and Dramatic Production 1570–1670', *Women's Writing*, special issue, ed. Marion Wynne-Davies (forthcoming). I directed a production of *The Concealed Fancies* with Jane Milling at Bretton Hall in December, 1994.
7 Margaret M. J. Ezell, '"To Be Your Daughter in Your Pen": The Social Functions of Literature in the Writings of Lady Elizabeth Brackley and Lady Jane Cavendish,' *Huntington Library Quarterly,* 51 (Autumn 1988), 281–96.
8 Dale B. J. Randall, *Winter Fruit: English Drama 1642–1660* (Lexington, KY: University Press of Kentucky, 1995), p. 326.
9 Richard Braithwait, *The English Gentlewoman* (London, 1631) reprinted (Amsterdam and New York: Da Capo Press, Theatrum Orbis Terrarum, 1970), p.131.
10 On Elizabeth's life and writings see Betty S. Travitsky, *Subordination and Authorship in Early Modern England: The Case of Elizabeth Egerton and her Loose Papers* (Tempe, AZ: Medieval and Renaissance Texts and Studies, forthcoming).
11 For further discussion of the performative nature of gender see my 'Playing the "scene self" in Jane Cavendish and Elizabeth Brackley's *The Concealed Fancies*', in *Enacting Gender on the English Renaissance Stage,* ed. Viviana Comensoli and Anne Russell (Urbana, IL: University of Illinois Press, 1998).
12 Bod. Rawl. MS Poet. 16, p. 1.
13 David Knowles, *The Religious Orders in England*, 3 vols (Cambridge: Cambridge University Press, 1948–59), 3, p. 43.
14 Robert Thoroton, *Antiquities of Nottinghamshire* (London, 1677), pp. 452–3.
15 Suzanne Westfall '"A Commonty a Christmas gambold or a tumbling trick": Household Theater', in *A New History of Early English Drama*, ed. John D. Cox and David Scott Kastan (New York: Columbia University Press, 1997), 39–67, p. 42. The house chapel is mentioned by Thoroton, p. 453.
16 Margaret Cavendish, *The Life of William Cavendish*, p. 84.
17 Cited in Nathan Comfort Starr, p. 803.
18 P. A. Faulkner, *Bolsover Castle* (London: English Heritage, 1985), p. 42.

19 See Nathan Comfort Starr, 'The Concealed Fansyes', p. 804.
20 On the relationship between imprisonment and literary production, see Marion Wynne-Davies's essay pp. 60–8.
21 Ezell, 'To Be Your Daughter in Your Pen', p. 287.
22 The full letter is cited in Starr, 'The Concealed Fansyes', p. 804. Elizabeth is mentioned in a postscript.
23 Bod. Rawl. MS Poet. 16, p. 127.
24 Ben Jonson, *Ben Jonson*, 7, p. 810.
25 Bod. Rawl. MS Poet 16, p. 141.
26 Kate Aughterson (ed.) *Renaissance Woman: Constructions of Femininity in England, A Sourcebook* (London: Routledge, 1995), p. 113.
27 Lorna Weatherill, 'A Possession of One's Own: Women and Consumer Behavior in England, 1660–1740', *Journal of British Studies*, 25 (1986), 131–56, pp. 155–6. The idea of material possessions as a source of women's pleasure and agency was explored by Lynnette McGrath, Lori Humphrey Newcomb and Allison Dean Spreuwenberg-Stewart in their inspiring workshop 'Tudor-Stuart Living: Domestic Style, Women's Pleasure', held at the conference *Attending to Early Modern Women: Crossing Boundaries* (University of Maryland, College Park, November 1997). I am especially indebted to the organizers of this workshop since the materials they provided for discussion have formed an invaluable starting point for the following reading of *The Concealed Fancies.*
28 Bod. Rawl. MS Poet. 16, p. 23.
29 Margaret Cavendish, *The Life of William Cavendish, Duke of Newcastle,* pp. 69–70.
30 See, for example, *With Faith and Physick: The Life of a Tudor Gentlewoman, Lady Grace Mildmay 1552–1620,* ed. Linda Pollock (London: Collins and Brown, 1993), *The Diary of Lady Margaret Hoby 1599–1605*, ed. Dorothy M. Meads (London: George Routledge and Sons, 1930) and Kim F. Hall, 'Culinary spaces, colonial spaces: the gendering of sugar in the seventeenth century', in *Feminist Readings of Early Modern Culture*, ed. Valerie Traub, Cora Kaplan and Dympna Callaghan (Cambridge: Cambridge University Press, 1996), 168–90, p. 176.
31 Bod. Rawl. MS Poet. 16, p. 12.
32 Marion Wynne-Davies notes this in *Renaissance Drama by Women*, p. 212, n. 51. *A Choice Manuall of Rare and Select Secrets in Physick and Chyrurgery* was published in 1653.
33 Margaret Cavendish, Duchess of Newcastle, *The Convent of Pleasure*, in *Plays, Never Before Printed* (London, 1668), pp. 13–16. On female pleasure in the convent, see Gweno Williams's essay pp. 95–107.
34 The manuscript assigns both speeches to Luceny but, given Tattiney's earlier identification with sadness in 3.2., it seems logical for her to speak these lines.
35 Christopher Breward, *The Culture of Fashion: A New History of Fashionable Dress* (Manchester: Manchester University Press, 1995), pp. 66–7. I am grateful to the organizers of the 'Tudor-Stuart Living' workshop for drawing my attention to this book.
36 Richard Braithwait, *Essays upon the five senses* (1620), in Aughterson (ed.) *Renaissance Woman*, p. 244.
37 Aughterson (ed.) *Renaissance Woman*, p. 97.
38 Peter Stallybrass, 'Worn worlds: clothes and identity on the Renaissance stage', in *Subject and Object in Renaissance Culture*, ed. Margreta De Grazia, Maureen Quilligan and Peter Stallybrass (Cambridge: Cambridge University Press, 1996), 289–320, pp. 294, 303.

13

'MY BRAIN THE STAGE'

Margaret Cavendish and the fantasy of female performance

Sophie Tomlinson

Sophie Tomlinson's essay, first published in 1992, was one of the key critiques of Margaret Cavendish's dramatic *oeuvre* which, by placing the plays in their historical and political contexts, was able to take seriously the possibility of female performance. Cavendish's plays had often suffered the same neglect and ridicule as her philosophical and scientific writings, but Tomlinson's essay, which deals with a substantial number of the dramatic writings (from *The Apocriphal Ladies* to *The Convent of Pleasure*), demonstrates categorically that women acting was a viable possibility for the Duchess both within the private world of her imagination and in the public arenas of the court and stage.

In one of her *Sociable Letters* (1664) written during her exile from the English Protectorate with her husband, the then Marquis of Newcastle, Margaret Cavendish describes to a female correspondent some of the 'several Sights and Shews' to be purchased at 'Carneval Time' in the city of Antwerp. From a medley of human and animal performers she singles out a female freak, half woman, half animal:

> amongst the rest there was a Woman brought to me, who was like a Shagg-dog, not in Shape, but Hair, as Grown all over her Body, which sight stay'd in my Memory, not for the Pleasantness, but Strangeness, as she troubled my Mind a Long time, but at last my Mind kick'd her Figure out, bidding it to be gone, as a Doglike Creature.[1]

Repressing in this way the psychological disturbance caused by this figure Cavendish recounts how she was further fascinated by an Italian mountebank, who had with him a man who 'did Act the part of a Fool', together with 'two Handsom Women Actors, both Sisters . . . one of [whom] was the Mountebank's, th'other the Fool's Wife'. The second of these women, in Cavendish's estimate, far outshone the other, both for her beauty and her skill in acting and dancing. 'Indeed', she writes,

> she was the Best Female Actor that ever I saw; and for Acting a Man's Part, she did it so Naturally as if she had been of that Sex, and yet she was of a Neat, Slender Shape; but being in her Dublet and Breeches, and a Sword hanging by her side, one would have believed she had never worn a Petticoat, and had been more used to Handle a Sword than a Distaff; and when she Danced in a Masculine Habit, she would Caper Higher, and Oftener than any of the Men, although they were great Masters of the Art of Dancing, and when she Danced after the Fashion of her own Sex, she Danced Justly, Evenly, Smoothly, and Gracefully.
>
> (pp. 406–7)

In the rest of the letter Cavendish explains how she took such delight in seeing 'this Woman, and the Fool her Husband' act, that she hired a room in the house next to the stage and went daily to watch them. However, in what seemed a short time, and 'to [her] great Grief', the itinerant troupe was commanded out of town by the local magistrate. To compensate for her loss Cavendish effected a characteristic gesture of interior withdrawal, in which

> to please me, my Fancy set up a Stage in my Brain . . . and the Incorporeal Thoughts were the several Actors, and my Wit play'd the Jack Fool, which Pleased me so much, as to make me Laugh Loud at the Actions in my Mind . . . but after my Thoughts had Acted, Danced, and Played the Fool, some several times of Contemplating, my Philosophical and Physical Opinions, which are as the Doctors of, and in the Mind, went to the Judgement, Reason, Discretion, Consideration, and the like, as to the Magistrates, and told them, it was very Unprofitable to let such Idle Company be in the Mind . . . whereupon the Magistrates of the Mind Commanded the Fancy-Stage to be taken down, and the Thought-Actors to go out, and would not suffer them to Cheat, or Fool any longer.
>
> (p. 408)

Subscribing herself, 'And so leaving my Mind Free of such Strangers', Cavendish brings her letter to a close.

Cavendish's writing is acutely conscious of 'Fancy's' power to substitute the scene of the mind for the theatre of the world. In this letter, however, it is a real theatre which is so transposed, and transposed twice over, from open-air stage to private room, from private room to a closet theatre of the mind. While the first of these retreats is occasioned by the joint constraints of Cavendish's class and gender, she is compelled to the second only by the magistrate's order to the players to leave. In another of the *Sociable Letters*, in which she defends her 'Retired Life', Cavendish claims that she prefers her fantasy stage to worldly recreations:

> and though I do not go Personally to Masks, Balls, and Playes, yet my Thoughts entertain my Mind with such Pleasures, for some of my Thoughts make Playes, and others Act those Playes on the Stage of the Imagination, where my Mind sits as a Spectator.[2]

But Cavendish's rapt viewing of the woman-actor undermines the integrity of this disavowal. 'Troubled for the Loss of that Pastime', she rehearses the scene in her head until her own regulatory controls intervene, suppressing the 'Fancy-Stage' and its cheating, fooling 'Strangers'. In a similar way her mind had earlier rid itself of the strange, amphibious 'Dog-like Creature'. I want to suggest that the acts of suppression are linked, and that Cavendish, in a manner appropriate to fantasy, was simultaneously enthralled and disturbed by the actress's ambidextrous shifting between sexes.[3]

One reason why the cross-dressing actress might be a disturbing as well as a pleasurable figure is that her performance seals the argument which Cavendish's texts constantly broach as to whether gender difference is natural or constructed.[4] Not only does the actress play a man 'so Naturally as if she had been of that Sex', she excels her male colleagues in the frequency and height of her capers. For Margaret, Duchess of Newcastle, at once pampered and constrained, wanting 'the Agility, Act, Courage [and] Liberty' to slide on the ice,[5] the female actor embodies a potent fantasy – not just of freedom from a natural femininity, but of litheness, aptitude, art and aspirations.

In the dedication to the first of her two books of plays, published respectively in 1662 and 1668, Cavendish traces her pleasure in 'making' plays to the imagined performance which accompanies their conception. She dedicates her book chiefly

> to my own Delight, for I did take
> Much pleasure and delight these Playes to make;
> For all the time my Playes a making were,
> My brain the Stage, my thoughts were acting there.[6]

The last line is redolent of Cavendish's creative resource, the power of her imagination to usurp the real. It gestures at the same time to the absence of a material stage, for as she goes on to indicate in one of her prefatory addresses, Cavendish wrote the plays which were published in her first volume during the Interregnum when public theatre performance was officially banned. One of the most striking features of Cavendish's plays is their use of performance as a metaphor of possibility for women. This embracing of the idea of acting as a means of becoming or self-realization is coupled in the first volume with a disparaging view of professional players, who counterfeit identities not truly their own.

As this attitude suggests, there are other contexts for Cavendish's engagement with female performance than the professional actress on the continent, or subsequently in Restoration England. In 1653, in the euphoria of her first publication, she proclaimed that 'this Age hath produced many effeminate Rulers, as well as Actors'.[7] One woman who belonged to the denomination of 'Royal Actors' was Charles I's French consort, Queen Henrietta Maria. Her practice of her native custom of performing, not just in masques, but in spoken drama at the Caroline court turned female acting into a fashionable and controversial issue in the period and inspired a growth in women's participation in private theatricals which continued into the Interregnum years. Acting formed part of the spectrum of the queen's social and religious interests, chief among which was a cult of platonic love, mediated through French romance and pastoral drama, which projected women centre-stage as the embodiment of ideal beauty.[8] The unprecedented feminine focus of court culture produced a division between an attitude which countenances the notion of women as theatrical, and one which stigmatizes female theatricality as sexually transgressive. The latter response is exemplified by the Puritan William Prynne's attack on women-actors as 'notorious whores' in his *Histrio-Mastix* (1633): the anti-theatrical tract which was construed as aiming at Henrietta Maria, and at the panoply of court culture and religion. The political furore caused by Prynne's book added fuel to a growing literary debate over the issue of women's cultural visibility and agency.[9]

One index of this debate is the new model of the court lady stereotype in Caroline drama, who is distinguished by her passion for acting and theatre. This figure is characterized by unruly behaviour, rising in degree from the frisky ladies-in-waiting who amuse themselves by acting Juniper and Danae in James Shirley's *The Bird in a Cage* (1633), to the woman-antic as homicide in John Ford's *Love's Sacrifice* (1633) to the actress as political subversive in William Cartwright's *The Lady-Errant* (1628–43?).

One can see a different kind of rapprochement with the notion of women as theatrical in the dramatic figure of the platonic mistress, whose role is essentially one of 'setting herselfe at gaze', playing prima donna to an audience of spectator servants whom she keeps at a distance through her artful language and wit. The discourse of acting and counterfeit attached to women within the platonic cult is clearly established in Jonson's *The New Inn* (1629) in the scenes in which Lady Frampul performs and so acts herself into her feeling for Lovel. This portrayal of the witty mistress as an actress persists in the series of capricious women in Shirley's comedies. In his play *The Ball* (1632) the demand for women-actors in England forms a fashionable talking point, while theatricality furnishes a standard for the behaviour of Lucilla, a rich young widow, who, entertaining three suitors in a row, jokes with her maid, 'Away, Scutilla, and / Laugh not [too] loud between our acts'.[10] A concept of theatricality as a necessary feminine ruse informs the household drama *The Concealed Fansyes*, written and perhaps performed in the mid-1640s by the sisters Lady Jane Cavendish and Lady Elizabeth Brackley. In their play the language of disguise and concealment expressed in the title is used consistently to characterize the two sisters' strategic obstruction of their lovers' address; their tormenting them, Beatrice-like, on the rack of their language: 'Sister pray tell mee in what humour thou wert wth thy servant yesterday, prethee tell mee how you acted yo^e^ Sceane.'[11]

When they wrote their play the Cavendish sisters were about to become stepdaughters to Margaret Lucas, who married their father, William Cavendish, in Paris in 1645. The fact that the sisters also authored a pastoral suggests that their dramatic writing, like that of their stepmother, was in part an effect of the culture set in motion by Henrietta Maria.[12]

Despite her disclaimers, the details of Cavendish's life support the more than passing acquaintance with theatre which is reflected in her work. In her autobiography she describes her family's manner of spending half of each year in London where they engaged in a typical range of 'town' recreations, one of which was 'in winter time to go sometimes to plays'.[13] Of crucial importance is Cavendish's volunteering as a maid of honour to Henrietta Maria in Oxford in 1643, a gesture which demonstrates her royalism, her social ambition and her identification with the queen's feminocentric culture.[14] At Oxford she would have witnessed the plays and other entertainments which continued to be staged in modified form.[15] The masque appears in her early work such as her prose fiction 'The Contract', in which two lovers are smitten during the dancing of the revels. The details of the occasion are carefully sketched, notably in the description of the tumult encountered by the heroine and her uncle as they attempt to gain access:

> and when they came to enter through the Door to the Masquing Room, there was such a Croud, and such a Noyse, the Officers beating the People back, the Women squeaking, and the Men cursing, the Officers threatening and the Enterers praying, which Confusion made her afraid.[16]

There is more evidence of Cavendish's colloquy with the culture surrounding the queen. The exiling of Henrietta's court to her native Paris supplied further contexts in which Cavendish could witness amateur and professional women actors, respectively in the distinctive French spectacle of the 'ballet de cour', and in performances by local and visiting theatre companies.[17] Her play *The Presence* (1668), which dramatizes this period of her life, ends with '*a Ball after the* French fashion', followed by '*an Anti-Mask*',[18] and in another play, *The Female Academy* (1662), a woman delivers an oration on the theme of 'a Theatre' in which she criticizes the 'feign'd and constrain'd acting of French and Italian players' (p. 671). It was in Paris too, while in the service of the queen, that Margaret met and married William Cavendish, Marquis of Newcastle, a man who brought with him a host of theatrical connections. One of the new breed of courtier dramatists encouraged by Charles and Henrietta Maria's theatrical interests, he patronized and received professional assistance from a number of playwrights spanning the Caroline and Restoration periods, including Jonson, Shirley, Flecknoe, Shadwell and Dryden. In the dedicatory epistle to her first volume of plays Cavendish states it was his reading his plays to her which made her take up the form (sig. A3R). The Marquis's dramatic leanings, moreover, were more than academic, as he was also involved in theatrical production. His plays *The Country Captain* and *The Varietie* had professional performances at the beginning of the 1640s. While he was in Paris he wrote 'several things' for the company of English players maintained by Prince Charles, and in 1658 the Newcastles gave a ball for Charles and his entourage in Antwerp involving four hours of dancing, speeches of welcome and farewell penned by Newcastle and delivered by the English actor Michael Mohun, and one of his songs, performed by 'Lady Moore, dressed in feathers.'[19] Finally, as we have seen, it was in Antwerp that Cavendish encountered women acting in street theatre, women for whom performance was a profession as opposed to a pastime. And once back in England this was the dispensation of the Restoration theatre, in which women-actors were a vital new force.[20]

In the rest of this essay I show how Cavendish's dramatic writing draws on this changing cultural and discursive status of female performance to enable fantasies of female self-representation. It is not my intention to suggest that Cavendish's plays were written for women actors. Rather I want to show that because of her particular historical position, performance – simulated in the mind of her reader – is a bookish but catalysing fantasy in her plays.

Cavendish's first book of plays contains a total of eleven prefatory addresses ranging from a justification of their deliberate structural disunity to a prescription for how they are to be read aloud. In two of these addresses she constantly raises and displaces the possibility of her plays being performed. They are, she tells her 'Lordship' in the dedicatory epistle,

> like dull dead statues, which is the reason I send them forth to be printed, rather than keep them concealed in hopes to have them first Acted; and this advantage I have, that is, I am out of the fear of having them hissed off the Stage, for they are not like to come thereon; but were they such as might deserve applause, yet if Envy did make a faction against them, they would have had a publick Condemnation . . . [and] it would have made me a little Melancholy to have my harmless and innocent Plays go weeping from the Stage, and whipt by malicious and hard-hearted censurers; but the truth is, I am careless, for so I have your applause I desire no more.
>
> (sigs A3R–V)

In dialogue with her 'Noble Readers', however, the reason Cavendish prints her plays,

> before they are Acted, is, first, that I know not when they will be Acted, by reason they are in English, and England doth not permit . . . of Playes . . . but the printing of my Playes spoils them for ever to be Acted (because what takes with the spectators is novelty) so that my Playes would seem lame or tired in action, and dull to hearing on the Stage, for which reason, I shall never desire they should be Acted.
>
> (sig. XIV)

At the end of this address Cavendish's 'reason' has come full circle and the reason she puts her plays out in print is because they will not be acted because she puts them out in print. As if to confirm this failure to squash the genie of performance Cavendish returns to the issue of acting in a further address. Here she refutes 'an erronious opinion got into this our Modern time and men . . . that it should be thought a crime or debasement for the nobler sort to Act Playes, especially on publick Theatres' (sig. X2R). Retaining the masculine bias of her previous address she argues for the edifying function of acting for 'the noblest youths':

> for it learns them gracefull behaviours and demeanors, it puts Spirit and Life into them, it teaches them Wit, and makes their Speech both voluble and tunable, besides it gives them Confidence, all which ought every man to have, that is of quality.
>
> (sig. X2R)

Cavendish contrasts this mode of acting, that is 'for Honour, and becoming' with the 'mercenary Players' who act solely for financial profit.

These passages are important because together they reveal that Cavendish did fantasize her plays as being performed, outside the theatre of her mind. Moreover they show that this fantasy remains couched within a masculine discourse. Even though her reference to the 'erronious opinion got into this our Modern time and men' might be construed as alluding to Prynne's attack on Henrietta Maria, the terms Cavendish uses, 'noblest youths', 'every man . . . of quality', indicate that she is speaking here of male-actors.

What apology for actors does Cavendish give? The concept of acting which she articulates in her address is scholastic and aristocratic. It views theatrical performance as a mode of self-enhancement, of becoming one's best self, stressing the reciprocity between actor and part. We can see this theory of acting applied to female performance in a letter from Richard Flecknoe's *A Relation of Ten Years Travells* (1654). Flecknoe describes to a female correspondent the play he is writing, a tragicomedy called *The Temple of Friendship*. The play deals with 'a Commonwealth of Amazons' who are clearly bound by ties of platonic love. The letter is worth quoting at length, both as an illustration of the aristocratic theory of *female* performance and for the light it sheds on the relation between this theory and the neo-platonic idealization of women:

> Frendship being our second Religion, and so main a part of our first, I have design'd to present it so beautiful to the Eye, as all should be ravisht with its Love and Admiration. To that end I have personated it in the loveliest Sex, and that betwixt persons of the same sex too, for avoiding all suspect; *Frendship being*

> *nothing but Love stript of suspition of Harm.* For representing it by Ladies, after the like example of the Queen and her Ladies here formerly, & of the greatest Ladies & Princesses in *Spain*, *France Flandres*, and elsewhere, I thought none reasonably could take exceptions, nor think me too ambitious in't, especially I having been long time train'd up & conversant in the Courts of the greatest Queens and Princesses in *Europe*, and consequently not altogether ignorant of personating and presenting them according to their dignity and quality.[21]

Consistent with his allusion to Henrietta Maria ('the Queen and her Ladies here formerly') Flecknoe's emphasis is on the presentational nature of aristocratic performance, the aptness or accord between the part and the person who plays it and the need for the dramatist to be schooled in noble society. This theory of performance depends on a rigid ideology of social order; the corollary is Cavendish's contempt for 'mercenary Players', who not only make 'a work of labour' that which should remain an exercise of 'honour' or 'delight' (sig. X2R), but who disrupt the social order by imitating noble status. Rather than viewing acting as an extension of the self, professional players engage in a form of *anti*-self-fashioning, or self-subversion: a deliberate fashioning of the self as other. We can see how Cavendish distrusts this protean theatricality and the social mobility it simulates by looking briefly at her play *The Apocriphal Ladies* (1662).

In this play, one of those which takes the form of a series of dialogues, the 'Unfortunate Dutchess' has been dispossessed of the right of her kingdom by her husband, the Duke Inconstancy. Living in exile, her woman brings her news of her husband's remarriage to the 'Apocriphal Dutchess', who is elsewhere termed the 'Comical Dutchess' (p. 649). The ensuing dialogue between the true Duchess and her woman elaborates the theatrical metaphor:

> *(Woman)*: She will be a Dutchess in a Play, she will only act the part of greatness.
> *(Unfortunate Dutchess)*: Indeed most Stage-Players are Curtizans.
> *(W)*: And most Curtizans are good Actors.
> *(UD)*: I make no question but she will now have enough Spectators.
> *(W)*: But I hope they will hiss her off from the Stage.
> (p. 641)

The passage uses the trope of female acting, or strictly, stage-playing, to signify social and sexual inauthenticity. Its obvious point of reference is Prynne's index entry, 'women-actors, notorious whores'. This critique of social imposture conducted through the metaphor of female acting or make-believe is repeated several times in the text: through the Creating Princess who marries beneath her, so 'creat[ing] [her] Husband to Honour', and the Imaginary Queen, who steps into a vacant throne but 'cannot act the part, for she appears like a good Country Housewife' (p. 646). It is further reinforced by a long oration delivered by the Lady True-Honour, who asks resoundingly 'shall Princes in Royal Courts, give place to Princes in Playes?' (p. 647).

The anti-feminist, anti-theatrical discourse articulated in *The Apocriphal Ladies* raises the question of why Cavendish couches her prefatory defence of noble performance in exclusively masculine terms. The explanation may lie in the passage from her dedicatory address to Newcastle quoted above (p. 140), in which she fantasizes, not simply her plays' performance, but their 'publick Condemnation'. The passage elaborates the fear from which Cavendish states she is saved by printing her plays, namely, 'the fear of having them hissed off from the Stage'. Her language personifies the plays as feminine, putting the case in which her 'harmless and innocent Plays' would be 'hissed off from the Stage'. As her echo of the last line in the dialogue from *The Apocriphal Ladies* confirms, Cavendish imagines her plays receiving the punitive treatment of a prostitute or public woman.[22] Her address aligns the female dramatist whose plays are performed with the actress-whore, each notorious by reason of her self-promotion.[23]

This dangerous proximity of the roles of public female dramatist and actress accounts for the divorce between the mooting of the issue of male performance in Cavendish's prefaces, and the feminine theatrical discourse of her plays. If we look at the place of this discourse in her 1662 volume we can see the positive constructions of female performance feasible within the enclosure of her 'Fancy-Stage'.

The use of theatrical metaphor to enable the performance of female identity is developed in *Youths Glory and Deaths Banquet.* Its protagonist, Lady Sanspareille, is blessed with a father who not only provides her with a rigorously learned, masculine education but also is willing to forgo his posterity in order to abet his daughter's quest for fame. Early in the play Cavendish characterizes Lady Sanspareille's unusual expressiveness in terms of a theatrical trope. As her daughter wafts in 'repeating some verses of her own making' Lady Sanspareille's mother accuses her, 'I am sure you are transformed from what you should be, from a sober young maid, to a Stage-player, as to act Parts, speak Speeches, rehearse Verses, sing Sonets, and the like' (p. 126). Lady Sanspareille replies with a speech which reiterates Cavendish's prefatory address, defending theatre as a means for 'the education of noble youth'. She rejects her mother's use of the term 'stage-player', drawing the same distinction we saw Cavendish make between noble amateurs and mercenary professionals: 'shall Kings, Princes or noble Persons, that dances, sings, or playes on Musick, or presents themselves in Masks, be thought, or called Dancers, or Fiddlers, Morris-dancers, Stage-players, or the like, as in their masking attire?' (p. 127). In view of her subsequent career as a woman-orator, Lady Sanspareille's omission of spoken acting from her defence of courtly performance can be construed only as a strategic display of daughterly tact. For later we learn that acting does indeed form part of her vocation, which involves the pervasive exercise of public speech. As a gentleman remarks,

> this lady Sanspareile hath a strange spreading wit, for she can plead causes at the Bar, decide causes in the court of Judicature, make Orations on publick Theatres, act parts, and speak speeches on the Stage, argue in the Schooles, preach in the Pulpits, either in Theology, Philosophy, moral and natural, and also phisick and Metaphysick.
>
> (p. 158)

Here Cavendish uses 'acting' simply as a metonym for female public utterance. Specifically, she affirms as a female trait the boldness or confidence that one of her Lady Speakers in *The Female Academy* describes as belonging to 'Preachers, Pleaders, and Players, that can present themselves, speak and act freely, in a publick Assembly' (p. 674).

Although stage acting is subsumed as one facet of Lady Sanspareille's verbal prowess the play leaves no doubt of the showiness of her orations. She speaks from a rostrum described as 'a place raised and railed with guilt rayles', and of which a philosopher remarks to her father, 'Sir, you have adorned her Theater to inthrone her wit' (p. 136). Apart from the attendance of Queen Attention at her oration on government Lady Sanspareille's audience is wholly male. Moreover the text emphatically marks the scopic nature of the event. For her first oration she appears '*drest all in black*'; upon her entrance the spectators are '*struck with amaze of her beauty*', one of them remarking to her father, 'Sir, we perceive now, you have invited us to feast our eyes, not our eares' (p. 136). For her final oration in which she justifies her vow never to marry, Lady Sanspareille enters '*all in white Satin, like as a Bride, and her Father and her audience, which are all Lovers; these stand gazing upon her*' (p. 158). At the end the lovers exit silently in various states of transport, '*some lifting up their eyes, others their hands, some striking their hands on their breast, and the like*' (p. 161). Susan Wiseman has commented on Cavendish's presentation of women who display themselves both educationally and erotically within a masculine preserve.[24] The erotic spectacle of Lady Sanspareille's final address echoes the role of women in the platonic theatre of cruelty in Caroline drama, in which, as I have indicated, the position of the platonic mistress is that of an actress. The platonic lady's power lies in her deployment of what *The Concealed Fansyes* calls her 'sceane self'. Lady Sanspareille's performance – dressed in white bridal satin before an audience of lovers, delivering an oration denouncing marriage as an impediment to the contemplative life – is the acme of sexual provocation and the platonic woman's 'will to power'.[25]

One may speculate about the topicality of Cavendish's fantasies of women's public speaking. Lois Potter cites as a precedent for her 'obsession with public orations' the academies offering public lectures which had existed for some time on the continent. In 1649 a similar institution had been opened in London by the royalist Sir Balthazar Gerbier, at which, 'by special request', a lecture was given for ladies, 'concerning the *Art of Well Speaking*'.[26] A remark by Francis Osborne in his *Historical memoires on the reigns of Queen Elizabeth, and King James* (1658) suggests a shift in attitude towards the kind of theatricality which Cavendish makes typical of Lady Sanspareille:

> Her Sex did beare out many impertinences in her words and actions, as *her making Latin speeches in the Universities*, and professing her selfe in publique *a Muse, then thought something too Theatrical for a virgine Prince.*
>
> (final italics mine)[27]

It is instructive to compare Cavendish's fantasy of public discoursing with her account of one of the few occasions in her life when she had the chance to make effective use of public speech. In her autobiography she describes her trip to England with her brother-in-law Sir Charles Cavendish in order to petition the parliamentary committee for compounding for a wife's share in Newcastle's sequestered estates. She received 'an absolute refusal' of her claim, being told in no uncertain terms that she had no entitlement to Newcastle's estate since she had married him after his delinquency, and moreover that she deserved nothing, her husband 'being the greatest traitor to the State'. Far from producing a show-stopping display of eloquence Cavendish

> whisperingly spoke to my brother to conduct me out of that ungentlemanly place, so without speaking to them one word good or bad, I returned to my lodgings, and as that committee was the first, so was it the last, I ever was at as a petitioner.[28]

In contrast to Dr Denton's commendation of the political usefulness of women's histrionic powers in a letter to Sir Ralph Verney, Cavendish patently failed, in his words, 'to act it with committees'.[29] In the self-defence which follows she ascribes her failure partly to bashfulness, but she precedes this by criticizing the contemporary state of affairs in England where 'women become pleaders, attornies, petitioners, and the like', an activity which she sees as a form of indecorous self-aggrandizement, 'nothing but jostl[ing] for the pre-eminence of words'.[30]

In considering this passage we should recall the type of bashfulness described by one of the Lady Speakers in *The Female Academy* as proceeding from the desire 'to out-act all others in Excellencies' (p. 674). Cavendish's stressing of her shyness is undoubtedly a symptom of what Elaine Hobby calls her 'highly repressive image of her own femininity',[31] but her attack on women who spoke in public could equally well be motivated by the bashfulness produced by 'aspiring Ambition'. As the correspondence between Lady Sanspareille's behaviour and Osborne's observation on Queen Elizabeth suggests, Cavendish's fantasies of action and expression are based on the figure of the female monarch. In his funeral oration for his daughter the first two things to which Sir Thomas Father Love compares her life are a masque and a monarchy. In the final play I wish to discuss from this volume, *Bell in Campo*, we can see Cavendish's identification with Queen Henrietta Maria as an actor in 'the Theatre of Warr' (p. 669).

In the play Lady Victoria persuades her husband the Lord General to allow her to accompany him to war, inspiring five or six thousand women to follow suit. When the men refuse to grant the women an active role Lady Victoria addresses the 'number of women of all sorts' who have imitated her example, and marshalling a panoply of rousing feminist arguments convinces them to form their own army, of which they elect her the 'Generaless'. Determined to prove themselves equal to men in constancy and valour the women 'surprize, seise and plunder' the garrison town, recruit its female population, and entrench themselves to practise their military manoeuvres. The chance arises to rescue their flagging male counterparts: the 'Amazonian Army' moves in, vanquishes the enemy forces and performs further military feats. When the men capitulate by sending the women 'a complemental letter' the female army delivers up its gains, happy with the honour of victory and passes the rest of the time in heroic sports on the frontiers while their husbands get on with conquering the 'Kingdom of Faction'. At the end of the play Lady Victoria is brought into the city in a military triumph and is greeted by the king. Several acts are then read: one grants all women in the kingdom precedence in the home; another ensures that Lady Victoria will be memorialized in history.

Bell in Campo gives full rein to Cavendish's fantasy of entering the male world of heroic action and honour. In constructing this fantasy she drew on a contemporary lexicon of female heroism, a lexicon expressed both in visual iconography and in a literature valorizing the heroic deeds of illustrious women. This cultural movement had an efflorescence in France in the 1640s, partly as a response to the participation in government and war of women like Anne of Austria, Queen Regent of France from 1643 to 1652, and her niece Anne Marie d'Orléans, the 'Grande Mademoiselle', who fought in the French civil wars known as the Fronde. As Ian Maclean has demonstrated, this movement was accompanied by an upsurge of feminist debate in France – a feminism he defines as 'a reassessment in women's favour of the relative capacities of the sexes'.[32]

While the image of the heroic woman flourished most visibly in France, it was also embodied in displaced form in England by Henrietta Maria. Decorous figures of female valour began to appear in Caroline masques and drama from the mid-1630s and with the onset of civil war Henrietta Maria embraced the chance to act out her role as a 'martial lady'. In her letters to Charles she draws amused attention to this role, dubbing herself 'her she-majesty, generalissima', while in Madame de Motteville's romantic transcription of the queen's account of 'the Troubles in England' she is compared to no less a figure than Alexander.[33] As Cavendish's two favourite heroes were Alexander and Caesar it is unsurprising that she should identify with this aspect of Henrietta Maria's persona.[34] It was Newcastle himself, as commander of the loyalist forces in the north, who met the queen on her landing from Holland and conducted her to York, from where she journeyed to Oxford with part of his army as escort. Cavendish was in Oxford with her family when the queen made what was reported as 'a most triumphant and magnificent entry' into the city and it was there that she conceived what she describes as 'a great desire to be one of her maids of honour.'[35] Rather than following the romantic model of the lone Lady Errant, or the solitary heroic endeavour of the '*femme forte*', Lady Victoria's desire to participate in her husband's actions seems more likely to be modelled on the conjugal team of Henrietta Maria and Charles. At one point Cavendish even makes fun of the queen's foibles. Early in the play a gentleman complains of the encumbrance of a woman in war, saying, 'and if her Dog should be left in any place, as being forgotten, all the whole Army must make a halt whilst the Dog is fetcht, and Trooper after Trooper must be sent to bring intelligence of the Dogs coming' (p. 583), a detail which rather dresses down the story of Henrietta Maria's heroic rescue of her lapdog during the bombardment of her dwelling at Bridlington Bay. As Madame de Motteville embroiders:

> She had an ugly Lap-Dog, nam'd *Mitte*, which she was very fond of; and remembering in the Middle of the Village, that she had left *Mitte* asleep in her Bed, she returned the Way she Came, and not fearing her Pursuers, she brought away her Favourite, and then retired as fast as she could from Cannon-Shot.[36]

The inflationary gesture of Lady Victoria's triumph can also be compared to the actual state entries in Europe of women like Queen Christina of Sweden, of which Henrietta Maria's Oxford entry may have been a modified version.[37]

Bell in Campo thus gives ample witness of Cavendish's imaginative investment in an ethic of female heroism, in the ostentation and bravura of a monarchist culture, and in the concept of individual sovereignty pertaining to it. While the play leaves us in no doubt of the apotheosis of its female hero, the nature of the gains won for women through her endeavors are rather more fragile. In the laws which are passed at the end of the play the changes affecting women's status are limited to the domestic sphere, where women are to be 'Mistris in their own Houses and Families', to sit above their husbands at the table, to keep the purse, to appoint the servants, to have ownership and management of the household goods, and lastly, to 'be of their Husband's Counsel' (p. 631).

These reforms first invert the structure of the patriarchal family, then backtrack pathetically to a provision for partnership in marriage. Their narrowing of scope in relation to the preceding action is echoed in the second plot, where in opposition to Lady Victoria's acting in the world and entering history, Madam Jantil, after the death of her husband, withdraws into his mausoleum and stages her own prolonged self-extinction, having first carefully arranged for the writing of her husband's *Life*. This division between the two plots, between Lady Victoria's public triumph and the rewards offered women in general is echoed by a division within the women's Act itself. There are four further clauses which unleash all the feminine frivolity which defies attempts to regulate and control women's existence:

Seventhly,	They shall wear what fashioned Clothes they will.
Eightly,	They shall go abroad when they will, without controul, or giving of any account thereof.
Ninthly,	They shall eat when they will, and of what they will, and as much as they will, and as often as they will.
Tenthly,	They shall go to Playes, Masks, Balls, Churchings, Christenings, Preachings, whensoever they will, and as finc and bravely attired as they will.

(p. 631)

These clauses show a glimpse of a Land of Cockayne, a world of inversion in which feminine folly and freedom have reign. In contrast to the inflationary fantasy of the foregoing play this vision of licence is disarmingly local and domestic. The freedom to eat, to roam, to indulge in the pleasures of self-display and theatrical, social pastimes forms a nucleus of resistance to women's entrenchment in the family. In the context of the play this fantasy is both deflationary and recuperative; in the context of the Act it is a relic of female survival.

Thus far I have been discussing Cavendish's use of a theatrical discourse to represent a particular kind of female identity. Cavendish uses theatrical tropes in her first volume of plays to legitimize a self which is envisaged not merely as authentic, but as fantastically inflated and absolute. This use of theatricality to supplement the self produces a subjectivity at once singular and sovereign because its boundaries are perceived as all-extensive. It would perhaps be useful to distinguish this fantasized subjectivity from the model of the female subject obtaining in Cavendish's non-dramatic writing.

Catherine Gallagher reads Cavendish as installing herself as absolute monarch of a fantasy microcosm, producing a self which is private, interior and infinitely recessive.[38] In Cavendish's plays, however, performance means crossing the boundary between inside and outside, animating the self in front of the gaze of others. This fantasy depends on self-projection, not self-withdrawal; even though the self is part of the audience. In her closet theatre of the mind Cavendish can marry the contrary impulses to solitude and sociability, bashfulness and exhibitionism, which inform the text of her life.

Cavendish's second volume of plays (1668) marks a shift from a fantasy of identity as static and sovereign to a fantasy of identity as dynamic and provisional. The single preface 'To the Readers' is a defiant rejoinder to the criticism which she implies had been heaped on her first volume. Cavendish makes no pretence that her plays conform either to the 'ancient Rules' or 'the modern Humor', but simply 'having pleased my Fancy in writing many Dialogues upon several Subjects, and having afterwards order'd them into Acts and Scenes, I will venture, in spight of the Criticks, to call them Plays' (sig. A2V).[39]

Ironically, despite this claim, the plays in this volume do conform more both to the dramatic and theatrical conventions: in the orthodox numbering of scenes within acts, in the restricted number of plots, in the use of dance and song, and in the more interactive nature of the writing.[40] The influence of Restoration drama is especially apparent in the first play in the volume, *The Sociable Companions; or, the Female Wits*, with its double-barrelled title and its use of personal first names like 'Peg Valorosa' for the female protagonists. The influence is most marked in the play's heightened awareness of a theatrical culture. At one point Will Fullwit is reported to have gone to the playhouse, or 'the Acting-house' as one character calls it (p. 15); when he returns he fools his friend into believing him first dead, then mad. Reverting to sanity he explains that he has 'only acted an Intrigue', a humour he got 'With seeing a new Play' (p. 18).

In keeping with this newly localized sense of theatre the play is constructed around a series of female-inspired intrigues in which dissembling and disguise are made concrete devices. Cavendish creates an unusually precise scenario showing a group of disbanded cavalier soldiers who, resentful of the poor reward of their loyalty, are squandering all the money they have in taverns. Frustrated by their brothers' lethargy in seeking 'some good Offices and Employments' that would 'maintain us according to our births and breedings' (p. 30), the sisters of the soldiers resolve to use their 'Wits and Honesty' to get rich husbands (p. 48). One of their designs involves Peg Valorosa testifying in a counterfeit spiritual court with the help of a fraudulent midwife that she has become platonically pregnant, the 'Idea of a Man' having created a child by conceit. In a parallel intrigue Jane Fullwit dresses as 'Jack Clerk' and enters the service of Lawyer Plead-all, whom she tricks into laying a charge against her brother. By counter-accusing Plead-all of keeping a gentlewoman in man's clothes sister and brother cozen the lawyer into marriage.

The Sociable Companions represents a major alteration in the status of acting and theatricality in Cavendish's texts. Whereas in her previous volume acting or disguise is used either metaphorically or as part of Cavendish's reworking of the codes of romance, this play inscribes theatricality as a distinctive practice, vindicating the resourceful use – by indigent cavaliers – of female counterfeit or intrigue. Though the nature of the women's necessitous marriages is never queried, their tactical use of intrigue and disguise is contrasted with the character Prudence, whose father Save-all abstained from fighting in the war and is therefore able to provide his daughter with a portion. In the manner of a similarly named character in the earlier play *The Publick Wooing* (1662), Prudence, granted her own choice by her father, hears the suits of potential lovers herself. The final scene of the play takes the form of a public assembly in which she delivers a speech to her suitors, simultaneously justifying her choice of an 'ancient man' for a husband and her act of exercising that choice:

> Concerning the Church and State, since they do allow of buying and selling young Maids to Men to be their Wives, they cannot condemn those Maids that make their bargains to their own advantage, and chuse rather to be bought then sold.
>
> (p. 95)

The discourse of authenticity which accrues to Prudence in the play, who is able through her father's dishonour to conduct her wooing in the open and to her own advantage, coexists with, rather than undermines, the other women's paradoxically 'honest' (because politically honourable) deployment of female deceit and disguise.

All of the four complete plays in Cavendish's 1668 volume make similarly concrete use of theatricality, in particular the device of cross-dressing for both sexes.[41] One might attribute the emphasis on female cross-dressing to the situation on the Restoration stage, where in contrast to the ornamental 'masculine' costuming adopted in female performances at the Caroline court, transvestite parts did involve the assumption of full masculine dress, including wearing breeches. The device of cross-dressing appears at its most complex in the final play in the book, *The Convent of Pleasure*, where it functions simultaneously as a form of male sexual expediency and as part of a feminine fantasy world. For this play Cavendish drew on an established romantic/comic plot in which a man enters a convent in female disguise.[42] What is appealing about her use of this plot is the way in which the male voyeurism made possible through the cross-dressing device is subordinated to the romantic perspective of Lady Happy, the founder of the convent, who fully believes that she has fallen in love with a woman.

In the play the heiress Lady Happy decides to 'incloister [her]self from the World', both to avoid the company of men, 'who make the Female Sex their slaves', and to enjoy the pleasures she can afford with her father's fortune (pp. 6–7). She defines her action in chaste and pragmatic opposition to orthodox sexual choice, for as she remarks, 'Marriage to those that are virtuous is a greater restraint than a Monastery' and 'should I quit Reputation and turn Courtizan, there would be more lost in my Health, then gained by my Lovers' (p. 3). Accordingly Lady Happy sets up cloister with 'a number of noble women, of greater birth than fortune', all of whom have vowed virginity, and together they embark on a life in which each sense is supplied, and as Madam Mediator remarks, 'every Lady . . . enjoyeth as much Pleasure as any absolute Monarch can do, without the Troubles and Cares, that wait on Royalty' (p. 17). In a lavish inventory, reminiscent of poetic invitations to the pastoral realm, Lady Happy describes to the women 'how I have order'd this our *Convent of Pleasure*'. The vision she creates is one of a domesticated golden world in which changes of season will merely bring increased sensual delights and in which luxury will extend to the smallest detail. Significantly, men are wholly excluded from this world: in contrast to the voyeuristic access granted men to the earlier Female Academy, Lady Happy's convent 'will admit none of the Masculine Sex, not so much as to a Grate' (p. 11).

In one scene however Cavendish portrays the comic eagerness of a group of gallants to invade and disrupt this community of women. Their designs include 'smoak[ing] them out, as they do a Swarm of Bees' (p. 18) and entering the convent 'in Womens apparel' (p. 20). This last idea is discounted by one of the gallants who argues that they would discover themselves by their masculine voices and behaviour, 'for we are as untoward to make Curtsies in Petticoats, as Women are to make Legs in Breeches' (p. 20). This assertion of sexual determinism goes hand in hand with the men's facile desire to create sexual havoc in the convent. Having raised this possibility the play then shifts into a romantic register which accommodates sexual ambiguity within a make-believe, theatrical world.

Shortly after the convent is established Lady Happy admits as a novice to her female community 'a great Foreign Princess', described as 'a Princely brave Woman truly, of a Masculine Presence' (p. 16), who hearing of the convent's fame has decided to 'quit a court of trouble for a *Convent of Pleasure*' (p. 22). The Princess tells Lady Happy that 'the greatest pleasure I could receive, were to have your Friendship', and desiring that Lady Happy 'would be my Mistress, and I your Servant' she makes one particular request:

> I observing in your several Recreations, some of your Ladies do accoustre [*sic*] Themselves in Masculine-Habits, and act Lovers-parts; I desire you will give me leave to be sometimes so accoustred and act the part of your loving Servant.
>
> (p. 22)

Lady Happy is delighted with the innocence of this request and sits down with the Princess to watch a play performed by the other women.[43] Rather than a gentle and decorous feminine pastoral, the play is a grim sequence of episodes depicting the miseries of marriage and the female condition, from the negligence and promiscuity of husbands, perpetual pregnancy, infant mortality, wife-abuse, the pains of childbirth, the irresponsibility of children, and death in childbirth to the sexual predatoriness of Lords. The epilogue hammers home the socially inclusive message of this feminist drama: '*Marriage is a Curse we find, / Especially to Womenkind: / From the Cobler's Wife we see, / To Ladies, they unhappie be*' (p. 30). This theatrical elaboration of the grotesqueness of the female condition in the workaday world functions as anti-masque to the recreative theatrical wooing of the Princess and Lady Happy. Just prior to their scene together Lady Happy enters 'drest as a Shepherdess', and debates with herself:

> My name is Happy, and so was my Condition, before I saw this Princess, but now I am like to be the most unhappy Maid alive: But why may I not love a Woman with the same affection I could a Man?
>
> (p. 32)

Lady Happy dissuades herself of this possibility by averring the unchanging laws of nature, after which the Princess enters 'in Masculine Shepherd's Clothes'. She responds to Lady Happy's doubts by asserting the virtuous, innocent and harmless nature of their love, in a discourse which draws on the tenets of platonic friendship: 'Let us please ourselves, as harmless Lovers use to do . . . as, to discourse, imbrace and kiss, so mingle souls together' (pp. 32–3). In answer to Lady Happy's objection, 'But innocent Lovers do not use to kiss', the Princess replies 'Not any act more frequent among us Women-kind; nay, it were a sin in friendship, should we not kiss', after which there is the stage description '*They imbrace and kiss, and hold each other in their Arms*', followed by the Princess's at once transgressive and salacious couplet: 'These my imbraces though of Femal kind, / May be as fervent as a Masculine mind.' Her couplet is followed by the extraordinary stage description:

> The Scene is open'd, the Princess and L. Happy go in
> A Pastoral within the Scene.
> The Scene is chang'd to a Green, or Plain, where Sheep
> are feeding, and a May-Pole in the middle.
> L. Happy as a Shepherdess, and the Princess as a Shepherd
> are sitting there.
>
> (p. 33)

In this transformation Cavendish shows us the moment of entry into the fictive theatrical world. In the ensuing scene the Princess and Lady Happy praise one another's wit and poetic genius, distinguishing their wooing from the 'amorous . . . Verse' of 'other Pastoral Lovers' (p. 37). The 'amorous' dimension of their courtship conveyed by Lady Happy's profession, 'I can neither deny you my Love nor Person' is channelled into the 'Rural Sports' which follow, at the end of which the Princess and Lady Happy are crowned 'King and Queen of the Shepherds' (p. 38). In a subsequent marine masque the Princess and Lady Happy appear as Neptune and a Sea-Goddess, surrounded by 'the rest of the Ladies . . . drest like Water-Nymphs' (p. 41).

At these points Cavendish's play takes on the infinitely recessive quality which Gallagher notes as peculiar to her writing.[44] Within her closet theatre of the mind she imagines a female convent within which there is a theatre in which women act out fantasy selves. Their acting, moreover, is freed from necessity, for within their self-enclosed female environment they mimic heterosexual conventions for pleasure. Though the Princess defines their love as harmless, Lady Happy has graver misgivings and bursts out shortly after the rural scene:

> O Nature, O you Gods above,
> Suffer me not to fall in Love;
> O Strike me dead here in this place
> Rather than fall into disgrace.
>
> (p. 40)

Because Lady Happy has already queried the legitimacy of her love for a woman, this last line must be read as referring to the disgrace, not simply of falling in love, but of falling in love with a woman. Cavendish seems to have married the cross-dressing convention of a female theatre with the chastity of platonic friendship derived from Henrietta Maria's feminized culture to allow a fleeting fantasy of what we would call lesbian love.[45] It is fleeting because the hints of the Princess's self-division which have already been laid are borne out immediately after the pastoral in a soliloquy:

> What have I on a petticoat, *Oh Mars*! thou God of War, pardon my sloth. . . . But what is a Kingdom in comparison of a Beautiful Mistress?
>
> (p. 39)

Yet with wonderful tenacity Cavendish will not abandon her view of the Princess's sex, for the stage description above the soliloquy reads 'Enter *the Princess Sola*, and walks a turn or two in a Musing posture, then views *her* Self and speaks' (p. 39, italics mine). Contrary to her earlier practice in *Loves Adventures* (1662) where the descriptions of the disguised Affectionata's soliloquies and asides revealing her true identity use feminine pronouns, Cavendish introduces a discrepancy between the prose description and the dramatic situation, in which the 'Princess' reveals himself as a man in disguise. The Princess is subsequently described as again 'in a Man's Apparel' (p. 44), producing the effect of an endlessly inhabitable series of sexual selves. This absolute uncertainty of the Princess's gender is sustained at the moment of catastrophe in which Madam Mediator interrupts the Princess and Lady Happy dancing. At this point the text moves into an extended passage of description:

> *And after they have Danced a little while, in comes Madam Mediator wringing her hands, and spreading her arms; and full of Passion cries out.*
>
> O Ladies Ladies! you're all betrayed, undone, undone; for there is a man in the Convent, search and you'l find it.
>
> *They all skip from each other, as afraid of each other; only the Princess and the Lady Happy stand still together.*
>
> (pp. 44–5)

Madam Mediator's use of the indefinite pronoun, 'search and you'l find it', registers at the climax of the play a moment of aporia, in which it is impossible to know whether the Princess is, as we are directed to believe, 'a Princely brave Woman, *truly* of a Masculine presence', or as Cavendish's comma has it, 'a Princely brave *Woman truly*, of a Masculine presence' (p. 16). In the dénouement the entrance of an 'embassador to the Prince' simultaneously forces the dissolution of the convent's fantasy feminine world and marks the decisive entry of a masculinist discourse into the play, as the 'Prince' declares that if his counsellors of state refuse him leave to marry Lady Happy he will 'have her by force of Arms' (p. 47).

Clearly *The Convent of Pleasure* offers different kinds of textual pleasure to different readers. The reader engaged in one way by Lady Happy's feminine world may share her credulity as to the Princess's gender and enjoy the suggestion of an erotic relationship between women. For other readers the story of a Prince who infiltrates a convent disguised as a woman who then acts as a man offers fantasies of voyeuristic access to a woman-centred world, and of the suspension of an essential masculine identity. We could see the play itself as caught in a conflict between these different, sexually determined modes of reading. For there is some doubt as to whether Cavendish's disposal of her female freak at the end of the play is a gesture motivated solely by her own reason. Rather than the infiltration of a man into the convent there is evidence that a man may have penetrated Cavendish's text. In some copies of the 1668 *Plays*,[46] the final two scenes after the revelation of the Princess as a man are headed with a pasted-in slip reading 'Written by my Lord Duke' (p. 47), but with no indication, as with similar instances elsewhere in Cavendish's texts, of where 'my Lord Duke's' ends. There are two ways of construing this textual anomaly: either Cavendish lost interest after the disclosure of the Princess as a man and left the writing of the rest of the play to her husband, or she did write the final two scenes, which poke fun at Puritan prurience and older women's sexual desires, but suspected they would be thought unseemly coming from a woman. Whoever wrote the final two scenes, it is Cavendish who has the last word on the Princess's gender, for in one of her breaks with tradition in this volume she prints the 'dramatis personae', or 'the Actors Names', at the end rather than at the beginning of the play, and if we look at the final page of the text of *The Convent of Pleasure* we will see that, contrary to the fool's assertion that 'the Prince has imitated a woman' (p. 51), in Cavendish's mind 'the Princess' was not an actor but an actress. We might speculate on Cavendish's placing of 'the Actors Names' at the end of three of the plays in this volume, as a means of deliberately enhancing the suspense enjoyed by the reader with respect to the gender of the characters. Certainly *The Convent of Pleasure* takes her experimentation with the closet drama form to the most sophisticated degree of the page becoming stage, producing the ultimate textual fantasy of female performance.

There is evidence that Cavendish herself in her rhetoric of dress and behaviour aimed at a blurring of the boundaries between genders similar to that produced by *The Convent of Pleasure*. Charles Lyttleton wrote of his meeting with the Newcastles on the way to York in 1665 that Margaret was 'dressed in a vest, and, instead of courtsies, made legs and bows to the ground with her hand and head'.[47] His description of her masculine dress and gestures echoes Bulstrode Whitelocke's account of the clothing and behaviour of Queen Christina of Sweden on his first reception at her court as Cromwell's ambassador. According to Whitelocke, Christina appeared soberly dressed in grey, with 'a jackett such as men weare' over her habit, and 'a black velvet cappe . . . which she used to put off and on as men doe their hattes'.[48] Whitelocke's representation of Christina's attitude suggests a social fantasy of her behaviour as sexually provocative and intimidating:

> The queen was very attentive whilst he spoke, and comming up close to him, by her looks and gestures (as was supposed) would have daunted him; butt those who

> have bin conversant in the late great affayres in England, are not so soon as others appaled, with the presence of a young lady and her servants.[49]

Whitelocke both evokes, and distances himself from, a form of seductiveness able to be manipulated by women in positions of power; an example of which is the overt sexual display characteristic of aristocratic female performance. Whitelocke saw Christina act 'a moorish lady' and 'a citizen's wife' in a court masque.[50] He also witnessed her abdication, after which she set off on an extravagant tour of Europe where her flamboyant conduct, particularly her masculine dress and behaviour, caused much amazed comment.[51] This contextualizes Samuel Pepys's remark that there was as much expectation of Cavendish's coming to court in London in 1667, 'that so [many] people may come to see her, as if it were the Queen of Sweden.'[52] Many details in Pepys's diary concur with Whitelocke's image of Queen Christina, which suggests that Cavendish may also have been trying to create an image of herself as 'a Princely brave Woman truly, of a Masculine Presence'. Pepys refers to Cavendish's 'velvet-cap', her 'many black patches', her décolletage, and her 'black juste-au-corps', a garment similar to a masculine riding coat, made popular as a fashion for women by Queen Catherine of Braganza. He also refers twice to her 'antic' dress and appearance.[53] Mary Evelyn's account of Cavendish as a spectacle viewed at close quarters confirms the hint that her presentation as a self-fashioned artifact using the discourse of dress should be seen as forming a continuum with her creation of fantasy selves in her writing:

> I was surprised to find so much extravagancy and vanity in any person not confined within four walls. Her habit particular, fantastical .... Her mien surpasses the imagination of poets, or the descriptions of a romance heroine's greatness: her gracious bows, seasonable nods, courteous stretching out of her hands, twinkling of her eyes, and various gestures of approbation, show what may be expected from her discourse, which is as airy, empty, whimsical and rambling as her books.[54]

This image of excess, of Cavendish bursting out of confinement, chimes with Colley Cibber's description of the actress Susannah Mountfort's performance as Melantha in Dryden's *Marriage à la Mode* (1673), as seeming 'to contain the most compleat System of Female Foppery that could possibly be crowded into the tortur'd form of a fine Lady'.[55] The comparison is enhanced by the fact that, with her gentry origins, Cavendish was herself an apocryphal lady.[56] Evelyn indicates that 'the theatre of Margaret' was the ultimate monologic performance: 'My part was not yet to speak, but to admire.'[57] Only at one point in her London visit did Cavendish engage in a performative act which had a semblance of the dialogic, during her visit with the Duke of Newcastle to the Lincoln's Inn Theatre for a performance of Newcastle's play *The Humourous Lovers* (1667). Pepys assumed that the play was by Cavendish and recorded how 'she at the end made her respect to the players from her box and did give them thanks.'[58] A contemporary letter alluding to this event describes the Duchess as 'all ye pageant now discoursed on: Her brests all laid out to view in a play house with scarlett trimd nipples.'[59] Cavendish's acting out the fantasy of having her plays performed was itself a piece of theatre. It seems appropriate that her acknowledgement of the art of female performance should have taken the form of such an outrageous upstaging.

Notes

1 Margaret Cavendish, *CCXI Sociable Letters* (London, 1664), no. CXCV, p. 405. The reference to 'Carneval Time' is from the preceding letter (no. CXCIV, p. 402), which is related in content to no. CXCV. Further references to letter no. CXCV are given in the text.

I am very grateful to Clare Brant, Diane Purkiss and Ruth Little for their scrupulous reading and editing of this essay.

2 Cavendish, *Letters*, no. XXIX, p. 57.

3 I use the word 'fantasy' here in the modern sense of the imaginary fulfilment of conscious or unconscious wishes (*OED*, 3b). In seventeenth-century usage the words 'fantasy' and 'fancy' were used interchangeably to signify the imaginative faculty or process. However the *OED* also gives as a possible meaning of 'fantasy' from the fourteenth century onwards, 'the fact or habit of deluding oneself by imaginary perceptions or reminiscences' (3a), which indicates an earlier form of the modern usage. Cavendish's letter, and the rest of her writing, testify to the fluidity between her concept of 'fancy', and 'fantasy' in its modern form.

4 A pertinent example is the series of 'Femal Orations' in Margaret Cavendish, *Orations of Divers Sorts, Accommodated to Divers Places* (London, 1662), pp. 225–32, especially p. 229.

5 Cavendish, *Letters*, no. CXCII, p. 400.

6 Margaret Cavendish, *Playes Written by the Thrice Noble, Illustrious and Excellent Princess, the Lady Marchioness of Newcastle* (London, 1662), sig. A2R. Further references to this volume are given in the text.

7 Margaret Cavendish, 'To all Writing Ladies', *Poems and Fancies* (London, 1653), sig. A1V [p. 161] (unnumbered page following p. 160). This epistle is omitted from the second impression of *Poems and Phancies* (London, 1664).

8 For a study of the queen's social fashions of platonic love and *préciosité*, which reads them in the context of her Catholic interests, see E. Veevers, *Images of Love and Religion: Queen Henrietta Maria and Court Entertainments*, (Cambridge: Cambridge University Press, 1988).

9 I discuss the material summarized in the next two paragraphs in my chapter, 'She that Plays the King: Henrietta Maria and the Threat of the Actress in Caroline Culture' in G. McMullan and J. Hope (eds) *The Politics of Tragicomedy: Shakespeare and After* (London: Routledge, 1991).

10 Ben Jonson, *The New Inn*, ed. M. Hattaway, *The Revels Plays* (Manchester: Manchester University Press, 1984), III.ii; IV.iv; James Shirley, *The Dramatic Works and Poems of James Shirley*, ed. W. Gifford and A. Dyce, 6 vols (London, 1833), III, pp. 79, 27.

11 N. C. Starr (ed.), '*The Concealed Fansyes*: A Play by Lady Jane Cavendish and Lady Elizabeth Brackley', *Proceedings of the Modern Languages Association* 1931, 46, p. 809.

12 Excerpts from *A Pastorall* are printed in Germaine Greer, Jeslyn Medoff, Melinda Sansone and Susan Hastings (eds) *Kissing the Rod: An Anthology of Seventeenth-Century Women's Verse* (London: Virago, 1988), pp. 109–15.

13 Margaret Cavendish, *The Life of William Cavendish, Duke of Newcastle, to Which is Added the True Relation of my Birth, Breeding and Life*, ed. C. H. Firth, 2nd edn (London: Routledge, 1906), p. 160.

14 Cavendish, *Life*, pp. 161–2; Kathleen Jones, *A Glorious Fame: The Life of Margaret Cavendish, Duchess of Newcastle, 1623–1673* (London: Bloomsbury, 1988), pp. 22–7; N. Cotton, *Women Playwrights in England c. 1363–1750* (London and Toronto: Associated University Presses, 1980), pp. 42–3; Sarah Heller Mendelson, *The Mental World of Stuart Women: Three Case Studies* (Brighton: Harvester, 1987), pp. 16–18.

15 C. Oman, *Henrietta Maria* (London: Hodder and Stoughton, 1936), p. 151; L. Hotson, *The Commonwealth and Restoration Stage* (Cambridge, MA: Harvard University Press, 1928), pp. 8–9.

16 Margaret Cavendish, *Natures Pictures drawn by Fancies Pencil to the Life* (London, 1656), p. 190.

17 On the entertainments of royalists in Paris and Holland see Hotson, pp. 21–3 and A. Harbage, *Cavalier Drama* (New York: Russell, 1964; first pub. 1936), pp. 207–8.

18 Margaret Cavendish, *Plays, Never Before Printed* (London, 1668), p. 92.

19 P. Edwards *et al.*, *The Revels History of Drama in English: Volume IV 1613–1660* (London and New York: Methuen, 1981), pp. 24, 278; Hotson, pp. 20–2; D. Grant, *Margaret the First: A Biography of Margaret Cavendish, Duchess of Newcastle* (London: Rupert Hart-Davies, 1957), pp. 173–4; *Calendar of State Papers Domestic*, 1657–8, pp. 296, 311.

20 See E. Howe, *Women and Drama: The First English Actresses* (Cambridge: Cambridge University Press, 1998).

21 Richard Flecknoe, *A Relation of Ten Years Travells in Europe, Asia, Affrique, and America* (London, 1654), p. 147; for details of Flecknoe's activity in Holland during the Interregnum and the suggestion that the duchess acted as his patron see Harbage, p. 207.

22 This was the treatment given to actresses belonging to the French troupe which visited London in 1629, who were 'hissed, hooted, and pippin-pelted from the stage' in one of their three performances; G. E. Bentley, *The Jacobean and Caroline Stage*, 7 vols (Oxford: Clarendon Press, 1941–68), 1, p. 25.

23 In an important essay Catherine Gallagher discusses Aphra Behn's very different self-alignment with the figure of the prostitute: see 'Who was that Masked Woman? The Prostitute and the Playwright in the Comedies of Aphra Behn', *Women's Studies*, 1988, 15, pp. 23–42.

24 Susan J. Wiseman, 'Gender and Status in Dramatic Discourse: Margaret Cavendish, Duchess of Newcastle', in Isobel Grundy and Susan J. Wiseman (eds) *Women/Writing/History 1640–1740* (London: Batsford, 1998). I have benefited much from Susan Wiseman's work on Cavendish.

25 Cf. Mendelson's observation that in Cavendish's fiction 'the focus is not on love *per se* but on a woman's "will to power", expressed as the chronicle of her extraordinary ambitions, or as her psychological conquest of a male protagonist', p. 22.

26 Edwards *et al.*, p. 278; Hotson, p. 136. See also Mendelson, p. 45.

27 Francis Osborne, *Historical Memoires on the Reigns of Queen Elizabeth, and King James* (London, 1658), p. 60. After one of Sanspareille's orations a poet declares that 'the Lady Muses are deposed' (p. 152), and she herself asks to be remembered among the Muses in her dying speech. After her death her statue is to be set up 'in every College, and in most publick places in the City' (p. 173).

28 Cavendish, *Life*, pp. 166–7.

29 Quoted in A. Clark, *Working Life of Women in the Seventeenth Century* (London: Routledge & Kegan Paul, 1982, first pub. 1919), p. 20.

30 Cavendish, *Life*, pp. 167–8.

31 Elaine Hobby, *Virtue of Necessity: English Women's Writing 1649–88* (London: Virago, 1988), p. 83; on Cavendish's bashfulness see also J. Pearson, *The Prostituted Muse: Images of Women and Women Dramatists 1642–1737* (Brighton: Harvester, 1988), pp. 128–9; Mendelson, pp. 17–18.

32 Ian Maclean, *Woman Triumphant: Feminism in French Literature 1610–1652* (Oxford: Oxford University Press, 1977), p. viii; Jones, pp. 56–7.

33 M. A. E. Green, *Letters of Queen Henrietta Maria* (London, 1857), p. 222; Françoise Bertaud de Motteville, 'A Short History of the Troubles in England', in *Memoirs for the History of Anne of Austria*, translated from the French, 5 vols, 1725 6, vol. I, p. 220.

34 See Cavendish, *Life*, p. 178, *Letters*, no. XXVII, pp. 52–3, 'To All Noble and Worthy Ladies', *The Description of a New World called the Blazing-World*, in *Observations upon Experimental Philosophy*, 1668, sig. A4V.

35 Cavendish, *Life*, pp. 18–19, 23, 161; Jones, pp. 22–3.

36 Motteville, vol. I, p. 220.

37 Following her abdication in 1654 and her conversion to Catholicism Christina embarked on a triumphal tour of Europe, beginning with the Italian papal states; see G. Masson, *Queen Christina* (London: Secker & Warburg, 1968), chs 7 and 8, *passim*.

38 Catherine Gallagher, 'Embracing the Absolute: The Politics of the Female Subject in Seventeenth-Century England', *Genders*, 1988, I, 1, pp. 25–33.

39 Cavendish, *Plays, Never Before Printed*, sig. A2V. Further references to this volume are given in the text. The plays in this volume are paginated individually.

40 Cf. Hobby, pp. 106–7.

41 See Pearson, pp. 140–2, and D. Paloma, 'Margaret Cavendish: Defining the Female Self', *Women's Studies*, 1980, 7, pp. 63–4.
42 Cavendish could have found this plot either in Fletcher's play *Monsieur Thomas* (performed 1610–16, published 1639) or in Fletcher's source, the French pastoral romance *L'Astrée* by Honoré d'Urfé, 1607–27, trans. 1620. I am grateful to Hester Jones for suggesting *Monsieur Thomas* as a source.
43 This play within a play evokes a medieval and Renaissance tradition of convent theatre and drama; see Cotton, pp. 27–8, 213, n. 2, and Elissa Weaver, 'Spiritual Fun: A Study of Sixteenth-Century Tuscan Convent Theatre', in Mary Beth Rose (ed.) *Women in the Middle Ages and the Renaissance: Literary and Historical Perspectives* (Syracuse, NY: Syracuse University Press, 1986), pp. 173–205.
44 Gallagher, 'Embracing the Absolute', pp. 30–3.
45 Cf. the use of a platonic discourse in *The Blazing-World*, pp. 89–92, 110. In making this statement I am trying to provide a historical explanation for what Moira Ferguson problematically describes as the play's 'sympathetic, tender, and natural portrayal of lesbian love', in *First Feminists: British Women Writers 1578–1799* (Bloomington, IN: Indiana University Press, 1985), p. 12. A context for the idea of love between women modelled on female friendship is Katherine Philips's poetry; see Hobby, pp. 128, 134–41.
46 The three copies of the 1668 *Plays* in the British Library, and the copy in the Cambridge University Library, all contain the pasted-in slip. It does not appear in the copy of the 1668 *Plays* in the Bodleian Library.
47 Cited in Grant, p. 184.
48 Bulstrode Whitelocke, *A Journal of the Swedish Embassy in the Years 1653 and 1654*, 2 vols (London, 1772), I, p. 234. I am grateful to Susan Wiseman for alerting me to this text.
49 Ibid., I, pp. 235–6.
50 Ibid., II, pp. 52–3.
51 See the accounts by Madame de Motteville and Anne Marie d'Orléans of Christina's appearance at the French court in 1656 in Masson, pp. 274–7.
52 Samuel Pepys, *The Diary of Samuel Pepys*, ed. Robert Latham and William Matthews, 11 vols (London: Bell, 1970–83), vol. VII, pp. 163–4. According to Kathleen Jones, p. 102, the Newcastles met Queen Christina briefly on her visit to Antwerp in 1654.
53 Pepys, vol. VII, pp. 186–7, 163, 243. Hero Chalmers shows that Cavendish's contemporary, Mary Carleton, invokes Queen Christina as a model for her self-portrayal as a romance heroine; see her chapter in this volume.
54 Quoted in Myra Reynolds, *The Learned Lady in England from 1650 to 1760* (Gloucester, MA: Peter Smith, 1964 [1920]), p. 51. Cf. Pepys's remark, 'The whole story of this Lady is a romance, and all she doth is romantic', vol. VII, p. 163.
55 B. R. Fone (ed.) *An Apology for the Life of Colley Cibber, With an Historical View of the Stage during his own Times* (Ann Arbor, MI: University of Michigan Press, 1968), p. 96.
56 See Mendelson, pp. 12, 22.
57 Quoted in Mendelson, p. 53. I owe the aperçu 'the theatre of Margaret' to Susan Wiseman.
58 Pepys, vol. VII, p. 163; Cotton, pp. 48–9.
59 Letter from Charles North to his father, 13 April 1667, Bodleian MS. North. c. 4., fol. 146. I am grateful to Robert Jordan for this reference.

14

'A WOMAN WRITE A PLAY!'

Jonsonian strategies and the dramatic writings of Margaret Cavendish; or, did the Duchess feel the anxiety of influence?

Julie Sanders

In this new essay on Margaret Cavendish's plays, Julie Sanders moves beyond the defensive approach often taken by critics writing about Early Modern women dramatists and successfully reintegrates Cavendish into the dominant dramatic discourses of her day. Sanders concludes that it is no longer adequate to separate women authors protectively from their male counterparts and that they must be understood as part of their historical and literary contexts, being influenced by – and influencing – the male playwrights of their age.

My title invokes in very obvious and overt ways a questioning of a type of critical reading that held sway in the 1970s in the wake of Harold Bloom's influential work, *The Anxiety of Influence*.[1] I used as my starting point in this project Sandra Gilbert and Susan Gubar's trenchant response to Bloom in their essay 'Infection in the sentence: the woman writer and the anxiety of authorship'.[2] In that essay, Gilbert and Gubar posed questions along the following lines:

> If the Queen's looking glass speaks with the King's own voice, how do its kingly admonitions affect the Queen's own voice? Since his is the chief voice she hears, does the Queen try to sound like the King, imitating his tone, his inflections, his phrasing, his point of view? Or does she 'talk back' to him in her own vocabulary, her own timbre, insisting on her own viewpoint?
>
> (Gilbert and Gubar, p. 290)

The king's own voice in the case of Margaret Cavendish could be interpreted as having a number of notional loci, not least in the often contradictory voices of the royalist cause and its attendant political philosophy, with which she was surrounded in Oxford during her time of service as a maid of honour to Queen Henrietta Maria, and in Paris and Antwerp during her period of exile in the 1640s and 1650s. The king's own voice might also be found in the authorial tones of the Duke of Newcastle himself, William Cavendish, tones heard after all in the indignant exclamation about women dramatists with which I have prefixed my title, a view expressed by the Second Gentleman in the Introduction Newcastle penned for the 1662 edition of Margaret's plays, and evident also in the various scenes he authored for her dramas, such as *The Lady Contemplation* and *The Convent of Pleasure*.[3] It could also be found perhaps in the terms and terminology of patriarchal authorship by which she was surrounded in terms of her husband's objects of patronage – amongst them the male dramatists Ben Jonson and James Shirley.

It is not my intention here to play some self-defeating game of 'proving' that Margaret Cavendish was influenced by patriarchal precursors and to claim that therefore this influence, this 'pollution' or 'infection' of her sentences, somehow devalues or de-individualizes the achievements of her literary projects. It is not to suggest that a literary world of nesting boxes in any way by their diminution of size represent a diminution in value or content.[4] Nor is it to deny in some way the possibility of female innovation in the seventeenth century.[5] What I am exploring is the possibility of a wholly more complex matrix of influence between these writers. I suggest that this model can be applied to other authors in the period, male and female, and therefore I am arguing for a model of interaction that consciously breaks down the easy binaries with which Gilbert and Gubar were working in the late 1970s, and which suggested that the 'patriarchal' literary inheritance was not available to women writers. This serves to complicate the landscape within which we are now operating as feminist critics. It is, I hope, a shifting of the parameters that affects not only our interpretations of Margaret Cavendish but also those of Jonson and Shirley, and other exponents of the 'Jonsonian' dramatic strategies I am discussing here, before her. The project then is one of reintegration rather than separation.

Criticism of Cavendish's writing, and in particular I would say her drama, has tended to emphasize its difference, even its strangeness; a detailed account of her responses to the Jonsonian theatrical inheritance suggests rather more parallels than differences. In the same way, the misogynist, absolutist, patriarchal labels that have been applied almost subconsciously to Ben Jonson's oeuvre are themselves subtly challenged by this exploration of influence.[6] As the retrieval of female agency, literary and social, gains force in the scholarship of the Early Modern period, it has become possible to argue for mutually beneficial lines of influence between Ben Jonson and female writers and patrons such as Lady Mary Wroth, Aemilia Lanyer, Lucy Russell, Countess of Bedford, Frances Howard, Countess of Essex and then Somerset, Elizabeth Cary, Viscountess Falkland, and Lady Anne Clifford: this influence extends to and pervades Jonson's work, particularly in its latter decades.[7] That expansive field of influence and interaction also incorporates James Shirley to the extent that not only was he deeply aware of the Jonsonian precedent for his dramatic writings (an awareness frequently articulated in the prefatory material to his printed plays), but also, as part of the feminocentric circle at court under the auspices of Queen Henrietta Maria, he looked to the likes of Mary Wroth for plotlines for plays such as *The Politician*.[8] Shirley of course co-authored plays with William Cavendish and, along with the Cavendish sisters, Lady Jane Cavendish and Lady Elizabeth Brackley, was part of the entourage of that theatrical family and household, which Susan Wiseman has stressed was very much a factor in Margaret Cavendish's personal theatrical inheritance:[9]

> Newcastle's daughters apparently wrote their two plays or fairly short entertainments with their father in mind, addressing passages directly to him. The Duke's

> first plays, co-written by Shirley, were published in 1649 and his daughters' plays seem to belong to the 1640s.
>
> (Wiseman, p. 162)

So here we have a family which writes plays or which in various ways participates in play-making, and we need to consider this deeply theatrical and theatricalized context for Cavendish's own oeuvre.[10]

Within her work, Cavendish repeatedly denies any working knowledge of theatrical methods and techniques. Perhaps most famously, she does so through the, admittedly filtered, mouthpiece of the Duchess in her utopian prose-text *The Blazing World*.[11] When the emperor requests assistance in establishing a theatre for plays in his 'metropolitan city', the duchess informs him that 'she knew nothing of erecting theatres or scenes' (*Blazing World*, p. 343) and that 'she had as little skill to form a play after the mode as she had to paint or make a scene for a show' (*Blazing World*, p. 343). It would be all too easy to invoke such statements in order to stress the eccentricity and singularity of Cavendish's 'drama' and to somehow extricate her from a more mainstream theatrical history.[12] However, as Susan Wiseman has stressed: 'A comparison of her plays with other contemporary plays, both within and without her immediate circle . . . makes her writing practice appear much less eccentric' (Wiseman, p. 161).

In truth, Cavendish's humble denials of an awareness of standard theatrical practices are effectively contradicted by the succeeding statements in *The Blazing World* on the topic of the disallowance of theatre at the time (Cavendish is of course referring to Puritan objections to the theatre and the 1642 closure and dismantling of the London playhouses – and possibly she invokes another metropolitan city in need of theatre in the process) in which she argues that her plays were simply not liked because of the nature of the times. That suggests an extensive knowledge on Cavendish's part not only of theatrical fashions but also of the contentious political issues accruing around the dramatic genre. There is an informed debate which follows within the pages of *The Blazing World* about the artificial nature of theatrical constructs and descriptions, which in turn indicates that Cavendish's theatrical awareness was far from limited, despite her aforementioned claims, but was rather extensive and complex.[13]

In *The Blazing World*, the Empress declares her fondness for farce, and, at that, farce which is curiously connotative of Jonsonian experiments within the form:

> Then the Empress told the Duchess that she loved a foolish farce added to a wise play. The Duchess answered that no world in nature had fitter creatures for it than the Blazing World. 'For,' said she, 'the louse-men, the bird-men, the spider and fox-men, the ape-men and satyrs appear in a farce extraordinary pleasant.'
>
> (*Blazing World*, p. 344)

Whilst there is an obvious kinship between these half-human, half-animal creatures and the types that populated the Jonsonian antimasques of his court-drama from *The Masque of Queens* (1609) onwards,[14] the dramatis personae of Jonson's farcical and satirical beast-fable of 1606, *Volpone the Fox* is surely recalled and recounted here – Mosca the flesh-fly or parasite in the louse-men; the predatory will-hunters, Corvino, Corbaccio, and Voltore, as well as the English visitants Sir Pol and Peregrine, in the bird-men (and readers will recall that the professed orators and logicians of the Blazing World are 'magpie, parrot and jack-daw men' in the Jonsonian vein).

These observations gain added credence when we consider the 'Piece of a Play' which Cavendish includes in her 1668 volume of *Playes never before Printed* and which she informs us had been originally intended for inclusion within *The Blazing World*. That play would have been a beast-fable along openly Jonsonian lines. It tells of various suitors – Sir Puppy Dog-man and Lord Bear-man who woo the Lady Monkey, and Monsieur Satyr and, most significantly, Sir Politick Fox-man who woo the Lady Leverit. Sir Politick woos Lady Leverit for her money and is assisted in this by Mr Worm-man his servant. As with *Volpone* then we are dealing with foxes and parasites, even if they lack a little of the Jonsonian subtlety.

Cavendish also seems to share in the aforementioned passages from *The Blazing World* Jonson's own frequently articulated understanding of the, ideally-speaking, instructive nature of the theatre. But it is an earlier reference that indicates most overtly Cavendish's acknowledgement of Jonsonian influence. In a section discussing the search for the Jews' Cabala, we hear of Dr John Dee and Edward Kelly who came nearest in the Jacobean period to finding it:

> but yet they proved at last mere cheats, and were described by one of their own country men, a famous poet named Ben Jonson, in a play called *The Alchemist*, where he expressed Kelly by Capt. Face and Dee by Dr Subtle, and their two wives by Doll Common and the widow. By the Spaniard in the play he meant the Spanish ambassador, and by Sir Epicure Mammon, a Polish lord.
>
> (*Blazing World*, p. 292)

Despite the slightly off-centre account of the role of Doll Common and Dame Pliant in *The Alchemist* Cavendish produces here an extremely astute reading of the play. The Empress goes on to remember the Anabaptist Ananias and to question which 'real-life' figure he represented within the drama: the spirits' memories fail them on this point, but it is important I think to register that Cavendish's is an inherently politicized reading of Jonsonian drama and that this in itself may lend credence to those who may wish to apply a topico-political picklock kind of approach to the text of *The Blazing World*: she appears almost to be instructing readers to do so in passages of this nature.

I have pondered for some time why it might be that Cavendish singles out both Jonson and *The Alchemist* in such overt fashion. Obviously the interest in a multivalent figure such as Dee is part of it, but one of my conclusions is that she did find in Jonson a paradigm and a model of authorship. In Jonson's canon there can be found a similarly problematical and paradoxical relationship between the multiplicity of dramatic meaning and the tyranny of the absolutist author; in Jonson, too, the acute agonizing over issues of social status and the status of genre. But also, in Jonson, and in *The Alchemist* in particular, there exists an awareness of the impact, effect, power, and danger of the theatrical. It can be no mere coincidence that *The Alchemist* is a play with a peculiar investment in questions of the feigned and the actual, and in utopian and dystopian visions. I wonder as well if it is any mere coincidence that it is dedicated to Lady Mary Wroth – another employer of theatrical tropes and a writer of theatre herself – and, as I have already argued, an influence, like Jonson, on James Shirley to whose theatrical practices and tendencies we can have little doubt Cavendish had access both before and after her marriage.

Cavendish's self-deprecating prefaces and addresses to readers from the two volumes of her plays are regularly cited but any reader of them should be struck by the prevalence of Ben Jonson in her thoughts when gathering her plays together for publication. There are obvious reasons why he might be the major precursor or precedent for her, not simply his association with her husband in earlier years. Jonson's 1616 Folio *Workes* offered a direct authority and precedent for Cavendish's own dramatic publications, and the paradoxical blend in Jonson of the authoritarian and the literary democrat may have been something she could identify with. What is clear is that Jonson provides an omnipresent measure for her work. In the 1662 *Playes* volume, there is a poem set there to serve as 'A General Prologue to all my Playes':

> Noble Spectators, do no think to see
> Such Playes, that's like Ben. Johnson's Alchymie,
> Nor Fox, nor Silent woman: for those Playes
> Did Crown the Author with exceeding praise:
> They were his Master-pieces, and were wrought
> By Wits Invention, and his labouring thought,
> (*Playes*, 1662: p. 7)[15]

She goes on to admire his classical learning and the time he took over the composition of his drama, describing his plays as like unto 'Forein Emperors, which do appear / Unto their Subjects, not 'bove once a year'. Cavendish deprecates her own plays by comparing them to Jonson's, but for the reader the experience of such observations may be to receive a tangible register of Cavendish's disingenuousness. These invocations of Jonson actually serve to link him with Cavendish in the reader's mind and therefore authenticate rather than diminish her own projects in both the theatrical and publishing worlds.

Shakespeare too is mentioned but less as a writer of labour and care than as a natural genius; interestingly Cavendish here repeats the tropes of Jonson's elegy on Shakespeare for the 1623 Folio. Shakespearean resonances can be traced in Cavendish's plays – not least *Twelfth Night* in the cross-dressing and twin-soaked play of *The Presence* – but it is significant that it is to Ben Jonson, the theorist of theatre and the publisher of theatre, that Cavendish looks most often. As a woman writer she was not unique in this: Aphra Behn, too, for all her surface rejections of Jonson, was troubled by his literary shadow and in her later plays went so far as to openly imitate his work.[16]

In some additional prefaces to the 1662 volume, Cavendish uses Jonson as a justification for her non-observation of the dramatic unities in her plays, saying that whilst he might on the surface have claimed to observe them the events of his plays could never have occurred in a single day.[17] Tellingly she adds: 'I hate constraint even in my works', but for all that she felt the need to seek authorities for her deviations; and, in her drama at least, it was to Jonson that she looked.

There are relatively easy ways of suggesting the presence of the Jonsonian paradigm within Cavendish's dramatic oeuvre – not least in her fondness for aptronyms – Sir Effeminate Lovely, Sir Golden Riches, and Sir Fancy Poet in *Lady Contemplation*, and Bridget Greasy the upwardly-mobile servant in the wonderfully funny *The Matrimoniall Trouble* (written in two parts). As a result, when I first came to Cavendish's drama, I wondered whether or not it was in fact early Jonson, the Jonson of the 'humours' plays, in which she found a particular point of identity – the writer of farce and comical satires as it were, as opposed to the author of the subtler romances and masque-inspired dramas for the private theatres of his later playwriting years. As already mentioned, however, in the antimasques of Jonson's elite Stuart drama Cavendish may have found characters akin to the satirical 'humours' characters of the public theatre plays, and I have traced very clear lines of connection through late Jonsonian drama and the 1630s and 1640s drama of James Shirley (itself Jonsonian-inspired) to Margaret Cavendish's work (with the additional filter of the theatrical writings of Newcastle's daughters, Lady Elizabeth and Lady Jane), pivoting in particular on questions about female performance, and women and theatre, that not only illuminate Cavendish's problematical relationship with this theme but also Jonson's and Shirley's involvement in and agitation for related debates.

There is a need to revise our critical tendency to regard women's involvement in performance culture in the Early Modern period as 'private'.[18] The gendered and supposedly non-performative sites of closets must be questioned as a concept: as critics we need to review them as sites of family and household politics and political representation. Closets are undoubtedly metonymic of 'private space' in the texts of this period and yet they are also politically charged spaces. Closet-drama, by extension, is a politically charged genre and the sites of retreat and withdrawal in Cavendish, such as the convent of noble ladies in *The Convent of Pleasure* can be read and interpreted in politicized fashion.[19] The trope of retreat in female-authored literature may contain within it implications for the public, political, or social space as much as it does in the poetry of withdrawal by Andrew Marvell such as 'The Garden' and 'Upon Appleton House'.[20]

As part of this related reconsideration of women and private space, and in particular the operations of female theatre within these supposedly 'private' enclosures, I propose to look in detail here at Margaret Cavendish's *The Convent of Pleasure* in the light of some of these reinvestigations of the significance of space and to relate them to what I see as linked plays within the Jonsonian and the Shirley canons: those plays being Jonson's 1629 *The New Inn* and Shirley's 1633 *The Bird in the Cage*.

There are obvious ways in which *The Convent of Pleasure* taps into the aforementioned framework of Jonsonian allusion in Cavendish's work: consider for example the description proffered by Lady Happy of the sensual pleasures that will be enjoyed by the inhabitants or votresses of this secular convent:

> Now give me leave to inform you, how I have ordered this our Convent of Pleasure; first, I have such things as are for our Ease and Conveniency; next for Pleasure, and Delight; as I have change of Furniture, for my house; according to the four Seasons of the year.
>
> (*The Convent of Pleasure*, II.ii. p. 15)[21]

These pleasures do clearly relate to Sir Epicure Mammon's epicurean and sensuous imaginings in *The Alchemist*:

> I will have all my beds blown up, not stuffed;
> Down is too hard. And then mine own oval room
> Filled with such pictures as Tiberius took
> From Elephantis, and dull Aretine
> But coldly imitated . . .
> . . . My mists
> I'll have of perfume, vapoured 'bout the room,

> To loose ourselves in; and my baths like pits
> To fall into, from whence we will come forth
> And roll us dry in gossamer and roses
> (*The Alchemist*, 2.2.41)[22]

But this is surely not an instance of mere allusion or direct reference. The very nature and scope of Mammon's dreaming is implicitly questioned and critiqued by Lady Happy's bioregional approach. Her household and bedchamber, and those of her female compatriots, will reflect the English seasons; the contents of the chambers will be taken only from the near environs – Mammon by contrast plunders the world (and, of course, in particular, the New World in a convincingly colonialist act of imagination):

> My meat shall come all in Indian shells,
> Dishes of agate, set in gold, and studded
> With emeralds, sapphires, hyacinths and rubies.
> The tongues of carps, dormice and camels' heels
> Boiled i'the spirit of Sol, and dissolved pearl
> (*The Alchemist*, 2.2.72)

Lady Happy reflects:

> also the Bedding and Pillows are ordered according to each Season; viz. to be stuft with Feathers in the Spring and Autumn, and with Downs in the Winter, but in the Summer only to be Quilts, either of Silk, or fine holland
> (*The Convent of Pleasure*, II.ii. p. 15)

Unlike Mammon's monomaniac excess, hers is an ordered and harmonious vision, in keeping with the natural environment and the locality:

> and my Gardens to be kept curiously, and flourish, in every Season of all sorts of Flowers, sweet Herbs and Fruits, and kept so as not to have a Weed in it, and all the Groves, Wildernesses, Bowers and Arbours pruned, and kept free from dead Boughs, Branches or Leaves
> (*The Convent of Pleasure*, II.ii. p. 16)

In some respects it might be more accurate here to suggest that Cavendish is drawing on the tropes and imagery of seventeenth-century country-house poetry, of which, of course, Jonson was the arch-exponent with his seminal paean to the Sidney family estate in Kent: 'To Penshurst'. There, the walls of the estate are constructed with 'no man's ruin, no man's groan' and the dwelling is distinctly harmonious and communal in its outlook. If the telling feature of the communities described in country-house poems is their enclosure and their self-sufficiency (and again the cloistered locale of Marvell's 'Upon Appleton House' can be recalled) then just such a community is Lady Happy's. If, however, as in Barbara Lewalski's thesis such poems are seen as inevitable 'celebrations of patriarchy' then perhaps Cavendish offers the potential here to realize an interior community of the kind described as being unhoused and dispossessed in Aemilia Lanyer's feminine variation on the genre (and arguably the first excursion into the form) in the 'Description of Cooke-ham'.[23]

What is certain is that Lady Happy's retreat enables female theatrical performance. The central positioning of the play-within-the-play performed for the foreign 'Princess' at Act III (a series of swift episodic scenes depicting typical women's experiences in life, in a vision that is cross-class and cross-generational in its scope) could again be viewed as an essentially or ostensibly Jonsonian strategy.[24] This was a technique he had himself learned from Aristophanic drama where the central act invariably introduces new movements, even new characters into the play. But an important source for this centrally positioned performance must surely have been Cavendish's own familiarity with the theatrical performances of Henrietta Maria and her court-ladies. The 'Princess' in *The Convent of Pleasure* reflects on the unusual nature of the convent inhabitants' theatrical practices:

> Why then, I observing in your several Recreations, some of your Ladies do accoustre Themselves in Masculine-Habits, and act Lovers-parts; I desire you will give me leave to be sometimes so accoustred and act the part of your loving Servant.
>
> (*The Convent of Pleasure*, III.i. p. 19)

Henrietta Maria's ladies were notorious, thanks to the Puritan pamphleteer William Prynne's vitriolic attacks, for attiring themselves as men as well as women in the context of their court performances in the 1620s and 1630s. James Shirley, as I have already mentioned, was a prominent member of the Catholic court coterie surrounding Henrietta Maria and it has been persuasively argued by Kim Walker that *The Bird in a Cage*, authored by him in 1633, was a direct response to Prynne's *Histriomastix* and its indexing of women actresses as 'notorious whores'.[25]

What seems most salient for our purposes here is that *The Bird in a Cage* constitutes another play that has as its centre a community of women; this time not residing in a self-imposed enclosure but one enforced by the Princess Eugenia's father. She and her ladies in waiting are made to live in a tower to prevent her from marrying against her father, the Duke's, desires. The tower imaginatively functions as a closet space and a site for closet-drama. To pass the time, the women stage a play: the story of Jupiter's rape of Danaë in the form of a shower of gold – a story which has obvious resonance for their own situation with its themes of patriarchal incarceration, sexual penetration, and female empowerment. In this performance the women take all the parts with Eugenia herself playing Danaë and her servant Donella performing Jupiter. This casting, as Valerie Traub has demonstrated, allows for scenes of homoerotic attraction and female liberation, albeit of a temporary nature.[26] The women are certainly not backwards in asserting their right to play all the roles; Donella instructs her companions: 'Wee? Doe not distrust your owne performance. I ha' knowne men ha' been insufficient, but women can play their parts.'[27]

The connections to Cavendish's *Convent of Pleasure* should already be evident: the female community, the female play-acting, the application to 'real-life' situations, the potential for same-sex love – witnessed in Cavendish's play in the touching kissing-scene between Lady Happy and the 'Princess'. (Interestingly whereas in Shirley's private theatre play all parts would in truth have been taken by men, Cavendish seems to envisage all-female performers for her 'play' of the mind – even in the case of the 'Princess'.)[28] The connections go deeper than that when we bear in mind that Shirley's play also catalogues with some humour the attempts by various men to penetrate the female enclosure of the tower. Morello attempts to do so in female dress, only to have his breeches uncovered in the very manner that the Advisor warns in *The Convent of Pleasure* will befall those men who attempt something similar in an effort to enter the convent:

> We cannot avoid it, for, our very Garb and Behaviour; besides, our Voices will discover us: for we are as untoward to make Courtsies in Petticoats, as Women are to make Legs in Breeches; and so it will be as great a difficulty to raise our voices to a Treble-sound, as for Women to press down their Voices to a Base
>
> (*The Convent of Pleasure*, II.iv. p. 18)

In Cavendish's play *The Bridals* the Fool Mimick emphasizes that only the assumption of costume allows the sexes to imitate each other successfully: 'I cannot speak like a Woman in Breeches and Doublet, unless I have a petticoat' (IV.v. p. 61) Other plays collected in her 1668 volume employ tropes of cross-dressing, including *The Presence* and *The Sociable Companions*. At that particular moment in her life, the question of female performance was clearly a pressing concern to her.

Other important connections must surely be drawn out with Lady Jane Cavendish and Lady Elizabeth Brackley's civil war drama *The Concealed Fancies* (*c.*1645). That play features a household under siege; there are obvious resonances in this of the real-life situation of the sisters at Welbeck Abbey, but it is intriguing that this play features women whose discourse is pervaded by the language of theatricality, who seem to act to pass the time whilst trapped inside the house, and who also temporarily act as nuns in a convent.[29]

In their entirety the intrinsic connections between all these dramas endorse readings that would argue for their agitations for, and illuminating interest in, female performance. There seem for example in the above quotation to be implicit attacks upon the tradition of boy-actors as much as females who impersonate the male. *The Bird in a Cage* contains an implicit argument for 'each sex to play their own' in a socio-theatrical context. Shirley, I would argue, has Jonsonian precedents of his own in the form of the masque-influenced later plays (remembering that many of Jonson's masque commissions were female and have, as a result, been read for subversive agency by a number of critics);[30] late plays such as *The New Inn* with its performing ladies in waiting and its quasi-pastoral day's sports, or *The Staple of News* with its allegory-made-flesh in the female form of Pecunia, would seem to offer a rich seam for comparison.[31]

'The Light Heart' inn in Jonson's *The New Inn* may be a more preferable enclosure than the ladies' tower in *The Bird in a Cage* but once again it is a space of theatrical free-play and of sensual enjoyment akin to Cavendish's convent – that epicurean aspect is embodied in the figure of Goodstock the Host. In *The New Inn* theatricality *per se* is noticeably associated with aristocratic female performers; in the opening scenes Prudence the chambermaid voices considerable anxiety about dressing up in her mistress's attire to play the Queen of the Revels in the day's sports in the inn and even more so about the dress then being handed on to a company of players: 'That were illiberal, madam, and mere sordid / In me, to let a suit of yours come there' (*The New Inn*, II.i.37–8).[32] Her mistress, Lady Frances Frampul, shares none of her concerns: 'Tut, all are players and but serve the scene, Pru' (*The New Inn*, II.i.39). Theatre then is subtly being presented as an acceptable domain for women of rank, and masque must be viewed as a contributing factor in this: in the empathetic portrait of Prudence though, who in an anti-romance gesture remains very much a chambermaid at the end of the play, Jonson may of course be suggesting an extension of that allowance downwards through society. The division of roles in *The Bird in a Cage*, where Eugenia assumes a role equivalent to her 'real-life' status in Mantua (and Henrietta Maria, like Anne of Denmark before her, for all her theatrical assertiveness never played 'beneath herself' at court) is actually considerably less subversive. Endorsement may then be being offered to aristocratic female theatre so long as rank, rather than gender, is not transgressed. The limitations of class must always be borne in mind as a factor in these texts, however liberating their theatrical agitations might seem.

Jonson's late plays can be seen then to register a shift in their treatment of women and female performance as a result of his experimentation within the masque form.[33] *The Convent of Pleasure* ends with further Jonson and masque-inspired resonances. Following the Act III play, the scene changes to reveal a pastoral scene of rural sports, in the midst of which the 'Princess' is now attired as a male shepherd. The Florizel-Perdita Bohemian sheep-shearing scenes of Shakespeare's *The Winter's Tale* are of course relevant here, but so are the pastoral-inspired Jacobean and Caroline court masques in some of which Ben Jonson had himself been involved – not least *Pan's Anniversary*.[34] This thought is further consolidated when we see the subsequent 'performance' in the convent – a full-blown masque with a watery theme and a debate about power which the Lady Happy seems to prove victor of. In this 'masque' she plays the role of a Sea-Goddess and the 'Princess' adopts another masculine role as Neptune, God of the Sea. This was a favourite role for the Stuart monarchs in their court masques and Jonson's cancelled masque of 1624, *Neptune's Triumph*, might be invoked as a precedent. The Cavendish family had obtained access to the intricacies of masque performance and politics within their own household with William Cavendish's 1634 commission of *Love's Welcome at Bolsover* from Ben Jonson. Whilst the date would not allow Margaret presence at this event, she would certainly have inherited a working awareness of the neoplatonic and performative operations of that text.

The play proper of *The Convent of Pleasure* ends with the revelation of the 'Princess''s cross-dressing and the marriage between 'him' and the Lady Happy, albeit amidst subtexts of force and rape. If these are the scenes the Marquis of Newcastle was involved in the penning of they raise intriguing notions of possible alternative endings to the play. For all her involvement in and confirmation of stereotypes of class Cavendish can be seen in the rest of the play to be enacting certain radical notions of alternative communities and alternative female communities for which she ironically finds her precedents in some male dramatic voices from the pre-war period of English theatre.

What I am only beginning to do then, and what I can only offer here in relation to a limited number of Cavendish texts, is to map out or chart ways in which we can not only trace Cavendish's engagement with the theatrical developments of her own century (including the onset of women professional performers and playwrights), but also, as a consequence, offer for consideration a more comprehensive field of literary influence and interaction between the dramatists of the time – pre-Civil War and beyond. This functions to reclaim Cavendish's drama for critical attention within the context of the dramatic mainstream. Women could write plays, and men read them and, as Jonson himself was not afraid to acknowledge in the case of Mary Wroth, learned from their literary examples.[35] Discussion of influence need not then make feminist critics anxious or cause them to demote the creative power of the individual to something shrunken and merely referential – it may rather release for discussion new and inherently more political aspects of the texts concerned and politicize the female space of closet-drama in the process.

Notes

1 Harold Bloom, *The Anxiety of Influence* (Oxford: Oxford University Press, 1973). An important critical influence of my own must be acknowledged: Jonathan Bate, 'Ovid and the Sonnets: Or, Did Shakespeare Feel the Anxiety of Influence?', *Shakespeare Survey*, 42(1990): 65–76.

2 In *Feminisms: An Anthology of Literary Theory and Criticism*, ed. Robyn R. Warhol and Diane Price Herndl (New Brunswick, NJ: Rutgers University Press, 1993), pp. 289–300. Further citations appear within parentheses within the text.

3 See Sophie Tomlinson, '"My Brain the Stage": Margaret Cavendish and the Fantasy of Female Performance', in *Women, Texts, and Histories, 1575–1760*, ed. Clare Brant and Diane Purkiss (London: Routledge, 1994), pp. 134–63.

4 The image is Cavendish's own, used in the *Poems and Fancies* to suggest the possibility of worlds within worlds in philosophical thought. See Sandra Sherman, 'Trembling Texts: Margaret Cavendish and the Dialectic of Authorship', *English Literary Renaissance*, 24 (1992): 184–210. I am reapplying the conceit here to suggest that Cavendish can be placed within the Jonsonian and Caroline dramatic worlds in terms of influence and inheritance.

5 Although I am wary of the usage of a term such as 'feminist' for the likes of Cavendish. See for example Hilda L. Smith, *Reason's Disciples: Seventeenth-Century English Feminists* (Urbana, IL: University of Illinois Press, 1982), in particular ch. 3: '"Daughters Are But Branches": English Feminists, 1650–80', pp. 75–95.

6 Cavendish herself has been subjected to such readings and categorization, at least of the absolutist kind, most notably in Catherine Gallagher's seminal article, 'Embracing the Absolute: The Politics of the Female Subject in Seventeenth Century England', *Genders*, 1 (1988): 24–39.

7 See for example, my 'Women and Theatre in the Late Plays of Ben Jonson', forthcoming.

8 Sections of this play's plotlines appear to derive from Wroth's *Urania*. See Josephine Roberts, 'Radigund Revisited: Perspectives on Women Rulers in Lady Mary Wroth's *Urania*', in *The Renaissance Englishwoman in Print: Counterbalancing the Canon*, ed. Anne M. Haselkorn and Betty S. Travitsky (Amherst, MA: University of Massachusetts, 1990), p. 198.

9 Susan Wiseman, 'Gender and Status in Dramatic Discourse: Margaret Cavendish, Duchess of Newcastle', in *Women, Writing, History*, ed. Isobel Grundy and Susan Wiseman (London: Batsford, 1992), pp. 159–77. Further citations appear within parentheses within the text.

10 See Margaret J.M. Ezell, '"To Be Your Daughter in Your Pen": The Social Functions of Literature in the Writings of Lady Elizabeth Brackley and Lady Jane Cavendish', *Huntington Library Quarterly*, 51 (1988): 281–96.

11 Margaret Cavendish, 'The Blazing World', in *An Anthology of Seventeenth-Century Fiction*, ed. Paul Salzman (Oxford: Oxford University Press, 1991). Further citations appear within parentheses in the text. Also reprinted in *The Blazing World and Other Writings*, ed. Kate Lilley (Harmondsworth: Penguin, 1994). See also Paul Salzman, *English Prose Fiction, 1558–1700: A Critical History* (Oxford: Clarendon Press, 1985) and Roger Pooley, *English Prose of the Seventeenth Century, 1590–1700* (London: Longman, 1992).

12 An operation which is in many respects performed by Linda R. Payne in her 'Dramatic Dreamscape: Women's Dreams and Utopian Vision in the Works of Margaret Cavendish, Duchess of Newcastle', in *Curtain Calls: British and American Women in the Theater, 1660–1820*, ed. Mary Anne Schofield and Cecilia Macheski (Athens, OH: Ohio University Press, 1991), pp. 18–33.

13 See Lee Cullen Khanna, 'Margaret Cavendish and her Blazing World', in *Utopian and Science Fiction by Women: Worlds of Difference*, ed. Jane L. Donawerth and Carol A. Kolmerten (Liverpool: Liverpool University Press, 1994), pp. 15–34.

14 For Inigo Jones's illustrations of these see John Peacock, *The Stage Designs of Inigo Jones* (Cambridge: Cambridge University Press, 1996).

15 Both the 1662 and 1668 volumes of Cavendish's play collections are held in the British Library. Further citations to these volumes are contained within parentheses in the text.

16 See Janet Todd (ed.) *Aphra Behn Studies* (Cambridge: Cambridge University Press, 1996) and her *The Secret Life of Aphra Behn* (London: Deutsch, 1996).

17 It is of course difficult to trace when exactly Jonson became associated in Restoration dramatic philosophy with the theory of the unities. He did in some respects defend them in the Folio revision of *Every Man In His Humour* when he added a prologue which attacked plays which strove to 'make a child, now swaddled, to proceed / Man' (ll. 7–8). However, the intricate association of Jonson and the unities appears on the whole to have been a posthumous invention. My thanks to Janet Todd for discussions on this issue.

18 See, for example, Jane Milling, 'Lady Contemplation's Philosophical Fancies: The Closet Drama of Margaret Cavendish', unpublished paper, Early Modern Closets Symposium, Wormleighton, Warwickshire, June 1995. My thanks to Jane for discussions of ideas expressed within this paper. See also my essay 'The Closet Opened: A Reconstruction of "Private" Space in the Writings of Margaret Cavendish', forthcoming in *A Princely Brave Woman: Collected Essays on Margaret Cavendish, Duchess of Newcastle*, edited by Stephen Clucas for the Scolar Press.

19 See Ezell, op. cit. See also Alan Stewart, 'The Early Modern Closet Discovered', *Representations*, 50 (1995): 76–100, and Lisa Jardine, *Reading Shakespeare Historically* (London: Routledge, 1996), especially pp. 126–7 and pp. 150–1.

20 See Thomas Healy, '"Dark All Without It Knits": Vision and Authority in Marvell's Upon Appleton House', in *Literature and the English Civil War*, ed. Thomas Healy and Jonathan Sawday (Cambridge: Cambridge University Press, 1990), pp. 170–88. I am indebted to Hero Chalmers's work on this theme and to our rich dialogue on the subject. See her 'The Politics of Female Retreat in Margaret Cavendish's *The Female Academy* and *The Convent of Pleasure*' forthcoming in *Women's Writing*.

21 The edition of *The Convent of Pleasure* used throughout is that edited by Jennifer Rowsell (Oxford: Seventeenth Century Press, 1995). Further citations appear within parentheses within the text.

22 The edition of *The Alchemist* referred to throughout is that edited by Gordon Campbell for the World's Classics series, *The Alchemist and Other Plays* (Oxford: Oxford University Press, 1995). Further citations appear within parentheses in the text.

23 See Barbara Kiefer Lewalski, *Writing Women in Jacobean England* (Cambridge, MA: Harvard University Press, 1994). See also Susanne Woods, *The Poems of Aemilia Lanyer* (Oxford: Oxford University Press, 1993) and her 'Aemilia Lanyer and Ben Jonson: Patronage, Authority, and Gender,' *Ben Jonson Journal* 1(1994): 15–30.

24 See Gweno Williams's essay in this volume, pp. 95–107.

25 See Kim Walker, '"New Prison": Representing the Female Actor in Shirley's *The Bird in a Cage* (1633)', *English Literary Renaissance*, 21 (1991): 385–400.

26 Valerie Traub, 'The (In)significance of "Lesbian" Desire in Early Modern England', in *Erotic Politics: Desire on the Renaissance Stage*, ed. Susan Zimmerman (London and New York: Routledge, 1992), pp. 150–69.

27 All quotations from *The Bird in a Cage* are taken from Frances Frazier Senescu, *James Shirley's The Bird in a Cage: A Critical Edition* (New York and London: Garland, 1980), II.1–3, p. 42.

28 See Sophie Tomlinson, op. cit. Tomlinson also suggests medieval sources for Cavendish's convent-trope as well as possible sources in Fletcher plays. It may be possible to add to that list certain seventeenth-century utopian texts by French women writers such as Mme D'Aulnoy's *L'Isle de la Félicité* to which Cavendish may have had access. See Ruth Varver Carpasso, 'Islands of Felicity: Women Seeing Utopia in Seventeenth-Century France', in Donawerth and Kolmerton, op. cit., pp. 35–53.

29 See Wiseman, op. cit. See also S.P. Cerasano and Marion Wynne-Davies (eds) *Renaissance Drama by Women: Texts and Documents* (London: Routledge, 1996).

30 See, for example, Lewalski, op. cit., pp. 15–44; Marion Wynne-Davies, 'The Queen's Masque: Renaissance Women and the Seventeenth-Century Court Masque', in *Gloriana's Face: Women, Public and Private in the English Renaissance*, ed. S. P. Cerasano and Marion Wynne-Davies (Hemel Hempstead: Harvester, 1992), pp. 79–104, and Clare McManus, '"Defacing the Carcass": Anne of Denmark and Jonson's *Masque of Blackness*', in *Refashioning Ben Jonson: Gender, Politics, and the Jonsonian Canon*, ed. Julie Sanders with Kate Chedgzoy and Susan Wiseman (London: Macmillan, 1998). Such arguments are however chal-

lenged by Suzanne Gossett's more normative account of the masques for Queen Anne in '"Man-maid begone!": Women in Masques', *English Literary Renaissance*, 18(1988), 96–113.

31 See my '"The Day's Sports Devised in the Inn": Jonson's *The New Inn* and Theatrical Politics', *Modern Language Review*, 91(1996): 545–60, and 'Print, Popular Culture, Consumption, and Commodity in *The Staple of News*', in Sanders, Chedgzoy and Wiseman, op. cit.

32 The edition of *The New Inn* used is that edited by Michael Hattaway for the Revels series (Manchester: Manchester University Press, 1984). Further citations are contained within parentheses in the text.

33 See Richard Allen Cave, *Ben Jonson* (London: Macmillan, 1991).

34 See Martin Butler, 'Ben Jonson's *Pan's Anniversary* and the Politics of Early Stuart Pastoral', *English Literary Renaissance* 22(1992): 369–403. The texts of all Jonson's court masques can be found in *Ben Jonson: The Complete Masques* ed. Stephen Orgel (Newhaven, CT: Yale University Press, 1969).

35 In his 'A Sonnet to the Noble Lady, the Lady Mary Worth', Ben Jonson records this view on Wroth's poetry: 'Since I exscribe your sonnets, am become / A better lover, and much better poet'. (II. 3–4); see *Ben Jonson*, ed. Ian Donaldson (Oxford: Oxford University Press, 1985). See also Mary Ellen Lamb, *Gender and Authorship in the Sidney Circle* (London and Madison, WI: University of Wisconsin Press, 1990), pp. 154–5.

CONTRIBUTORS

Leeds Barroll is Presidential Research Professor at the University of Maryland (Baltimore). Editor of *Shakespeare Studies*, he is also the author of numerous books and articles on Renaissance drama and literature. His *Politics, Plague, and Shakespeare's Theatre* (Ithaca, NY: Cornell University Press, 1991) was awarded the Bernard Hewitt Prize by the American Society for Theatre Research in 1992. He has most recently published articles on the Jacobean regulation of drama, and he is presently completing a book on the Jacobean court masque.

Elaine V. Beilin is Professor of English at Framingham State College. She edited Anne Askew's *Examinations* for the series Women Writers in English, 1350–1850 (Oxford University Press, 1996) and is currently working on *Creating a Commonwealth: Early Modern Women Writers and History.*

David M. Bergeron, Professor of English at the University of Kansas, is the author of several books on Renaissance drama and Tudor-Stuart culture, including the edited volume *Reading and Writing in Shakespeare* (Newark, DE: University of Delaware Press, 1996). Since 1973 he has been editor of *Research Opportunities in Renaissance Drama.*

S. P. Cerasano, Professor of English at Colgate University, is currently writing a biography of the Renaissance actor and theatre entrepreneur Edward Alleyn. With Marion Wynne-Davies she is co-editor of *Gloriana's Face: Women, Public and Private in the English Renaissance* (Hemel Hempstead: Harvester, 1992) and of *Renaissance Drama by Women: Texts and Documents* (London: Routledge, 1996).

Nancy Cotton is Professor and Chair of English at Wake Forest at Wake Forest University. She is the author of *John Fletcher's Chastity Plays* (Lewisburg, PA: Bucknell University Press, 1973) and *Women Playwrights in England c. 1363–1750* (Lewisburg, PA: Bucknell University Press, 1980). She writes and lectures on English and American drama.

Margaret J. M. Ezell is the John Paul Abbott Professor of Liberal Arts at Texas A & M University. She is author of *The Patriarch's Wife: Literary Evidence and the History of the Family* (Chapel Hill, NC: University of North Carolina Press, 1987), *Writing Women's Literary History* (Baltimore, MD: Johns Hopkins University Press, 1993) and editor of *The Poems and Prose of Mary, Lady Chudleigh* (New York: Oxford University Press, 1993) and, with Katherine O'Brien O'Keefe, *Cultural Artifacts and the Production of Meaning: The Page, The Image, and the Body* (Ann Arbor, MI: University of Michigan Press, 1994). Recently she completed a collection on print and manuscript cultures in Early Modern Britain and is at work on Volume V of the new *Oxford English Literary History.*

Margaret Ferguson, Professor of English at the University of California at Davis, has taught at Yale, Columbia, and the University of Colorado. She has co-edited Elizabeth Cary's *The Tragedy of Mariam* as well as volumes on Milton, feminism and postmodernism, and the discourses of sexual difference in Early Modern Europe. Author of *Trials of Desire: Renaissance Defenses of Poetry* (New Haven, CT: Yale University Press, 1983) and numerous articles, she is currently completing a book entitled *Female Literacies and Emergent Empires: Studies in French and English Cultural History, 1400–1700.*

Alison Findlay lectures at Lancaster University where she teaches Renaissance drama and women's writing. She is author of *Illegitimate Power: Bastards in Renaissance Drama* (Manchester University Press, 1994) and has edited a collection of critical writing on Jacobean and Caroline Drama for *Biblioteca Elizabethana*, ed. Susan Brock and Stanley Wells (Keero Microfilms). She has just completed a feminist introduction to Renaissance drama which uses women's writing from the period to read mainstream plays by Shakespeare and his contemporaries. With Stephanie Hodgson-Wright and Gweno Williams, she is co-director of Women and Dramatic Production, 1550–1670, an interdisciplinary research project designed to explore the interface between women's writing and performance. A co-authored article, '"The Play is Ready to be Acted", Women and Dramatic Production', *Women's Writing* 5(1998), discusses the project's premiere productions of Renaissance plays by women. She is also the author of '"Playing the Scene Self" in Jane Cavendish and Elizabeth Brackley's *The Concealed Fancies*' in *Enacting Gender on the English Renaissance Stage*, ed. Viviana Comensoli and Anne Russell (University of Illinois Press, 1998).

Margaret P. Hannay, Professor of English Literature at Siena College, is the author of *Philip's Phoenix: Mary Sidney, Countess of Pembroke* (New York: Oxford University Press, 1990) and editor of *Silent but for the Word: Tudor Women as Patrons, Translators and Writers of Religious Works* (Kent, OH: Kent State University Press, 1985). She is currently editing *The Collected Works of Mary Sidney Herbert, Countess of Pembroke* with Noel J. Kinnamon and Michael G. Brennan for the Oxford English Texts series.

Jean E. Howard is Professor of English at Columbia University and Director of the Institute for Research on Women and Gender. Her publications include *The Stage and Social Struggle in Early Modern England* (London: Routledge, 1994) and, with Phyllis Rackin, *Engendering a Nation: A Feminist Account of Shakespeare's English Histories* (London: Routledge, 1997). She is one of the editors of *The Norton Shakespeare* (New York: W. W. Norton, 1997).

Tina Krontiris, Assistant Professor of English at Aristotle University in Thessaloniki, Greece, is the author of *Oppositional Voices: Women as Writers and Translators of Literature in the English Renaissance* (London: Routledge, 1992) and of several essays on women and literature. At present she is maintaining the chapter on 'Renaissance and Early Seventeenth-Century Women's Writing' in a new series – *Annotated Bibliography for English Studies* on CD-ROM (Lise: Swets & Zeitlinger, 1997). She is also working on issues of gender in Shakespeare.

Carole Levin is Professor of History at University of Nebraska. She is the author of *Heart and Stomach of a King: Elizabeth I and the Politics of Sex and Power* (Philadelphia, PA: University of Pennsylvania Press, 1994) and *Propaganda in the English Reformation:*

Heroic and Villainous Images of King John (Lewiston: E. Mellen Press, 1988). She is co-editor of *Ambiguous Realities: Women in the Middle Ages and Renaissance* (1987), *Sexuality and Politics in Renaissance Drama* (1991) and *Political Rhetoric, Power, and Renaissance Women* (1995). She has held long-term fellowships at Newberry Library and Folger Shakespeare Library and has received the SUNY Chancellor's Award for Excellence in Teaching.

Barbara Kiefer Lewalski is William R. Kenan Professor of English at Harvard University. Among her numerous publications in Early Modern literature are *Writing Women in Jacobean England* (Cambridge, MA: Harvard University Press, 1993), *Paradise Lost and the Rhetoric of Literary Forms* (Princeton, NJ: Princeton University Press, 1987), *Protestant Poetics and the Seventeenth-Century Religious Lyric* (Princeton, NJ: Princeton University Press, 1979) and *The Polemics and Poems of Rachel Speght* (New York: Oxford University Press, 1996). She is now completing a biography of Milton.

Margaret Anne McLaren has taught since 1982, including two years at a girls' school in Tanzania located on Mt Kilimanjaro. She has presently settled back in New Zealand where she is involved in management and pastoral care roles, as well as curriculum development.

Julie Sanders is Lecturer in the Department of English at Keele University. She is the author of *Ben Jonson's Theatrical Republics* (London: Macmillan Press, 1998) and co-editor with Kate Chedgzoy and Susan Wiseman of *Refashioning Ben Jonson* (London: Macmillan, 1998). She is currently researching a book on Caroline Drama.

Sophie Tomlinson is Lecturer in English at the University of Auckland, New Zealand. She is currently at work on a book provisionally entitled *Theatrical Women: The Female Actor in Early Modern English Drama.*

Gary Waller is Vice-President for Academic Affairs and Professor of Literature and Cultural Studies at Purchase College, SUNY. He is the author of some twenty books, mainly on Renaissance and Early Modern literature and culture, including *English Poetry of the Sixteenth Century* (London: Longman, 1986), *The Sidney Family Romance* (Detroit, MI: Wayne State University Press, 1993), *Edmund Spenser: a Literary Life* (London: Macmillan, 1994) and *Reading Texts* (Lexington, KY: D.C. Heath, 1987). His current work focuses on Early Modern sexuality and trans-gendering, especially in Shakespeare, and he is completing a third collection of his own poetry.

Gweno Williams is Senior Lecturer in Literature Studies at the University College of Ripon and York St John. She is currently preparing an edition of Margaret Cavendish's plays. With Alison Findlay and Stephanie Hodgson-Wright she co-founded the interdisciplinary research project Women and Dramatic Production, 1550–1670. A co-authored account of the project, 'The Play is Ready to be Acted' is in *Women's Writing* 5 (1998) and a book on the subject is forthcoming in the Longman Medieval and Renaissance Library. She has a teaching video of the world premiere production of *The Convent of Pleasure* (forthcoming).

Stephanie Hodgson-Wright is Senior Lecturer in English Studies at the University of Sunderland. She has published an edition of Elizabeth Cary's *The Tragedy of Mariam* and is preparing an edition of Jane Lumley's *Iphigenia at Aulis*, having also directed premiere productions of both plays. She is currently working on a co-authored study of Women and Dramatic Production, 1550–1670, together with Alison Findlay and Gweno Williams.

Marion Wynne-Davies is Senior Lecturer in the English Department at the University of Dundee. Her published works include *Women and Arthurian Literature: Seizing the Sword* (London: Macmillan, 1996) and *Renaissance Women Poets* (1998), and she has co-edited, with S. P. Cerasano, *Gloriana's Face: Women, Public and Private in the English Renaissance* (1992) and *Renaissance Drama by Women: Texts and Documents* (1996).

BIBLIOGRAPHY OF SECONDARY SOURCES

Bainton, Rolan H. 'Learned Women in the Sixteenth Century', in Patricia Labalme (ed.) *Beyond Their Sex*, New York: New York University Press, 1980.

Ballard, George. *Memoirs of Several Ladies of Great Britain* 1752, rpt Detroit, MI: Wayne State University Press, 1985.

Beauchamp, V. W. 'Sidney's Sister as Translator of Garnier', *Renaissance Notes* 10 (1957), pp. 8–13.

Beilin, Elaine V. *Redeeming Eve: Women Writers of the English Renaissance*, Princeton, NJ: Princeton University Press, 1987.

—— 'Current Bibliography of English Women Writers, 1500–1640', in Anne M. Haselkorn and Betty S. Travitsky (eds) *The Renaissance Englishwoman in Print: Counterbalancing the Canon*, Amherst, MA: University of Massachusetts Press, 1990.

Bell, Maureen, Parfitt, George and Shepherd, Simon (eds) *A Biographical Dictionary of English Women Writers 1580–1720*, Brighton: Harvester, 1990.

Bergeron, David. 'Women as Patrons of English Renaissance Drama', in G. F. Lytle and S. Orgel (eds) *Patronage in the Renaissance*, Princeton, NJ: Princeton University Press, 1981.

Bickley, Francis. *The Cavendish Family*, London: Constable, 1911.

Bowerbank, Sylvia. 'The Spider's Delight: Margaret Cavendish and the "Female" Imagination', *English Literary Renaissance* 14(1984), pp. 392–408.

Brennan, Michael. *Literary Patronage in the English Renaissance: The Pembroke Family*, London: Routledge, 1988.

Burner, Sandra A. *James Shirley: A Study of Literary Coteries and Patronage*, London: University Presses of America, 1988.

Callaghan, Dympna. 'Re-Reading Elizabeth Cary's *The Tragedie of Mariam, Faire Queene of Jewry*', in Margo Hendricks and Patricia Parker (eds) *Women, 'Race,' and Writing in the Early Modern Period*, New York: Routledge, 1994.

Camden, Carroll. *The Elizabethan Woman*, New York: Paul Appel, 1975.

Cerasano, S. P. and Wynne-Davies, Marion (eds) *Gloriana's Face: Women, Public and Private, in the English Renaissance*, Hemel Hempstead: Harvester, 1992.

—— (eds) *Renaissance Drama by Women: Texts and Documents*, London and New York: Routledge, 1996.

Cotton, Nancy. 'Elizabeth Cary, Renaissance Playwright', *Texas Studies in Literature and Language* 18(1977), pp. 601–8.

—— *Women Playwrights in England: c.1363–1750*, London: Associated University Presses, 1980.

Ezell, Margaret J. M. '"To Be Your Daughter in Your Pen": The Social Functions of Literature in the Writings of Lady Elizabeth Brackley and Lady Jane Cavendish', *Huntington Library Quarterly* 51(1988), pp. 281–96.

—— *Writing Women's Literary History*, Baltimore, MD: Johns Hopkins University Press, 1996.

Ferguson, Margaret W. 'The Spectre of Resistance: *The Tragedy of Mariam (1613)*', in David

Scott Kastan and Peter Stallybrass (eds), *Staging the Renaissance: Reinterpretations of Elizabethan and Jacobean Drama*, London: Routledge, 1991.

—— 'Running On with Almost Public Voice: The Case of "E. C."' in Florence Howe (ed.) *Tradition and the Talents of Women*, Urbana, IL: University of Illinois Press, 1991.

Ferguson, Moira. 'A "Wise, Wittie and Learned Lady": Margaret Lucas Cavendish', in Katharina M. Wilson and Frank J. Warnke (eds) *Women Writers of the Seventeenth Century*, Athens, GA: University of Georgia Press, 1989.

Findley, Sandra and Elaine Hobby. 'Seventeenth-Century Women's Biography' in F. Barker (ed.) *1642: Literature and Power in the Seventeenth Century*, Colchester: Essex University, 1981.

Fischer, Sandra K. 'Elizabeth Cary and Tyranny, Domestic and Religious', in Margaret Hannay (ed.) *Silent but for the Word: Tudor Women as Patrons, Translators, and Writers of Religious Works*, Kent, OH: Kent State University Press, 1985.

Fisher, Sheila and Halley, Janet E. (eds) *Seeking the Woman in Late Medieval and Renaissance Writings*, Knoxville, TN: University of Tennessee Press, 1989.

Flügel, Ewald. 'Die Gedichte der Königin Elisabeth', *Anglia* 14 (1892), pp. 346–52.

Freer, Coburn. 'Mary Sidney: Countess of Pembroke', in Katharina M. Wilson (ed.) *Women Writers of the Renaissance and Reformation*, Athens, GA: University of Georgia Press, 1987.

Fullerton, Georgianna. *Life of Elizabeth Cary, Lady Falkland 1582–1639*, London: Burns and Oates, 1883.

Gossett, Suzanne. '"Man-Maid, Begone!": Women in Masques', in Kirby Farrell, Elizabeth H. Hageman and Arthur F. Kinney (eds) *Women in the Renaissance*, Amherst, MA: University of Massachusetts Press, 1988.

Grant, Douglas. *Mary the First: A Biography of Margaret Cavendish, Duchess of Newcastle, 1623–1673*, London: Rupert Hart-Davis, 1957.

Gutierrez, Nancy A. 'Valuing Mariam: Genre Study and Feminist Analysis', *Tulsa Studies in Women's Literature* 10(1991), pp. 233–51.

Hannay, Margaret P. *Silent but for the Word: Tudor Women as Patrons, Translators, and Writers of Religious Works*, Kent, OH: Kent State University Press, 1986.

—— 'Mary Sidney: Lady Wroth', in Katharina M. Wilson (ed.) *Women Writers of the Renaissance and Reformation*, Athens, GA: University of Georgia Press, 1987.

—— *Philip's Phoenix: Mary Sidney, Countess of Pembroke*, Oxford: Oxford University Press, 1990.

Haselkorn, Anne M. and Travitsky, Betty S. (eds) *The Renaissance Englishwoman in Print*, Amherst, MA: University of Massachusetts Press, 1990.

Hay, Millicent V. *The Life of Robert Sidney, Earl of Leicester (1563–1626)*, Washington, DC: Folger Books, 1984.

Hopkins, Lisa. 'Judith Shakespeare's Reading: Teaching *The Concealed Fancies*', *Shakespeare Quarterly* 47(1996), pp. 396–406.

Howard, Jean E. 'Women as Spectators, Spectacles, and Paying Customers' in David Scott Kastan and Peter Stallybrass (eds), *Staging the Renaissance*, London: Routledge, 1991.

Kemp, Theresa D. 'The Family is a Little Commonwealth: Teaching *Mariam* and *Othello* in a Special-Topics Course on Domestic England', *Shakespeare Quarterly* 47(1996), pp. 451–60.

Krontiris, Tina. 'Breaking Barriers of Genre and Gender', *English Literary Renaissance* 18 (1988), pp. 19–39.

—— 'Style and Gender in Elizabeth Cary's *Edward II*', in Anne M. Haselkorn and Betty Travitsky (eds) *The Renaissance Englishwoman in Print: Counterbalancing the Canon*, Amherst, MA: University of Massachusetts Press, 1990.

—— *Oppositional Voices: Women as Writers and Translators of Literature in the English Renaissance*, London: Routledge, 1992.

—— 'Reading with the Author's Sex: A Comparison of Two Seventeenth-Century Texts', *Gramma* 1(1993), pp. 123–36.

Lamb, Mary Ellen. 'The Myth of the Countess of Pembroke: The Dramatic Circle', *The Year's Work in English Studies* 11(1981), pp. 194–202.

—— 'The Countess of Pembroke's Patronage', *English Literary Renaissance* 12(1982), pp. 162–79.

—— 'The Countess of Pembroke and the Art of Dying', in Mary Beth Rose (ed.) *Women in the Middle Ages and the Renaissance*, Syracuse, NY: Syracuse University Press, 1986.

—— *Gender and Authorship in the Sidney Circle*, Madison, WI: University of Wisconsin Press, 1990.

Levin, Carole. 'Power, Politics, and Sexuality: Images of Elizabeth I', in Jean R. Brink, Allison P. Coudert, and Maryanne C. Horowitz (eds) *The Politics of Gender in Early Modern Europe*, Kinksville, MO: Sixteenth Century Journal Publications, 1989.

—— *The Heart and Stomach of a King: Elizabeth I and the Politics of Sex and Power*, Philadelphia, PA: University of Pennsylvania Press, 1994.

Levin, Carole and Patricia A. Sullivan (eds) *Political Rhetoric, Power, and Renaissance Women*, Albany, NY: State University of New York Press, 1995.

Lewalski, Barbara. 'Lucy, Countess of Bedford', in Kevin Sharpe and Steven N. Zwicker (eds) *Politics of Discourse*, Los Angeles: University of California Press, 1987.

—— 'Mary Wroth's *Love's Victory* and Pastoral Tragicomedy', in Naomi J. Miller and Gary Waller (eds) *Reading Mary Wroth: Representing Alternatives in Early Modern England*, Knoxville, TN: University of Tennessee Press, 1991.

—— *Writing Women in Jacobean England*, Cambridge, MA: Harvard University Press, 1993.

Luce, Alice. 'The Countess of Pembroke's *Antonie*' in *Literarhistorische Forschungen*, Weimar: Verlag von Emil Felber, 1897.

McLaren, Margaret Anne. 'An Unknown Continent: Lady Mary Wroth's Forgotten Pastoral Drama, "Loves Victorie"', in Anne M. Haselkorn and Betty Travitsky (eds) *The Renaissance Englishwoman in Print*, Amherst, MA: University of Massachusetts Press, 1990.

Mahl, Mary R. and Koon, Helene (eds) *The Female Spectator: English Women Writers Before 1800*, Bloomington, IN: Indiana University Press, 1977.

Mendelson, Sarah Heller. *The Mental World of Stuart Women: Three Studies*, Brighton: Harvester, 1987.

Miller, Naomi J. and Waller, Gary (eds) *Reading Mary Wroth: Representing Alternatives in Early Modern England*, Knoxville, TN: University of Tennessee Press, 1991.

—— *Changing the Subject: Mary Wroth and Figurations of Gender in Early Modern England*, Lexington, KY: University Press of Kentucky, 1996.

Morrison, Mary. 'Some Aspects of the Treatment of the Theme of Antony and Cleopatra in Tragedies of the Sixteenth Century', *Journal of English Studies* 4 (1974), pp. 113–25.

Murdoch, Kenneth B. *Sun at Noon: Three Biographical Sketches*, New York: Macmillan, 1939.

Nichols, John. *The Progresses and Public Processions of Queen Elizabeth*, London: J. Nichols and Son, 1823.

—— *The Progresses, Processions, and Magnificent Festivities of King James the First*, London: J. B. Nichols, 1828.

Patrick, J. Max. 'The Cleopatra Theme in World Literature up to 1700', in J. R. Conway Perkin (ed.) *The Undoing of Babel: Watson Kirkconnell, the Man and his Work*, Toronto: MacLelland and Stewart, 1975.

Payne, Linda R. 'Dramatic Dreamscape: Women's Drama and Utopian Vision in the Works of Margaret Cavendish, Duchess of Newcastle' in Mary Anne Schofield and Cecilia Macheski (eds) *Curtain Calls: British and American Women and the Theater, 1660–1820*, Athens, OH: Ohio University Press, 1991.

Quilligan, Maureen. 'Staging Gender: William Shakespeare and Elizabeth Cary', in James Grantham Turner (ed.) *Sexuality and Gender in Early Modern Europe: Institutions, Texts, Images*, Cambridge: Cambridge University Press, 1993.

Raber, Karen L. 'Gender and the Political Subject in *Tragedy of Mariam*', *Studies in English Literature* 35(1995), pp. 321–43.

Roberts, Josephine. 'The Huntington Manuscript of Lady Mary Wroth's Play, *Loves Victorie*', *Huntington Library Quarterly* 46(1983), pp. 156–74.

—— *The Poems of Lady Mary Wroth*, Baton Rouge, LA: Louisiana State University Press, 1983.

—— 'Recent Studies in Women Writers of Tudor England: Mary Sidney, Countess of Pembroke', *English Literary Renaissance* 14 (1984), pp. 426–39.

Rose, Mary Beth (ed.) *Women in the Middle Ages and the Renaissance: Literary and Historical Perspectives*, Syracuse, NY: Syracuse University Press, 1986.

Shannon, Laurie J. '*The Tragedie of Mariam*: Cary's Critique of the Terms of Founding Social Discourses', *English Literary Renaissance* 24(1994), pp. 135–53.

Shapiro, Michael. 'Lady Mary Wroth Describes a "Boy Actress"', *MARDIE* 4(1989), pp. 187–94.

Shattock, Joanne. *The Oxford Guide to British Women Writers*, Oxford: Oxford University Press, 1993.

Shepherd, Simon. *Amazons and Warrior Women: Varieties of Feminism in Seventeenth Century Drama*, Brighton: Harvester, 1981.

Simpson, Richard (ed.) *The Lady Falkland, Her life From a MS in the Imperial Archives at Lisle*, London: Catholic Publishing and Bookselling, 1861.

Skura, Meredith. 'The Reproduction of Mothering in *Mariam, Queen of Jewry*: A Defense of "Biographical" Criticism', *Tulsa Studies in Women's Literature* 16 (1997), pp. 27–56.

Straznicky, Marta. '"Profane Stoical Paradoxes": *The Tragedie of Mariam* and Sidnean Closet Drama', *English Literary Renaissance* 24(1994), pp. 104–34.

—— 'Reading the Stage: Margaret Cavendish and Commonwealth Closet Drama', *Criticism* 37(1995), pp. 355–90.

Smith, C. Fell. *Mary Rich: Countess of Warwick, 1625–1678*, London: Longmans, Green, 1901.

Swift, Carolyn Ruth. 'Feminine Identity in Lady Mary Wroth's Romance *Urania*', in Kirby Farrell, Elizabeth Hageman and Arthur F. Kinney (eds) *Women in the Renaissance. Selections from 'English Literary Renaissance'*, Amherst, MA: University of Massachusetts Press, 1988.

—— 'Feminine Self-Definition in Lady Mary Wroth's *Love's Victorie* (c.1621)', *English Literary Renaissance* 19 (1989), pp. 171–88.

Teague, Frances. 'Elizabeth I', in Katharina M. Wilson (ed.) *Women Writers of the Renaissance and Reformation*, Athens, GA: University of Georgia Press, 1987.

Tomlinson, Sophie. '"My Brain the Stage": Margaret Cavendish and the Fantasy of Female Performance', in Clare Brant and Diane Purkiss (eds) *Women, Texts and Histories 1575–1760*, London: Routledge, 1992.

Travitsky, Betty. *The Paradise of Women: Writings by Englishwomen of the Renaissance*, London: Greenwood Press, 1981.

—— 'The *Feme Covert* in Elizabeth Cary's *Mariam*', in Carole Levin and Jeanie Watson (eds) *Ambiguous Realities: Women in the Middle Ages and Renaissance*, Detroit, MI: Wayne State University Press, 1987.

—— 'His Wife's Prayers and Meditations; MS Egerton 607', in Anne M. Haselkorn and Betty Travitsky (eds) *The Renaissance Englishwoman in Print: Counterbalancing the Canon*, Amherst, MA: University of Massachusetts Press, 1990.

Turberville A. S. *A History of Welbeck Abbey and its Owners*, London: Faber and Faber, 1937.

Valency, Maurice. *The Tragedies of Herod and Mariamne*, New York: Columbia University Press, 1940.

Waller, Gary F. 'Struggling into Discourse: The Emergence of Renaissance Women's Writing', in Margaret Hannay (ed.) *Silent but for the Word: Tudor Women as Patrons, Translators, and Writers of Religious Works*, Kent, OH: Kent State University Press, 1985.

—— *Mary Sidney Countess of Pembroke, A Critical Study of her Writings and Literary Milieu*, Salzburg: Salzburg Studies in English Literature, 1987.

—— 'Mary Wroth and the Sidney Family Romance: Gender Construction in Early Modern England', in Naomi J. Miller and Gary Waller (eds) *Reading Mary Wroth: Representing Alternatives in Early Modern England*, Knoxville, TN: University of Tennessee Press, 1991.

—— *The Sidney Family Romance: Mary Wroth, William Herbert, and The Early Modern Construction of Gender*, Detroit, MI: Wayne State University Press, 1993.

Walpole, Horatio. *A Catalogue of the Royal and Noble Authors of England, Scotland, and Ireland; with Lists of their Works*, London: John Scott, 1806.

Weller, Barry and Ferguson, Margaret W. (eds) *Elizabeth Cary, Lady Falkland/ 'The Tragedy of Mariam, the Fair Queen of Jewry' with 'The Lady Falkland: Her Life by One of Her Daughters'*, Berkeley: University of California Press, 1994.

Wiesner, Merry. 'Women in the Sixteenth Century: A Bibliography', *Sixteenth-Century Bibliography* 23 (1983), pp. 1–65.

Wilcox, Helen (ed.) *Women and Literature in Britain, 1500–1700*, Cambridge: Cambridge University Press, 1996.

Wilson, Jean. *Entertainments for Elizabeth I*, Woodbridge: D. S. Brewer, 1980.

Wilson, Katharina M. (ed.) *Women Writers of the Renaissance and Reformation*, Athens, GA: University of Georgia Press, 1987.

Wiseman, Susan. 'Gender and Status in Dramatic Discourse: Margaret Cavendish, Duchess of Newcastle', in Isobel Grundy and Susan Wiseman (eds) *Women, Writing and History*, London: Batsford, 1992.

Witherspoon, Alexander. *The Influence of Robert Garnier on Elizabethan Drama*, New Haven, CT: Archon, 1924.

Wynne-Davies, Marion. 'The Queen's Masque: Renaissance Women and the Seventeenth-Century Court Masque', in S. P. Cerasano and M. Wynne-Davies (eds) *Gloriana's Face: Women, Public and Private, in the English Renaissance*, Hemel Hempstead: Harvester, 1992.

Young, Frances B. *Mary Sidney, Countess of Pembroke*, London: David Nutt, 1912.

INDEX

The following index records surnames, titles, place names, and some subjects. It does not include note references.